Edmund Burke

Selected Writings and Speeches

Peter J. Stanlis, a native of New Jersey, took his B.A., at Middlebury College (1942), his M.A. at the Bread Loaf School of English (1944), and his Ph.D. at the University of Michigan (1951). He has taught in various American colleges and universities for over forty years, and has been a guest lecturer in three European universities. He has published over 100 articles on political, historical, legal, and literary subjects, and has edited a law journal. His publications on Burke include many articles, editing *The Burke Newsletter* and *Studies in Burke and His Time* for thirteen years, and six books on various aspects of Burke's thought and politics. His best known book, *Edmund Burke and the Natural Law* (1958), revolutionized modern scholarship on Burke. His most recent book, co-authored with Clara I. Gandy, *Edmund Burke: A Bibliography of Secondary Studies to 1982* (1983), reviews all scholarship and writings on Burke for the past two centuries.

Peter J. Stanlis has also been active in practical politics, having been a city councilman for six years, and serving on the constitutional commission for the state of Michigan, which resulted in a new constitution being adopted by that state. In 1982 he was appointed by President Ronald Reagan to the National Council for the Humanities, for a six year term.

Edmund Burke

Selected Writings and Speeches

Edited by Peter J. Stanlis

A Gateway Edition
Regnery Gateway

Copyright © 1963 by Peter J. Stanlis
All Rights Reserved

Cover photo: J. Jones' mezzotint is taken from George Romney's
portrait of Edmund Burke, dated 1776.

Published by Regnery Gateway
360 West Superior Street
Chicago, Illinois 60610-0890

Manufactured in the United States of America

ISBN: 0-89526-834-5

Library of Congress Catalog Card Number: 83–63119

To the memory of Louis I. Bredvold

Preface

William Hazlitt once remarked that the only fair specimen of Burke's writing is all that he wrote, because each new work shows additional evidence of his power in thought and brilliance in expression. Only an editor of Burke's writings and speeches, who has experienced the painful task of deleting passages and omitting entire works, can appreciate the full force of Hazlitt's perceptive observation.

The selections from Burke's writings and speeches in this volume have been chosen from the entire canon of his works, from his earliest to his last writings. Special attention has been paid to Burke's early writings, which have been unduly neglected. This is the first anthology of Burke to include selections from his *An Abridgment of English History* and his early book reviews in the *Annual Register*.

The main purpose of these selections is to present extensive and in the main unbroken samples of Burke's most representative thought in his most characteristic style, on a great variety of subjects. By this procedure a balance has been maintained in covering all of Burke's great concerns, and a sense of proportion has been observed in the length of the selections on each subject.

From the works that have had to be abridged, I have often omitted passages containing purely local references, digressions that include inert materials not functional to Burke's main purpose in writing, and those copious illustrations that enrich Burke's main line of argument beyond what is necessary to understand his themes clearly. I am well aware that such deletions create difficult problems of transition, and that they invite the serious danger of dislocating the detailed texture and organic structure of Burke's compositions, and of oversimplifying his thought. I have done my best to avoid all of these pitfalls.

In keeping only what I considered essential, I have not abstracted Burke's political ideas out of their concrete historical context. Nothing could be more foreign to Burke's character and temper than to treat his thought in an abstract manner. I have also tried to avoid the other great danger, that of treating long dead political and historical issues as though they were, in themselves, philosophically important. In the introductions to each work I have summarized the essential circumstances surrounding the historical occasion that prompted Burke to write or speak. But, as Matthew Arnold said, "Burke saturated politics with thought," so that we read him for his reflective wisdom in combining philosophical principles and historical circumstances and facts. We read Burke not merely for his illumination of past political and historical events, but for the perennial vitality of his ideas and principles, and for his skill in combining principles with the concrete historical circumstances and occasions that called forth his reflections on man as a political animal. By any reasonable judgment, Burke has to be considered one of the world's outstanding thinkers on politics.

Except for the early writings of Burke, which are a unit based on the time of composition, the basis of division for selections in this volume has been to group them according to subject—the American Colonies, Ireland, Economic Reform, Constitutional Affairs, India, and the French Revolution. I have followed a chronological principle of arrangement for selections within each subject group.

The basic text used in making selections, including Burke's speeches, is *The Works of the Rt. Hon. Edmund Burke* (Boston: Little, Brown & Company, 1865–67), in twelve volumes. A few selections, such as Burke's *Letter to M. Depont* (1789), were taken from *Correspondence of the Rt. Hon. Edmund Burke* (London: Rivington, 1844), in four volumes.

The University of Michigan Press has granted permission to include certain passages in the general introduction which appeared originally in the editor's book, *Edmund Burke and the Natural Law* (Ann Arbor: University of Michigan Press, 1958).

I am grateful to Mrs. Bernice Winter of Detroit, Michigan, for her help in typing the manuscript and in proofreading the text.

Peter J. Stanlis

University of Detroit
March 1, 1963

Contents

Edmund Burke

1729	Born in Dublin, January 12.
1741	Educated at Ballitore.
1743–48	Educated at Trinity College, Dublin.
1746	Founded Trinity College Historical Society.
1747	Began to write *The Sublime and Beautiful*.
1748	Entered at the Middle Temple, London.
1750	Arrived in London to study law.
1756	*A Vindication of Natural Society*.
1757	Marriage with Jane Nugent.
	An Account of European Settlements in America.
	The Sublime and Beautiful.
	An Abridgment of English History (published in 1811).
	Newcastle Ministry.
1758	Birth of Burke's son, Richard.
	Became acquainted with Dr. Johnson and Reynolds.
1759	First *Annual Register* published (Burke continued as editor to 1765–66).
	Introduced to William Hamilton.
	Became acquainted with Hume.
1761	Bute Ministry.
	Spent winters, 1761–62 and 1762–63 in Dublin as Hamilton's assistant.
	Fragment on Irish Penal Laws (published posthumously).
1763	Grenville Ministry.
1763–64	Founded Literary Club with Dr. Johnson and Reynolds.
1765	First Rockingham Ministry.
	Secretary to Lord Rockingham.
	Elected to House of Commons for Wendover.
1766	Burke entered House of Commons.
	Chatham Ministry.
1768	Grafton Ministry.
	Burke purchased Gregories, estate at Beaconsfield.
1769	*Observations on Present State of Nation*.
1770	*Thoughts on Present Discontents*.
	North Ministry.
1771–74	Burke as agent for New York.
1772	Opposed Petition of Clergy against Subscription.
	Speech on Protestant Dissenters.

Edmund Burke: Selected Writings and Speeches

Introduction

I. BURKE'S EARLY LIFE

Edmund Burke was born on January 12, 1729, in Dublin, and died on July 9, 1797, at his country home in Beaconsfield, England, where he lies buried. His father was a modestly successful Irish attorney, descended from the family of the poet Edmund Spenser, and a member of the Church of England. His mother was of the eminent Irish Nagle family, and a Roman Catholic. Undoubtedly, Burke's mixed religious background played a key role in determining his whole intellectual, moral, aesthetic, and social temperament and character. Also, beginning in 1741, his education at Ballitore in County Kildare, at the school of a humane and liberal Quaker, Abraham Shackleton, contributed much toward Burke's sense of the pieties of life, and helped to shape his lifelong intense dislike of religious intolerance. Throughout his life Burke revealed a humanity toward *all* forms of sincere religious belief. For example, in 1781, when he learned that some Hindu Brahmins in London could not find the proper means of practicing the rituals of their faith, and had become the objects of derision of some rationalist freethinkers and wits, Burke placed his home at the disposal of the Hindus. Burke and his brother Richard were brought up in the Church of England; his sister was brought up as a Catholic, in the religion of his mother and maternal uncles. Burke always remained a loyal adherent of the Church of England, and defended her privileged position whenever she was attacked by freethinkers or dissenters. Yet he was intensely aware of the penal laws against Roman Catholics, and the civil disabilities against Protestant dissenters, and throughout his twenty-nine years in Parliament did his best to establish equal constitutional rights for British subjects of all faiths. He always believed that "all the three religions prevalent . . . in various parts of these islands, ought all, in subordination to the legal establishments, as they stand in the several countries, to be all countenanced, protected, and cherished." Burke's mixed religious background was undoubtedly an important factor in the interests and conduct of his public life. It also probably contributed strongly to his lifelong habit of reticence about his private life.

From 1743 to 1748 Burke attended Trinity College, Dublin, where he was a fellow student with Oliver Goldsmith. Burke received the usual liberal arts education of his time, centered in the study of such classical authors as Homer, Pindar, Aristotle, Virgil, Horace, Tacitus, Ovid, and Cicero. He found in Cicero an author whose thought and style appealed deeply to him, and quoted or alluded to Cicero more frequently than to any ancient writer. Aristotle's political thought also left a permanent positive effect on him. In 1746, as a junior, he commented upon his college education in a letter to his friend, Richard Shackleton (the son of Abraham Shackleton):

> *All my studies have rather proceeded from sallies of passion, than from the preference of sound reason; and, like all other natural appetites, have been very violent for a season, and very soon cooled, and quite absorbed in the succeeding. I have often thought it a humorous consideration to observe and sum up all the madness of this kind I have fallen into, this two years past. First, I was greatly taken with natural philosophy; which, while I should have given my mind to logic, employed me incessantly. This I call my* furor mathematicus. *But this worked off as soon as I began to read it in the college, as men by repletion cast off their stomachs all they have eaten. Then I turned back to logic and metaphysics. Here I remained a good while, and with much pleasure, and this was my* furor logicus, *a disease very common in the days of ignorance, and very uncommon in these enlightened times. Next succeeded the* furor historicus, *which also had its day, but is now no more, being entirely absorbed in the* furor poeticus.

Burke confessed that he spent "three hours almost every day in the public library," pursuing his regular studies in a "desultory and excursive" manner, and striving "to get a little into the accounts of this, our own poor country." Shortly after this period he founded a student debating club, which still exists today as the Trinity College Historical Society. The minute book of this debating society, mainly written by him, reveals his arguments in the undergraduate debates. Clearly, while at Trinity Burke acquired a substantial body of liberal knowledge and some literary skill, and laid the foundations of his future achievements in literature and politics.

As a freshman at Trinity, in his reaction to his text in logic, Burke first revealed what was to become a lifelong deep distrust of speculative mathematical reasoning in political and practical affairs. Like Swift many years earlier, he reacted violently against Bergersdicius's *Institutionum libri duo* (Leyden, 1626). This famous compendium was based upon refutations of Aristotle's *Organon* by the followers of Peter Ramus, a Calvinist French philosopher. Burke reacted with instinctive horror against such "metaphysicians" and "refining speculatists." To his friend Richard Shackleton he wrote: "Never look Burgy in the face! . . . The blackguard stuff, the hoard of exploded nonsense, the scum of pedantry and the refuse of the Boghouse school of Philosophy. . . . I assure you I stink of that crabbed stuff as any vile fresh. in the Univ. and I believe it will ruin me in my next examination." This youthful outburst is highly significant in the light of Burke's later constant opposition to the use of scholastic logic and mathematical reasoning in politics. In 1775 he invoked Aristotle in maintaining that neither *a priori* reasoning nor inductive empirical experience analytically arranged could ever attain a geometric certainty in moral and political affairs: "Man acts from adequate motives relative to his interests; and not on metaphysical speculations. Aristotle . . . cautions us against this species of delusive geometrical accuracy in moral arguments, as the most fallacious of all sophistry." One of the great themes of Burke's *Reflections* was to be that "in politics the most fallacious of all things [is] geometrical demonstration." It is important to note that as a college freshman he had rejected with disgust the use of scholastic and mathematical logic in practical affairs, and that as a junior he had considered the *furor logicus* "a disease very common in the days of ignorance," but "very uncommon in these enlightened times." To his great despair he was to learn better. But as an undergraduate he was blissfully unaware of the war he was to wage with the Cartesian rationalism of the "Enlightenment," which dominated eighteenth-century politics. After he entered Parliament in 1766 Burke discovered that even more than in "the days of ignorance" his "enlightened times" were addicted to an innovating *furor logicus* aimed at attaining mathematical accuracy in politics.

II. BURKE'S LEGAL ERUDITION

In 1748, just before Burke graduated from college, his father entered his name at the Middle Temple, and early in 1750, at age twenty-one, he was sent to London to study law. He was strongly repelled by the "narrow and contracted notions" of his teachers, whose methods were mechanical and whose aims were pragmatic and materialistic. Much to his father's displeasure, Burke soon abandoned his legal studies for a career in literature. Although he gave up formal study of the law, he nevertheless acquired early in life a profound and very extensive knowledge of European and English jurisprudence, from the ancient Roman law to the common law of England down to his own age. In 1780 Burke stated that since "very early youth" he had "been conversant in reading and thinking upon the subject of our laws and constitution, as well as upon those of other times and other countries." A decade before his death Burke stated in Parliament that he "had in the course of his life looked frequently into law books on different subjects." Undoubtedly, his initial interest in the law began at least by 1750, but his legal erudition grew and was well advanced long before he entered politics.

Burke's knowledge of the law is evidenced in the volumes in his library, which included the works of many writers, both ancient and modern, on Natural Law jurisprudence. Among 664 known items in his library were works containing discussions of Natural Law by Aristotle, such as his *Ethics* and *Politics* and by Cicero, such as *De officiis* and *De legibus*, all of which he read. There is the philosophy of Epictetus (known through his pupil, Flavius Arrian), and works by Francis Bacon, Coke, Delolme, Prynne, Blackstone, and many others, including such classics as Grotius's *On the Law of War and Peace*, Pufendorf's *On the Law of Nature and Nations*, and Vattel's *Droit des gens*. In a parliamentary report Burke once wrote that "much has been written by persons learned in the Roman law, particularly in modern times." Among the jurists who helped to form the Roman law Burke knew the work of Paulus and the Athenian, Callistratus; he was also familiar with Gravinia's *Origines juris civilis* and with the compilations of Justinian. All of these works on Roman jurisprudence breathe the spirit of Cicero and the Roman Stoics, and are based on the Classical Natural Law.

Among legal philosophers on the Continent, Burke had certainly read Sigonio's *De antiquo jure provinciarum,* Calvin's *Institutes of the Christian Religion,* Suarez' *Tractatus de legibus,* and the works of Grotius and Pufendorf. He made direct use of Montesquieu's *L'esprit des lois* and Vattel's *Droit des gens.* From the first he learned the historical method of treating ideas; the second was his most frequently quoted modern authority on the law of nations. Burke also knew the work of the famous Jansenist jurist, Jean Domat, whose *Civil Laws in Their Natural Order* established him, according to Burke's *Reflections* (1790), as "one of the greatest lawyers" in the French National Assembly.

Burke's particular awareness of English legal history and his general knowledge of the Natural Law were enormously increased by his role as editor and writer of Dodsley's *Annual Register,* from 1758 to at least 1765. In 1757 Burke wrote a fragmentary "Essay Towards an History of the Laws of England," as a supplement to his *Abridgment of English History.* His interest in English legal and constitutional thought was strongly reflected in the large number of book reviews on legal works which he wrote for the early numbers of the *Annual Register.* Burke certainly reviewed the following books on law that appeared in Britain from 1758 to 1765: Blackstone's *Discourses on the Study of Law* (1759), Wallace's *Laws of Scotland* (1760), Grey's *Debates of the House of Commons* (1763), and Elly's *Liberty of Subjects in England* (1765). He probably severed his official connection as editor of the *Annual Register* in 1765–66. Yet he reviewed Blackstone's *Commentaries* (1767–68), Beccaria's *Essay on Crimes and Punishments* (1767), Dalrymple's *Memoirs of Great Britain and Ireland* (1771), and Sullivan's *Lectures on the Feudal and English Laws* (1773). All of these reviews of books on law reveal that early in his public life Burke had acquired an encyclopedic knowledge of civil, criminal, constitutional, and Natural Law.

But his knowledge of the law is most clearly evident in his innumerable quotations and references to the ancient records, charters, legal treatises, statutes, procedures, and decisions which comprised the common law of England. In 1773 he said in Parliament: "I have studied . . . God knows: hard have I studied, even to the making dog-ears of almost every statute book in the kingdom . . . the letter as well as the spirit of the laws, the liberties, and the constitution of this country." Burke's references to the laws of England begin with Ina of Wessex, late in the seventh century, and continue through the long line of English kings from Alfred on, who recorded the body of common law precedents down to his own era. The enormous labor that he expended in mastering English law is well summarized by Arthur L. Woehl in his doctoral dissertation, "Burke's Reading" (Cornell University, 1928): "Burke evidently ransacked legal and historical documents of all kinds, including the Journals of the Lords and Commons, the Rolls and Laws of Parliament, State Trials, Statutes of Jeofails, Woodfall's Parliamentary Debates, the legal decisions of Chief-Barons and Justices Hardwicke, Willes, Parker, Raymond, Vaughan, Holt, Lee, Mansfield and Wilmot." In addition to reading these records and masters of English jurisprudence, he read widely and used digests of English common law.

While debating in the House of Commons, Burke frequently made good extemporaneous use of his legal knowledge: "In this part of his speech," the Commons clerk once recorded, "Mr. Burke entered into a detail of legal authority, which he traced so far back as the reign of Richard II, and followed up with different instances to the reign of George the First, with much learning and ingenuity." It is no exaggeration to say that from his early studies of the law he knew well the chief works on European jurisprudence, and especially on English common law, from the Code of Justinian down to his own time.

Among the great body of writers on English law there were several whom he particularly admired. "Bracton," he said in a speech, "is allowed by all to be a good authority," and Hooker was for Burke the great fountainhead of post-Reformation English canon law. Next to Cicero, no legal theorist had quite the same authority for him as Sir Edward Coke, whom he quotes nine times in his works and to whom he alludes in speeches more frequently—and in general with unreserved admiration—than to any other legal writer. In the *Reflections* Burke said that he venerated "Sir Edward Coke, that great oracle of our law, and indeed all the great men, who follow him, to Blackstone," because Coke had inspired his seventeenth-century successors in legal theory to give a strong moral and constitutional basis to English civil liberty under the common law. Among the men who followed Coke was Selden, whom Burke called "a great ornament of the common law." He also admired the moderate lawyers who produced the Revolution of 1688. Burke's interpretation of that important event was an important part of the opening section of the

Reflections and of *An Appeal from the New to the Old Whigs* (1791). In 1770 he said in the House of Commons: "No man here has a greater veneration than I have for the doctors of the law," and four years later, in his *Speech on American Taxation*, he voiced his greatest tribute to great lawyers and the law: "The law . . . is, in my opinion, one of the first and noblest of human sciences; a science which does more to quicken and invigorate the understanding than all other kinds of learning put together; but it is not apt, except in persons very happily born, to open and to liberate the mind in the same proportion." Burke always believed that nothing sharpened the mind as did the study of law; therefore, he cautioned his colleagues in March 1775 not to underestimate the resources of the American colonists, who had bought as many copies of Blackstone's *Commentaries* as the British: "This study renders men acute, inquisitive, dexterous, prompt in attack, ready in defence, full of resources." His legal erudition was so well known and highly respected in the House of Commons, his mastery of English common law was so complete, that his colleagues considered him the fittest man among them to handle the enormous legal problems entailed in the impeachment of Warren Hastings.

In summary, although Burke never concluded his formal legal studies, and was never admitted to the bar, his mastery of the laws of Europe and England was of the greatest practical value to him throughout his later political career. His great knowledge of law enhanced his value to the Rockingham Whigs. It is also important to note that his legal erudition, which includes the traditions of Natural Law, the law of nations, English common law, criminal law, and the precedents of prescription in positive law, all infuse and inform his political philosophy, his sense of Europe as a great commonwealth of nations with a common moral and legal inheritance, and his faith in the historical processes of tradition. It is therefore of the greatest importance, in reading Burke's writings and speeches, to keep in mind his legal erudition.

III. BURKE'S LITERARY CAREER

After abandoning his formal study of the law, Burke in his middle twenties turned to a career in literature. On March 12, 1757, he married Jane Nugent, the daughter of an eminent physician who had attended him during an illness. In anticipation of his marriage, as a means of supporting his family, literature and journalism offered Burke the double opportunity of making good use of his extensive store of knowledge and of developing his writing talents. It would also make him known in the London world of letters, which could open up new opportunities for advancement.

In May 1756 Burke became an author by publishing *A Vindication of Natural Society*. This work was an ironical satire on the religious rationalism of Lord Bolingbroke's "natural" religion, applied to society by an assumed antithesis between the "natural" and "artificial" political institutions of man. Burke's imitation of Bolingbroke's famous prose style was such a masterful parody that many readers took his satire as a posthumous work of Bolingbroke.

While still an undergraduate at Trinity, Burke had read "On the Sublime," ascribed to Longinus, and at about age nineteen, and certainly by 1747, he had sketched out the essentials of a similar speculative aesthetic study. Shortly after he published *A Vindication of Natural Society*, during the winter of 1756–57, he revised and completed this early work and published it on April 21, 1757, as *A Philosophical Inquiry into the Origin of our Ideas of the Sublime and Beautiful*. Burke's study was the earliest attempt to examine the psychological basis of art, originating in the variety of sensory observations rather than in deductions drawn from accepted "rules." In Britain, despite an adverse review by his friend Goldsmith in the *Monthly Review* (May 1757), Burke's pioneering effort brought him considerable immediate recognition. Burke's *Sublime and Beautiful* went through nine English editions during his lifetime. In Germany, Lessing translated and annotated Burke's aesthetic theory, and this helped to spread his fame on the Continent.

Burke's marriage and early literary activities led to the establishment of a household in Queen Anne Street, London, that included several persons besides Burke, his wife, and their son Richard, who was born on February 9, 1758. Mrs. Burke's father, Dr. Nugent, and for a while her brother, Jack Nugent, lived with them. They were joined by Burke's brother, Richard, who had recently come over from Ireland, and by Will Burke, a man whom Edmund described as his "kinsman." This entire family circle, known as "the Burkes," was always very congenial and intimate, and even at times shared a common purse in their economic necessities. Burke's relationship to Will Burke was particularly close. They even took excursions together in the country, for health and diversion.

It was largely through the generous help of Will Burke, who was on intimate terms with Lord Verney, that Burke was first able to enter the House of Commons in 1766.

Just before Burke published his *Sublime and Beautiful,* there appeared on April 12, 1757, an anonymous two-volume work called *An Account of the European Settlements in America.* Although the book was probably written largely by Will Burke, it appears that Edmund had a share in writing or revising it, and certainly he was thoroughly familiar with its contents. Fortunately, the work appeared when the Seven Years' War had brought political interest in America to a high level, so that in November 1757 a second edition was published, and before the end of the American Revolution seven editions had appeared. Although the book was weak in factual details concerning the Spanish, French, Portuguese, and English settlements in America, it revealed a sympathetic understanding of the problems of the European colonies. It emphasized particularly the blessings of political liberty enjoyed by the English colonies, and even warned against imposing too restrictive trade regulations. Also, in a manner that anticipated Burke's speeches eighteen years later, the author recognized the importance of the common bonds of language, culture, and economic interests that united the English colonies to Britain. Burke's share in writing the *European Settlements* may never be known, but it is clear that in contributing to this book he enriched his knowledge of the colonies and was aware of an attitude toward the problems of empire that he was to champion years later.

On April 24, 1758, Burke contracted with Robert Dodsley to "write, collect and compile" an annual book of about five hundred octavo pages, reviewing the year's "history, politics and literature." For this undertaking Burke received one hundred pounds. The first *Annual Register* was published in May 1759, and contained five sections edited by Burke, consisting of important state papers, character sketches drawn from books, fictional adventures, a literary miscellany of essays and scientific discoveries, and selected quotations of poetry. In addition, there were three sections of personal contributions by Burke—a historical account of the year's events, the book reviews, and a history of the Seven Years' War to that time. Beginning in 1762–63, there was a historical article covering the history of Europe for the previous year. Burke's labors on the *Annual Register* greatly extended his already broad and deep knowledge of the politics, science, and literature of his time, and sharpened his growing literary talents.

Burke's connection with the *Annual Register* deserves special notice beyond his function as general editor and his important contributions of book reviews and historical articles. Under Burke's editorship, the *Annual Register* was a brilliant success, and some of its early issues ran to nine editions. From the beginning Burke's journal was recognized as a valuable and objective historical source, and it has continued to be an influential journal for over two hundred years, down to the present. Yet Burke preferred to keep his connection with the *Annual Register* anonymous, even after he gave up being the active editor in 1765 or 1766. However, for the next thirty years the *Annual Register* continued to be edited and written by a succession of Burke's friends and political disciples. Thomas English (c. 1725–1798), who always retained Burke's highest confidence, replaced Burke as the chief active editor in 1766, and continued in this role for about thirty years. For about two decades, beginning in the early 1780's, English received much help from Walker King (c. 1755–1827), one of Burke's literary executors, who later edited half of Burke's collected works, and also from his brother John King. Two other close friends, Dr. French Laurence, and his brother Richard, also wrote for the *Annual Register*. Therefore, although Burke gave up his official connection with the *Annual Register* soon after he entered Parliament, throughout the rest of his life he continued to exercise considerable control over the policy of the journal he had founded. A comparison between Burke's speeches in Parliament and articles in the *Annual Register* dealing with the same subjects reveals a great similarity in the ideas and temper, so that it is clear the *Annual Register* remained a valuable literary asset for Burke's political and party interests.

During the first year of work on the *Annual Register*, 1758–59, Burke also worked on his "Essay towards an Abridgment of the English History," but it was never completed beyond the reign of King John, and was published posthumously in 1811. However, through such literary activities, and his friendship with the Dodsleys, in his first decade in England Burke became well known among the chief lights in the London literary and theatrical world. He enjoyed the close friendships of Arthur Murphy and David Garrick for over two decades. At Robert Dodsley's shop, under the sign of Tully's Head, Burke met Thomas Warton, professor of poetry at Oxford, and his brother Joseph, a well-known literary critic, both prominent in the growing movement in Romantic literature. Burke also came to know well the minor Romantic poet William Shenstone. About 1758 Burke met two of his most cherished friends, Dr. Samuel Johnson and Sir Joshua Reynolds. With them, in the winter of 1763–64, he helped to found the famous Literary Club of the Johnson circle, which met for good food and delightful talk at seven o'clock every Monday evening at the Turk's Head on Gerard Street. On several occasions Burke had Christmas dinner with Arthur Murphy, Dr. Johnson, and Garrick. In 1758, at the home of Reynolds, Burke renewed acquaintance with his Trinity College colleague, Oliver Goldsmith. Among other members of the Johnson circle whom Burke came to know was Mrs. Elizabeth Carter, the great master of languages, in 1756, and Bennet Langton, in 1758. Mrs. Elizabeth Montagu, the very wealthy "Queen" of the bluestocking set, welcomed Burke cordially within her Mayfair circle, and was pleased to introduce him among her many influential friends. Even a decade later, when she wrote her famous essay on Shakespeare (1769), she valued Burke's literary judgment enough to consult him about it. Mrs. Vesey, another bluestocking, was instrumental through her husband in bringing about not only a "reconciliation" between Burke and his father, over the lapsed law studies, but a much-needed remittance as well. In 1759, through his *Sublime and Beautiful,* Burke secured the high regard of David Hume and Lord Lyttleton. A good summary description of how Burke struck some of his contemporaries is provided by Horace Walpole. On July 22, 1761, Walpole wrote to George Montagu of having dined with David Garrick. There he met "a young Mr. Burk, who wrote a book in the style of Lord Bolingbroke that was much admired. He is a sensible man, but has not worn off his authorism yet—and thinks there is nothing so charming as writers and to be one—he will know better one of these days." In short, at age thirty-two, after a decade in England, Burke was recognized and accepted as an eager, bright, successful, and rising writer.

IV. BURKE'S PROSE STYLE

The literary qualities which later made Burke famous as an orator and master of prose style were already fully developed by the early 1760's. Burke's successful parody of Bolingbroke's masterful English prose in 1756 shows that he had brought his own power over words and language to a high degree of perfection. Burke's contemporaries show remarkable agreement about his powers of oral and written expression. According to Dr. Johnson, the chief characteristic of Burke's conversation was "copiousness and fertility of allusion, a power of diversifying his matter by placing it in various relations." Johnson admired Burke's sheer weight of knowledge and "the ebullition of his mind." Johnson noted that "his stream of mind is perpetual. He talks not from a desire to excel, but because his mind is full." After hearing Burke speak in the House of Commons, Boswell wrote: "It was astonishing how all kinds of figures of speech crowded upon him. He was like a man in an orchard where boughs loaded with fruit hung around him, and he pulled apples as fast as he pleased and pelted the ministry." Seven months before Burke's death, during Christmas 1796, Sir James Mackintosh visited him and recorded his observations: "[I] found Burke, despite his infirmities, playing with children on the carpet, rolling about with them and pouring out in his gambols the sublimest images, mingled with the most wretched puns." When he left Beaconsfield Mackintosh was so impressed with Burke's powers of conversation that he remarked "Gibbon might have been cut out of a corner of Burke's mind without anyone noticing the excision." Gibbon himself, who disliked Burke's Christian orthodoxy, called him "the most eloquent and rational madman that I ever knew." Reynolds and Malone thought him superior to Johnson, both as a thinker and conversationalist. Johnson himself, despite his partisan political differences with Burke, paid a generous tribute to his friend and called him "the first man in the House of Commons . . . the first man everywhere." Johnson also noted that he was "the *only* man whose common conversation corresponds with the fame which he has in the world," because "the pulse beat [is] higher in Burke's tongue at two o'clock in the morning than in that of any other man at nine at night." On one occasion when Johnson was ill he refused to see Burke because he feared the excitement of Burke's talk would cause a relapse. Johnson added that if a stranger were to stop under a shed during a shower, and found himself with Burke, upon leaving he would say to himself that he had been with a most remarkable man. Boswell took special pains in his *Life of Johnson* that Burke should not supplant Johnson in the center of the stage. Therefore Burke is seldom mentioned by name, but is commonly introduced as "an eminent friend of ours," or as "one of the most luminous minds of the present age," or some such expression.

But the most remarkable insight into the unique manner of Burke's thought and expression came from Goldsmith, who once remarked in conversation that Burke "wound into his subject like a serpent." This simile reflects perfectly Burke's most characteristic method of treating a subject—his mind grasped it, penetrated to its core, and enveloped it in a three-dimensional hold that included his senses, his intuitional reason, and his emotions and imagination. His desire to grasp the whole reality of life lay behind his complex style of expression. His conviction that "reason is but a part of human nature" made him distrust a merely rational or logical approach to any subject, and to suspect easy definitions. In his "Essay on Taste," prefixed to the second edition of his *Sublime and Beautiful* (1759), he wrote: "When we define, we seem in danger of circumscribing nature within the bounds of our notions . . . instead of extending our ideas to take in all that Nature comprehends, according to her manner of combining." In a sketch called "The Character of a Fine Gentleman," written between 1750–54 and now found in the Burke papers in the Sheffield City Library in England, he wrote: "A character is too complex a thing to be drawn into a definition. We may acquire a much better idea of it from viewing it in as great a variety of lights as the subject will bear." The same principle in handling a subject, by combining all the various ways it can be considered, is also found in Burke's three-page listing of details in "A Plan for Arguing," which was written during this period. In short, Burke's prose style appeals to the total nature of man and comprehends the whole reality of each subject. This is the main point in Edward Dowden's summary of what distinguished Burke's prose style from that of most other good writers:

> *In a well-known canon of style Burke lays it down that the master sentence of every paragraph should involve, first, a thought, second, an image, and thirdly, a sentiment. The rule . . . expresses the character of his mind. A thought, an image, a sentiment, and all bearing upon action—it gives us an intimation that the writer who set forth such a canon was a complete nature, no fragment of a man . . . and that when he came to write or speak, he put his total manhood into his utterance. This is, indeed, Burke's first and highest distinction.*

Burke did indeed appeal to man's reason, to the senses and emotions, but the mere presence of these ingredients in his speeches and writings did not, in themselves, make his style great. His imaginative fusion of all these ingredients, his skill in converting an image into a state of mind and feeling, enabled his readers to leap from sight to insight, from the physical sense to the metaphysical essence of his subject or theme, so that at once they saw, understood, and felt profoundly the point of his argument.

Among his predecessors in English literature, Burke esteemed John Dryden's prose style very highly. Dryden's prose embodied all the best qualities but none of the vices of excessive ornateness of his chief seventeenth-century predecessors, such as John Donne, Robert Burton, Isaak Walton, and Sir Thomas Browne. Dryden's colloquial ease and manly vigor, his copiousness, amplitude, and variety, the energetic power of his sure accents, are all found in Burke's writing, but greatly heightened by his more intense and elastic intelligence, and by a richer texture in his range of learning. The parallelism, balance, and antithesis in the structure of Dryden's prose, which give his rhythms their characteristic cadence and tone, are also found in his style, but complicated by a greater use of expanded analogies and sustained comparisons. Burke's prose appears more discursive than Dryden's, because it is more complex in the structure of its form and the texture of its technique. Also, he is much more the poet in his prose than was Dryden. His writing contains far more figures of speech, images, similes, simple and extended metaphors, etc., all of which are functional in illuminating his theme. As John Morley noted, Burke was a great phrasemaker, because "even in the coolest and driest of his pieces there is the mark of greatness, of grasp, of comprehension. . . . In the midst of discussions on the local and the accidental, he scatters apophthegms that take us into the regions of lasting wisdom." If Swift is the greatest master of the simple style, and Dryden's predecessors perfected the ornate style, Burke can be considered the most polished writer in the complex style. In the literature of enduring power, Thomas De Quincey, Edward Bulwer-Lytton, Sir Leslie Stephen, Matthew Arnold, John Morley, and James Russell Lowell all considered Burke the foremost writer of English prose.

V. BURKE'S POLITICAL CAREER

Early in 1759 an event occurred which diverted Burke from the literary career he was pursuing, and placed him on the road that led ultimately to his career in politics. Either through Joseph Warton or his friend Lord Charlemont, he was introduced to William Gerard Hamilton, a wealthy young man exactly his own age, with influential connections, already in Parliament, and with ambitions to go much further in politics. Hamilton soon noted Burke's outstanding talents in literature and extensive knowledge of public affairs, and immediately recognized the value of having such a man as Burke in his service. He offered Burke political patronage in exchange for an informal personal arrangement which included duties as his private secretary and political assistant. The financial terms of their arrangement are unknown, although several years later, after they had quarreled, Hamilton wrote a note to himself: "Took Mr. B. up, unknown £2,000," and added, "Did I ever refuse him money." Whatever the terms, whether a salary or gifts, Burke needed money and accepted Hamilton's offer, on condition he would be free during summers for his literary work. Their relationship lasted almost six years. It was finally dissolved after a bitter argument which grew out of Hamilton's attempt to bind Burke to him more firmly and completely, through a pension of three hundred pounds per year drawn on the Irish establishment, and Burke's refusal to give up his independence.

In April 1761, while Burke and Hamilton were on very good terms, the Earl of Halifax was made Lord Lieutenant of Ireland, and appointed Hamilton as his secretary. Hamilton knew that Burke's extensive knowledge of Ireland would be very valuable to him, and induced him to accompany him back to his native land as his secretary. After eleven years in England, Burke was pleased to return to Ireland in a position of influence. He and his family lived in Dublin Castle for the winters of 1761–62 and 1762–63, returning to London during the summers.

During the autumn of 1761, while in Ireland with Hamilton, Burke began to compose his *Tracts Relative to the Laws against Popery in Ireland*. This important work reveals much that is most significant in the development of Burke's political philosophy. Yet it remained a fragment and was not published until after his death in 1797. His other writings up to this time made clear the historical basis of his political conservatism, his reverence for the processes of history, the continuity of social traditions, and the prescriptive and legal foundations of civil society. But in his tract on the Popery laws, for the first time he set forth the essential moral and philosophical principles of his later political philosophy, based on the Natural Law.

Burke's Irish experience under Hamilton was a sound initiation into politics and a necessary prelude to what was probably the most important political decision of his life—his identification of himself with the Rockingham Whigs. This connection led directly to a life in politics and a career in the House of Commons from 1766 to 1794. Very shortly after his quarrel with Hamilton, Burke was recommended by William Fitzherbert to the Marquis of Rockingham. On July 10, 1765, shortly after the fall of the Grenville ministry, George III reluctantly made Rockingham Prime Minister. Within a week of this event Burke became Rockingham's private secretary. Late in 1765 Burke was elected to the House of Commons for Wendover, and took his seat for the session of 1766. For the next seventeen years, until Rockingham's death in 1782, Burke and Rockingham remained the closest of personal friends and political associates. Burke soon became the intellectual guide, the public voice in the Commons, and the official pamphleteer of the Rockingham branch of the Whig party.

To many of Burke's close literary friends it appeared that he was giving up to politics and to party what was meant for mankind. In reality, he was exchanging a precarious *belles lettres* literary career, and journalistic hack work, for Rockingham's secure political patronage and a stormy political life. In his new public life, Burke's literary talents were to truly serve mankind, not in the closeted security of ornamental, reflective, "pure" literature, but in the far more challenging context of the broad stage of the world, in the practical affairs of the American colonies, Ireland, England, India, and France. But before summarizing his active political career it is important briefly to note several points, often overlooked, concerning the relationship between Burke's literary career and his new life in party politics.

Certain twentieth-century historians, particularly of the Namier school, have sometimes charged Burke with pure political expediency and calculated self-interest in the arguments he advanced in defense of the Rockingham party. These charges are made on the assumption that he created his arguments *ad hoc,* to serve some political occasion at the time they were advanced. But no just appraisal of Burke's partisan political arguments, both in and out of the House of Commons, can be made without studying the political convictions he had expressed in his early literary works, prior to entering politics in 1765. The influence of his education and reading in classical literature and the law is evident in his political philosophy, and these are important factors in his career in active politics. Burke's reading, as reflected in his early writings, was an immense factor in ripening his political thought and in preparing him for the ideas he was to advance in the rough-and-tumble partisan politics of his era. His reading infused a humanistic temper into his political principles, and lifted his approach to politics above the ordinary mechanical formulas and processes of his time.

Throughout Burke's *Abridgment of English History* (1757) and the early volumes of the *Annual Register* (1759–65), his veneration for the historical diversity and continuity of civil society, so like that of Montesquieu, is everywhere evident. He stressed the importance of legal prescription and the common law, of a balanced growth and change, combining past inheritance and present needs, and of the "wisdom of our ancestors," as embodied in living social traditions and civil manners. In these early works he had voiced his faith in the gradual development of a constitutional system of government in England, based on the principle of the division of power within and between Church and State, and aimed at establishing the maximum of civil liberty, under which man as a political animal could fulfill his highest capabilities in the corporate life of his society. In addition to these vital appeals to the historical inheritance of society, in his *Tract on the Popery Laws* Burke had set forth the cardinal philosophical principles of his conception of man and civil society, centered in the ethical norms and political sovereignty of the Natural Law. Thus, his three early literary works reveal that history as a preceptor of prudence, and the Natural Law as an ethical norm, provided him with the two most important positive ingredients in his mature political philosophy.

But perhaps of equal significance, Burke's youthful satire on Bolingbroke also reveals the negative side of his later political philosophy—his extreme distrust toward the two most important political traditions against which he was to struggle throughout his life. Long before he entered Parliament, he had rejected the *a priori*, abstract, analytical type of reasoning in politics, centered in mathematical logic and metaphysical speculation, as represented by Descartes, Hobbes, and Locke. Burke always looked with deep distrust on any speculative theories which aimed at human perfectibility through scientific methodology, or through a rearrangement of social machinery. In his book reviews of Rousseau's early work, he rejected wholly the antithesis between "art" and "Nature," and the assumed doctrine of the natural or instinctive goodness of man in a supposed state of nature, before history or without civil society. His early literary writings prove that even before he entered politics he had allied himself firmly to the ancient Classical and Christian view of man and society, and had declared war on both the scientific rationalism and the Romantic sensibility of the Enlightenment philosophy of man and society. The arguments he used to criticize the ministers of George III, and the ideas which fill his speeches and writings on government from 1765 to his death in 1797, reveal that he remained consistent to this position throughout his life.

Burke's active political career extended from 1765 to 1794, and involved him actively in the affairs of the American colonies, Ireland, economic reforms and parliamentary reforms in England, India, and revolutionary France. Except for a year in 1765–66 and a few months in 1782, when the Rockingham Whigs were in power, most of his twenty-nine years in the House of Commons were spent in opposition to the administrations of George III, on behalf of unpopular causes which almost always, at least at the time, went down to defeat. His opposition to the innovating policy to tax the American colonies, initiated by the Grenville ministry in 1764 and supported thereafter by George III, met with no success. Yet John Morley wrote of Burke's writings and speeches on American colonial affairs: "They compose the most perfect manual in our literature or in any literature, for one who approaches the study of public affairs, whether for knowledge or for practice. They are an example without fault of all the qualities which the critic, whether a theorist or an actor, of great political situations should strive by night and by day to possess." Burke also fought for twenty-nine years against the whole English system of government which proscribed Ireland and prevented her from enjoying the benefits of the English constitution. What little economic freedom Ireland gained during the eighteenth century, to develop her industry and commerce, came from the constant efforts of Burke and his friends. His attempts to bring relief to the Catholics of Ireland from the tyrannical penal laws were largely unsuccessful, but his principles were gradually fulfilled after his death. His bill in 1780 to reform the abuses of royal patronage was defeated, although a modified and largely ineffectual measure was passed in 1782. After Rockingham's death in that year, Burke's once eminent position in the House of Commons rapidly declined. Although he succeeded in impeaching Warren Hastings, Governor General of India, for misgovernment in India, the trial ended in acquittal before the House of Lords, and at best Burke's efforts served as a warning to future British governors. His opposition to the radicals and liberal Whigs who wished to reform the representation of the House of Commons earned him the intense enmity of many members of his own party. The great crisis of the French Revolution further alienated him and the "new Whigs," who followed Charles James Fox, while Burke led the anti-revolution old Whigs into a coalition with the Tory party of Pitt the Younger.

By the vulgar standards of immediate success and external appearances, it would seem that Burke's political career was largely wasted in serving lost causes. But in his constant efforts to establish an orderly, just, and free society, under constitutional and moral law, he set forth the vital ideas and principles of his political philosophy, which has continued to influence men throughout history long after the partisan causes which triumphed over him were buried in the graveyard of dead politics. But before considering Burke's living political philosophy it will be worthwhile to examine briefly the one outstanding personal triumph Burke achieved during his lifetime—his writings on the French Revolution, which won most of the British nation, and much of Europe, to his interpretation of that event.

VI. BURKE AND THE FRENCH REVOLUTION

The French Revolution is without question one of the two or three most important historical events of modern times, and signalized a great and enduring change in the world's affairs. Burke's sympathetic position toward the American Revolution has in general met with the warm approval of posterity, but his intense opposition to the French Revolution has been the subject of intense controversy ever since his publication of the *Reflections on the Revolution in France* (1790). The most frequent charge of his critics has been that after a lifetime of defending the oppressed, in America, Ireland, India, and at home, he betrayed his love of liberty by defending the old regime in France, and in so doing was inconsistent with the political principles he had always professed.

This charge of inconsistency shows an ignorance of Burke or the French Revolution or both. When Coleridge finally came to understand him he stated that Burke's principles always remained the same. John Morley disposed of this charge as follows: "There is no difference in social spirit and doctrine between his protests against the maxims of the English common people as to the colonists, and his protests against the maxims of the French common people as to the court and the nobles; and it is impossible to find a single principle either asserted or implied in the speeches on the American revolution which was afterwards repudiated in the writings on the revolution in France." It was not that Burke was inconsistent in principle, but that the sources of oppression in the two revolutions were altogether different—in the American, from the King and Parliament against the colonies, and in the French, from the revolutionaries, in the name of the people, against the King, nobles, clergy, and the whole legal, social, political, religious, and economic inheritance of France, and even of all Europe. As Morley said, Burke "changed his front, but he never changed his ground." Woodrow Wilson also defended Burke's consistency: "He was applying the same principles to the case of France and to the case of India that he had applied to the case of the colonies." The key to his consistency is his insistence that civil liberty, in whatever form of government, is under a political sovereignty based on Natural Law. "If I were to describe slavery," he once wrote, "I would say with those who hate it, it is living under will, not under law." This principle applied equally to the Americans and the Irish, living under the arbitrary will of George III's ministers, to the people of India under Hastings' oligarchical arbitary will, and to the French, under the arbitrary "general will" of the National Assembly. Burke opposed Dr. Price, Priestley, and Paine, and the revolutionaries in France, on exactly the same grounds on which he had opposed George III and Warren Hastings.

Another common charge against Burke's position toward the French Revolution is that although undoubtedly his political principles were the same as ever, he did not know enough about the specific economic and social evils existing in France to apply his principles validly. Although he knew more about the internal conditions of France than most of his contemporaries in England, this charge is true in those cases where his knowledge was insufficient. But the same objection applies to those who favored the Revolution without sufficient historical knowledge. But the issue of Burke and the French Revolution is not to be settled by considering the condition of France in 1789. As he noted in the *Reflections,* when the Revolution began practically all men were of one mind that the existing order needed badly to be reformed, so that long-standing economic and social inequities could be eliminated, and a more free, just, and well-ordered society established. But after the clergy, nobility, and third estate were merged into a unicameral National Assembly, with votes told by the head, serious differences arose among the members—differences in philosophical principles, in the methods of procedure for reforms, in the substantive content of what was to be reformed, and in the great ultimate objects to be realized by the Revolution. It is in these vital areas that Burke found himself more and more alienated from the French Revolution, and it is in these areas that we are to look for the reasons why he became the greatest single antagonist of the Revolution.

As the course of the French Revolution gradually unfolded, Burke became convinced that it was aimed not at reforming the ills of the existing society of France, but at destroying the whole inherited structure and order of European civilization, and of the principles on which European institutions stood. In short, the Revolution was a movement founded on an entirely new and revolutionary theory of man and civil society. Burke was the first public man in Europe to perceive the ideological basis of the Revolution, centered in a materialistic conception of man and a mechanistic conception of society. In this, and in its spirit, it differed completely from the moderate English Revolution of 1688 and in essentials from the American Revolution of 1775. These earlier revolutions modified certain details in the structure of society, or in the means of succession to power and the methods of administrating government. Otherwise, they were in perfect conformity with the common law of England, and with the religion, laws, manners, and customs of basic European institutions.

The principles and the fanatical spirit of the French Revolution were precisely the things Burke had always feared and opposed. The Revolution, he noted in the *Reflections,* involved primarily "a revolution in sentiments, manners, and moral opinions." In his *Thoughts on French Affairs* (1791),

he called it "a revolution of doctrine and theoretical dogma."
In a letter to his son, written in November 1792, Burke called
the Revolution "an event which has nothing to match it, or in
the least to resemble it, in history." He believed that the Revolution violated "the whole system of policy on which the general state of Europe has hitherto stood," that the revolutionists
wished to make themselves "paramount to every known principle of public law in Europe," and that they sought to establish "principles subversive of the whole political, civil, and
religious system of Europe." In his *Letter to a Noble Lord*
(1795), he referred to the Revolution as "a subject of awful
meditation. Before this of France," he continued, "the annals
of all time have not furnished an instance of a *complete* revolution. That Revolution seems to have extended even to the
constitution of the mind of man." Also in 1796, in his second
Letter on a Regicide Peace, Burke said that "a silent revolution in the moral world preceded the political, and prepared
it." Burke summarized his impressions of the strange and
powerful effect the Revolution had produced on the imaginations of men; he found it "a vast, tremendous, unformed
spectre" which "subdued the fortitude of man," and went
"straight forward to its end, unappaled by peril, unchecked by
remorse, despising all common maxims and all common
means." For him, the events of 1789 initiated "a revolution
in dogma"; they were "a total departure . . . from every one
of the ideas and usages, religious, legal, moral, or social, of
this civilized world." So catastrophic was the French Revolution that it compelled Burke, against his will and temperament, to become a political philosopher in defense of the traditional principles of European civilized society.

Undoubtedly, Burke achieved the most notable success of
his life with the publication of his justly famous work, *Reflections on the Revolution in France,* which appeared in November 1790. He took exactly a year to write this book. As a
literary composition, despite its discursiveness and unevenness,
it is his greatest single claim to enduring fame, and its historical importance can hardly be overestimated. Alfred Cobban
did not exaggerate in calling the *Reflections* "the greatest and
most influential political pamphlet ever written." If we consider only Burke's immediate practical intention—to warn his
countrymen and Europeans who cherished a Christian and
Natural Law conception of civil society against the rationalism
and the *a priori,* speculative, anti-historical ideology and doctrinaire spirit underlying the Revolution, the *Reflections* was

the most successful book of the eighteenth-century "Enlightenment," and it was almost totally opposed to the prevailing spirit of the age.

Before the *Reflections* appeared, the predominant attitude in Britain toward the Revolution was one of amazement and enthusiastic satisfaction that the French were emancipating themselves from the tyranny of the old regime, which had been Britain's chief enemy for centuries, and which had helped the rebellious Americans gain their independence. Burke's *Reflections* shattered this facile view of the French Revolution. So clearly and eloquently did he analyze the basic issues and social theories raised by the Revolution, that the people of Britain were almost immediately divided into two distinct groups for or against it. The first British edition sold twelve thousand copies in the first month; in less than a year there were eleven editions, and by 1796 over thirty thousand official copies had been sold. For that era, when a book was circulated among many readers and was frequently read to public groups, this was a phenomenal achievement. So remarkable was the immediate effect of the *Reflections* that it became the focal point for all private and public discussions of the Revolution. Wilberforce, the ardent advocate of emancipation for slaves, praised Burke as the man who "had stood between the living and the dead until the plague was stayed." Reynolds and Gibbon greatly admired the *Reflections,* the latter writing of it: "Burke's book is an admirable medicine against the French disease. I admire his eloquence; I approve his politics; I adore his chivalry; and I can almost forgive his reverence for church establishments." In November 1796, Earl Fitzwilliam wrote to Burke and estimated the practical effect his *Reflections* and other writings on French affairs had produced in Britain: "You, my dear Burke, by the exertion of your great powers, have carried three-fourths of the public. . . . Your labours . . . have produced an effect in the country beyond expectation." The French translation, reputed to have been done in part by the imprisoned Louis XVI, enjoyed an even greater contemporary triumph throughout Europe. In over a century and a half the *Reflections* and Burke's other writings on the French Revolution have been studied extensively, and remain as great a source of political wisdom as when they first appeared.

Over forty replies were written to Burke's *Reflections* in Britain, and his book was the center of perhaps the greatest debate ever carried on in English over the first principles of

politics. Almost from the beginning he knew that the old
"Christian commonwealth of Europe" was under attack by the
coming age of "sophisters, economists, and calculators," and
that the French Revolution had permanently altered the inherited traditional order of Europe. In this he saw the inscrutable hand of Divine intervention in human affairs, and in
Thoughts on French Affairs (1791), he wrote one of his most
memorable passages accepting this fact: "If a great change
is to be made in human affairs, the minds of men will be fitted
to it, the general opinions and feelings will draw that way.
Every fear, every hope, will forward it; and then they who
persist in opposing this mighty current in human affairs will
appear rather to resist the decrees of Providence itself than
the mere designs of men. They will not be resolute and firm,
but perverse and obstinate." This passage shows Burke's acceptance of the coming historical changes that the French Revolution had wrought; but he never accepted the political
principles of the Revolution, principles which were the very
reverse of his own political philosophy.

VII.   INTERPRETATIONS OF BURKE'S POLITICAL PHILOSOPHY

Since Burke's death in 1797 a great many scholars have discussed in great detail various aspects of his basic political principles, and there has been a broad range of interpretations
placed on his political philosophy. Considering the complexity
of his thought, the large number of political and historical issues in which he was involved, and the changing patterns of
philosophical belief among his scholars, it is not surprising that
at various times Burke has been claimed by both liberals and
conservatives. In general, his nineteenth-century commenta-
tors interpreted him as a liberal; during the past several decades most writers on Burke have found in him the great
founder of modern political conservatism. A descriptive account of the various important interpretations of his political
philosophy over the past century should be of great value to
every reader of this volume.

It is a commonplace of scholarship on Burke that his political genius consisted of an extraordinary ability to understand the complex relationships between the constantly changing empirical and historical conditions of practical politics,
and the basic principles of common morality. During most of
the nineteenth century, and until around 1940, studies of

Burke's political philosophy have been concerned mainly with what has been called the "empirical," "utilitarian," and "pragmatic" elements in his thought, or with the historical rather than the ethical foundations of his politics. His own explicit words, that "the principles of true politics are those of morality enlarged," have been generally subordinated to non-ethical considerations.

Ever since Henry Buckle published *The History of Civilization in England* (1857–61), it has been universally assumed by utilitarian and positivist writers, and by some Christian humanists, that Burke's political philosophy rests upon a purely empirical, utilitarian, and pragmatic foundation. John Morley, the outstanding Victorian disciple of Bentham and Mill, and the recognized authority on Burke during the late nineteenth century, wrote two books on him, in which he emphasized "Burke's utilitarian liberalism," and praised him for having overthrown "the baneful superstition that politics . . . is a province of morals." According to Morley, Burke refused "to reason downwards from high sounding ideas of Right, Sovereignty, Property, and so forth," because such ideas "have no invariable conformity to facts, and . . . are only treated with reverence because they are absurdly supposed to be ultimate, eternal entities." Thus Morley interpreted him as a political liberal and relativist, whose strict regard for "circumstances," "expediency," and "prudence" made "the standard of convenience," rather than appeals to absolute ethical principles, the ultimate foundation of his politics.

The path charted by Morley's interpretation of Burke was followed, with some slight variations, by William Lecky, Sir Leslie Stephen, and a whole host of Victorian and early twentieth-century writers in the liberal tradition of politics. Charles E. Vaughan, a learned political scientist and recognized authority on Burke, applied the usual Benthamite antithesis between "natural rights" and "expediency," and concluded that in Burke's politics "the last appeal is not to Rights but to expediency." Vaughan noted that Burke's "expediency" differed from that of Hume and Bentham, because it was qualified by "higher principles" and "a tissue of moral and religious ideals," but like Morley, he concluded that Burke made "expediency the ultimate principle of politics." In 1913, John MacCunn, an excellent Burke scholar, also argued that Burke was a utilitarian, and concluded: "To Burke, as to Bentham, all rights . . . are not ultimate but derivative." Elie Halévy supplied a variation on this theme in 1928: "From a utilitarian

philosophy Burke deduced an anti-democratic political theory.
. . . The utilitarian morality led Burke to social views which
were profoundly different from those to which it led Bentham." In 1934, Lois Whitney, a noted eighteenth-century literary scholar, contended: "Priestley, Burke, and Bentham are
in harmony in their utilitarianism, Burke developing the doctrine in the form of a philosophy of expediency." Two years
later, Henry V. S. Ogden, in a Ph.D. thesis, extended this
common conviction concerning Burke: "The repudiation of
natural rights was implicit not only in his utilitarian conviction
that the end of government is the happiness and welfare of
the people governed, but also in his reliance on experience and
in his rejection of all abstract doctrines of political theory.
. . . Burke's opposition to the theory of natural rights and
to the use of nature as the norm in political theory was . . .
a conviction unshaken during his whole career." In 1940,
John H. Randall repeated this point, and during the 1940's
two other writers on Burke, Annie M. Osborn and John A.
Lester, added their voices to this chorus of scholars who supposed he was a utilitarian, a relativist, and a pragmatist in his
political philosophy.

Thus, for the past century scholars in the liberal tradition
of politics have always interpreted Burke's political philosophy
by resorting to formulas based on "utility" versus "natural
rights," and have interpreted his frequent attacks on metaphysical abstract rights as a rejection of belief in absolute
moral principles. They have made much of his strict regard
for "circumstances," and have praised his "expediency" and
"prudence," and his appeals to consider the practical consequences of following a given political policy to its logical but
fatal conclusion. All these elements in his political thought
have been praised by liberal writers as the ultimate in political
wisdom, and the basis for his enduring appeal.

Certain conservative writers, such as Professor Richard M.
Weaver, have accepted the utilitarian and pragmatic frame of
reference of those who have interpreted Burke as a liberal,
and have denied that he has any real claim to be considered
a conservative political philosopher:

> *Burke is widely respected as a conservative who was intelli-*
> *gent enough to provide solid philosophical foundations for*
> *his conservatism. It is perfectly true that many of his ob-*
> *servations upon society have a conservative basis; but if one*
> *studies the kind of argument which Burke regularly employed*
> *when at grips with concrete policies, one discovers a strong*

*addiction to the argument from circumstance. Now . . . the
argument from circumstance is the argument philosophically
appropriate to the liberal. Indeed, one can go much further
and say that it is the argument fatal to conservatism.*

Since Burke always argued from circumstances, rather than
from "the nature of things," Professor Weaver concluded that
"Burke should not be taken as prophet by the political conservatives." The basic assumption in this argument is that
Burke argued *only* from circumstances, and that his strict
regard for circumstances is merely a matter of empirical observation and rational analysis, and wholly disconnected from
any legal or ethical principles. Professor Weaver interprets
Burke's principle of political prudence in the same way as
Morley and Lord Acton, both of whom identified his "prudence" with the calculated expediency of utilitarianism, and
did not note its vital connection with legal equity and with the
ethical norms of the Natural Law in his political philosophy.

Quite apart from the utilitarian and liberal tradition of
Morley, many recent writers who have claimed Burke as a
conservative have laid great stress upon the historical elements
in his political philosophy. They have emphasized the importance of his appeals to social traditions and manners, to legal
prescription and laws, to his passion for liberty connected with
civil order and legal justice, to his veneration of "the wisdom
of our ancestors," as embodied in Church and State, to his
defense of the constitutional safeguards to life, liberty, and
property, to his praise of "prejudice" and duty as against abstract reason and "rights," and to his conception of man as a
civil or political animal, who finds his self-fulfillment in the
gradually unfolding corporate life of his nation. This conception of Burke as a historical conservative takes into stricter
account a larger number of the ingredients found in his political philosophy, as these were discussed by Burke in his concern with the practical issues of his age, so that this view of
his politics has illuminated many of the most vital principles in
his complex thought. Yet the ultimate basis of Burke's political philosophy, as he himself made clear in an important
passage, is not to be found in history or in legal prescription,
but in moral principles:

*My principles enable me to form my judgment upon men and
actions in history, just as they do in common life, and are
not formed out of events and characters, either present or
past. History is a preceptor of prudence, not of principles.*

The principles of true politics are those of morality enlarged; and I neither now do, nor ever will, admit of any other.

In the light of this key passage it is clear that all the elements perceived by utilitarian liberals and historical conservatives in Burke's political thought do not in themselves alone, or in any combination, constitute the ultimate principles of his political philosophy. Some account must also be given to his normative moral principles. Writers who have converted the empirical and historical elements in his thought into his basic political philosophy have invariably reduced the scope and complexity of his thought to the measure of their own ideas and temperament. Thus, both liberals and conservatives have praised or condemned Burke for insufficient reasons, on a consideration of those parts of his political philosophy which fitted or failed to fit into their own thought.

Since history is descriptive, not normative; since, as Burke said, "history is a preceptor of prudence, not of principles," to fully understand the basis of his political philosophy it is necessary to look beyond history to his religious and ethical principles. But before doing this it is necessary to understand in what sense "history is a preceptor of prudence," and why it was that he considered prudence to be "in all things a virtue, in politics the first of virtues." For the past century, the most common single error of writers on Burke has been the failure to understand the nature and function of "prudence" in his political philosophy.

For Burke, political philosophy was the practical art of governing man as a moral agent in civil society. It was not and could not be a speculative science dealing with abstract truth. The politician, by his definition, was "the philosopher in action," and he could never assume *a priori* knowledge that would enable him to attain exact mathematical certainty of the consequences of his decisions. Politics was a part of practical reason, not of theoretical reason; it was concerned with the good, not with the true. The nature and actions of men are under general laws of moral necessity, but because the will of man is free to obey or defy the moral law, and because his social circumstances are infinitely varied, in contingent matters and details there can be no general laws. Although justice must always be observed, the determination of what is just in each particular instance, under the different institutions and conditions of mankind, must always vary in its means, according to the infinite variations of men's temporal circumstances. The common nature of man is infinitely modified by climate, geography, history, religion, nationality, and race; by institutions, customs, manners, and habits; by all the civil circumstances of time, place, and occasions, which cut across and qualify, but do not impair the different means by which the moral ends of society are fulfilled through government. "The progressive sagacity that keeps company with times and occasions," Burke wrote, "and decides upon things in their existing position, is that alone which can give true propriety, grace, and effect to a man's conduct. It is very hard to anticipate the occasion, and to live by a rule more general." To Burke, "no moral questions are ever abstract questions." Prudence was for him not primarily an intellectual but a moral virtue; as such it was a corrective and the best positive alternative to the errors of metaphysical abstraction and intellectual speculation:

> *Nothing universal can be rationally affirmed on any moral or political subject. Pure metaphysical abstraction does not belong to these matters. The lines of morality are not like ideal lines of mathematics. They are broad and deep as well as long. They admit of exceptions; they demand modifications. These exceptions and modifications are not made by the process of logic, but by the rules of prudence. Prudence is not only the first in rank of the virtues political and moral, but she is the director, the regulator, the standard of them all.*

Burke always maintained that "the exercise of competent jurisdiction is a matter of moral prudence," because "moral necessity is not like metaphysical, or even physical." Tyranny was a more common abuse in government than usurpation, he believed, because even under legitimate legislatures, "if rules of benignity and prudence are not observed" oppressive actions may result. Prudence, or a strict regard for circumstances, is not merely a matter of empirical observation and intellectual calculation; it is morally imperative to regard circumstances, because otherwise political action, however right on principle, could mortally injure those whom the statesman wishes to serve.

In Burke's attempted economical reform of 1780, he distinguished between his principle of prudence and moral weakness or equivocation:

> *It is much more easy to reconcile this measure to humanity, than to bring it to any agreement with prudence. I do not mean that little, selfish, pitiful, bastard thing, which sometimes goes by the name of a family in which it is not legitimate, and to which it is a disgrace—I mean that public and*

enlarged prudence, which, apprehensive of being disabled from rendering acceptable service to the world, withholds itself from those that are invidious.

His remark, "If I cannot reform with equity I will not reform at all," and his statement, "I am not possessed of an exact measure between real service and its reward," provoked Jeremy Bentham to reply: "Except Edmund Burke, no man is thus ignorant." Bentham's willingness to compute the ratio between public service and reward illustrates one of the great differences between Burke's principle of prudence and the utilitarian idea of "expediency." To Burke, prudence is the general regulator of social changes, including the reforms of abuses in society, according to the legal norms of the constitution and the moral principles of Natural Law. As such, prudence is the cardinal political virtue because it supplies the practical means by which Natural Law principles are fulfilled in the various concrete circumstances of man's social life. Burke's prudence is not the utilitarian computation of circumstances, a calculation of how far political power might be utilized before provoking opposition. Nor is prudence merely the social virtue of tact. To him, prudence is part of God's "divine tactic" fulfilled in man's moral temperance and political tact.

Understood in this profoundly Aristotelian sense, Burke's principle of prudence is nothing less than the universal, eternal, and unchangeable Natural Law applied in practice through politics to each particular man, at every moment and in all circumstances, under the constitutional sovereignty of various nations. Since "the situation of man is the preceptor of his duty," prudence tells us when we should "abate our demands in favor of moderation and justice, and tenderness to individuals." Prudence is not intellectual calculation, but the moral discretion which enables men to live by the spirit of the law.

The claim of utilitarian writers that Burke belongs to their camp has obscured the absolute difference between his principle of prudence and their conception of expediency. He had a principle of utility, but he was no utilitarian. In the *Tracts Relative to the Laws Against Popery in Ireland,* Burke indicated that he derived utility from Cicero's principle of moral equity, which was based upon "original justice." It was a utility "connected with and derived directly from our rational nature; for any other utility may be the utility of a robber."

In his attack on Warren Hastings' "system of corruption," he noted the governor's "attempts to justify it on the score of utility," and added, "God forbid that prudence, which is the supreme guide, and indeed stands first of all virtues, should ever be the guide of vices." Burke distinguished carefully between a true and false adherent of moral prudence: "Our love to the occasionalist, but not server of occasions." In any conflict between merely utilitarian convenience and law, his stand was clear: "What the law respects shall be sacred to me. If the barriers of law should be broken down upon ideas of convenience, even of public convenience, we shall have no longer any thing certain among us." When rulers follow true moral prudence they are perfectly in accord with Natural and constitutional law, from which men's true natural and civil rights are derived. He believed that when claims to individual "rights" conflicted with moral expediency or prudence they were not really "rights," and not, as Morley said, that they were rights but had to yield to public expediency.

Burke once described prudence as "the god of this lower world." Professor Leo Strauss has wisely seen fit to note that "prudence and 'this lower world' cannot be seen properly without some knowledge of 'the higher world'—without genuine *theorie*." Through the Natural Law and political prudence, Burke combined his eloquent religious mysticism and stark concrete practicality. As a normative code of ethics, the Natural Law was the basis of his political philosophy in "the higher world" of principle. As a practical means of applying the Natural Law in "this lower world" of civil society, prudence underlies Burke's sensitive regard for men's differences, his reverence for local loyalties and prejudices, his intense dislike for *a priori* abstract absolutes in doctrinaire theory, and his skepticism of ideal, simple plans of government. His ability to combine the Natural Law and prudence made his political philosophy thoroughly consistent, yet almost wholly unsystematic. Natural Law and prudence enabled him to fuse to the limit of their valence the most sublime moral precepts and the most concrete empirical facts, details, and circumstances, so that political theory and practice were one: "A statesman, never losing sight of principles, is to be guided by circumstances; and judging contrary to the exigencies of the moment he may ruin his country for ever." This is the key statement behind Burke's definition of the politician as "a philosopher in action." As a philosopher, Burke drew his absolute ethical principles from the Natural Law; as a politician, he applied his principles in the concrete, with a full regard to historical circumstances, through his principle of prudence.

For Burke, history is "the preceptor of prudence" because it reveals "the known march of the ordinary providence of God." History was for him a secondary form of divine revelation, supplementing Scripture. History taught practical ethics, not directly through moral principles, but indirectly, by inculcating the spirit of morality through temperance and moderation: "Our physical well-being, our moral worth, our social happiness, our political tranquillity, all depend on that control of our appetites and passions, which the ancients designated by the cardinal virtue of Temperance." Burke believed that "the restraints on men are to be reckoned among their rights." In civil society, the moral law alone was insufficient to restrain the passions of men. The most immediate restraints on men came from the established institutions and legal processes of society, regardless of its political structure. In every just social order, sound ethical norms are embodied in its established institutions, so that in ordinary cases, within "the ordinary providence of God" which constitutes the historical process, society provided the practical means of solving its political problems by political and legal norms, in harmony with the moral law. Since for Burke "the actual and the present is the rational," prudence was a sufficient guide in the ordinary political problems of man. It was not necessary to appeal to transcendental moral standards in every political conflict; such appeals were reserved for extraordinary violations of the moral law, as in the cases of British misrule in Ireland and India, and the Jacobin tyranny in France.

It was the cardinal error of Morley and the utilitarians, and even of Christians such as Lord Acton, that they interpreted Burke's prudence as identical with utilitarian expediency, which was based on empirical philosophy and analytical reason. Morley and those who followed him saw nothing of the ethical norms of the Natural Law in his principle of prudence. They were quite unaware that the Natural Law was the ultimate moral foundation of his political philosophy. Morley admired the blooming flowers of Burke's politics, without noting the philosophical ground in which they were rooted. He enjoyed the taste of the stream without going back to its source. Consequently, Morley made a *tabula rasa* of the moral principles in Burke's political philosophy, expunging the Natural Law in favor of history. Thus, Morley praised and Acton condemned Burke as a shrewd political activist who had no ultimate philosophical principles to guide his actions. Burke's definition, "a philosopher in action," was split in half, with Morley insisting on the self-sufficiency of *ad hoc* pragmatic action, and Acton insisting that the politician be a moral philosopher. Both Morley and Acton fully appreciated his practical genius in politics, but neither man understood the philosophical basis of his political philosophy.

The two most important questions to be answered concerning Burke's political philosophy are (1) What, to Burke, were the basic principles of sound morality? and (2) How could moral principles be man's guide in practical politics? The second question has already been answered in considering his principle of moral prudence. For purposes of convenience, these questions can be stated separately. But in the close fusion of theory and practice in politics, they are ideally one and the same question, although man as a finite and fallible creature can approximate this ideal fusion only according to the purity of his understanding, the determination of his will, and the means at his disposal. His actions as a practicing statesman, and the dialectical means by which he defended his actions or advocated political policy, are much more evident than his basic ethical principles. There are several good reasons for this.

For Burke, in ordinary political issues, the practical instruments for realizing moral ends in civil society are not found in an abstract code, but in the constitutional means and institutional arrangements inherited from the past. It is a common error to construe his refusal to appeal to universal and eternal absolute moral principles at every point as a denial of belief in such principles. Also, as a practicing politician his basic political principles were never presented in a systematic treatise. His essential ethical and political beliefs, more or less explicit or assumed, are to be found scattered throughout his voluminous writings and recorded speeches. They are never stated abstractly, but are imbedded in his various responses to the particular circumstances and political situations which confronted him during his twenty-nine years in Parliament.

Yet nothing is more evident than that Burke never approached the immediate contingencies of particular political problems in an *ad hoc*, arbitrary, or unprincipled way. Quite the contrary, he always raised each political issue above its empirical circumstances, to the level of constitutional principles, and when necessary, to the level of moral principles. Matthew Arnold's remark that "Burke saturated politics with thought" can be refined into the higher claim that he saturated politics with historical, legal, and ethical principles. In so do-ing, he continuously achieved a close reciprocal fusion of the particular and the universal. If Burke did not reason down-ward from high-sounding metaphysical abstractions, as Mor-ley said, it was not because he had rejected moral absolutes, as Morley assumed, but because for Burke, as for Aristotle, transcendental moral truths possess reality only in so far as they are immanent in human affairs, and self-evident to right reason. The empirical actions of men are judged according to their conformity to or violation of basic ethical norms, as these are embodied in man's civil institutions, or in the revela-tions of religion and right reason.

Burke's politics involves much more than his initial response and subsequent method of reasoning on concrete political situations. Without his faith in the Natural Law, his responses and reasoning in politics would have had no order or cohesion, since there is no ultimate principle of organic unity in empiri-cal, utilitarian, and historical political appeals. The much be-labored question of his political consistency can never be re-solved on the political level alone, within history, without recourse to the moral principles which underlie his politics. He changed his partisan political front, but he never changed his moral ground.

The utilitarians and positivists of the nineteenth and twen-tieth centuries have persistently misunderstood or ignored Burke's appeals to the Natural Law. Because they held Natu-ral Law in contempt, as unscientific, their frequent ignorance of what it had meant to men in previous periods resulted in a serious failure to distinguish between the traditional meaning of Classical and Scholastic Natural Law, and eighteenth-century aberrations from "Nature" put forth by revolution-aries under slogans such as the "natural rights of man." As Jacques Maritain has said: "The idea of natural law . . . does not go back to the philosophy of the eighteenth century, which more or less deformed it." To the utilitarians, all appeals to "nature" as an ethical norm were anathema. Since it was well known that Burke was an enemy of the revolutionary "rights of man" doctrines, utilitarian writers assumed that he rejected the whole tradition of Natural Law in favor of expediency, social utility, and an appeal to history. Morley wrote two books on Burke and never mentioned the Natural Law. Sir Leslie Stephen noted Burke's appeals to "natural rights," but dismissed all such passages as mere rhetoric. Vaughan and

MacCunn also noted his "natural rights," but insisted that what he really meant was "civil rights," based upon conventions rather than on ethical norms. Following his secondary sources, George Sabine, an outstanding authority in the history of political theory, in *A History of Political Theory* refined upon these long-prevailing convictions concerning Burke:

> *Burke made an important contribution to the nineteenth century proposal to replace the system of natural law. . . . In a sense Burke showed precisely . . . the reaction that was to follow upon Hume's destruction of the eternal verities of reason and natural law. . . . It is true that he never denied the reality of natural rights. . . . However, like Hume, he believed that they were purely conventional. . . . They arise not from anything belonging to nature or to the human species at large, but solely from civil society. . . . Accordingly, Burke not only cleared away, as Hume had done, the pretense that social institutions depend on reason or nature, but far more than Hume he reversed the scheme of values implied by the system of natural law.*

With such a universal chorus of learned authorities proclaiming Burke an apostle of expediency and a deadly enemy of Natural Law, it is not surprising that in many contemporary reference and textbooks he is commonly still enlisted as the foremost British political thinker opposed to belief in the Natural Law. "The reaction of the nineteenth century against natural law formulae," wrote Georges Gurvitch in the *Encyclopedia of the Social Sciences,* "is traceable ultimately to Edmund Burke." Reliance on the high and reverend authorities in the tradition of Morley has caused many eminent writers of textbooks in history and politics to be overwhelmed in "the great Serbonian bog" of positivist scholarship on Burke. Thus Professor Oscar Handlin writes: "Intellectually, the weightiest attacks upon the conception of a natural and universal law took their points of departure in the writings of Burke and Montesquieu." The unawareness of his works revealed in such statements is clearly evident to anyone familiar with all the recent scholarship on Burke.

Recent studies of Burke's political philosophy have established beyond any reasonable doubt that far from being an empiricist, utilitarian, and pragmatist, and therefore an enemy of Natural Law, he was in principle and practice one of the most eloquent and profound defenders of Natural Law morality and politics in Western civilization. In 1948, in the preface to *Burke's Politics,* Professor Ross Hoffman took conscious issue with all previous scholarship on Burke in the Morley tradition:

> *Burke's politics . . . were grounded on recognition of the universal natural law of reason and justice ordained by God as the foundation of a good community. In this recognition the Machiavellian schism between politics and morality is closed, and it is exactly in this respect that Burke stands apart from the modern positivists and pragmatists, who in claiming him have diminished him. His thought, to be sure, worked mostly on concrete and practical questions and he was not fond of adverting to first principles of public morality; but affirmation of the natural law is implicit in all his works, and when he criticized radically—when he attacked at the roots such heinous systems as the anti-Catholic penal code of Ireland and the tyrannical rule of Hastings in Bengal—it became explicit.*

Professor Hoffman was among the first writers to realize, and the first to say in print, that the foundations of Burke's political philosophy rested upon the Natural Law. Since 1948, at least a half dozen major publications have proved this thesis to the hilt.

In "Burke and Natural Rights," *The Review of Politics* (October 1951), Russell Kirk argued that Burke's "theory of natural law and natural rights made him the founder of philosophical conservatism" in politics. In *Natural Right and History* (1953), Professor Leo Strauss presented a brilliantly condensed analysis of Burke's basic principles, and extended further the evidence of Burke's adherence to the ethical norms of traditional Natural Law. Strauss avoided the common pitfalls of the positivists by distinguishing sharply between Burke's Classical or "premodern conception of natural right," and the "imaginary rights of men" theories of the eighteenth-century revolutionaries, who based their doctrines on Hobbes, Locke, and Rousseau, or on their own arbitrary theories. In 1956 Charles Parkin's *The Moral Basis of Burke's Political Thought* was published, in which he demonstrated the close relationship in Burke's political philosophy between Natural Law and Burke's conception of the social contract. Parkin's book clearly showed that the moral order in Burke's political philosophy does not derive from history, but rather from a religious and Natural Law basis. To enumerate the extent and variety of Burke's appeals to the Natural Law during his twenty-nine years in Parliament is far beyond the scope of this introduction. A full-length study of the Natural Law in

Burke's political philosophy is available in this author's *Edmund Burke and the Natural Law* (1958). Francis Canavan's *The Political Reason of Edmund Burke* (1960), has extended the main thesis of these recent studies: "There is not to be found in Burke's writing a formal treatise on the natural law . . . but the doctrine is alluded to throughout his works and furnishes the premises of his most profound arguments." A counter-revolution on traditional grounds has characterized scholarship on Burke since 1948, and has completely reversed the utilitarian-positivist interpretation of his political philosophy. All the outstanding scholars on Burke now agree that in the final analysis of his complex thought the Natural Law is the most fundamental moral element in his political philosophy. As Burke so beautifully summarized his position: "The principles of true politics are those of morality enlarged; and I neither now do, nor ever will, admit of any other."

Peter J. Stanlis

University of Detroit
March 1, 1963

I

EARLY WRITINGS

A Vindication of Natural Society
or,
*A View of the Miseries and Evils Arising to Mankind
from Every Species of Artificial Society
In a Letter to Lord * * * *
by a Late Noble Writer
1756*

It is remarkably prophetic that Burke's first important work in political thought, his *A Vindication of Natural Society* (1756), was directed against the same doctrines of a primitive or simple state of nature, and against the private, speculative, abstract, and geometrical type of reasoning about man and society, so characteristic of Descartes and Hobbes and the Enlightenment, which was to call forth his dying protests against the French Revolution. With characteristic insight, even at age twenty-seven, he perceived the essential philosophical assumptions and rationalist principles of the Enlightenment which in his last years were to destroy the established order of European society.

Burke's *A Vindication of Natural Society* was primarily a satire of Lord Bolingbroke's deism and rationalism. Bolingbroke had died in 1751, and his posthumous collected philosophical writings were published by David Mallet in 1754, the same year as Rousseau's *Discourse on Inequality*. The literary and political world had long anticipated a great intellectual contribution from the mature reflections of the old friend of Swift, Pope, and the Queen Anne Wits, the brilliant Tory statesman whose powerful prose style and "enlightened" political ideas had made him an almost legendary figure for much of the first half of the eighteenth century. Like his friend Dr. Johnson, Burke read enough of Bolingbroke's work to be thoroughly disappointed with it. He was strongly repelled by Bolingbroke's methodology, which was based on speculative and self-sufficient analytical reason, and which Burke considered as dangerous to civil society. Burke's satire purported to be a serious posthumous work by Bolingbroke, anonymously published as by a "late Noble Writer." By pre-

tending to assume Bolingbroke's Cartesian rationalism, and by
a perfect imitation of his prose style, through a sustained
reductio ad absurdum, he wrote an ironical parody of Bolingbroke's principles and arguments.

A few of Burke's readers, such as the reviewer in the
Monthly Review (1756), XV, p. 21, perceived what he was
about and expressed appreciation of "this writer's talents at
imitation." But unfortunately for Burke, his satire so perfectly reproduced the thought, method, and style of Bolingbroke that many of his readers, including such sophisticated
men as Lord Chesterfield and Bishop Warburton, did not perceive his irony. Most of the reading public, which two years
earlier had accepted at face value Rousseau's paradox that
man in a simple state, close to nature, was morally superior
to man in a polished state of society, had no difficulty in
reading his satire as serious discourse, in which what was
said was meant. Late in the eighteenth century William Godwin even advanced the proposition that Burke's satire had
demonstrated what was literally true: "In Burke's *Vindication of Natural Society* . . . the evils of the existing political
institutions are displayed with incomparable force of reasoning and lustre of eloquence." In the twentieth century Elie
Halévy, in commenting upon Godwin's indictment of civil society, seems not even to have been aware that the *Vindication*
was a satire: "Godwin perhaps drew his inspiration from
Burke, who, in a youthful work, a curious essay devoted to
the defence of natural society, had contrasted the state of
nature . . . with the state of 'artificial' society." An implicit
faith in the superiority of a state of nature to civil society is
contained in J. B. Bury's comparison of Rousseau's *Discourse
on Inequality* and Burke's satire:

*In truth, a more powerful and comprehensive case against
civilized society was drawn up about the same time, by one
whose thought represented all that was opposed to Rousseau's
teaching. Burke's early work,* A Vindication of Natural Society, *worked out in detail a historical picture of the evils of
civilization which is far more telling than Rousseau's generalities.*

Woodrow Wilson's comment on the *Vindication* reveals a
more profound appreciation of Burke's ironical method and
serious position toward his subject: "Much that Burke urges
against civil society he could urge in good faith, and his mind
works soberly upon it. It is only the main thesis that he does
not seriously mean." The main thesis of the satire was the
Rousseauist paradox that a simple society, close to "nature,"
was morally superior to the complex and refined "artificial"
society of eighteenth-century Europe. Burke did not believe
that man was intrinsically moral by his instincts and that he

became corrupted by the external refinements and demands of his civil institutions. Quite the reverse. As an Aristotelian he believed that man is by nature a political or social animal, that "art is man's nature." To Burke, civil society however imperfect was superior to any hypothetical simple "state of nature," without organized institutions. His satire merely proved that he understood and could present the arguments of his philosophical opponents better than they could themselves, and that he rejected totally any serious consideration of a state of nature.

Burke's analogical method supplies the key to an understanding of his satire. In attacking Bolingbroke's deism, he made use of the method used by Bishop Joseph Butler in *The Analogy of Religion* (1736). Just as Butler had shown that the deist objections to revealed Christianity applied as well to "natural" religion, Burke argued that Bolingbroke's attacks on artificial religion applied equally to political institutions and to organized civil society itself:

Show me an absurdity in religion, and I will undertake to show you an hundred for one in political laws and institutions. . . . If after all, you should confess all these things, yet plead the necessity of political institutions, weak and wicked as they are, I can argue with equal, perhaps superior, force, concerning the necessity of artificial religion; and every step you advance in your argument, you add a strength to mine.

In short, without irony, Burke believed that "artificial" institutions such as Church and State are "natural" to man, and that a state of "natural society," without institutions, was a fictitious and dangerous illusion when applied to man. But for the purposes of his satire he had to invert his real convictions. In order to show that the same type of self-sufficient rationalism which was employed for the destruction of organized religion could also be employed for the subversion of organized government, he pretended to vindicate "natural society" as a state in which men were free, good, and happy, and to condemn civil or "artificial" society as a state in which men are tyrannized, corrupted, and made miserable by their institutions.

Burke believed that when men such as Bolingbroke assumed an antithesis between "nature" and "art," their logical arguments in favor of the supposed superiority of a state of nature could be made to appear very plausible. For this reason he attacked Bolingbroke's rationalism, and argued seriously that the civil world of man would be destroyed "if the practice of all moral duties, and the foundations of society, rested upon having their reasons made clear and demonstrative to every individual." His satire attacked the theory that if every individual was free to speculate upon political and moral subjects, with no sense of self-restraint arising from an awareness of the limitations and fallibility of his private reason, and from his subordinate place in the moral universe, then everything among all the excellent achievements of men throughout history was subject to the destructive analysis of rationalistic criticism. Burke perceived that this is precisely what the rationalist philosophers of the Enlightenment encouraged men to do. The *Vindication* is an important document for an understanding of his political career and philosophy, because it reveals that even in his twenties he was keenly aware of the chief philosophical assumptions and methods that were shaping eighteenth-century revolutionary theory.

The speculative rationalism that Burke satirized in the *Vindication* he attacked again and again throughout his political writings, in American, Irish, Indian, and French affairs, up to the time of his death. His attacks on *a priori* reasoning in politics, his contempt for metaphysical abstractions, his fear of "the contagion of project and system," his deep skepticism toward the "species of delusive geometrical accuracy in moral arguments" and conviction that "mathematical demonstration" in politics is "the most fallacious of all sophistry," and his belief that "politics ought to be adjusted, not to human reasonings, but to human nature" and to history and moral and legal principles, all these grand themes that run through almost everything he ever wrote become doubly clear in the light of his early satire.

It is worth noting that the more than forty pamphleteers who replied to Burke's *Reflections on the Revolution in France* (1790), put forth in perfect seriousness many ideas that Burke had argued ironically thirty-four years earlier. The author of *Pearls Cast Before Swine* (London, 1793), one of his many anonymous critics, tried to prove by contrasting quotations from his early satire and his later works that after 1790 he was inconsistent.

Although in 1756 Burke had no way of anticipating these later developments, from the very beginning he realized that satirical irony and intellectual paradox are dangerous weapons with which to combat plausible theories of primitive or natural society. He understood the strength of the appeal of speculative rationalism; he noted that such "pleasing impressions on the imagination subsist and produce their effect, even after the understanding has been satisfied of their unsubstantial nature." In 1757, when Burke published a second edition of his *Vindication,* he wrote a preface to assure his readers that it was a satire, that there was "no reason to conceal the design" of it "any longer." The following selections include portions of the preface to the second edition as well as of the satire.

PREFACE

Before the philosophical works of Lord Bolingbroke had appeared, great things were expected from the leisure of a man, who, from the splendid scene of action in which his talents had enabled him to make so conspicuous a figure, had retired to employ those talents in the investigation of truth. Philosophy began to congratulate herself upon such a proselyte from the world of business, and hoped to have extended her power under the auspices of such a leader. In the midst of these pleasing expectations, the works themselves at last appeared in *full body,* and with great pomp. Those who searched in them for new discoveries in the mysteries of nature; those who expected something which might explain or direct the operations of the mind; those who hoped to see morality illustrated and enforced; those who looked for new helps to society and government; those who desired to see the characters and passions of mankind delineated; in short, all who consider such things as philosophy, and require some of them at least in every philosophical work, all these were certainly disappointed; they found the landmarks of science precisely in their former places: and they thought they received but a poor recompense for this disappointment, in seeing every mode of religion attacked in a lively manner, and the foundation of every virtue, and of all government, sapped with great art and much ingenuity. What advantage do we derive from such writings? What delight can a man find in employing a capacity which might be usefully exerted for the noblest purposes, in a sort of sullen labor, in which, if the author could succeed, he is obliged to own, that nothing could be more fatal to mankind than his success?

I cannot conceive how this sort of writers propose to compass the designs they pretend to have in view, by the instruments which they employ. Do they pretend to exalt the mind of man, by proving him no better than a beast? Do they think to enforce the practice of virtue, by denying that vice and virtue are distinguished by good or ill fortune here, or by happiness or misery hereafter? Do they imagine they shall increase our piety, and our reliance on God, by exploding his providence, and insisting that he is neither just nor good? Such are the doctrines which, sometimes concealed, sometimes openly and fully avowed, are found to prevail throughout the writings of Lord Bolingbroke; and such are the reasonings which this noble writer and several others have been pleased to dignify with the name of philosophy. If these are delivered in a specious manner, and in a style above the common, they cannot want a number of admirers of as much docility as can be wished for in disciples. To these the editor of the following little piece has addressed it: there is no reason to conceal the design of it any longer.

The design was to show that, without the exertion of any considerable forces, the same engines which were employed for the destruction of religion, might be employed with equal success for the subversion of government; and that specious arguments might be used against those things which they, who doubt of everything else, will never permit to be questioned. It is an observation which I think Isocrates makes in one of his orations against the sophists, that it is far more easy to maintain a wrong cause, and to support paradoxical opinions to the satisfaction of a common auditory, than to establish a doubtful truth by solid and conclusive arguments. When men find that something can be said in favor of what, on the very proposal, they have thought utterly indefensible, they grow doubtful of their own reason; they are thrown into a sort of pleasing surprise; they run along with the speaker, charmed and captivated to find such a plentiful harvest of reasoning, where all seemed barren and unpromising. This is the fairy land of philosophy. And it very frequently happens, that those pleasing impressions on the imagination subsist and produce their effect, even after the understanding has been satisfied of their unsubstantial nature. There is a sort of gloss upon ingenious falsehoods that dazzles the imagination, but which neither belongs to, nor becomes the sober aspect of truth. . . . The editor is satisfied that a mind which has no restraint from a sense of its own weakness, of its subordinate rank in the creation, and of the extreme danger of letting the imagination loose upon some subjects, may very plausibly attack everything the most excellent and venerable; that it would not be difficult to criticise the creation itself; and that if we were to examine the divine fabrics by our ideas of reason and fitness, and to use the same method of attack by which some men have assaulted revealed religion, we might with as good color, and with the same success, make the wisdom and power of God in his creation appear to many no better than foolishness. There is an air of plausibility which accompanies vulgar reasonings and notions, taken from the beaten circle of ordinary experience, that is admirably suited to the narrow capacities of some, and to the laziness of others. But this advantage is in a great measure lost, when a painful, comprehensive survey of a very complicated matter, and which requires a great variety of considerations, is to be made; when we must seek in a profound subject, not only for arguments, but for new materials of argument, their measures and their method of arrangement; when we must go out of the sphere of our ordinary ideas, and when we can never walk surely, but by being sensible of our blindness. And this we must do, or we do nothing, whenever we examine the result of a reason which is not our own. Even in matters which are, as it were, just within our reach, what would become of the world, if the practice of all moral duties, and the foundations of society, rested upon having their reasons made clear and demonstrative to every individual?

The editor knows that the subject of this letter is not so fully handled as obviously it might; it was not his design to say all that could possibly be said. It had been inexcusable to fill a large volume with the abuse of reason; nor would such an abuse have been tolerable, even for a few pages, if some under-plot, of more consequence than the apparent design, had not been carried on.

Some persons have thought that the advantages of the state of nature ought to have been more fully displayed. This had undoubtedly been a very ample subject for declamation; but they do not consider the character of the piece. The writers against religion, whilst they oppose every system, are wisely careful never to set up any of their own. If some inaccuracies in calculation, in reasoning, or in method, be found, perhaps these will not be looked upon as faults by the admirers of Lord Bolingbroke; who will, the editor is afraid, observe much more of his lordship's character in such particulars of the following letter, than they are likely to find of that rapid torrent of an impetuous and overbearing eloquence, and the variety of rich imagery for which that writer is justly admired.

A LETTER TO LORD * * * *

Shall I venture to say, my lord, that in our late conversation, you were inclined to the party which you adopted rather by the feelings of your good nature, than by the conviction of your judgment? We laid open the foundations of society; and you feared that the curiosity of this search might endanger the ruin of the whole fabric. You would readily have allowed my principle, but you dreaded the consequences; you thought, that having once entered upon these reasonings, we might be carried insensibly and irresistibly farther than at first we could either have imagined or wished. But for my part, my lord, I then thought, and am still of the same opinion, that error, and not truth of any kind, is dangerous; that ill conclusions can only flow from false propositions; and that, to know whether any proposition be true or false, it is a preposterous method to examine it by its apparent consequences.

These were the reasons which induced me to go so far into that inquiry; and they are the reasons which direct me in all my inquiries. . . .

On considering political societies, their origin, their constitution, and their effects, I have sometimes been in a good deal more than doubt, whether the Creator did ever really intend man for a state of happiness. He has mixed in his cup a number of natural evils, (in spite of the boasts of stoicism they are evils,) and every endeavor which the art and policy of mankind has used from the beginning of the world to this day, in order to alleviate or cure them, has only served to introduce new mischiefs, or to aggravate and inflame the old. . . .

In the state of nature, without question, mankind was subjected to many and great inconveniences. Want of union, want of mutual assistance, want of a common arbitrator to resort to in their differences. These were evils which they could not but have felt pretty severely on many occasions. The original children of the earth lived with their brethren of the other kinds in much equality. Their diet must have been confined almost wholly to the vegetable kind; and the same tree, which in its flourishing state produced them berries, in its decay gave them an habitation. The mutual desires of the sexes uniting their bodies and affections, and the children which are the results of these intercourses, introduced first the notion of society, and taught its conveniences. This society, founded in natural appetites and instincts, and not in any positive institution, I shall call *natural society*. Thus far nature went and succeeded: but man would go farther. The great error of our nature is, not to know where to stop, not to be satisfied with any reasonable acquirement; not to compound with our condition; but to lose all we have gained by an insatiable pursuit after more. Man found a considerable advantage by this union of many persons to form one family; he therefore judged that he would find his account proportionably in an union of many families into one body politic. And as nature has formed no bond of union to hold them together, he supplied this defect by *laws*.

This is *political society*. And hence the sources of what are usually called states, civil societies, or governments; into some form of which, more extended or restrained, all mankind have gradually fallen. And since it has so happened, and that we owe an implicit reverence to all the institutions of our ancestors, we shall consider these institutions with all that modesty with which we ought to conduct ourselves in examining a received opinion; but with all that freedom and candor which we owe to truth wherever we find it, or however it may contradict our own notions, or oppose our own interests. There is a most absurd and audacious method of reasoning avowed by some bigots and enthusiasts, and through fear assented to by some wiser and better men; it is this: they argue against a fair discussion of popular prejudices, because, say they, though they would be found without any reasonable support, yet the discovery might be productive of the most dangerous consequences. Absurd and blasphemous notion! as if all happiness was not connected with the practice of virtue, which necessarily depends upon the knowledge of truth; that is, upon the knowledge of those unalterable relations which Providence has ordained that every thing should bear to every other. These relations, which are truth itself, the foundation of virtue, and consequently the only measures of happiness, should be likewise the only measures by which we should direct our reasoning. To these we should conform in good earnest; and not think to force nature, and the whole order of her system, by a compliance with our pride and folly, to conform to our artificial regulations. It is by a conformity to this method we owe the discovery of the few truths we know, and the little liberty and rational happiness we enjoy. We have something fairer play than a reasoner could have expected formerly; and we derive advantages from it which are very visible.

The fabric of superstition has in this our age and nation received much ruder shocks than it had ever felt before; and through the chinks and breaches of our prison, we see such glimmerings of light, and feel such refreshing airs of liberty, as daily raise our ardor for more. The miseries derived to mankind from superstition under the name of religion, and of ecclesiastical tyranny under the name of church government, have been clearly and usefully exposed. We begin to think and to act from reason and from nature alone. This is true of several, but by far the majority is still in the same old state of blindness and slavery; and much is it to be feared that we shall perpetually relapse, whilst the real productive cause of all this superstitious folly, enthusiastical nonsense, and holy tyranny, holds a reverend place in the estimation even of those who are otherwise enlightened.

Civil government borrows a strength from ecclesiastical; and artificial laws receive a sanction from artificial revelations. The ideas of religion and government are closely connected; and whilst we receive government as a thing necessary, or even useful to our well-being, we shall in spite of us draw in, as a necessary, though undesirable consequence, an artificial religion of some kind or other. To this the vulgar will always be voluntary slaves; and even those of a rank of understanding superior, will now and then involuntarily feel its influence. It is therefore of the deepest concernment to us to be set right in this point; and to be well satisfied whether civil government be such a protector from natural evils, and such a nurse and increaser of blessings, as those of warm imaginations promise. . . .

In looking over any state to form a judgment on it, it presents itself in two lights; the external, and the internal. The first, that relation which it bears in point of friendship or enmity to other states. The second, that relation which its component parts, the governing and the governed, bear to each other. The first part of the external view of all states, their relation as friends, makes so trifling a figure in history, that I am very sorry to say, it affords me but little matter on which to expatiate. The good offices done by one nation to its neighbor; the support given in public distress; the relief afforded in general calamity; the protection granted in emergent danger; the mutual return of kindness and civility, would afford a very ample and very pleasing subject for history. But, alas! all the history of all times, concerning all nations, does not afford matter enough to fill ten pages . . . The glaring side is that of enmity. War is the matter which fills all history, and consequently the only or almost the only view in which we can see the external of political society is in a hostile shape; and the only actions to which we have always seen, and still see all of them intent, are such as tend to the destruction of one another. "War," says Machiavel, "ought to be the only study of a prince"; and by a prince, he means every sort of state, however constituted. "He ought," says this great political doctor, "to consider peace only as a breathing-time, which gives him leisure to contrive, and furnishes ability to execute military plans." A meditation on the conduct of political societies made old Hobbes imagine, that war was the state of nature; and truly, if a man judged of the individuals of our race by their conduct when united and packed into nations and kingdoms, he might imagine that every sort of virtue was unnatural and foreign to the mind of man.

The first accounts we have of mankind are but so many accounts of their butcheries. All empires have been cemented in blood; and, in those early periods, when the race of mankind began first to form themselves into parties and combinations, the first effect of the combination, and indeed the end for which it seems purposely formed, and best calculated, was their mutual destruction. . . .

I go upon a naked and moderate calculation, just enough, without a pedantical exactness, to give your lordship some feeling of the effects of political society. I charge the whole of these effects on political society. . . . The numbers I particularized are about thirty-six millions. . . .

Political society is justly chargeable with much the greatest part of this destruction of the species. To give the fairest play to every side of the question, I will own that there is a haughtiness and fierceness in human nature, which will cause innumerable broils, place men in what situation you please; but owning this, I still insist in charging it to political regulations, that these broils are so frequent, so cruel, and attended with consequences so deplorable. In a state of nature, it had been impossible to find a number of men, sufficient for such slaughters, agreed in the same bloody purpose; or allowing that they might have come to such an agreement (an impossible supposition), yet the means that simple nature has supplied them with, are by no means adequate to such an end; many scratches, many bruises undoubtedly would be received upon all hands; but only a few, a very few deaths. Society and politics, which have given us these destructive views, have given us also the means of satisfying them. From the earliest dawnings of policy to this day, the invention of men has been sharpening and improving the mystery of murder, from the first rude essays of clubs and stones, to the present perfection of gunnery, cannoneering, bombarding, mining, and all those species of artificial, learned, and refined cruelty, in which we are now so expert, and which make a principal part of what politicians have taught us to believe is our principal glory.

How far mere nature would have carried us, we may judge

by the example of those animals who still follow her laws, and even of those to whom she has given dispositions more fierce, and arms more terrible than ever she intended we should use. It is an incontestable truth that there is more havoc made in one year by men of men, than has been made by all the lions, tigers, panthers, ounces, leopards, hyenas, rhinoceroses, elephants, bears and wolves, upon their several species, since the beginning of the world; though these agree ill enough with each other, and have a much greater proportion of rage and fury in their composition than we have. But with respect to you, ye legislators, ye civilizers of mankind! ye Orpheuses, Moseses, Minoses, Solons, Theseuses, Lycurguses, Numas! with respect to you be it spoken, your regulations have done more mischief in cold blood, than all the rage of the fiercest animals in their greatest terrors, or furies, has ever done, or ever could do!

These evils are not accidental. Whoever will take the pains to consider the nature of society will find that they result directly from its constitution. For as *subordination,* or, in other words, the reciprocation of tyranny and slavery, is requisite to support these societies; the interest, the ambition, the malice, or the revenge, nay, even the whim and caprice of one ruling man among them, is enough to arm all the rest, without any private views of their own, to the worst and blackest purposes . . .

This artificial division of mankind into separate societies is a perpetual source in itself of hatred and dissension among them. The names which distinguish them are enough to blow up hatred and rage. Examine history; consult present experience; and you will find that far the greater part of the quarrels between several nations had scarce any other occasion than that these nations were different combinations of people, and called by different names: to an Englishman, the name of a Frenchman, a Spaniard, an Italian, much more a Turk, or a Tartar, raises of course ideas of hatred and contempt. If you would inspire this compatriot of ours with pity or regard for one of these, would you not hide that distinction? You would not pray him to compassionate the poor Frenchman, or the unhappy German. Far from it; you would speak of him as a *foreigner;* an accident to which all are liable. You would represent him as a *man;* one partaking with us of the same common nature, and subject to the same law. There is something so averse from our nature in these artificial political distinctions, that we need no other trumpet to kindle us to war and destruction. But there is something so benign and healing in the general voice of humanity that, maugre all our regulations to prevent it, the simple name of man applied properly, never fails to work a salutary effect.

This natural unpremeditated effect of policy on the unpossessed passions of mankind appears on other occasions. The very name of a politician, a statesman, is sure to cause terror and hatred; it has always connected with it the ideas of treachery, cruelty, fraud, and tyranny . . . The case of Machiavel seems at first sight something hard in that respect. He is obliged to bear the iniquities of those whose maxims and rules of government he published. His speculation is more abhorred than their practice.

But if there were no other arguments against artificial society than this I am going to mention, methinks it ought to fall by this one only. All writers on the science of policy are agreed, and they agree with experience, that all governments must frequently infringe the rules of justice to support themselves; that truth must give way to dissimulation; honesty to convenience; and humanity itself to the reigning interest. The whole of this mystery of iniquity is called the reason of state. It is a reason which I own I cannot penetrate. What sort of a protection is this of the general right, that is maintained by infringing the rights of particulars? What sort of justice is this, which is enforced by breaches of its own laws? These paradoxes I leave to be solved by the able heads of legislators and politicians. For my part, I say what a plain man would say on such an occasion. I can never believe that any institution, agreeable to nature, and proper for mankind, could find it necessary, or even expedient, in any case whatsoever, to do what the best and worthiest instincts of mankind warn us to avoid. But no wonder, that what is set up in opposition to the state of nature should preserve itself by trampling upon the law of nature.

To prove that these sorts of policed societies are a violation offered to nature, and a constraint upon the human mind, it needs only to look upon the sanguinary measures, and instruments of violence, which are everywhere used to support them. Let us take a review of the dungeons, whips, chains, racks, gibbets, with which every society is abundantly stored; by which hundreds of victims are annually offered up to support a dozen or two in pride and madness, and millions in an abject servitude and dependence. There was a time when I looked with a reverential awe on these mysteries of policy;

but age, experience, and philosophy, have rent the veil; and I view this *sanctum sanctorum,* at least, without any enthusiastic admiration. I acknowledge, indeed, the necessity of such a proceeding in such institutions; but I must have a very mean opinion of institutions where such proceedings are necessary.

It is a misfortune that in no part of the globe natural liberty and natural religion are to be found pure, and free from the mixture of political adulterations. Yet we have implanted in us by Providence, ideas, axioms, rules, of what is pious, just, fair, honest, which no political craft, nor learned sophistry can entirely expel from our breasts. By these we judge, and we cannot otherwise judge, of the several artificial modes of religion and society, and determine of them as they approach to or recede from this standard.

The simplest form of government is *despotism,* where all the inferior orbs of power are moved merely by the will of the Supreme, and all that are subjected to them directed in the same manner, merely by the occasional will of the magistrate. This form, as it is the most simple, so it is infinitely the most general. Scarcely any part of the world is exempted from its power. And in those few places where men enjoy what they call liberty, it is continually in a tottering situation, and makes greater and greater strides to that gulf of despotism which at last swallows up every species of government. . . .

In this kind of government human nature is not only abused and insulted, but it is actually degraded and sunk into a species of brutality. The consideration of this made Mr. Locke say, with great justice, that a government of this kind was worse than anarchy: indeed it is so abhorred and detested by all who live under forms that have a milder appearance, that there is scarcely a rational man in Europe that would not prefer death to Asiatic despotism. Here then we have the acknowledgment of a great philosopher, that an irregular state of nature is preferable to such a government; we have the consent of all sensible and generous men, who carry it yet further, and avow that death itself is preferable; and yet this species of government, so justly condemned, and so generally detested, is what infinitely the greater part of mankind groan under, and have groaned under from the beginning. So that, by sure and uncontested principles, the greatest part of the governments on earth must be concluded tyrannies, impostures, violations of the natural rights of mankind, and worse than the most disorderly anarchies. How much other forms exceed this we shall consider immediately.

In all parts of the world, mankind, however debased, retains still the sense of *feeling;* the weight of tyranny at last becomes insupportable . . . In some countries . . . were found men of . . . penetration, who discovered *"that to live by one man's will was the cause of all men's misery."* They therefore changed their former method, and assembling the men in their several societies the most respectable for their understanding and fortunes, they confided to them the charge of the public welfare. This originally formed what is called an *aristocracy.* They hoped it would be impossible that such a number could ever join in any design against the general good; and they promised themselves a great deal of security and happiness from the united counsels of so many able and experienced persons. But it is now found by abundant experience, that an *aristocracy,* and a *despotism,* differ but in name; and that a people who are in general excluded from any share of the legislative, are, to all intents and purposes, as much slaves, when twenty, independent of them, govern, as when but one domineers. The tyranny is even more felt, as every individual of the nobles has the haughtiness of a sultan . . . In short, the regular and methodical proceedings of an *aristocracy* are more intolerable than the very excesses of a *despotism,* and, in general, much further from any remedy. . . .

However, the fruitful policy of man was not yet exhausted. He had yet another farthing candle to supply the deficiencies of the sun. This was the third form, known by political writers under the name of *democracy.* Here the people transacted all public business, or the greater part of it, in their own persons; their laws were made by themselves, and, upon any failure of duty, their officers were accountable to themselves, and to them only. In all appearance, they had secured by this method the advantages of order and good government without paying their liberty for the purchase. . . . Republics have many things in the spirit of absolute monarchy, but none more than this. A shining merit is ever hated or suspected in a popular assembly, as well as in a court . . . A republic, as an ancient philosopher has observed, is no one species of government, but a magazine of every species; here you find every sort of it, and that in the worst form. As there is a perpetual change, one rising and the other falling, you have all the violence and wicked policy by which a beginning power must always acquire its strength, and all the weakness by which falling states are brought to a complete destruction. . . .

We are now at the close of our review of the three simple

forms of artificial society; and we have shown them, however they may differ in name, or in some slight circumstances, to be all alike in effect: in effect, to be all tyrannies. . . .

After so fair an examen, wherein nothing has been exaggerated; no fact produced which cannot be proved, and none which has been produced in any wise forced or strained, while thousands have, for brevity, been omitted; after so candid a discussion in all respects; what slave so passive, what bigot so blind, what enthusiast so headlong, what politician so hardened, as to stand up in defence of a system calculated for a curse to mankind? a curse under which they smart and groan to this hour, without thoroughly knowing the nature of the disease, and wanting understanding or courage to supply the remedy.

I need not excuse myself to your lordship, nor, I think, to any honest man, for the zeal I have shown in this cause . . . I have defended natural religion against a confederacy of atheists and divines. I now plead for natural society against politicians, and for natural reason against all three. . . . My antagonists have already done as much as I could desire. Parties in religion and politics make sufficient discoveries concerning each other, to give a sober man a proper caution against them all. The monarchic, and aristocratical, and popular partisans, have been jointly laying their axes to the root of all government, and have, in their turns, proved each other absurd and inconvenient. In vain you tell me that artificial government is good, but that I fall out only with the abuse. The thing! the thing itself is the abuse! . . .

I have purposely avoided the mention of the mixed form of government, for reasons that will be very obvious to your lordship. But my caution can avail me but little. You will not fail to urge it against me in favor of political society. You will not fail to show how the errors of the several simple modes are corrected by a mixture of all of them, and a proper balance of the several powers in such a state. I confess, my lord, that this has been long a darling mistake of my own; and that of all the sacrifices I have made to truth, this has been by far the greatest. . . . There are few with whom I can communicate so freely as with Pope. But Pope cannot bear every truth. He has a timidity which hinders the full exertion of his faculties, almost as effectually as bigotry cramps those of the general herd of mankind. But whoever is a genuine follower of truth keeps his eye steady upon his guide, indifferent whither he is led, provided that she is the leader. . . . Let us therefore

freely, and without fear or prejudice, examine this last contrivance of policy. . . .

First, then, all men are agreed that this junction of regal,
aristocratic, and popular power, must form a very complex,
nice, and intricate machine, which being composed of such a
variety of parts, with such opposite tendencies and movements,
it must be liable on every accident to be disordered. To speak
without metaphor, such a government must be liable to frequent cabals, tumults, and revolutions, from its very constitution. These are undoubtedly as ill effects as can happen in a
society; for in such a case, the closeness acquired by community, instead of serving for mutual defence, serves only to
increase the danger. . . .

In the second place, the several constituent parts having
their distinct rights, and these many of them so necessary to
be determined with exactness, are yet so indeterminate in their
nature, that it becomes a new and constant source of debate
and confusion. Hence it is, that whilst the business of government should be carrying on, the question is, Who has a right
to exercise this or that function of it, or what men have power
to keep their offices in any function? Whilst this contest continues, and whilst the balance in any sort continues, it has never
any remission; all manner of abuses and villainies in officers
remain unpunished; the greatest frauds and robberies in the
public revenues are committed in defiance of justice; and
abuses grow, by time and impunity, into customs; until they
prescribe against the laws, and grow too inveterate often to
admit a cure, unless such as may be as bad as the disease.

Thirdly, the several parts of this species of government,
though united, preserve the spirit which each form has separately. Kings are ambitious; the nobility haughty; and the
populace tumultuous and ungovernable. Each party, however
in appearance peaceable, carries on a design upon the others;
and it is owing to this, that in all questions, whether concerning
foreign or domestic affairs, the whole generally turns more
upon some party-matter than upon the nature of the thing itself; whether such a step will diminish or augment the power
of the crown, or how far the privileges of the subject are likely
to be extended or restricted by it. And these questions are
constantly resolved, without any consideration of the merits of
the cause, merely as the parties who uphold these jarring interests may chance to prevail; and as they prevail, the balance
is overset, now upon one side, now upon the other. The government is, one day, arbitrary power in a single person; an-

other, a juggling confederacy of a few to cheat the prince and enslave the people; and the third, a frantic and unmanageable democracy. The great instrument of all these changes, and what infuses a peculiar venom into all of them, is party. It is of no consequence what the principles of any party, or what their pretensions are; the spirit which actuates all parties is the same; the spirit of ambition, of self-interest, of oppression and treachery. This spirit entirely reverses all the principles which a benevolent nature has erected within us; all honesty, all equal justice, and even the ties of natural society, the natural affections. . . .

I have done with the forms of government. During the course of my inquiry you may have observed a very material difference between my manner of reasoning and that which is in use amongst the abettors of artificial society. They form their plans upon what seems most eligible to their imaginations, for the ordering of mankind. I discover the mistakes in those plans, from the real known consequences which have resulted from them. They have enlisted reason to fight against itself, and employ its whole force to prove that it is an insufficient guide to them in the conduct of their lives. But unhappily for us, in proportion as we have deviated from the plain rule of our nature, and turned our reason against itself, in that proportion have we increased the follies and miseries of mankind. The more deeply we penetrate into the labyrinth of art, the further we find ourselves from those ends for which we entered it. This has happened in almost every species of artificial society, and in all times. We found, or we thought we found, an inconvenience in having every man the judge of his own cause. Therefore judges were set up, at first, with discretionary powers. But it was soon found a miserable slavery to have our lives and properties precarious, and hanging upon the arbitrary determination of any one man, or set of men. We fled to laws as a remedy for this evil. By these we persuaded ourselves we might know with some certainty upon what ground we stood. But lo! differences arose upon the sense and interpretation of these laws. Thus were we brought back to our old incertitude. . . . In this uncertainty, (uncertain even to the professors, an Egyptian darkness to the rest of mankind), the contending parties felt themselves more effectually ruined by the delay, than they could have been by the injustice of any decision. Our inheritances are become a prize for disputation; and disputes and litigations are become an inheritance.

The professors of artificial law have always walked hand in

hand with the professors of artificial theology. As their end, in confounding the reason of man, and abridging his natural freedom, is exactly the same, they have adjusted the means to that end in a way entirely similar. The divine thunders out his *anathemas* with more noise and terror against the breach of one of his positive institutions, or the neglect of some of his trivial forms, than against the neglect or breach of those duties and commandments of natural religion, which by these forms and institutions he pretends to enforce. . . .

Ask of politicians the end for which laws were originally designed; and they will answer, that the laws were designed as a protection for the poor and weak, against the oppression of the rich and powerful. But surely no pretence can be so ridiculous; a man might as well tell me he has taken off my load, because he has changed the burden. If the poor man is not able to support his suit, according to the vexatious and expensive manner established in civilized countries, has not the rich as great an advantage over him as the strong has over the weak in a state of nature? But we will not place the state of nature, which is the reign of God, in competition with political society, which is the absurd usurpation of man. In a state of nature, it is true that a man of superior force may beat or rob me; but then it is true, that I am at full liberty to defend myself, or make reprisal by surprise or by cunning, or by any other way in which I may be superior to him. But in political society, a rich man may rob me in another way. I cannot defend myself; for money is the only weapon with which we are allowed to fight. And if I attempt to avenge myself the whole force of that society is ready to complete my ruin.

A good parson once said, that where mystery begins, religion ends. Cannot I say, as truly at least, of human laws, that where mystery begins, justice ends? It is hard to say, whether the doctors of law or divinity have made the greater advances in the lucrative business of mystery. The lawyers, as well as the theologians, have erected another reason besides natural reason; and the result has been, another justice besides natural justice. They have so bewildered the world and themselves in unmeaning forms and ceremonies, and so perplexed the plainest matters with metaphysical jargon, that it carries the highest danger to a man out of that profession, to make the least step without their advice and assistance. Thus, by confining to themselves the knowledge of the foundation of all men's lives and properties, they have reduced all mankind into the most abject and servile dependence. We are tenants at the will of these gentlemen for everything; and a metaphysical quibble is to decide whether the greatest villain breathing shall meet his deserts, or escape with impunity, or whether the best man in the society shall not be reduced to the lowest and most despicable condition it affords. In a word, my lord, the injustice, delay, puerility, false refinement, and affected mystery of the law are such, that many who live under it come to admire and envy the expedition, simplicity, and equality of arbitrary judgments. . . .

Before we finish our examination of artificial society, I shall lead your lordship into a closer consideration of the relations which it gives birth to, and the benefits, if such they are, which result from these relations. The most obvious division of society is into rich and poor; and it is no less obvious, that the number of the former bear a great disproportion to those of the latter. The whole business of the poor is to administer to the idleness, folly, and luxury of the rich; and that of the rich, in return, is to find the best methods of confirming the slavery and increasing the burdens of the poor. In a state of nature, it is an invariable law, that a man's acquisitions are in proportion to his labors. In a state of artificial society, it is a law as constant and as invariable, that those who labor most enjoy the fewest things; and that those who labor not at all have the greatest number of enjoyments. A constitution of things this, strange and ridiculous beyond expression! . . . On considering the strange and unaccountable fancies and contrivances of artificial reason, I have somewhere called this earth the Bedlam of our system. Looking now upon the effects of some of those fancies, may we not with equal reason call it likewise the Newgate and the Bridewell of the universe? Indeed the blindness of one part of mankind co-operating with the frenzy and villainy of the other, has been the real builder of this respectable fabric of political society: and as the blindness of mankind has caused their slavery, in return their state of slavery is made a pretence for continuing them in a state of blindness; for the politician will tell you gravely, that their life of servitude disqualifies the greater part of the race of man for a search of truth, and supplies them with no other than mean and insufficient ideas. This is but too true; and this is one of the reasons for which I blame such institutions.

In a misery of this sort, admitting some few lenitives, and those too but a few, nine parts in ten of the whole race of mankind drudge through life. It may be urged perhaps, in palliation of this, that at least the rich few find a considerable and real benefit from the wretchedness of the many. But is this so in fact? Let us examine the point with a little more attention. For this purpose the rich in all societies may be thrown into two classes. The first is of those who are powerful as well as rich, and conduct the operations of the vast political machine. The other is of those who employ their riches wholly in the acquisition of pleasure. As to the first sort, their continual care and anxiety, their toilsome days, and sleepless nights, are next to proverbial. These circumstances are sufficient almost to level their condition to that of the unhappy majority; but there are other circumstances which place them in a far lower condition. Not only their understandings labor continually, which is the severest labor, but their hearts are torn by the worst, most troublesome, and insatiable of all passions, by avarice, by ambition, by fear and jealousy. No part of the mind has rest. Power gradually extirpates from the mind every humane and gentle virtue. Pity, benevolence, friendship, are things almost unknown in high stations. . . . And indeed courts are the schools were cruelty, pride, dissimulation, and treachery are studied and taught in the most vicious perfection. This is a point so clear and acknowledged, that if it did not make a necessary part of my subject, I should pass it by entirely. And this has hindered me from drawing at full length, and in the most striking colors, this shocking picture of the degeneracy and wretchedness of human nature, in that part which is vulgarly thought its happiest and most amiable state. . . .

Let us now view the other species of the rich, those who devote their time and fortunes to idleness and pleasure. How much happier are they? The pleasures which are agreeable to nature are within the reach of all, and therefore can form no distinction in favor of the rich. The pleasures which art forces up are seldom sincere, and never satisfying. What is worse, this constant application to pleasure takes away from the enjoyment, or rather turns it into the nature of a very burdensome and laborious business. It has consequences much more fatal. It produces a weak valetudinary state of body, attended by all those horrid disorders, and yet more horrid methods of cure, which are the result of luxury on the one hand, and the weak and ridiculous efforts of human art on the other. The pleasures of such men are scarcely felt as pleasures; at the same time that they bring on pains and diseases, which are felt but too severely. The mind has its share of the misfortune; it grows lazy and enervate, unwilling and unable to search for truth, and utterly uncapable of knowing, much less of relishing, real happiness. The poor by their excessive labor, and the rich by their enormous luxury, are set upon a level, and rendered equally ignorant of any knowledge which might conduce to their happiness. A dismal view of the interior of all civil society! The lower part broken and ground down by the most cruel oppression; and the rich by their artificial method of life bringing worse evils on themselves than their tyranny could possibly inflict on those below them. Very different is the prospect of the natural state. Here there are no wants which nature gives, and in this state men can be sensible of no other wants, which are not to be supplied by a very moderate degree of labor; therefore there is no slavery. Neither is there any luxury, because no single man can supply the materials of it. Life is simple, and therefore it is happy.

I am conscious, my lord, that your politician will urge in his defence, that this unequal state is highly useful. That without dooming some part of mankind to extraordinary toil, the arts which cultivate life could not be exercised. But I demand of this politician, how such arts came to be necessary? He answers, that civil society could not well exist without them. So that these arts are necessary to civil society, and civil society necessary again to these arts. Thus are we running in a circle, without modesty, and without end, and making one error and extravagance an excuse for the other. My sentiments about these arts and their cause, I have often discoursed with my friends at large. Pope has expressed them in good verse, where he talks with so much force of reason and elegance of language, in praise of the state of nature:

> *Then was not pride, nor arts that pride to aid,*
> *Man walked with beast, joint tenant of the shade.*

On the whole, my lord, if political society, in whatever form, has still made the many the property of the few; if it has introduced labors unnecessary, vices and diseases unknown, and pleasures incompatible with nature; if in all countries it abridges the lives of millions, and renders those of millions more utterly abject and miserable, shall we still worship so destructive an idol, and daily sacrifice to it our health, our liberty, and our peace? Or shall we pass by this monstrous heap of absurd notions, and abominable practices, thinking we have sufficiently discharged our duty in exposing the trifling cheats, and ridiculous juggles of a few mad, designing, or ambitious priests? Alas! my lord, we labor under a mortal consumption, whilst we are so anxious about the cure of a sore finger. For has not this leviathan of civil power overflowed the earth with a deluge of blood, as if he were made to disport and play therein? We have shown that political society, on a moderate calculation, has been the means of murdering several times the number of inhabitants now upon the earth, during its short existence, not upwards of four thousand years in any accounts to be depended on. But we have said nothing of the other, and perhaps as bad, consequence of these wars, which have spilled such seas of blood, and reduced so many millions to a merciless slavery. But these are only the ceremonies performed in the porch of the political temple. Much more horrid ones are seen as you enter it. The several species of government vie with each other in the absurdity of their constitutions, and the oppression which they make their subjects endure. Take them under what form you please, they are in effect but a despotism, and they fall, both in effect and appearance too, after a very short period, into that cruel and detestable species of tyranny: which I rather call it, because we have been educated under another form, than that this is of worse consequences to mankind. For the free governments, for the point of their space, and the moment of their duration, have felt more confusion, and committed more flagrant acts of tyranny, than the most perfect despotic governments which we have ever known. Turn your eye next to the labyrinth of the law, and the iniquity conceived in its intricate recesses. Consider the ravages committed in the bowels of all commonwealths by ambition, by avarice, envy, fraud, open injustice, and pretended friendship; vices which could draw little support from a state of nature, but which blossom and flourish in the rankness of political society. Revolve our whole discourse; add to it all those reflections which your own good understanding shall suggest, and make a strenuous effort beyond the reach of vulgar philosophy, to confess that the cause of artificial society is more defenceless even than that of artificial religion; that it is as derogatory from the honor of the Creator, as subversive of human reason, and productive of infinitely more mischief to the human race.

If pretended revelations have caused wars where they were opposed, and slavery where they were received, the pretended wise inventions of politicians have done the same. But the slavery has been much heavier, the wars far more bloody, and both more universal by many degrees. Show me any mischief produced by the madness or wickedness of theologians, and I will show you a hundred resulting from the ambition and villainy of conquerors and statesmen. Show me an absurdity in religion, and I will undertake to show you a hundred for one in political laws and institutions. If you say that natural religion is a sufficient guide without the foreign aid of revelation, on what principle should political laws become necessary? Is not the same reason available in theology and in politics? If the laws of nature are the laws of God, is it consistent with the Divine wisdom to prescribe rules to us, and leave the enforcement of them to the folly of human institutions? Will you follow truth but to a certain point?

We are indebted for all our miseries to our distrust of that guide which Providence thought sufficient for our condition, our own natural reason, which rejecting both in human and divine things, we have given our necks to the yoke of political and theological slavery. We have renounced the prerogative of man, and it is no wonder that we should be treated like beasts. But our misery is much greater than theirs, as the crime we commit in rejecting the lawful dominion of our reason is greater than any which they can commit. If, after all, you should confess all these things, yet plead the necessity of political institutions, weak and wicked as they are, I can argue with equal, perhaps superior, force, concerning the necessity of artificial religion; and every step you advance in your argument, you add a strength to mine. So that if we are resolved to submit our reason and our liberty to civil usurpation, we have nothing to do but to conform as quietly as we can to the vulgar notions which are connected with this, and take up the theology of the vulgar as well as their politics. But if we think this necessity rather imaginary than real, we should renounce their dreams of society, together with their visions of religion, and vindicate ourselves into perfect liberty. . . .

*An Essay
towards an
Abridgment of the English History
in Three Books*
[1757]

Among Burke's early literary projects was a one-volume
history of England, which he contracted with Robert Dodsley
to complete by 1759. Burke worked hard on this literary
work, but for various reasons he only carried it through the
reign of King John, and then abandoned it; in his lifetime
only forty-eight pages of his history were published. After his
death the entire history, comprising over three hundred pages,
was published in 1811, under the title *Essay towards an
Abridgment of the English History*.

This work has been unduly neglected by most Burke scholars. Yet its importance in understanding his early intellectual
development can hardly be overestimated. Burke's history revealed an extensive knowledge of European and English affairs, from the Ancients to the late Middle Ages; Lord Acton
found much in his history of value for historical insight.
But more important than the knowledge it contained, Burke's
history supplies the first explicit evidence of his profound respect for the historical method of Montesquieu, which was to
permeate almost every page of all that he was later to write on
politics. His appeal to history includes a recognition of the
chief elements that, in various combinations in different areas
of Europe, comprised the foundations of European civilization—Roman civil law, Christian morality, and Teutonic customs and manners. These basic ingredients of Western civilization, which always commanded his veneration and respect,
were embodied in Church and State and infused even the
subordinate corporate orders of society.

Burke had no explicit or systematic philosophy of history.
But his *Abridgment of English History* reveals a conception
of man's place in temporal events, under the mysterious dispensations of God, that connects his view of history with
his religious and political philosophy. The common unity
throughout the "Christian commonwealth of Europe" of laws,
morals, and customs, though modified by the particular cir-

cumstances of each nation, was for him the product of slow historical development. As a member of the Christian commonwealth, Burke found his primary source of ethical principles in Divine revelation. As a British subject he based his legal principles upon the common law and equity of the English constitution. But history was for him a secondary source of moral and legal truths. The revelations of historical continuity were for Burke "the known march of the ordinary providence of God," and they took complete precedence over social knowledge acquired through immediate sense perception and private analytical reason. Through moral, legal, political, and literary documents and social monuments, through the accumulated knowledge of the practical arts and sciences, and through the growth of civil institutions, history revealed the will of God in man's temporal affairs. But unlike religion and the law, history was not a depository of principles. It was "a preceptor of prudence" which taught men humbly to subordinate their private will and reason to the general pattern of God's reason and will as revealed in human temporal events. Refining upon Aristotle, Burke contended that man was by nature not only a social and political animal, but also a religious animal; and religion was for him the foundation of civil society. His conception of historical continuity included a principle of development and change, under the immediate and conscious direction of man's corporate reason and free will, but guided also by the mysterious hand of Providence. His veneration of antiquity, his awareness of the slow organic growth of institutions and nations and of man's subordination to moral and civil laws, and, above all, his sense of the intricacy and mystery at the core of man's life on earth, flowed from his faith in historical revelation.

Burke's theory of England's constitutional development, which forms the grand theme of *An Abridgment of English History*, is a particular manifestation of his more general view of history. He believed that as English sovereigns with doubtful claims to the throne granted subordinate orders in the state civil rights and privileges, in order to secure allegiance, a legal system of liberty, order, and justice gradually developed. This, in essence, was how constitutional government based on division of powers grew in England. Burke never tired of pointing out that it was not on any rational system or plan that England developed civil liberty beyond that of any other nation, but by "working after the pattern of Nature," and through "a deliberate election of ages and generations." In this light, a close reading of *An Abridgment of English History* will supply rich insights into his writings on English constitutional problems, particularly concerning the American colonies and Ireland, and also on the French Revolution, which totally violated his conception of history.

. . . It is very difficult, at this distance of time, and with so little information, to discern clearly what sort of civil government prevailed among the ancient Britons. In all very uncultivated countries, as society is not close nor intricate, nor property very valuable, liberty subsists with few restraints. The natural equality of mankind appears and is asserted, and therefore there are but obscure lines of any form of government. In every society of this sort the natural connections are the same as in others, though the political ties are weak. Among such barbarians, therefore, though there is little authority in the magistrate, there is often great power lodged, or rather left, in the father: for, as among the Gauls, so among the Britons, he had the power of life and death in his own family, over his children and his servants.

But among freemen and heads of families, causes of all sorts seem to have been decided by the Druids: they summoned and dissolved all the public assemblies; they alone had the power of capital punishments, and indeed seem to have had the sole execution and interpretation of whatever laws subsisted among this people. In this respect the Celtic nations did not greatly differ from others, except that we view them in an earlier stage of society. Justice was in all countries originally administered by the priesthood: nor, indeed, could laws in their first feeble state have either authority or sanction, so as to compel men to relinquish their natural independence, had they not appeared to come down to them enforced by beings of more than human power. The first openings of civility have been everywhere made by religion. Amongst the Romans, the custody and interpretation of the laws continued solely in the college of the pontiffs for above a century.

The time in which the Druid priesthood was instituted is unknown. It probably rose, like other institutions of that kind, from low and obscure beginnings, and acquired from time, and the labors of able men, a form by which it extended itself so far, and attained at length so mighty an influence over the minds of a fierce and otherwise ungovernable people. Of the place where it arose there is somewhat less doubt: Cæsar mentions it as the common opinion that this institution began in Britain, that there it always remained in the highest perfection, and that from thence it diffused itself into Gaul. I own I find it not easy to assign any tolerable cause why an order of so much authority and a discipline so exact should have passed from the more barbarous people to the more civilized, from the younger to the older, from the colony to the mother country: but it is not wonderful that the early extinction of this order, and that general contempt in which the Romans held all the barbarous nations, should have left these matters obscure and full of difficulty.

The Druids were kept entirely distinct from the body of the people; and they were exempted from all the inferior and burdensome offices of society, that they might be at leisure to attend the important duties of their own charge. They were chosen out of the best families, and from the young men of the most promising talents: a regulation which placed and preserved them in a respectable light with the world. None were admitted into this order but after a long and laborious novitiate, which made the character venerable in their own eyes by the time and difficulty of attaining it. They were much devoted to solitude, and thereby acquired that abstracted and thoughtful air which is so imposing upon the vulgar; and when they appeared in public, it was seldom, and only on some great occasion—in the sacrifices of the gods, or on the seat of judgment. They prescribed medicine; they formed the youth; they paid the last honors to the dead; they foretold events; they exercised themselves in magic. They were at once the priests, lawgivers, and physicians of their nation, and consequently concentred in themselves all that respect that men have diffusively for those who heal their diseases, protect their property, or reconcile them to the Divinity. What contributed not a little to the stability and power of this order was the extent of its foundation, and the regularity and proportion of its structure. It took in both sexes; and the female Druids were in no less esteem for their knowledge and sanctity than the males. It was divided into several subordinate ranks and classes; and they all depended upon a chief or Arch-Druid, who was elected to his place with great authority and preeminence for life. They were further armed with a power of interdicting from their sacrifices, or excommunicating, any obnoxious persons. This interdiction, so similar to that used by the ancient Athenians, and to that since practised among Christians, was followed by an exclusion from all the benefits of civil community; and it was accordingly the most dreaded of all punishments. This ample authority was in general usefully exerted; by the interposition of the Druids differences were composed, and wars ended; and the minds of the fierce Northern people, being reconciled to each other under the influence of religion, united with signal effect against their common enemies. . . .

It is impossible not to perceive a great conformity between

this and the ancient orders which have been established for the purposes of religion in almost all countries. For, to say nothing of the resemblance which many have traced between this and the Jewish priesthood, the Persian Magi, and the Indian Brahmans, it did not so greatly differ from the Roman priesthood, either in the original objects or in the general mode of worship, or in the constitution of their hierarchy. . . . When the order of Druids was suppressed by the Emperors, it was rather from a dread of an influence incompatible with the Roman government than from any dislike of their religious opinions. . . .

When Vespasian arrived to the head of affairs, he caused the vigor of his government to be felt in Britain, as he had done in all the other parts of the Empire. . . . But its final reduction and perfect settlement were reserved for Julius Agricola, a man by whom it was a happiness for the Britons to be conquered. He was endued with all those bold and popular virtues which would have given him the first place in the times of the free Republic; and he joined to them all that reserve and moderation which enabled him to fill great offices with safety . . .

After reducing some tribes, Mona became the principal object of his attention. . . . Here Agricola observed a conduct very different from that of his predecessor, Paulinus: the island, when he had reduced it, was treated with great lenity. Agricola was a man of humanity and virtue: he pitied the condition and respected the prejudices of the conquered. This behavior facilitated the progress of his arms, insomuch that in less than two campaigns all the British nations comprehended in what we now call England yielded themselves to the Roman government, as soon as they found that peace was no longer to be considered as a dubious blessing. . . .

In the interval between his campaigns Agricola was employed in the great labors of peace. He knew that the general must be perfected by the legislator, and that the conquest is neither permanent nor honorable which is only an introduction to tyranny. . . . He eased the tribute of the province, not so much by reducing it in quantity as by cutting off all those vexatious practices which attended the levying of it, far more grievous than the imposition itself. Every step in securing the subjection of the conquered country was attended with the utmost care in providing for its peace and internal order. Agricola reconciled the Britons to the Roman government by reconciling them to the Roman manners. He moulded that fierce nation by degrees to soft and social customs, leading them imperceptibly into a fondness for baths, for gardens, for grand houses, and all the commodious elegancies of a cultivated life. He diffused a grace and dignity over this new luxury by the introduction of literature. He invited instructors in all the arts and sciences from Rome; and he sent the principal youth of Britain to that city to be educated at his own expense. In short, he subdued the Britons by civilizing them, and made them exchange a savage liberty for a polite and easy subjection. His conduct is the most perfect model for those employed in the unhappy, but sometimes necessary task, of subduing a rude and free people. . . .

Rome extended herself by her colonies into every part of her empire, and was everywhere present. . . .

There were few countries of any considerable extent in which all these different modes of government and different shades and gradations of servitude did not exist together. There were allies, *municipia*, provinces, and colonies in this island, as elsewhere; and those dissimilar parts, far from being discordant, united to make a firm and compact body, the motion of any member of which could only serve to confirm and establish the whole; and when time was given to this structure to coalesce and settle, it was found impossible to break any part of it from the Empire.

By degrees the several parts blended and softened into one another. And as the remembrance of enmity, on the one hand, wore away by time, so, on the other, the privileges of the Roman citizens at length became less valuable. When nothing throughout so vast an extent of the globe was of consideration but a single man, there was no reason to make any distinction amongst his subjects. Claudius first gave the full rights of the city to all the Gauls. Under Antoninus Rome opened her gates still wider. All the subjects of the Empire were made partakers of the same common rights. . . .

But Constantine made a much greater change with regard to religion by the establishment of Christianity. At what time the Gospel was first preached in this island I believe it impossible to ascertain, as it came in gradually, and without, or rather contrary to, public authority. It was most probably first introduced among the legionary soldiers; for we find St. Alban, the first British martyr, to have been of that body. As it was introduced privately, so its growth was for a long time insensible; but it shot up at length with great vigor, and spread itself widely, at first under the favor of Constantius and the protection of Helena, and at length under the establishment of Constantine. From this time it is to be considered as the ruling religion; though heathenism subsisted long after, and at last expired imperceptibly, and with as little noise as Christianity had been at first introduced. . . .

The Empire was perishing by the vices of its constitution. . . .

As the Empire on the continent was now attacked on all sides, and staggered under the innumerable shocks which it received, [it] ventured to recall the Roman forces from Britain . . .

When the Romans deserted this island, they left a country, with regard to the arts of war or government, in a manner barbarous, but destitute of that spirit or those advantages with which sometimes a state of barbarism is attended. They carried out of each province its proper and natural strength, and supplied it by that of some other, which had no connection with the country. The troops raised in Britain often served in Egypt; and those which were employed for the protection of this island were sometimes from Batavia or Germany, sometimes from provinces far to the east. Whenever the strangers were withdrawn, as they were very easily, the province was left in the hands of men wholly unpractised in war. After a peaceable possession of more than three hundred years, the Britons derived but very few benefits from their subjection to the conquerors and civilizers of mankind. Neither does it appear that the Roman people were at any time extremely numerous in this island, or had spread themselves, their manners, or their language as extensively in Britain as they had done in the other parts of their Empire. . . .

After having been so long subject to a foreign dominion, there was among the Britons no royal family, no respected order in the state, none of those titles to government, confirmed by opinion and long use, more efficacious than the wisest schemes for the settlement of the nation. Mere personal merit was then the only pretence to power. But this circumstance only added to the misfortunes of a people who had no orderly method of election, and little experience of merit in any of the candidates. During this anarchy, whilst they suffered the most dreadful calamities from the fury of barbarous nations which invaded them, they fell into that disregard of religion, and those loose, disorderly manners, which are sometimes the consequence of desperate and hardened wretchedness, as well as the common distempers of ease and prosperity. . . .

But having been long habituated to defeats, neither relying on their king nor on themselves, and fatigued with the obstinate attacks of an enemy whom they sometimes checked, but could never remove, in one of their national assemblies it was resolved to call in the mercenary aid of the Saxons, a powerful nation of Germany, which had been long by their piratical incursions terrible not only to them, but to all the adjacent countries. . . .

The army which came over under Hengist did not exceed fifteen hundred men. . . .

Hengist and his Saxons, who had obtained by the free vote of the Britons that introduction into this island they had so long in vain attempted by arms, saw that by being necessary they were superior to their allies. They discovered the character of the king; they were eye-witnesses of the internal weakness and distraction of the kingdom. This state of Britain was represented with so much effect to the Saxons in Germany, that another and much greater embarkation followed the first; new bodies daily crowded in. . . . Hengist, with very little opposition, subdued the province of Kent, and there laid the foundation of the first Saxon kingdom. . . .

The news of his success had roused all Saxony. Five great bodies of that adventurous people, under different and independent commanders, very nearly at the same time broke in upon as many different parts of the island. They came no longer as pirates, but as invaders. Whilst the Britons contended with one body of their fierce enemies, another gained ground, and filled with slaughter and desolation the whole country from sea to sea. A devouring war, a dreadful famine, a plague, the most wasteful of any recorded in our history, united to consummate the ruin of Britain. The ecclesiastical writers of that age, confounded at the view of those complicated calamities, saw nothing but the arm of God stretched out for the punishment of a sinful and disobedient nation. And truly, when we set before us in one point of view the condition of almost all the parts which had lately composed the Western Empire—of Britain, of Gaul, of Italy, of Spain, of Africa—at once overwhelmed by a resistless inundation of most cruel barbarians, whose inhuman method of war made but a small part of the miseries with which these nations were afflicted, we are almost driven out of the circle of political inquiry: we are in a manner compelled to acknowledge the hand of God in those immense revolutions by which at certain periods He so signally asserts His supreme dominion, and brings about that great system of change which is perhaps as necessary to the moral as it is found to be in the natural world.

But whatever was the condition of the other parts of Europe, it is generally agreed that the state of Britain was the worst of all. . . .

That they were much more broken and reduced than any other nation which had fallen under the German power I think may be inferred from two considerations. First, that in all other parts of Europe the ancient language subsisted after the conquest, and at length incorporated with that of the conquerors; whereas in England the Saxon language received little or no tincture from the Welsh; and it seems, even among the lowest people, to have continued a dialect of pure Teutonic to the time in which it was itself blended with the Norman. Secondly, that on the continent the Christian religion, after the Northern irruptions, not only remained, but flourished. It was very early and universally adopted by the ruling people. In England it was so entirely extinguished, that, when Augustin undertook his mission, it does not appear that among all the Saxons there was a single person professing Christianity. . . .

The Anglo-Saxons . . . were, until their conversion, ignorant of the use of letters. . . .

Light scarce begins to dawn until the introduction of Christianity, which, bringing with it the use of letters and the arts of civil life, affords at once a juster account of things and facts that are more worthy of relation: nor is there, indeed, any revolution so remarkable in the English story.

The bishops of Rome had for some time meditated the conversion of the Anglo-Saxons. Pope Gregory, who is surnamed the Great, affected that pious design with an uncommon zeal; and he at length found a circumstance highly favorable to it in the marriage of a daughter of Charibert, a king of the Franks, to the reigning monarch of Kent. This opportunity induced Pope Gregory to commission Augustin, a monk of Rheims, and a man of distinguished piety, to undertake this arduous enterprise.

It was in the year of Christ 600, and 150 years after the coming of the first Saxon colonies into England, that Ethelbert, king of Kent, received intelligence of the arrival in his dominions of a number of men in a foreign garb, practising several strange and unusual ceremonies, who desired to be conducted to the king's presence, declaring that they had things to communicate to him and to his people of the utmost importance to their eternal welfare. This was Augustin, with forty of the associates of his mission, who now landed in the Isle of Thanet, the same place by which the Saxons had before entered, when they extirpated Christianity. . . .

The king was among their first converts. The principal of his nobility, as usual, followed that example . . . Paganism, after a faint resistance, everywhere gave way. And, indeed, the chief difficulties which Christianity had to encounter did not arise so much from the struggles of opposite religious prejudices as from the gross and licentious manners of a barbarous people. . . .

As to the manners of the Anglo-Saxons, they were such as might be expected in a rude people—fierce, and of a gross simplicity. Their clothes were short. As all barbarians are much taken with exterior form, and the advantages and distinctions which are conferred by Nature, the Saxons set an high value on comeliness of person, and studied much to improve it. . . .

They dwelt in cottages of wicker-work plastered with clay and thatched with rushes, where they sat with their families, their officers and domestics, round a fire made in the middle of the house. In this manner their greatest princes lived amidst the ruins of Roman magnificence. But the introduction of Christianity, which, under whatever form, always confers such inestimable benefits on mankind, soon made a sensible change in these rude and fierce manners.

It is by no means impossible, that, for an end so worthy, Providence on some occasions might directly have interposed. The books which contain the history of this time and change are little else than a narrative of miracles—frequently, however, with such apparent marks of weakness or design that they afford little encouragement to insist on them. They were then received with a blind credulity: they have been since rejected with as undistinguishing a disregard. But as it is not in my design nor inclination, nor indeed in my power, either to establish or refute these stories, it is sufficient to observe, that the reality or opinion of such miracles was the principal cause of the early acceptance and rapid progress of Christianity in this island. Other causes undoubtedly concurred; and it will be more to our purpose to consider some of the human and politic ways by which religion was advanced in this nation, and those more particularly by which the monastic institution, then interwoven with Christianity, and making an equal progress with it, attained to so high a pitch of property and power, so as, in a time extremely short, to form a kind of order, and that not the least considerable, in the state. . . .

In the change of religion, care was taken to render the transition from falsehood to truth as little violent as possible. Though the first proselytes were kings, it does not appear that there was any persecution. It was a precept of Pope Gregory, under whose auspices this mission was conducted, that the heathen temples should not be destoyed, especially where they were well built—but that, first removing the idols, they should be consecrated anew by holier rites and to better purposes, in order that the prejudices of the people might not be too rudely shocked by a declared profanation of what they had so long held sacred, and that, everywhere beholding the same places to which they had formerly resorted for religious comfort, they might be gradually reconciled to the new doctrines and ceremonies which were there introduced; and as the sacrifices used in the Pagan worship were always attended with feasting, and consequently were highly grateful to the multitude, the Pope ordered that oxen should as usual be slaughtered near the church, and the people indulged in their ancient festivity. Whatever popular customs of heathenism were found to be absolutely not incompatible with Christianity were retained; and some of them were continued to a very late period. Deer were at a certain season brought into St. Paul's church in London, and laid on the altar; and this custom subsisted until the Reformation. The names of some of the Church festivals were, with a similar design, taken from those of the heathen which had been celebrated at the same time of the year. Nothing could have been more prudent than these regulations: they were, indeed, formed from a perfect understanding of human nature. . . .

If the monks contributed to the fall of science in the Roman Empire, it is certain that the introduction of learning and civility into this Northern world is entirely owing to their labors. It is true that they cultivated letters only in a secondary way, and as subsidiary to religion. But the scheme of Christianity is such that it almost necessitates an attention to many kinds of learning. For the Scripture is by no means an irrelative system of moral and divine truths; but it stands connected with so many histories, and with the laws, opinions, and manners of so many various sorts of people, and in such different times, that it is altogether impossible to arrive to any tolerable knowledge of it without having recourse to much exterior inquiry: for which reason the progress of this religion has always been marked by that of letters. . . .

The Christian religion, having once taken root in Kent, spread itself with great rapidity throughout all the other Saxon kingdoms in England. The manners of the Saxons underwent a notable alteration by this change in their religion: their ferocity was much abated; they became more mild and sociable; and their laws began to partake of the softness of their manners . . .

Several kings resigned their crowns to devote themselves to religious contemplation in monasteries—more at that time and in this nation than in all other nations and in all times. This, as it introduced great mildness into the tempers of the people, made them less warlike . . .

If people so barbarous as the Germans have no laws, they have yet customs that serve in their room; and these customs operate amongst them better than laws, because they become a sort of Nature both to the governors and the governed. This circumstance in some measure removed all fear of the abuse of authority, and induced the Germans to permit their chiefs to decide upon matters of lesser moment, their private differences . . . These chiefs were a sort of judges, but not legislators; nor do they appear to have had a share in the superior branches of the executive part of government—the business of peace and war, and everything of a public nature, being determined . . . by the whole body of the people, according to a maxim general among the Germans, that what concerned all ought to be handled by all. Thus were delineated the faint and incorrect outlines of our Constitution, which has since been so nobly fashioned and so highly finished. This fine system, says Montesquieu, was invented in the woods; but whilst it remained in the woods, and for a long time after, it was far from being a fine one—no more, indeed, than a very imperfect attempt at government, a system for a rude and barbarous people, calculated to maintain them in their barbarity. . . .

The ancient German people, as all the other Northern tribes, consisted of freemen and slaves: the freemen professed arms, the slaves cultivated the ground. But men were not allowed to profess arms at their own will, nor until they were admitted to that dignity by an established order . . . No man could stand out as an independent individual, but must have enlisted in one of these military fraternities; and as soon as he had so enlisted, immediately he became bound to his leader in the strictest dependence, which was confirmed by an oath, and to his brethren in a common vow for their mutual support in all dangers, and for the advancement and the honor of their common chief. This chief was styled Senior, Lord, and the like terms, which marked out a superiority in age and merit; the followers were called Ambacti, Comites, Leudes, Vassals, and other terms, marking submission and dependence. This was the very first origin of civil, or rather, military government, amongst the ancient people of Europe; and it arose from the connection that necessarily was created between the person who gave the arms, or knighted the young man, and him that received them; which implied that they were to be occupied in his service who originally gave them. These principles it is necessary strictly to attend to, because they will serve much to explain the whole course both of government and real property, wherever the German nations obtained a settlement . . .

In no other bonds, I conceive, were they united before they quitted Germany. In this ancient state we know them from Tacitus. Then follows an immense gap, in which undoubtedly some changes were made by time; and we hear little more of them until we find them Christians, and makers of written laws.

In this interval of time the origin of kings may be traced out. . . .

What rights the king had in this assembly is a matter of equal uncertainty. The laws generally run in his name, with the assent of his wise men, &c. But considering the low estimation of royalty in those days, this may rather be considered as the voice of the executive magistrate, of the person who compiled the law and propounded it to the Witenagemote for their consent, than of a legislator dictating from his own proper authority. For then, it seems, the law was digested by the king or his council for the assent of the general assembly. That order is now reversed. All these things are, I think, sufficient to show of what a visionary nature those systems are which would settle the ancient Constitution in the most remote times exactly in the same form in which we enjoy it at this day—not considering that such mighty changes in manners, during so many ages, always must produce a considerable change in laws, and in the forms as well as the powers of all governments. . . .

The Saxons were extremely imperfect in their ideas of law—

the civil institutions of the Romans, who were the legislators of mankind, having never reached them. The order of our courts, the discipline of our jury, by which it is become so elaborate a contrivance, and the introduction of a sort of scientific reason in the law, have been the work of ages. . . .

The Saxons were extremely moderate in their punishments. Murder and treason were compounded, and a fine set for every offence. . . . The Saxon government did little more than act the part of arbitrator between the contending parties, exacted the payment of this composition, and reduced it to a certainty. However, the king, as the sovereign of all, and the sheriff, as the judicial officer, had their share in those fines. This unwillingness to shed blood, which the Saxon customs gave rise to, the Christian religion confirmed. . . .

. . . EUROPE AT THE TIME OF THE NORMAN INVASION

Before the period of which we are going to treat, England was little known or considered in Europe. Their situation, their domestic calamities, and their ignorance circumscribed the views and politics of the English within the bounds of their own island. But the Norman conqueror threw down all these barriers. The English laws, manners, and maxims were suddenly changed; the scene was enlarged; and the communication with the rest of Europe, being thus opened, has been preserved ever since in a continued series of wars and negotiations. That we may, therefore, enter more fully into the matters which lie before us, it is necessary that we understand the state of the neighboring continent at the time when this island first came to be interested in its affairs.

The Northern nations who had overran the Roman Empire were at first rather actuated by avarice than ambition, and were more intent upon plunder than conquest; they were carried beyond their original purposes, when they began to form regular governments, for which they had been prepared by no just ideas of legislation. For a long time, therefore, there was little of order in their affairs or foresight in their designs. The Goths, the Burgundians, the Franks, the Vandals, the Suevi, after they had prevailed over the Roman Empire, by turns prevailed over each other in continual wars, which were carried on upon no principles of a determinate policy, entered into upon motives of brutality and caprice, and ended as fortune and rude violence chanced to prevail. Tumult, anarchy, confusion, overspread the face of Europe; and an obscurity rests upon the transactions of that time which suffers us to discover nothing but its extreme barbarity. . . .

Italy, who had so long sat the mistress of the world, was by turns the slave of all nations. The possession of that fine country was hotly disputed between the Greek Emperor and the Lombards, and it suffered infinitely by that contention. Germany, the parent of so many nations, was exhausted by the swarms she had sent abroad.

However, in the midst of this chaos there were principles at work which reduced things to a certain form, and gradually unfolded a system in which the chief movers and main springs were the Papal and the Imperial powers—the aggrandizement or diminution of which have been the drift of almost all the politics, intrigues, and wars which have employed and distracted Europe to this day.

From Rome the whole Western world had received its Christianity; she was the asylum of what learning had escaped the general desolation; and even in her ruins she preserved something of the majesty of her ancient greatness. On these accounts she had a respect and a weight which increased every day amongst a simple religious people, who looked but a little way into the consequences of their actions. The rudeness of the world was very favorable for the establishment of an empire of opinion. The moderation with which the Popes at first exerted this empire made its growth unfelt until it could no longer be opposed; and the policy of later Popes, building on the piety of the first, continually increased it: and they made use of every instrument but that of force. . . .

Charlemagne . . . received from the hand of the Pope the Imperial crown, sanctified by the authority of the Holy See, and with it the title of Emperor of the Romans, a name venerable from the fame of the old Empire, and which was supposed to carry great and unknown prerogatives; and thus the Empire rose again out of its ruins in the West, and, what is remarkable, by means of one of those nations which had helped to destroy it. . . . From Charlemagne the Pope received in return an enlargement and a confirmation of his new territory. Thus the Papal and Imperial powers mutually gave birth to each other. They continued for some ages, and in some measure still continue, closely connected, with a variety of pretensions upon each other, and on the rest of Europe. . . .

The Pope, because he first revived the Imperial dignity, claimed a right of disposing of it, or at least of giving validity to the election of the Emperor. The Emperor, on the other hand, remembering the rights of those sovereigns whose title he bore, and how lately the power which insulted him with such demands had arisen from the bounty of his predecessors, claimed the same privileges in the election of a Pope. The claims of both were somewhat plausible; and they were supported, the one by force of arms, and the other by ecclesiastical influence, powers which in those days were very nearly balanced. . . . In every city the parties in favor of each of the opponents were not far from an equality in their numbers and strength. Whilst these parties disagreed in the choice of a master, by contending for a choice in their subjection they grew imperceptibly into freedom, and passed through the medium of faction and anarchy into regular commonwealths. Thus arose the republics of Venice, of Genoa, of Florence, Sienna, and Pisa, and several others. . . .

All the kingdoms on the continent of Europe were governed nearly in the same form; from whence arose a great similitude in the manners of their inhabitants. . . .

REIGN OF WILLIAM THE CONQUEROR

. . . William . . . fortified his throne . . . strongly by the policy of good government. To London he confirmed by charter the liberties it had enjoyed under the Saxon kings, and endeavored to fix the affections of the English in general by governing them with equity according to their ancient laws, and by treating them on all occasions with the most engaging deportment. He set up no pretences which arose from absolute conquest. He confirmed their estates to all those who had not appeared in arms against him, and seemed not to aim at subjecting the English to the Normans, but to unite the two nations under the wings of a common parental care. . . .

[Henry I] confirmed and enlarged the privileges of the city of London, and gave to the whole kingdom a charter of liberties, which was the first of the kind, and laid the foundation of those successive charters which at last completed the freedom of the subject. . . .

In imitation of the measures of the late king, . . . [Stephen] concluded all by giving a charter of liberties as ample as the people at that time aspired to. This charter contained a renunciation of the forests made by his predecessor, a grant to the ecclesiastics of a jurisdiction over their own vassals, and to the people in general an immunity from un-

just tallages and exactions. It is remarkable, that the oath of
allegiance taken by the nobility on this occasion was condi-
tional: it was to be observed so long as the king observed the
terms of his charter . . .

At the Conquest there were very few fortifications in the
kingdom. William found it necessary for his security to erect
several. During the struggles of the English, the Norman nobility were permitted (as in reason it could not be refused)
to fortify their own houses. It was, however, still understood
that no new fortress could be erected without the king's special license. These private castles began very early to embarrass the government. The royal castles were scarcely less
troublesome: for, as everything was then in tenure, the governor held his place by the tenure of castle-guard; and thus,
instead of a simple officer, subject to his pleasure, the king
had to deal with a feudal tenant, secure against him by law, if
he performed his services, and by force, if he was unwilling to
perform them. Every resolution of government required a
sort of civil war to put it in execution. The two last kings had
taken and demolished several of these castles; but when they
found the reduction of any of them difficult, their custom frequently was, to erect another close by it, tower against tower,
ditch against ditch: these were called Malvoisins, from their
purpose and situation. Thus, instead of removing, they in fact
doubled the mischief. Stephen, perceiving the passion of the
barons for these castles, among other popular acts in the beginning of his reign, gave a general license for erecting them.
Then was seen to arise in every corner of the kingdom, in every petty seigniory, an inconceivable multitude of strongholds,
the seats of violence, and the receptacles of murderers, felons,
debasers of the coin, and all manner of desperate and abandoned villains. Eleven hundred and fifteen of these castles were
built in this single reign. The barons, having thus shut out the
law, made continual inroads upon each other, and spread war,
rapine, burning, and desolation throughout the whole kingdom. They infested the highroads, and put a stop to all trade
by plundering the merchants and travellers. Those who dwelt
in the open country they forced into their castles, and after
pillaging them of all their visible substance, these tyrants held
them in dungeons, and tortured them with a thousand cruel
inventions to extort a discovery of their hidden wealth. The
lamentable representation given by history of those barbarous
times justifies the pictures in the old romances of the castles
of giants and magicians. A great part of Europe was in the

same deplorable condition. It was then that some gallant spirits, struck with a generous indignation at the tyranny of these miscreants, blessed solemnly by the bishop, and followed by the praises and vows of the people, sallied forth to vindicate the chastity of women and to redress the wrongs of travellers and peaceable men. The adventurous humor inspired by the Crusade heightened and extended this spirit; and thus the idea of knight-errantry was formed. . . .

It was grown into a custom for the king to grant a charter of liberties on his accession to the crown. Henry [II] also granted a charter of that kind, confirming that of his grandfather; but as his situation was very different from that of his predecessors, his charter was different—reserved, short, dry, conceived in general terms—a gift, not a bargain. And, indeed, there seems to have been at that juncture but little occasion to limit a power which seemed not more than sufficient to correct all the evils of an unlimited liberty. . . .

REIGN OF JOHN

We are now arrived at one of the most memorable periods in the English story . . .

[King John] also . . . paid court to the cities and boroughs, which is the first instance of that policy: but several of these communities now happily began to emerge from their slavery, and, taking advantage of the necessities and confusion of the late reign, increased in wealth and consequence, and had then first attained a free and regular form of administration. The towns new to power declared heartily in favor of a prince who was willing to allow that their declaration could confer a right. The nobility, who saw themselves beset by the Church, the law, and the burghers, had taken no measures, nor even a resolution, and therefore had nothing left but to concur in acknowledging the title of John, whom they knew and hated. But though they were not able to exclude him from the succession, they had strength enough to oblige him to a solemn promise of restoring those liberties and franchises which they had always claimed without having ever enjoyed or even perfectly understood. . . .

John, by virtue of a prerogative hitherto undisputed, summoned his English barons to attend him into France; but instead of a compliance with his orders, he was surprised with a solemn demand of their ancient liberties. It is astonishing that the barons should at that time have ventured on a resolution

of such dangerous importance, as they had provided no sort
of means to support them. But the history of those times
furnishes many instances of the like want of design in the
most momentous affairs, and shows that it is in vain to look
for political causes for the actions of men, who were most
commonly directed by a brute caprice, and were for the
greater part destitute of any fixed principles of obedience or
resistance. . . .

John, at the head of one of the finest armies in the world,
trembled inwardly, when he reflected how little he possessed
or merited their confidence. Wounded by the consciousness of
his crimes, excommunicated by the Pope, hated by his subjects, in danger of being at once abandoned by heaven and
earth, he was filled with the most fearful anxiety. . . .

Cardinal Langton . . . became the first mover in all the
affairs which distinguish the remainder of this reign. In the
oath which he administered to John on his absolution, he did
not confine himself solely to the ecclesiastical grievances, but
made him swear to amend his civil government, to raise no
tax without the consent of the Great Council, and to punish
no man but by the judgment of his court. In these terms we
may see the Great Charter traced in miniature. . . .

The English barons had privileges, which they knew to have
been violated; they had always kept up the memory of the
ancient Saxon liberty; and if they were the conquerors of
Britain, they did not think that their own servitude was the
just fruit of their victory. They had, however, but an indis-
tinct view of the object at which they aimed; they rather felt
their wrongs than understood the cause of them; and having
no head nor council, they were more in a condition of dis-
tressing their king and disgracing their country by their disobedience than of applying any effectual remedy to their
grievances. Langton saw these dispositions, and these wants.
He had conceived a settled plan for reducing the king, and all
his actions tended to carry it into execution. This prelate,
under pretence of holding an ecclesiastical synod, drew together privately some of the principal barons to the Church
of St. Paul in London. There, having expatiated on the miseries which the kingdom suffered, and having explained at the
same time the liberties to which it was entitled, he produced
the famous charter of Henry the First, long concealed, and
of which, with infinite difficulty, he had procured an authentic copy. This he held up to the barons as the standard about
which they were to unite. These were the liberties which their

ancestors had received by the free concession of a former king, and these the rights which their virtue was to force from the present, if (which God forbid!) they should find it necessary to have recourse to such extremities. The barons, transported to find an authentic instrument to justify their discontent and to explain and sanction their pretensions, covered the Archbishop with praises, [and] readily confederated to support their demands . . .

The barons of England . . . appeared in a body before him [John] at London. All in complete armor, and in the guise of defiance, they presented a petition, very humble in the language, but excessive in the substance, in which they declared their liberties, and prayed that they might be formally allowed and established by the royal authority. . . .

The instruments by which the barons secured their liberties were drawn up in form of charters, and in the manner by which grants had been usually made to monasteries . . . For the place of solemnizing this remarkable act they chose a large field, overlooked by Windsor, called Running-mede, which, in our present tongue, signifies the Meadow of Council—a place long consecrated by public opinion, as that wherein the quarrels and wars which arose in the English nation, when divided into kingdoms or factions, had been terminated from the remotest times. Here it was that King John, on the 15th day of June, in the year of our Lord 1215, signed those two memorable instruments which first disarmed the crown of its unlimited prerogatives, and laid the foundation of English liberty. . . .

In the preamble to the Great Charter it is stipulated that the barons shall *hold* the liberties there granted *to them and their heirs, from the king and his heirs;* which shows that the doctrine of an unalienable tenure was always uppermost in their minds. Their idea even of liberty was not (if I may use the expression) perfectly free; and they did not claim to possess their privileges upon any natural principle or independent bottom, but just as they held their lands from the king. This is worthy of observation. . . .

There were other provisions made in the Great Charter that went deeper than the feudal tenure, and affected the whole body of the civil government. A great part of the king's revenue then consisted in the fines and amercements which were imposed in his courts. A fine was paid there for liberty to commence or to conclude a suit. The punishment of offences by fine was discretionary; and this discretionary power had been very much abused. But by Magna Charta things were so ordered, that a delinquent might be punished, but not ruined, by a fine or amercement; because the degree of his offence, and the rank he held, were to be taken into consideration. His freehold, his merchandise, and those instruments by which he obtained his livelihood were made sacred from such impositions.

A more grand reform was made with regard to the administration of justice. The kings in those days seldom resided long in one place, and their courts followed their persons. This erratic justice must have been productive of infinite inconvenience to the litigants. It was now provided that civil suits, called *Common Pleas*, should be fixed to some certain place. Thus one branch of jurisdiction was separated from the king's court, and detached from his person. They had not yet come to that maturity of jurisprudence as to think this might be made to extend to criminal law also, and that the latter was an object of still greater importance. But even the former may be considered as a great revolution. A tribunal, a creature of mere law, independent of personal power, was established; and this separation of a king's authority from his person was a matter of vast consequence towards introducing ideas of freedom, and confirming the sacredness and majesty of laws.

But the grand article, and that which cemented all the parts of the fabric of liberty, was this—that "no freeman shall be taken, or imprisoned, or disseized, or outlawed, or banished, or in any wise destroyed, but by judgment of his peers."

There is another article of nearly as much consequence as the former, considering the state of the nation at that time, by which it is provided that the barons shall grant to their tenants the same liberties which they had stipulated for themselves. This prevented the kingdom from degenerating into the worst imaginable government, a feudal aristocracy. The English barons . . . were not in a condition to set up for petty sovereigns by an usurpation equally detrimental to the crown and the people. They were able to act only in confederacy; and this common cause made it necessary to consult the common good, and to study popularity by the equity of their proceedings. This was a very happy circumstance to the growing liberty. . . .

AN ESSAY TOWARDS AN HISTORY OF THE LAWS OF ENGLAND

. . . What can be more instructive than to search out the first obscure and scanty fountains of that jurisprudence which now waters and enriches whole nations with so abundant and copious a flood—to observe the first principles of RIGHT springing up, involved in superstition and polluted with violence, until by length of time and favorable circumstances it has worked itself into clearness: the laws sometimes lost and trodden down in the confusion of wars and tumults, and sometimes overruled by the hand of power; then, victorious over tyranny, growing stronger, clearer, and more decisive by the violence they had suffered; enriched even by those foreign conquests which threatened their entire destruction; softened and mellowed by peace and religion; improved and exalted by commerce, by social intercourse, and that great opener of the mind, ingenuous science? . . .

The sources of our English law are not well, nor indeed fairly, laid open . . .

Of this defect I think there were two principal causes. The first, a persuasion, hardly to be eradicated from the minds of our lawyers, that the English law has continued very much in the same state from an antiquity to which they will allow hardly any sort of bounds. The second is, that it was formed and grew up among ourselves; that it is in every respect peculiar to this island; and that, if the Roman or any foreign laws attempted to intrude into its composition, it has always had vigor enough to shake them off, and return to the purity of its primitive constitution.

These opinions are flattering to national vanity and professional narrowness . . . If these principles are admitted, the history of the law must in a great measure be deemed superfluous. For to what purpose is a history of a law of which it is impossible to trace the beginning, and which during its continuance has admitted no essential changes? . . .

The opinions which have drawn the law into such narrowness, as they are weakly founded, so they are very easily refuted. . . . It is obvious, on the very first view of the Saxon laws, that we have entirely altered the whole frame of our jurisprudence since the Conquest. Hardly can we find in these old collections a single title which is law at this day; and one may venture to assert, without much hazard, that, if there were at present a nation governed by the Saxon laws, we should find it difficult to point out another so entirely different from everything we now see established in England. . . .

Nothing has been a larger theme of panegyric with all our writers on politics and history than the Anglo-Saxon government . . . These monuments of our pristine rudeness still subsist; and they stand out of themselves indisputable evidence to confute the popular declamations of those writers who would persuade us that the crude institutions of an unlettered people had reached a perfection which the united efforts of inquiry, experience, learning, and necessity have not been able to attain in many ages.

But the truth is, the present system of our laws, like our language and our learning, is a very mixed and heterogeneous mass: in some respects our own; in more borrowed from the policy of foreign nations, and compounded, altered, and variously modified, according to the various necessities which the manners, the religion, and the commerce of the people have at different times imposed. . . .

The Law of the Romans seems utterly to have expired in this island together with their empire, and that, too, before the Saxon establishment. The Anglo-Saxons came into England as conquerors. They brought their own customs with them, and doubtless did not take laws from, but imposed theirs upon, the people they had vanquished. . . . The best image we have of them is to be found in Tacitus. But there is reason to believe that some changes were made suitable to the circumstances of their new settlement, and to the change their constitution must have undergone by adopting a kingly government, not indeed with unlimited sway, but certainly with greater powers than their leaders possessed whilst they continued in Germany. However, we know very little of what was done in these respects until their conversion to Christianity, a revolution which made still more essential changes in their manners and government. For immediately after the conversion of Ethelbert, King of Kent, the missionaries . . . came from Rome full of the ideas of the Roman civil establishment . . .

We have observed the progress of the Saxon laws, which, conformably to their manners, were rude and simple, . . . and though in some degree, yet not very considerably, improved by foreign communication. However, we can plainly discern its three capital sources. First, the ancient traditionary customs of the North, which, coming upon this and the other civilized parts of Europe with the impetuosity of a conquest, bore down all the ancient establishments, and, by being suited to the genius of the people, formed, as it were, the great body and main stream of the Saxon laws. The second source was the canons of the Church. As yet, indeed, they were not reduced into system and a regular form of jurisprudence; but they were the law of the clergy, and consequently influenced considerably a people over whom that order had an almost unbounded authority. They corrected, mitigated, and enriched those rough Northern institutions; and the clergy having once bent the stubborn necks of that people to the yoke of religion, they were the more easily susceptible of other changes introduced under the same sanction. These formed the third source—namely, some parts of the Roman civil law, and the customs of other German nations. . . .

Selections from Book Reviews in the Annual Register

Burke's book reviews in the *Annual Register* reveal the diversity of his intellectual interests and the catholicity of his literary taste and judgment. He had a remarkable gift for choosing to review books which were to endure and become an important part of eighteenth-century thought.

Among the following reviews, of special interest are those on Rousseau, which should be read in conjunction with Burke's later attack on Rousseau in his *Letter to a Member of the National Assembly* (January 1791). His review of Wallace's *Laws of Scotland* shows that he was aware early in life that the law of Scotland, far more than that of England, was founded upon Roman law, and therefore was more consciously related to Natural Law. Burke knew that Coke was the most eminent modern English jurist to defend the Natural Law. This is the point of his statement that "The laws of Scotland are here referred to, and grounded upon, those of nature and of nations; and the author has endeavoured to do, what, if it had been done with regard to the law of England, might be considered as a union of Lord Coke with Grotius and Puffendorf." As Burke well knew, English common law supplied for Coke the bridge which connected statutes with the Natural Law. In this light, Burke's general legal erudition takes on added significance as a measure of his knowledge of Natural Law. Finally, his review of Hume's *History of England* contains comments on the limits of the royal prerogative under the Stuarts and Tudors, which are very significant when reading his arguments in opposition to George III during the period of the American Revolution.

FROM THE *Annual Register* (1759–62)

The History of Rasselas, Prince of Abissinia.　　The instruction which is found in most works of this kind, when they convey any instruction at all, is not the predominant part, but arises accidentally in the course of a story planned only to please. But in this novel the moral is the principal object, and the story is a mere vehicle to convey the instruction.

Accordingly the tale is not near so full of incidents, nor so diverting in itself, as the ingenious author, if he had not had higher views, might easily have made it; neither is the distinction of characters sufficiently attended to: but with these defects, perhaps no book ever inculcated a purer and sounder morality; no book ever made a more just estimate of human life, its pursuits, and its enjoyments. The descriptions are rich and luxuriant, and show a poetic imagination not inferior to our best writers in verse. The style, which is peculiar and characteristical of the author, is lively, correct, and harmonious. It has however in a few places an air too exact and studied.

The ideas which travellers have given us of a mountain in which the branches of the royal family of Abissinia are confined, though it may not be very well founded in fact, affords a ground for the most striking description of a terrestrial paradise, which has ever been drawn; in this the author places the hero of his tale . . .

He contrives to escape out of the valley; but if the hero of the tale was not happy in this situation, we are not to be surprised, that he did not find happiness in his excursion into the world at large.

Though the author has not put his name to this work, there is no doubt that he is the same who has before done so much for the improvement of our taste and our morals, and employed a great part of his life in an astonishing work for the fixing the language of this nation; whilst this nation, which admires his works, and profits by them, has done nothing for the author.

A Letter from M. Rousseau of Geneva, to M. d'Alembert, of Paris, concerning the effects of theatrical entertainments on the manners of mankind.   None of the present writers have a greater share of talents and learning than Rousseau; yet it has been his misfortune and that of the world, that those of his works which have made the greatest noise, and acquired to their author the highest reputation, have been of little real use or emolument to mankind. A tendency to paradox, which is always the bane of solid learning, and threatens now to destroy it, a splenetic disposition carried to misanthropy, and an austere virtue pursued to an unsociable fierceness, have prevented a great deal of the good effects which might be expected from such a genius. A satire upon civilized society, a satire upon learning, may make a tolerable sport for an ingenious fancy; but if carried farther it can do no more (and that in such a way is surely too much) than to unsettle our notions of right and wrong, and lead by degrees to universal scepticism. His having before attempted two such subjects, must make his attack upon the stage far less formidable than otherwise it would have been. This last subject has been often discussed before him; more good pieces have been written against the stage than in its favour; but this is by far the most ingenious, spirited, and philosophical performance that ever appeared on theatrical entertainments. The author has placed the matter in a light almost wholly new. So far as his remarks relate to small and indigent states in general, and to that of Geneva in particular, they are as just as they are ingenious; but with regard to the stage writers and performers in nations not so circumstanced, he seems to have pushed his objections much too far. There are certainly plays which show, that the stage may at least be made as innocent as any other public entertainments; as innocent as his favourite entertainment of dancing; and there are actors of both sexes, who (though it must be admitted their situation is a little dangerous) have proved by their conduct the injustice of his assertion, which makes vice inseparable from their profession, and its infamy not created, but only declared by the laws . . .

The Theory of Moral Sentiments, by Adam Smith.   It is very difficult, if not impossible, consistently with the brevity of our design, to give the reader a proper idea of this excellent work. A dry abstract of the system would convey no juster idea of it, than the skeleton of a departed beauty would of her form when she was alive; at the same time the work is so well methodized, the parts grow so naturally and gracefully out of each other, that it would be doing it equal injustice to show it by broken and detached pieces . . .

There have been of late many books written on our moral duties, and our moral sensations. One would have thought the matter had been exhausted. But this author has struck out a new, and at the same time a perfectly natural road of speculation on this subject. Had it been only an ingenious novelty on any other subject, it might have been praised; but with regard to morals, nothing could be more dangerous. We conceive, that here the theory is in all its essential parts just, and founded on truth and nature. The author seeks for the foundation of the just, the fit, the proper, the decent, in our most common and most allowed passions; and making approbation and disapprobation the tests of virtue and vice, and showing that those are founded on sympathy, he raises from this simple truth, one of the most beautiful fabrics of moral theory, that has perhaps ever appeared. The illustrations are numerous and happy, and show the author to be a man of uncommon observation. His language is easy and spirited, and puts things before you in the fullest light; it is rather painting than writing . . .

FROM THE *Annual Register* (1760)

Fragments of ancient Poetry collected in the Highlands of Scotland, and translated from the Gallic, or Erse language. The love and study of antiquities is one of the most prevailing tastes of this age. With great expence and pains, and no less honour, some travellers have penetrated into the deserts of the East, and have presented Europe with those magnificent scenes of the ruins of Palmyra and Balbec; some have given us an idea of the antient grandeur of Egypt; some dig out those immense treasures of classical antiquity from the mines of Herculaneum; and from some we still expect the genuine remains of Athens; others, at the same time, have been searching into our northern antiquities; and these fragments are no mean specimen of the effects of their labours.

The northern nations have always been highly celebrated for their skill in poetry. We have seen specimens of that of Lapland and Denmark; but, before these, no piece from the Erse (the language of the Highland Scots and Irish) has appeared. Much has been said concerning the genuineness of these remarkable fragments. A discussion of this kind is attended with great difficulties, and makes the inquirer run the risk of falling perpetually into mistakes; as we have not sufficient monuments of the arts, customs, and manners, of the times and countries in which these scenes are laid, to judge how far they agree with, or transgress, those only standards for that sort of criticism. But there is far less doubt of the merit, than of the authenticity, of these pieces. They are mostly dirges; and are animated with a wild, passionate, and pathetic spirit of poetry . . .

A System of the principles of the Laws of Scotland. By George Wallace. The work before us is a piece of uncommon labour, research, and reach of thought. The laws of Scotland are here referred to, and grounded upon, those of nature and nations; and the author has endeavoured to do, what, if it had been done with regard to the law of England, might be considered as an union of Lord Coke, with Grotius and Puffendorf. Tho' his plan has limited him principally to the municipal laws of Scotland, there are several parts of so general a nature, and so well reasoned, that they cannot fail of giving general entertainment and instruction . . .

FROM THE *Annual Register* (1761)

Fingal, an ancient epic poem, in six books, together with several other poems, composed by Ossian the son of Fingal; translated from the Gallic language, by James Macpherson. From the publication of these extraordinary poems, the ingenious editor has a double claim to literary applause. One, as having with equal industry and taste recovered from the obscurity of barbarism, the rust of fifteen hundred years, and the last breath of a dying language, these inestimable relicks of the genuine spirit of poetry: and the other, for presenting them to the world in an English translation, whose expressive singularity evidently retains the majestic air, and native simplicity of a sublime original. The venerable author, and his elegant translator, thus have mutually conferred immortality on each other . . .

Whether this poem, and the smaller ones which accompany it, were composed by the real or some fictitious Ossian, they have that primitive air, which, were we not informed they can't at the utmost be more than fifteen centuries old, would naturally incline us to fix their date in the earliest period of society. The style so consonant to the ideas, the ideas so agreeable to the simple manners of remote ages, and both of a cast so different from the modern modes of expression and thinking; hunting the subsistence, and war the occupation of this pristine people; the savage grossness of their vices; and the wild sublimity of their virtues; the extravagant heroism of the principal characters; that spirit of hospitality which invited the stranger seven different ways; their tokens of submission by delivering the spouse and dog; their superstitious notions so beautifully poetic; the feast of shells; the signal of battle by striking the shield; the songs of the bards which make so many interesting episodes; all these, whilst they give us a striking picture of the manners, the customs, the superstitions of the times; whilst they affect us with all that is pathetic, and elevate with all that is sublime; these, we think, are impressed with such genuine, such peculiar, such original marks of antiquity, as seem utterly beyond the reach of any modern invention . . .

But whilst the uncommon merit of Fingal, as the extraordinary production of uncultivated genius, is universally admitted, its degree of perfection, as an epic poem, seems not to be so well established. Some insist it has not only the superior parts, but even the very *minutiae* so essential to this exalted species of poetry; while others hold it defective in the most capital articles, the fable, the manners, and characters . . .

On the whole, the imperfections of this poem, which will not bear the test of critical examination, are naturally accounted for by the disadvantages of an ignorant and barbarous age . . . Indeed, both its defects and excellencies speak loudly in favour of its antiquity; its defects, as the natural result of barbarism; its excellencies, as the efforts of a great genius, which, like light bursting from darkness, shine the brighter for the night of ignorance, through which they blaze. But if, notwithstanding these marks of antique genuineness, which add so much weight to the editor's assertion, this extraordinary piece should prove, after all, a modern composition; then would its faults admit of little extenuation, its beauties sink in that peculiar value which they derive from primitive simplicity; and the poem, however well imagined, and happily executed, and with all the merit of a fine original, be nevertheless esteemed but as a grand imposture . . .

The History of England, from the Invasion of Julius Caesar to the Accession of Henry VII . . . By David Hume. Our writers had commonly so ill succeeded in history, the Italians and even the French had so long continued our acknowledged superiors, that it was almost feared that the British genius, which had so happily displayed itself in every other kind of writing, and had gained the prize in most, yet could not enter the lists in this. The historical work Mr. Hume first published, discharged our country from this opprobrium.

This very ingenious and elegant writer is certainly a very profound thinker. The idea of the growth, as I may call it, of our present constitution seems to be the principle of the whole work completed by the part now published, which is written in the same bold masterly manner as the two formerly published; and though in point of time it precedes them, is possibly, in reason, but a consequence of the other two; and the three parts, we imagine, may with propriety enough be read in the order the ingenious author has chosen to publish them.

It is natural that the line, which is always kept to its utmost length, must break at last; and probably in its recoil hurt them who endeavour to keep it at full stretch; and so it fared with the Stuarts, who, we imagine with this ingenious author, erred not so much in extending the prerogative, as in not having had sagacity enough to see that they had fallen in the times, when, from the opinions and fashions of the age, it behoved them to slacken and remit of the authority exercised by their predecessors.

The second work, which appeared, certainly showed that the Tudors had not left it in the power of any other family to carry the prerogative higher than they had done. They left it to their successors, adorned and supported with every sanction, which custom, and which, in many cases, legal institution, could give it.

The third part seems to evince, that this pitch, which the prerogative had attained, was not the effect of the abilities, or the violence, of this or that family, so much as the natural course of things.

If the periods of the history first published interested our passions more, the curiosity of the learned will be more gratified in that now before us. It will be curious to observe from what a strange chaos of liberty and tyranny, of anarchy and order, the constitution, we are now blessed with, has at length arisen . . .

No man perhaps has come nearer to that so requisite and so rare a quality in an historian of unprejudiced partiality . . .

FROM THE *Annual Register* (1762)

Emilius and Sophia: or, A new System of Education. Translated from the French of J. J. Rousseau, Citizen of Geneva.   The fault most generally observed in discourses upon education, is a tendency to commonplace. Nothing, in fact, can be more trite, than the greatest part of the observations, which have been retailed upon that subject from Quintilian down to Monsieur Rollin. This is however the fault, into which the ingenious author of Emilius is, of all others, in the least danger of falling. To know what the received notions are upon any subject, is to know with certainty what those of Rousseau are not. In his treatise on the inequality amongst mankind, he has shown his man in a natural state; in his Emilius he undertakes to educate him. In the prosecution of this design he begins early, and carefully attends his pupil from his cradle to his marriage-bed. He forms him to morals, to science, to knowledge of men, and to natural labour, and at length gives him a wife, whom he has previously educated for him according to ideas a little different from that model which he has formed in his Eloise.

In this system of education there are some very considerable parts that are impracticable, others that are chimerical; and not a few highly blameable, and dangerous both to piety and morals. It is easy to discern how it has happened, that this book should be censured as well at Geneva as in Paris. However, with those faults in the design, with the whimsies into which his paradoxical genius continually hurries him, there are a thousand noble hints relative to his subject, grounded on a profound knowledge of the human mind, and the order of its operations. There are many others, which, though they have little relation to the subject, are admirable on their own account; and even, in his wildest sallies, we now and then discover strokes of the most solid sense, and instructions of the most useful nature. Indeed he very seldom thinks himself bound to adhere to any settled order or design, but is borne away by every object started by his vivid imagination, and hurries continually from system to system, in the career of an animated, glowing, exuberant style, which paints everything with great minuteness, yet with infinite spirit.

There is, it must be acknowledged, one considerable defect in his judgment, which infects both his matter and his style. He never knows where to stop. He seldom can discover that precise point in which excellence consists, where to exceed is almost as bad as to fall short, and which every step you go beyond, you grow worse and worse. He is therefore frequently tiresome and disgusting by pushing his notions to excess; and by repeating the same thing in a thousand different ways. Poverty can hardly be more vicious than such an abundance . . .

II

AMERICA AND THE BRITISH EMPIRE

A Short Account
of
A Late Short Administration
1766

In December 1765, shortly after becoming Lord Rockingham's secretary, Burke was elected to the House of Commons for the pocket borough of Wendover. Two years earlier, the Treaty of Paris had put an end to the Seven Years' War (1756–63), in which the elder William Pitt's direction as leader of the House of Commons and virtual Prime Minister had brought Great Britain immense gains in her overseas empire. But the new king, George III, had dismissed Pitt in 1761 and had appointed as Prime Minister a royal favorite, the Scottish Earl of Bute, whose unpopularity with the English and personal ineptitude forced him to resign in 1763. Bute was succeeded by George Grenville, who proceeded to tax the American colonies and to restrict their trade in favor of English merchants. When the Americans complained, further restrictions were imposed, this time upon their civil liberty, by general warrants and restraints on public discussions of grievances. In the year of Burke's election, the Grenville administration passed the Stamp Act, which so intensified colonial discontent that public reaction forced the King to recall Grenville. From the beginning the Rockingham Whigs had strongly opposed the Grenville policy, which the King approved, so that reluctantly, on July 10, 1765, George III appointed Rockingham his Prime Minister.

The first Rockingham administration lasted only a year and twenty days, until July 30, 1766, when the King's opposition to its repeal of the Stamp Act and the opportunism of the Bedford Whigs combined with the ambition of Pitt to force it out of office. During its brief tenure the Rockingham administration had conciliated the Colonies by reversing completely the Grenville policies. Of its positive achievements John Morley wrote: "Nothing so good was done in an English parliament for nearly twenty years to come."

Upon Rockingham's dismissal Burke published *A Short Account of a Late Short Administration* (1766), the first of his many defenses of the Rockingham Whigs. His aim was to show the British public that in one year Rockingham had succeeded in restoring the confidence of the Colonies in the British government, and that the Rockingham policy was the only sound and proven method of at once maintaining British sovereignty and Colonial civil and commercial liberty.

The late administration came into employment, under the mediation of the Duke of Cumberland, on the tenth day of July, 1765; and was removed, upon a plan settled by the Earl of Chatham, on the thirtieth day of July, 1766, having lasted just one year and twenty days.

In that space of time:

The distractions of the British empire were composed, by *the repeal of the American stamp act;*

But the constitutional superiority of Great Britain was preserved by *the act for securing the dependence of the colonies.*

Private houses were relieved from the jurisdiction of the excise, by *the repeal of the cider tax.*

The personal liberty of the subject was confirmed, by *the resolution against general warrants.*

The lawful secrets of business and friendship were rendered inviolable, by *the resolution for condemning the seizure of papers.*

The trade of America was set free from injudicious and ruinous impositions—its revenue was improved, and settled upon a rational foundation—its commerce extended with foreign countries; while all the advantages were secured to Great Britain, by *the act for repealing certain duties, and encouraging, regulating, and securing the trade of this kingdom, and the British dominions in America.* . . .

That administration was the first which proposed and encouraged public meetings and free consultations of merchants from all parts of the kingdom; by which means the truest lights have been received; great benefits have been already derived to manufactures and commerce; and the most extensive prospects are opened for further improvement.

Under them, the interests of our northern and southern colonies, before that time jarring and dissonant, were understood, compared, adjusted, and perfectly reconciled. The passions and animosities of the colonies, by judicious and lenient measures, were allayed and composed, and the foundation laid for a lasting agreement amongst them. . . .

They treated their sovereign with decency; with reverence.

They discountenanced, and, it is hoped, forever abolished, the dangerous and unconstitutional practice of removing military officers for their votes in Parliament. They firmly adhered to those friends of liberty, who had run all hazards in its cause; and provided for them in preference to every other claim.

With the Earl of Bute they had no personal connection; no correspondence of councils. They neither courted him nor persecuted him. They practised no corruption; nor were they even suspected of it. They sold no offices. They obtained no reversions or pensions, either coming in or going out, for themselves, their families, or their dependents.

In the prosecution of their measures they were traversed by an opposition of a new and singular character; an opposition of placemen and pensioners. They were supported by the confidence of the nation. And having held their offices under many difficulties and discouragements, they left them at the express command, as they had accepted them at the earnest request, of their royal master.

These are plain facts; of a clear and public nature; neither extended by elaborate reasoning, nor heightened by the coloring of eloquence. They are the services of a single year.

The removal of that administration from power is not to them premature; since they were in office long enough to accomplish many plans of public utility; and, by their perseverance and resolution, rendered the way smooth and easy to their successors; having left their king and their country in a much better condition than they found them. By the temper they manifest, they seem to have now no other wish than that their successors may do the public as real and as faithful service as they have done.

Thoughts

on

The Cause of the Present Discontents. . . .
1770

A pamphlet by George Grenville, accusing the Rockingham Whigs of ruining Britain by reversing his policy of taxing America, provoked Burke's reply, *Observations on 'The
Present State of the Nation'* (1769). In Burke's second defense of his party, he attributed Britain's misfortunes in the
Colonies to "the injudicious tampering of bold, improvident,
and visionary ministers," such as Grenville, whose "grand
scheme" of taxing the Colonies he denounced as contrary to
experience and based upon metaphysical speculation in politics:

*In this great work he proceeds with a facility equally aston-
ishing and pleasing. Never was financier less embarrassed by
the burden of establishments, or with the difficulty of finding
ways and means. If an establishment is troublesome to him,
he lops off at a stroke just as much of it as he chooses. He
mows down, without giving quarter, or assigning reason, army,
navy, ordnance, ordinary, extraordinaries; nothing can stand
before him. Then, when he comes to provide . . . he pours
out with an inexhaustible bounty, taxes, duties, loans, and
revenues, without uneasiness to himself, or burden to the
public . . .*

Burke's characteristic distrust of *a priori* reasoning in politics
is everywhere evident in his strictures against Grenville. He
objected to Grenville's "high talk of Parliamentary rights, of
the universality of legislative powers, and of uniform taxation," without regard to the circumstances of each colony, or
to the consequences of his acts, as a violation of moral prudence. He cautioned: "An attempt towards a compulsory
equality in all circumstances, and an exact practical definition
of the supreme rights in every case, is the most dangerous and
chimerical of all enterprises." Burke disapproved of Grenville's "introduction into a discourse relating to . . . practical
government" and such "speculative inquiries," because like

Aristotle he held that politics was a practical science aimed at the good, not a theoretical science to establish what is true. Grenville's series of trade regulations, "which caused an universal consternation throughout the colonies," and his system of taxation, were wholly untried schemes based not on experience but upon "mere abstract principles of government." He then asserted one of his most fundamental political principles: "Politics ought to be adjusted, not to human reasonings, but to human nature; of which the reason is but a part, and by no means the greatest part." This is one of the grand themes in all his writings and speeches on the practical politics of the American colonies, Ireland, India, and France. Burke concluded that unless such speculative theories as Grenville's were abandoned, and "until the ideas of 1766 are resumed," and Rockingham's policies were once more followed, that Britain and the Colonies would become increasingly alienated. His *Observations* contains in summary the essential principles, policies, and arguments he was to advance concerning the American colonies from 1769 to their independence from Britain.

The year after his attack on Grenville's American policy Burke wrote his first great pamphlet in the literature of politics, *Thoughts on the Cause of the Present Discontents* (1770). When Burke entered Parliament the Whigs were not a united party. Indeed, the very conception of a political party, in any modern sense, did not exist until it was formulated by him during the 1770's. The Whigs were split into sections such as the Pelhams, who came to form the core of Rockingham's party; the Bedfords, under the Duke of Bedford; the Grenvilles, under Earl Temple; the followers of the elder William Pitt, and other small groups. George III, who wished to maintain personal control of the government, found it greatly to his advantage to keep the Whigs divided, by playing off each group against the others. The Rockingham Whigs regarded themselves as different from the other Whigs, because they acted as a party, upon publicly declared political principles and policies, and not merely as placemen seeking royal pensions and pursuing economic self-interest. This unique claim is borne out by the special aversion George III always held for the Rockingham Whigs. But many of their contemporaries, and the Namier historians of the twentieth century, have regarded the Rockinghams in general, and Burke their chief spokesman in particular, as hypocrites who cleverly disguised their ambitions and self-interest under the cloak of appeals to constitutional principles, party policy, and political reforms.

One of the immediate objects in writing *Thoughts on the Cause of the Present Discontents,* as Burke wrote to Rockingham, was to show the British public how their party differed from "the Bedfords, the Grenvilles, and other knots, who are combined for no public purpose, but only as a means of furthering with joint strength their private and individual advantage." Therefore, the pamphlet was in part a manifesto of the Rockingham Whigs. But there was a far greater purpose behind Burke's pamphlet, centered in the constitutional crisis which, from 1765 to 1782, involved the King and the House of Commons in a struggle over policies concerning the American colonies, the use of the royal prerogative, and economic reforms to limit the extent of royal patronage. Burke opposed the King's plans to again tax the Colonies. John Morley has well summarized how Burke met the King's appeal to prerogative: "The revival of high doctrines of prerogative in the Crown was accompanied by the revival of high doctrines of privilege in the House of Commons." But according to Burke's analysis, the main source of discontent was the King's desire to establish personal rule. The appointment as Prime Minister of the royal favorite Bute had been an utter failure. But Burke believed that George III sought to achieve the same result by creating a "double cabinet"; the one in Parliament exercising only nominal power, but the other, the "King's friends" behind the throne, having real powers over policy. Undoubtedly, in his eagerness to assert the independence of Parliament from the Crown, Burke overstated his case. Some twentieth-century historians, taking the "double cabinet" as a formal arrangement within the government, have denied that it existed, except in Burke's imagination. But he meant no more than that a clique of political courtiers close to the King wished to weaken the influence of independent members of Parliament, to extend royal power at the expense of representative government, and that this was against "the spirit of the whole constitution." Since ministers appointed by the Crown had no direct responsibility to the people, or even to Parliament, they were far more prone than elected members of Parliament to introduce "a great spirit of innovation" in government. This made government "at once odious and feeble"; it resulted in disorder and created discontent at home and in the Colonies. The practical alternative urged by Burke was to replace royal influence through favoritism with party government in the House of Commons. Only then would constitutional government, responsible to the electorate, prevail again in England.

. . . Nations are not primarily ruled by laws: less by violence. Whatever original energy may be supposed either in force or regulation, the operation of both is, in truth, merely instrumental. Nations are governed by the same methods, and on the same principles, by which an individual without authority is often able to govern those who are his equals or his superiors; by a knowledge of their temper, and by a judicious management of it; I mean—when public affairs are steadily and quietly conducted; not when government is nothing but a continued scuffle between the magistrate and the multitude; in which sometimes the one and sometimes the other is uppermost; in which they alternately yield and prevail, in a series of contemptible victories, and scandalous submissions. The temper of the people amongst whom he presides ought therefore to be the first study of a statesman. And the knowledge of this temper it is by no means impossible for him to attain, if he has not an interest in being ignorant of what it is his duty to learn.

To complain of the age we live in, to murmur at the present possessors of power, to lament the past, to conceive extravagant hopes of the future, are the common dispositions of the greatest part of mankind; indeed the necessary effects of the ignorance and levity of the vulgar. Such complaints and humors have existed in all times; yet as all times have *not* been alike, true political sagacity manifests itself in distinguishing that complaint which only characterizes the general infirmity of human nature, from those which are symptoms of the particular distemperature of our own air and season.

Nobody, I believe, will consider it merely as the language of spleen or disappointment, if I say, that there is something particularly alarming in the present conjuncture. There is hardly a man, in or out of power, who holds any other language. That government is at once dreaded and contemned; that the laws are despoiled of all their respected and salutary terrors; that their inaction is a subject of ridicule, and their exertion of abhorrence; that rank, and office and title, and all the solemn plausibilities of the world, have lost their reverence and effect; that our foreign politics are as much deranged as our domestic economy; that our dependencies are slackened in their affection, and loosened from their obedience; that we know neither how to yield nor how to enforce; that hardly anything above or below, abroad or at home, is sound and entire; but that disconnection and confusion, in offices, in parties, in families, in Parliament, in the nation, prevail beyond the disorders of any former time: these are facts universally admitted and lamented.

This state of things is the more extraordinary, because the great parties which formerly divided and agitated the kingdom are known to be in a manner entirely dissolved. No great external calamity has visited the nation; no pestilence or famine. We do not labor at present under any scheme of taxation new or oppressive in the quantity or in the mode. Nor are we engaged in unsuccessful war; in which, our misfortunes might easily pervert our judgment; and our minds, sore from the loss of national glory, might feel every blow of fortune as a crime in government.

It is impossible that the cause of this strange distemper should not sometimes become a subject of discourse. It is a compliment due, and which I willingly pay, to those who administer our affairs, to take notice in the first place of their speculation. Our ministers are of opinion, that the increase of our trade and manufactures, that our growth by colonization, and by conquest, have concurred to accumulate immense wealth in the hands of some individuals; and this again being dispersed among the people, has rendered them universally proud, ferocious, and ungovernable; that the insolence of some from their enormous wealth, and the boldness of others from a guilty poverty, have rendered them capable of the most atrocious attempts; so that they have trampled upon all subordination, and violently borne down the unarmed laws of a free government; barriers too feeble against the fury of a populace so fierce and licentious as ours. They contend, that no adequate provocation has been given for so spreading a discontent; our affairs having been conducted throughout with remarkable temper and consummate wisdom. The wicked industry of some libellers, joined to the intrigues of a few disappointed politicians, have, in their opinion, been able to produce this unnatural ferment in the nation.

Nothing indeed can be more unnatural than the present convulsions of this country, if the above account be a true one. I confess I shall assent to it with great reluctance, and only on the compulsion of the clearest and firmest proofs; because their account resolves itself into this short, but discouraging proposition, "That we have a very good ministry, but that we are a very bad people"; that we set ourselves to bite the hand that feeds us; that with a malignant insanity, we oppose the measures, and ungratefully vilify the persons, of those whose sole object is our own peace and prosperity. If a few puny libellers, acting under a knot of factious politicians, without virtue, parts, or character, (such they are constantly represented by these gentlemen,) are sufficient to excite this disturbance, very perverse must be the disposition of that people, amongst whom such a disturbance can be excited by such means. It is besides no small aggravation of the public misfortune, that the disease, on this hypothesis, appears to be without remedy. If the wealth of the nation be the cause of its turbulence, I imagine it is not proposed to introduce poverty, as a constable to keep the peace. If our dominions abroad are the roots which feed all this rank luxuriance of sedition, it is not intended to cut them off in order to famish the fruit. If our liberty has enfeebled the executive power, there is no design, I hope, to call in the aid of despotism, to fill up the deficiencies of law. Whatever may be intended, these things are not yet professed. We seem therefore to be driven to absolute despair; for we have no other materials to work upon, but those out of which God has been pleased to form the inhabitants of this island. . . . I hear it indeed sometimes asserted, that a steady perseverance in the present measures, and a rigorous punishment of those who oppose them, will in course of time infallibly put an end to these disorders. But this, in my opinion, is said without much observation of our present disposition, and without any knowledge at all of the general nature of mankind. . . .

I am not one of those who think that the people are never in the wrong. They have been so, frequently and outrageously, both in other countries and in this. But I do say, that in all disputes between them and their rulers, the presumption is at least upon a par in favor of the people. Experience may perhaps justify me in going further. When popular discontents have been prevalent, it may well be affirmed and supported, that there has been generally something found amiss in the constitution, or in the conduct of government. The people have no interest in disorder. When they do wrong, it is their error, and not their crime. But with the governing part of the state, it is far otherwise. They certainly may act ill by design, as well as by mistake. . . .

Upon a supposition, therefore, that, in the opening of the cause, the presumptions stand equally balanced between the parties, there seems sufficient ground to entitle any person to a fair hearing, who attempts some other scheme beside that easy one which is fashionable in some fashionable companies, to account for the present discontents. It is not to be argued that we endure no grievance, because our grievances are not of the same sort with those under which we labored formerly; not precisely those which we bore from the Tudors, or vindicated on the Stuarts. A great change has taken place in the affairs of this country. For in the silent lapse of events as material alterations have been insensibly brought about in the policy and character of governments and nations, as those which have been marked by the tumult of public revolutions.

It is very rare indeed for men to be wrong in their feelings concerning public misconduct; as rare to be right in their speculation upon the cause of it. I have constantly observed, that the generality of people are fifty years, at least, behindhand in their politics. There are but very few who are capable of comparing and digesting what passes before their eyes at different times and occasions, so as to form the whole into a distinct system. But in books everything is settled for them, without the exertion of any considerable diligence or sagacity. For which reason men are wise with but little reflection, and good with little self-denial, in the business of all times except their own. We are very uncorrupt and tolerably enlightened judges of the transactions of past ages; where no passions deceive, and where the whole train of circumstances, from the trifling cause to the tragical event, is set in an orderly series before us. Few are the partisans of departed tyranny; and to be a Whig on the business of an hundred years ago, is very consistent with every advantage of present servility. This retrospective wisdom, and historical patriotism, are things of wonderful convenience, and serve admirably to reconcile the old quarrel between speculation and practice. Many a stern republican, after gorging himself with a full feast of admiration of the Grecian commonwealths and of our true Saxon constitution, and discharging all the splendid bile of his virtuous indignation on King John and King James, sits down perfectly satisfied to the coarsest work and homeliest job of the day he lives in. I believe there was no professed admirer of Henry the Eighth among the instruments of the last King James; nor in the court of Henry the Eighth was there, I dare say, to be found a single advocate for the favorites of Richard the Second.

No complaisance to our court, or to our age, can make me believe nature so changed, but that public liberty will be among us as among our ancestors, obnoxious to some person or other; and that opportunities will be furnished for attempting, at least, some alteration to the prejudice of our constitution. These attempts will naturally vary in their mode according to times and circumstances. For ambition, though it has ever the same general views, has not at all times the same means, nor the same particular objects. A great deal of the furniture of ancient tyranny is worn to rags; the rest is entirely out of fashion. Besides, there are few statesmen so very clumsy and awkward in their business, as to fall into the identical snare which has proved fatal to their predecessors. . . .

Every age has its own manners, and its politics dependent upon them; and the same attempts will not be made against a constitution fully formed and matured, that were used to destroy it in the cradle, or to resist its growth during its infancy.

Against the being of Parliament, I am satisfied, no designs have ever been entertained since the revolution. Every one must perceive, that it is strongly the interest of the court, to have some second cause interposed between the ministers and the people. The gentlemen of the House of Commons have an interest equally strong in sustaining the part of that intermediate cause. . . . Accordingly those who have been of the most known devotion to the will and pleasure of a court have, at the same time, been most forward in asserting a high authority in the House of Commons. When they knew who were to use that authority, and how it was to be employed, they thought it never could be carried too far. It must be always the wish of an unconstitutional statesman, that a House of Commons, who are entirely dependent upon him, should have every right of the people entirely dependent upon their pleasure. It was soon discovered, that the forms of a free, and the ends of an arbitrary government, were things not altogether incompatible.

The power of the crown, almost dead and rotten as Prerogative, has grown up anew, with much more strength, and far less odium, under the name of Influence. An influence, which operated without noise and without violence; an influence, which converted the very antagonist into the instrument of power; which contained in itself a perpetual principle of growth and renovation; and which the distresses and the prosperity of the country equally tended to augment, was an admirable substitute for a prerogative, that, being only the offspring of antiquated prejudices, had moulded in its original stamina irresistible principles of decay and dissolution. The ignorance of the people is a bottom but for a temporary system; the interest of active men in the state is a foundation perpetual and infallible. . . .

At the revolution, the crown, deprived, for the ends of the revolution itself, of many prerogatives, was found too weak to struggle against all the difficulties which pressed so new and unsettled a government. The court was obliged therefore to delegate a part of its powers to men of such interest as could support, and of such fidelity as would adhere to, its establishment. Such men were able to draw in a greater number to a concurrence in the common defence. This connection, necessary at first, continued long after convenient; and properly conducted might indeed, in all situations, be an useful instrument of government. At the same time, through the intervention of men of popular weight and character, the people possessed a security for their just proportion of importance in the state. But as the title to the crown grew stronger by long possession, and by the constant increase of its influence, these helps have of late seemed to certain persons no better than incumbrances. The powerful managers for government were not sufficiently submissive to the pleasure of the possessors of immediate and personal favor, sometimes from a confidence in their own strength, natural and acquired; sometimes from a fear of offending their friends, and weakening that lead in the country which gave them a consideration independent of the court. Men acted as if the court could receive, as well as confer, an obligation. The influence of government, thus divided in appearance between the court and the leaders of parties, became in many cases an accession rather to the popular than to the royal scale; and some part of that influence, which would otherwise have been possessed as in a sort of mortmain and unalienable domain, returned again to the great ocean from whence it arose, and circulated among the people. This method, therefore, of governing by men of great natural interest or great acquired consideration was viewed in a very invidious light by the true lovers of absolute monarchy. It is the nature of despotism to abhor power held by any means but its own momentary pleasure; and to annihilate all intermediate situations between boundless strength on its own part, and total debility on the part of the people.

To get rid of all this intermediate and independent importance, and *to secure to the court the unlimited and uncontrolled use of its own vast influence, under the sole direction of its own private favor,* has for some years past been the great object of policy. If this were compassed, the influence of the crown must of course produce all the effects which the most sanguine partisans of the court could possibly desire. Government might then be carried on without any concurrence on the part of the people; without any attention to the dignity of the greater, or to the affections of the lower sorts. A new project was therefore devised by a certain set of intriguing men, totally different from the system of administration which had prevailed since the accession of the House of Brunswick. This project, I have heard, was first conceived by some persons in the court of Frederick Prince of Wales.

The earliest attempt in the execution of this design was to set up for minister, a person, in rank indeed respectable, and very ample in fortune; but who, to the moment of this vast and sudden elevation, was little known or considered in the kingdom. To him the whole nation was to yield an immediate and implicit submission. But whether it was from want of firmness to bear up against the first opposition; or that things were not yet fully ripened, or that this method was not found the most eligible; that idea was soon abandoned. The instrumental part of the project was a little altered, to accommodate it to the time and to bring things more gradually and more surely to the one great end proposed.

The first part of the reformed plan was to draw *a line which should separate the court from the ministry.* Hitherto these names had been looked upon as synonymous; but for the future, court and administration were to be considered as things totally distinct. By this operation, two systems of administration were to be formed; one which should be in the real secret and confidence; the other merely ostensible to perform the official and executory duties of government. The latter were alone to be responsible; whilst the real advisers, who enjoyed all the power, were effectually removed from all the danger.

Secondly, *A party under these leaders was to be formed in favor of the court against the ministry:* this party was to have a large share in the emoluments of government, and to hold it totally separate from, and independent of, ostensible administration.

The third point, and that on which the success of the whole scheme ultimately depended, was *to bring Parliament to an acquiescence in this project.* Parliament was therefore to be taught by degrees a total indifference to the persons, rank, influence, abilities, connections, and character of the ministers of the crown . . . that body was to be habituated to the most opposite interests, and the most discordant politics. All connections and dependencies among subjects were to be entirely dissolved. As, hitherto, business had gone through the hands of leaders of Whigs or Tories, men of talents to conciliate the people, and to engage their confidence; now the method was to be altered: and the lead was to be given to men of no sort of consideration or credit in the country. This want of natural importance was to be their very title to delegated power. Members of Parliament were to be hardened into an insensibility to pride as well as to duty. Those high and haughty sentiments, which are the great support of independence, were to be let down gradually. Points of honor and precedence were no more to be regarded in Parliamentary decorum than in a Turkish army. It was to be avowed, as a constitutional maxim, that the king might appoint one of his footmen, or one of your footmen for minister; and that he ought to be, and that he would be, as well followed as the first name for rank or wisdom in the nation. Thus Parliament was to look on as if perfectly unconcerned, while a cabal of the closet and back-stairs was substituted in the place of a national administration.

With such a degree of acquiescence, any measure of any court might well be deemed thoroughly secure. The capital objects, and by much the most flattering characteristics of arbitrary power, would be obtained. Everything would be drawn from its holdings in the country to the personal favor and inclination of the prince. This favor would be the sole introduction to power, and the only tenure by which it was to be held; so that no person looking towards another, and all looking towards the court, it was impossible but that the motive which solely influenced every man's hopes must come in time to govern every man's conduct; till at last the servility became universal, in spite of the dead letter of any laws or institutions whatsoever.

How it should happen that any man could be tempted to venture upon such a project of government, may at first view appear surprising. But the fact is that opportunities very inviting to such an attempt have offered; and the scheme itself was not destitute of some arguments, not wholly unplausible, to recommend it. These opportunities and these arguments, the use that has been made of both, the plan for carrying this new scheme of government into execution, and the effects which it has produced, are, in my opinion, worthy of our serious consideration.

His Majesty came to the throne of these kingdoms with more advantages than any of his predecessors since the revolution. Fourth in descent, and third in succession of his royal family, even the zealots of hereditary right, in him, saw something to flatter their favorite prejudices; and to justify a transfer of their attachments, without a change in their principles.

The person and cause of the Pretender were become contemptible; his title disowned throughout Europe; his party disbanded in England. His Majesty came, indeed, to the inheritance of a mighty war; but, victorious in every part of the globe, peace was always in his power, not to negotiate, but to dictate. No foreign habitudes or attachments withdrew him from the cultivation of his power at home. His revenue for the civil establishment, fixed (as it was the thought) at a large, but definite sum, was ample without being invidious. His influence, by additions from conquest, by an augmentation of debt, by an increase of military and naval establishment, much strengthened and extended. And coming to the throne in the prime and full vigor of youth, as from affection there was a strong dislike, so from dread there seemed to be a general averseness, from giving anything like offence to a monarch, against whose resentment opposition could not look for a refuge in any sort of reversionary hope.

These singular advantages inspired his Majesty only with a more ardent desire to preserve unimpaired the spirit of that national freedom, to which he owed a situation so full of glory. But to others it suggested sentiments of a very different nature. They thought they now beheld an opportunity (by a certain sort of statesmen never long undiscovered or unemployed) of drawing themselves by the aggrandizement of a court faction, a degree of power which they could never hope to derive from natural influence or from honorable service; and which it was impossible they could hold with the least security, whilst the system of administration rested upon its former bottom. In order to facilitate the execution of their design, it was necessary to make many alterations in political arrangement, and a signal change in the opinions, habits, and connections of the greatest part of those who at that time acted in public. . . .

To reconcile the minds of the people to all these movements, principles correspondent to them had been preached up with great zeal. Every one must remember that the cabal set out with the most astonishing prudery, both moral and political. Those, who in a few months after soused over head and ears into the deepest and dirtiest pits of corruption, cried out violently against the indirect practices in the electing and managing of Parliaments, which had formerly prevailed. This marvellous abhorrence which the court had suddenly taken to all influence, was not only circulated in conversation through the kingdom, but pompously announced to the public, with many other extraordinary things, in a pamphlet which had all the appearance of a manifesto preparatory to some considerable enterprise. . . .

In this piece appeared the first dawning of the new system: there first appeared the idea (then only in speculation) of *separating the court from the administration;* of carrying everything from national connection to personal regards; and of forming a regular party for that purpose, under the name of *king's men.*

To recommend this system to the people, a perspective view of the court, gorgeously painted, and finely illuminated from within, was exhibited to the gaping multitude. Party was to be totally done away, with all its evil works. Corruption was to be cast down from court, as *Atè* was from heaven. Power was thenceforward to be the chosen residence of public spirit; and no one was to be supposed under any sinister influence, except those who had the misfortune to be in disgrace at court, which was to stand in lieu of all vices and all corruptions. A scheme of perfection to be realized in a monarchy far beyond the visionary republic of Plato. The whole scenery was exactly disposed to captivate those good souls, whose credulous morality is so invaluable a treasure to crafty politicians. . . . Now was the time to unlock the sealed fountain of royal bounty, which had been infamously monopolized and huckstered, and to let it flow at large upon the whole people. The time was come, to restore royalty to its original splendor. . . . And it was constantly in the mouths of all the runners of the court, that nothing could preserve the balance of the constitution from being overturned by the rabble, or by a faction of the nobility, but to free the sovereign effectually from that ministerial tyranny under which the royal dignity had been oppressed in the person of his Majesty's grandfather. . . .

One of the principal topics which was then, and has been since, much employed by that political school, is an affected terror of the growth of an aristocratic power, prejudicial to the rights of the crown, and the balance of the constitution. . . .

It is true, that the peers have a great influence in the kingdom, and in every part of the public concerns. . . . If any particular peers, by their uniform, upright, constitutional conduct, by their public and their private virtues, have acquired an influence in the country; the people, on whose favor that influence depends, and from whom it arose, will never be duped into an opinion, that such greatness in a peer is the despotism of an aristocracy, when they know and feel it to be the effect and pledge of their own importance.

I am no friend to aristocracy, in the sense at least in which that word is usually understood. If it were not a bad habit to moot cases on the supposed ruin of the constitution, I should be free to declare, that if it must perish, I would rather by far see it resolved into any other form, than lost in that austere and insolent domination. But, whatever my dislikes may be, my fears are not upon that quarter. The question, on the influence of a court, and of a peerage, is not, which of the two dangers is the more eligible, but which is the more imminent. He is but a poor observer, who has not seen, that the generality of peers, far from supporting themselves in a state of independent greatness, are but too apt to fall into an oblivion of their proper dignity, and to run headlong into an abject servitude. Would to God it were true, that the fault of our peers were too much spirit. It is worthy of some observation that these gentlemen, so jealous of aristocracy, make no complaints of the power of those peers (neither few nor inconsiderable) who are always in the train of a court, and whose whole weight must be considered as a portion of the settled influence of the crown. This is all safe and right; but if some peers (I am very sorry they are not as many as they ought to be) set themselves, in the great concern of peers and commons, against a back-stairs influence and clandestine government, then the alarm begins; then the constitution is in danger of being forced into an aristocracy.

I rest a little the longer on this court topic, because it was much insisted upon at the time of the great change, and has been since frequently revived by many of the agents of that party; for, whilst they are terrifying the great and opulent with the horrors of mob-government, they are by other managers attempting (though hitherto with little success) to alarm the people with a phantom of tyranny in the nobles. All this is done upon their favorite principle of disunion, of sowing jealousies amongst the different orders of the state, and of disjointing the natural strength of the kingdom; that it may be rendered incapable of resisting the sinister designs of wicked men, who have engrossed the royal power.

Thus much of the topics chosen by the courtiers to recommend their system; it will be necessary to open a little more at large the nature of that party which was formed for its support. . . . As a powerful party, and a party constructed on a new principle, it is a very inviting object of curiosity.

It must be remembered, that since the revolution, until the period we are speaking of, the influence of the crown had been always employed in supporting the ministers of state, and in carrying on the public business according to their opinions. But the party now in question is formed upon a very different idea. It is to intercept the favor, protection, and confidence of the crown in the passage to its ministers; it is to come between them and their importance in Parliament; it is to separate them from all their natural and acquired dependencies; it is intended as the control, not the support, of administration. The machinery of this system is perplexed in its movements, and false in its principle. It is formed on a supposition that the king is something external to his government; and that he may be honored and aggrandized, even by its debility and disgrace. The plan proceeds expressly on the idea of enfeebling the regular executory power. It proceeds on the idea of weakening the state in order to strengthen the court. . . .

As a foundation of their scheme, the cabal have established a sort of *rota* in the court. All sorts of parties, by this means, have been brought into administration; from whence few have had the good fortune to escape without disgrace; none at all without considerable losses. In the beginning of each arrangement no professions of confidence and support are wanting, to induce the leading men to engage. But while the ministers of the day appear in all the pomp and pride of power, while they have all their canvas spread out to the wind, and every sail filled with the fair and prosperous gale of royal favor, in a short time they find, they know not how, a current, which sets directly against them: which prevents all progress, and even drives them backwards. They grow ashamed and mortified in a situation, which, by its vicinity to power, only serves to remind them the more strongly of their insignificance. They are obliged either to execute the orders of their inferiors, or to see themselves opposed by the natural instruments of their office. With the loss of their dignity they lose their temper. In their turn they grow troublesome to that cabal which, whether it supports or opposes, equally disgraces and equally betrays them. It is soon found necessary to get rid of the heads only. As there always are many rotten members belonging to the best connections, it is not hard to persuade several to continue in office without their leaders. By this means the party goes out much thinner than it came in; and is only reduced in strength by its temporary possession of power. . . .

They contrive to form in the outward administration two parties at the least; which, whilst they are tearing one another to pieces, are both competitors for the favor and protection of the cabal; and, by their emulation, contribute to throw everything more and more into the hands of the interior managers.

A minister of state will sometimes keep himself totally estranged from all his colleagues; will differ from them in their councils, will privately traverse, and publicly oppose, their measures. He will, however, continue in his employment. Instead of suffering any mark of displeasure, he will be distinguished by an unbounded profusion of court rewards and caresses; because he does what is expected, and all that is expected, from men in office. He helps to keep some form of administration in being, and keeps it at the same time as weak and divided as possible.

However, we must take care not to be mistaken, or to imagine that such persons have any weight in their opposition. When, by them, administration is convinced of its insignificancy, they are soon to be convinced of their own. They never are suffered to succeed in their opposition. They and the world are to be satisfied, that neither office, nor authority, nor property, nor ability, eloquence, counsel, skill, or union, are of the least importance; but that the mere influence of the court, naked of all support, and destitute of all management, is abundantly sufficient for all its own purposes.

When any adverse connection is to be destroyed, the cabal seldom appear in the work themselves. They find out some person of whom the party entertains a high opinion. Such a person they endeavor to delude with various pretences. They teach him first to distrust, and then to quarrel with his friends; among whom, by the same arts, they excite a similar diffidence of him; so that in this mutual fear and distrust, he may suffer himself to be employed as the instrument in the change which is brought about. Afterwards they are sure to destroy him in his turn, by setting up in his place some person in whom he had himself reposed the greatest confidence, and who serves to carry off a considerable part of his adherents. . . . They have so contrived matters, that people have a greater hatred to the subordinate instruments than to the principal movers. . . .

That this body may be enabled to compass all the ends of its institution, its members are scarcely ever to aim at the high and responsible offices of the state. They are distributed

with art and judgment through all the secondary, but efficient, departments of office, and through the households of
all the branches of the royal family: so as on one hand to
occupy all the avenues to the throne; and on the other to
forward or frustrate the execution of any measure, according
to their own interests. . . .

The members of the court faction are fully indemnified for
not holding places on the slippery heights of the kingdom,
not only by the lead in all affairs, but also by the perfect security in which they enjoy less conspicuous, but very advantageous situations. Their places are in express legal tenure, or,
in effect, all of them for life. Whilst the first and most respectable persons in the kingdom are tossed about like tennis-balls,
the sport of a blind and insolent caprice, no minister dares
even to cast an oblique glance at the lowest of their body. If
an attempt be made upon one of this corps, immediately he
flies to sanctuary, and pretends to the most inviolable of all
promises. No conveniency of public arrangement is available
to remove any one of them from the specific situation he
holds; and the slightest attempt upon one of them, by the
most powerful minister, is a certain preliminary to his own
destruction. . . .

Here is a sketch, though a slight one, of the constitution,
laws, and policy of this new court corporation. The name by
which they choose to distinguish themselves, is that of *king's
men* or the *king's friends,* by an invidious exclusion of the rest
of his Majesty's most loyal and affectionate subjects. The
whole system, comprehending the exterior and interior administrations, is commonly called, in the technical language
of the court, *double cabinet;* in French or English, as you
choose to pronounce it.

Whether all this be a vision of a distracted brain, or the
invention of a malicious heart, or a real faction in the country, must be judged by the appearances which things have
worn for eight years past. Thus far I am certain, that there is
not a single public man, in or out of office, who has not, at
some time or other, borne testimony to the truth of what I
have now related. . . .

It may appear somewhat affected, that in so much discourse upon this extraordinary party, I should say so little of
the Earl of Bute, who is the supposed head of it. But this
was neither owing to affectation nor inadvertence. I have
carefully avoided the introduction of personal reflections of
any kind. Much the greater part of the topics which have been

used to blacken this nobleman are either unjust or frivolous. At best, they have a tendency to give the resentment of this bitter calamity a wrong direction, and to turn a public grievance into a mean, personal, or a dangerous national quarrel. Where there is a regular scheme of operations carried on, it is the system, and not any individual person who acts in it, that is truly dangerous. This system has not arisen solely from the ambition of Lord Bute, but from the circumstances which favored it, and from an indifference to the constitution which had been for some time growing among our gentry. We should have been tried with it, if the Earl of Bute had never existed; . . . It is not, therefore, to rail at Lord Bute, but firmly to embody against this court party and its practices, which can afford us any prospect of relief in our present condition. . . .

It is this unnatural infusion of a *system of favoritism* into a government which in a great part of its constitution is popular, that has raised the present ferment in the nation. The people, without entering deeply into its principles, could plainly perceive its effects, in much violence, in a great spirit of innovation, and a general disorder in all the functions of government. I keep my eye solely on this system; if I speak of those measures which have arisen from it, it will be so far only as they illustrate the general scheme. This is the fountain of all those bitter waters of which, through an hundred different conduits, we have drunk until we are ready to burst. The discretionary power of the crown in the formation of ministry, abused by bad or weak men, has given rise to a system, which, without directly violating the letter of any law, operates against the spirit of the whole constitution.

A plan of favoritism for our executory government is essentially at variance with the plan of our legislature. One great end undoubtedly of a mixed government like ours, composed of monarchy, and of controls, on the part of the higher people and the lower, is that the prince shall not be able to violate the laws. This is useful and indeed fundamental. But this, even at first view, is no more than a negative advantage; an armor merely defensive. It is therefore next in order, and equal in importance, *that the discretionary powers which are necessarily vested in the monarch, whether for the execution of the laws, or for the nomination to magistracy and office, or for conducting the affairs of peace and war, or for ordering the revenue, should all be exercised upon public principles and national grounds, and not on the likings or prejudices, the intrigues or policies, of a court.* This, I said, is equal in importance to the securing a government according to law. The laws reach but a very little way. Constitute government how you please, infinitely the greater part of it must depend upon the exercise of the powers which are left at large to the prudence and uprightness of ministers of state. Even all the use and potency of the laws depends upon them. Without them, your commonwealth is no better than a scheme upon paper; and not a living, active, effective constitution. It is possible that through negligence, or ignorance, or design artfully conducted, ministers may suffer one part of government to languish, another to be perverted from its purposes, and every valuable interest of the country to fall into ruin and decay, without possibility of fixing any single act on which a criminal prosecution can be justly grounded. The due arrangement of men in the active part of the state, far from being foreign to the purposes of a wise government, ought to be among its very first and dearest objects. When, therefore, the abettors of the new system tell us, that between them and their opposers there is nothing but a struggle for power, and that therefore we are no ways concerned with it; we must tell those who have the impudence to insult us in this manner, that, of all things, we ought to be the most concerned who, and what sort of men they are that hold the trust of everything that is dear to us. Nothing can render this a point of indifference to the nation, but what must render us totally desperate, or soothe us into the security of idiots. We must soften into a credulity below the milkiness of infancy to think all men virtuous. We must be tainted with a malignity truly diabolical to believe all the world to be equally wicked and corrupt. Men are in public life as in private, some good, some evil. The elevation of the one, and the depression of the other, are the first objects of all true policy. But that form of government, which, neither in its direct institutions, nor in their immediate tendency, has contrived to throw its affairs into the most trustworthy hands, but has left its whole executory system to be disposed of agreeably to the uncontrolled pleasure of any one man, however excellent or virtuous, is a plan of polity defective not only in that member, but consequentially erroneous in every part of it.

In arbitrary governments, the constitution of the ministry follows the constitution of legislature. Both the law and the magistrate are the creatures of will. It must be so. Nothing, indeed, will appear more certain, on any tolerable consideration of this matter, than that *every sort of government ought to have its administration correspondent to its legislature.* If it should be otherwise, things must fall into an hideous disorder. The people of a free commonwealth, who have taken such care that their laws should be the result of general consent, cannot be so senseless as to suffer their executory system to be composed of persons on whom they have no dependence, and whom no proofs of the public love and confidence have recommended to those powers, upon the use of which the very being of the state depends.

The popular election of magistrates, and popular disposition of rewards and honors, is one of the first advantages of a free state. Without it, or something equivalent to it, perhaps the people cannot long enjoy the substance of freedom; certainly none of the vivifying energy of good government. The frame of our commonwealth did not admit of such an actual election: but it provided as well, and (while the spirit of the constitution is preserved) better for all the effects of it than by the method of suffrage in any democratic state whatsoever. It had always, until of late, been held the first duty of Parliament *to refuse to support government, until power was in the hands of persons who were acceptable to the people, or while factions predominated in the court in which the nation had no confidence.* Thus all the good effects of popular election were supposed to be secured to us, without the mischiefs attending on perpetual intrigue, and a distinct canvass for every particular office throughout the body of the people. This was the most noble and refined part of our constitution. The people, by their representatives and grandees, were intrusted with a deliberative power in making laws; the king with the control of his negative. The king was intrusted with the deliberative choice and the election to office; the people had the negative in a Parliamentary refusal to support. Formerly this power of control was what kept ministers in awe of Parliaments, and Parliaments in reverence with the people. If the use of this power of control on the system and persons of administration is gone, everything is lost, Parliament and all. We may assure ourselves, that if Parliament will tamely see evil men take possession of all the strongholds of their country, and allow them time and means to fortify themselves, under a pretence of giving them a fair trial, and upon a hope of discovering, whether they will not be reformed by power, and whether their measures will not be better than their morals; such a Parliament will give countenance to their measures also, whatever that Parliament may pretend, and whatever those measures may be.

Every good political institution must have a preventive operation as well as a remedial. It ought to have a natural tendency to exclude bad men from government, and not to trust for the safety of the state to subsequent punishment alone; punishment, which has ever been tardy and uncertain; and which, when power is suffered in bad hands, may chance to fall rather on the injured than the criminal.

Before men are put forward into the great trusts of the state, they ought by their conduct to have obtained such a degree of estimation in their country, as may be some sort of pledge and security to the public, that they will not abuse those trusts. It is no mean security for a proper use of power, that a man has shown by the general tenor of his actions, that the affection, the good opinion, the confidence of his fellow-citizens have been among the principal objects of his life; and that he has owed none of the gradations of his power or fortune to a settled contempt, or occasional forfeiture of their esteem.

That man who before he comes into power has no friends, or who coming into power is obliged to desert his friends, or who losing it has no friends to sympathize with him; he who has no sway among any part of the landed or commercial interest, but whose whole importance has begun with his office, and is sure to end with it, is a person who ought never to be suffered by a controlling Parliament to continue in any of those situations which confer the lead and direction of all our public affairs; because such a man *has no connection with the interest of the people*.

Those knots or cabals of men who have got together, avowedly without any public principle, in order to sell their conjunct iniquity at the higher rate, and are therefore universally odious, ought never to be suffered to domineer in the state; because they have *no connection with the sentiments of the people*.

These are considerations which in my opinion enforce the necessity of having some better reason, in a free country, and a free Parliament, for supporting the ministers of the crown, than that short one, *That the king has throught proper to appoint them*. There is something very courtly in this. But it is a principle pregnant with all sorts of mischief, in a constitution like ours, to turn the views of active men from the country to the court. Whatever be the road to power, that is the

road which will be trod. . . . Whether it will be right, in a
state so popular in its constitution as ours, to leave ambition
without popular motives, and to trust all to the operation of
pure virtue in the minds of kings, and ministers, and public
men, must be submitted to the judgment and good sense of
the people of England.

Cunning men are here apt to break in, and, without directly controverting the principle, to raise objections from the
difficulty under which the sovereign labors, to distinguish the
genuine voice and sentiments of his people, from the clamor of
faction, by which it is so easily counterfeited. The nation, they
say, is generally divided into parties, with views and passions
utterly irreconcilable. If the king should put his affairs into the
hands of any one of them, he is sure to disgust the rest; if he
select particular men from among them all, it is a hazard that
he disgusts them all. Those who are left out, however divided
before, will soon run into a body of opposition; which, being
a collection of many discontents into one focus, will without
doubt be hot and violent enough. Faction will make its cries
resound through the nation, as if the whole were in an uproar,
when by far the majority, and much the better part, will seem
for a while as it were annihilated by the quiet in which their
virtue and moderation incline them to enjoy the blessings of
government. Besides that the opinion of the mere vulgar is a
miserable rule even with regard to themselves, on account of
their violence and instability. So that if you were to gratify
them in their humor today, that very gratification would be a
ground of their dissatisfaction on the next. Now as all these
rules of public opinion are to be collected with great difficulty,
and to be applied with equal uncertainty as to the effect, what
better can a king of England do, than to employ such men as
he finds to have views and inclinations most conformable to
his own; who are least infected with pride and self-will; and
who are least moved by such popular humors as are perpetually traversing his designs, and disturbing his service; trusting
that, when he means no ill to his people, he will be supported
in his appointments, whether he chooses to keep or to change,
as his private judgment or his pleasure leads him? He will find
a sure resource in the real weight and influence of the crown,
when it is not suffered to become an instrument in the hands
of a faction.

I will not pretend to say, that there is nothing at all in this
mode of reasoning; because I will not assert that there is no
difficulty in the art of government. Undoubtedly the very best

administration must encounter a great deal of opposition; and the very worst will find more support than it deserves. Sufficient appearances will never be wanting to those who have a mind to deceive themselves. It is a fallacy in constant use with those who would level all things, and confound right with wrong, to insist upon the inconveniences which are attached to every choice, without taking into consideration the different weight and consequence of those inconveniences. The question is not concerning *absolute* discontent or *perfect* satisfaction in government; neither of which can be pure and unmixed at any time, or upon any system. The controversy is about that degree of good humor in the people, which may possibly be attained, and ought certainly to be looked for. While some politicians may be waiting to know whether the sense of every individual be against them, accurately distinguishing the vulgar from the better sort, drawing lines between the enterprises of a faction and the efforts of a people, they may chance to see the government, which they are so nicely weighing, and dividing, and distinguishing, tumble to the ground in the midst of their wise deliberation. Prudent men, when so great an object as the security of government, or even its peace, is at stake, will not run the risk of a decision which may be fatal to it. They who can read the political sky will see a hurricane in a cloud no bigger than a hand at the very edge of the horizon, and will run into the first harbor. No lines can be laid down for civil or political wisdom. They are a matter incapable of exact definition. But, though no man can draw a stroke between the confines of day and night, yet light and darkness are upon the whole tolerably distinguishable. Nor will it be impossible for a prince to find out such a mode of government, and such persons to administer it, as will give a great degree of content to his people; without any curious and anxious research for that abstract, universal, perfect harmony, which while he is seeking, he abandons those means of ordinary tranquility which are in his power without any research at all. . . .

Here it is that the people must on their part show themselves sensible of their own value. Their whole importance, in the first instance, and afterwards their whole freedom, is at stake. Their freedom cannot long survive their importance. Here it is that the natural strength of the kingdom, the great peers, the leading landed gentlemen, the opulent merchants and manufacturers, the substantial yeomanry, must interpose, to rescue their prince, themselves, and their posterity.

We are at present at issue upon this point. We are in the great crisis of this contention; and the part which men take, one way or other, will serve to discriminate their characters and their principles. Until the matter is decided, the country will remain in its present confusion. For while a system of administration is attempted, entirely repugnant to the genius of the people, and not conformable to the plan of their government, everything must necessarily be disordered for a time, until this system destroys the constitution, or the constitution gets the better of this system.

There is, in my opinion, a peculiar venom and malignity in this political distemper beyond any that I have heard or read of. In former times the projectors of arbitrary government attacked only the liberties of their country; a design surely mischievous enough to have satisfied a mind of the most unruly ambition. But a system unfavorable to freedom may be so formed, as considerably to exalt the grandeur of the state; and men may find, in the pride and splendor of that prosperity, some sort of consolation for the loss of their solid privileges. Indeed the increase of the power of the state has often been urged by artful men, as a pretext for some abridgment of public liberty. But the scheme of the junto under consideration, not only strikes a palsy into every nerve of our free constitution, but in the same degree benumbs and stupefies the whole executive power: rendering government in all its grand operations languid, uncertain, ineffective; making ministers fearful of attempting, and incapable of executing any useful plan of domestic arrangement, or of foreign politics. It tends to produce neither the security of a free government, nor the energy of a monarchy that is absolute. . . .

These are the consequences inevitable to our public peace, from the scheme of rendering the executory government at once odious and feeble; or freeing administration from the constitutional and salutary control of Parliament, and inventing for it a *new control*, unknown to the constitution, an *interior cabinet;* which brings the whole body of government into confusion and contempt. . . .

There remains only . . . to say something of the grand principle which first recommended this system at court. The pretence was, to prevent the king from being enslaved by a faction, and made a prisoner in his closet. This scheme might have been expected to answer at least its own end, and to indemnify the king, in his personal capacity, for all the confusion into which it has thrown his government. But has it in reality answered this purpose? I am sure, if it had, every affectionate subject would have one motive for enduring with patience all the evils which attend it.

In order to come at the truth in this matter, it may not be amiss to consider it somewhat in detail. I speak here of the king, and not of the crown; the interests of which we have already touched. Independent of that greatness which a king possesses merely by being a representative of the national dignity, the things in which he may have an individual interest seem to be these:—wealth accumulated; wealth spent in magnificence, pleasure, or beneficence; personal respect and attention; and, above all, private ease and repose of mind. . . .

Suppose then we were to ask, whether the king has been richer than his predecessors in accumulated wealth, since the establishment of the plan of favoritism? I believe it will be found that the picture of royal indigence, which our court has presented until this year, has been truly humiliating. Nor has it been relieved from this unseemly distress, but by means which have hazarded the affection of the people, and shaken their confidence in Parliament. If the public treasures had been exhausted in magnificence and splendor, this distress would have been accounted for, and in some measure justified. Nothing would be more unworthy of this nation, than with a mean and mechanical rule, to mete out the splendor of the crown. Indeed I have found very few persons disposed to so ungenerous a procedure. But the generality of people, it must be confessed, do feel a good deal mortified, when they compare the wants of the court with its expenses. They do not behold the cause of this distress in any part of the apparatus of royal magnificence. In all this, they see nothing but the operations of parsimony, attended with all the consequences of profusion. Nothing expended, nothing saved. Their wonder is increased by their knowledge, that besides the revenue settled on his Majesty's civil list to the amount of 800,000*l.* a year, he has a farther aid from a large pension list, near 90,000*l.* a year, in Ireland; from the produce of the duchy of Lancaster (which we are told has been greatly improved); from the revenue of the duchy of Cornwall; from the American quit-rents; from the four and a half per cent duty in the Leeward Islands; this last worth to be sure considerably more than 40,000*l.* a year. The whole is certainly not much short of a million annually.

These are revenues within the knowledge and cognizance of our national councils. We have no direct right to examine

into the receipts from his Majesty's German dominions, and
the bishopric of Osnaburg. This is unquestionably true. But
that which is not within the province of Parliament, is yet
within the sphere of every man's own reflection. If a foreign
prince resided amongst us, the state of his revenues could
not fail of becoming the subject of our speculation. Filled with
an anxious concern for whatever regards the welfare of our
sovereign, it is impossible, in considering the miserable circumstances into which he has been brought, that this obvious
topic should be entirely passed over. There is an opinion universal, that these revenues produce something not inconsiderable, clear of all charges and establishments. This produce the
people do not believe to be hoarded, nor perceive to be spent.
It is accounted for in the only manner it can, by supposing
that it is drawn away, for the support of that court faction,
which, whilst it distresses the nation, impoverishes the prince
in every one of his resources. . . .

Has this system provided better for the treatment becoming
his high and sacred character, and secured the king from those
disgusts attached to the necessity of employing men who are
not personally agreeable? This is a topic upon which for many
reasons I could wish to be silent; but the pretence of securing
against such causes of uneasiness, is the corner-stone of the
court-party. It has however so happened, that if I were to fix
upon any one point, in which this system has been more particularly and shamefully blamable, the effects which it has
produced would justify me in choosing for that point its tendency to degrade the personal dignity of the sovereign, and
to expose him to a thousand contradictions and mortifica-
tions. . . .

If therefore this system has so ill answered its own grand
pretence of saving the king from the necessity of employing
persons disagreeable to him, has it given more peace and
tranquility to his Majesty's private hours? No, most certainly.
The father of his people cannot possibly enjoy repose, while
his family is in such a state of distraction. Then what has the
crown or the king profited by all this fine-wrought scheme?
Is he more rich, or more splendid, or more powerful, or more
at his ease, by so many labors and contrivances? Have they
not beggared his exchequer, tarnished the splendor of his
court, sunk his dignity, galled his feelings, discomposed the
whole order and happiness of his private life?

It will be very hard, I believe, to state in what respect the king has profited by that faction which presumptuously choose to call themselves his friends. . . .

So far I have considered the effect of the court system, chiefly as it operates upon the executive government, on the temper of the people, and on the happiness of the sovereign. It remains that we should consider, with a little attention, its operation upon Parliament.

Parliament was indeed the great object of all these politics, the end at which they aimed, as well as the instrument by which they were to operate. But, before Parliament could be made subservient to a system, by which it was to be degraded from the dignity of a national council into a mere member of the court, it must be greatly changed from its original character.

In speaking of this body, I have my eye chiefly on the House of Commons. I hope I shall be indulged in a few observations on the nature and character of that assembly; not with regard to its *legal form and power,* but to its *spirit,* and to the purposes it is meant to answer in the constitution.

The House of Commons was supposed originally to be *no part of the standing government of this country*. It was considered as a *control,* issuing *immediately* from the people, and speedily to be resolved into the mass from whence it arose. In this respect it was in the higher part of government what juries are in the lower. The capacity of magistrate being transitory, and that of a citizen permanent, the latter capacity it was hoped would of course preponderate in all discussions, not only between the people and the standing authority of the crown, but between the people and the fleeting authority of the House of Commons itself. It was hoped that, being of a middle nature between subject and government, they would feel with a more tender and a nearer interest everything that concerned the people, than the other remoter and more permanent parts of legislature.

Whatever the alterations time and the necessary accommodation of business may have introduced, this character can never be sustained, unless the House of Commons shall be made to bear some stamp of the actual disposition of the people at large. It would (among public misfortunes) be an evil more natural and tolerable, that the House of Commons should be infected with every epidemical frenzy of the people, as this would indicate some consanguinity, some sympathy of nature with their constituents, than that they should in all cases be wholly untouched by the opinions and feelings of the people out of doors. By this want of sympathy they would cease to be a House of Commons. For it is not the derivation of the power of that House from the people, which makes it in a distinct sense their representative. The king is the representative of the people; so are the lords; so are the judges. They all are trustees for the people, as well as the commons; because no power is given for the sole sake of the holder; and although government certainly is an institution of divine authority, yet its forms, and the persons who administer it, all originate from the people.

A popular origin cannot therefore be the characteristical distinction of a popular representative. This belongs equally to all parts of government and in all forms. The virtue, spirit, and essence of a House of Commons consists in its being the express image of the feelings of the nation. It was not instituted to be a control *upon* the people, as of late it has been taught, by a doctrine of the most pernicious tendency. It was designed as a control *for* the people. Other institutions have been formed for the purpose of checking popular excesses; and they are, I apprehend, fully adequate to their object. If not, they ought to be made so. The House of Commons, as it was never intended for the support of peace and subordination, is miserably appointed for that service; having no stronger weapon than its mace, and no better officer than its serjeant-at-arms, which it can command of its own proper authority. A vigilant and jealous eye over executory and judicial magistracy; an anxious care of public money; an openness, approaching towards facility, to public complaint: these seem to be the true characteristics of a House of Commons. But an addressing House of Commons, and a petitioning nation; a House of Commons full of confidence, when the nation is plunged in despair; in the utmost harmony with ministers, whom the people regard with the utmost abhorrence; who vote thanks, when the public opinion calls upon them for impeachments; who are eager to grant, when the general voice demands account; who, in all disputes between the people and administration, presume against the people; who punish their disorders, but refuse even to inquire into the provocations to them; this is an unnatural, a monstrous state of things in this constitution. Such an assembly may be a great, wise, awful senate; but it is not, to any popular purpose, a House of Commons. This change from an immediate state of procuration and delegation to a course of acting as from original power, is the way in which all the popular magistracies in the world have been perverted from their purposes. It is indeed their greatest and sometimes their incurable corruption. For there is a material distinction between that corruption by which particular points are carried against reason, (this is a thing which cannot be prevented by human wisdom, and is of less consequence,) and the corruption of the principle itself. For then the evil is not accidental, but settled. The distemper becomes the natural habit.

For my part, I shall be compelled to conclude the principle of Parliament to be totally corrupted, and therefore its ends entirely defeated, when I see two symptoms: first, a rule of indiscriminate support to all ministers; because this destroys the very end of Parliament as a control, and is a general, previous sanction to misgovernment: and secondly, the setting up any claims adverse to the right of free election; for this tends to subvert the legal authority by which the House of Commons sits.

I know that, since the Revolution, along with many dangerous, many useful powers of government have been weakened. It is absolutely necessary to have frequent recourse to the legislature. Parliaments must therefore sit every year, and for great part of the year. The dreadful disorders of frequent elections have also necessitated a septennial instead of a triennial duration. . . . The constant habit of authority, and the unfrequency of elections, have tended very much to draw the House of Commons towards the character of a standing senate. It is a disorder which has arisen from the cure of greater disorders; it has arisen from the extreme difficulty of reconciling liberty under a monarchical government, with external strength and with internal tranquility.

It is very clear that we cannot free ourselves entirely from this great inconvenience; but I would not increase an evil, because I was not able to remove it; and because it was not in my power to keep the House of Commons religiously true to its first principles, I would not argue for carrying it to a total oblivion of them. This has been the great scheme of power in our time. They, who will not conform their conduct to the public good, and cannot support it by the prerogative of the crown, have adopted a new plan. They have totally abandoned the shattered and old-fashioned fortress of prerogative, and made a lodgment in the stronghold of Parliament itself. If they have any evil design to which there is no ordinary legal power commensurate, they bring it into Parliament. In Parliament the whole is executed from the beginning to the end. In

Parliament the power of obtaining their object is absolute; and the safety in the proceeding perfect: no rules to confine, no after-reckonings to terrify. Parliament cannot, with any great propriety, punish others for things in which they themselves have been accomplices. Thus the control of Parliament upon the executory power is lost; because Parliament is made to partake in every considerable act of government. *Impeachment, that great guardian of the purity of the constitution, is in danger of being lost, even to the idea of it.*

By this plan several important ends are answered to the cabal. If the authority of Parliament supports itself, the credit of every act of government, which they contrive, is saved; but if the act be so very odious that the whole strength of Parliament is insufficient to recommend it, then Parliament is itself discredited; and this discredit increases more and more that indifference to the constitution, which it is the constant aim of its enemies, by their abuse of Parliamentary powers, to render general among the people. Whenever Parliament is persuaded to assume the offices of executive government, it will lose all the confidence, love, and veneration, which it has ever enjoyed whilst it was supposed the *corrective and control* of the acting powers of the state. This would be the event, though its conduct in such a perversion of its functions should be tolerably just and moderate; but if it should be iniquitous, violent, full of passion, and full of faction, it would be considered as the most intolerable of all the modes of tyranny.

For a considerable time this separation of the representatives from their constituents went on with a silent progress; and had those, who conducted the plan for their total separation, been persons of temper and abilities any way equal to the magnitude of their design, the success would have been infallible: but by their precipitancy they have laid it open in all its nakedness; the nation is alarmed at it: and the event may not be pleasant to the contrivers of the scheme. In the last session, the corps called the *king's friends* made a hardy attempt, all at once, *to alter the right of election itself;* to put it into the power of the House of Commons to disable any person disagreeable to them from sitting in Parliament, without any other rule than their own pleasure; to make incapacities, either general for descriptions of men, or particular for individuals; and to take into their body, persons who avowedly had never been chosen by the majority of legal electors, nor agreeably to any known rule of law. . . .

A violent rage for the punishment of Mr. Wilkes was the

pretence of the whole. This gentleman, by setting himself strongly in opposition to the court cabal, had become at once an object of their persecution, and of the popular favor. The hatred of the court party pursuing, and the countenance of the people protecting him, it very soon became not at all a question on the man, but a trial of strength between the two parties. The advantage of the victory in this particular contest was the present, but not the only, nor by any means the principal object. Its operation upon the character of the House of Commons was the great point in view. The point to be gained by the cabal was this; that a precedent should be established, tending to show, *That the favor of the people was not so sure a road as the favor of the court even to popular honors and popular trusts.* A strenuous resistance to every appearance of lawless power; a spirit of independence carried to some degree of enthusiasm; an inquisitive character to discover, and a bold one to display, every corruption and every error of government; these are the qualities which recommend a man to a seat in the House of Commons, in open and merely popular elections. An indolent and submissive disposition; a disposition to think charitably of all the actions of men in power, and to live in a mutual intercourse of favors with them; an inclination rather to countenance a strong use of authority, than to bear any sort of licentiousness on the part of the people; these are unfavorable qualities in an open election for members of Parliament.

The instinct which carries the people towards the choice of the former, is justified by reason; because, a man of such a character, even in its exorbitances, does not directly contradict the purposes of a trust, the end of which is a control on power. The latter character, even when it is not in its extreme, will execute this trust but very imperfectly; and, if deviating to the least excess, will certainly frustrate instead of forwarding the purposes of a control on government. But when the House of Commons was to be new modelled, this principle was not only to be changed but reversed. Whilst any errors committed in support of power were left to the law, with every advantage of favorable construction, of mitigation, and finally of pardon; all excesses on the side of liberty, or in pursuit of popular favor, or in defence of popular rights and privileges, were not only to be punished by the rigor of the known law, but by a *discretionary* proceeding, which brought on *the loss of the popular object itself.* Popularity was to be rendered, if not directly penal, at least highly dangerous. The favor of the people might lead even to a disqualification of representing them. . . . Until this time, the opinion of the people, through the power of an assembly, still in some sort popular, led to the greatest honors and emoluments in the gift of the crown. Now the principle is reversed; and the favor of the court is the only sure way of obtaining and holding those honors which ought to be in the disposal of the people. . . .

I will not believe, what no other man living believes, that Mr. Wilkes was punished for the indecency of his publications, or the impiety of his ransacked closet. If he had fallen in a common slaughter of libellers and blasphemers, I could well believe that nothing more was meant than was pretended. But when I see, that, for years together full as impious, and perhaps more dangerous writings to religion, and virtue, and order, have not been punished, nor their authors discountenanced; that the most audacious libels on royal majesty have passed without notice; that the most treasonable invectives against the laws, liberties, and constitution of the country, have not met with the slightest animadversion; I must consider this as a shocking and shameful pretence. . . .

When therefore I reflect upon this method pursued by the cabal in distributing rewards and punishments, I must conclude that Mr. Wilkes is the object of persecution, not on account of what he has done in common with others who are the objects of reward, but for that in which he differs from many of them: that he is pursued for the spirited dispositions which are blended with his vices; for his unconquerable firmness, for his resolute, indefatigable, strenuous resistance against oppression. . . .

It behooves the people of England to consider how the House of Commons, under the operation of these examples, must of necessity be constituted. On the side of the court will be, all honors, offices, emoluments; every sort of personal gratification to avarice or vanity; and, what is of more moment to most gentlemen, the means of growing, by innumerable petty services to individuals, into a spreading interest in their country. On the other hand, let us suppose a person unconnected with the court, and in opposition to its system. For his own person, no office, or emolument, or title; no promotion, ecclesiastical, or civil, or military, or naval, for children, or brothers, or kindred. In vain an expiring interest in a borough calls for offices, or small livings, for the children of mayors, and aldermen, and capital burgesses. His court rival has them all. He can do an infinite number of acts of generosity and kindness, and even of public spirit. He can procure indemnity from quarters. He can procure advantages in trade. He can get pardons for offences. He can obtain a thousand favors, and avert a thousand evils. He may, while he betrays every valuable interest of the kingdom, be a bene-factor, a patron, a father, a guardian angel to his borough. The unfortunate independent member has nothing to offer, but harsh refusal, or pitiful excuse, or despondent representation of a hopeless interest. Except from his private fortune, in which he may be equalled, perhaps exceeded, by his court competitor, he has no way of showing any one good quality, or of making a single friend. In the House, he votes forever in a dispirited minority. If he speaks, the doors are locked. A body of loquacious placemen go out to tell the world that all he aims at is to get into office. . . . Can we conceive a more discouraging post of duty than this? Strip it of the poor reward of popularity; suffer even the excesses committed in defence of the popular interest to become a ground for the majority of that House to form a disqualification out of the line of the law, and at their pleasure, attended not only with the loss of the franchise, but with every kind of personal dis-grace:—If this shall happen, the people of this kingdom may be assured that they cannot be firmly or faithfully served by any man. It is out of the nature of men and things that they should; and their presumption will be equal to their folly if they expect it. The power of the people, within the laws, must show itself sufficient to protect every representative in ani-mated performance of his duty, or that duty cannot be per-formed. The House of Commons can never be a control on other parts of government, unless they are controlled them-selves by their constituents; and unless these constituents pos-sess some right in the choice of that House, which it is not in the power of that House to take away. If they suffer this power of arbitrary incapacitation to stand, they have utterly perverted every other power of the House of Commons. . . .

The people indeed have been told, that this power of dis-cretionary disqualification is vested in hands that they may trust, and who will be sure not to abuse it to their prejudice. Until I find something in this argument differing from that on which every mode of despotism has been defended, I shall not be inclined to pay it any great compliment. The people are satisfied to trust themselves with the exercise of their own privileges, and do not desire this kind of intervention of the

House of Commons to free them from the burden. They are certainly in the right. They ought not to trust the House of Commons with a power over their franchises; because the constitution, which placed two other co-ordinate powers to control it, reposed no such confidence in that body. . . .

When the House of Commons, in an endeavor to obtain new advantages at the expense of the other orders of the state, for the benefit of the *commons at large,* have pursued strong measures; if it were not just, it was at least natural, that the constituents should connive at all their proceedings; because we were ourselves ultimately to profit. But when this submission is urged to us, in a contest between the representatives and ourselves, and where nothing can be put into their scale which is not taken from ours, they fancy us to be children when they tell us they are our representatives, our own flesh and blood, and that all the stripes they give us are for our good. The very desire of that body to have such a trust contrary to law reposed in them, shows that they are not worthy of it. They certainly will abuse it; because all men possessed of an uncontrolled discretionary power leading to the aggrandizement and profit of their own body have always abused it: and I see no particular sanctity in our times, that is at all likely, by a miraculous operation, to overrule the course of nature.

But we must purposely shut our eyes, if we consider this matter merely as a contest between the House of Commons and the electors. The true contest is between the electors of the kingdom and the crown; the crown acting by an instrumental House of Commons. . . .

If once members of Parliament can be practically convinced that they do not depend on the affection or opinion of the people for their political being, they will give themselves over, without even an appearance of reserve, to the influence of the court.

Indeed a Parliament unconnected with the people is essential to a ministry unconnected with the people; and therefore those who saw through what mighty difficulties the interior ministry waded, and the exterior were dragged, in this business, will conceive of what prodigious importance, the new corps of *king's men* held this principle of occasional and personal incapacitation, to the whole body of their design.

When the House of Commons was thus made to consider itself as the master of its constituents, there wanted but one thing to secure that House against all possible future deviation towards popularity: an *unlimited* fund of money to be laid out according to the pleasure of the court.

To complete the scheme of bringing our court to a resemblance to the neighboring monarchies, it was necessary, in effect, to destroy those appropriations of revenue, which seem to limit the property, as the other laws had done the powers, of the crown. An opportunity for this purpose was taken, upon an application to Parliament for payment of the debts of the civil list; which in 1769 had amounted to 513,000*l.* Such application had been made upon former occasions; but to do it in the former manner would by no means answer the present purpose. . . .

A deficiency of the civil list duties for several years before was stated as the principal, if not the sole ground on which an application to Parliament could be justified. . . .

To have exceeded the sum given for the civil list, and to have incurred a debt without special authority of Parliament, was *prima facie,* a criminal act . . .

But, in order firmly to establish the precedent of *payment previous to account,* and to form it into a settled rule of the House, the god in the machine was brought down, nothing less than the wonder-working *law of Parliament.* It was alleged, that it is the law of Parliament, when any demand comes from the crown, that the House must go immediately into the committee of supply; in which committee it was allowed, that the production and examination of accounts would be quite proper and regular. It was therefore carried, that they should go into the committee without delay, and accounts, in order to examine with great order and regularity things that could not possibly come before them. After this stroke of orderly and Parliamentary wit and humor, they went into the committee; and very generously voted the payment. . . .

Five hundred thousand pounds is a serious sum. But it is nothing to the prolific principle upon which the sum was voted: a principle that may be well called, *the fruitful mother of an hundred more.* . . . The power of discretionary disqualification by one law of Parliament, and the necessity of paying every debt of the civil list by another law of Parliament, if suffered to pass unnoticed, must establish such a fund of rewards and terrors as will make Parliament the best appendage and support of arbitrary power that ever was invented by the wit of man. . . .

I know the diligence with which my observations on our public disorders have been made; I am very sure of the in-

tegrity of the motives on which they are published: I cannot
be equally confident in any plan for the absolute cure of those
disorders, or for their certain future prevention. . . .

The first ideas which generally suggest themselves, for the
cure of Parliamentary disorders, are, to shorten the duration
of Parliaments; and to disqualify all, or a great number of
placemen, from a seat in the House of Commons. Whatever
efficacy there may be in those remedies, I am sure in the present state of things it is impossible to apply them. A restoration
of the right of free election is a preliminary indispensable to
every other reformation. What alterations ought afterwards
to be made in the constitution, is a matter of deep and difficult
research.

If I wrote merely to please the popular palate, it would
indeed be as little troublesome to me as to another, to extol
these remedies, so famous in speculation, but to which their
greatest admirers have never attempted seriously to resort in
practice. I confess then, that I have no sort of reliance upon
either a triennial Parliament, or a place-bill. With regard to
the former, perhaps it might rather serve to counteract, than
to promote the ends that are proposed by it. To say nothing of
the horrible disorders among the people attending frequent
elections, I should be fearful of committing, every three years,
the independent gentlemen of the country into a contest with
the treasury. It is easy to see which of the contending parties
would be ruined first. Whoever has taken a careful view of
public proceedings, so as to endeavor to ground his speculations on his experience, must have observed how prodigiously
greater the power of ministry is in the first and last session of
a Parliament, than it is in the intermediate period, when members sit a little firm on their seats. The persons of the greatest
Parliamentary experience, with whom I have conversed, did
constantly, in canvassing the fate of questions, allow something to the court side, upon account of the elections depend-
ing or imminent. The evil complained of, if it exists in the
present state of things, would hardly be removed by a triennial Parliament: for unless the influence of government in
elections can be entirely taken away, the more frequently they
return, the more they will harass private independence; the
more generally men will be compelled to fly to the settled
systematic interest of government, and to the resources of a
boundless civil list. Certainly something may be done, and
ought to be done, towards lessening that influence in elections;

and this will be necessary upon a plan either of longer or shorter duration of Parliament. . . .

The next favorite remedy is a place-bill. The same principle guides in both; I mean, the opinion which is entertained by many, of the infallibility of laws and regulations, in the cure of public distempers. Without being as unreasonably doubtful as many are unwisely confident, I will only say, that this also is a matter very well worthy of serious and mature reflection. It is not easy to foresee, what the effect would be, of disconnecting with Parliament the greatest part of those who hold civil employments, and of such mighty and important bodies as the military and naval establishments. It were better, perhaps, that they should have a corrupt interest in the forms of the constitution, than that they should have none at all. This is a question altogether different from the disqualification of a particular description of revenue-officers from seats in Parliament; or, perhaps, of all the lower sorts of them from votes in elections. In the former case, only the few are affected; in the latter, only the inconsiderable. But a great official, a great professional, a great military and naval interest, all necessarily comprehending many people of the first weight, ability, wealth, and spirit, has been gradually formed in the kingdom. These new interests must be let into a share of representation, else possibly they may be inclined to destroy those institutions of which they are not permitted to partake. This is not a thing to be trifled with; nor is it every well-meaning man that is fit to put his hands to it. Many other serious considerations occur. I do not open them here, because they are not directly to my purpose; proposing only to give the reader some taste of the difficulties that attend all capital changes in the constitution; just to hint the uncertainty, to say no worse, of being able to prevent the court, as long as it has the means of influence abundantly in its power, of applying that influence to Parliament; and perhaps, if the public method were precluded, of doing it in some worse and more dangerous method. Underhand and oblique ways would be studied. The science of evasion, already tolerably understood, would then be brought to the greatest perfection. It is no inconsiderable part of wisdom, to know how much of an evil ought to be tolerated; lest, by attempting a degree of purity impracticable in degenerate times and manners, instead of cutting off the subsisting ill-practices, new corruptions might be produced for the concealment and security of the old. It were better, undoubtedly, that no influence at all could affect the mind of a member of Parliament. But of all modes of influence, in my opinion, a place under the government is the least disgraceful to the man who holds it, and by far the most safe to the country. I would not shut out that sort of influence which is open and visible, which is connected with the dignity and the service of the state, when it is not in my power to prevent the influence of contracts, of subscriptions, of direct bribery, and those innumerable methods of clandestine corruption, which are abundantly in the hands of the court, and which will be applied as long as these means of corruption, and the disposition to be corrupted, have existence amongst us. Our constitution stands on a nice equipoise, with steep precipices and deep waters upon all sides of it. In removing it from a dangerous leaning towards one side, there may be a risk of oversetting it on the other. Every project of a material change in a government so complicated as ours, combined at the same time with external circumstances still more complicated, is a matter full of difficulties: in which a considerate man will not be too ready to decide; a prudent man too ready to undertake; or an honest man too ready to promise. They do not respect the public nor themselves, who engage for more than they are sure that they ought to attempt, or that they are able to perform. . . .

Indeed, in the situation in which we stand, with an immense revenue, an enormous debt, mighty establishments, government itself a great banker and a great merchant, I see no other way for the preservation of a decent attention to public interest in the representatives, but *the interposition of the body of the people itself*, whenever it shall appear, by some flagrant and notorious act, by some capital innovation, that these representatives are going to overlap the fences of the law, and to introduce an arbitrary power. This interposition is a most unpleasant remedy. But, if it be a legal remedy, it is intended on some occasion to be used; to be used then only, when it is evident that nothing else can hold the constitution to its true principles.

The distempers of monarchy were the greatest subjects of apprehension and redress, in the last century; in this the distemper of Parliament. It is not in Parliament alone that the remedy for Parliamentary disorders can be completed; hardly indeed can it begin there. Until a confidence in government is re-established, the people ought to be excited to a more strict and detailed attention to the conduct of their representatives. Standards for judging more systematically upon their conduct ought to be settled in the meetings of counties and corporations. Frequent and correct lists of the voters in all important questions ought to be procured.

By such means something may be done. By such means it may appear who those are, that, by an indiscriminate support of all administrations, have totally banished all integrity and confidence out of public proceedings; have confounded the best men with the worst; and weakened and dissolved, instead of strengthening and compacting, the general frame of government. If any person is more concerned for government and order, than for the liberties of his country; even he is equally concerned to put an end to this course of indiscriminate support. It is this blind and undistinguishing support, that feeds the spring of those very disorders, by which he is frightened into the arms of the faction which contains in itself the source of all disorders, by enfeebling all the visible and regular authority of the state. . . .

Let us learn from our experience. It is not support that is wanting to government, but reformation. When ministry rests upon public opinion, it is not indeed built upon a rock of adamant; it has, however, some stability. But when it stands upon private humor, its structure is of stubble, and its foundation is on quicksand. I repeat it again—He that supports every administration subverts all government. The reason is this: The whole business in which a court usually takes an interest goes on at present equally well, in whatever hands, whether high or low, wise or foolish, scandalous or reputable; there is nothing therefore to hold it firm to any one body of men, or to any one consistent scheme of politics. Nothing interposes, to prevent the full operation of all the caprices and all the passions of a court upon the servants of the public. The system of administration is open to continual shocks and changes, upon the principles of the meanest cabal, and the most contemptible intrigue. . . .

Such are the consequences of the division of court from the administration; and of the division of public men among themselves. By the former of these, lawful government is undone; by the latter, all opposition to lawless power is rendered impotent. Government may in a great measure be restored, if any considerable bodies of men have honesty and resolution enough never to accept administration, unless this garrison of *king's men*, which is stationed, as in a citadel, to control and enslave it, be entirely broken and disbanded, and every work they have thrown up be levelled with the ground.

The disposition of public men to keep this corps together, and to act under it, or to co-operate with it, is a touchstone by which every administration ought in future to be tried. There has not been one which has not sufficiently experienced the utter incompatibility of that faction with the public peace, and with all the ends of good government: since, if they opposed it, they soon lost every power of serving the crown; if they submitted to it, they lost all the esteem of their country. . . . In this particular, it ought to be the electors' business to look to their representatives. The electors ought to esteem it no less culpable in their member to give a single vote in Parliament to such an administration, than to take an office under it; to endure it, than to act in it. The notorious infidelity and versatility of members of Parliament, in their opinions of men and things, ought in a particular manner to be considered by the electors in the inquiry which is recommended to them. This is one of the principal holdings of that destructive system, which has endeavored to unhinge all the virtuous, honorable, and useful connections in this kingdom.

This cabal has, with great success, propagated a doctrine which serves for a color to those acts of treachery; and whilst it receives any degree of countenance it will be utterly senseless to look for a vigorous opposition to the court party. The doctrine is this: That all political connections are in their nature factious, and as such ought to be dissipated and destroyed; and that the rule for forming administrations is mere personal ability, rated by the judgment of this cabal upon it, and taken by draughts from every division and denomination of public men. This decree was solemnly promulgated by the head of the court corps, the Earl of Bute himself, in a speech which he made, in the year 1766, against the then administration, the only administration which he has ever been known directly and publicly to oppose.

It is indeed in no way wonderful, that such persons should make such declarations. That connection and faction are equivalent terms, is an opinion which has been carefully inculcated at all times by unconstitutional statesmen. The reason is evident. Whilst men are linked together, they easily and speedily communicate the alarm of any evil design. They are enabled to fathom it with common counsel, and to oppose it with united strength. Whereas, when they lie dispersed, without concert, order, or discipline, communication is uncertain, counsel difficult, and resistance impracticable. Where men are not acquainted with each other's principles, nor experienced in each other's talents, nor at all practised in their mutual habitudes and dispositions by joint efforts in business; no personal confidence, no friendship, no common interest, subsisting among them; it is evidently impossible that they can act a public part with uniformity, perseverance, or efficacy. In a connection, the most inconsiderable man, by adding to the weight of the whole, has his value, and his use; out of it, the greatest talents are wholly unserviceable to the public. No man, who is not inflamed by vainglory into enthusiasm, can flatter himself that his single, unsupported, desultory, unsystematic endeavors are of power to defeat the subtle designs and united cabals of ambitious citizens. When bad men combine, the good must associate; else they will fall, one by one, an unpitied sacrifice in a contemptible struggle.

It is not enough in a situation of trust in the commonwealth, that a man means well to his country; it is not enough that in his single person he never did an evil act, but always voted according to his conscience, and even harangued against every design which he apprehended to be prejudicial to the interests of his country. This innoxious and ineffectual character, that seems formed upon a plan of apology and disculpation, falls miserably short of the mark of public duty. That duty demands and requires, that what is right should not only be made known, but made prevalent; that what is evil should not only be detected, but defeated. When the public man omits to put himself in a situation of doing his duty with effect, it is an omission that frustrates the purposes of his trust almost as much as if he had formally betrayed it. It is surely no very rational account of a man's life, that he has always acted right; but has taken special care, to act in such a manner that his endeavors could not possibly be productive of any consequence.

I do not wonder that the behavior of many parties should have made persons of tender and scrupulous virtue somewhat out of humor with all sorts of connection in politics. I admit that people frequently acquire in such confederacies a narrow, bigoted, and proscriptive spirit; that they are apt to sink the idea of the general good in this circumscribed and partial interest. But, where duty renders a critical situation a necessary one, it is our business to keep free from the evils attendant upon it; and not to fly from the situation itself. If a fortress is seated in an unwholesome air, an officer of the garrison is obliged to be attentive to his health, but he must not desert his station. Every profession, not excepting the glorious one of a soldier, or the sacred one of a priest, is liable to its own particular vices; which, however, form no argument against those ways of life; nor are the vices themselves inevitable to every individual in those professions. Of such a nature are connections in politics; essentially necessary for the full performance of our public duty, accidentally liable to degenerate into faction. Commonwealths are made of families, free commonwealths of parties also; and we may as well affirm, that our natural regards and ties of blood tend inevitably to make men bad citizens, as that the bonds of our party weaken those by which we are held to our country. . . .

Certain it is, the best patriots in the greatest commonwealths have always commended and promoted such connections. . . . The Romans carried this principle a great way. Even the holding of offices together, the disposition of which arose from chance, not selection, gave rise to a relation which continued for life. . . . Breaches of any of these kinds of civil relation were considered as acts of the most distinguished turpitude. The whole people was distributed into political societies, in which they acted in support of such interests in the state as they severally affected. For it was then thought no crime to endeavor by every honest means to advance to superiority and power those of your own sentiments and opinions. This wise people was far from imagining that those connections had no tie, and obliged to no duty; but that men might quit them without shame, upon every call of interest. They believed private honor to be the great foundation of public trust; that friendship was no mean step towards patriotism; that he who, in the common intercourse of life, showed he regarded somebody besides himself, when he came to act in a public situation, might probably consult some other interest than his own. . . . In one of the most fortunate periods of our history this country was governed by a *connection;* I mean, the great connection of Whigs in the reign of Queen Anne. . . .

The Whigs of those days believed that the only proper method of rising into power was through hard essays of practised friendship and experimented fidelity. At that time it was not imagined, that patriotism was a bloody idol, which required the sacrifice of children and parents, or dearest connections in private life, and of all the virtues that rise from those relations. They were not of that ingenious paradoxical morality, to imagine that a spirit of moderation was properly shown in patiently bearing the sufferings of your friends; or that disinterestedness was clearly manifested at the expense of other people's fortune. They believed that no men could act in concert, who did not act with confidence, who were not bound together by common opinions, common affections, and common interests. . . .

Party is a body of men united for promoting by their joint endeavors the national interest upon some particular principle in which they are all agreed. For my part, I find it impossible to conceive, that any one believes in his own politics, or thinks them to be of any weight, who refuses to adopt the means of having them reduced into practice. It is the business of the speculative philosopher to mark the proper ends of government. It is the business of the politician, who is the philosopher in action, to find out proper means towards those ends, and to employ them with effect. Therefore every honorable connection will avow it is their first purpose, to pursue every just method to put the men who hold their opinions into such a condition as may enable them to carry their common plans into execution, with all the power and authority of the state. As this power is attached to certain situations, it is their duty to contend for these situations. Without a proscription of others, they are bound to give to their own party the preference in all things; and by no means, for private considerations, to accept any offers of power in which the whole body is not included; nor to suffer themselves to be led, or to be controlled, or to be overbalanced, in office or in council, by those who contradict the very fundamental principles on which their party is formed, and even those upon which every fair connection must stand. Such a generous contention for power, on such manly and honorable maxims, will easily be distinguished from the mean and interested struggle for place and emolument. . . .

It is an advantage to all narrow wisdom and narrow morals, that their maxims have a plausible air: and, on a cursory view, appear equal to first principles. They are light and portable. They are as current as copper coin; and about as valuable. They serve equally the first capacities and the lowest; and they are, at least, as useful to the worst men as to the best. Of this stamp is the cant of *Not men, but measures;* a sort of charm by which many people get loose from every honorable engagement. When I see a man acting this desultory and disconnected part, with as much detriment to his own fortune as prejudice to the cause of any party, I am not persuaded that he is right; but I am ready to believe he is in earnest. I respect virtue in all its situations; even when it is found in the unsuitable company of weakness. I lament to see qualities, rare and valuable, squandered away without any public utility. But when a gentleman with great visible emoluments abandons the party in which he has long acted, and tells you, it is because he proceeds upon his own judgment; that he acts on the merits of the several measures as they arise; and that he is obliged to follow his own conscience, and not that of others; he gives reasons which it is impossible to controvert, and discovers a character which it is impossible to mistake. What shall we think of him who never differed from a certain set of men until the moment they lost their power, and who never agreed with them in a single instance afterwards? Would not such a coincidence of interest and opinion be rather fortunate? . . . Whether a *measure* of government be right or wrong, is *no matter of fact,* but a mere affair of opinion, on which men may, as they do, dispute and wrangle without end. But whether the individual *thinks* the measure right or wrong, is a point at still a greater distance from the reach of all human decision. It is therefore very convenient to politicians, not to put the judgment of their conduct on overt acts, cognizable in any ordinary court, but upon such matter as can be triable only in that secret tribunal, where they are sure of being heard with favor, or where at worst the sentence will be only private whipping. . . .

In order to throw an odium on political connection, these politicians suppose it a necessary incident to it, that you are blindly to follow the opinions of your party, when in direct opposition to your own clear ideas; a degree of servitude that no worthy man could bear the thought of submitting to; and such as, I believe, no connections (except some court factions) ever could be so senselessly tyrannical as to impose. Men thinking freely, will, in particular instances, think differently. But still as the greater part of the measures which arise in the course of public business are related to, or dependent on, some great, *leading, general principles in government,* a man must be peculiarly unfortunate in the choice of his political company, if he does not agree with them at least nine times in ten. If he does not concur in these general principles upon which the party is founded, and which necessarily draw on a concurrence in their application, he ought from the beginning to have chosen some other, more conformable to his opinions. When the question is in its nature doubtful, or not very material, the modesty which becomes an individual, and, (in spite of our court moralists) that partiality which becomes a well-chosen friendship, will frequently bring on an acquiescence in the general sentiment. Thus the disagreement will naturally be rare; it will be only enough to indulge freedom, without violating concord, or disturbing arrangement. And this is all that ever was required for a character of the greatest uniformity and steadiness in connection. How men can proceed without any connection at all, is to me utterly incomprehensible. . . .

I remember an old scholastic aphorism, which says, "that the man who lives wholly detached from others, must be either an angel or a devil." When I see in any of these detached gentlemen of our times the angelic purity, power, and beneficence, I shall admit them to be angels. In the mean time we are born only to be men. We shall do enough if we form ourselves to be good ones. It is therefore our business carefully to cultivate in our minds, to rear to the most perfect vigor and maturity, every sort of generous and honest feeling, that belongs to our nature. To bring the dispositions that are lovely in private life into the service and conduct of the commonwealth; so to be patriots, as not to forget we are gentlemen. To cultivate friendships, and to incur enmities. To have both strong, but both selected: in the one, to be placable; in the other immovable. To model our principles to our duties and our situation. To be fully persuaded, that all virtue which is impracticable is spurious; and rather to run the risk of falling into faults in a course which leads us to act with effect and energy, than to loiter out our days without blame, and without use. Public life is a situation of power and energy; he trespasses against his duty who sleeps upon his watch, as well as he that goes over to the enemy.

There is, however, a time for all things. It is not every conjuncture which calls with equal force upon the activity of honest men; but critical exigencies now and then arise; and I am mistaken, if this be not one of them. Men will see the necessity of honest combination; but they may see it when it is too late. They may embody, when it will be ruinous to themselves, and of no advantage to the country; when, for want of such a timely union as may enable them to oppose in favor of the laws, with the laws on their side, they may at length find themselves under the necessity of conspiring, instead of consulting. The law, for which they stand, may become a weapon in the hands of its bitterest enemies; and they will be cast, at length, into that miserable alternative between slavery and civil confusion, which no good man can look upon without horror; an alternative in which it is impossible he should take either part, with a conscience perfectly at repose. To keep that situation of guilt and remorse at the utmost distance is, therefore, our first obligation. Early activity may prevent late and fruitless violence. As yet we work in the light. The scheme of the enemies of public tranquility has disarranged, it has not destroyed us.

If the reader believes that there really exists such a faction as I have described; a faction ruling by the private inclinations of a court, against the general sense of the people; and that this faction, whilst it pursues a scheme for undermining all the foundations of our freedom, weakens (for the present at least) all the powers of executory government, rendering us abroad contemptible, and at home distracted; he will believe also, that nothing but a firm combination of public men against this body, and that, too, supported by the hearty concurrence of the people at large, can possibly get the better of it. The people will see the necessity of restoring public men to an attention to the public opinion, and of restoring the constitution to its original principles. Above all, they will endeavor to keep the House of Commons from assuming a character which does not belong to it. They will endeavor to keep that House, for its existence, for its powers, and its privileges, as independent of every other, and as dependent upon themselves, as possible. . . . When, through the medium of this just connection with their constituents, the genuine dignity of the House of Commons is restored, it will begin to think of casting from it, with scorn, as badges of servility, all the false ornaments of illegal power, with which it has been, for some time, disgraced. It will begin to think of its old office of CONTROL. It will not suffer that last of evils to predominate in the country: men without popular confidence, public opinion, natural connection, or mutual trust, invested with all the powers of government.

When they have learned this lesson themselves, they will be willing and able to teach the court, that it is the true interest of the prince to have but one administration; and that one composed of those who recommend themselves to their sovereign through the opinion of their country, and not by their obsequiousness to a favorite. Such men will serve their sovereign with affection and fidelity; because his choice of them, upon such principles, is a compliment to their virtue. They will be able to serve him effectually; because they will add the weight of the country to the force of the executory power. They will be able to serve their king with dignity; because they will never abuse his name to the gratification of their private spleen or avarice. This, with allowances for human frailty, may probably be the general character of a ministry, which thinks itself accountable to the House of Commons; when the House of Commons thinks itself accountable to its constituents. If other ideas should prevail, things must remain in their present confusion, until they are hurried into all the rage of civil violence, or until they sink into the dead repose of despotism.

Speech on
Moving His Resolutions for
Conciliation with the Colonies
March 22, 1775

Burke was not able to persuade the British government or the public of the folly of trying to raise revenue by taxing the American colonies. In 1767 the Townshend Acts put new duties on imports and produced new violent reactions in the Colonies, who responded by boycotting British goods and re-sisting the payment of customs. To enforce its authority the British government sent troops to ports that had resisted, and in 1770 the "Boston massacre" occurred. In the same year Lord North became Prime Minister, and remained in office as the King's personal minister until 1782. From 1767 to 1782 Burke drew up all the principal protests of his party against the King's policies. During that period his warnings that Britain was following a disastrous colonial policy were fulfilled.

In May 1771 Burke became the agent in Britain for the New York Colonial Assembly, at seven hundred pounds per year, a post he retained until hostilities began. As one of "the real well-wishers to the Colonies," he did everything in his power to prevent the outbreak of hostilities, by reconciling British sovereignty and American liberty in its internal affairs, including the power of the Colonies to tax themselves. In a letter to the New York Committee of Correspondence, April 6, 1774, he repeated his long-held conviction that the "real essential rights" of the Colonies were perfectly compatible with British sovereignty, and that both were grounded in mutual self-interest.

Burke believed that the whole object of the King's ministers was to subordinate the Colonies not to the constitutional sovereignty of the Empire, but to the arbitrary will of the Crown. This policy was first tried with success against the East India Company. He wrote to the New York Assembly that even the dividends of the East India Company were brought "into an entire dependence upon the Crown." It was in the light of such policy that Burke interpreted the Mutiny Act, the Restraining Act, the Boston Port Bill, the revocation of the Massachusetts Bay Charter, the suspension of habeas corpus, and the priority given to claims by Quebec over land grants in northern New York. Without inflaming passions, he cautioned the New York Assembly to be vigilant against such trespasses of their legitimate interests and constitutional rights. He hoped they would be of "the party that resisted but would not revolt." As agent for New York Burke held himself responsible *only* to the Assembly which had hired him, not to the Crown. He opposed the Board of Trade, acting for the King, to make the nomination of colonial agents depend upon the royal governor, because such an agent "will be to all intents and purposes an officer of the Crown." Should his appointment be made subject to the royal governor, Burke wrote to the New York Assembly that he would resign. By such practical means he sought to preserve the principle of the balance of power within the colony, and to keep royal prerogative within constitutional bounds.

In his *Speech on American Taxation* (April 19, 1774), Burke reviewed the series of blunders that accompanied the imprudent and untried schemes to tax the Colonies. He pointed out that under the Act of Navigation, which had been from 1660 to 1764 "the cornerstone of the policy of this country with regard to its colonies," a Parliamentary revenue from America "was never once in contemplation." Up to 1764 Britain was content with "commercial regulation" without revenue from taxes. A revenue tax was a radical innovation which the Colonies had resisted, and which had alienated and might lose the Colonies. The extent of this loss to Britain Burke set forth in a great passage:

Nothing in the history of mankind is like their progress. For my part, I never cast an eye on their flourishing commerce, and their cultivated and commodious life, but they seem to me rather ancient nations grown to perfection through a long series of fortunate events, and a train of successful industry, accumulating wealth in many centuries, than the colonies of yesterday . . .

This enormous and swift growth of the Colonies, Burke observed, had "raised the trade" of England "at least fourfold." This was accomplished while America had "every characteristic mark of a free people in all her internal concerns. She had the image of the British Constitution. She had the substance. She was taxed by her own representatives. She chose most of her own magistrates. She paid them all. She had in effect the sole disposal of her own internal government." All the peace and prosperity which Britain and her Colonies had enjoyed together had been disrupted by the speculative theories initiated in 1764. Burke urged his colleagues to "oppose the ancient practice of the empire as a rampart against the speculations of innovators." Toward the end of his speech he put forward his characteristic faith in tradition and experience and his intense dislike of political metaphysics:

The spirit of practicality, of moderation, and mutual convenience will never call in geometrical exactness as the arbitrator of an amicable settlement. Consult and follow your experience. . . . Revert to your old principles. . . . Leave America, if she has taxable matter in her, to tax herself. I am not here going into the distinctions of rights, nor attempting to mark their boundaries. I do not enter into these metaphysical distinctions; I hate the very sound of them. Leave the Americans as they anciently stood, and these distinctions, born of our unhappy contest, will die along with it.

Britain could reconcile her sovereignty and colonial freedom only by reverting to the system in force prior to 1764. But if colonial expressions of particular grievances were treated by Parliament as a denial of the entire sovereignty of Britain, and led to the rejection of real grievances, the Colonies would be left with the impression that Parliament desired not peace through conciliation but unconditional submission. "If that sovereignty and their freedom cannot be reconciled," Burke asked, "which will they take? They will cast your sovereignty in your face. Nobody will be argued into slavery." The ideas and even the language of his *Speech on American Taxation* anticipate much that he was to say the following year in his *Speech on Conciliation with the Colonies.*

Burke's efforts to preserve the unity of the British empire by preventing war with the Colonies proved fruitless. After the North ministry passed additional restrictive laws, the Colonies sent delegates to the First Continental Congress in Philadelphia. Parliament was dissolved in October 1774, and Burke was asked to stand for election for the city of Bristol. On October 13, in a speech to the Bristol electors, he said: "I have held, and ever shall maintain, to the best of my power, unimpaired and undiminished, the just, wise, and necessary constitutional superiority of Great Britain. This is necessary for America as well as for us. . . . But . . . this superiority is consistent with all the liberties a sober and spirited American ought to desire. I never mean to put any colonist, or any human creature, in a situation not becoming a free man. To reconcile British superiority with American liberty shall be my great object. . . . I am far from thinking that both, even yet, may not be preserved."

But Burke was painfully aware that time was running out for Britain. On March 22, 1775, less than a month before hostilities began on April 19 at Lexington and Concord, he delivered his *Speech on Conciliation with the Colonies.* This speech has been studied and admired more frequently than any of his other writings. In it his principles of government are stated in a more simple and understandable form than in his writings on the French Revolution, and the structure of his form and the logic of his reasoning are more coherently organized and expressed. The factual thoroughness behind his argument carries a weight and power of its own. John Morley said that Burke's *Speech on American Taxation* (1774), his *Speech on Conciliation* (1775), and his *Letter to the Sheriffs of Bristol* (1777), taken together, "compose the most perfect manual in our literature, or in any literature, for one who approaches the study of public affairs, whether for knowledge or for practice."

. . . We are . . . called upon, as it were by a superior warning voice, again to attend to America—to attend to the whole of it together—and to review the subject with an unusual degree of care and calmness.

Surely it is an awful subject—or there is none so on this side of the grave. When I first had the honor of a seat in this House, the affairs of that continent pressed themselves upon us as the most important and most delicate object of Parliamentary attention. My little share in this great deliberation oppressed me. I found myself a partaker in a very high trust; and having no sort of reason to rely on the strength of my natural abilities for the proper execution of that trust, I was obliged to take more than common pains to instruct myself in everything which relates to our colonies. I was not less under the necessity of forming some fixed ideas concerning the general policy of the British empire. Something of this sort seemed to be indispensable, in order, amidst so vast a fluctuation of passions and opinions, to concentre my thoughts, to ballast my conduct, to preserve me from being blown about by every wind of fashionable doctrine. I really did not think it safe or manly to have fresh principles to seek upon every fresh mail which should arrive from America.

At that period I had the fortune to find myself in perfect concurrence with a large majority in this House. Bowing under that high authority, and penetrated with the sharpness and strength of that early impression, I have continued ever since, without the least deviation, in my original sentiments. Whether this be owing to an obstinate perseverance in error, or to a religious adherence to what appears to me truth and reason, it is in your equity to judge.

Sir, Parliament, having an enlarged view of objects, made, during this interval, more frequent changes in their sentiments and their conduct than could be justified in a particular person upon the contracted scale of private information. But though I do not hazard anything approaching to a censure on the motives of former Parliaments to all those alterations, one fact is undoubted—that under them the state of America has been kept in continual agitation. Everything administered as remedy to the public complaint, if it did not produce, was at least followed by, an heightening of the distemper, until, by a variety of experiments, that important country has been brought into her present situation—a situation which I will not miscall, which I dare not name, which I scarcely know how to comprehend in the terms of any description.

In this posture, Sir, things stood at the beginning of the session. About that time, a worthy member, of great Parliamentary experience, who in the year 1766 filled the chair of the American Committee with much ability, took me aside, and, lamenting the present aspect of our politics, told me, things were come to such a pass that our former methods of proceeding in the House would be no longer tolerated—that the public tribunal (never too indulgent to a long and unsuccessful opposition) would now scrutinize our conduct with unusual severity—that the very vicissitudes and shiftings of ministerial measures, instead of convicting their authors of inconstancy and want of system, would be taken as an occasion of charging us with a predetermined discontent which nothing could satisfy, whilst we accused every measure of vigor as cruel and every proposal of lenity as weak and irresolute. The public, he said, would not have patience to see us play the game out with our adversaries; we must produce our hand: it would be expected that those who for many years had been active in such affairs should show that they had formed some clear and decided idea of the principles of colony government, and were capable of drawing out something like a platform of the ground which might be laid for future and permanent tranquillity.

I felt the truth of what my honorable friend represented; but I felt my situation, too. His application might have been made with far greater propriety to many other gentlemen. No man was, indeed, ever better disposed, or worse qualified, for such an undertaking, than myself. Though I gave so far into his opinion, that I immediately threw my thoughts into a sort of Parliamentary form, I was by no means equally ready to produce them. It generally argues some degree of natural impotence of mind, or some want of knowledge of the world, to hazard plans of government, except from a seat of authority. Propositions are made, not only ineffectually, but somewhat disreputably, when the minds of men are not properly disposed for their reception; and for my part, I am not ambitious of ridicule, not absolutely a candidate for disgrace.

Besides, Sir, to speak the plain truth, I have in general no very exalted opinion of the virtue of paper government, nor of any politics in which the plan is to be wholly separated from the execution. But when I saw that anger and violence prevailed every day more and more, and that things were hastening towards an incurable alienation of our colonies, I confess my caution gave way. I felt this as one of those few moments in which decorum yields to an higher duty. Public calamity is a mighty leveller; and there are occasions when any, even the slightest, chance of doing good must be laid hold on, even by the most inconsiderable person.

To restore order and repose to an empire so great and so distracted as ours is, merely in the attempt, an undertaking that would ennoble the flights of the highest genius, and obtain pardon for the efforts of the meanest understanding. Struggling a good while with these thoughts, by degrees I felt myself more firm. I derived, at length, some confidence from what in other circumstances usually produces timidity. I grew less anxious, even from the idea of my own insignificance. For, judging of what you are by what you ought to be, I persuaded myself that you would not reject a reasonable proposition because it had nothing but its reason to recommend it. . . .

The proposition is peace. Not peace through the medium

of war; not peace to be hunted through the labyrinth of intricate and endless negotiations; not peace to arise out of universal discord, fomented from principle, in all parts of the empire; not peace to depend on the juridical determination of perplexing questions, or the precise marking the shadowy boundaries of a complex government. It is simple peace, sought in its natural course and in its ordinary haunts. . . . I propose, by removing the ground of the difference, and by restoring the *former unsuspecting confidence of the colonies in the mother country,* to give permanent satisfaction to your people . . .

My idea is nothing more. Refined policy ever has been the parent of confusion—and ever will be so, as long as the world endures. Plain good intention, which is as easily discovered at the first view as fraud is surely detected at last, is, let me say, of no mean force in the government of mankind. Genuine simplicity of heart is an healing and cementing principle. My plan, therefore, being formed upon the most simple grounds imaginable, may disappoint some people, when they hear it. It has nothing to recommend it to the pruriency of curious ears. There is nothing at all new and captivating in it. . . .

The idea of conciliation is admissible. . . .

I take my ground on the admitted principle. I mean to give peace. Peace implies reconciliation; and where there has been a material dispute, reconciliation does in a manner always imply concession on the one part or on the other. In this state of things I make no difficulty in affirming that the proposal ought to originate from us. Great and acknowledged force is not impaired, either in effect or in opinion, by an unwillingness to exert itself. The superior power may offer peace with honor and with safety. Such an offer from such a power will be attributed to magnanimity. But the concessions of the weak are the concessions of fear. When such a one is disarmed, he is wholly at the mercy of his superior; and he loses forever that time and those chances which, as they happen to all men, are the strength and resources of all inferior power.

The capital leading questions on which you must this day decide are these two: First, whether you ought to concede; and secondly, what your concession ought to be. . . . To enable us to determine both on the one and the other of these great questions with a firm and precise judgment, I think it may be necessary to consider distinctly the true nature and the peculiar circumstances of the object which we have before us: because, after all our struggle, whether we will or not, we must govern America according to that nature and to those circumstances, and not according to our own imaginations, not according to abstract ideas of right, by no means according to mere general theories of government, the resort to which appears to me, in our present situation, no better than arrant trifling. I shall therefore endeavor, with your leave, to lay before you some of the most material of these circumstances in as full and as clear a manner as I am able to state them.

The first thing that we have to consider with regard to the nature of the object is the number of people in the colonies. I have taken for some years a good deal of pains on that point. I can by no calculation justify myself in placing the number below two millions of inhabitants of our own European blood and color—besides at least 500,000 others, who form no inconsiderable part of the strength and opulence of the whole. . . . But whether I put the present numbers too high or too low is a matter of little moment. Such is the strength with which population shoots in that part of the world, that, state the numbers as high as we will, whilst the dispute continues, the exaggeration ends. Whilst we are discussing any given magnitude, they are grown to it. Whilst we spend our time in deliberating on the mode of governing two millions, we shall find we have millions more to manage. Your children do not grow faster from infancy to manhood than they spread from families to communities, and from villages to nations.

I put this consideration of the present and the growing numbers in the front of our deliberation, because, Sir, this consideration will make it evident to a blunter discernment than yours, that no partial, narrow, contracted, pinched, occasional system will be at all suitable to such an object. . . . It will prove that some degree of care and caution is required in the handling such an object; it will show that you ought not, in reason, to trifle with so large a mass of the interests and feelings of the human race. You could at no time do so without guilt; and be assured you will not be able to do it long with impunity.

But the population of this country, the great and growing population, though a very important consideration, will lose much of its weight, if not combined with other circumstances. The commerce of your colonies is out of all proportion beyond the numbers of the people. . . .

I have in my hand two accounts: one a comparative state

of the export trade of England to its colonies, as it stood in the year 1704, and as it stood in the year 1772; the other a state of the export trade of this country to its colonies alone, as it stood in 1772, compared with the whole trade of England to all parts of the world (the colonies included) in the year 1704. . . .

The trade with America alone is now within less than 500,-000*l.* of being equal to what this great commercial nation, England, carried on at the beginning of this century with the whole world! . . . But, it will be said, is not this American trade an unnatural protuberance, that has drawn the juices from the rest of the body? The reverse. It is the very food that has nourished every other part into its present magnitude. Our general trade has been greatly augmented, and augmented more or less in almost every part to which it ever extended, but with this material difference: that of the six millions which in the beginning of the century constituted the whole mass of our export commerce the colony trade was but one twelfth part; it is now (as a part of sixteen millions) considerably more than a third of the whole. This is the relative proportion of the importance of the colonies at these two periods: and all reasoning concerning our mode of treating them must have this proportion as its basis, or it is a reasoning weak, rotten, and sophistical. . . .

Let us . . . reflect that this growth of our national prosperity has happened within the short period of the life of man. It has happened within sixty-eight years. . . .

So far, Sir, as to the importance of the object in the view of its commerce, as concerned in the exports from England. If I were to detail the imports, I could show how many enjoyments they procure which deceive the burden of life, how many materials which invigorate the springs of national industry and extend and animate every part of our foreign and domestic commerce. This would be a curious subject indeed —but I must prescribe bounds to myself in a matter so vast and various.

I pass, therefore, to the colonies in another point of view—their agriculture. This they have prosecuted with such a spirit, that, besides feeding plentifully their own growing multitude, their annual export of grain, comprehending rice, has some years ago exceeded a million in value. Of their last harvest, I am persuaded, they will export much more. At the beginning of the century some of these colonies imported corn from the mother country. For some time past the Old World has been fed from the New. . . .

As to the wealth which the colonies have drawn from the sea by their fisheries, you had all that matter fully opened at your bar. You surely thought those acquisitions of value, for they seemed even to excite your envy; and yet the spirit by which that enterprising employment has been exercised ought rather, in my opinion, to have raised your esteem and admiration. And pray, Sir, what in the world is equal to it? Pass by the other parts, and look at the manner in which the people of New England have of late carried on the whale-fishery. Whilst we follow them among the tumbling mountains of ice, and behold them penetrating into the deepest frozen recesses of Hudson's Bay and Davis's Straits, whilst we are looking for them beneath the arctic circle, we hear that they have pierced into the opposite region of polar cold, that they are at the antipodes, and engaged under the frozen serpent of the South. Falkland Island, which seemed too remote and romantic an object for the grasp of national ambition, is but a stage and resting-place in the progress of their victorious industry. Nor is the equinoctial heat more discouraging to them than the accumulated winter of both the poles. We know, that, whilst some of them draw the line and strike the harpoon on the coast of Africa, others run the longitude, and pursue their gigantic game along the coast of Brazil. No sea but what is vexed by their fisheries. No climate that is not witness to their toils. Neither the perseverance of Holland, nor the activity of France, nor the dexterous and firm sagacity of English enterprise, ever carried this most perilous mode of hardy industry to the extent to which it has been pushed by this recent people —a people who are still, as it were, but in the gristle, and not yet hardened into the bone of manhood. When I contemplate these things—when I know that the colonies in general owe little or nothing to any care of ours, and that they are not squeezed into this happy form by the constraints of watchful and suspicious government, but that, through a wise and salutary neglect, a generous nature has been suffered to take her own way to perfection—when I reflect upon these effects, when I see how profitable they have been to us, I feel all the pride of power sink, and all presumption in the wisdom of human contrivances melt and die away within me—my rigor relents—I pardon something to the spirit of liberty. . . .

America, gentlemen say, is a noble object—it is an object well worth fighting for. Certainly it is, if fighting a people be the best way of gaining them. Gentlemen in this respect will be led to their choice of means by their complexions and their habits. Those who understand the military art will of course have some predilection for it. Those who wield the thunder of the state may have more confidence in the efficacy of arms. But I confess, possibly for want of this knowledge, my opinion is much more in favor of prudent management than of force—considering force not as an odious, but a feeble instrument, for preserving a people so numerous, so active, so growing, so spirited as this, in a profitable and subordinate connection with us.

First, Sir, permit me to observe, that the use of force alone is but *temporary*. It may subdue for a moment; but it does not remove the necessity of subduing again: and a nation is not governed which is perpetually to be conquered.

My next objection is its *uncertainty*. Terror is not always the effect of force, and an armament is not a victory. If you do not succeed, you are without resource: for, conciliation failing, force remains; but, force failing, no further hope of reconciliation is left. Power and authority are sometimes bought by kindness; but they can never be begged as alms by an impoverished and defeated violence.

A further objection to force is, that you *impair the object* by your very endeavors to preserve it. The thing you fought for is not the thing which you recover, but depreciated, sunk, wasted, and consumed in the contest. Nothing less will content me than *whole America*. I do not choose to consume its strength along with our own; because in all parts it is the British strength that I consume. I do not choose to be caught by a foreign enemy at the end of this exhausting conflict, and still less in the midst of it. I may escape, but I can make no insurance against such an event. Let me add, that I do not choose wholly to break the American spirit; because it is the spirit that has made the country.

Lastly, we have no sort of *experience* in favor of force as an instrument in the rule of our colonies. Their growth and their utility has been owing to methods altogether different. Our ancient indulgence has been said to be pursued to a fault. It may be so; but we know, if feeling is evidence, that our fault was more tolerable than our attempt to mend it, and our sin far more salutary than our penitence.

These, Sir, are my reasons for not entertaining that high opinion of untried force by which many gentlemen, for whose sentiments in other particulars I have great respect, seem to be so greatly captivated. But there is still behind a third consideration concerning this object, which serves to determine my opinion on the sort of policy which ought to be pursued in the management of America, even more than its population and its commerce: I mean its *temper and character*.

In this character of the Americans a love of freedom is the predominating feature which marks and distinguishes the whole: and as an ardent is always a jealous affection, your colonies become suspicious, restive, and untractable, whenever they see the least attempt to wrest from them by force, or shuffle from them by chicane, what they think the only advantage worth living for. This fierce spirit of liberty is stronger in the English colonies, probably, than in any other people of the earth, and this from a great variety of powerful causes; which, to understand the true temper of their minds, and the direction which this spirit takes, it will not be amiss to lay open somewhat more largely.

First, the people of the colonies are descendants of Englishmen. England, Sir, is a nation which still, I hope, respects, and formerly adored, her freedom. The colonists emigrated from you when this part of your character was most predominant; and they took this bias and direction the moment they parted from your hands. They are therefore not only devoted to liberty, but to liberty according to English ideas and on English principles. Abstract liberty, like other mere abstractions, is not to be found. Liberty inheres in some sensible object; and every nation has formed to itself some favorite point, which by way of eminence becomes the criterion of their happiness. It happened, you know, Sir, that the great contests for freedom in this country were from the earliest times chiefly upon the question of taxing. Most of the contests in the ancient commonwealths turned primarily on the right of election of magistrates, or on the balance among the several orders of the state. The question of money was not with them so immediate. But in England it was otherwise. On this point of taxes the ablest pens and most eloquent tongues have been exercised, the greatest spirits have acted and suffered. In order to give the fullest satisfaction concerning the importance of this point, it was not only necessary for those who in argument defended the excellence of the English Constitution to insist on this privilege of granting money as a dry point of fact, and to prove that the right had been acknowledged in ancient parchments and blind usages to reside in a certain body called an House of Commons: they went much further: they attempted to prove, and they succeeded, that in theory it ought to be so, from the particular nature of a House of Commons, as an immediate representative of the people, whether the old records had delivered this oracle or not. They took infinite pains to inculcate, as a fundamental principle, that in all monarchies the people must in effect themselves, mediately or immediately, possess the power of granting their own money, or no shadow of liberty could subsist. The colonies draw from you, as with their life-blood, these ideas and principles. Their love of liberty, as with you, fixed and attached on this specific point of taxing. Liberty might be safe or might be endangered in twenty other particulars without their being much pleased or alarmed. Here they felt its pulse; and as they found that beat, they thought themselves sick or sound. I do not say whether they were right or wrong in applying your general arguments to their own case. It is not easy, indeed, to make a monopoly of theorems and corollaries. The fact is, that they did thus apply those general arguments; and your mode of governing them, whether through lenity or indolence, through wisdom or mistake, confirmed them in the imagination, that they, as well as you, had an interest in these common principles.

They were further confirmed in this pleasing error by the form of their provincial legislative assemblies. Their governments are popular in an high degree: some are merely popular; in all, the popular representative is the most weighty; and this share of the people in their ordinary government never fails to inspire them with lofty sentiments, and with a strong aversion from whatever tends to deprive them of their chief importance.

If anything were wanting to this necessary operation of the form of government, religion would have given it a complete effect. Religion, always a principle of energy, in this new people is no way worn out or impaired; and their mode of professing it is also one main cause of this free spirit. The people are Protestants, and of that kind which is the most adverse to all implicit submission of mind and opinion. This is a persuasion not only favorable to liberty, but built upon it. I do not think, Sir, that the reason of this averseness in the dissenting churches from all that looks like absolute government is so much to be sought in their religious tenets as in their history. Every one knows that the Roman Catholic religion is at least coeval with most of the governments where it prevails, that it has generally gone hand in hand with them, and received great favor and every kind of support from author-

ity. The Church of England, too, was formed from her cradle
under the nursing care of regular government. But the dissenting interests have sprung up in direct opposition to all the
ordinary powers of the world, and could justify that opposition only on a strong claim to natural liberty. Their very existence depended on the powerful and unremitted assertion of
that claim. All Protestantism, even the most cold and passive,
is a sort of dissent. But the religion most prevalent in our
northern colonies is a refinement on the principle of resistance: it is the dissidence of dissent, and the protestantism of
the Protestant religion. This religion, under a variety of denominations agreeing in nothing but in the communion of the
spirit of liberty, is predominant in most of the northern provinces, where the Church of England, notwithstanding its legal
rights, is in reality no more than a sort of private sect, not
composing, most probably, the tenth of the people. The colonists left England when this spirit was high, and in the emi-
grants was the highest of all; and even that stream of foreigners which has been constantly flowing into these colonies
has, for the greatest part, been composed of dissenters from
the establishments of their several countries, and have brought
with them a temper and character far from alien to that of the
people with whom they mixed.

Sir, I can perceive, by their manner, that some gentlemen
object to the latitude of this description, because in the southern colonies the Church of England forms a large body, and
has a regular establishment. It is certainly true. There is, however, a circumstance attending these colonies, which, in my
opinion, fully counterbalances this difference, and makes the
spirit of liberty still more high and haughty than in those to the
northward. It is, that in Virginia and the Carolinas they have a
vast multitude of slaves. Where this is the case in any part of
the world, those who are free are by far the most proud and
jealous of their freedom. Freedom is to them not only an
enjoyment, but a kind of rank and privilege. Not seeing there,
that freedom, as in countries where it is a common blessing,
and as broad and general as the air, may be united with much
abject toil, with great misery, with all the exterior of servitude,
liberty looks, amongst them, like something that is more noble
and liberal. I do not mean, Sir, to commend the superior
morality of this sentiment, which has at least as much pride as
virtue in it; but I cannot alter the nature of man. The fact is
so; and these people of the southern colonies are much more
strongly, and with an higher and more stubborn spirit, at-

tached to liberty, than those to the northward. Such were all the ancient commonwealths; such were our Gothic ancestors; such in our days were the Poles; and such will be all masters of slaves, who are not slaves themselves. In such a people, the haughtiness of domination combines with the spirit of freedom, fortifies it, and renders it invincible.

Permit me, Sir, to add another circumstance in our colonies, which contributes no mean part towards the growth and effect of this untractable spirit: I mean their education. In no country, perhaps, in the world is the law so general a study. The profession itself is numerous and powerful, and in most provinces it takes the lead. The greater number of the deputies sent to the Congress were lawyers. But all who read, and most do read, endeavor to obtain some smattering in that science. I have been told by an eminent bookseller, that in no branch of his business, after tracts of popular devotion, were so many books as those on the law exported to the plantations. The colonists have now fallen into the way of printing them for their own use. I hear that they have sold nearly as many of Blackstone's "Commentaries" in America as in England. General Gage marks out this disposition very particularly in a letter on your table. He states, that all the people in his government are lawyers, or smatterers in law—and that in Boston they have been enabled, by successful chicane, wholly to evade many parts of one of your capital penal constitutions. The smartness of debate will say, that this knowledge ought to teach them more clearly the rights of legislature, their obligations to obedience, and the penalties of rebellion. All this is mighty well. But my honorable and learned friend on the floor, who condescends to mark what I say for animadversion, will disdain that ground. He has heard, as well as I, that, when great honors and great emoluments do not win over this knowledge to the service of the state, it is a formidable adversary to government. If the spirit be not tamed and broken by these happy methods, it is stubborn and litigious. *Abeunt studia in mores.* This study renders men acute, inquisitive, dexterous, prompt in attack, ready in defence, full of resources. In other countries, the people, more simple, and of a less mercurial cast, judge of an ill principle in government only by an actual grievance; here they anticipate the evil, and judge of the pressure of the grievance by the badness of the principle. They augur misgovernment at a distance, and snuff the approach of tyranny in every tainted breeze.

The last cause of this disobedient spirit in the colonies is hardly less powerful than the rest, as it is not merely moral, but laid deep in the natural constitution of things. Three thousand miles of ocean lie between you and them. No contrivance can prevent the effect of this distance in weakening government. Seas roll, and months pass, between the order and the execution; and the want of a speedy explanation of a single point is enough to defeat an whole system. You have, indeed, winged ministers of vengeance, who carry your bolts in their pounces to the remotest verge of the sea: but there a power steps in, that limits the arrogance of raging passions and furious elements, and says, "So far shalt thou go, and no farther." Who are you, that should fret and rage, and bite the chains of Nature? Nothing worse happens to you than does to all nations who have extensive empire; and it happens in all the forms into which empire can be thrown. In large bodies, the circulation of power must be less vigorous at the extremities. Nature has said it. The Turk cannot govern Egypt, and Arabia, and Kurdistan, as he governs Thrace; nor has he the same dominion in Crimea and Algiers which he has at Brusa and Smyrna. Despotism itself is obliged to truck and huckster. The Sultan gets such obedience as he can. He governs with a loose rein, that he may govern at all; and the whole of the force and vigor of his authority in his centre is derived from a prudent relaxation in all his borders. Spain, in her provinces, is perhaps not so well obeyed as you are in yours. She complies, too; she submits; she watches times. This is the immutable condition, the eternal law, of extensive and detached empire.

Then, Sir, from these six capital sources, of descent, of form of government, of religion in the northern provinces, of manners in the southern, of education, of the remoteness of situation from the first mover of government—from all these causes a fierce spirit of liberty has grown up. It has grown with the growth of the people in your colonies, and increased with the increase of their wealth: a spirit, that, unhappily meeting with an exercise of power in England, which, however lawful, is not reconcilable to any ideas of liberty, much less with theirs, has kindled this flame that is ready to consume us.

I do not mean to commend either the spirit in this excess, or the moral causes which produce it. Perhaps a more smooth and accommodating spirit of freedom in them would be more acceptable to us. Perhaps ideas of liberty might be desired more reconcilable with an arbitrary and boundless authority. Perhaps we might wish the colonists to be persuaded that their liberty is more secure when held in trust for them by us (as their guardians during a perpetual minority) than with any part of it in their own hands. But the question is not, whether their spirit deserves praise or blame—what, in the name of God, shall we do with it? You have before you the object, such as it is—with all its glories, with all its imperfections on its head. You see the magnitude, the importance, the temper, the habits, the disorders. By all these considerations we are strongly urged to determine something concerning it. We are called upon to fix some rule and line for our future conduct, which may give a little stability to our politics, and prevent the return of such unhappy deliberations as the present. . . . Until very lately, all authority in America seemed to be nothing but an emanation from yours. Even the popular part of the colony constitution derived all its activity, and its first vital movement, from the pleasure of the crown. We thought, Sir, that the utmost which the discontented colonists could do was to disturb authority; we never dreamt they could of themselves supply it, knowing in general what an operose business it is to establish a government absolutely new. But having, for our purposes in this contention, resolved that none but an obedient assembly should sit, the humors of the people there, finding all passage through the legal channel stopped, with great violence broke out another way. Some provinces have tried their experiment, as we have tried ours; and theirs has succeeded. They have formed a government sufficient for its purposes, without the bustle of a revolution, or the troublesome formality of an election. Evident necessity and tacit consent have done the business in an instant. . . . Obedience is what makes government, and not the names by which it is called: not the name of Governor, as formerly, or Committee, as at present. This new government has originated directly from the people, and was not transmitted through any of the ordinary artificial media of a positive constitution. It was not a manufacture ready formed, and transmitted to them in that condition from England. The evil arising from hence is this: that the colonists having once found the possibility of enjoying the advantages of order in the midst of a struggle for liberty, such struggles will not henceforward seem so terrible to the settled and sober part of mankind as they had appeared before the trial.

Pursuing the same plan of punishing by the denial of the

exercise of government to still greater lengths, we wholly abrogated the ancient government of Massachusetts. We were confident that the first feeling, if not the very prospect of anarchy, would instantly enforce a complete submission. The experiment was tried. A new, strange, unexpected face of things appeared. Anarchy is found tolerable. A vast province has now subsisted, and subsisted in a considerable degree of health and vigor, for near a twelvemonth, without governor, without public council, without judges, without executive magistrates. How long it will continue in this state, or what may arise out of this unheard-of situation, how can the wisest of us conjecture? Our late experience has taught us that many of those fundamental principles formerly believed infallible are either not of the importance they were imagined to be, or that we have not at all adverted to some other far more important and far more powerful principles which entirely overrule those we had considered as omnipotent. I am much against any further experiments which tend to put to the proof any more of these allowed opinions which contribute so much to the public tranquillity. In effect, we suffer as much at home by this loosening of all ties, and this concussion of all established opinions, as we do abroad. For, in order to prove that the Americans have no right to their liberties, we are every day endeavoring to subvert the maxims which preserve the whole spirit of our own. To prove that the Americans ought not to be free, we are obliged to depreciate the value of freedom itself; and we never seem to gain a paltry advantage over them in debate, without attacking some of those principles, or deriding some of those feelings, for which our ancestors have shed their blood. . . .

As far as I am capable of discerning, there are but three ways of proceeding relative to this stubborn spirit which prevails in your colonies and disturbs your government. These are—to change that spirit, as inconvenient, by removing the causes—to prosecute it, as criminal—or to comply with it, as necessary. I would not be guilty of an imperfect enumeration; I can think of but these three. Another has, indeed, been started—that of giving up the colonies; but it met so slight a reception that I do not think myself obliged to dwell a great while upon it. . . .

As the growing population of the colonies is evidently one cause of their resistance, it was last session mentioned in both Houses, by men of weight, and received not without applause, that, in order to check this evil, it would be proper for the crown to make no further grants of land. But to this scheme there are two objections. The first, that there is already so much unsettled land in private hands as to afford room for an immense future population, although the crown not only withheld its grants, but annihilated its soil. If this be the case, then the only effect of this avarice of desolation, this hoarding of a royal wilderness, would be to raise the value of the possessions in the hands of the great private monopolists, without any adequate check to the growing and alarming mischief of population.

But if you stopped your grants, what would be the consequence? The people would occupy without grants. They have already so occupied in many places. You cannot station garrisons in every part of these deserts. If you drive the people from one place, they will carry on their annual tillage, and remove with their flocks and herds to another. Many of the people in the back settlements are already little attached to particular situations. Already they have topped the Appalachian mountains. From thence they behold before them an immense plain, one vast, rich, level meadow: a square of five hundred miles. Over this they would wander without a possibility of restraint; they would change their manners with the habits of their life; would soon forget a government by which they were disowned; would become hordes of English Tartars, and, pouring down upon your unfortified frontiers a fierce and irresistible cavalry, become masters of your governors and your counsellors, your collectors and comptrollers, and of all the slaves that adhered to them. Such would, and, in no long time, must be, the effect of attempting to forbid as a crime, and to suppress as an evil, the command and blessing of Providence, "Increase and multiply." Such would be the happy result of an endeavor to keep as a lair of wild beasts that earth which God by an express charter has given to the children of men. Far different, and surely much wiser, has been our policy hitherto. Hitherto we have invited our people, by every kind of bounty, to fixed establishments. We have invited the husbandman to look to authority for his title. We have taught him piously to believe in the mysterious virtue of wax and parchment. We have thrown each tract of land, as it was peopled, into districts, that the ruling power should never be wholly out of sight. . . .

I think this new project of hedging in population to be neither prudent nor practicable.

To impoverish the colonies in general, and in particular to

arrest the noble course of their marine enterprises, would be a more easy task. I freely confess it. We have shown a disposition to a system of this kind—a disposition even to continue the restraint after the offence—looking on ourselves as rivals to our colonies, and persuaded that of course we must gain all that they shall lose. Much mischief we may certainly do. The power inadequate to all other things is often more than sufficient for this. I do not look on the direct and immediate power of the colonies to resist our violence as very formidable. In this, however, I may be mistaken. But when I consider that we have colonies for no purpose but to be serviceable to us, it seems to my poor understanding a little preposterous to make them unserviceable, in order to keep them obedient. It is, in truth, nothing more than the old, and, as I thought, exploded problem of tyranny, which proposes to beggar its subjects into submission. But remember, when you have completed your system of impoverishment, that Nature still proceeds in her ordinary course; that discontent will increase with misery; and that there are critical moments in the fortune of all states, when they who are too weak to contribute to your prosperity may be strong enough to complete your ruin. . . .

The temper and character which prevail in our colonies are, I am afraid, unalterable by any human art. We cannot, I fear, falsify the pedigree of this fierce people, and persuade them that they are not sprung from a nation in whose veins the blood of freedom circulates. The language in which they would hear you tell them this tale would detect the imposition; your speech would betray you. An Englishman is the unfittest person on earth to argue another Englishman into slavery.

I think it is nearly as little in our power to change their republican religion as their free descent, or to substitute the Roman Catholic as a penalty, or the Church of England as an improvement. The mode of inquisition and dragooning is going out of fashion in the Old World, and I should not confide much to their efficacy in the New. The education of the Americans is also on the same unalterable bottom with their religion. You cannot persuade them to burn their books of curious science, to banish their lawyers from their courts of law, or to quench the lights of their assemblies by refusing to choose those persons who are best read in their privileges. It would be no less impracticable to think of wholly annihilating the popular assemblies in which these lawyers sit. The army, by which we must govern in their place, would be far more chargeable to us, not quite so effectual, and perhaps, in the end, full as difficult to be kept in obedience.

With regard to the high aristocratic spirit of Virginia and the southern colonies, it has been proposed, I know, to reduce it by declaring a general enfranchisement of their slaves. This project has had its advocates and panegyrists; yet I never could argue myself into any opinion of it. Slaves are often much attached to their masters. A general wild offer of liberty would not always be accepted. History furnishes few instances of it. It is sometimes as hard to persuade slaves to be free as it is to compel freemen to be slaves; and in this auspicious scheme we should have both these pleasing tasks on our hands at once. But when we talk of enfranchisement, do we not perceive that the American master may enfranchise, too, and arm servile hands in defence of freedom?—a measure to which other people have had recourse more than once, and not without success, in a desperate situation of their affairs.

Slaves as these unfortunate black people are, and dull as all men are from slavery, must they not a little suspect the offer of freedom from that very nation which has sold them to their present masters—from that nation, one of whose causes of quarrel with those masters is their refusal to deal any more in that inhuman traffic? An offer of freedom from England would come rather oddly, shipped to them in an African vessel, which is refused an entry into the ports of Virginia or Carolina, with a cargo of three hundred Angola negroes. It would be curious to see the Guinea captain attempting at the same instant to publish his proclamation of liberty and to advertise his sale of slaves.

But let us suppose all these moral difficulties got over. The ocean remains. You cannot pump this dry; and as long as it continues in its present bed, so long all the causes which weaken authority by distance will continue. . . .

If, then, Sir, it seems almost desperate to think of any alternative course for changing the moral causes (and not quite easy to remove the natural) which produce prejudices irreconcilable to the late exercise of our authority, but that the spirit infallibly will continue, and, continuing, will produce such effects as now embarrass us—the second mode under consideration is, to prosecute that spirit in its overt acts, as *criminal*.

At this proposition I must pause a moment. The thing seems a great deal too big for my ideas of jurisprudence. It should seem, to my way of conceiving such matters, that there is a very wide difference, in reason and policy, between the mode of proceeding on the irregular conduct of scattered individuals, or even of bands of men, who disturb order within the state, and the civil dissensions which may, from time to time, on great questions, agitate the several communities which compose a great empire. It looks to me to be narrow and pedantic to apply the ordinary ideas of criminal justice to this great public contest. I do not know the method of drawing up an indictment against an whole people. I cannot insult and ridicule the feelings of millions of my fellow-creatures . . . I am not ripe to pass sentence on the gravest public bodies, intrusted with magistracies of great authority and dignity, and charged with the safety of their fellow-citizens, upon the very same title that I am. I really think that for wise men this is not judicious, for sober men not decent, for minds tinctured with humanity not mild and merciful.

Perhaps, Sir, I am mistaken in my idea of an empire, as distinguished from a single state or kingdom. But my idea of it is this: than an empire is the aggregate of many states under one common head, whether this head be a monarch or a presiding republic. It does, in such constitutions, frequently happen (and nothing but the dismal, cold, dead uniformity of servitude can prevent its happening) that the subordinate parts have many local privileges and immunities. Between these privileges and the supreme common authority the line may be extremely nice. Of course disputes, often, too, very bitter disputes, and much ill blood, will arise. But though every privilege is an exemption (in the case) from the ordinary exercise of the supreme authority, it is no denial of it. The claim of a privilege seems rather, *ex vi termini,* to imply a superior power: for to talk of the privileges of a state or of a person who has no superior is hardly any better than speaking nonsense. Now in such unfortunate quarrels among the component parts of a great political union of communities, I can scarcely conceive anything more completely imprudent than for the head of the empire to insist, that if any privilege is pleaded against his will or his acts, that his whole authority is denied—instantly to proclaim rebellion, to beat to arms, and to put the offending provinces under the ban. Will not this, Sir, very soon teach the provinces to make no distinctions on their part? Will it not teach them that the government against which a claim of liberty is tantamount to high treason is a government to which submission is equivalent to slavery? It may not always be quite convenient to impress dependent communities with such an idea.

We are, indeed, in all disputes with the colonies, by the necessity of things, the judge. It is true, Sir. But I confess that the character of judge in my own cause is a thing that frightens me. Instead of filling me with pride, I am exceedingly humbled by it. I cannot proceed with a stern, assured judicial confidence, until I find myself in something more like a judicial character. I must have these hesitations as long as I am compelled to recollect, that, in my little reading upon such contests as these, the sense of mankind has at least as often decided against the superior as the subordinate power. Sir, let me add, too, that the opinion of my having some abstract right in my favor would not put me much at my ease in passing sentence, unless I could be sure that there were no rights which, in their exercise under certain circumstances, were not the most odious of all wrongs and the most vexatious of all injustice. Sir, these considerations have great weight with me, when I find things so circumstanced that I see the same party at once a civil litigant against me in a point of right and a culprit before me, while I sit as criminal judge on acts of his whose moral quality is to be decided upon the merits of that very litigation. Men are every now and then put, by the complexity of human affairs, into strange situations; but justice is the same, let the judge be in what situation he will.

There is, Sir, also a circumstance which convinces me that this mode of criminal proceeding is not (at least in the present stage of our contest) altogether expedient—which is nothing less than the conduct of those very persons who have seemed to adopt that mode, by lately declaring a rebellion in Massachusetts Bay, as they had formerly addressed to have traitors brought hither, under an act of Henry the Eighth, for trial. For, though rebellion is declared, it is not proceeded against as such; nor have any steps been taken towards the apprehension or conviction of any individual offender, either on our late or our former address; but modes of public coercion have been adopted, and such as have much more resemblance to a sort of qualified hostility towards an independent power than the punishment of rebellious subjects. All this seems rather inconsistent; but it shows how difficult it is to apply these juridical ideas to our present case.

In this situation, let us seriously and coolly ponder. What is it we have got by all our menaces, which have been many and ferocious? What advantage have we derived from the penal laws we have passed, and which, for the time, have been severe and numerous? What advances have we made towards our object, by the sending of a force, which, by land and sea, is no contemptible strength? Has the disorder abated? Nothing less. —When I see things in this situation, after such confident hopes, bold promises, and active exertions, I cannot, for my life, avoid a suspicion that the plan itself is not correctly right.

If, then, the removal of the causes of this spirit of American liberty be, for the greater part, or rather entirely, impracticable—if the ideas of criminal process be inapplicable, or, if applicable, are in the highest degree inexpedient, what way yet remains? No way is open, but the third and last—to comply with the American spirit as necessary, or, if you please, to submit to it as a necessary evil.

If we adopt this mode, if we mean to conciliate and concede, let us see of what nature the concession ought to be. To ascertain the nature of our concession, we must look at their complaint. The colonies complain that they have not the characteristic mark and seal of British freedom. They complain that they are taxed in a Parliament in which they are not represented. If you mean to satisfy them at all, you must satisfy them with regard to this complaint. . . .

I am resolved this day to have nothing at all to do with the question of the right of taxation. Some gentlemen startle—but it is true: I put it totally out of the question. It is less than nothing in my consideration. I do not indeed wonder, nor will you, Sir, that gentlemen of profound learning are fond of displaying it on this profound subject. But my consideration is narrow, confined, and wholly limited to the policy of the question. I do not examine whether the giving away a man's money be a power excepted and reserved out of the general trust of government, and how far all mankind, in all forms of polity, are entitled to an exercise of that right by the charter of Nature—or whether, on the contrary, a right of taxation is necessarily involved in the general principle of legislation, and inseparable from the ordinary supreme power. These are deep questions, where great names militate against each other, where reason is perplexed, and an appeal to authorities only thickens the confusion: for high and reverend authorities lift up their heads on both sides, and there is no sure footing in the middle. This point is the *great Serbonian bog, betwixt Damiata and Mount Casius old, where armies whole have sunk*. I do not intend to be overwhelmed in that bog, though in such respectable company. The question with me is, not whether you have a right to render your people miserable, but whether it is not your interest to make them happy. It is not what a lawyer tells me I *may* do, but what humanity, reason, and justice tell me I ought to do. Is a politic act the worse for being a generous one? Is no concession proper, but that which is made from your want of right to keep what you grant? Or does it lessen the grace or dignity of relaxing in the exercise of an odious claim, because you have your evidence-room full of titles, and your magazines stuffed with arms to enforce them? What signify all those titles and all those arms? Of what avail are they, when the reason of the thing tells me that the assertion of my title is the loss of my suit, and that I could do nothing but wound myself by the use of my own weapons?

Such is steadfastly my opinion of the absolute necessity of keeping up the concord of this empire by a unity of spirit, though in a diversity of operations, that, if I were sure the colonists had, at their leaving this country, sealed a regular compact of servitude, that they had solemnly abjured all the rights of citizens, that they had made a vow to renounce all ideas of liberty for them and their posterity to all generations, yet I should hold myself obliged to conform to the temper I found universally prevalent in my own day, and to govern two million of men, impatient of servitude, on the principles of freedom. I am not determining a point of law; I am restoring tranquillity; and the general character and situation of a people must determine what sort of government is fitted for them. . . .

My idea, therefore, without considering whether we yield as matter of right or grant as matter of favor, is, *to admit the people of our colonies into an interest in the Constitution,* and, by recording that admission in the journals of Parliament, to give them as strong an assurance as the nature of the thing will admit that we mean forever to adhere to that solemn declaration of systematic indulgence. . . .

I have taken a very incorrect measure of the disposition of the House, if this proposal in itself would be received with dislike. I think, Sir, we have few American financiers. But our misfortune is, we are too acute, we are too exquisite in our conjectures of the future, for men oppressed with such great and present evils. The more moderate among the opposers of Parliamentary concession freely confess that they hope no good from taxation; but they apprehend the colonists have further views, and if this point were conceded, they would instantly attack the trade laws. These gentlemen are convinced that this was the intention from the beginning, and the quarrel of the Americans with taxation was no more than a cloak and cover to this design. . . .

One fact is clear and indisputable: the public and avowed origin of this quarrel was on taxation. This quarrel has, indeed, brought on new disputes on new questions, but certainly the least bitter, and the fewest of all, on the trade laws. To judge which of the two be the real, radical cause of quarrel, we have to see whether the commercial dispute did, in order of time, precede the dispute on taxation. There is not a shadow of evidence for it. Next, to enable us to judge whether at this moment a dislike to the trade laws be the real cause of quarrel, it is absolutely necessary to put the taxes out of the question by a repeal. See how the Americans act in this position, and then you will be able to discern correctly what is the true object of the controversy, or whether any controversy at all will remain. Unless you consent to remove this cause of difference, it is impossible, with decency, to assert that the dispute is not upon what it is avowed to be. And I would, Sir, recommend to your serious consideration, whether it be prudent to form a rule for punishing people, not on their own acts, but on your conjectures. Surely it is preposterous, at the very best. It is not justifying your anger by their misconduct, but it is converting your ill-will into their delinquency. . . .

When will this speculating against fact and reason end? What will quiet these panic fears which we entertain of the hostile effect of a conciliatory conduct? Is it true that no case can exist in which it is proper for the sovereign to accede to the desires of his discontented subjects? Is there anything peculiar in this case, to make a rule for itself? Is all authority of course lost, when it is not pushed to the extreme? Is it a certain maxim, that, the fewer causes of dissatisfaction are left by government, the more the subject will be inclined to resist and rebel?

All these objections being in fact no more than suspicions, conjectures, divinations, formed in defiance of fact and experience, they did not, Sir, discourage me from entertaining the idea of a conciliatory concession, founded on the principles which I have just stated.

In forming a plan for this purpose, I endeavored to put myself in that frame of mind which was the most natural and the most reasonable, and which was certainly the most probable means of securing me from all error. I set out with a perfect distrust of my own abilities, a total renunciation of every speculation of my own, and with a profound reverence for the wisdom of our ancestors, who have left us the inheritance of so happy a Constitution and so flourishing an empire, and, what is a thousand times more valuable, the treasury of the maxims and principles which formed the one and obtained the other. . . .

I am sure that I shall not be misled, when, in a case of constitutional difficulty, I consult the genius of the English Constitution. Consulting at that oracle, (it was with all due humility and piety,) I found four capital examples in a similar case before me: those of Ireland, Wales, Chester, and Durham.

Ireland, before the English conquest, though never governed by a despotic power, had no Parliament. How far the English Parliament itself was at that time modelled according to the present form is disputed among antiquarians. But we have all the reason in the world to be assured, that a form of Parliament, such as England then enjoyed, she instantly communicated to Ireland; and we are equally sure that almost every successive improvement in constitutional liberty, as fast as it was made here, was transmitted thither. The feudal baronage, and the feudal knighthood, the roots of our primitive Constitution, were early transplanted into that soil, and grew and flourished there. Magna Charta, if it did not give us originally the House of Commons, gave us at least an House of Commons of weight and consequence. But your ancestors did not churlishly sit down alone to the feast of Magna Charta. Ireland was made immediately a partaker. This benefit of English laws and liberties, I confess, was not at first extended to *all* Ireland. Mark the consequence. English authority and English liberty had exactly the same boundaries. . . . It was not English arms, but the English Constitution, that conquered Ireland. . . .

My next example is Wales. This country was said to be reduced by Henry the Third. It was said more truly to be so by Edward the First. But though then conquered, it was not looked upon as any part of the realm of England. Its old Constitution, whatever that might have been, was destroyed; and no good one was substituted in its place. . . . The manners of the Welsh nation followed the genius of the government: the people were ferocious, restive, savage, and uncultivated; sometimes composed, never pacified. Wales, within itself, was in perpetual disorder; and it kept the frontier of

England in perpetual alarm. Benefits from it to the state there were none. Wales was only known to England by incursion and invasion.

Sir, during that state of things, Parliament was not idle. They attempted to subdue the fierce spirit of the Welsh by all sorts of rigorous laws. They prohibited by statute the sending all sorts of arms into Wales, as you prohibit by proclamation (with something more of doubt on the legality) the sending arms to America. They disarmed the Welsh by statute, as you attempted (but still with more question on the legality) to disarm New England by an instruction. They made an act to drag offenders from Wales into England for trial, as you have done (but with more hardship) with regard to America. By another act, where one of the parties was an Englishman, they ordained that his trial should be always by English. They made acts to restrain trade, as you do; and they prevented the Welsh from the use of fairs and markets, as you do the Americans from fisheries and foreign ports. . . .

Here we rub our hands—A fine body of precedents for the authority of Parliament and the use of it!—I admit it fully; and pray add likewise to these precedents, that all the while Wales rid this kingdom like an *incubus;* that it was an unprofitable and oppressive burden; and that an Englishman travelling in that country could not go six yards from the highroad without being murdered.

The march of the human mind is slow. Sir, it was not until after two hundred years discovered, that, by an eternal law, Providence had decreed vexation to violence, and poverty to rapine. Your ancestors did, however, at length open their eyes to the ill husbandry of injustice. They found that the tyranny of a free people could of all tyrannies the least be endured, and that laws made against an whole nation were not the most effectual methods for securing its obedience. Accordingly, in the twenty-seventh year of Henry the Eighth the course was entirely altered. With a preamble stating the entire and perfect rights of the crown of England, it gave to the Welsh all the rights and privileges of English subjects. A political order was established; the military power gave way to the civil; the marches were turned into counties. But that a nation should have a right to English liberties, and yet no share at all in the fundamental security of these liberties—the grant of their own property—seemed a thing so incongruous, that eight years after, that is, in the thirty-fifth of that reign, a complete and not ill-proportioned representation by counties and boroughs was bestowed upon Wales by act of Parliament. From that moment, as by a charm, the tumults subsided; obedience was restored; peace, order, and civilization followed in the train of liberty. . . .

The very same year the County Palatine of Chester received the same relief from its oppressions, and the same remedy to its disorders. Before this time Chester was little less distempered than Wales. . . . The people of Chester applied to Parliament in a petition . . .

What did Parliament with this audacious address? . . . —They took the petition of grievance, all rugged as it was, without softening or temperament, unpurged of the original bitterness and indignation of complaint; they made it the very preamble to their act of redress, and consecrated its principle to all ages in the sanctuary of legislation. . . .

It was attended with the success of the two former. Chester, civilized as well as Wales, has demonstrated that freedom, and not servitude, is the cure of anarchy; as religion, and not atheism, is the true remedy for superstition. Sir, this pattern of Chester was followed in the reign of Charles the Second with regard to the County Palatine of Durham, which is my fourth example. This county had long lain out of the pale of free legislation. So scrupulously was the example of Chester followed, that the style of the preamble is nearly the same with that of the Chester act; and, without affecting the abstract extent of the authority of Parliament, it recognizes the equity of not suffering any considerable district, in which the British subjects may act as a body, to be taxed without their own voice in the grant.

Now if the doctrines of policy contained in these preambles, and the force of these examples in the acts of Parliament, avail anything, what can be said against applying them with regard to America? Are not the people of America as much Englishmen as the Welsh? . . . Is America in rebellion? Wales was hardly ever free from it. Have you attempted to govern America by penal statutes? You made fifteen for Wales. But your legislative authority is perfect with regard to America: was it less perfect in Wales, Chester, and Durham? But America is virtually represented. What! does the electric force of virtual representation more easily pass over the Atlantic than pervade Wales, which lies in your neighborhood? or than Chester and Durham, surrounded by abundance of representation that is actual and palpable? But, Sir, your ancestors thought this sort of virtual representation, however ample, to be totally insufficient for the freedom of the inhabitants of territories that are so near, and comparatively so inconsiderable. How, then, can I think it sufficient for those which are infinitely greater, and infinitely more remote?

You will now, Sir, perhaps imagine that I am on the point of proposing to you a scheme for a representation of the colonies in Parliament. Perhaps I might be inclined to entertain some such thought; but a great flood stops me in my course. *Opposuit Natura.* I cannot remove the eternal barriers of the creation. The thing, in that mode, I do not know to be possible. As I meddle with no theory, I do not absolutely assert the impracticability of such a representation; but I do not see my way to it; and those who have been more confident have not been more successful. However, the arm of public benevolence is not shortened; and there are often several means to the same end. What Nature has disjoined in one way wisdom may unite in another. When we cannot give the benefit as we would wish, let us not refuse it altogether. If we cannot give the principal, let us find a substitute. . . .

Fortunately, I am not obliged, for the ways and means of this substitute, to tax my own unproductive invention. I am not even obliged to go to the rich treasury of the fertile framers of imaginary commonwealths: not to the Republic of Plato, not to the Utopia of More, not to the Oceana of Harrington. It is before me—it is at my feet—

> *And the rude swain*
> *Treads daily on it with his clouted shoon.*

I only wish you to recognize, for the theory, the ancient constitutional policy of this kingdom with regard to representation, as that policy has been declared in acts of Parliament—and as to the practice, to return to that mode which an uniform experience has marked out to you as best, and in which you walked with security, advantage, and honor, until the year 1763.

My resolutions, therefore, mean to establish the equity and justice of a taxation of America by *grant,* and not by *imposition;* to mark the *legal competency* of the colony assemblies for the support of their government in peace, and for public aids in time of war; to acknowledge that this legal competency has had *a dutiful and beneficial exercise,* and that experience has shown *the benefit of their grants,* and *the futility of Parliamentary taxation, as a method of supply.*

These solid truths compose six fundamental propositions.

. . . I think these six massive pillars will be of strength sufficient to support the temple of British concord. I have no more doubt than I entertain of my existence, that, if you admitted these, you would command an immediate peace, and, with but tolerable future management, a lasting obedience in America. . . .

The first is a resolution—"That the colonies and plantations of Great Britain in North America, consisting of fourteen separate governments, and containing two millions and upwards of free inhabitants, have not had the liberty and privilege of electing and sending any knights and burgesses, or others, to represent them in the high court of Parliament."

This is a plain matter of fact, necessary to be laid down, and (excepting the description) it is laid down in the language of the Constitution; it is taken nearly *verbatim* from acts of Parliament.

The second is like unto the first—"That the said colonies and plantations have been made liable to, and bounden by, several subsidies, payments, rates, and taxes, given and granted by Parliament, though the said colonies and plantations have not their knights and burgesses in the said high court of Parliament, of their own election, to represent the condition of their country; by lack whereof they have been oftentimes touched and grieved by subsidies, given, granted, and assented to, in the said court, in a manner prejudicial to the commonwealth, quietness, rest, and peace of the subjects inhabiting within the same."

Is this description too hot or too cold, too strong or too weak? Does it arrogate too much to the supreme legislature? Does it lean too much to the claims of the people? If it runs into any of these errors, the fault is not mine. It is the language of your own ancient acts of Parliament. . . . It is the genuine produce of the ancient, rustic, manly, home-bred sense of this country. I did not dare to rub off a particle of the venerable rust that rather adorns and preserves than destroys the metal. It would be a profanation to touch with a tool the stones which construct the sacred altar of peace. I would not violate with modern polish the ingenuous and noble roughness of these truly constitutional materials. Above all things, I was resolved not to be guilty of tampering—the odious vice of restless and unstable minds. I put my foot in the tracks of our forefathers, where I can neither wander nor stumble. Determining to fix articles of peace, I was resolved not to be wise beyond what was written . . .

The next proposition is—"That, from the distance of the said colonies, and from other circumstances, no method hath hitherto been devised for procuring a representation in Parliament for the said colonies."

This is an assertion of a fact. I go no further on the paper; though, in my private judgment, an useful representation is impossible; I am sure it is not desired by them, nor ought it, perhaps, by us: but I abstain from opinions.

The fourth resolution is—"That each of the said colonies hath within itself a body, chosen, in part or in the whole, by the freemen, freeholders, or other free inhabitants thereof, commonly called the General Assembly, or General Court, with powers legally to raise, levy, and assess, according to the several usages of such colonies, duties and taxes towards defraying all sorts of public services."

This competence in the colony assemblies is certain. It is proved by the whole tenor of their acts of supply in all the assemblies, in which the constant style of granting is, "An aid to his Majesty"; and acts granting to the crown have regularly, for near a century, passed the public offices without dispute. Those who have been pleased paradoxically to deny this right, holding that none but the British Parliament can grant to the crown, are wished to look to what is done, not only in the colonies, but in Ireland, in one uniform, unbroken tenor, every session. . . .

The fifth resolution is also a resolution of fact—"That the said general assemblies, general courts, or other bodies legally qualified as aforesaid, have at sundry times freely granted several large subsidies and public aids for his Majesty's service, according to their abilities, when required thereto by letter from one of his Majesty's principal Secretaries of State; and that their right to grant the same, and their cheerfulness and sufficiency in the said grants, have been at sundry times acknowledged by Parliament."

To say nothing of their great expenses in the Indian wars, and not to take their exertion in foreign ones, so high as the supplies in the year 1695, not to go back to their public contributions in the year 1710, I shall begin to travel only where the journals give me light—resolving to deal in nothing but fact authenticated by Parliamentary record, and to build myself wholly on that solid basis.

On the 4th of April, 1748, a committee of this House came to the following resolution:—

"*Resolved*, That it is the opinion of this committee, *that it is just and reasonable,* that the several provinces and colonies of Massachusetts Bay, New Hampshire, Connecticut, and Rhode Island be reimbursed the expenses they have been at in taking and securing to the crown of Great Britain the island of Cape Breton and its dependencies."

These expenses were immense for such colonies. They were above 200,000*l.* sterling: money first raised and advanced on their public credit.

On the 28th of January, 1756, a message from the king came to us, to this effect:—"His Majesty, being sensible of the zeal and vigor with which his faithful subjects of certain colonies in North America have exerted themselves in defence of his Majesty's just rights and possessions, recommends it to this House to take the same into their consideration, and to enable his Majesty to give them such assistance as may be a *proper reward and encouragement.*"

On the 3d of February, 1756, the House came to a suitable resolution, expressed in words nearly the same as those of the message; but with the further addition, that the money then voted was as an *encouragement* to the colonies to exert themselves with vigor. . . .

Sir, here is the repeated acknowledgment of Parliament, that the colonies not only gave, but gave to satiety. This nation has formally acknowledged two things: first, that the colonies had gone beyond their abilities, Parliament having thought it necessary to reimburse them; secondly, that they had acted legally and laudably in their grants of money, and their maintenance of troops, since the compensation is expressly given as reward and encouragement. Reward is not bestowed for acts that are unlawful; and encouragement is not held out to things that deserve reprehension. My resolution, therefore, does nothing more than collect into one proposition what is scattered through your journals. I give you nothing but your own; and you cannot refuse in the gross what you have so often acknowledged in detail. . . .

I think, then, I am, from those journals, justified in the sixth and last resolution, which is—"That it hath been found by experience, that the manner of granting the said supplies and aids by the said general assemblies hath been more agreeable to the inhabitants of the said colonies, and more beneficial and conducive to the public service, than the mode of giving and granting aids and subsidies in Parliament, to be raised and paid in the said colonies."

This makes the whole of the fundamental part of the plan.

The conclusion is irresistible. You cannot say that you were driven by any necessity to an exercise of the utmost rights of legislature. You cannot assert that you took on yourselves the task of imposing colony taxes, from the want of another legal body that is competent to the purpose of supplying the exigencies of the state without wounding the prejudices of the people. Neither is it true that the body so qualified, and having that competence, had neglected the duty.

The question now, on all this accumulated matter, is— Whether you will choose to abide by a profitable experience or a mischievous theory? whether you choose to build on imagination or fact? whether you prefer enjoyment or hope? satisfaction in your subjects, or discontent?

If these propositions are accepted, everything which has been made to enforce a contrary system must, I take it for granted, fall along with it. . . .

I wish, Sir, to repeal the Boston Port Bill, because (independently of the dangerous precedent of suspending the rights of the subject during the king's pleasure) it was passed, as I apprehend, with less regularity, and on more partial principles, than it ought. The corporation of Boston was not heard before it was condemned. . . .

Ideas of prudence and accommodation to circumstances prevent you from taking away the charters of Connecticut and Rhode Island, as you have taken away that of Massachusetts Colony, though the crown has far less power in the two former provinces than it enjoyed in the latter, and though the abuses have been full as great and as flagrant in the exempted as in the punished. The same reasons of prudence and accommodation have weight with me in restoring the charter of Massachusetts Bay. . . . It is shameful to behold such a regulation standing among English laws.

The act for bringing persons accused of committing murder under the orders of government to England for trial is but temporary. . . . I would hasten the happy moment of reconciliation, and therefore must, on my principle, get rid of that most justly obnoxious act. . . .

I do not know that the colonies have, in any general way, or in any cool hour, gone much beyond the demand of immunity in relation to taxes. It is not fair to judge of the temper or dispositions of any man or any set of men, when they are composed and at rest, from their conduct or their expressions in a state of disturbance and irritation. It is, besides, a very great mistake to imagine that mankind follow up practically any speculative principle, either of government or of freedom, as far as it will go in argument and logical illation. We Englishmen stop very short of the principles upon which we support any given part of our Constitution, or even the whole of it together. . . . All government, indeed every human benefit and enjoyment, every virtue and every prudent act, is founded on compromise and barter. We balance inconveniences; we give and take; we remit some rights, that we may enjoy others; and we choose rather to be happy citizens than subtle disputants. As we must give away some natural liberty, to enjoy civil advantages, so we must sacrifice some civil liberties, for the advantages to be derived from the communion and fellowship of a great empire. But, in all fair dealings, the thing bought must bear some proportion to the purchase paid. None will barter away the immediate jewel of his soul. Though a great house is apt to make slaves haughty, yet it is purchasing a part of the artificial importance of a great empire too dear, to pay for it all essential rights, and all the intrinsic dignity of human nature. None of us who would not risk his life rather than fall under a government purely arbitrary. But although there are some amongst us who think our Constitution wants many improvements to make it a complete system of liberty, perhaps none who are of that opinion would think it right to aim at such improvement by disturbing his country and risking everything that is dear to him. In every arduous enterprise, we consider what we are to lose, as well as what we are to gain; and the more and better stake of liberty every people possess, the less they will hazard in a vain attempt to make it more. These are *the cords of man*. Man acts from adequate motives relative to his interest, and not on metaphysical speculations. Aristotle, the great master of reasoning, cautions us, and with great weight and propriety, against this species of delusive geometrical accuracy in moral arguments, as the most fallacious of all sophistry.

The Americans will have no interest contrary to the grandeur and glory of England, when they are not oppressed by the weight of it; and they will rather be inclined to respect the acts of a superintending legislature, when they see them the acts of that power which is itself the security, not the rival, of their secondary importance. In this assurance my mind most perfectly acquiesces, and I confess I feel not the least alarm from the discontents which are to arise from putting people at their ease; nor do I apprehend the destruction of this empire from giving, by an act of free grace and indulgence, to two millions of my fellow-citizens some share of those rights upon which I have always been taught to value myself.

It is said, indeed, that this power of granting, vested in American assemblies, would dissolve the unity of the empire . . . I do not know what this unity means; nor has it ever been heard of, that I know, in the constitutional policy of this country. The very idea of subordination of parts excludes this notion of simple and undivided unity. England is the head; but she is not the head and the members too. Ireland has ever had from the beginning a separate, but not an independent legislature, which, far from distracting, promoted the union of the whole. Everything was sweetly and harmoniously disposed through both islands for the conservation of English dominion and the communication of English liberties. I do not see that the same principles might not be carried into twenty islands, and with the same good effect. This is my model with regard to America, as far as the internal circumstances of the two countries are the same. I know no other unity of this empire than I can draw from its example during these periods, when it seemed to my poor understanding more united than it is now, or than it is likely to be by the present methods. . . .

You have heard me with goodness. May you decide with wisdom! For my part, I feel my mind greatly disburdened by what I have done to-day. I have been the less fearful of trying your patience, because on this subject I mean to spare it altogether in future. I have this comfort—that, in every stage of the American affairs, I have steadily opposed the measures that have produced the confusion, and may bring on the destruction, of this empire. I now go so far as to risk a proposal of my own. If I cannot give peace to my country, I give it to my conscience.

But what (says the financier) is peace to us without money? Your plan gives us no revenue.—No! But it does: for it secures to the subject the power of REFUSAL—the first of all revenues. Experience is a cheat, and fact a liar, if this power in the subject, of proportioning his grant, or of not granting at all, has not been found the richest mine of revenue ever discovered by the skill or by the fortune of man. It does not, indeed, vote you £152,750: 11: 2 3/4ths, nor any other paltry limited sum; but it gives the strong-box itself, the fund, the bank, from whence only revenues can arise amongst a people sensible of freedom . . . Cannot you in England, cannot you at this time of day, cannot you, an House of Commons, trust to the principle which has raised so mighty a revenue, and accumulated a debt of near 140 millions in this country? Is this principle to be true in England and false everywhere else? Is it not true in Ireland? Has it not hitherto been true in the colonies? Why should you presume, that, in any country, a body duly constituted for any function will neglect to perform its duty, and abdicate its trust? Such a presumption would go against all government in all modes. But, in truth, this dread of penury of supply from a free assembly has no foundation in Nature. For first observe, that, besides the desire which all men have naturally of supporting the honor of their own government, that sense of dignity, and that security to property, which ever attends freedom, has a tendency to increase the stock of the free community. Most may be taken where most is accumulated. And what is the soil or climate where experience has not uniformly proved that the voluntary flow of heaped-up plenty, bursting from the weight of its own rich luxuriance, has ever run with a more copious stream of revenue than could be squeezed from the dry husks of oppressed indigence by the straining of all the politic machinery in the world?

Next, we know that parties must ever exist in a free country. We know, too, that the emulations of such parties, their contradictions, their reciprocal necessities, their hopes, and their fears, must send them all in their turns to him that holds the balance of the state. The parties are the gamesters; but government keeps the table, and is sure to be the winner in the end. When this game is played, I really think it is more to be feared that the people will be exhausted than that government will not be supplied. Whereas whatever is got by acts of absolute power ill obeyed because odious, or by contracts ill kept because constrained, will be narrow, feeble, uncertain, and precarious. . . .

But to clear up my ideas on this subject—a revenue from America transmitted hither. Do not delude yourselves: you can never receive it—no, not a shilling. We have experience that from remote countries it is not to be expected. If, when you attempted to extract revenue from Bengal, you were obliged to return in loan what you had taken in imposition, what can you expect from North America? For, certainly, if ever there was a country qualified to produce wealth, it is India; or an institution fit for the transmission, it is the East India Company. America has none of these aptitudes. If America gives you taxable objects on which you lay your duties here, and gives you at the same time a surplus by a foreign sale of her commodities to pay the duties on these objects which you tax at home, she has performed her part to the British revenue. But with regard to her own internal establishments, she may, I doubt not she will, contribute in moderation. I say in moderation; for she ought not to be permitted to exhaust herself. She ought to be reserved to a war; the weight of which, with the enemies that we are most likely to have, must be considerable in her quarter of the globe. There she may serve you, and serve you essentially.

For that service, for all service, whether of revenue, trade, or empire, my trust is in her interest in the British Constitution. My hold of the colonies is in the close affection which grows from common names, from kindred blood, from similar privileges, and equal protection. These are ties which, though light as air, are as strong as links of iron. Let the colonies always keep the idea of their civil rights associated with your government—they will cling and grapple to you, and no force under heaven will be of power to tear them from their allegiance. But let it be once understood that your government may be one thing and their privileges another, that these two things may exist without any mutual relation—the cement is gone, the cohesion is loosened, and everything hastens to decay and dissolution. As long as you have the wisdom to keep the sovereign authority of this country as the sanctuary of liberty, the sacred temple consecrated to our common faith, wherever the chosen race and sons of England worship freedom, they will turn their faces towards you. The more they multiply, the more friends you will have; the more ardently they love liberty, the more perfect will be their obedience. Slavery they can have anywhere. It is a weed that grows in every soil. They may have it from Spain, they may have it from Prussia. But, until you become lost to all feeling of your true interest and your natural dignity, freedom they can have from none but you. This is the commodity of price, of which you have the monopoly. This is the true Act of Navigation, which binds to you the commerce of the colonies, and through them secures to you the wealth of the world. Deny them this participation of freedom, and you break that sole bond which originally made, and must still preserve, the unity of the empire. Do not entertain so weak an imagination as that your registers and your bonds, your affidavits and your sufferances, your cockets and your clearances, are what form the great securities of your commerce. Do not dream that your letters of office, and your instructions, and your suspending clauses are the things that hold together the great contexture of this mysterious whole. These things do not make your government. Dead instruments, passive tools as they are, it is the spirit of the English communion that gives all their life and efficacy to them. It is the spirit of the English Constitution, which, infused through the mighty mass, pervades, feeds, unites, invigorates, vivifies every part of the empire, even down to the minutest member.

Is it not the same virtue which does everything for us here in England? Do you imagine, then, that it is the Land-Tax Act which raises your revenue? that it is the annual vote in the Committee of Supply which gives you your army? or that it is the Mutiny Bill which inspires it with bravery and discipline? No! surely, no! It is the love of the people; it is their attachment to their government, from the sense of the deep stake they have in such a glorious institution, which gives you your army and your navy, and infuses into both that liberal obedience without which your army would be a base rabble and your navy nothing but rotten timber.

All this, I know well enough, will sound wild and chimerical to the profane herd of those vulgar and mechanical politicians who have no place among us: a sort of people who think that nothing exists but what is gross and material—and who, therefore, far from being qualified to be directors of the great movement of empire, are not fit to turn a wheel in the machine. But to men truly initiated and rightly taught, these ruling and master principles, which in the opinion of such men as I have mentioned have no substantial existence, are in truth everything, and all in all. Magnanimity in politics is not seldom the truest wisdom; and a great empire and little minds go ill together. If we are conscious of our situation, and glow with zeal to fill our place as becomes our station and ourselves, we ought to auspicate all our public proceedings on America with the old warning of the Church, *Sursum corda!* We ought to elevate our minds to the greatness of that trust to which the order of Providence has called us. By adverting to the dignity of this high calling our ancestors have turned a savage wilderness into a glorious empire, and have made the most extensive and the only honorable conquests, not by destroying, but by promoting the wealth, the number, the happiness of the human race. . . .

*A Letter to
John Farr and John Harris, Esqrs.
Sheriffs of the City of Bristol
on the
Affairs of America
1777*

During the eighteenth century, among English cities Bristol
was second in size, wealth, and commercial importance only
to London. Certain influential Bristol merchants had come to
recognize that Burke's "tried abilities and known commercial
knowledge" would make him a powerful representative of
their interests in Parliament. They also agreed with his policy
of conciliation toward America. Therefore, in October 1774 a
deputation from Bristol went to London to see Burke, found
he had gone to Malton in Yorkshire, followed him there, and
despite his recent election from Malton, invited him to Bristol, where the election was already in progress. Burke was
aware of the singular honor in being asked to stand for such
a great constituency. He accepted immediately, drove the 270
miles to Bristol in forty hours, and after an intense and tedious
campaign was declared elected on November 3, having run
second to his fellow Whig, Henry Cruger.

In the acceptance speeches following their election, Burke's
colleague declared that he regarded himself bound by the
coercive authority of his constituents. Burke had an altogether
different conception of the relationship between a representative in Parliament and his constituents, and in his acceptance
speech he put forth the classic expression of his doctrine of
representation:

*Certainly, gentlemen, it ought to be the happiness and
glory of a representative to live in the strictest union, the closest correspondence, and the most unreserved communication
with his constituents. Their wishes ought to have great weight
with him; their opinions high respect; their business unremitted attention. It is his duty to sacrifice his repose, his pleasure, his satisfactions, to theirs—and above all, ever, and in all
cases, to prefer their interest to his own.*

But his unbiased opinion, his mature judgment, his enlightened conscience, he ought not to sacrifice to you, to any man, or to any set of men living. These he does not derive from your pleasure—no, nor from the law and the Constitution. They are a trust from Providence, for the abuse of which he is deeply answerable. Your representative owes you, not his industry only, but his judgment; and he betrays, instead of serving you, if he sacrifices it to your opinion.

My worthy colleague says, his will ought to be subservient to yours. If that be all, the thing is innocent. If government were a matter of will upon any side, yours, without question, ought to be superior. But government and legislation are matters of reason and judgment, and not of inclination; and what sort of reason is that in which the determination precedes the discussion, in which one set of men deliberate and another decide, and where those who form the conclusion are perhaps three hundred miles distant from those who hear the arguments?

To deliver an opinion is the right of all men; that of constituents is a weighty and respectable opinion, which a representative . . . ought always most seriously to consider. But authoritative *instructions,* mandates *issued,* which the member is bound blindly and implicitly to obey, to vote, and to argue for, though contrary to the clearest convictions of his judgment and conscience—these are things utterly unknown to the laws of this land, and which arise from a fundamental mistake of the whole order and tenor of our constitution.

Parliament is not a congress of ambassadors from different and hostile interests, which interests each must maintain, as an agent and advocate, against other agents and advocates; but *Parliament is a* deliberative *assembly of* one *nation, with* one *interest, that of the whole—where not local purposes, not local prejudices, ought to guide, but the general good, resulting from the general reason of the whole. You choose a member, indeed; but when you have chosen him, he is not a member of Bristol, but he is a member of* Parliament.

Burke represented Bristol in this manly spirit of duty and independence from 1774 to 1780. Ultimately, his refusal to maintain trade restrictions against Ireland, and to continue the penal laws against Catholics, and some lesser matters, alienated him from Bristol. From 1780 to 1794 he represented the pocket borough of Malton.

But in 1777 Burke's relationship with his Bristol constituents was as yet unimpaired. The outbreak of hostilities in the Colonies, with initial British victories late in 1776, had strengthened North's administration and the King's determination to subdue the Colonies by force. The opposition of Rockingham's party to the administration had grown so weak that when American affairs were discussed, to dramatize their disapproval, Burke and his friends "seceded" from the proceedings, and returned only for other business. Bolstered by victories abroad, early in 1777 North used his great majority in Parliament to restrict his critics by passing a bill to partially suspend the Habeas Corpus Act in Britain. Burke had noted on several occasions that the American war was creating a constitutional crisis in Britain, that success abroad would result in restrictions against civil liberty at home. North's action was the occasion for writing *A Letter to the Sheriffs of Bristol* (April 3, 1777), but Burke enlarged upon his theme of defending constitutional liberty by reviewing the effects of political policies conceived in metaphysical speculations rather than in experience and moral prudence.

LETTER

. . . I have the honor of sending you the two last acts which have been passed with regard to the troubles in America. . . . It affords no matter for very pleasing reflection to observe that our subjects diminish as our laws increase.

If I have the misfortune of differing with some of my fellow-citizens on this great and arduous subject, it is no small consolation to me that I do not differ from you. With you I am perfectly united. We are heartily agreed in our detestation of a civil war. We have ever expressed the most unqualified disapprobation of all the steps which have led to it, and of all those which tend to prolong it. And I have no doubt that we feel exactly the same emotions of grief and shame on all its miserable consequences, whether they appear, on the one side or the other, in the shape of victories or defeats, of captures made from the English on the continent or from the English in these islands, of legislative regulations which subvert the liberties of our brethren or which undermine our own.

Of the first of these statutes (that for the letter of marque) I shall say little. . . . The other (for a partial suspension of the *Habeas Corpus*) appears to me of a much deeper malignity. . . .

It seems to have in view two capital objects: the first, to enable administration to confine, as long as it shall think proper, those whom that act is pleased to qualify by the name of *pirates*. Those so qualified I understand to be the commanders and mariners of such privateers and ships of war belonging to the colonies as in the course of this unhappy contest may fall into the hands of the crown. They are there-

fore to be detained in prison, under the criminal description
of piracy, to a future trial and ignominious punishment, whenever circumstances shall make it convenient to execute
vengeance on them, under the color of that odious and infamous offence.

To this first purpose of the law I have no small dislike, because the act does not (as all laws and all equitable transactions ought to do) fairly describe its object. The persons who
make a naval war upon us, in consequence of the present
troubles, may be rebels; but to call and treat them as pirates
is confounding not only the natural distinction of things, but
the order of crimes—which, whether by putting them from a
higher part of the scale to the lower or from the lower to the
higher, is never done without dangerously disordering the
whole frame of jurisprudence. Though piracy may be, in the
eye of the law, a *less* offence than treason, yet, as both are, in
effect, punished with the same death, the same forfeiture, and
the same corruption of blood, I never would take from any
fellow-creature whatever any sort of advantage which he may
derive to his safety from the pity of mankind, or to his reputation from their general feelings, by degrading his offence,
when I cannot soften his punishment. The general sense of
mankind tells me that those offences which may possibly arise
from mistaken virtue are not in the class of infamous actions.
Lord Coke, the oracle of the English law, conforms to that
general sense, where he says that "those things which are of
the highest criminality may be of the least disgrace." The act
prepares a sort of masked proceeding, not honorable to the
justice of the kingdom, and by no means necessary for its
safety. . . .

Besides, I must honestly tell you that I could not vote for,
or countenance in any way, a statute which stigmatizes with
the crime of piracy these men whom an act of Parliament
had previously put out of the protection of the law. When
the legislature of this kingdom had ordered all their ships and
goods, for the mere new-created offence of exercising trade,
to be divided as a spoil among the seamen of the navy—to consider the necessary reprisal of an unhappy, proscribed, inter-
dicted people, as the crime of piracy, would have appeared,
in any other legislature than ours, a strain of the most insulting and most unnatural cruelty and injustice. I assure you
I never remember to have heard of anything like it in any
time or country.

The second professed purpose of the act is to detain in

England for trial those who shall commit high treason in America.

That you may be enabled to enter into the true spirit of the present law, it is necessary, Gentlemen, to apprise you that there is an act, made so long ago as in the reign of Henry the Eighth, before the existence or thought of any English colonies in America, for the trial in this kingdom of treasons committed out of the realm. In the year 1769 Parliament thought proper to acquaint the crown with their construction of that act in a formal address, wherein they entreated his Majesty to cause persons charged with high treason in America to be brought into this kingdom for trial. By this act of Henry the Eighth, *so construed and so applied,* almost all that is substantial and beneficial in a trial by jury is taken away from the subject in the colonies. . . . To try a man under that act is, in effect, to condemn him unheard. A person is brought hither in the dungeon of a ship's hold; thence he is vomited into a dungeon on land, loaded with irons, unfurnished with money, unsupported by friends, three thousand miles from all means of calling upon or confronting evidence, where no one local circumstance that tends to detect perjury can possibly be judged of;—such a person may be executed according to form, but he can never be tried according to justice.

I therefore could never reconcile myself to the bill I send you, which is expressly provided to remove all inconveniences from the establishment of a mode of trial which has ever appeared to me most unjust and most unconstitutional. Far from removing the difficulties which impede the execution of so mischievous a project, I would heap new difficulties upon it, if it were in my power. All the ancient, honest, juridical principles and institutions of England are so many clogs to check and retard the headlong course of violence and oppression. They were invented for this one good purpose, that what was not just should not be convenient. Convinced of this, I would leave things as I found them. The old, cool-headed, general law is as good as any deviation dictated by present heat.

I could see no fair, justifiable expedience pleaded to favor this new suspension of the liberty of the subject. . . .

But it really appears to me that the means which this act employs are at least as exceptionable as the end. Permit me to open myself a little upon this subject; because it is of importance to me, when I am obliged to submit to the power without acquiescing in the reason of an act of legislature, that I should justify my dissent by such arguments as may be supposed to have weight with a sober man.

The main operative regulation of the act is to suspend the Common Law and the statute *Habeas Corpus* (the sole securities either for liberty or justice) with regard to all those who have been out of the realm, or on the high seas, within a given time. The rest of the people, as I understand, are to continue as they stood before.

I confess, Gentlemen, that this appears to me as bad in the principle, and far worse in its consequence, than an universal suspension of the *Habeas Corpus* Act; and the limiting qualification, instead of taking out the sting, does in my humble opinion sharpen and envenom it to a greater degree. Liberty, if I understand it at all, is a *general* principle, and the clear right of all the subjects within the realm, or of none. Partial freedom seems to me a most invidious mode of slavery. But, unfortunately, it is the kind of slavery the most easily admitted in times of civil discord: for parties are but too apt to forget their own future safety in their desire of sacrificing their enemies. People without much difficulty admit the entrance of that injustice of which they are not to be the immediate victims. In times of high proceeding it is never the faction of the predominant power that is in danger: for no tyranny chastises its own instruments. It is the obnoxious and the suspected who want the protection of law; and there is nothing to bridle the partial violence of state factions but this —"that, whenever an act is made for a cessation of law and justice, the whole people should be universally subjected to the same suspension of their franchises." The alarm of such a proceeding would then be universal. It would operate as a sort of *call of the nation*. It would become every man's immediate and instant concern to be made very sensible of *the absolute necessity* of this total eclipse of liberty. They would more carefully advert to every renewal, and more powerfully resist it. These great determined measures are not commonly so dangerous to freedom. They are marked with too strong lines to slide into use. No plea, nor pretence, of *inconvenience or evil example* (which must in their nature be daily and ordinary incidents) can be admitted as a reason for such mighty operations. But the true danger is when liberty is nibbled away, for expedients, and by parts. The *Habeas Corpus* Act supposes, contrary to the genius of most other laws, that the lawful magistrate may see particular men with a malignant eye, and it provides for that identical case. But when men, in particular descriptions, marked out by the magistrate himself, are delivered over by Parliament to this possible malignity, it is not the *Habeas Corpus* that is occasionally suspended, but its spirit that is mistaken, and its principle that is subverted. Indeed, nothing is security to any individual but the common interest of all.

This act, therefore, has this distinguished evil in it, that it is the first *partial* suspension of the *Habeas Corpus* that has been made. The precedent, which is always of very great importance, is now established. For the first time a distinction is made among the people within this realm. Before this act, every man putting his foot on English ground, every stranger owing only a local and temporary allegiance, even negro slaves who had been sold in the colonies and under an act of Parliament, became as free as every other man who breathed the same air with them. Now a line is drawn, which may be advanced further and further at pleasure, on the same argument of mere expedience on which it was first described. There is no equality among us; we are not fellow-citizens, if the mariner who lands on the quay does not rest on as firm legal ground as the merchant who sits in his counting-house. Other laws may injure the community; this dissolves it. As things now stand, every man in the West Indies, every one inhabitant of three unoffending provinces on the continent, every person coming from the East Indies, every gentleman who has travelled for his health or education, every mariner who has navigated the seas, is, for no other offence, under a temporary proscription. Let any of these facts (now become presumptions of guilt) be proved against him, and the bare suspicion of the crown puts him out of the law. It is even by no means clear to me whether the negative proof does not lie upon the person apprehended on suspicion, to the subversion of all justice. . . .

The act of which I speak is among the fruits of the American war—a war in my humble opinion productive of many mischiefs, of a kind which distinguish it from all others. Not only our policy is deranged, and our empire distracted, but our laws and our legislative spirit appear to have been totally perverted by it. We have made war on our colonies, not by arms only, but by laws. As hostility and law are not very concordant ideas, every step we have taken in this business has been made by trampling on some maxim of justice or some capital principle of wise government. What precedents were established, and what principles overturned, (I will not say of English privilege, but of general justice,) in the Boston Port, the Massachusetts Charter, the Military Bill, and all that long array of hostile acts of Parliament by which the war with America has been begun and supported! Had the principles of any of these acts been first exerted on English ground, they would probably have expired as soon as they touched it. But by being removed from our persons, they have rooted in our laws, and the latest posterity will taste the fruits of them.

Nor is it the worst effect of this unnatural contention, that our *laws* are corrupted. Whilst *manners* remain entire, they will correct the vices of law, and soften it at length to their own temper. But we have to lament that in most of the late proceedings we see very few traces of that generosity, humanity, and dignity of mind, which formerly characterized this nation. War suspends the rules of moral obligation, and what is long suspended is in danger of being totally abrogated. Civil wars strike deepest of all into the manners of the people. They vitiate their politics; they corrupt their morals; they pervert even the natural taste and relish of equity and justice. By teaching us to consider our fellow-citizens in an hostile light, the whole body of our nation becomes gradually less dear to us. The very names of affection and kindred, which were the bond of charity whilst we agreed, become new incentives to hatred and rage when the communion of our country is dissolved. We may flatter ourselves that we shall not fall into this misfortune. But we have no charter of exemption, that I know of, from the ordinary frailties of our nature.

What but that blindness of heart which arises from the frenzy of civil contention could have made any persons conceive the present situation of the British affairs as an object of triumph to themselves or of congratulation to their sovereign? Nothing surely could be more lamentable to those who remember the flourishing days of this kingdom than to see the insane joy of several unhappy people, amidst the sad spectacle which our affairs and conduct exhibit to the scorn of Europe. We behold (and it seems some people rejoice in beholding) our native land, which used to sit the envied arbiter of all her neighbors, reduced to a servile dependence on their mercy—acquiescing in assurances of friendship which she does not trust—complaining of hostilities which she dares not resent—deficient to her allies, lofty to her subjects, and submissive to her enemies—whilst the liberal government of this free nation is supported by the hireling sword of German boors and vassals, and three millions of the subjects of Great Britain are seeking for protection to English privileges in the arms of France!

These circumstances appear to me more like shocking prodigies than natural changes in human affairs. Men of firmer minds may see them without staggering or astonishment. Some may think them matters of congratulation and complimentary addresses; but I trust your candor will be so indulgent to my weakness as not to have the worse opinion of me for my declining to participate in this joy, and my rejecting all share whatsoever in such a triumph. I am too old, too stiff in my inveterate partialities, to be ready at all the fashionable evolutions of opinion. I scarcely know how to adapt my mind to the feelings with which the Court Gazettes mean to impress the people. It is not instantly that I can be brought to rejoice, when I hear of the slaughter and captivity of long lists of those names which have been familiar to my ears from my infancy, and to rejoice that they have fallen under the sword of strangers, whose barbarous appellations I scarcely know how to pronounce. The glory acquired at the White Plains by Colonel Rahl has no charms for me, and I fairly acknowledge that I have not yet learned to delight in finding Fort Kniphausen in the heart of the British dominions.

It might be some consolation for the loss of our old regards, if our reason were enlightened in proportion as our honest prejudices are removed. Wanting feelings for the honor of our country, we might then in cold blood be brought to think a little of our interests as individual citizens and our private conscience as moral agents.

Indeed, our affairs are in a bad condition. I do assure those gentlemen who have prayed for war, and obtained the blessing they have sought, that they are at this instant in very great straits. The abused wealth of this country continues a little longer to feed its distemper. As yet they, and their German allies of twenty hireling states, have contended only with the unprepared strength of our own infant colonies. But America is not subdued. Not one unattacked village which was originally adverse throughout that vast continent has yet submitted from love or terror. You have the ground you encamp on, and you have no more. The cantonments of your troops and your dominions are exactly of the same extent. You spread devastation, but you do not enlarge the sphere of authority.

The events of this war are of so much greater magnitude

than those who either wished or feared it ever looked for, that this alone ought to fill every considerate mind with anxiety and diffidence. Wise men often tremble at the very things which fill the thoughtless with security. . . .

The way still before you is intricate, dark, and full of perplexed and treacherous mazes. Those who think they have the clew may lead us out of this labyrinth. We may trust them as amply as we think proper; but as they have most certainly a call for all the reason which their stock can furnish, why should we think it proper to disturb its operation by inflaming their passions? . . . A conscientious man would be cautious how he dealt in blood. He would feel some apprehension at being called to a tremendous account for engaging in so deep a play without any sort of knowledge of the game. It is no excuse for presumptuous ignorance, that it is directed by insolent passion. The poorest being that crawls on earth, contending to save itself from injustice and oppression, is an object respectable in the eyes of God and man. . . .

I can well conceive a country completely overrun, and miserably wasted, without approaching in the least to settlement. In my apprehension, as long as English government is attempted to be supported over Englishmen by the sword alone, things will thus continue. I anticipate in my mind the moment of the final triumph of foreign military force. When that hour arrives, (for it may arrive,) then it is that all this mass of weakness and violence will appear in its full light. If we should be expelled from America, the delusion of the partisans of military government might still continue. They might still feed their imaginations with the possible good consequences which might have attended success. Nobody could prove the contrary by facts. But in case the sword should do all that the sword can do, the success of their arms and the defeat of their policy will be one and the same thing. You will never see any revenue from America. Some increase of the means of corruption, without ease of the public burdens, is the very best that can happen. Is it for this that we are at war—and in such a war?

As to the difficulties of laying once more the foundations of that government which, for the sake of conquering what was our own, has been voluntarily and wantonly pulled down by a court faction here, I tremble to look at them. Has any of these gentlemen who are so eager to govern all mankind shown himself possessed of the first qualification towards government, some knowledge of the object, and of the difficulties which occur in the task they have undertaken?

I assure you, that, on the most prosperous issue of your arms, you will not be where you stood when you called in war to supply the defects of your political establishment. Nor would any disorder or disobedience to government which could arise from the most abject concession on our part ever equal those which will be felt after the most triumphant violence. You have got all the intermediate evils of war into the bargain.

I think I know America—if I do not, my ignorance is incurable, for I have spared no pains to understand it—and I do most solemnly assure those of my constituents who put any sort of confidence in my industry and integrity, that everything that has been done there has arisen from a total misconception of the object: that our means of originally holding America, that our means of reconciling with it after quarrel, of recovering it after separation, of keeping it after victory, did depend, and must depend, in their several stages and periods, upon a total renunciation of that unconditional submission which has taken such possession of the minds of violent men. The whole of those maxims upon which we have made and continued this war must be abandoned. Nothing, indeed, (for I would not deceive you,) can place us in our former situation. That hope must be laid aside. But there is a difference between bad and the worst of all. Terms relative to the cause of the war ought to be offered by the authority of Parliament. An arrangement at home promising some security for them ought to be made. By doing this, without the least impairing of our strength, we add to the credit of our moderation, which, in itself, is always strength more or less.

I know many have been taught to think that moderation in a case like this is a sort of treason—and that all arguments for it are sufficiently answered by railing at rebels and rebellion, and by charging all the present or future miseries which we may suffer on the resistance of our brethren. But I would wish them, in this grave matter, and if peace is not wholly removed from their hearts, to consider seriously, first, that to criminate and recriminate never yet was the road to reconciliation, in any difference amongst men. In the next place, it would be right to reflect that the American English (whom they may abuse, if they think it honorable to revile the absent) can, as things now stand, neither be provoked at our railing or bettered by our instruction. All communication is cut off between us. But this we know with certainty, that, though we cannot reclaim them, we may reform ourselves. If measures of peace are necessary, they must begin somewhere; and a conciliatory temper must precede and prepare every plan of reconciliation. Nor do I conceive that we suffer anything by thus regulating our own minds. We are not disarmed by being disencumbered of our passions. Declaiming on rebellion never added a bayonet or a charge of powder to your military force; but I am afraid that it has been the means of taking up many muskets against you. . . .

I know it is said, that your kindness is only alienated on account of their resistance, and therefore, if the colonies surrender at discretion, all sort of regard, and even much indulgence, is meant towards them in future. But can those who are partisans for continuing a war to enforce such a surrender be responsible (after all that has passed) for such a future use of a power that is bound by no compacts and restrained by no terror? Will they tell us what they call indulgences? Do they not at this instant call the present war and all its horrors a lenient and merciful proceeding?

No conqueror that I ever heard of has *professed* to make a cruel, harsh, and insolent use of his conquest. No! The man of the most declared pride scarcely dares to trust his own heart with this dreadful secret of ambition. But it will appear in its time; and no man who professes to reduce another to the insolent mercy of a foreign arm ever had any sort of goodwill towards him. . . .

When any community is subordinately connected with another, the great danger of the connection is the extreme pride and self-complacency of the superior, which in all matters of controversy will probably decide in its own favor. It is a powerful corrective to such a very rational cause of fear, if the inferior body can be made to believe that the party inclination or political views of several in the principal state will induce them in some degree to counteract this blind and tyrannical partiality. There is no danger that any one acquiring consideration or power in the presiding state should carry this leaning to the inferior too far. The fault of human nature is not of that sort. Power, in whatever hands, is rarely guilty of too strict limitations on itself. . . .

If the colonies . . . could see that in Great Britain the mass of the people is melted into its government, and that every dispute with the ministry must of necessity be always a quarrel with the nation, they can stand no longer in the equal and friendly relation of fellow-citizens to the subjects of this kingdom. Humble as this relation may appear to some, when it is once broken, a strong tie is dissolved. Other sort of connections will be sought. For there are very few in the world who will not prefer an useful ally to an insolent master.

Such discord has been the effect of the unanimity into which so many have of late been seduced or bullied, or into the appearance of which they have sunk through mere despair. They have been told that their dissent from violent measures is an encouragement to rebellion. Men of great presumption and little knowledge will hold a language which is contradicted by the whole course of history. *General* rebellions and revolts of an whole people never were *encouraged,* now or at any time. They are always *provoked.* . . . Does anybody seriously maintain, that, charged with my share of the public councils, I am obliged not to resist projects which I think mischievous, lest men who suffer should be encouraged to resist? The very tendency of such projects to produce rebellion is one of the chief reasons against them. Shall that reason not be given? Is it, then, a rule, that no man in this nation shall open his mouth in favor of the colonies, shall defend their rights, or complain of their sufferings—or when war finally breaks out, no man shall express his desires of peace? . . .

I have always wished, that as the dispute had its apparent origin from things done in Parliament, and as the acts passed there had provoked the war, that the foundations of peace should be laid in Parliament also. I have been astonished to find that those whose zeal for the dignity of our body was so hot as to light up the flames of civil war should even publicly declare that these delicate points ought to be wholly left to the crown. Poorly as I may be thought affected to the authority of Parliament, I shall never admit that our constitutional rights can ever become a matter of ministerial negotiation.

I am charged with being an American. If warm affection towards those over whom I claim any share of authority be a crime, I am guilty of this charge. But I do assure you, (and they who know me publicly and privately will bear witness to me,) that, if ever one man lived more zealous than another for the supremacy of Parliament and the rights of this imperial crown, it was myself. Many others, indeed, might be more knowing in the extent of the foundation of these rights. I do not pretend to be an antiquary, a lawyer, or qualified for the chair of professor in metaphysics. I never ventured to put your solid interests upon speculative grounds. My having constantly declined to do so has been attributed to my incapacity for such disquisitions; and I am inclined to believe it is partly the cause. I never shall be ashamed to confess, that, where I am ignorant, I am diffident. I am, indeed, not very solicitous to clear myself of this imputed incapacity; because men even less conversant than I am in this kind of subtleties, and placed in stations to which I ought not to aspire, have, by the mere force of civil discretion, often conducted the affairs of great nations with distinguished felicity and glory.

When I first came into a public trust, I found your Parliament in possession of an unlimited legislative power over the colonies. I could not open the statute-book without seeing the actual exercise of it, more or less, in all cases whatsoever. This possession passed with me for a title. It does so in all human affairs. No man examines into the defects of his title to his paternal estate or to his established government. Indeed, common sense taught me that a legislative authority not actually limited by the express terms of its foundation, or by its own subsequent acts, cannot have its powers parcelled out by argumentative distinctions, so as to enable us to say that here they can and there they cannot bind. . . .

I had, indeed, very earnest wishes to keep the whole body of this authority perfect and entire as I found it—and to keep it so, not for our advantage solely, but principally for the sake of those on whose account all just authority exists: I mean the people to be governed. For I thought I saw that many cases might well happen in which the exercise of every power comprehended in the broadest idea of legislature might become, in its time and circumstances, not a little expedient for the peace and union of the colonies amongst themselves, as well as for their perfect harmony with Great Britain. Thinking so, . . . I was at the same time very sure that the authority of which I was so jealous could not, under the actual circumstances of our plantations, be at all preserved in any of its members, but by the greatest reserve in its application, particularly in those delicate points in which the feelings of mankind are the most irritable. They who thought otherwise have found a few more difficulties in their work than (I hope) they were thoroughly aware of, when they undertook the present business. I must beg leave to observe, that it is not only the invidious branch of taxation that will be resisted, but that no other given part of legislative rights can be exercised, without regard to the general opinion of those who are to be governed. That general opinion is the vehicle and organ of legislative omnipotence. Without this, it may be a theory to entertain the mind, but it is nothing in the direction of affairs. The completeness of the legislative authority of Parliament *over this kingdom* is not questioned; and yet many things indubitably included in the abstract idea of that power, and which carry no absolute injustice in themselves, yet being contrary to the opinions and feelings of the people, can as little be exercised as if Parliament in that case had been possessed of no right at all. I see no abstract reason, which can be given, why the same power which made and repealed the High Commission Court and the Star-Chamber might not revive them again; and these courts, warned by their former fate, might possibly exercise their powers with some degree of justice. But the madness would be as unquestionable as the competence of that Parliament which should attempt such things. If anything can be supposed out of the power of human legislature, it is religion; I admit, however, that the established religion of this country has been three or four times altered by act of Parliament, and therefore that a statute binds even in that case. But we may very safely affirm, that, notwithstanding this apparent omnipotence, it would be now found as impossible for King and Parliament to alter the established religion of this country as it was to King James alone, when he attempted to make such an alteration without a Parliament. In effect, to follow, not to force, the public inclination—to give a direction, a form, a technical dress, and a specific sanction, to the general sense of the community, is the true end of legislature.

It is so with regard to the exercise of all the powers which our Constitution knows in any of its parts, and indeed to the substantial existence of any of the parts themselves. The king's negative to bills is one of the most indisputed of the royal prerogatives; and it extends to all cases whatsoever. I am far from certain, that if several laws, which I know, had fallen under the stroke of that sceptre, that the public would have had a very heavy loss. But it is not the *propriety* of the exercise which is in question. The exercise itself is wisely forborne. Its repose may be the preservation of its existence; and its existence may be the means of saving the Constitution itself, on an occasion worthy of bringing it forth.

As the disputants whose accurate and logical reasonings have brought us into our present condition think it absurd that powers or members of any constitution should exist, rarely, if ever, to be exercised, I hope I shall be excused in mentioning another instance that is material. We know that the Convocation of the Clergy had formerly been called, and sat with nearly as much regularity to business as Parliament itself. It is now called for form only. It sits for the purpose of making some polite ecclesiastical compliments to the king, and, when that grace is said, retires and is heard of no more. It is, however, *a part of the Constitution,* and may be called out into act and energy, whenever there is occasion, and whenever those who conjure up that spirit will choose to abide the consequences. It is wise to permit its legal existence: it is much wiser to continue it a legal existence only. So truly has prudence (constituted as the god of this lower world) the entire dominion over every exercise of power committed into its hands! And yet I have lived to see prudence and conformity to circumstances wholly set at nought in our late controversies, and treated as if they were the most contemptible and irrational of all things. I have heard it an hundred times very gravely alleged, that, in order to keep power in mind, it was necessary, by preference, to exert it in those very points in which it was most likely to be resisted and the least likely to be productive of any advantage.

These were the considerations, Gentlemen, which led me early to think, that, in the comprehensive dominion which the Divine Providence had put into our hands, instead of troubling our understandings with speculations concerning the unity of empire and the identity or distinction of legislative powers, and inflaming our passions with the heat and pride of controversy, it was our duty, in all soberness, to conform our government to the character and circumstances of the several people who composed this mighty and strangely diversified mass. I never was wild enough to conceive that one method would serve for the whole, that the natives of Hindostan and those of Virginia could be ordered in the same manner, or that the Cutchery court and the grand jury of Salem could be regulated on a similar plan. I was persuaded that government was a practical thing, made for the happiness of mankind, and not to furnish out a spectacle of uniformity to gratify the schemes of visionary politicians. Our business was to rule, not to wrangle; and it would have been a poor compensation that we had triumphed in a dispute, whilst we lost an empire.

If there be one fact in the world perfectly clear, it is this—"that the disposition of the people of America is wholly averse to any other than a free government"; and this is indication enough to any honest statesman how he ought to adapt whatever power he finds in his hands to their case. If any ask me what a free government is, I answer, that, for any practical purpose, it is what the people think so—and that they, and not I, are the natural, lawful, and competent judges of this matter. If they practically allow me a greater degree of authority over them than is consistent with any correct ideas of perfect freedom, I ought to thank them for so great a trust, and not to endeavor to prove from thence that they have reasoned amiss, and that, having gone so far, by analogy they must hereafter have no enjoyment but by my pleasure.

If we had seen this done by any others, we should have concluded them far gone in madness. It is melancholy, as well as ridiculous, to observe the kind of reasoning with which the public has been amused, in order to divert our minds from the common sense of our American policy. There are people who have split and anatomized the doctrine of free government, as if it were an abstract question concerning metaphysical liberty and necessity, and not a matter of moral prudence and natural feeling. They have disputed whether liberty be a positive or a negative idea; whether it does not consist in being governed by laws, without considering what are the laws, or who are the makers; whether man has any rights by Nature; and whether all the property he enjoys be not the alms of his government, and his life itself their favor and indulgence. Others, corrupting religion as these have perverted philosophy, contend that Christians are redeemed into captivity, and the blood of the Saviour of mankind has been shed to make them the slaves of a few proud and insolent sinners. These shocking extremes provoking to extremes of another kind, speculations are let loose as destructive to all authority as the former are to all freedom; and every government is called tyranny and usurpation which is not formed on their fancies. In this manner the stirrers-up of this contention, not satisfied with distracting our dependencies and filling them with blood and slaughter, are corrupting our understandings: they are endeavoring to tear up, along with practical liberty, all the foundations of human society, all equity and justice, religion and order.

Civil freedom, Gentlemen, is not, as many have endeavored to persuade you, a thing that lies hid in the depth of abstruse science. It is a blessing and a benefit, not an abstract speculation; and all the just reasoning that can be upon it is of so coarse a texture as perfectly to suit the ordinary capacities of those who are to enjoy, and of those who are to defend it. Far from any resemblance to those propositions in geometry and metaphysics which admit no medium, but must be true or false in all their latitude, social and civil freedom, like all other things in common life, are variously mixed and modified, enjoyed in very different degrees, and shaped into an infinite diversity of forms, according to the temper and circumstances of every community. The *extreme* of liberty (which is its abstract perfection, but its real fault) contains nowhere, nor ought to obtain anywhere; because extremes, as we all know, in every point which relates either to our duties or satisfactions in life, are destructive both to virtue and enjoyment. Liberty, too, must be limited in order to be possessed. The degree of restraint it is impossible in any case to settle precisely. But it ought to be the constant aim of every wise public counsel to find out by cautious experiments, and rational, cool endeavors, with how little, not how much, of this restraint the community can subsist: for liberty is a good to be improved, and not an evil to be lessened. It is not only a private blessing of the first order, but the vital spring and energy of the state itself, which has just so much life and vigor as there is liberty in it. But whether liberty be advantageous or not, (for I know it is a fashion to decry the very principle,) none will dispute that peace is a blessing; and peace must, in the course of human affairs, be frequently bought by some indulgence and toleration at least to liberty: for, as the Sabbath (though of divine institution) was made for man, not man for the Sabbath, government, which can claim no higher origin or authority, in its exercise at least, ought to conform to the exigencies of the time, and the temper and character of the people with whom it is concerned, and not always to attempt violently to bend the people to their theories of subjection. The bulk of mankind, on their part, are not excessively curious concerning any theories whilst they are really happy; and one sure symptom of an ill-conducted state is the propensity of the people to resort to them.

But when subjects, by a long course of such ill conduct, are once thoroughly inflamed, and the state itself violently distempered, the people must have some satisfaction to their feelings more solid than a sophistical speculation on law and government. Such was our situation: and such a satisfaction was necessary to prevent recourse to arms; it was necessary towards laying them down; it will be necessary to prevent the taking them up again and again. Of what nature this satisfaction ought to be I wish it had been the disposition of Parliament seriously to consider. It was certainly a deliberation that called for the exertion of all their wisdom.

I am, and ever have been, deeply sensible of the difficulty of reconciling the strong presiding power, that is so useful towards the conservation of a vast, disconnected, infinitely diversified empire, with that liberty and safety of the provinces which they must enjoy, (in opinion and practice at least,) or they will not be provinces at all. I know, and have long felt, the difficulty of reconciling the unwieldy haughtiness of a great ruling nation, habituated to command, pampered by enormous wealth, and confident from a long course of prosperity and victory, to the high spirit of free dependencies, animated with the first glow and activity of juvenile heat, and assuming to themselves, as their birthright, some part of that very pride which oppresses them. They who perceive no difficulty in reconciling these tempers (which, however, to make peace, must some way or other be reconciled) are much above my capacity, or much below the magnitude of the business. Of one thing I am perfectly clear: that it is not by deciding the suit, but by compromising the difference, that peace can be restored or kept. They who would put an end to such quarrels by declaring roundly in favor of the whole demands of either party have mistaken, in my humble opinion, the office of a mediator.

The war is now of full two years' standing: the controversy of many more. In different periods of the dispute, different methods of reconciliation were to be pursued. I mean to trouble you with a short state of things at the most important of these periods, in order to give you a more distinct idea of our policy with regard to this most delicate of all objects. The colonies were from the beginning subject to the legislature of Great Britain on principles which they never examined; and we permitted to them many local privileges, without asking how they agreed with that legislative authority. Modes of administration were formed in an insensible and very unsystematic manner. But they gradually adapted themselves to the varying condition of things. What was first a single kingdom stretched into an empire; and an imperial superintendency, of some kind or other, became necessary. Parliament, from a mere representative of the people, and a guardian of popular privileges for its own immediate constituents, grew into a mighty sovereign. Instead of being a control on the crown on its own behalf, it communicated a sort of strength to the royal authority, which was wanted for the conservation of a new object, but which could not be safely trusted to the crown alone. On the other hand, the colonies, advancing by equal steps, and governed by the same necessity, had formed within themselves, either by royal instruction or royal charter, assemblies so exceedingly resembling a parliament, in all their forms, functions, and powers, that it was impossible they should not imbibe some opinion of a similar authority.

At the first designation of these assemblies, they were probably not intended for anything more (nor perhaps did they think themselves much higher) than the municipal corporations within this island, to which some at present love to compare them. But nothing in progression can rest on its original plan. We may as well think of rocking a grown man in the cradle of an infant. Therefore, as the colonies prospered and increased to a numerous and mighty people, spreading over a very great tract of the globe, it was natural that they should attribute to assemblies so respectable in their formal constitution some part of the dignity of the great nations which they represented. No longer tied to by-laws, these assemblies made acts of all sorts and in all cases whatsoever. They levied money, not for parochial purposes, but upon regular grants to the crown, following all the rules and principles of a parliament, to which they approached every day more and more nearly. Those who think themselves wiser than Providence and stronger than the course of Nature may complain of all this variation, on the one side or the other, as their several humors and prejudices may lead them. But things could not be otherwise; and English colonies must be had on these terms, or not had at all. In the mean time neither party felt any inconvenience from this double legislature, to which they had been formed by imperceptible habits, and old custom, the great support of all the governments in the world. Though these two legislatures were sometimes found perhaps performing the very same functions, they did not very grossly or systematically clash. In all likelihood this arose from mere neglect, possibly from the natural operation of things, which, left to themselves, generally fall into their proper order. But whatever was the cause, it is certain that a regular revenue, by the authority of Parliament, for the support of civil and military establishments, seems not to have been thought of until the colonies were too proud to submit, too strong to be forced, too enlightened not to see all the consequences which must arise from such a system.

If ever this scheme of taxation was to be pushed against the inclinations of the people, it was evident that discussions must arise, which would let loose all the elements that composed this double constitution, would show how much each of their members had departed from its original principles, and would discover contradictions in each legislature, as well to its own first principles as to its relation to the other, very difficult, if not absolutely impossible, to be reconciled.

Therefore, at the first fatal opening of this contest, the wisest course seemed to be to put an end as soon as possible to the immediate causes of the dispute, and to quiet a discussion, not easily settled upon clear principles, and arising from claims which pride would permit neither party to abandon, by resorting as nearly as possible to the old, successful course. A mere repeal of the obnoxious tax, with a declaration of the legislative authority of this kingdom, was then fully sufficient to procure peace to *both sides*. Man is a creature of habit, and, the first breach being of very short continuance, the colonies fell back exactly into their ancient state. The Congress has used an expression with regard to this pacification which appears to me truly significant. After the repeal of the Stamp Act, "the colonies fell," says this assembly, "into their ancient state of *unsuspecting confidence in the mother country*." This unsuspecting confidence is the true centre of gravity amongst mankind, about which all the parts are at rest. It is this *unsuspecting confidence* that removes all difficulties, and reconciles all the contradictions which occur in the complexity of all ancient puzzled political establishments. Happy are the rulers which have the secret of preserving it! . . .

I hope there are none of you corrupted with the doctrine taught by wicked men for the worst purposes, and received by the malignant credulity of envy and ignorance, which is, that the men who act upon the public stage are all alike, all equally corrupt, all influenced by no other views than the sordid lure of salary and pension. The thing I know by experience to be false. Never expecting to find perfection in men, and not looking for divine attributes in created beings, in my commerce with my contemporaries I have found much human virtue. . . . They who raise suspicions on the good on account of the behavior of ill men are of the party of the latter. . . . A conscientious person would rather doubt his own judgment than condemn his species. . . . I should much rather admit those whom at any time I have disrelished the most to be patterns of perfection than seek a consolation to my own unworthiness in a general communion of depravity with all about me.

That this ill-natured doctrine should be preached by the missionaries of a court I do not wonder. It answers their purpose. But that it should be heard among those who pretend to be strong assertors of liberty is not only surprising, but hardly natural. This moral levelling is a *servile principle*. It leads to practical passive obedience far better than all the doctrines which the pliant accommodation of theology to power has ever produced. It cuts up by the roots, not only all idea of forcible resistance, but even of civil opposition. It disposes men to an abject submission, not by opinion, which may be shaken by argument or altered by passion, but by the strong ties of public and private interest. For, if all men who act in a public situation are equally selfish, corrupt, and venal, what reason can be given for desiring any sort of change, which, besides the evils which must attend all changes, can be productive of no possible advantage? The active men in the state are true samples of the mass. If they are universally depraved, the commonwealth itself is not sound. We may amuse ourselves with talking as much as we please of the virtue of middle or humble life; that is, we may place our confidence in the virtue of those who have never been tried. But if the persons who are continually emerging out of that sphere be no better than those whom birth has placed above it, what hopes are there in the remainder of the body which is to furnish the perpetual succession of the state? All who have ever written on government are unanimous, that among a people generally corrupt liberty cannot long exist. . . .

I am aware that the age is not what we all wish. But I am sure that the only means of checking its precipitate degeneracy is heartily to concur with whatever is the best in our time . . .

This, Gentlemen, has been from the beginning the rule of my conduct; and I mean to continue it, as long as such a body as I have described can by any possibility be kept together; for I should think it the most dreadful of all offences, not only towards the present generation, but to all the future, if I were to do anything which could make the minutest breach in this great conservatory of free principles. . . .

Liberty is in danger of being made unpopular to Englishmen. Contending for an imaginary power, we begin to acquire the spirit of domination, and to lose the relish of honest equality. The principles of our forefathers become suspected to us, because we see them animating the present opposition of our children. The faults which grow out of the luxuriance of freedom appear much more shocking to us than the base vices which are generated from the rankness of servitude. Accordingly, the least resistance to power appears more inexcusable in our eyes than the greatest abuses of authority. All dread of a standing military force is looked upon as a superstitious panic. All shame of calling in foreigners and savages in a civil contest is worn off. We grow indifferent to the consequences inevitable to ourselves from the plan of ruling half the empire by a mercenary sword. We are taught to believe that a desire of domineering over our countrymen is love to our country, that those who hate civil war abet rebellion, and that the amiable and conciliatory virtues of lenity, moderation, and tenderness to the privileges of those who depend on this kingdom are a sort of treason to the state.

It is impossible that we should remain long in a situation which breeds such notions and dispositions without some great alteration in the national character. Those ingenuous and feeling minds who are so fortified against all other things, and so unarmed to whatever approaches in the shape of disgrace, finding these principles, which they considered as sure means of honor, to be grown into disrepute, will retire disheartened and disgusted. Those of a more robust make, the bold, able, ambitious men, who pay some of their court to power through the people, and substitute the voice of transient opinion in the place of true glory, will give into the general mode; and those superior understandings which ought to correct vulgar prejudice will confirm and aggravate its errors. Many things have been long operating towards a gradual change in our principles; but this American war has done more in a very few years than all the other causes could have effected in a century. It is therefore not on its own separate account, but because of its attendant circumstances, that I consider its continuance, or its ending in any way but that of an honorable and liberal accommodation, as the greatest evils which can befall us. . . . Let us not be amongst the first who renounce the maxims of our forefathers. . . .

III

IRELAND AND CATHOLIC EMANCIPATION

*Fragments of a Tract
Relative to
the Laws against Popery
in Ireland*
[1765]

John Morley has written perhaps the best summary of the
historical origins of the penal laws against Irish Catholics,
and of their effect upon Ireland during the eighteenth century:
"After the suppression of the great rebellion of Tyrconnel by
William of Orange, nearly the whole of the land was confiscated, the peasants were made beggars and outlaws, the
Penal Laws against the Catholics were enacted and enforced,
and the grand reign of Protestant Ascendancy began in all its
vileness and completeness. The Protestants and landlords
were supreme; the peasants and the Catholics were prostrate
in despair. The Revolution brought about in Ireland just the
reverse of what it effected in England. Here it delivered the
body of the nation from the attempted supremacy of a small
sect. There it made a small sect supreme over the body of the
nation." Burke's writings on Irish affairs, and especially his
Tract on the Popery Laws, are a detailed elaboration of what
Morley has here summarized.

As Burke was well aware, the "popery laws" had two general purposes: to persecute Catholics for adhering to their religion, and to reduce them to extreme poverty and ignorance by
proscribing them from the social rights and political benefits
of the British constitution. In the first section of his *Tract on
the Popery Laws,* he described how particular statutes prohibited the rights of inheritance; encouraged children "to revolt against their parents" by going to court to secure their
estate; gave wives who became Protestants power over the
children and property of their Catholic husbands; and excluded
Catholics from all the professions. He also noted that the
penal laws prevented Catholics from attending schools, or establishing their own, or even from sending their children
abroad to be educated. These laws even extended to the keeping of arms for "the right of self-defence," which Burke called
"one of the rights by the law of Nature." He noted: "In order
to enforce this regulation, the whole spirit of the Common

Law is changed, very severe penalties are enjoined, the largest powers are vested in the lowest magistrates." The whole system of the penal laws was fed by "informers," who received a share of the fines levied or of property confiscated. In addition, many of the Catholic clergy were "banished the kingdom," and "should they return from exile" they were "to be hanged, drawn, and quartered." All of these unjust statutes, Burke insisted, violated the natural and civil rights of Catholics, and kept Ireland in a perpetual state of unrest.

In the second part of his *Tract on the Popery Laws,* which follows, Burke turned to the larger questions of the nature and purpose of law, government, and civil society. Here he examined not the particular provisions and evil effects of the penal laws, but the legal and moral implications of their principles. Here, for the first time in his political writings, Burke set forth his belief in the Natural Law as the basis of a just and free social order.

. . . The reader has now before him a tolerably complete view of the Popery laws relative to property by descent or acquisition, to education, to defence, and to the free exercise of religion, which may be necessary to enable him to form some judgment of the spirit of the whole system, and of the subsequent reflections that are to be made upon it.

The system which we have just reviewed, and the manner in which religious influence on the public is made to operate upon the laws concerning property in Ireland, is in its nature very singular, and differs, I apprehend, essentially, and perhaps to its disadvantage, from any scheme of religious persecution now existing in any other country in Europe, or which has prevailed in any time or nation with which history has made us acquainted. I believe it will not be difficult to show that it is unjust, impolitic, and inefficacious; that it has the most unhappy influence on the prosperity, the morals, and the safety of that country; that this influence is not accidental, but has flowed as the necessary and direct consequence of the laws themselves, first on account of the object which they affect, and next by the quality of the greatest part of the instruments they employ. . . .

The first and most capital consideration with regard to this, as to every object, is the extent of it. And here it is necessary to premise, this system of penalty and incapacity has for its object no small sect or obscure party, but a very numerous body of men—a body which comprehends at least two thirds of that whole nation: it amounts to 2,800,000 souls, a number sufficient for the materials constituent of a great people. . . .

This consideration of the magnitude of the object ought to attend us through the whole inquiry: if it does not always affect the reason, it is always decisive on the importance of the question. It not only makes in itself a more leading point, but complicates itself with every other part of the matter, giving every error, minute in itself, a character and significance from its application. . . .

In the making of a new law it is undoubtedly the duty of the legislator to see that no injustice be done even to an individual: for there is then nothing to be unsettled, and the matter is under his hands to mould it as he pleases; and if he finds it untractable in the working, he may abandon it without incurring any new inconvenience. But in the question concerning the repeal of an old one, the work is of more difficulty; because laws, like houses, lean on one another, and the operation is delicate, and should be necessary: the objection, in such a case, ought not to arise from the natural infirmity of human institutions, but from substantial faults which contradict the nature and end of law itself—faults not arising from the imperfection, but from the misapplication and abuse of our reason. As no legislators can regard the *minima* of equity, a law may in some instances be a just subject of censure without being at all an object of repeal. But if its transgressions against common right and the ends of just government should be considerable in their nature and spreading in their effects, as this objection goes to the root and principle of the law, it renders it void in its obligatory quality on the mind, and therefore determines it as the proper object of abrogation and repeal, so far as regards its civil existence. The objection here is, as we observed, by no means on account of the imperfection of the law; it is on account of its erroneous principle: for if this be fundamentally wrong, the more perfect the law is made, the worse it becomes. It cannot be said to have the properties of genuine law, even in its imperfections and defects. The true weakness and opprobrium of our best general constitutions is, that they cannot provide beneficially for every particular case, and thus fill, adequately to their intentions, the circle of universal justice. But where the principle is faulty, the erroneous part of the law is the beneficial, and justice only finds refuge in those holes and corners which had escaped the sagacity and inquisition of the legislator. The happiness or misery of multitudes can never be a thing indifferent. A law against the majority of the people is in substance a law against the people itself; its extent determines its invalidity; it even changes its character as it enlarges its operation: it is not particular injustice, but general oppression; and can no longer be considered as a private hardship, which might be borne, but spreads and grows up into the unfortunate importance of a national calamity.

Now as a law directed against the mass of the nation has not the nature of a reasonable institution, so neither has it the authority: for in all forms of government the people is the true legislator; and whether the immediate and instrumental cause of the law be a single person or many, the remote and efficient cause is the consent of the people, either actual or implied; and such consent is absolutely essential to its validity. To the solid establishment of every law two things are essentially requisite: first, a proper and sufficient human power to declare and modify the matter of the law; and next, such a fit and equitable constitution as they have a right to declare and render binding. With regard to the first requisite, the human authority, it is their judgment they give up, not their right. The people, indeed, are presumed to consent to whatever the legislature ordains for their benefit; and they are to acquiesce in it, though they do not clearly see into the propriety of the means by which they are conducted to that desirable end. This they owe as an act of homage and just deference to a reason which the necessity of government has made superior to their own. But though the means, and indeed the nature, of a public advantage may not always be evident to the understanding of the subject, no one is so gross and stupid as not to distinguish between a benefit and an injury. No one can imagine, then, an exclusion of a great body of men, not from favors, privileges, and trusts, but from the common advantages of society, can ever be a thing intended for their good, or can ever be ratified by any implied consent of theirs. If, therefore, at least an implied human consent is necessary to the existence of a law, such a constitution cannot in propriety be a law at all.

But if we could suppose that such a ratification was made, not virtually, but actually, by the people, not representatively, but even collectively, still it would be null and void. They have no right to make a law prejudicial to the whole community, even though the delinquents in making such an act should be themselves the chief sufferers by it; because it would be made against the principle of a superior law, which it is not in the power of any community, or of the whole race of man, to alter—I mean the will of Him who gave us our nature, and in giving impressed an invariable law upon it. It would be hard to point out any error more truly subversive of all the order and beauty, of all the peace and happiness of human society, than the position, that any body of men have a right to make what laws they please—or that laws can derive any authority from their institution merely, and independent of the quality of the subject-matter. No arguments of policy, reason of state, or preservation of the constitution can be pleaded in favor of such a practice. They may, indeed, impeach the frame of that constitution, but can never touch this immovable principle. This seems to be, indeed, the doctrine which Hobbes broached in the last century, and which was then so frequently and so ably refuted. Cicero exclaims with the utmost indignation and contempt against such a notion: he considers it not only as unworthy of a philosopher, but of an illiterate peasant; that of all things this was the most truly absurd, to fancy that the rule of justice was to be taken from the constitutions of commonwealths, or that laws derived their authority from the statutes of the people, the edicts of princes, or the decrees of judges. If it be admitted that it is not the black-letter and the king's arms that makes the law, we are to look for it elsewhere.

In reality there are two, and only two, foundations of law; and they are both of them conditions without which nothing can give it any force: I mean equity and utility. With respect to the former, it grows out of the great rule of equality, which is grounded upon our common nature, and which Philo, with propriety and beauty, calls the mother of justice. All human laws are, properly speaking, only declaratory; they may alter the mode and application, but have no power over the substance of original justice. The other foundation of law, which is utility, must be understood, not of partial or limited, but of general and public utility, connected in the same manner with, and derived directly from, our rational nature: for any other utility may be the utility of a robber, but cannot be that of a citizen—the interest of the domestic enemy, and not that of a member of the commonwealth. This present equality can never be the foundation of statutes which create an artificial difference between men, as the laws before us do, in order to induce a consequential inequality in the distribution of justice. Law is a mode of human action respecting society, and must be governed by the same rules of equity which govern every private action; and so Tully considers it in his Offices as the only utility agreeable to that nature. . . .

If any proposition can be clear in itself, it is this: that a law which shuts out from all secure and valuable property the bulk of the people cannot be made for the utility of the party so excluded. This, therefore, is not the utility which Tully mentions. But if it were true (as it is not) that the real interest of any part of the community could be separated from the happiness of the rest, still it would afford no just foundation for a statute providing exclusively for that interest at the expense of the other; because it would be repugnant to the essence of law, which requires that it be made as much as possible for the benefit of the whole. If this principle be denied or evaded, what ground have we left to reason on? We must at once make a total change in all our ideas, and look for a new definition of law. Where to find it I confess myself at a loss. If we resort to the fountains of jurisprudence, they will not supply us with any that is for our purpose. . . .

It would be far more easy to heap up authorities on this article than to excuse the prolixity and tediousness of producing any at all in proof of a point which, though too often practically denied, is in its theory almost self-evident. For Suarez, handling this very question . . . does not hesitate a moment, finding no ground in reason or authority to render the affirmative in the least degree disputable. . . .

Partiality and law are contradictory terms. Neither the merits nor the ill deserts, neither the wealth and importance nor the indigence and obscurity, of the one part or of the other, can make any alteration in this fundamental truth. On any other scheme, I defy any man living to settle a correct standard which may discriminate between equitable rule and the most direct tyranny. For if we can once prevail upon ourselves to depart from the strictness and integrity of this principle in favor even of a considerable party, the argument will hold for one that is less so; and thus we shall go on, narrowing the bottom of public right, until step by step we arrive, though after no very long or very forced deduction, at what one of our poets calls the *enormous faith*—the faith of the many, created for the advantage of a single person.* I cannot see a glimmering of distinction to evade it; nor is it possible to al-

---

* Who first taught souls enslaved, and realms undone,
 Th' enormous faith of many made for one?
  Pope, *An Essay on Man*, Epistle III

lege any reason for the proscription of so large a part of the kingdom, which would not hold equally to support, under parallel circumstances, the proscription of the whole.

I am sensible that these principles, in their abstract light, will not be very strenuously opposed. Reason is never inconvenient, but when it comes to be applied. Mere general truths interfere very little with the passions. They can, until they are roused by a troublesome application, rest in great tranquillity, side by side with tempers and proceedings the most directly opposite to them. Men want to be reminded, who do not want to be taught; because those original ideas of rectitude, to which the mind is compelled to assent when they are proposed, are not always as present to it as they ought to be. When people are gone, if not into a denial, at least into a sort of oblivion of those ideas, when they know them only as barren speculations, and not as practical motives for conduct, it will be proper to press, as well as to offer them to the understanding; and when one is attacked by prejudices which aim to intrude themselves into the place of law, what is left for us but to vouch and call to warranty those principles of original justice from whence alone our title to everything valuable in society is derived? Can it be thought to arise from a superfluous, vain parade of displaying general and uncontroverted maxims, that we should revert at this time to the first principles of law, when we have directly under our consideration a whole body of statutes, which, I say, are so many contradictions, which their advocates allow to be so many exceptions from those very principles? Take them in the most favorable light, every exception from the original and fixed rule of equality and justice ought surely to be very well authorized in the reason of their deviation, and very rare in their use. For, if they should grow to be frequent, in what would they differ from an abrogation of the rule itself? By becoming thus frequent, they might even go further, and, establishing themselves into a principle, convert the rule into the exception. It cannot be dissembled that this is not at all remote from the case before us, where the great body of the people are excluded from all valuable property—where the greatest and most ordinary benefits of society are conferred as privileges, and not enjoyed on the footing of common rights.

The clandestine manner in which those in power carry on such designs is a sufficient argument of the sense they inwardly entertain of the true nature of their proceedings. Seldom is the title or preamble of the law of the same import with the body and enacting part; but they generally place some other color uppermost, which differs from that which is afterwards to appear, or at least one that is several shades fainter. Thus, the penal laws in question are not called laws to oblige men baptized and educated in Popery to renounce their religion or their property, but are called laws to prevent the growth of Popery; as if their purpose was only to prevent conversions to that sect, and not to persecute a million of people already engaged in it. But of all the instances of this sort of legislative artifice, and of the principles that produced it, I never met with any which made a stronger impression on me than that of Louis the Fourteenth, in the revocation of the Edict of Nantes. That monarch had, when he made that revocation, as few measures to keep with public opinion as any man. In the exercise of the most unresisted authority at home, in a career of uninterrupted victory abroad, and in a course of flattery equal to the circumstances of his greatness in both these particulars, he might be supposed to have as little need as disposition to render any sort of account to the world of his procedure towards his subjects. But the persecution of so vast a body of men as the Huguenots was too strong a measure even for the law of pride and power. It was too glaring a contradiction even to those principles upon which persecution itself is supported. Shocked at the naked attempt, he had recourse, for a palliation of his conduct, to an unkingly denial of the fact which made against him. In the preamble, therefore, to his Act of Revocation, he sets forth that the Edict of Nantes was no longer necessary, as the object of it (the Protestants of his kingdom) were then reduced to a very small number. The refugees in Holland cried out against this misrepresentation. They asserted, I believe with truth, that this revocation had driven two hundred thousand of them out of their country, and that they could readily demonstrate there still remained six hundred thousand Protestants in France. If this were the fact, (as it was undoubtedly,) no argument of policy could have been strong enough to excuse a measure by which eight hundred thousand men were despoiled, at one stroke, of so many of their rights and privileges. Louis the Fourteenth confessed, by this sort of apology, that, if the number had been large, the revocation had been unjust. But, after all, is it not most evident that this act of injustice, which let loose on that monarch such a torrent of invective and reproach, and which threw so dark a cloud over all the splendor of a most illustrious reign, falls far short of the case in Ireland? The privileges which the Protestants of that kingdom enjoyed antecedent to this revocation were far greater than the Roman Catholics of Ireland ever aspired to under a contrary establishment. The number of their sufferers, if considered absolutely, is not half of ours; if considered relatively to the body of each community, it is not perhaps a twentieth part. And then the penalties and incapacities which grew from that revocation are not so grievous in their nature, nor so certain in their execution, nor so ruinous by a great deal to the civil prosperity of the state, as those which we have established for a perpetual law in our unhappy country. . . .

In putting this parallel, I take it for granted that we can stand for this short time very clear of our party distinctions. . . . I flatter myself that not a few will be found who do not think that the names of Protestant and Papist can make any change in the nature of essential justice. Such men will not allow that to be proper treatment to the one of these denominations which would be cruelty to the other, and which converts its very crime into the instrument of its defence: they will hardly persuade themselves that what was bad policy in France can be good in Ireland, or that what was intolerable injustice in an arbitrary monarch becomes, only by being more extended and more violent, an equitable procedure in a country professing to be governed by law. It is, however, impossible not to observe with some concern, that there are many also of a different disposition—a number of persons whose minds are so formed that they find the communion of religion to be a close and an endearing tie, and their country to be no bond at all—to whom common altars are a better relation than common habitations and a common civil interest—whose hearts are touched with the distresses of foreigners, and are abundantly awake to all the tenderness of human feeling on such an occasion, even at the moment that they are inflicting the very same distresses, or worse, on their fellow-citizens, without the least sting of compassion or remorse. To commiserate the distresses of all men suffering innocently, perhaps meritoriously, is generous, and very agreeable to the better part of our nature—a disposition that ought by all means to be cherished. But to transfer humanity from its natural basis, our legitimate and home-bred connections—to lose all feeling for those who have grown up by our sides, in our eyes, the benefit of whose cares and labors we have partaken from our birth, and meretriciously to hunt abroad after foreign affections, is such a disarrangement of the whole system of our duties, that

I do not know whether benevolence so displaced is not almost the same thing as destroyed, or what effect bigotry could have produced that is more fatal to society. This no one could help observing, who has seen our doors kindly and bountifully thrown open to foreign sufferers for conscience, whilst through the same ports were issuing fugitives of our own, driven from their country for a cause which to an indifferent person would seem to be exactly similar, whilst we stood by, without any sense of the impropriety of this extraordinary scene, accusing and practising injustice. . . . These observations, which are a digression, but hardly, I think, can be considered as a departure from the subject, have detained us some time: we will now come more directly to our purpose.

It has been shown, I hope with sufficient evidence, that a constitution against the interest of the many is rather of the nature of a grievance than of a law; that of all grievances it is the most weighty and important; that it is made without due authority, against all the acknowledged principles of jurisprudence, against the opinions of all the great lights in that science; and that such is the tacit sense even of those who act in the most contrary manner. These points are, indeed, so evident, that I apprehend the abettors of the penal system will ground their defence on an admission, and not on a denial of them. They will lay it down as a principle, that the Protestant religion is a thing beneficial for the whole community, as well in its civil interests as in those of a superior order. From thence they will argue, that, the end being essentially beneficial, the means become instrumentally so; that these penalties and incapacities are not final causes of the law, but only a discipline to bring over a deluded people to their real interest, and therefore, though they may be harsh in their operation, they will be pleasant in their effects; and be they what they will, they cannot be considered as a very extraordinary hardship, as it is in the power of the sufferer to free himself when he pleases, and that only by converting to a better religion . . .

I shall be very short, without being, I think, the less satisfactory, in my answer to these topics, because they never can be urged from a conviction of their validity, and are, indeed, only the usual and impotent struggles of those who are unwilling to abandon a practice which they are unable to defend. First, then, I observe, that, if the principle of their final and beneficial intention be admitted as a just ground for such proceedings, there never was, in the blamable sense of the word, nor ever can be, such a thing as a religious persecution in the world. Such an intention is pretended by all men—who all not only insist that their religion has the sanction of Heaven, but is likewise, and for that reason, the best and most convenient to human society. All religious persecution, Mr. Bayle well observes, is grounded upon a miserable *petitio principii.* You are wrong, I am right; you must come over to me, or you must suffer. Let me add, that the great inlet by which a color for oppression has entered into the world is by one man's pretending to determine concerning the happiness of another, and by claiming a right to use what means he thinks proper in order to bring him to a sense of it. It is the ordinary and trite sophism of oppression. But there is not yet such a convenient ductility in the human understanding as to make us capable of being persuaded that men can possibly mean the ultimate good of the whole society by rendering miserable for a century together the greater part of it—or that any one has such a reversionary benevolence as seriously to intend the remote good of a late posterity, who can give up the present enjoyment which every honest man must have in the happiness of his contemporaries. Everybody is satisfied that a conservation and secure enjoyment of our natural rights is the great and ultimate purpose of civil society, and that therefore all forms whatsoever of government are only good as they are subservient to that purpose to which they are entirely subordinate. Now to aim at the establishment of any form of government by sacrificing what is the substance of it, to take away or at least to suspend the rights of Nature in order to an approved system for the protection of them, and for the sake of that about which men must dispute forever to postpone those things about which they have no controversy at all, and this not in minute and subordinate, but large and principal objects, is a procedure as preposterous and absurd in argument as it is oppressive and cruel in its effect. For the Protestant religion, nor (I speak it with reverence, I am sure) the truth of our common Christianity, is not so clear as this proposition—that all men, at least the majority of men in the society, ought to enjoy the common advantages of it. You fall, therefore, into a double error: first, you incur a certain mischief for an advantage which is comparatively problematical, even though you were sure of obtaining it; secondly, whatever the proposed advantage may be, were it of a certain nature, the attainment of it is by no means certain; and such deep gaming for stakes so valuable ought not to be admitted: the risk is of too much consequence to society. If no other country furnished examples of this risk, yet our laws and our country are enough fully to demonstrate the fact: Ireland, after almost a century of persecution, is at this hour full of penalties and full of Papists. . . .

Now as to the other point, that the objects of these laws suffer voluntarily: this seems to me to be an insult rather than an argument. For, besides that it totally annihilates every characteristic and therefore every faulty idea of persecution, just as the former does, it supposes, what is false in fact, that it is in a man's moral power to change his religion whenever his convenience requires it. If he be beforehand satisfied that your opinion is better than his, he will voluntarily come over to you, and without compulsion, and then your law would be unnecessary; but if he is not so convinced, he must know that it is his duty in this point to sacrifice his interest here to his opinion of his eternal happiness, else he could have in reality no religion at all. In the former case, therefore, as your law would be unnecessary, in the latter it would be persecuting: that is, it would put your penalty and his ideas of duty in the opposite scales; which is, or I know not what is, the precise idea of persecution. If, then, you require a renunciation of his conscience, as a preliminary to his admission to the rights of society, you annex, morally speaking, an impossible condition to it. In this case, in the language of reason and jurisprudence, the condition would be void, and the gift absolute; as the practice runs, it is to establish the condition, and to withhold the benefit. The suffering is, then, not voluntary. . . .

The second head upon which I propose to consider those statutes with regard to their object, and which is the next in importance to the magnitude, and of almost equal concern in the inquiry into the justice of these laws, is its possession. It is proper to recollect that this religion, which is so persecuted in its members, is the old religion of the country, and the once established religion of the state—the very same which had for centuries received the countenance and sanction of the laws, and from which it would at one time have been highly penal to have dissented. In proportion as mankind has become enlightened, the idea of religious persecution, under any circumstances, has been almost universally exploded by all good and thinking men. The only faint shadow of difficulty which remains is concerning the introduction of new opinions. Experience has shown, that, if it has been favorable to the cause of truth, it has not been always conducive to the peace of society. Though a new religious sect should even be totally free in itself from any tumultuous and disorderly zeal, which, however, is rarely the case, it has a tendency to create a resistance from the establishment in possession, productive of great disorders, and thus becomes, innocently indeed, but yet very certainly, the cause of the bitterest dissensions in the commonwealth. To a mind not thoroughly saturated with the tolerating maxims of the Gospel, a preventive persecution, on such principles, might come recommended by strong, and, apparently, no immoral motives of policy, whilst yet the contagion was recent, and had laid hold but on a few persons. The truth is, these politics are rotten and hollow at bottom, as all that are founded upon any however minute a degree of positive injustice must ever be. But they are specious, and sufficiently so to delude a man of sense and of integrity. But it is quite otherwise with the attempt to eradicate by violence a widespreading and established religious opinion. If the people are in an error, to inform them is not only fair, but charitable; to drive them is a strain of the most manifest injustice. If not the right, the presumption, at least, is ever on the side of possession. Are they mistaken? If it does not fully justify them, it is a great alleviation of guilt, which may be mingled with their misfortune, that the error is none of their forging—that they received it on as good a footing as they can receive your laws and your legislative authority, because it was handed down to them from their ancestors. The opinion may be erroneous, but the principle is undoubtedly right; and you punish them for acting upon a principle which of all others is perhaps the most necessary for preserving society, an implicit admiration and adherence to the establishments of their forefathers.

If, indeed, the legislative authority was on all hands admitted to be the ground of religious persuasion, I should readily allow that dissent would be rebellion. In this case it would make no difference whether the opinion was sucked in with the milk or imbibed yesterday; because the same legislative authority which had settled could destroy it with all the power of a creator over his creature. But this doctrine is universally disowned, and for a very plain reason. Religion, to have any force on men's understandings, indeed to exist at all, must be supposed paramount to laws, and independent for its substance upon any human institution—else it would be the absurdest thing in the world, an acknowledged cheat. Religion, therefore, is not believed because the laws have established it, but it is established because the leading part of the community have previously believed it to be true. . . .

However, we are warranted to go thus far. The people often actually do (and perhaps they cannot in general do better) take their religion, not on the coercive, which is impossible, but on the influencing authority of their governors, as wise and informed men. But if they once take a religion on the word of the state, they cannot in common sense do so a second time, unless they have some concurrent reason for it. The prejudice in favor of your wisdom is shook by your change. You confess that you have been wrong, and yet you would pretend to dictate by your sole authority; whereas you disengage the mind by embarrassing it. For why should I prefer your opinion of to-day to your persuasion of yesterday? If we must resort to prepossessions for the ground of opinion, it is in the nature of man rather to defer to the wisdom of times past, whose weakness is not before his eyes, than to the present, of whose imbecility he has daily experience. Veneration of antiquity is congenial to the human mind. When, therefore, an establishment would persecute an opinion in possession, it sets against it all the powerful prejudices of human nature. It even sets its own authority, when it is of most weight, against itself in that very circumstance in which it must necessarily have the least; and it opposes the stable prejudice of time against a new opinion founded on mutability: a consideration that must render compulsion in such a case the more grievous, as there is no security, that, when the mind is settled in the new opinion, it may not be obliged to give place to one that is still newer, or even to a return of the old. But when an ancient establishment begins early to persecute an innovation, it stands upon quite other grounds, and it has all the prejudices and presumptions on its side. It puts its own authority, not only of compulsion, but prepossession, the veneration of past age, as well as the activity of the present time, against the opinion only of a private man or set of men. If there be no reason, there is at least some consistency in its proceedings. Commanding to constancy, it does nothing but that of which it sets an example itself. But an opinion at once new and persecuting is a monster; because, in the very instant in which it takes a liberty of change, it does not leave to you even a liberty of perseverance.

Is, then, no improvement to be brought into society? Undoubtedly; but not by compulsion—but by encouragement—but by countenance, favor, privileges, which are powerful, and are lawful instruments. The coercive authority of the state is limited to what is necessary for its existence. . . .

But, say the abettors of our penal laws, this old possessed superstition is such in its principles, that society, on its general principles, cannot subsist along with it. Could a man think such an objection possible, if he had not actually heard it made—an objection contradicted, not by hypothetical reasonings, but the clear evidence of the most decisive facts? Society not only exists, but flourishes at this hour, with this superstition, in many countries, under every form of government—in some established, in some tolerated, in others upon an equal footing. And was there no civil society at all in these kingdoms before the Reformation? To say it was not as well constituted as it ought to be is saying nothing at all to the purpose; for that assertion evidently regards improvement, not existence. It certainly did then exist; and it as certainly then was at least as much to the advantage of a very great part of society as what we have brought in the place of it: which is, indeed, a great blessing to those who have profited of the change; but to all the rest, as we have wrought, that is, by blending general persecution with partial reformation, it is the very reverse. We found the people heretics and idolaters; we have, by way of improving their condition, rendered them slaves and beggars: they remain in all the misfortune of their old errors, and all the superadded misery of their recent punishment. They were happy enough, in their opinion at least, before the change; what benefits society then had, they partook of them all. They are now excluded from those benefits; and, so far as civil society comprehends them, and as we have managed the matter, our persecutions are so far from being necessary to its existence, that our very reformation is made in a degree noxious. If this be improvement, truly I know not what can be called a depravation of society. . . .

Even if these laws could be supposed agreeable to those of Nature . . . on another and almost as strong a principle they are yet unjust, as being contrary to positive compact, and the public faith most solemnly plighted. On the surrender of Limerick, and some other Irish garrisons, in the war of the Revolution, the Lords Justices of Ireland and the commander-in-chief of the king's forces signed a capitulation with the Irish, which was afterwards ratified by the king himself . . . under the great seal of England. It contains some public articles relative to the whole body of the Roman Catholics in that kingdom . . . The first is of this tenor:—"The Roman Catholics of this kingdom [Ireland] shall enjoy such privileges in the exercise of their religion as are consistent with the laws of Ireland, or as they did enjoy in the reign of King Charles the Second. And their Majesties, as soon as affairs will permit them to summon a Parliament in this kingdom, will endeavor to procure the said Roman Catholics such farther security in that particular as may preserve them from any disturbance upon the account of their said religion." The ninth article is to this effect:—"The oath to be administered to such Roman Catholics as submit to their Majesties' government shall be the oath abovesaid, and no other,"—viz., the oath of allegiance, made by act of Parliament in England, in the first year of their then Majesties; as required by the second of the Articles of Limerick. Compare this latter article with the penal laws, . . . and judge whether they seem to be the public acts of the same power, and observe whether other oaths are tendered to them, and under what penalties. Compare the former with the same laws, from the beginning to the end, and judge whether the Roman Catholics have been preserved, agreeably to the sense of the article, from any disturbance upon account of their religion—or rather, whether on that account there is a single right of Nature or benefit of society which has not been either totally taken away or considerably impaired. . . .

The great prop of this whole system is not pretended to be its justice or its utility, but the supposed danger to the state, which gave rise to it originally, and which, they apprehend, would return, if this system were overturned. Whilst, say they, the Papists of this kingdom were possessed of landed property, and of the influence consequent to such property, their allegiance to the crown of Great Britain was ever insecure, the public peace was ever liable to be broken, and Protestants never could be a moment secure either of their properties or of their lives. Indulgence only made them arrogant, and power daring; confidence only excited and enabled them to exert their inherent treachery; and the times which they generally selected for their most wicked and desperate rebellions were those in which they enjoyed the greatest ease and the most perfect tranquillity.

Such are the arguments that are used, both publicly and privately, in every discussion upon this point. They are generally full of passion and of error, and built upon facts which in themselves are most false. It cannot, I confess, be denied, that those miserable performances which go about under the names of Histories of Ireland do, indeed, represent those events after this manner; and they would persuade us, contrary to the known order of Nature, that indulgence and moderation in governors is the natural incitement in subjects to rebel. But there is an interior history of Ireland, the genuine voice of its records and monuments, which speaks a very different language from these histories, from Temple and from Clarendon: these restore Nature to its just rights, and policy to its proper order. For they even now show to those who have been at the pains to examine them, and they may show one day to all the world, that these rebellions were not produced by toleration, but by persecution—that they arose not from just and mild government, but from the most unparalleled oppression. These records will be far from giving the least countenance to a doctrine so repugnant to humanity and good sense as that the security of any establishment, civil or religious, can ever depend upon the misery of those who live under it, or that its danger can arise from their quiet and prosperity. God forbid that the history of this or any country should give such encouragement to the folly or vices of those who govern! If it can be shown that the great rebellions of Ireland have arisen from attempts to reduce the natives to the state to which they are now reduced, it will show that an attempt to continue them in that state will rather be disadvantageous to the public peace than any kind of security to it. These things have in some measure begun to appear already; and as far as regards the argument drawn from former rebellions, it will fall readily to the ground. But, for my part, I think the real danger to every state is, to render its subjects justly discontented; nor is there in politics or science any more effectual secret for their security than to establish in their people a firm opinion that no change can be for their advantage. It is true that bigotry and fanaticism may for a time draw great multitudes of people from a knowledge of their true and substantial interest. But upon this I have to remark three things. First, that such a temper can never become universal, or last for a long time. . . . The majority of men are in no persuasion bigots; they are not willing to sacrifice, on every vain imagination that superstition or enthusiasm holds forth, or that even zeal and piety recommend, the certain possession of their temporal happiness. And if such a spirit has been at any time roused in a society, after it has had its paroxysm it commonly subsides and is quiet, and is even the weaker for the violence of its first exertion: security and ease are its mortal enemies. But, secondly, if anything can tend to revive and keep it up, it is to keep alive the passions of men by ill

usage. This is enough to irritate even those who have not a
spark of bigotry in their constitution to the most desperate
enterprises; it certainly will inflame, darken, and render
more dangerous the spirit of bigotry in those who are possessed by it. Lastly, by rooting out any sect, you are never
secure against the effects of fanaticism; it may arise on the
side of the most favored opinions; and many are the instances
wherein the established religion of a state has grown ferocious
and turned upon its keeper, and has often torn to pieces the
civil establishment that had cherished it, and which it was
designed to support: France—England—Holland. . . .

A Letter to
A Peer of Ireland
on the
Penal Laws against Irish Catholics,
Previous to
The Late Repeal of a Part Thereof in
The Session of the Irish Parliament
Held A.D. 1782

During the 1770's, when England was increasingly involved
in American affairs, some of the anti-Catholic penal laws of
Ireland were partially rescinded. Small economic rights were
extended in 1771 and in 1774. But in 1778, under pressure
from the Dublin Association, a group of Catholic merchants,
the English Parliament passed the Savile Act, removing some
important disabilities against the ownership and inheritance of
land by Catholics. For supporting these measures, and others
aimed at helping Ireland to participate in trade, Burke found
himself the target of criticism of some of his Bristol constituents. In 1778 he wrote *Two Letters to Gentlemen in Bristol,*
defending his support of the Savile Act. Burke lamented that
the new statutes fell "extremely short" of the freedom needed
to be granted to Ireland. He noted that he supported the principle of free trade for Ireland just as he had done for the

American colonies, and that the "resolutions in favor of Ireland are trifling and insignificant, when compared with the concessions to the Americans." After Scotland had been allowed to participate in English trade, wrote Burke, the trade of England had greatly increased; and so it would be with Ireland. He believed that the permanent interests of communities grew with a mutual increase in wealth. But this, he reminded his constituents in an eloquent passage, required a liberal view of the advantages of free trade:

I know that it is but too natural for us to see our own certain ruin in the possible prosperity of other people. It is hard to persuade us that everything which is got by another is not taken from ourselves. But it is fit that we should get the better of these suggestions, which come from what is not the best and soundest part of our nature, and that we should form to ourselves a way of thinking, more rational, more just, and more religious. Trade is not a limited thing: as if the objects of mutual demand and consumption could not stretch beyond the bounds of our jealousies. God has given the earth to the children of men, and He has undoubtedly, in giving it to them, given them what is abundantly sufficient for all their exigencies: not a scanty, but a most liberal, provision for them all. The Author of our nature has written it strongly in that nature, and has promulgated the same law in His written word, that man shall eat his bread by his labor; and I am persuaded that no man, and no combination of men, for their own ideas of their particular profit, can, without great impiety, undertake to say that he shall not do so—that they have no sort of right either to prevent the labor or to withhold the bread. Ireland having received no compensation, directly or indirectly, for any restraints on their trade, ought not, in justice or common honesty, to be made subject to such restraints.

Two years after Burke wrote these words, in his *Letter to Thomas Burgh, Esq.* (1780), he was again obliged to explain his parliamentary conduct concerning Ireland. But this time the criticism came from his Irish friends, who misunderstood his gradualism and prudence and charged him with not having been diligent enough in securing economic concessions for Ireland that went beyond Lord North's "six resolutions." He wrote to Burgh: "I was in hopes that we might obtain gradually and by parts what we might attempt at once and in the whole without success . . . and that the people of England discovering by progressive experience that none of the concessions actually made were followed by the consequences they had dreaded, their fears from what they were yet to yield would considerably diminish." Burke stated that his main object, as always, was "to fix *the principle* of a free trade in all the ports of these islands, as founded in justice, and beneficial to the whole . . ."

In January 1782, Luke Gardiner, a member of the Irish House of Commons and an undersecretary to the lord-lieutenant, introduced a bill to further extend relief to Catholics. But as Gardiner's bill retained many of the old disabilities, Burke found much in it that was objectionable. On February 21, 1782, he expressed his views in *A Letter to a Peer of Ireland on the Penal Laws against the Irish Catholics.*

CHARLES STREET, LONDON, Feb. 21, 1782.

My Lord,   I am obliged to your Lordship for your communication of the heads of Mr. Gardiner's bill. . . .

I have read the heads of the bill, with the amendments. Your Lordship is too well acquainted with men, and with affairs, to imagine that any true judgment can be formed on the value of a great measure of policy from the perusal of a piece of paper. At present I am much in the dark with regard to the state of the country which the intended law is to be applied to. It is not easy for me to determine whether or no it was wise (for the sake of expunging the black letter of laws which, menacing as they were in the language, were every day fading into disuse) solemnly to reaffirm the principles and to re-enact the provisions of a code of statutes by which you are totally excluded from the privileges of the COMMONWEALTH, from the highest to the lowest, from the most material of the civil professions, from the army, and even from education, where alone education is to be had.

Whether this scheme of indulgence, grounded at once on contempt and jealousy, has a tendency gradually to produce something better and more liberal, I cannot tell, for want of having the actual map of the country. If this should be the case, it was right in you to accept it, such as it is. But if this should be one of the experiments which have sometimes been made before the temper of the nation was ripe for a real reformation, I think it may possibly have ill effects, by disposing the penal matter in a more systematic order, and thereby fixing a permanent bar against any relief that is truly substantial. The whole merit or demerit of the measure depends upon the plans and dispositions of those by whom the act was made, concurring with the general temper of the Protestants of Ireland, and their aptitude to admit in time of some part of that equality without which you never can be FELLOW-CITIZENS. . . .

To look at the bill in the abstract, it is neither more nor less than a renewed act of UNIVERSAL, UNMITIGATED, INDISPENSABLE, EXCEPTIONLESS DISQUALIFICATION.

One would imagine that a bill inflicting such a multitude of incapacities had followed on the heels of a conquest made by a very fierce enemy, under the impression of recent animosity and resentment. No man, on reading that bill, could imagine he was reading an act of amnesty and indulgence, following a recital of the good behavior of those who are the objects of it—which recital stood at the head of the bill, as it was first introduced, but, I suppose for its incongruity with the body of the piece, was afterwards omitted. This I say on memory. It, however, still recites the oath, and that Catholics ought to be considered as good and loyal subjects to his Majesty, his crown and government. Then follows an universal exclusion of those GOOD and LOYAL subjects from every (even the lowest) office of trust and profit—from any vote at an election —from any privilege in a town corporate—from being even a freeman of such a corporation—from serving on grand juries —from a vote at a vestry—from having a gun in his house— from being a barrister, attorney, or solicitor, &c., &c., &c.

This has surely much more the air of a table of proscription than an act of grace. What must we suppose the laws concerning those *good* subjects to have been, of which this is a relaxation? I know well that there is a cant language current, about the difference between an exclusion from employments, even to the most rigorous extent, and an exclusion from the natural benefits arising from a man's own industry. I allow, that, under some circumstances, the difference is very material in point of justice, and that there are considerations which may render it advisable for a wise government to keep the leading parts of every branch of civil and military administration in hands of the best trust; but a total exclusion from the commonwealth is a very different thing. When a government subsists (as governments formerly did) on an estate of its own, with but few and inconsiderable revenues drawn from the subject, then the few officers which existed in such establishments were naturally at the disposal of that government, which paid the salaries out of its own coffers: there an exclusive preference could hardly merit the name of proscription. Almost the whole produce of a man's industry at that time remained in his own purse to maintain his family. But times alter, and the *whole* estate of government is from private contribution. When a very great portion of the labor of individuals goes to the state, and is by the state again refunded to individuals, through the medium of offices, and in this circuitous progress from the private to the public, and from the public again to the private fund, the families from whom the revenue is taken are indemnified, and an equitable balance between the government and the subject is established. But if a great body of the people who contribute to this state lottery are excluded from all the prizes, the stopping the circulation with regard to them may be a most cruel hardship, amounting in effect to being double and treble taxed; and it will be felt as such to the very quick, by all the families, high and low, of those hundreds of thousands who are denied their chance in the returned fruits of their own industry. This is the thing meant by those who look upon the public revenue only as a spoil, and will naturally wish to have as few as possible concerned in the division of the booty. If a state should be so unhappy as to think it cannot subsist without such a barbarous proscription, the persons so proscribed ought to be indemnified by the remission of a large part of their taxes, by an immunity from the offices of public burden, and by an exemption from being pressed into any military or naval service.

Common sense and common justice dictate this at least, as some sort of compensation to a people for their slavery. . . . This hardship is the more intolerable because the professions are shut up. The Church is so of course. Much is to be said on that subject, in regard to them, and to the Protestant Dissenters. But that is a chapter by itself. I am sure I wish well to that Church, and think its ministers among the very best citizens of your country. However, such as it is, a great walk in life is forbidden ground to seventeen hundred thousand of the inhabitants of Ireland. Why are they excluded from the law? Do not they expend money in their suits? Why may not they indemnify themselves, by profiting, in the persons of some, for the losses incurred by others? Why may not they have persons of confidence, whom they may, if they please, employ in the agency of their affairs? The exclusion from the law, from grand juries, from sheriffships and under-sheriffships, as well as from freedom in any corporation, may subject them to dreadful hardships, as it may exclude them wholly from all that is beneficial and expose them to all that is mischievous in a trial by jury. This was manifestly within my own observation, for I was three times in Ireland from the year 1760 to the year 1767, where I had sufficient means of information concerning the inhuman proceedings (among which were many cruel murders, besides an infinity of outrages and oppressions unknown before in a civilized age) which prevailed during that period, in consequence of a pretended conspiracy among *Roman Catholics* against the king's government. I could dilate upon the mischiefs that may happen, from those which have happened, upon this head of disqualification, if it were at all necessary.

The head of exclusion from votes for members of Parliament is closely connected with the former. When you cast your eye on the statute-book, you will see that no *Catholic*, even in the ferocious acts of Queen Anne, was disabled from voting on account of his religion. The only conditions required for that privilege were the oaths of allegiance and abjuration —both oaths relative to a civil concern. Parliament has since added another oath of the same kind; and yet a House of Commons, adding to the securities of government in proportion as its danger is confessedly lessened, and professing both confidence and indulgence, in effect takes away the privilege left by an act full of jealousy and professing persecution.

The taking away of a vote is the taking away the shield which the subject has, not only against the oppression of power, but that worst of all oppressions, the persecution of private society and private manners. No candidate for Parliamentary influence is obliged to the least attention towards them, either in cities or counties. On the contrary, if they should become obnoxious to any bigoted or malignant people amongst whom they live, it will become the interest of those who court popular favor to use the numberless means which always reside in magistracy and influence to oppress them. . . . The Protestants of Ireland feel well and naturally on the hardship of being bound by laws in the enacting of which they do not directly or indirectly vote. The bounds of these matters are nice, and hard to be settled in theory, and perhaps they have been pushed too far. But how they can avoid the necessary application of the principles they use in their disputes with others to their disputes with their fellow-citizens, I know not. . . .

The laws against foreign education are clearly the very worst part of the old code. Besides your laity, you have the succession of about four thousand clergymen to provide for. These, having no lucrative objects in prospect, are taken very much out of the lower orders of the people. At home they have no means whatsoever provided for their attaining a clerical education, or indeed any education at all. . . .

It has been the custom of poor persons in Ireland to pick up such knowledge of the Latin tongue as, under the general discouragements, and occasional pursuits of magistracy, they were able to acquire; and receiving orders at home, were sent abroad to obtain a clerical education. By officiating in petty chaplainships, and performing now and then certain offices of religion for small gratuities, they received the means of maintaining themselves until they were able to complete their education. Through such difficulties and discouragements, many of them have arrived at a very considerable proficiency, so as to be marked and distinguished abroad. These persons afterwards, by being sunk in the most abject poverty, despised and ill-treated by the higher orders among Protestants, and not much better esteemed or treated even by the few persons of fortune of their own persuasion, and contracting the habits and ways of thinking of the poor and uneducated, among whom they were obliged to live, in a few years retained little or no traces of the talents and acquirements which distinguished them in the early periods of their lives. Can we with justice cut them off from the use of places of education founded for the greater part from the economy of poverty and exile, without providing something that is equivalent at home?

Whilst this restraint of foreign and domestic education was part of an horrible and impious system of servitude, the members were well fitted to the body. To render men patient under a deprivation of all the rights of human nature, everything which could give them a knowledge or feeling of those rights was rationally forbidden. To render humanity fit to be insulted, it was fit that it should be degraded. But when we profess to restore men to the capacity for property, it is equally irrational and unjust to deny them the power of improving their minds as well as their fortunes. Indeed, I have ever thought the prohibition of the means of improving our rational nature to be the worst species of tyranny that the insolence and perverseness of mankind ever dared to exercise. This goes to all men, in all situations, to whom education can be denied.

Your Lordship mentions a proposal which came from my friend, the Provost, whose benevolence and enlarged spirit I am perfectly convinced of—which is, the proposal of erecting a few sizarships in the college, for the education (I suppose) of Roman Catholic clergymen. He certainly meant it well; but, coming from such a man as he is, it is a strong instance of the danger of suffering any description of men to fall into entire contempt. The charities intended for them are not perceived to be fresh insults; and the true nature of their wants and necessities being unknown, remedies wholly unsuitable to the nature of their complaint are provided for them. . . . If the other parts of the university were open to them, as well on the foundation as otherwise, the offering of sizarships would be a proportioned part of a *general* kindness. But when everything *liberal* is withheld, and only that which is *servile* is permitted, it is easy to conceive upon what footing they must be in such a place. . . .

When we are to provide for the education of any body of men, we ought seriously to consider the particular functions they are to perform in life. A Roman Catholic clergyman is the minister of a very ritual religion, and by his profession subject to many restraints. His life is a life full of strict observances; and his duties are of a laborious nature towards himself, and of the highest possible trust towards others. The duty of confession alone is sufficient to set in the strongest light the necessity of his having an appropriated mode of education. The theological opinions and peculiar rites of one religion never can be properly taught in universities founded for the purposes and on the principles of another which in many points are directly opposite. If a Roman Catholic clergyman, intended for celibacy and the function of confession, is not strictly bred in a seminary where these things are respected, inculcated, and enforced, as sacred, and not made the subject of derision and obloquy, he will be ill fitted for the former, and the latter will be indeed in his hands a terrible instrument. . . .

The Council of Trent has wisely introduced the discipline of seminaries, by which priests are not trusted for a clerical institution even to the severe discipline of their colleges, but, after they pass through them, are frequently, if not for the greater part, obliged to pass through peculiar methods, having their particular ritual function in view. It is in a great measure to this, and to similar methods used in foreign education, that the Roman Catholic clergy of Ireland, miserably provided for, living among low and ill-regulated people, without any discipline of sufficient force to secure good manners, have been prevented from becoming an intolerable nuisance to the country, instead of being, as I conceive they generally are, a very great service to it.

The ministers of Protestant churches require a different mode of education, more liberal, and more fit for the ordinary intercourse of life. That religion having little hold on the minds of people by external ceremonies and extraordinary observances, or separate habits of living, the clergy make up the deficiency by cultivating their minds with all kinds of ornamental learning, which the liberal provision made in England and Ireland for the parochial clergy, (to say nothing of the ample Church preferments, with little or no duties annexed,) and the comparative lightness of parochial duties, enables the greater part of them in some considerable degree to accomplish.

This learning, which I believe to be pretty general, together with an higher situation, and more chastened by the opinion of mankind, forms a sufficient security for the morals of the established clergy, and for their sustaining their clerical character with dignity. It is not necessary to observe, that all these things are, however, collateral to their function, and that, except in preaching, which may be and is supplied, and often best supplied, out of printed books, little else is necessary for a Protestant minister than to be able to read the English language—I mean for the exercise of his function, not to the qualification of his admission to it. But a Popish parson in Ireland may do very well without any considerable classical erudition, or any proficiency in pure or mixed mathematics, or any knowledge of civil history. Even if the Catholic clergy should possess those acquisitions, as at first many of them do, they soon lose them in the painful course of professional and parochial duties: but they must have all the knowledge, and, what is to them more important than the knowledge, the discipline, necessary to those duties. All modes of education conducted by those whose minds are cast in another mould, as I may say, and whose original ways of thinking are formed upon the reverse pattern, must be to them not only useless, but mischievous. Just as I should suppose the education in a Popish ecclesiastical seminary would be ill fitted for a Protestant clergyman. To educate a Catholic priest in a Protestant seminary would be much worse. The Protestant educated amongst Catholics has only something to reject: what he keeps may be useful. But a Catholic parish priest learns little for his peculiar purpose and duty in a Protestant college.

All this, my Lord, I know very well, will pass for nothing

with those who wish that the Popish clergy should be illiterate, and in a situation to produce contempt and detestation. Their minds are wholly taken up with party squabbles, and I have neither leisure nor inclination to apply any part of what I have to say to those who never think of religion or of the commonwealth in any other light than as they tend to the prevalence of some faction in either. I speak on a supposition that there is a disposition *to take the state in the condition in which it is found,* and to improve it *in that state* to the best advantage. Hitherto the plan for the government of Ireland has been to sacrifice the civil prosperity of the nation to its religious improvement. But if people in power there are at length come to entertain other ideas, they will consider the good order, decorum, virtue, and morality of every description of men among them as of infinitely greater importance than the struggle (for it is nothing better) to change those descriptions by means which put to hazard objects which, in my poor opinion, are of more importance to religion and to the state than all the polemical matter which has been agitated among men from the beginning of the world to this hour.

On this idea, an education fitted *to each order and division of men, such as they are found,* will be thought an affair rather to be encouraged than discountenanced . . .

Before I had written thus far, I heard of a scheme of giving to the Castle the patronage of the presiding members of the Catholic clergy. At first I could scarcely credit it; for I believe it is the first time that the presentation to other people's alms has been desired in any country. If the state provides a suitable maintenance and temporality for the governing members of the Irish Roman Catholic Church, and for the clergy under them, I should think the project, however improper in other respects, to be by no means unjust. But to deprive a poor people, who maintain a second set of clergy, out of the miserable remains of what is left after taxing and tithing, to deprive them of the disposition of their own charities among their own communion, would, in my opinion, be an intolerable hardship. Never were the members of one religious sect fit to appoint the pastors to another. Those who have no regard for their welfare, reputation, or internal quiet will not appoint such as are proper. The seraglio of Constantinople is as equitable as we are, whether Catholics or Protestants—and where their own sect is concerned, full as religious. But the sport which they make of the miserable dignities of the Greek Church, the little factions of the harem to which they make them subservient, the continual sale to which they expose and reëxpose the same dignity, and by which they squeeze all the inferior orders of the clergy, is (for I have had particular means of being acquainted with it) nearly equal to all the other oppressions together, exercised by Mussulmen over the unhappy members of the Oriental Church. It is a great deal to suppose that even the present Castle would nominate bishops for the Roman Church of Ireland with a religious regard for its welfare. Perhaps they cannot, perhaps they dare not do it.

But suppose them to be as well inclined as I know that I am to do the Catholics all kind of justice, I declare I would not, if it were in my power, take that patronage on myself. I know I ought not to do it. I belong to another community . . .

How can the Lord-Lieutenant form the least judgment of their merits, so as to discern which of the Popish priests is fit to be made a bishop? It cannot be: the idea is ridiculous. He will hand them over to lords-lieutenant of counties, justices of the peace, and other persons, who, for the purpose of vexing and turning to derision this miserable people, will pick out the worst and most obnoxious they can find amongst the clergy to set over the rest. Whoever is complained against by his brother will be considered as persecuted; whoever is censured by his superior will be looked upon as oppressed; whoever is careless in his opinions and loose in his morals will be called a liberal man, and will be supposed to have incurred hatred because he was not a bigot. Informers, tale-bearers, perverse and obstinate men, flatterers, who turn their back upon their flock and court the Protestant gentlemen of the country, will be the objects of preferment. And then I run no risk in foretelling that whatever order, quiet, and morality you have in the country will be lost. A Popish clergy who are not restrained by the most austere subordination will become a nuisance, a real public grievance of the heaviest kind, in any country that entertains them; and instead of the great benefit which Ireland does and has long derived from them, if they are educated without any idea of discipline and obedience, and then put under bishops who do not owe their station to their good opinion, and whom they cannot respect, that nation will see disorders, of which, bad as things are, it has yet no idea. I do not say this, as thinking the leading men in Ireland would exercise this trust worse than others. Not at all. No man, no set of men living are fit to administer the affairs or regulate the interior economy of a church to which they are enemies. . . .

The act, as far as it goes, is good undoubtedly. It amounts, I think, very nearly to a *toleration,* with respect to religious ceremonies; but it puts a new bolt on civil rights, and rivets it to the old one in such a manner, that neither, I fear, will be easily loosened. What I could have wished would be, to see the civil advantages take the lead; the other, of a religious toleration, I conceive, would follow, (in a manner,) of course. From what I have observed, it is pride, arrogance, and a spirit of domination, and not a bigoted spirit of religion, that has caused and kept up those oppressive statutes. I am sure I have known those who have oppressed Papists in their civil rights exceedingly indulgent to them in their religious ceremonies, and who really wished them to continue Catholics, in order to furnish pretences for oppression. These persons never saw a man (by converting) escape out of their power, but with grudging and regret. I have known men to whom I am not uncharitable in saying (though they are dead) that they would have become Papists in order to oppress Protestants, if, being Protestants, it was not in their power to oppress Papists. It is injustice, and not a mistaken conscience, that has been the principle of persecution . . .

*A Letter to
Sir Hercules Langrishe, Bart., M.P.
on the Subject of
The Roman Catholics of Ireland
and
The Propriety of Admitting Them to the
Elective Franchise, Consistently with
the Principles of the Constitution
as Established at the Revolution
1792*

In 1782, during the second Rockingham administration, Henry Grattan had secured for the Irish Parliament complete legislative independence from the jurisdiction of the English Parliament. Burke was pleased with this development, because it at least raised Ireland from the legal subordination to England which had made possible the worst economic and religious disabilities. But he and his friends in Ireland were well aware that this new independence was more nominal than real. The Crown continued to appoint Irish ministers; the lord-lieutenant of Ireland was still responsible to the English government; the administrative structure and personnel of Dublin Castle continued to be dominated by England.

The general discontent throughout Ireland over the failure to obtain a genuine control over her own internal affairs received strong encouragement in 1789 by the French Revolution. To many Irishmen it appeared that the only way to secure their basic civil rights was to follow the example of revolutionary France. In 1791 the Society of United Irishmen was formed, which included revolutionaries and radical reformers from both Presbyterian and Catholic groups. The United Irishmen sympathized with the French Jacobins, and hoped by violence to overthrow the English government in Ireland, and to establish a democracy similar to that of France.

From 1782 to 1791 there had been almost no interest

among the ruling Protestants of Ireland to allow any political rights to Catholics, and Catholics themselves had shown little interest in obtaining such rights. But with the model of the French Revolution before them, many Catholics began to demand the rights of political franchise, and they supported the United Irishmen as the means to that end. Faced with the formidable combined opposition of Presbyterian Irish Jacobins and intensely discontented Catholics, the English government of the younger William Pitt saw the need of conciliating the Catholics in order to prevent a Jacobin revolution in Britain. In England, Pitt's government passed laws in 1791 giving Catholics the legal right to conduct religious services, and to practice law, although they were still excluded from the franchise and from holding elective or appointive offices. In Ireland the question of how far political rights should be extended to Catholics was hotly debated in the Irish Parliament. Burke was aware that even on the part of those in the Irish Parliament who wished to see the worst religious and civil disabilities abolished, there remained many persistent misunderstandings of the Irish question, which would require patient, humane, and wise statesmanship to overcome. He remembered the violence of the Whiteboy insurrections in 1761, and in 1792 feared that continued economic and religious discontent in Ireland would drive many into following the violence of the French Jacobins. He was anxious that a policy of reconciliation be adopted, which would grant Ireland substantial rights under the British constitution, including a generous extension of political rights to Catholics. Justice and equity, quite as much as political considerations, demanded it. Burke was convinced that a continuation of the old tyrannical proscriptions would drive the Irish into the arms of revolutionary France, with disastrous results to Britain and Europe. It was against the background of these historical developments, and with these political considerations, that on January 3, 1792, he wrote his *Letter to Sir Hercules Langrishe, Bart., M.P., on the subject of the Roman Catholics of Ireland and the propriety of admitting them to the elective franchise, consistently with the principles of the Constitution, as established at the Revolution.*

My Dear Sir,   Your remembrance of me, with sentiments of so much kindness, has given me the most sincere satisfaction. . . .

The case upon which your letter of the 10th of December turns is hardly before me with precision enough to enable me to form any very certain judgment upon it. It seems to be some plan of further indulgence proposed for the Catholics of Ireland. . . .

In my present state of imperfect information, you will pardon the errors into which I may easily fall. The principles you lay down are, "that the Roman Catholics should enjoy everything *under* the state, but should not be *the state itself.*" And you add, "that, when you exclude them from being *a part of the state,* you rather conform to the spirit of the age than to any abstract doctrine"; but you consider the Constitution as already established—that our state is Protestant. "It was declared so at the Revolution. It was so provided in the acts for settling the succession of the crown:—the king's coronation oath was enjoined in order to keep it so. The king, as first magistrate of the state, is obliged to take the oath of abjuration, and to subscribe the Declaration; and by laws subsequent, every other magistrate and member of the state, legislative and executive, are bound under the same obligation."

As to the plan to which these maxims are applied, I cannot speak, as I told you, positively about it: because neither from your letter, nor from any information I have been able to collect, do I find anything settled, either on the part of the Roman Catholics themselves, or on that of any persons who may wish to conduct their affairs in Parliament. But if I have leave to conjecture, something is in agitation towards admitting them, under *certain qualifications,* to have *some share* in the election of members of Parliament. This I understand is the scheme of those who are entitled to come within your description of persons of consideration, property, and character —and firmly attached to the king and Constitution, as by "law established, with a grateful sense of your former concessions, and a patient reliance on the benignity of Parliament for the further mitigation of the laws that still affect them."—As to the low, thoughtless, wild, and profligate, who have joined themselves with those of other professions, but of the same character, you are not to imagine that for a moment I can suppose them to be met with anything else than the manly and enlightened energy of a firm government, supported by the united efforts of all virtuous men, if ever their proceedings should become so considerable as to demand its notice. I really think that such associations should be crushed in their very commencement.

Setting, therefore, this case out of the question, it becomes an object of very serious consideration, whether, because wicked men of *various* descriptions are engaged in seditious courses, the rational, sober, and valuable part of *one* description should not be indulged in their sober and rational expectations. You, who have looked deeply into the spirit of the Popery laws, must be perfectly sensible that a great part of the present mischief which we abhor in common (if it at all exists) has arisen from them. Their declared object was, to reduce the Catholics of Ireland to a miserable populace, without property, without estimation, without education. The professed object was, to deprive the few men, who, in spite of those laws, might hold or obtain any property amongst them, of all sort of influence or authority over the rest. They divided the nation into two distinct bodies, without common interest, sympathy, or connection. One of these bodies was to possess *all* the franchises, *all* the property, *all* the education: the other was to be composed of drawers of water and cutters of turf for them. Are we to be astonished, when, by the efforts of so much violence in conquest, and so much policy in regulation, continued without intermission for near an hundred years, we had reduced them to a mob, that, whenever they came to act at all, many of them would act exactly like a mob, without temper, measure, or foresight? Surely it might be just now a matter of temperate discussion, whether you ought not to apply a remedy to the real cause of the evil. If the disorder you speak of be real and considerable, you ought to raise an aristocratic interest, that is, an interest of property and education, amongst them—and to strengthen, by every prudent means, the authority and influence of men of that description. . . .

If the absurd persons you mention find no way of providing for liberty, but by overturning this happy Constitution, and introducing a frantic democracy, let us take care how we prevent better people from any rational expectations of partaking in the benefits of that Constitution *as it stands*. The maxims you establish cut the matter short. . . .

You begin by asserting, that "the Catholics ought to enjoy all things *under* the state, but that they ought not to *be the state*": a position which, I believe, in the latter part of it, and in the latitude there expressed, no man of common sense has ever thought proper to dispute; because the contrary implies that the state ought to be in them *exclusively*. But before you have finished the line, you express yourself as if the other member of your proposition, namely, that "they ought not to be *a part* of the state," were necessarily included in the first— whereas I conceive it to be as different as a part is from the whole, that is, just as different as possible. I know, indeed, that it is common with those who talk very differently from you, that is, with heat and animosity, to confound those things, and to argue the admission of the Catholics into any, however minute and subordinate, parts of the state, as a surrender into their hands of the whole government of the kingdom. To them I have nothing at all to say.

Wishing to proceed with a deliberative spirit and temper in so very serious a question, I shall attempt to analyze, as well as I can, the principles you lay down, in order to fit them for the grasp of an understanding so little comprehensive as mine.—"State"—"Protestant"—"Revolution." These are terms which, if not well explained, may lead us into many errors. In the word *State* I conceive there is much ambiguity. The state is sometimes used to signify *the whole commonwealth*, comprehending all its orders, with the several privileges belonging to each. Sometimes it signifies only *the higher and ruling part* of the commonwealth, which we commonly call *the Government*. In the first sense, to be under the state, but not the state itself, *nor any part of it*, that is, to be nothing at all in the commonwealth, is a situation perfectly intelligible—but to those who fill that situation, not very pleasant, when it is understood. It is a state of *civil servitude*, by the very force of the definition. . . . This servitude, which makes men *subject* to a state without being *citizens*, may be more or less tolerable from many circumstances; but these circumstances, more or less favorable, do not alter the nature of the thing. The mildness by which absolute masters exercise their dominion leaves them masters still. . . .

In the other sense of the word *State*, by which is understood the *Supreme Government* only, I must observe this upon the question: that to exclude whole classes of men entirely from this *part* of government cannot be considered as *absolute slavery*. It only implies a lower and degraded state of citizenship: such is (with more or less strictness) the condition of all countries in which an hereditary nobility possess the exclusive rule. This may be no bad mode of government—provided that the personal authority of individual nobles be kept in due bounds, that their cabals and factions are guarded against with a severe vigilance, and that the people (who have no share in granting their own money) are subjected to but light impositions, and are otherwise treated with attention, and with indulgence to their humors and prejudices. . . .

Between the extreme of *a total exclusion*, to which your

maxim goes, and *an universal unmodified capacity,* to which the fanatics pretend, there are many different degrees and stages, and a great variety of temperaments, upon which prudence may give full scope to its exertions. For you know that the decisions of prudence (contrary to the system of the insane reasoners) differ from those of judicature; and that almost all the former are determined on the more or the less, the earlier or the later, and on a balance of advantage and inconvenience, of good and evil.

In all considerations which turn upon the question of vesting or continuing the state solely and exclusively in some one description of citizens, prudent legislators will consider how far *the general form and principles of their commonwealth render it fit to be cast into an oligarchical shape, or to remain always in it.* We know that the government of Ireland (the same as the British) is not in its constitution *wholly* aristocratical; and as it is not such in its form, so neither is it in its spirit. If it had been inveterately aristocratical, exclusions might be more patiently submitted to. The lot of one plebeian would be the lot of all; and an habitual reverence and admiration of certain families might make the people content to see government wholly in hands to whom it seemed naturally to belong. But our Constitution has *a plebeian member,* which forms an essential integrant part of it. A plebeian oligarchy is a monster; and no people, not absolutely domestic or predial slaves, will long endure it. The Protestants of Ireland are not *alone* sufficiently the people to form a democracy; and they are *too numerous* to answer the ends and purposes of *an aristocracy.* Admiration, that first source of obedience, can be only the claim or the imposture of the few. I hold it to be absolutely impossible for two millions of plebeians, composing certainly a very clear and decided majority in that class, to become so far in love with six or seven hundred thousand of their fellow-citizens (to all outward appearance plebeians like themselves, and many of them tradesmen, servants, and otherwise inferior to some of them) as to see with satisfaction, or even with patience, an exclusive power vested in them, by which *constitutionally* they become the absolute masters, and by the *manners* derived from their circumstances, must be capable of exercising upon them, daily and hourly, an insulting and vexatious superiority. Neither are the majority of the Irish indemnified (as in some aristocracies) for this state of humiliating vassalage (often inverting the nature of things and relations) by having the lower walks of industry wholly abandoned to them. They are rivalled, to say the least of the matter, in every laborious and lucrative course of life; while every franchise, every honor, every trust, every place, down to the very lowest and least confidential, (besides whole professions,) is reserved for the master caste.

Our Constitution is not made for great, general, and proscriptive exclusions; sooner or later it will destroy them, or they will destroy the Constitution. In our Constitution there has always been a difference beween *a franchise* and *an office*, and between the capacity for the one and for the other. Franchises were supposed to belong to the *subject*, as *a subject*, and not *as a member of the governing part of the state*. The policy of government has considered them as things very different; for, whilst Parliament excluded by the test acts (and for a while these test acts were not a dead letter, as now they are in England) Protestant Dissenters from all civil and military employments, they *never touched their right of voting for members of Parliament or sitting in either House:* a point I state, not as approving or condemning, with regard to them, the measure of exclusion from employments, but to prove that the distinction has been admitted in legislature, as, in truth, it is founded in reason.

I will not here examine whether the principles of the British [the Irish] Constitution be wise or not. I must assume that they are, and that those who partake the franchises which make it partake of a benefit. They who are excluded from votes (under proper qualifications inherent in the Constitution that gives them) are excluded, not from *the state*, but from *the British Constitution*. They cannot by any possibility, whilst they hear its praises continually rung in their ears, and are present at the declaration which is so generally and so bravely made by those who possess the privilege, that the best blood in their veins ought to be shed to preserve their share in it— they, the disfranchised part, cannot, I say, think themselves in an *happy* state, to be utterly excluded from all its direct and all its consequential advantages. The popular part of the Constitution must be to them by far the most odious part of it. To them it is not an *actual*, and, if possible, still less a *virtual* representation. It is, indeed, the direct contrary. It is power unlimited placed in the hands of *an adverse* description *because it is an adverse description*. And if they who compose the privileged body have not an interest, they must but too frequently have motives of pride, passion, petulance, peevish jealousy, or tyrannic suspicion, to urge them to treat the excluded people with contempt and rigor.

This is not a mere theory; though, whilst men are men, it is a theory that cannot be false. . . .

This universal exclusion seems to me a serious evil—because many collateral oppressions . . . have arisen from it. . . .

I have said enough of the question of state, *as it affects the people merely as such.* But it is complicated with a political question relative to religion, to which it is very necessary I should say something—because the term *Protestant*, which you apply, is too general for the conclusions which one of your accurate understanding would wish to draw from it, and because a great deal of argument will depend on the use that is made of that term.

It is *not* a fundamental part of the settlement at the Revolution that the state should be Protestant *without any qualification of the term.* With a qualification it is unquestionably true; not in all its latitude. With the qualification, it was true before the Revolution. Our predecessors in legislation were not so irrational (not to say impious) as to form an operose ecclesiastical establishment, and even to render the state itself in some degree subservient to it, when their religion (if such it might be called) was nothing but a mere *negation* of some other—without any positive idea, either of doctrine, discipline, worship, or morals, in the scheme which they professed themselves, and which they imposed upon others, even under penalties and incapacities. No! No! This never could have been done, even by reasonable atheists. They who think religion of no importance to the state have abandoned it to the conscience or caprice of the individual . . . There never has been a religion of the state (the few years of the Parliament only excepted) but that of *the Episcopal Church of England:* the Episcopal Church of England, before the Reformation, connected with the see of Rome; since then, disconnected, and protesting against some of her doctrines, and against the whole of her authority, as binding in our national church: nor did the fundamental laws of this kingdom (in Ireland it has been the same) ever know, at any period, any other church *as an object of establishment*—or, in that light, any other Protestant religion. Nay, our Protestant *toleration* itself, at the Revolution, and until within a few years, required a signature of thirty-six, and a part of the thirty-seventh, out of the Thirty-Nine Articles. So little idea had they at the Revolution of *establishing* Protestantism indefinitely, that they did not indefinitely *tolerate* it under that name. I do not mean to praise that strictness, where nothing more than merely religious toleration is concerned. Toleration, being a part of moral and political prudence, ought to be tender and large. . . .

The Church of Scotland knows as little of Protestantism *undefined* as the Church of England and Ireland do. She has by the articles of union secured to herself the perpetual establishment of *the Confession of Faith*, and the *Presbyterian* Church government. In England, even during the troubled interregnum, it was not thought fit to establish a *negative* religion; but the Parliament settled the *Presbyterian* as the Church *discipline*, the *Directory* as the rule of public *worship*, and the *Westminster Catechism* as the institute of *faith*. This is to show that at no time was the Protestant religion, *undefined*, established here or anywhere else . . .

As to the coronation oath, to which you allude, as opposite to admitting a Roman Catholic to the use of any franchise whatsoever, I cannot think that the king would be perjured, if he gave his assent to any regulation which Parliament might think fit to make with regard to that affair. The king is bound by law, as clearly specified in several acts of Parliament, to be in communion with the Church of England. It is a part of the tenure by which he holds his crown; and though no provision was made till the Revolution, which could be called positive and valid in law, to ascertain this great principle, I have always considered it as in fact fundamental, that the king of England should be of the Christian religion, according to the national legal church for the time being. I conceive it was so before the Reformation. Since the Reformation it became doubly necessary; because the king is the head of that church, in some sort an ecclesiastical person—and it would be incongruous and absurd to have the head of the Church of one faith, and the members of another. The king may *inherit* the crown as a *Protestant;* but he cannot *hold it*, according to law, without being a Protestant *of the Church of England*.

Before we take it for granted that the king is bound by his coronation oath not to admit any of his Catholic subjects to the rights and liberties which ought to belong to them as Englishmen, (not as religionists,) or to settle the conditions or proportions of such admission by an act of Parliament, I wish you to place before your eyes that oath itself, as it is settled in the act of William and Mary.

"Will you to the utmost of your power maintain the laws of God, the true profession of the Gospel, and the Protestant Reformed Religion *established by law?* And will you preserve unto the *bishops* and clergy of this realm, and to the churches committed to *their* charge, all such rights and privileges as by law do or shall appertain unto them, or any of them?—All this I promise to do."

Here are the coronation engagements of the king. In them I do not find one word to preclude his Majesty from consenting to any arrangement which Parliament may make with regard to the civil privileges of any part of his subjects.

It may not be amiss, on account of the light which it will throw on this discussion, to look a little more narrowly into the matter of that oath—in order to discover how far it has hitherto operated, or how far in future it ought to operate, as a bar to any proceedings of the crown and Parliament in favor of those against whom it may be supposed that the king has engaged to support the Protestant Church of England in the two kingdoms in which it is established by law. First, the king swears he will maintain to the utmost of his power "the laws of God." I suppose it means the natural moral laws.— Secondly, he swears to maintain "the true profession of the Gospel." By which I suppose is understood *affirmatively* the Christian religion.—Thirdly, that he will maintain "the Protestant reformed religion." This leaves me no power of supposition or conjecture; for that Protestant reformed religion is defined and described by the subsequent words, "established by law"; and in this instance, to define it beyond all possibility of doubt, he swears to maintain the "bishops and clergy, and the churches committed to their charge," in their rights present and future. . . .

All this shows that the religion which the king is bound to maintain has a positive part in it, as well as a negative—and that the positive part of it (in which we are in perfect agreement with the Catholics and with the Church of Scotland) is infinitely the most valuable and essential. . . .

For reasons forcible enough at all times, but at this time particularly forcible with me, I dwell a little the longer upon this matter, and take the more pains, to put us both in mind that it was not settled at the Revolution that the state should be Protestant, in the latitude of the term, but in a defined and limited sense only, and that in that sense only the king is sworn to maintain it. To suppose that the king has sworn with his utmost power to maintain what it is wholly out of his power to discover, or which, if he could discover, he might discover to consist of things directly contradictory to each other, some of them perhaps impious, blasphemous, and seditious upon principle, would be not only a gross, but a most mischievous absurdity. If mere dissent from the Church of Rome be a merit, he that dissents the most perfectly is the most meritorious. In many points we hold strongly with that church. He that dissents throughout with that church will dissent with the Church of England, and then it will be a part of his merit that he dissents with ourselves: a whimsical species of merit for any set of men to establish. . . . A man is certainly the most perfect Protestant who protests against the whole Christian religion. Whether a person's having no Christian religion be a title to favor, in exclusion to the largest description of Christians, who hold all the doctrines of Christianity, though holding along with them some errors and some superfluities, is rather more than any man, who has not become recreant and apostate from his baptism, will, I believe, choose to affirm. The countenance given from a spirit of controversy to that negative religion may by degrees encourage light and unthinking people to a total indifference to everything positive in matters of doctrine, and, in the end, of practice too. If continued, it would play the game of that sort of active, proselytizing, and persecuting atheism which is the disgrace and calamity of our time . . .

Now let us fairly see what course has been taken relative to those against whom, in part at least, the king has sworn to maintain a church, *positive in its doctrine and its discipline*. The first thing done, even when the oath was fresh in the mouth of the sovereigns, was to give a toleration to Protestant Dissenters *whose doctrines they ascertained*. As to the mere civil privileges which the Dissenters held as subjects before the Revolution, these were not touched at all. The laws have fully permitted, in a qualification for all offices, to such Dissenters, *an occasional conformity:* a thing I believe singular, where tests are admitted. The act, called the Test Act, itself, is, with regard to them, grown to be hardly anything more than a dead letter. Whenever the Dissenters cease by their conduct to give any alarm to the government, in Church and State, I think it very probable that even this matter, rather disgustful than inconvenient to them, may be removed, or at least so modified as to distinguish the qualification to those offices which really *guide the state* from those which are *merely instrumental,* or that some other and better tests may be put in their place.

So far as to England. In Ireland you have outran us. Without waiting for an English example, you have totally, and without any modification whatsoever, repealed the test as to Protestant Dissenters. . . .

By this unqualified repeal you certainly did not mean to deny that it was the duty of the crown to preserve the Church against Protestant Dissenters; or taking this to be the true sense of the two Revolution acts of King William, and of the previous and subsequent Union acts of Queen Anne, you did not declare by this most unqualified repeal, by which you broke down all the barriers, not invented, indeed, but carefully preserved, at the Revolution—you did not then and by that proceeding declare that you had advised the king to perjury towards God and perfidy towards the Church. No! far, very far from it! You never would have done it, if you did not think it could be done with perfect repose to the royal conscience, and perfect safety to the national established religion. You did this upon a full consideration of the circumstances of your country. Now, if circumstances required it, why should it be contrary to the king's oath, his Parliament judging on those circumstances, to restore to his Catholic people, in such measure and with such modifications as the public wisdom shall think proper to add, *some part* in these franchises which they formerly had held without any limitation at all, and which, upon no sort of urgent reason at the time, they were deprived of? If such means can with any probability be shown, from circumstances, rather to add strength to our mixed ecclesiastical and secular Constitution than to weaken it, surely they are means infinitely to be preferred to penalties, incapacities, and proscriptions, continued from generation to generation. They are perfectly consistent with the other parts of the coronation oath, in which the king swears to maintain "the laws of God and the true profession of the Gospel, and to govern the people according to the statutes in Parliament agreed upon, and the laws and customs of the realm." In consenting to such a statute, the crown would act at least as agreeable to the laws of God, and to the true profession of the Gospel, and to the laws and customs of the kingdom . . .

I cannot conceive how anything worse can be said of the Protestant religion of the Church of England than this—that, wherever it is judged proper to give it a legal establishment, it becomes necessary to deprive the body of the people, if they adhere to their old opinions, of "their liberties and of all their free customs," and to reduce them to a state of *civil* servitude.

There is no man on earth, I believe, more willing than I am to lay it down as a fundamental of the Constitution, that the Church of England should be united and even identified with it; but, allowing this, I cannot allow that all *laws of regulation*, made from time to time, in support of that fundamental law, are of course equally fundamental and equally unchangeable. This would be to confound all the branches of legislation and of jurisprudence. The *crown* and the personal safety of the monarch are *fundamentals* in our Constitution: yet I hope that no man regrets that the rabble of statutes got together during the reign of Henry the Eighth, by which treasons are multiplied with so prolific an energy, have been all repealed in a body; although they were all, or most of them, made in support of things truly fundamental in our Constitution. So were several of the acts by which the crown exercised its supremacy: such as the act of Elizabeth for making the *high commission courts,* and the like; as well as things made treason in the time of Charles the Second. None of this species of *secondary and subsidiary laws* have been held fundamental. They have yielded to circumstances; particularly where they were thought, even in their consequences, or obliquely, to affect other fundamentals. How much more, certainly, ought they to give way, when, as in our case, they affect, not here and there, in some particular point, or in their consequence, but universally, collectively, and directly, the fundamental franchises of a people equal to the whole inhabitants of several respectable kingdoms and states . . . This way of proscribing men by whole nations, as it were, from all the benefits of the Constitution to which they were born, I never can believe to be politic or expedient, much less necessary for the existence of any state or church in the world. . . .

Recollect, my dear friend, that it was a fundamental principle in the French monarchy, whilst it stood, that the state should be Catholic; yet the Edict of Nantes gave, not a full ecclesiastical, but a complete civil *establishment,* with places of which only they were capable, to the Calvinists of France—and there were very few employments, indeed, of which they were not capable. The world praised the Cardinal de Richelieu, who took the first opportunity to strip them of their fortified places and cautionary towns. The same world held and does hold in execration (so far as that business is concerned) the memory of Louis the Fourteenth, for the total repeal of that favorable edict; though the talk of "fundamental laws, established religion, religion of the prince, safety to the state," &c., &c., was then as largely held, and with as bitter a revival of the animosities of the civil confusions during the struggles between the parties, as now they can be in Ireland.

Perhaps there are persons who think that the same reason does not hold, when the religious relation of the sovereign and subject is changed; but they who have their shop full of false weights and measures, and who imagine that the adding or taking away the name of Protestant or Papist, Guelph or Ghibelline, alters all the principles of equity, policy, and prudence, leave us no common data upon which we can reason. I therefore pass by all this, which on you will make no impression, to come to what seems to be a serious consideration in your mind: I mean the dread you express of "reviewing, for the purpose of altering, the *principles of the Revolution.*" This is an interesting topic, on which I will, as fully as your leisure and mine permits, lay before you the ideas I have formed.

First, I cannot possibly confound in my mind all the things which were done at the Revolution with the *principles* of the Revolution. As in most great changes, many things were done from the necessities of the time, well or ill understood, from passion or from vengeance, which were not only not perfectly agreeable to its principles, but in the most direct contradiction to them. I shall not think that the *deprivation of some millions of people of all the rights of citizens, and all interest in the Constitution, in and to which they were born,* was a thing conformable to the *declared principles* of the Revolution. This I am sure is true relatively to England (where the operation of these *anti-principles* comparatively were of little extent); and some of our late laws, in repealing acts made immediately after the Revolution, admit that some things then done were not done in the true spirit of the Revolution. But the Revolution operated differently in England and Ireland, in many, and these essential particulars. . . . In England it was the struggle of the *great body* of the people for the establishment of their liberties, against the efforts of a very *small faction,* who would have oppressed them. In Ireland it was the establishment of the power of the smaller number, at the expense of the civil liberties and properties of the far greater part, and at the expense of the political liberties of the whole. It was, to say the truth, not a revolution, but a conquest: which is not to say a great deal in its favor. To insist on everything done in Ireland at the Revolution would be to insist on the severe and jealous policy of a conqueror, in the crude settlement of his new acquisition, as a *permanent* rule for its future government. This no power, in no country that ever I heard of, has done or professed to do—except in Ireland; where it is done, and possibly by some people will be professed. Time has, by degrees, in all other places and periods, blended and coalited the conquered with the conquerors. So, after some time, and after one of the most rigid conquests that we read of in history, the Normans softened into the English. . . .

For a much longer period . . . the Protestants settled in Ireland considered themselves in no other light than that of a sort of a colonial garrison, to keep the natives in subjection to the other state of Great Britain. The whole spirit of the Revolution in Ireland was that of not the mildest conqueror. In truth, the spirit of those proceedings did not commence at that era, nor was religion of any kind their primary object. What was done was not in the spirit of a contest between two religious factions, but between two adverse nations. The statutes of Kilkenny show that the spirit of the Popery laws, and some even of their actual provisions, as applied between Englishry and Irishry, had existed in that harassed country before the words *Protestant* and *Papist* were heard of in the world. If we read Baron Finglas, Spenser, and Sir John Davies, we cannot miss the true genius and policy of the English government there before the Revolution, as well as during the whole reign of Queen Elizabeth. Sir John Davies boasts the benefits received by the natives, by extending to them the English law, and turning the whole kingdom into shire ground. But the appearance of things alone was changed. The original scheme was never deviated from for a single hour. Unheard-of confiscations were made in the northern parts, upon grounds of plots and conspiracies, never proved upon their supposed authors. The war of chicane succeeded to the war of arms and of hostile statutes; and a regular series of operations was carried on, particularly from Chichester's time, in the ordinary courts of justice, and by special commissions and inquisitions —first under pretence of tenures, and then of titles in the crown, for the purpose of the total extirpation of the interest of the natives in their own soil—until this species of subtle ravage, being carried to the last excess of oppression and insolence under Lord Strafford, it kindled the flames of that rebellion which broke out in 1641. By the issue of that war, by the turn which the Earl of Clarendon gave to things at the Restoration, and by the total reduction of the kingdom of Ireland in 1691, the ruin of the native Irish, and, in a great measure, too, of the first races of the English, was completely accomplished. The new English interest was settled with as solid a stability as anything in human affairs can look for. All the penal laws of that unparalleled code of oppression, which were made after the last event, were manifestly the effects of national hatred and scorn towards a conquered people, whom the victors delighted to trample upon and were not at all afraid to provoke. They were not the effect of their fears, but of their security. They who carried on this system looked to the irresistible force of Great Britain for their support in their acts of power. They were quite certain that no complaints of the natives would be heard on this side of the water with any other sentiments than those of contempt and indignation. . . . Whilst that temper prevailed, (and it prevailed in all its force to a time within our memory,) every measure was pleasing and popular just in proportion as it tended to harass and ruin a set of people who were looked upon as enemies to God and man, and, indeed, as a race of bigoted savages who were a disgrace to human nature itself.

However, as the English in Ireland began to be domiciliated, they began also to recollect that they had a country. The *English interest*, at first by faint and almost insensible degrees, but at length openly and avowedly, became an *independent Irish interest*—full as independent as it could ever have been if it had continued in the persons of the native Irish; and it was maintained with more skill and more consistency than probably it would have been in theirs. With their views, the *Anglo-Irish* changed their maxims: it was necessary to demonstrate to the whole people that there was something, at least, of a common interest, combined with the independency, which was to become the object of common exertions. The mildness of government produced the first relaxation towards the Irish; the necessities, and, in part, too, the temper that predominated at this great change, produced the second and the most important of these relaxations. English government and Irish legislature felt jointly the propriety of this measure. The Irish Parliament and nation became independent.

The true revolution to you, that which most intrinsically and substantially resembled the English Revolution of 1688, was the Irish Revolution of 1782. . . .

Great Britain, finding the Anglo-Irish highly animated with a spirit which had indeed shown itself before, though with little energy and many interruptions, and therefore suffered a multitude of uniform precedents to be established against it, acted, in my opinion, with the greatest temperance and wisdom. She saw that the disposition of the *leading part* of the nation would not permit them to act any longer the part of a *garrison*. She saw that true policy did not require that they ever should have appeared in that character; or if it had done so formerly, the reasons had now ceased to operate. She saw that the Irish of her race were resolved to build their Constitution and their politics upon another bottom. With those things under her view, she instantly complied with the whole of your demands, without any reservation whatsoever. She surrendered that boundless superiority, for the preservation of which, and the acquisition, she had supported the English colonies in Ireland for so long a time, and at so vast an expense (according to the standard of those ages) of her blood and treasure.

When we bring before us the matter which history affords for our selection, it is not improper to examine the spirit of the several precedents which are candidates for our choice. Might it not be as well for your statesmen, on the other side of the water, to take an example from this latter and surely more conciliatory revolution, as a pattern for your conduct towards your own fellow-citizens, than from that of 1688, when a paramount sovereignty over both you and them was more loftily claimed and more sternly exerted than at any former or at any subsequent period? Great Britain in 1782 rose above the vulgar ideas of policy, the ordinary jealousies of state, and all the sentiments of national pride and national ambition. . . .

At that time, on your part, you were not afraid to review what was done at the Revolution of 1688, and what had been continued during the subsequent flourishing period of the British empire. The change then made was a great and fundamental alteration. In the execution, it was an operose business on both sides of the water. It required the repeal of several laws, the modification of many, and a new course to be given to an infinite number of legislative, judicial, and official practices and usages in both kingdoms. This did not frighten any of us. You are now asked to give, in some moderate measure, to your fellow-citizens, what Great Britain gave to you without any measure at all. Yet, notwithstanding all the difficulties at the time, and the apprehensions which some very well-meaning people entertained, through the admirable temper in which this revolution (or restoration in the nature of a revolution) was conducted in both kingdoms, it has hitherto produced no inconvenience to either; and I trust, with the continuance of the same temper, that it never will. I think that this small, inconsiderable change, (relative to an exclusive statute not made at the Revolution,) for restoring the people to the benefits from which the green soreness of a civil war had not excluded them, will be productive of no sort of mischief whatsoever. Compare what was done in 1782 with what is wished in 1792; consider the spirit of what has been done at the several periods of reformation; and weigh maturely whether it be exactly true that conciliatory concessions are of good policy only in discussions between nations, but that among descriptions in the same nation they must always be irrational and dangerous. . . .

I do not mean to trouble you with anything to remove the objections, I will not call them arguments, against this measure, taken from a ferocious hatred to all that numerous description of Christians. It would be to pay a poor compliment to your understanding or your heart. Neither *your* religion nor *your* politics consist "in odd, perverse antipathies." You are not resolved to persevere in proscribing from the Constitution so many millions of your countrymen, because, in contradiction to experience and to common sense, you think proper to imagine that their principles are subversive of common human society. . . .

As little shall I detain you with matters that can as little obtain admission into a mind like yours: such as the fear, or pretence of fear, that, in spite of your own power and the trifling power of Great Britain, you may be conquered by the Pope; or that this commodious bugbear (who is of infinitely more use to those who pretend to fear than to those who love him) will absolve his Majesty's subjects from their allegiance, and send over the Cardinal of York to rule you as his viceroy; or that, by the plenitude of his power, he will take that fierce tyrant, the king of the French, out of his jail, and arm that nation (which on all occasions treats his Holiness so very politely) with his bulls and pardons, to invade poor old Ireland, to reduce you to Popery and slavery, and to force the free-born, naked feet of your people into the wooden shoes of that arbitrary monarch. I do not believe that discourses of this kind are held, or that anything like them will be held, by any who walk about without a keeper. . . .

There is another way of taking an objection to this concession, which I admit to be something more plausible, and worthy of a more attentive examination. It is, that this numerous class of people is mutinous, disorderly, prone to sedition, and easy to be wrought upon by the insidious arts of wicked and designing men; that, conscious of this, the sober, rational, and wealthy part of that body, who are totally of another character, do by no means desire any participation for themselves, or for any one else of their description, in the franchises of the British Constitution.

I have great doubt of the exactness of any part of this observation. But let us admit that the body of the Catholics are prone to sedition, (of which, as I have said, I entertain much doubt,) is it possible that any fair observer or fair reasoner can think of confining this description to them only? I believe it to be possible for men to be mutinous and seditious who feel no grievance, but I believe no man will assert seriously, that, when people are of a turbulent spirit, the best way to keep them in order is to furnish them with something substantial to complain of.

You separate, very properly, the sober, rational, and substantial part of their description from the rest. You give, as you ought to do, weight only to the former. What I have always thought of the matter is this—that the most poor, illiterate, and uninformed creatures upon earth are judges of a *practical* oppression. It is a matter of feeling; and as such persons generally have felt most of it, and are not of an over-lively sensibility, they are the best judges of it. But for *the real cause*, or *the appropriate remedy*, they ought never to be called into council about the one or the other. They ought to be totally shut out: because their reason is weak; because, when once roused, their passions are ungoverned; because they want information; because the smallness of the property which individually they possess renders them less attentive to the consequence of the measures they adopt in affairs of moment. . . .

The object pursued by the Catholics is, I understand, and have all along reasoned as if it were so, in some degree or measure to be again admitted to the franchises of the Constitution. Men are considered as under some derangement of their intellects, when they see good and evil in a different light from other men—when they choose nauseous and unwholesome food, and reject such as to the rest of the world seems pleasant and is known to be nutritive. I have always considered the British Constitution not to be a thing in itself so vicious as that none but men of deranged understanding and turbulent tempers could desire a share in it: on the contrary, I should think very indifferently of the understanding and temper of any body of men who did not wish to partake of this great and acknowledged benefit. . . .

As to the means which the Catholics employ to obtain this object, so worthy of sober and rational minds, I do admit that such means may be used in the pursuit of it as may make it proper for the legislature, in this case, to defer their compliance until the demandants are brought to a proper sense of their duty. A concession in which the governing power of our country loses its dignity is dearly bought even by him who obtains his object. All the people have a deep interest in the dignity of Parliament. But as the refusal of franchises which are drawn out of the first vital stamina of the British Constitution is a very serious thing, we ought to be very sure that the manner and spirit of the application is offensive and dangerous indeed, before we ultimately reject all applications of this nature. The mode of application, I hear, is by petition. It is the manner in which all the sovereign powers of the world are approached; and I never heard (except in the case of James the Second) that any prince considered this manner of supplication to be contrary to the humility of a subject or to the respect due to the person or authority of the sovereign. . . .

Since you have given to all other Dissenters these privileges without limit which are hitherto withheld without any limitation whatsoever from the Catholics—since no nation in the world has ever been known to exclude so great a body of men (not born slaves) from the civil state, and all the benefits of its Constitution—the whole question comes before Parliament as a matter for its prudence. I do not put the thing on a question of right. That discretion, which in judicature is well said by Lord Coke to be a crooked cord, in legislature is a golden rule. Suppliants ought not to appear too much in the character of litigants. If the subject thinks so highly and reverently of the sovereign authority as not to claim anything of right, so that it may seem to be independent of the power and free choice of its government—and if the sovereign, on his part, considers the advantages of the subjects as their right, and all their reasonable wishes as so many claims—in the fortunate conjunction of these mutual dispositions are laid the foundations of a happy and prosperous commonwealth. For my own part, desiring of all things that the authority of the legislature under which I was born, and which I cherish, not only with a dutiful awe, but with a partial and cordial affection, to be maintained in the utmost possible respect, I never will suffer myself to suppose that at bottom their discretion will be found to be at variance with their justice.

The whole being at discretion, I beg leave just to suggest some matters for your consideration:—Whether the government in Church or State is likely to be more secure by continuing causes of grounded discontent to a very great number (say two millions) of the subjects? or whether the Constitution, combined and balanced as it is, will be rendered more solid by depriving so large a part of the people of all concern or interest or share in its representation, actual or *virtual?* I here mean to lay an emphasis on the word *virtual*. Virtual representation is that in which there is a communion of interests and a sympathy in feelings and desires between those who act in the name of any description of people and the people in whose name they act, though the trustees are not actually chosen by them. This is virtual representation. Such a representation I think to be in many cases even better than the actual. It possesses most of its advantages, and is free from many of its inconveniences; it corrects the irregularities in the literal representation, when the shifting current of human affairs or the acting of public interests in different ways carry it obliquely from its first line of direction. The people may err in their choice; but common interest and common sentiment are rarely mistaken. But this sort of virtual representation cannot have a long or sure existence, if it has not a substratum in the actual. The member must have some relation to the constituent. As things stand, the Catholic, as a Catholic, and belonging to a description, has no *virtual* relation to the representative—but the *contrary*. There is a relation in mutual obligation. Gratitude may not always have a very lasting power; but the frequent recurrence of an application for favors will revive and refresh it, and will necessarily produce some degree of mutual attention. It will produce, at least, acquaintance. The several descriptions of people will not be kept so much apart as they now are, as if they were not only separate nations, but separate species. The stigma and reproach, the hideous mask will be taken off, and men will see each other as they are. Sure I am that there have been thousands in Ireland who have never conversed with a Roman Catholic in their whole lives, unless they happened to talk to their gardener's workmen, or to ask their way, when they had lost it in their sports—or, at best, who had known them only as footmen, or other domestics, of the second and third order: and so averse were they, some time ago, to have them near their persons, that they would not employ even those who could never find their way beyond the stable. . . .

Reduced to a question of discretion, and that discretion exercised solely upon what will appear best for the conservation of the state on its present basis, I should recommend it to your serious thoughts, whether the narrowing of the foundation is always the best way to secure the building? The body of disfranchised men will not be perfectly satisfied to remain always in that state. If they are not satisfied, you have two millions of subjects in your bosom full of uneasiness: not that they cannot overturn the Act of Settlement, and put themselves and you under an arbitrary master; or that they are not permitted to spawn a hydra of wild republics, on principles of a pretended natural equality in man; but because you will not suffer them to enjoy the ancient, fundamental, tried advantages of a British Constitution—that you will not permit them to profit of the protection of a common father or the freedom of common citizens, and that the only reason which can be assigned for this disfranchisement has a tendency more deeply to ulcerate their minds than the act of exclusion itself. What the consequence of such feelings must be it is for you to look to. To warn is not to menace.

I am far from asserting that men will not excite disturbances without just cause. I know that such an assertion is not true. But neither is it true that disturbances have never just complaints for their origin. I am sure that it is hardly prudent to furnish them with such causes of complaint as every man who thinks the British Constitution a benefit may think at least colorable and plausible. . . .

Think whether this be the way to prevent or dissolve factious combinations against the Church or the State. Reflect seriously on the possible consequences of keeping in the heart of your country a bank of discontent, every hour accumulating, upon which every description of seditious men may draw at pleasure. They whose principles of faction will dispose them to the establishment of an arbitrary monarchy will find a nation of men who have no sort of interest in freedom, but who will have an interest in that equality of justice or favor with which a wise despot must view all his subjects who do not attack the foundations of his power. Love of liberty itself may, in such men, become the means of establishing an arbitrary domination. On the other hand, they who wish for a democratic republic will find a set of men who have no choice between civil servitude and the entire ruin of a mixed Constitution. . . .

You mention that the minds of some gentlemen are a good deal heated, and that it is often said, that, rather than submit to such persons, having a share in their franchises, they would throw up their independence, and precipitate an union with Great Britain. I have heard a discussion concerning such an union amongst all sorts of men ever since I remember anything. For my own part, I have never been able to bring my mind to anything clear and decisive upon the subject. There cannot be a more arduous question. As far as I can form an opinion, it would not be for the mutual advantage of the two kingdoms. Persons, however, more able than I am think otherwise. But whatever the merits of this union may be, to make it a *menace,* it must be shown to be an *evil,* and an evil more particularly to those who are threatened with it than to those who hold it out as a terror. I really do not see how this threat of an union can operate, or that the Catholics are more likely to be losers by that measure than the churchmen.

The humors of the people, and of politicians too, are so variable in themselves, and are so much under the occasional influence of some leading men, that it is impossible to know what turn the public mind here would take on such an event. There is but one thing certain concerning it. Great divisions and vehement passions would precede this union, both on the measure itself and on its terms; and particularly, this very question of a share in the representation for the Catholics, from whence the project of an union originated, would form a principal part in the discussion; and in the temper in which some gentlemen seem inclined to throw themselves, by a sort of high, indignant passion, into the scheme, those points would not be deliberated with all possible calmness.

From my best observation, I should greatly doubt, whether, in the end, these gentlemen would obtain their object, so as to make the exclusion of two millions of their countrymen a fundamental article in the union. The demand would be of a nature quite unprecedented. You might obtain the union; and yet a gentleman, who, under the new union establishment, would aspire to the honor of representing his county, might possibly be as much obliged, as he may fear to be under the old separate establishment, to the unsupportable mortification of asking his neighbors, who have a different opinion concerning the elements in the sacrament, for their votes.

I believe, nay, I am sure, that the people of Great Britain, with or without an union, might be depended upon, in cases of any real danger, to aid the government of Ireland, with the same cordiality as they would support their own, against any wicked attempts to shake the security of the happy Constitution in Church and State. But before Great Britain engages in any quarrel, the *cause of the dispute* would certainly be a part of her consideration. If confusions should arise in that kingdom from too steady an attachment to a proscriptive, monopolizing system, and from the resolution of regarding the franchise, and in it the security of the subject, as belonging rather to religious opinions than to civil qualification and civil conduct, I doubt whether you might quite certainly reckon on obtaining an aid of force from hence for the support of that system. We might extend your distractions to this country by taking part in them. England will be indisposed, I suspect, to send an army for the conquest of Ireland. What was done in 1782 is a decisive proof of her sentiments of justice and moderation. She will not be fond of making another American war in Ireland. The principles of such a war would but too much resemble the former one. The well-disposed and the ill-disposed in England would (for different reasons perhaps) be equally averse to such an enterprise. The confiscations, the public auctions, the private grants, the plantations, the transplantations, which formerly animated so many adventurers, even among sober citizens, to such Irish expeditions, and which possibly might have animated some of them to the American, can have no existence in the case that we suppose.

Let us form a supposition, (no foolish or ungrounded supposition,) that, in an age when men are infinitely more disposed to heat themselves with political and religious controversies, the former should entirely prevail, as we see that in some places they have prevailed, over the latter—and that the Catholics of Ireland, from the courtship paid them on the one hand, and the high tone of refusal on the other, should, in order to enter into all the rights of subjects, all become Protestant Dissenters, and, as the others do, take all your oaths. They would all obtain their civil objects; and the change, for anything I know to the contrary, (in the dark as I am about the Protestant Dissenting tenets,) might be of use to the health of their souls. But what security our Constitution, in Church or State, could derive from that event, I cannot possibly discern. Depend upon it, it is as true as Nature is true, that, if you force them out of the religion of habit, education, or opinion, it is not to yours they will ever go. Shaken in their minds, they will go to that where the dogmas are fewest—where they are the most uncertain—where they lead them the least to a consideration of what they have abandoned. They will go to that uniformly democratic system to whose first movements they owed their emancipation. I recommend you seriously to turn this in your mind. Believe that it requires your best and maturest thoughts. . . .

It is a consideration of great moment, that you make the desired admission without altering the system of your representation in the smallest degree or in any part. You may leave that deliberation of a Parliamentary change or reform, if ever you should think fit to engage in it, uncomplicated and unembarrassed with the other question. Whereas, if they are mixed and confounded, as some people attempt to mix and confound them, no one can answer for the effects on the Constitution itself.

There is another advantage in taking up this business singly and by an arrangement for the single object. It is that you may proceed by *degrees*. We must all obey the great law of change. It is the most powerful law of Nature, and the means perhaps of its conservation. All we can do, and that human wisdom can do, is to provide that the change shall proceed by insensible degrees. This has all the benefits which may be in change, without any of the inconveniences of mutation. Everything is provided for as it arrives. This mode will, on the one hand, prevent the *unfixing old interests at once:* a thing which is apt to breed a black and sullen discontent in those who are at once dispossessed of all their influence and consideration. This gradual course, on the other side, will prevent men long under depression from being intoxicated with a large draught of new power, which they always abuse with a licentious insolence. But, wishing, as I do, the change to be gradual and cautious, I would, in my first steps, lean rather to the side of enlargement than restriction.

It is one excellence of our Constitution, that all our rights of provincial election regard rather property than person. It is another, that the rights which approach more nearly to the personal are most of them corporate, and suppose a restrained and strict education of seven years in some useful occupation. In both cases the practice may have slid from the principle. The standard of qualification in both cases may be so low, or not so judiciously chosen, as in some degree to frustrate the end. But all this is for your prudence in the case before you. You may rise a step or two the qualification of the Catholic voters. But if you were to-morrow to put the Catholic freeholder on the footing of the most favored forty-shilling Protestant Dissenter, you know, that, such is the actual state of Ireland, this would not make a sensible alteration in almost any *one* election in the kingdom. The effect in their favor, even defensively, would be infinitely slow. But it would be healing; it would be satisfactory and protecting. The stigma would be removed. By admitting settled, permanent substance in lieu of the numbers, you would avoid the great danger of our time, that of setting up number against property. The numbers ought never to be neglected, because (besides what is due to them as men) collectively, though not individually, they have great property: they ought to have, therefore, protection; they ought to have security; they ought to have even consideration: but they ought not to predominate.

My dear Sir, I have nearly done. I meant to write you a long letter: I have written a long dissertation. . . . Though my hand but signs it, my heart goes with what I have written. Since I could think at all, those have been my thoughts. You know that thirty-two years ago they were as fully matured in my mind as they are now. . . . Time has more and more confirmed me in them all. The present circumstances fix them deeper in my mind.

I voted last session, if a particular vote could be distinguished in unanimity, for an establishment of the Church of England *conjointly* with the establishment, which was made some years before by act of Parliament, of the Roman Catholic, in the French conquered country of Canada. At the time of making this English ecclesiastical establishment, we did not think it necessary for its safety to destroy the former Gallican Church settlement. In our first act we settled a government altogether monarchical, or nearly so. In that system, the Canadian Catholics were far from being deprived of the advantages or distinctions, of any kind, which they enjoyed under their former monarchy. It is true that some people, and amongst them one eminent divine, predicted at that time that by this step we should lose our dominions in America. He foretold that the Pope would send his indulgences hither; that

the Canadians would fall in with France, would declare independence, and draw or force our colonies into the same
design. The independence happened according to his prediction; but in directly the reverse order. All our English Protestant colonies revolted. They joined themselves to France;
and it so happened that Popish Canada was the only place
which preserved its fidelity, the only place in which France
got no footing, the only peopled colony which now remains
to Great Britain. Vain are all the prognostics taken from ideas
and passions, which survive the state of things which gave rise
to them. When last year we gave a popular representation to
the same Canada by the choice of the landholders, and an
aristocratic representation at the choice of the crown, neither
was the choice of the crown nor the election of the landholders limited by a consideration of religion. We had no
dread for the Protestant Church which we settled there, because we permitted the French Catholics, in the utmost latitude of the description, to be free subjects. They are good
subjects, I have no doubt; but I will not allow that any French
Canadian Catholics are better men or better citizens than the
Irish of the same communion. . . . I should not know how to
show my face, here or in Ireland, if I should say that all the
Pagans, all the Mussulmen, and even all the Papists, (since
they must form the highest stage in the climax of evil,) are
worthy of a liberal and honorable condition, except those of
one of the descriptions, which forms the majority of the inhabitants of the country in which you and I were born. . . .

You hated the old system as early as I did. . . . You abhorred it, as I did, for its vicious perfection. For I must do it
justice: it was a complete system, full of coherence and consistency, well digested and well composed in all its parts. It
was a machine of wise and elaborate contrivance, and as well
fitted for the oppression, impoverishment, and degradation of
a people, and the debasement, in them, of human nature itself, as ever proceeded from the perverted ingenuity of man.
. . . My opinion ever was, (in which I heartily agree with
those that admired the old code,) that it was so constructed,
that, if there was once a breach in any essential part of it,
the ruin of the whole, or nearly of the whole, was, at some
time or other, a certainty. For that reason I honor and shall
forever honor and love you, and those who first caused it to
stagger, crack, and gape. Others may finish; the beginners
have the glory . . .

A Letter to
Richard Burke, Esq.
on
Protestant Ascendency in Ireland
1793

Despite Pitt's urgent plea to grant the franchise to Catholics, the Irish Parliament refused to change its historical policy of exclusion. It was known that King George III bitterly opposed such a measure, and this gave strength to the lord-lieutenant of Ireland (the Earl of Westmoreland), and the Dublin Castle administration, to maintain what they called their "Protestant ascendency." Pitt's insistence that the failure to act would bring on revolution finally compelled the Irish Parliament to grant Catholics the right to vote in parliamentary elections, but not to hold any important public office. Even this partial political enfranchisement was strongly opposed by those who insisted upon a complete "Protestant ascendency."

In 1792 Burke's son, Richard, had gone to Dublin as the agent of the Catholic Committee, to help secure the franchise for Catholics. He had failed in his mission, largely because he lacked the tact and prudence necessary to carry through such a delicate and complex negotiation. In 1793 Burke wrote a letter to his son on the nature of the "Protestant ascendency," and expressed his fear that its policy would contribute to the downfall of all Christian religions, and help to bring about the triumph of the Jacobin revolutionaries.

. . . This system, in its real nature, and under its proper appellations, is odious and unnatural, especially when a constitution is admitted which not only, as all constitutions do profess, has a regard to the good of the multitude, but in its theory makes profession of their power also. . . . A word has been lately struck in the mint of the Castle of Dublin; thence it was conveyed to the Tholsel, or City-Hall, where, having passed the touch of the corporation, so respectably stamped and vouched, it soon became current in Parliament, and was carried back by the Speaker of the House of Commons in great pomp, as an offering of homage from whence it came. The word is *ascendency*. . . . This Protestant ascendency means nothing less than . . . an *ascendency,* in public assemblies in England, that is, by a liberal distribution of places and pensions, and other graces of government. This last is wide indeed of the signification of the word. New *ascendency* is the old *mastership*. It is neither more nor less than the resolution of one set of people in Ireland to consider themselves as the sole citizens in the commonwealth, and to keep a dominion over the rest by reducing them to absolute slavery under a military power, and, thus fortified in their power, to divide the public estate, which is the result of general contribution, as a military booty, solely amongst themselves.

The poor word *ascendency* . . . is large enough in its comprehension. I cannot conceive what mode of oppression in civil life, or what mode of religious persecution, may not come within the methods of preserving an *ascendency*. In plain old English, as they apply it, it signifies *pride and dominion* on the one part of the relation, and on the other *subserviency and contempt*—and it signifies nothing else. . . .

This ascendency, by being a *Protestant* ascendency, does not better it from the combination of a note or two more in this anti-harmonic scale. If Protestant ascendency means the proscription from citizenship of by far the major part of the people of any country, then Protestant ascendency is a bad thing, and it ought to have no existence. But there is a deeper evil. By the use that is so frequently made of the term, and the policy which is engrafted on it, the name Protestant becomes nothing more or better than the name of a persecuting faction, with a relation of some sort of theological hostility to others, but without any sort of ascertained tenets of its own upon the ground of which it persecutes other men: for the patrons of this Protestant ascendency neither do nor can, by anything positive, define or describe what they mean by the word Protestant. It is defined, as Cowley defines wit, not by what it is, but by what it is not. It is not the Christian religion as professed in the Churches holding communion with Rome, the majority of Christians: that is all which, in the latitude of the term, is known about its signification. This makes such persecutors ten times worse than any of that description that hitherto have been known in the world. The old persecutors, whether Arian or Orthodox, whether Catholics, Anglicans, or Calvinists, actually were, or at least had the decorum to pretend to be, strong dogmatists. They pretended that their religious maxims were clear and ascertained, and so useful that they were bound, for the eternal benefit of mankind, to defend or diffuse them, though by any sacrifices of the temporal good of those who were the objects of their system of experiment.

The bottom of this theory of persecution is false. It is not permitted to us to sacrifice the temporal good of any body of men to our own ideas of the truth and falsehood of any religious opinions. By making men miserable in this life, they counteract one of the great ends of charity, which is, in as much as in us lies, to make men happy in every period of their existence, and most in what most depends upon us. But give to these old persecutors their mistaken principle, in their reasoning they are consistent, and in their tempers they may be even kind and good-natured. But whenever a faction would render millions of mankind miserable, some millions of the race coëxistent with themselves, and many millions in their succession, without knowing or so much as pretending to ascertain the doctrines of their own school, (in which there is much of the lash and nothing of the lesson,) the errors which the persons in such a faction fall into are not those that are natural to human imbecility, nor is the least mixture of mistaken kindness to mankind an ingredient in the severities they inflict. The whole is nothing but pure and perfect malice. It is, indeed, a perfection in that kind belonging to beings of an higher order than man, and to them we ought to leave it.

This kind of persecutors without zeal, without charity, know well enough that religion, to pass by all questions of the truth or falsehood of any of its particular systems, (a matter I abandon to the theologians on all sides,) is a source of great comfort to us mortals, in this our short, but tedious journey through the world. They know, that, to enjoy this consolation, men must believe their religion upon some principle or other, whether of education, habit, theory, or authority. When men are driven from any of those principles on which they have received religion, without embracing with the same assurance and cordiality some other system, a dreadful void is left in their minds, and a terrible shock is given to their morals. They lose their guide, their comfort, their hope. None but the most cruel and hardhearted of men, who had banished all natural tenderness from their minds, such as those beings of iron, the atheists, could bring themselves to any persecution like this. . . .

The harsh methods in use with the old class of persecutors were to make converts, not apostates only. If they perversely hated other sects and factions, they loved their own inordinately. But in this Protestant persecution there is anything but benevolence at work. What do the Irish statutes? They do not make a conformity to the *established* religion, and to its doctrines and practices, the condition of getting out of servitude. No such thing. Let three millions of people but abandon all that they and their ancestors have been taught to believe sacred, and to forswear it publicly in terms the most degrading, scurrilous, and indecent for men of integrity and virtue, and to abuse the whole of their former lives, and to slander the education they have received, and nothing more is required of them. There is no system of folly, or impiety, or blasphemy, or atheism, into which they may not throw themselves, and which they may not profess openly, and as a system, consistently with the enjoyment of all the privileges of a free citizen in the happiest constitution in the world.

Some of the unhappy assertors of this strange scheme say they are not persecutors on account of religion. In the first place, they say what is not true. For what else do they disfranchise the people? If the man gets rid of a religion through which their malice operates, he gets rid of all their penalties and incapacities at once. They never afterwards inquire about him. I speak here of their pretexts, and not of the true spirit of the transaction, in which religious bigotry, I apprehend, has little share. Every man has his taste; but I think, if I were so miserable and undone as to be guilty of premeditated and continued violence towards any set of men, I had rather that my conduct was supposed to arise from wild conceits concerning their religious advantages than from low and ungenerous motives relative to my own selfish interest. I had rather be thought insane in my charity than rational in my malice. This much, my dear son, I have to say of this Protestant persecution—that is, a persecution of religion itself.

A very great part of the mischiefs that vex the world arises from words. People soon forget the meaning, but the impression and the passion remain. The word Protestant is the charm that locks up in the dungeon of servitude three millions of your people. It is not amiss to consider this spell of potency, this abracadabra, that is hung about the necks of the unhappy, not to heal, but to communicate disease. We sometimes hear of a Protestant *religion,* frequently of a Protestant *interest.* We hear of the latter the most frequently, because it has a positive meaning. The other has none. We hear of it the most frequently, because it has a word in the phrase which, well or ill understood, has animated to persecution and oppression at all times infinitely more than all the dogmas in dispute between religious factions. These are, indeed, well formed to perplex and torment the intellect, but not half so well calculated to inflame the passions and animosities of men.

I do readily admit that a great deal of the wars, seditions, and troubles of the world did formerly turn upon the contention between *interests* that went by the names of Protestant and Catholic. But I imagined that at this time no one was weak enough to believe, or impudent enough to pretend, that questions of Popish and Protestant opinions or interest are the things by which men are at present menaced with crusades by foreign invasion, or with seditions which shake the foundations of the state at home. It is long since all this combination of things has vanished from the view of intelligent observers. The existence of quite another system of opinions and interests is now plain to the grossest sense. Are these the questions that raise a flame in the minds of men at this day? If ever the Church and the Constitution of England should fall in these islands, (and they will fall together,) it is not Presbyterian discipline nor Popish hierarchy that will rise upon their ruins. It will not be the Church of Rome nor the Church of Scotland, not the Church of Luther nor the Church of Calvin. On the contrary, all these churches are menaced, and menaced alike. It is the new fanatical religion, now in the heat of its first ferment, of the Rights of Man, which rejects all establishments, all discipline, all ecclesiastical, and in truth all civil order, which will triumph, and which will lay prostrate your Church, which will destroy your distinctions, and which will put all your properties to auction, and disperse you over the earth. If the present establishment should fall, it is this religion which will triumph in Ireland and in England, as it has triumphed in France. This religion, which laughs at creeds and dogmas and confessions of faith, may be fomented equally amongst all descriptions and all sects—amongst nominal Catholics, and amongst nominal Churchmen, and amongst those Dissenters who know little and care less about a presbytery, or any of its discipline, or any of its doctrine. Against this new, this growing, this exterminatory system, all these churches have a common concern to defend themselves. How the enthusiasts of this rising sect rejoice to see you of the old churches play their game, and stir and rake the cinders of animosities sunk in their ashes, in order to keep up the execution of their plan for your common ruin! . . .

I do not pretend to take pride in an extravagant attachment to any sect. Some gentlemen in Ireland affect that sort of glory. It is to their taste. Their piety, I take it for granted, justifies the fervor of their zeal, and may palliate the excess of it. . . . Yet . . . not one of those zealots for a Protestant interest wishes more sincerely than I do, perhaps not half so sincerely, for the support of the Established Church in both these kingdoms. It is a great link towards holding fast the connection of religion with the State, and for keeping these two islands, in their present critical independence of constitution, in a close connection of *opinion and affection*. I wish it well, as the religion of the greater number of the primary land-proprietors of the kingdom, with whom all establishments of Church and State, for strong political reasons, ought in my opinion to be firmly connected. I wish it well, because it is more closely combined than any other of the church systems with the *crown*, which is the stay of the mixed Constitution—because it is, as things now stand, the sole connecting *political* principle between the constitutions of the two independent kingdoms. I have another and infinitely a stronger reason for wishing it well: it is, that in the present time I consider it as one of the main pillars of the Christian religion itself. The body and substance of every religion I regard much more than any of the forms and dogmas of the particular sects. Its fall would leave a great void, which nothing else, of which I can form any distinct idea, might fill. I respect the Catholic hierarchy and the Presbyterian republic; but I know that the hope or the fear of establishing either of them is, in these kingdoms, equally chimerical, even if I preferred one or the other of them to the Establishment, which certainly I do not. . . .

The legislature of Ireland, like all legislatures, ought to frame its laws to suit the people and the circumstances of the country, and not any longer to make it their whole business to force the nature, the temper, and the inveterate habits of a nation to a conformity to speculative systems concerning any kind of laws. Ireland has an established government, and a religion legally established, which are to be preserved. It has a people who are to be preserved too, and to be led by reason, principle, sentiment, and interest to acquiesce in that government. Ireland is a country under peculiar circumstances. The people of Ireland are a very mixed people; and the quantities of the several ingredients in the mixture are very much disproportioned to each other. Are we to govern this mixed body as if it were composed of the most simple elements, comprehending the whole in one system of benevolent legislation? or are we not rather to provide for the several parts according to the various and diversified necessities of the heterogeneous nature of the mass? Would not common reason and common honesty dictate to us the policy of regulating the people, in the several descriptions of which they are composed, according to the natural ranks and classes of an orderly civil society, under a common protecting sovereign, and under a form of constitution favorable at once to authority and to freedom—such as the British Constitution boasts to be, and such as it is to those who enjoy it?

You have an ecclesiastical establishment, which, though the religion of the prince, and of most of the first class of landed proprietors, is not the religion of the major part of the inhabitants, and which consequently does not answer to *them* any one purpose of a religious establishment. This is a state of things which no man in his senses can call perfectly happy. But it is the state of Ireland. Two hundred years of experiment show it to be unalterable. Many a fierce struggle has passed between the parties. The result is, you cannot make the people Protestants, and they cannot shake off a Protestant government. This is what experience teaches, and what all men of sense of all descriptions know. To-day the question is this: Are we to make the best of this situation, which we cannot alter? The question is: Shall the condition of the body of the people be alleviated in other things, on account of their necessary suffering from their being subject to the burdens of two religious establishments, from one of which they do not partake the least, living or dying, either of instruction or of consolation—or shall it be aggravated, by stripping the people thus loaded of everything which might support and indemnify them in this state, so as to leave them naked of every sort of right and of every name of franchise, to outlaw them from the Constitution, and to cut off (perhaps) three millions of plebeian subjects, without reference to property, or any other qualification, from all connection with the popular representation of the kingdom?

As to religion, it has nothing at all to do with the proceeding. Liberty is not sacrificed to a zeal for religion, but a zeal for religion is pretended and assumed to destroy liberty. The Catholic religion is completely free. It has no establishment—but it is recognized, permitted, and, in a degree, protected by the laws. If a man is satisfied to be a slave, he may be a Papist with perfect impunity. He may say mass, or hear it, as he pleases; but he must consider himself as an outlaw from the British Constitution. If the constitutional liberty of the subject were not the thing aimed at, the direct reverse course would be taken. The franchise would have been permitted, and the mass exterminated. But the conscience of a man left, and a tenderness for it hypocritically pretended, is to make it a trap to catch his liberty.

So much is this the design, that the violent partisans of this scheme fairly take up all the maxims and arguments, as well as the practices, by which tyranny has fortified itself at all times. Trusting wholly in their strength and power . . . they abandon all pretext of the general good of the community. . . . Therefore, they cannot so much as listen to any arguments drawn from equity or from national or constitutional policy . . .

The language of tyranny has been invariable: "The general good is inconsistent with my personal safety." Justice and liberty seem so alarming to these gentlemen, that they are not ashamed even to slander their own titles, to calumniate and call in doubt their right to their own estates, and to consider themselves as novel disseizors, usurpers, and intruders, rather than lose a pretext for becoming oppressors of their fellow-citizens, whom they (not I) choose to describe themselves as having robbed.

Instead of putting themselves in this odious point of light, one would think they would wish to let Time draw his oblivious veil over the unpleasant modes by which lordships and demesnes have been acquired in theirs, and almost in all other countries upon earth. . . .

The people desire the privileges inseparably annexed, since Magna Charta, to the freehold which they have by descent or obtain as the fruits of their industry. They call for no man's estate; they desire not to be dispossessed of their own. . . .

I shall never praise confiscations or counterconfiscations as long as I live. When they happen by necessity, I shall think the necessity lamentable and odious: I shall think that anything done under it ought not to pass into precedent, or to be adopted by choice, or to produce any of those shocking retaliations which never suffer dissensions to subside. Least of all would I fix the transitory spirit of civil fury by perpetuating and methodizing it in tyrannic government. If it were permitted to argue with power, might one not ask these gentlemen whether it would not be more natural, instead of wantonly mooting these questions concerning their property, as if it were an exercise in law, to found it on the solid rock of prescription —the soundest, the most general, and the most recognized title between man and man that is known in municipal or in public jurisprudence?—a title in which not arbitrary institutions, but the eternal order of things, gives judgment; a title which is not the creature, but the master, of positive law; a title which, though not fixed in its term, is rooted in its principle in the law of Nature itself, and is indeed the original ground of all known property: for all property in soil will always be traced back to that source, and will rest there. . . . All titles terminate in prescription . . .

*A Letter to
William Smith, Esq.
on the Subject of
Catholic Emancipation
January 29, 1795*

Burke saw in organized Christianity, and especially in Catholicism, the chief barrier to the spread of triumphant French Jacobinism throughout Europe. In Ireland, where Catholics consisted of over four-fifths of the Christian community, nothing could be more fatal to the cause of Christianity, nor more favorable to Jacobinism, than the policy of those Protestants who wished to continue to exclude Catholics from the political franchise. Burke believed that many such Protestants were not aware that they faced in Jacobinism an alternative to Catholicism which would utterly destroy "the present order of things." It was to make this point crystal clear that he wrote to an Irish friend his *Letter to William Smith, Esq.*, on January 29, 1795.

. . . My whole politics, at present, centre in one point, and to this the merit or demerit of every measure (with me) is referable—that is, what will most promote or depress the cause of Jacobinism. What is Jacobinism? It is an attempt (hitherto but too successful) to eradicate prejudice out of the minds of men, for the purpose of putting all power and authority into the hands of the persons capable of occasionally enlightening the minds of the people. For this purpose the Jacobins have resolved to destroy the whole frame and fabric of the old societies of the world, and to regenerate them after their fashion. To obtain an army for this purpose, they everywhere engage the poor by holding out to them as a bribe the spoils of the rich. This I take to be a fair description of the principles and leading maxims of the enlightened of our day who are commonly called Jacobins.

As the grand prejudice, and that which holds all the other

prejudices together, the first, last, and middle object of their hostility is religion. With that they are at inexpiable war. They make no distinction of sects. A Christian, as such, is to them an enemy. What, then, is left to a real Christian, (Christian as a believer and as a statesman,) but to make a league between all the grand divisions of that name, to protect and to cherish them all, and by no means to proscribe in any manner, more or less, any member of our common party? The divisions which formerly prevailed in the Church, with all their overdone zeal, only purified and ventilated our common faith, because there was no common enemy arrayed and embattled to take advantage of their dissensions; but now nothing but inevitable ruin will be the consequence of our quarrels. I think we may dispute, rail, persecute, and provoke the Catholics out of their prejudices; but it is not in ours they will take refuge. If anything is, one more than another, out of the power of man, it is to *create* a prejudice. Somebody has said, that a king may make a nobleman, but he cannot make a gentleman.

All the principal religions in Europe stand upon one common bottom. The support that the whole or the favored parts may have in the secret dispensations of Providence it is impossible to tell; but, humanly speaking, they are all *prescriptive* religions. They have all stood long enough to make prescription and its chain of legitimate prejudices their main stay. The people who compose the four grand divisions of Christianity have now their religion as an habit, and upon authority, and not on disputation—as all men who have their religion derived from their parents and the fruits of education *must* have it, however the one more than the other may be able to reconcile his faith to his own reason or to that of other men. Depend upon it, they must all be supported, or they must all fall in the crash of a common ruin. The Catholics are the far more numerous part of the Christians in your country; and how can Christianity (that is now the point in issue) be supported under the persecution, or even under the discountenance, of the greater number of Christians? It is a great truth, and which in one of the debates I stated as strongly as I could to the House of Commons in the last session, that, if the Catholic religion is destroyed by the infidels, it is a most contemptible and absurd idea, that this, or any Protestant Church, can survive that event. Therefore my humble and decided opinion is, that all the three religions prevalent more or less in various parts of these islands ought all, in subordination to the legal establishments as they stand in the several countries, to be all countenanced, protected, and cherished, and that in Ireland particularly the Roman Catholic religion should be upheld in high respect and veneration, and should be, in its place, provided with all the means of making it a blessing to the people who profess it—that it ought to be cherished as a good, (though not as the most preferable good, if a choice was now to be made,) and not tolerated as an inevitable evil. If this be my opinion as to the Catholic religion as a sect, you must see that I must be to the last degree averse to put a man, upon that account, upon a bad footing with relation to the privileges which the fundamental laws of this country give him as a subject. I am the more serious on the positive encouragement to be given to this religion, (always, however, as secondary,) because the serious and earnest belief and practice of it by its professors forms, as things stand, the most effectual barrier, if not the sole barrier, against Jacobinism. The Catholics form the great body of the lower ranks of your community, and no small part of those classes of the middling that come nearest to them. You know that the seduction of that part of mankind from the principles of religion, morality, subordination, and social order is the great object of the Jacobins. Let them grow lax, skeptical, careless, and indifferent with regard to religion, and, so sure as we have an existence, it is not a zealous Anglican or Scottish Church principle, but direct Jacobinism, which will enter into that breach. Two hundred years dreadfully spent in experiments to force that people to change the form of their religion have proved fruitless. You have now your choice, for full four fifths of your people, of the Catholic religion or Jacobinism. If things appear to you to stand on this alternative, I think you will not be long in making your option.

You have made, as you naturally do, a very able analysis of powers, and have separated, as the things are separable, civil from political powers. You start, too, a question, whether the civil can be secured without some share in the political. For my part, as abstract questions, I should find some difficulty in an attempt to resolve them. But as applied to the state of Ireland, to the form of our commonwealth, to the parties that divide us, and to the dispositions of the leading men in those parties, I cannot hesitate to lay before you my opinion, that, whilst any kind of discouragements and disqualifications remain on the Catholics, an handle will be made by a factious power utterly to defeat the benefits of any civil

rights they may apparently possess. I need not go to very remote times for my examples. It was within the course of about
a twelvemonth, that, after Parliament had been led into a
step quite unparalleled in its records, after they had resisted
all concession, and even hearing, with an obstinacy equal to
anything that could have actuated a party domination in the
second or eighth of Queen Anne, after the strange adventure
of the Grand Juries, and after Parliament had listened to the
sovereign pleading for the emancipation of his subjects—it was
after all this, that such a grudging and discontent was expressed as must justly have alarmed, as it did extremely alarm,
the whole of the Catholic body: and I remember but one
period in my whole life (I mean the savage period between
1761 and 1767) in which they have been more harshly or
contumeliously treated than since the last partial enlargement.
And thus I am convinced it will be, by paroxysms, as long
as any stigma remains on them, and whilst they are considered
as no better than half citizens. If they are kept such for any
length of time, they will be made whole Jacobins. Against
this grand and dreadful evil of our time (I do not love to
cheat myself or others) I do not know any solid security whatsoever; but I am quite certain that what will come nearest to
it is to interest as many as you can in the present order of
things, religiously, civilly, politically, by all the ties and principles by which mankind are held. This is like to be effectual
policy: I am sure it is honorable policy: and it is better to
fail, if fail we must, in the paths of direct and manly than of
low and crooked wisdom. . . .

Second Letter to
Sir Hercules Langrishe
on the
Catholic Question
May 26, 1795

Irish affairs continued to absorb Burke's attention almost to the day of his death. For a while during the first two months of 1795, when his close friend Fitzwilliam was viceroy of Ireland, Burke held high hopes that his policy of Catholic emancipation would be extended. But George III's inveterate opposition and the equivocation of Pitt resulted in Fitzwilliam's sudden recall. When Grattan's attempt to put some of Fitzwilliam's policies into effect was voted down by the Irish Parliament, Burke expressed his despair in one of his last statements of importance on Irish affairs, when on May 26, 1795, he wrote his *Second Letter to Sir Hercules Langrishe*.

. . . I think I can hardly overrate the malignity of the principles of Protestant ascendency, as they affect Ireland—or of Indianism, as they affect these countries, and as they affect Asia—or of Jacobinism, as they affect all Europe and the state of human society itself. The last is the greatest evil. But it readily combines with the others, and flows from them. Whatever breeds discontent at this time will produce that great master-mischief most infallibly. Whatever tends to persuade the people that the *few*, called by whatever name you please, religious or political, are of opinion that their interest is not compatible with that of the *many*, is a great point gained to Jacobinism. Whatever tends to irritate the talents of a country, which have at all times, and at these particularly, a mighty influence on the public mind, is of infinite service to that formidable cause. Unless where Heaven has mingled uncommon ingredients of virtue in the composition . . . talents naturally gravitate to Jacobinism. Whatever ill-humors are afloat in the state, they will be sure to discharge themselves in a mingled torrent in the *Cloaca Maxima* of Jacobinism. Therefore people ought well to look about them. First, the physicians are to take care that they do nothing to irritate this epidemical distemper. It is a foolish thing to have the better of the patient in a dispute. The complaint or its cause ought to be removed, and wise and lenient arts ought to precede the measures of vigor. They ought to be the *ultima,* not the *prima,* not the *tota* ratio of a wise government. God forbid, that, on a worthy occasion, authority should want the means of force, or the disposition to use it! But where a prudent and enlarged policy does not precede it, and attend it too, where the hearts of the better sort of people do not go with the hands of the soldiery, you may call your Constitution what you will, in effect it will consist of three parts, (orders, if you please,) cavalry, infantry, and artillery—and of nothing else or better. . . .

The worst of the matter is this: you are partly leading, partly driving into Jacobinism that description of your people whose religious principles, church polity, and habitual discipline might make them an invincible dike against that inundation. . . . In the present state of men's minds and affairs, do not flatter yourselves that they will piously look to the head of our Church in the place of that Pope whom you make them forswear, and out of all reverence to whom you bully and rail and buffoon them. Perhaps you may succeed in the same manner with all the other tenets of doctrine and usages of discipline amongst the Catholics; but what security have you, that, in the temper and on the principles on which they have made this change, they will stop at the exact sticking-places you have marked in *your* articles? You have no security for anything, but that they will become what are called *Franco-Jacobins,* and reject the whole together. No converts now will be made in a considerable number from one of our sects to the other upon a really religious principle. Controversy moves in another direction.

Next to religion, *property* is the great point of Jacobin attack. Here many of the debaters in your majority, and their writers, have given the Jacobins all the assistance their hearts can wish. When the Catholics desire places and seats, you tell them that this is only a pretext, (though Protestants might suppose it just *possible* for men to like good places and snug boroughs for their own merits,) but that their real view is, to strip Protestants of their property. To my certain knowledge, till those Jacobin lectures were opened in the House of

Commons, they never dreamt of any such thing; but now the great professors may stimulate them to inquire (on the new principles) into the foundation of that property, and of all property. If you treat men as robbers, why, robbers, sooner or later, they will become.

A third point of Jacobin attack is on *old traditionary constitutions.* . . . It passes my comprehension, in what manner it is that men can be reconciled to the *practical* merits of a constitution, the theory of which is in litigation, by being *practically* excluded from any of its advantages. Let us put ourselves in the place of these people, and try an experiment of the effects of such a procedure on our own minds. Unquestionably, we should be perfectly satisfied, when we were told that Houses of Parliament, instead of being places of refuge for popular liberty, were citadels for keeping us in order as a conquered people. These things play the Jacobin game to a nicety. . . .

IV

ECONOMICAL REFORM

Speech
on Presenting to the House of Commons
(on the 11th February, 1780)
A Plan
for
The Better Security of the Independence of
Parliament, and the Economical Reformation
of the Civil and Other Establishments

The defeat of the British under Burgoyne on October 17, 1777, at Saratoga, was the turning point of the war with the American colonies, and also marked the first step in the weakening of George III's system of personal rule. First France and then Spain and Holland joined the Colonies in the war with Britain. The states of northern Europe and Russia sympathized with the Colonies and put economic pressures on Britain. British commerce was nearly swept from the seas as British naval supremacy declined. Ireland saw her chance, in the midst of these developments, and secured legislative independence from Britain. For a few years it appeared that India might also be lost to the French and to native princes. At home, during 1779–80, long-simmering political discontent at last boiled over in a series of county movements aimed at reforming Parliament, by extending the franchise and by eliminating Crown influence over members. Resolutions and petitions were submitted to the House of Commons by political associations, condemning the abuses of the civil pension list and sinecures for friends and relations of royal favorites.

Burke had long believed that abuses in the royal prerogative were made possible mainly by the King's access to large sums of public money. In December 1779 he felt the time was ripe for action, and informed the House of Commons that after the Christmas recess he would submit a plan for reforming the civil and domestic expenditures of the Crown. His object was to describe and analyze the incredible waste and antiquated arrangements of the King's household, and to show how this "cumbrous . . . Gothic establishment" supported the inefficiency of civil administration and the corruption of Parliament by the King. By removing some of the financial resources of the King, through which George III secured the election of men friendly to his Administration, and had patronage for pensions and sinecures for the Lords, Burke hoped to establish greater independence of Parliament from the Crown.

The objectives and principles of Burke's *Speech on Economical Reform* (1780), were lost in debate for two years, until the King was forced to appoint Lord Rockingham Prime Minister in 1782. Under the Civil Establishment Act of 1782 some of Burke's original proposals were passed.

Mr. Speaker—I rise, in acquittal of my engagement to the House, in obedience to the strong and just requisition of my constituents, and, I am persuaded, in conformity to the unanimous wishes of the whole nation, to submit to the wisdom of Parliament "A Plan of Reform in the Constitution of Several Parts of the Public Economy."

I have endeavored that this plan should include, in its execution, a considerable reduction of improper expense; that it should effect a conversion of unprofitable titles into a productive estate; that it should lead to, and indeed almost compel, a provident administration of such sums of public money as must remain under discretionary trusts; that it should render the incurring debts on the civil establishment (which must ultimately affect national strength and national credit) so very difficult as to become next to impracticable.

But what, I confess, was uppermost with me, what I bent the whole force of my mind to, was the reduction of that corrupt influence which is itself the perennial spring of all prodigality and of all disorder—which loads us more than millions of debt—which takes away vigor from our arms, wisdom from our councils, and every shadow of authority and credit from the most venerable parts of our Constitution. . . .

I enter perfectly into the nature and consequences of my attempt, and I advance to it with a tremor that shakes me to the inmost fibre of my frame. I feel that I engage in a business, in itself most ungracious, totally wide of the course of prudent conduct, and, I really think, the most completely adverse that can be imagined to the natural turn and temper of my own mind. I know that all parsimony is of a quality approaching to unkindness, and that (on some person or other) every reform must operate as a sort of punishment. Indeed, the whole class of the severe and restrictive virtues are at a market almost too high for humanity. What is worse, there are very few of those virtues which are not capable of being imitated, and even outdone in many of their most striking effects, by the worst of vices. Malignity and envy will carve much more deeply, and finish much more sharply, in the work of retrenchment, than frugality and providence. I do not, therefore, wonder that gentlemen have kept away from such a task, as well from good-nature as from prudence. Private feeling might, indeed, be overborne by legislative reason; and a man of a long-sighted and a strong-nerved humanity might bring himself not so much to consider from whom he takes a superfluous enjoyment as for whom in the end he may preserve the absolute necessaries of life.

But it is much more easy to reconcile this measure to humanity than to bring it to any agreement with prudence. I do not mean that little, selfish, pitiful, bastard thing which sometimes goes by the name of a family in which it is not legitimate and to which it is a disgrace;—I mean even that public and enlarged prudence, which, apprehensive of being disabled from rendering acceptable services to the world, withholds itself from those that are invidious. . . .

The private enemies to be made in all attempts of this kind are innumerable; and their enmity will be the more bitter, and the more dangerous too, because a sense of dignity will oblige them to conceal the cause of their resentment. Very few men of great families and extensive connections but will feel the smart of a cutting reform, in some close relation, some bosom friend, some pleasant acquaintance, some dear, protected dependant. Emolument is taken from some; patronage from others; objects of pursuit from all. Men forced into an involuntary independence will abhor the authors of a blessing which in their eyes has so very near a resemblance to a curse. . . . So that, for the present at least, the reformation will operate against the reformers; and revenge . . . will produce all the effects of corruption. . . .

Nothing, you know, is more common than for men to wish, and call loudly too, for a reformation, who, when it arrives, do by no means like the severity of its aspect. Reformation is one of those pieces which must be put at some distance in order to please. Its greatest favorers love it better in the abstract than in the substance. . . .

The apology for my undertaking . . . is not grounded on my want of the fullest sense of the difficult and invidious nature of the task I undertake. I risk odium, if I succeed, and contempt, if I fail. My excuse must rest in mine and your conviction of the absolute, urgent *necessity* there is that something of the kind should be done. . . . It is necessary from our own political circumstances; it is necessary from the operations of the enemy; it is necessary from the demands of the people, whose desires, when they do not militate with the stable and eternal rules of justice and reason, (rules which are above us and above them,) ought to be as a law to a House of Commons. . . .

I do most seriously put it to administration to consider the wisdom of a timely reform. Early reformations are amicable arrangements with a friend in power; late reformations are terms imposed upon a conquered enemy: early reformations are made in cool blood; late reformations are made under a state of inflammation. In that state of things the people behold in government nothing that is respectable. They see the abuse, and they will see nothing else. They fall into the temper of a furious populace provoked at the disorder of a house of ill-fame; they never attempt to correct or regulate; they go to work by the shortest way: they abate the nuisance, they pull down the house.

This is my opinion with regard to the true interest of government. But as it is the interest of government that reformation should be early, it is the interest of the people that it should be temperate. It is their interest, because a temperate reform is permanent, and because it has a principle of growth. Whenever we improve, it is right to leave room for a further improvement. It is right to consider, to look about us, to examine the effect of what we have done. Then we can proceed with confidence, because we can proceed with intelligence. Whereas in hot reformations, in what men more zealous than considerate call *making clear work,* the whole is generally so crude, so harsh, so indigested, mixed with so much imprudence and so much injustice, so contrary to the whole course of human nature and human institutions, that the very people who are most eager for it are among the first to grow disgusted at what they have done. Then some part of the abdicated grievance is recalled from its exile in order to become a corrective of the correction. Then the abuse assumes all the credit and popularity of a reform. The very idea of purity and disinterestedness in politics falls into disrepute, and is considered as a vision of hot and inexperienced men; and thus disorders become incurable, not by the virulence of their own quality, but by the unapt and violent nature of the remedies.

A great part, therefore, of my idea of reform is meant to operate gradually: some benefits will come at a nearer, some at a more remote period. We must no more make haste to be rich by parsimony than by intemperate acquisition. . . .

Sir, before I proceed further, I will lay these principles fairly before you, that afterwards you may be in a condition to judge whether every object of regulation, as I propose it, comes fairly under its rule. This will exceedingly shorten all discussion between us, if we are perfectly in earnest in establishing a system of good management. I therefore lay down to myself seven fundamental rules: they might, indeed, be reduced to two or three simple maxims; but they would be too general, and their application to the several heads of the business before us would not be so distinct and visible. I conceive, then,

First, That all jurisdictions which furnish more matter of expense, more temptation to oppression, or more means and instruments of corrupt influence, than advantage to justice or political administration, ought to be abolished.

Secondly, That all public estates which are more subservient to the purposes of vexing, overawing, and influencing those who hold under them, and to the expense of perception and management, than of benefit to the revenue, ought, upon every principle both of revenue and of freedom, to be disposed of.

Thirdly, That all offices which bring more charge than proportional advantage to the state, that all offices which may be engrafted on others, uniting and simplifying their duties, ought, in the first case, to be taken away, and, in the second, to be consolidated.

Fourthly, That all such offices ought to be abolished as obstruct the prospect of the general superintendent of finance, which destroy his superintendency, which disable him from foreseeing and providing for charges as they may occur, from preventing expense in its origin, checking it in its progress, or securing its application to its proper purposes. A minister, under whom expenses can be made without his knowledge, can never say what it is that he can spend, or what it is that he can save.

Fifthly, That it is proper to establish an invariable order in all payments, which will prevent partiality, which will give preference to services, not according to the importunity of the demandant, but the rank and order of their utility or their justice.

Sixthly, That it is right to reduce every establishment and every part of an establishment (as nearly as possible) to certainty, the life of all order and good management.

Seventhly, That all subordinate treasuries, as the nurseries of mismanagement, and as naturally drawing to themselves as much money as they can, keeping it as long as they can, and accounting for it as late as they can, ought to be dissolved. They have a tendency to perplex and distract the public accounts, and to excite a suspicion of government even beyond the extent of their abuse.

Under the authority and with the guidance of those principles I proceed—wishing that nothing in any establishment may be changed, where I am not able to make a strong, direct, and solid application of those principles, or of some one of them. An economical constitution is a necessary basis for an economical administration.

First, with regard to the sovereign jurisdictions, I must observe, Sir, that whoever takes a view of this kingdom in a cursory manner will imagine that he beholds a solid, compacted, uniform system of monarchy, in which all inferior jurisdictions are but as rays diverging from one centre. But on examining it more nearly, you find much eccentricity and confusion. It is not a *monarchy* in strictness. But, as in the Saxon times this country was an heptarchy, it is now a strange sort of *pentarchy*. It is divided into five several distinct principalities, besides the supreme. There is, indeed, this difference from the Saxon times—that, as in the itinerant exhibitions of the stage, for want of a complete company, they are obliged to throw a variety of parts on their chief performer, so our sovereign condescends himself to act not only the principal, but all the subordinate parts in the play. He condescends to dissipate the royal character, and to trifle with those light, subordinate, lacquered sceptres in those hands that sustain the ball representing the world, or which wield the trident that commands the ocean. Cross a brook, and you lose the King of England; but you have some comfort in coming again under his Majesty, though "shorn of his beams," and no more than Prince of Wales. Go to the north, and you find him dwindled to a Duke of Lancaster; turn to the west of that north, and he pops upon you in the humble character of Earl of Chester. Travel a few miles on, the Earl of Chester disappears, and the king surprises you again as Count Palatine of Lancaster. If you travel beyond Mount Edgecombe, you find him once more in his incognito, and he is Duke of Cornwall. So that, quite fatigued and satiated with this dull variety, you are infinitely refreshed when you return to the sphere of his proper splendor, and behold your amiable sovereign in his true, simple, undisguised, native character of Majesty.

In every one of these five principalities, duchies, palatinates, there is a regular establishment of considerable expense and most domineering influence. As his Majesty submits to appear in this state of subordination to himself, his loyal peers and faithful commons attend his royal transformations, and are not so nice as to refuse to nibble at those crumbs of emoluments which console their petty metamorphoses. Thus every one of those principalities has the apparatus of a kingdom for the jurisdiction over a few private estates; and the formality and charge of the Exchequer of Great Britain for collecting the rents of a country squire. Cornwall is the best of them; but when you compare the charge with the receipt, you will find that it furnishes no exception to the general rule. The Duchy and County Palatine of Lancaster do not yield, as I have reason to believe, on an average of twenty years, four thousand pounds a year clear to the crown. As to Wales, and the County Palatine of Chester, I have my doubts whether their productive exchequer yields any returns at all. . . .

When a government is rendered complex, (which in itself is no desirable thing,) it ought to be for some political end which cannot be answered otherwise. Subdivisions in government are only admissible in favor of the dignity of inferior princes and high nobility, or for the support of an aristocratic confederacy under some head, or for the conservation of the franchises of the people in some privileged province. For the two former of these ends, such are the subdivisions in favor of the electoral and other princes in the Empire; for the latter of these purposes are the jurisdictions of the Imperial cities and the Hanse towns. For the latter of these ends are also the countries of the States (*Pays d'États*) and certain cities and orders in France. These are all regulations with an object, and some of them with a very good object. But how are the principles of any of these subdivisions applicable in the case before us?

Do they answer any purpose to the king? The Principality of Wales was given by patent to Edward the Black Prince on the ground on which it has since stood. Lord Coke sagaciously observes upon it, "That in the charter of creating the Black Prince Edward Prince of Wales there is a *great mystery:* for *less* than an estate of inheritance so *great* a prince *could* not

have, and an *absolute estate of inheritance* in so *great* a principality as Wales (this principality being *so dear* to him) he
should not have; and therefore it was made *sibi et heredibus
suis regibus Angliæ,* that by his decease, or attaining to the
crown, it might be extinguished in the crown."

For the sake of this foolish *mystery,* of what a great prince
could not have *less* and *should* not have *so much,* of a principality which was too *dear* to be given and too *great* to be
kept—and for no other cause that ever I could find—this form
and shadow of a principality, without any substance, has been
maintained. That you may judge in this instance (and it serves
for the rest) of the difference between a great and a little
economy, you will please to recollect, Sir, that Wales may
be about the tenth part of England in size and population,
and certainly not a hundredth part in opulence. Twelve judges
perform the whole of the business, both of the stationary and
the itinerant justice of this kingdom; but for Wales there are
eight judges. There is in Wales an exchequer, as well as in all
the duchies, according to the very best and most authentic
absurdity of form. There are in all of them a hundred more
difficult trifles and laborious fooleries, which serve no other
purpose than to keep alive corrupt hope and servile dependence.

These principalities are so far from contributing to the ease
of the king, to his wealth, or his dignity, that they render both
his supreme and his subordinate authority perfectly ridiculous. It was but the other day, that that pert, factious fellow,
the Duke of Lancaster, presumed to fly in the face of his
liege lord, our gracious sovereign, and, *associating* with a par-
cel of lawyers, as factious as himself, to the destruction of *all
law and order,* and *in committees leading directly to rebellion,* presumed to go to law with the king. The object is neither your business nor mine. Which of the parties got the
better I really forget. I think it was (as it ought to be) the
king. The material point is, that the suit cost about fifteen
thousand pounds. But as the Duke of Lancaster is but a sort
of *Duke Humphrey,* and not worth a groat, our sovereign
was obliged to pay the costs of both. Indeed, this art of converting a great monarch into a little prince, this royal mas-
querading, is a very dangerous and expensive amusement,
and one of the king's *menus plaisirs,* which ought to be reformed. This duchy, which is not worth four thousand pounds
a year at best to *revenue,* is worth forty or fifty thousand to
influence. . . .

If, therefore, we aim at regulating this household, the question will be, whether we ought to economize by *detail* or by *principle*. The example we have had of the success of an attempt to economize by detail, and under establishments adverse to the attempt, may tend to decide this question.

At the beginning of his Majesty's reign, Lord Talbot came to the administration of a great department in the household. I believe no man ever entered into his Majesty's service, or into the service of any prince, with a more clear integrity, or with more zeal and affection for the interest of his master, and, I must add, with abilities for a still higher service. Economy was then announced as a maxim of the reign. This noble lord, therefore, made several attempts towards a reform. In the year 1777, when the king's civil list debts came last to be paid, he explained very fully the success of his undertaking. He told the House of Lords that he had attempted to reduce the charges of the king's tables and his kitchen. . . . Frugality, Sir, is founded on the principle, that all riches have limits. A royal household, grown enormous, even in the meanest departments, may weaken and perhaps destroy all energy in the highest offices of the state. The gorging a royal kitchen may stint and famish the negotiations of a kingdom. Therefore the object was worthy of his, was worthy of any man's attention.

In consequence of this noble lord's resolution, (as he told the other House,) he reduced several tables, and put the persons entitled to them upon board wages, much to their own satisfaction. But, unluckily, subsequent duties requiring constant attendance, it was not possible to prevent their being fed where they were employed: and thus this first step towards economy doubled the expense.

There was another disaster far more doleful than this. I shall state it, as the cause of that misfortune lies at the bottom of almost all our prodigality. Lord Talbot attempted to reform the kitchen; but such, as he well observed, is the consequence of having duty done by one person whilst another enjoys the emoluments, that he found himself frustrated in all his designs. On that rock his whole adventure split, his whole scheme of economy was dashed to pieces. His department became more expensive than ever; the civil list debt accumulated. Why? It was truly from a cause which, though perfectly adequate to the effect, one would not have instantly guessed. It was because *the turnspit in the king's kitchen was a member of Parliament!* The king's domestic servants were all undone, his tradesmen remained unpaid and became bankrupt—*because the turnspit of the king's kitchen was a member of Parliament*. His Majesty's slumbers were interrupted, his pillow was stuffed with thorns, and his peace of mind entirely broken—*because the king's turnspit was a member of Parliament*. The judges were unpaid, the justice of the kingdom bent and gave way, the foreign ministers remained inactive and unprovided, the system of Europe was dissolved, the chain of our alliances was broken, all the wheels of government at home and abroad were stopped—*because the king's turnspit was a member of Parliament*.

Such, Sir, was the situation of affairs, and such the cause of that situation, when his Majesty came a second time to Parliament to desire the payment of those debts which the employment of its members in various offices, visible and invisible, had occasioned. I believe that a like fate will attend every attempt at economy by detail, under similar circumstances, and in every department. A complex, operose office of account and control is, in itself, and even if members of Parliament had nothing to do with it, the most prodigal of all things. The most audacious robberies or the most subtle frauds would never venture upon such a waste as an over-careful detailed guard against them will infallibly produce. In our establishments, we frequently see an office of account of an hundred pounds a year expense, and another office of an equal expense to control that office, and the whole upon a matter that is not worth twenty shillings.

To avoid, therefore, this minute care, which produces the consequences of the most extensive neglect, and to oblige members of Parliament to attend to public cares, and not to the servile offices of domestic management, I propose, Sir, to *economize by principle* . . .

Sir, I think myself bound to give you my reasons as clearly and as fully for stopping in the course of reformation as for proceeding in it. My limits are the rules of law, the rules of policy, and the service of the state. This is the reason why I am not able to intermeddle with another article, which seems to be a specific object in several of the petitions: I mean the reduction of exorbitant emoluments to efficient offices. If I knew of any real efficient office which did possess exorbitant emoluments, I should be extremely desirous of reducing them. Others may know of them: I do not. I am not possessed of an exact common measure between real service and its reward. I am very sure that states do sometimes receive services which is hardly in their power to reward according to their worth. If I were to give my judgment with regard to this country, I do not think the great efficient offices of the state to be overpaid. The service of the public is a thing which cannot be put to auction and struck down to those who will agree to execute it the cheapest. When the proportion between reward and service is our object, we must always consider of what nature the service is, and what sort of men they are that must perform it. What is just payment for one kind of labor, and full encouragement for one kind of talents, is fraud and discouragement to others. Many of the great offices have much duty to do, and much expense of representation to maintain. A Secretary of State, for instance, must not appear sordid in the eyes of the ministers of other nations; neither ought our ministers abroad to appear contemptible in the courts where they reside. In all offices of duty, there is almost necessarily a great neglect of all domestic affairs. A person in high office can rarely take a view of his family-house. If he sees that the state takes no detriment, the state must see that his affairs should take as little.

I will even go so far as to affirm, that, if men were willing to serve in such situations without salary, they ought not to be permitted to do it. Ordinary service must be secured by the motives to ordinary integrity. I do not hesitate to say that that state which lays its foundation in rare and heroic virtues will be sure to have its superstructure in the basest profligacy and corruption. An honorable and fair profit is the best security against avarice and rapacity; as in all things else, a lawful and regulated enjoyment is the best security against debauchery and excess. For as wealth is power, so all power will infallibly draw wealth to itself by some means or other; and when men are left no way of ascertaining their profits but by their means of obtaining them, those means will be increased to infinity. This is true in all the parts of administration, as well as in the whole. If any individual were to decline his appointments, it might give an unfair advantage to ostentatious ambition over unpretending service; it might breed invidious comparisons; it might tend to destroy whatever little unity and agreement may be found among ministers. And, after all, when an ambitious man had run down his competitors by a fallacious show of disinterestedness, and fixed himself in power by that means, what security is there that he would not change his course, and claim as an indemnity ten times more than he has given up?

This rule, like every other, may admit its exceptions. When a great man has some one great object in view to be achieved in a given time, it may be absolutely necessary for him to walk out of all the common roads, and, if his fortune permits it, to hold himself out as a splendid example. I am told that something of this kind is now doing in a country near us. But this is for a short race, the training for a heat or two, and not the proper preparation for the regular stages of a methodical journey. I am speaking of establishments, and not of men.

It may be expected, Sir, that, when I am giving my reasons why I limit myself in the reduction of employments, or of their profits, I should say something of those which seem of eminent inutility in the state: I mean the number of officers who, by their places, are attendant on the person of the king. Considering the commonwealth merely as such, and considering those officers only as relative to the direct purposes of the state, I admit that they are of no use at all. But there are many things in the constitution of establishments, which appear of little value on the first view, which in a secondary and oblique manner produce very material advantages. It was on full consideration that I determined not to lessen any of the offices of honor about the crown, in their number or their emoluments. These emoluments, except in one or two cases, do not much more than answer the charge of attendance. Men of condition naturally love to be about a court; and women of condition love it much more. But there is in all regular attendance so much of constraint, that, if it were a mere charge, without any compensation, you would soon have the court deserted by all the nobility of the kingdom.

Sir, the most serious mischiefs would follow from such a desertion. Kings are naturally lovers of low company. They are so elevated above all the rest of mankind that they must look upon all their subjects as on a level. They are rather apt to hate than to love their nobility, on account of the occasional resistance to their will which will be made by their virtue, their petulance, or their pride. It must, indeed, be admitted that many of the nobility are as perfectly willing to act the part of flatterers, tale-bearers, parasites, pimps, and buffoons, as any of the lowest and vilest of mankind can possibly be. But they are not properly qualified for this object of their ambition. The want of a regular education, and early habits, and some lurking remains of their dignity, will never permit them to become a match for an Italian eunuch, a mountebank, a fiddler, a player, or any regular practitioner of that tribe. The Roman emperors, almost from the beginning, threw themselves into such hands; and the mischief increased every day till the decline and final ruin of the empire. It is therefore of very great importance (provided the thing is not overdone) to contrive such an establishment as must, almost whether a prince will or not, bring into daily and hourly offices about his person a great number of his first nobility; and it is rather an useful prejudice that gives them a pride in such a servitude. Though they are not much the better for a court, a court will be much the better for them. I have therefore not attempted to reform any of the offices of honor about the king's person. . . .

Sir, I move for leave to bring in a bill, "For the better regulation of his Majesty's civil establishments, and of certain public offices; for the limitation of pensions, and the suppression of sundry useless, expensive, and inconvenient places, and for applying the moneys saved thereby to the public service."

V

MISCELLANEOUS CONSTITUTIONAL AFFAIRS

The following selections comprise miscellaneous works dealing with Burke's reflections on various constitutional problems. In one way or another they reveal his basic convictions about such vital elements in his revered English constitution as the nature and role of legal prescription, and the position and function of the Church of England and the House of Commons as parts of the constitutional establishment. In each case his thoughts are his response to some particular historical event or reform movement which vitally affected the constitution.

The first constitutional issue to arise after Burke was elected to the House of Commons was the Wilkes affair. In 1764 John Wilkes, an anti-royalist demagogue, had gotten into legal difficulties over some political and pornographic publications. In 1768, while still outlawed by a court conviction, Wilkes was elected to the House of Commons for the County of Middlesex, but the House voted to expel him as morally unfit to take his seat. He was quickly re-elected three times and was expelled again each time. On the fourth expulsion the House of Commons also incapacitated him, altered the results of the election, and declared the defeated candidate, Colonel Luttrell, to be duly elected. Although Burke had no regard for Wilkes' personal character, he responded to the House of Commons' action with his *Speech on . . . the Middlesex Election,* in which he challenged the constitutional right to reverse election results.

Burke's speeches *On the Acts of Uniformity* (1772), *On Relief of Protestant Dissenters* (1773), and *On the Petition of the Unitarian Society* (1792), are all concerned with the intricate and delicate position of the Church of England as a legally established part of the English constitution, and the problems raised by English subjects, in and out of the Church, who dissented from its doctrines and objected to its privileged position. In all three speeches he defended the Church of England as an integral part of the English constitution, and insisted that its existence and privileges were in perfect harmony with humane principles of religious toleration and with the rights of private conscience. The *Speech on the Acts of Uniformity* was occasioned by two Church of England clergymen, who petitioned Parliament to be relieved of subscribing to certain doctrines of their Church, on the grounds of conscience. Burke's rebuttal to the petition turns upon his important distinction between "the original rights of nature" and ventions, a distinction which runs throughout his political philosophy. In the *Speech on Relief of Protestant Dissenters* he emphasized what all Christians have in common, and favored relief from civil disabilities for Protestant dissenters on the same grounds that he had favored eliminating the penal laws against Roman Catholics in Ireland. In this speech Burke anticipated by seventeen years his eloquent defense of the Church of England in the *Reflections*. In the *Speech on the Petition of the Unitarian Society* he denied that an appeal to conscience justified regarding the very existence of the Church of England as a personal grievance, as contrary to Christianity, illegal, and idolatrous.

Burke's response to the county parliamentary reform movements of 1779–82 produced three notable works, *Letter on Parliamentary Reform* (April 12, 1780), *Speech on the Duration of Parliaments* (1780), and *Speech on the Representation of the Commons in Parliament* (1782). In the first of these works, he objected to any reform of the franchise that stressed numbers at the expense of the corporate nature of man. A mere enlargement in the numbers of representatives would not assure better government. His organic view of the English constitution in its full complexity, as a product of many generations through history, is evident in his caution that any fundamental change in the constitution must come gradually. In his *Speech on the Duration of Parliaments* he objected to any return to triennial parliaments, and even more to the proposed innovation of annual parliaments. He showed how the reformers who favored these projects, in order to restrict Crown influence, would in fact unwittingly further impair the independence and integrity of the House of Commons. In his final speech Burke did not merely defend the English constitutional state as a prescriptive corporate authority; he assumed the offensive against those reformers whose desire to extend the franchise involved drastic innovations in the whole conception of the House of Commons. Burke favored the purging of Parliament of corrupt influence from without; he did not favor a basic change in its structure. There is a tone of growing alarm in the *Speech on the Representation of the Commons in Parliament* that indicates his deep suspicion that the main body of reformers of representation was, in fact, heading a revolutionary movement based upon speculative theories that could destroy the constitution. Burke distinguished between two groups of reformers: the "rights of man" radicals, who demanded personal representation, and the "equal representation" liberals, who aimed at arithmetical exactness in extending the franchise. Since these were precisely the same two groups who differed so strongly from him in 1790 over the French Revolution, it is important for an understanding of his political philosophy to study carefully his position on parliamentary reform in 1780–82.

The "rights of man" theory was held by Thomas Paine, Mary Wollstonecraft, Mrs. Catharine Macaulay, Charles Pigott, Joseph Priestley, Francis Stone, and Joseph Thelwall, all of whom later wrote replies to Burke's *Reflections*. This theory took its norms for individual liberty from an idyllic conception of a primitive or pre-civil state of nature. It made the social contract revocable at the arbitrary will of each disaffected individual. From Burke's point of view the "rights of man" theory was based on philosophical anarchy, and made an antithesis between "Nature" and civil society that denied Aristotle's great precept that man is by nature a political or social animal. Such a conception of man and society, Burke always believed, destroyed not only the very idea of political representation, but the very existence of corporate civil institutions.

The theory of equal representation was an assumed political principle of the secular liberals in the Whig party, such as William Belsham, Sir Brooke Boothby, Benjamin Bousfield, Sir James Mackintosh, George Rous, and Christopher Wyvill. A decade after the county reform movements all of these men wrote replies to Burke's *Reflections* or to his *An Appeal from the New to the Old Whigs*. In the main they rejected the radical "rights of man" theories, although some elements of primitivist doctrines are found in their frequent appeals to "simplicity" in government. These "new Whigs" were sympathetic to Dr. Richard Price, whose sermon provoked Burke to write his *Reflections*. But above all they looked to Charles James Fox as their political leader. To those who read with attention Burke's three works on the county reform movements of 1779–82, there should be nothing unexpected about his split with Fox and the "new Whigs" in 1790–91. Fox was among those who strongly favored annual parliaments and the addition of a hundred county members in the House of Commons. Burke's strong opposition to these and other objectives of Fox and his friends reveals a basic difference in political principles which reached the breaking point during the French Revolution.

Speech
on . . .
the Middlesex Election
[1771]

.   .   .   .   .

In every complicated constitution (and every free constitution is complicated) cases will arise when the several orders of the state will clash with one another, and disputes will arise about the limits of their several rights and privileges. . . .

Carry the principle on by which you expelled Mr. Wilkes, there is not a man in the House, hardly a man in the nation, who may not be disqualified. That this House should have no power of expulsion is an hard saying: that this House should have a general discretionary power of disqualification is a dangerous saying. That the people should not choose their own representative is a saying that shakes the Constitution: that this House should name the representative is a saying which, followed by practice, subverts the Constitution. They have the right of electing; you have a right of expelling: they of choosing; you of judging, and only of judging, of the choice. What bounds shall be set to the freedom of that choice? Their right is prior to ours: we all originate there. They are the mortal enemies of the House of Commons who would persuade them to think or to act as if they were a self-originated magistracy, independent of the people, and unconnected with their opinions and feelings. Under a pretence of exalting the dignity, they undermine the very foundations of this House. . . .

The substance of the question is, to put bounds to your own power by the rules and principles of law. This is, I am sensible, a difficult thing to the corrupt, grasping, and ambitious part of human nature. But the very difficulty argues and enforces the necessity of it. First, because the greater the power, the more dangerous the abuse. Since the Revolution, at least, the power of the nation has all flowed with a full tide into the House of Commons. Secondly, because the House of Commons, as it is the most powerful, is the most corruptible part of the whole Constitution. Our public wounds cannot be concealed; to be cured, they must be laid open. The public does think we are a corrupt body. In our *legislative capacity*, we are, in most instances, esteemed a very wise body; in our judicial, we have no credit, no character at all. . . .

This House has not by itself alone a legislative authority in any case whatsoever. . . . The power of occasional incapacitation, on discretionary grounds, is a legislative power. . . .

A legislative act has no reference to any rule but these two—original justice, and discretionary application. Therefore it can give rights—rights where no rights existed before; and it can take away rights where they were before established. . . . But a judge, a person exercising a judicial capacity, is neither to apply to original justice nor to a discretionary application of it. He goes to justice and discretion only at second hand, and through the medium of some superiors. He is to work neither upon his opinion of the one nor of the other, but upon a fixed rule, of which he has not the making, but singly and solely the *application* to the case.

The power assumed by the House neither is nor can be judicial power exercised according to known law. . . .

The question is over, if this is shown not to be a legislative act.

But what is very usual and natural is, to corrupt judicature into legislature. On this point it is proper to inquire whether a court of judicature which decides without appeal has it as a necessary incident of such judicature, that whatever it decides is *de jure* law. Nobody will, I hope, assert this; because the direct consequence would be the entire extinction of the difference between true and false judgments. For if the judgment makes the law, and not the law directs the judgment, it is impossible there should be such a thing as an illegal judgment given. . . .

Speech

on

the Acts of Uniformity

[1772]

. . . We all know that those who loll at their ease in high dignities, whether of the Church or of the State, are commonly averse to all reformation. It is hard to persuade them that there can be anything amiss in establishments which by feeling experience they find to be so very comfortable. It is as true, that, from the same selfish motives, those who are struggling upwards are apt to find everything wrong and out of order. These are truths upon one side and on the other; and neither on the one side or the other in argument are they worth a single farthing. . . .

Two honorable gentlemen . . . assert, that, if you alter her symbols, you destroy the being of the Church of England. This, for the sake of the liberty of that Church, I must absolutely deny. The Church, like every body corporate, may alter her laws without changing her identity. As an independent church, professing fallibility, she has claimed a right of acting without the consent of any other; as a church, she claims, and has always exercised, a right of reforming whatever appeared amiss in her doctrine, her discipline, or her rites. . . .

In the reign of Charles the First a violent and ill-considered attempt was made unjustly to establish the platform of the government and the rites of the Church of England in Scotland, contrary to the genius and desires of far the majority of that nation. This usurpation excited a most mutinous spirit in that country. It produced that shocking fanatical Covenant (I mean the Covenant of '36) for forcing their ideas of religion on England, and indeed on all mankind. This became the occasion, at length, of other covenants, and of a Scotch army marching into England to fulfil them; and the Parliament of England (for its own purposes) adopted their scheme, took their last covenant, and destroyed the Church of England. The Parliament, in their ordinance of 1643, expressly assign their desire of conforming to the Church of Scotland as a motive for their alteration.

To prevent such violent enterprises on the one side or on the other, . . . the Act of Union provided that presbytery should continue the Scotch, as episcopacy the English establishment, and that this separate and mutually independent Church-government was to be considered as a part of the Union, without aiming at putting the regulation within each Church out of its own power, without putting both Churches out of the power of the State. It could not mean to forbid us to set anything ecclesiastical in order, but at the expense of tearing up all foundations, and forfeiting the inestimable benefits (for inestimable they are) which we derive from the happy union of the two kingdoms. To suppose otherwise is to suppose that the act intended we could not meddle at all with the Church, but we must as a preliminary destroy the State. . . .

If ever there was anything to which, from reason, nature, habit, and principle, I am totally averse, it is persecution for conscientious difference in opinion. If these gentlemen complained justly of any compulsion upon them on that article, I would hardly wait for their petitions; as soon as I knew the evil, I would haste to the cure; I would even run before their complaints.

I will not enter into the abstract merits of our Articles and Liturgy. Perhaps there are some things in them which one would wish had not been there. They are not without the marks and characters of human frailty.

But it is not human frailty and imperfection, and even a considerable degree of them, that becomes a ground for your alteration; for by no alteration will you get rid of those errors, however you may delight yourselves in varying to infinity the fashion of them. . . .

It ill becomes your gravity, on the petition of a few gentlemen, to listen to anything that tends to shake one of the capital pillars of the state, and alarm the body of your people upon that one ground, in which every hope and fear, every interest, passion, prejudice, everything which can affect the human breast, are all involved together. If you make this a season for religious alterations, depend upon it, you will soon find it a season of religious tumults and religious wars.

These gentlemen complain of hardship. No considerable number shows discontent; but, in order to give satisfaction to any number of respectable men, who come in so decent and constitutional a mode before us, let us examine a little what that hardship is. They want to be preferred clergymen in the Church of England as by law established; but their consciences will not suffer them to conform to the doctrines and practices of that Church: that is, they want to be teachers in a church to which they do not belong; and it is an odd sort of hardship. They want to receive the emoluments appropriated for teaching one set of doctrines, whilst they are teaching another. A church, in any legal sense, is only a certain system of religious doctrines and practices fixed and ascertained by some law—by the difference of which laws different churches (as different commonwealths) are made in various parts of the world; and the establishment is a tax laid by the same sovereign authority for payment of those who so teach and so practise: for no legislature was ever so absurd as to tax its people to support men for teaching and acting as they please, but by some prescribed rule.

The hardship amounts to this—that the people of England are not taxed two shillings in the pound to pay them for teaching, as divine truths, their own particular fancies. . . .

The laws of toleration provide for every real grievance that these gentlemen can rationally complain of. Are they hindered from professing their belief of what they think to be truth? If they do not like the Establishment, there are an hundred different modes of Dissent in which they may teach. But even if they are so unfortunately circumstanced that of all that variety none will please them, they have free liberty to assemble a congregation of their own; and if any persons think their fancies (they may be brilliant imaginations) worth paying for, they are at liberty to maintain them as their clergy: nothing hinders it. But if they cannot get an hundred people together who will pay for their reading a liturgy after their form, with what face can they insist upon the nation's conforming to their ideas, for no other visible purpose than the enabling them to receive with a good conscience the tenth part of the produce of your lands? . . .

But how do you ease and relieve? How do you know, that, in making a new door into the Church for these gentlemen, you do not drive ten times their number out of it? . . . Alter your Liturgy—will it please all even of those who wish an alteration? will they agree in what ought to be altered? And after it is altered to the mind of every one, you are no further advanced than if you had not taken a single step; because a large body of men will then say you ought to have no liturgy at all: and then these men, who now complain so bitterly that they are shut out, will themselves bar the door against thousands of others. Dissent, not satisfied with toleration, is not conscience, but ambition. . . .

Nor can you content other men's conscience, real or pretended, by any concessions: follow your own; seek peace and ensue it. You have no symptoms of discontent in the people to their Establishment. The churches are too small for their congregations. The livings are too few for their candidates. The spirit of religious controversy has slackened by the nature of things: by act you may revive it. I will not enter into the question, how much truth is preferable to peace. Perhaps truth may be far better. But as we have scarcely ever the same certainty in the one that we have in the other, I would, unless the truth were evident indeed, hold fast to peace, which has in her company charity, the highest of the virtues. . . .

I know many gentlemen think that the very essence of liberty consists in being governed according to law, as if grievances had nothing real and intrinsic; but I cannot be of that opinion. Grievances may subsist by law. Nay, I do not know whether any grievance can be considered as intolerable, until it is established and sanctified by law. . . .

The matter . . . does not concern toleration, but establishment; and it is not the rights of private conscience that are in question, but the propriety of the terms which are proposed by law as a title to public emoluments: so that the complaint is not, that there is not toleration of diversity in opinion, but that diversity in opinion is not rewarded by bishoprics, rectories, and collegiate stalls. When gentlemen complain of the subscription as matter of grievance, the complaint arises from confounding private judgment, whose rights are anterior to law, and the qualifications which the law creates for its own magistracies, whether civil or religious. To take away from men their lives, their liberty, or their property, those things for the protection of which society was introduced, is great hardship and intolerable tyranny; but to annex any condition you please to benefits artificially created is the most just, natural, and proper thing in the world. . . .

In all human institutions, a great part, almost all regulations, are made from the mere necessity of the case, let the theoretical merits of the question be what they will. . . .

When tyranny is extreme, and abuses of government intolerable, men resort to the rights of Nature to shake it off. When they have done so, the very same principle of necessity of human affairs to establish some other authority, which shall preserve the order of this new institution, must be obeyed, until they grow intolerable; and you shall not be suffered to plead original liberty against such an institution. . . .

If you will have religion publicly practised and publicly taught, you must have a power to say what that religion will be which you will protect and encourage, and to distinguish it by such marks and characteristics as you in your wisdom shall think fit. . . . Your determination may be unwise in this as in other matters; but it cannot be unjust, hard, or oppressive, or contrary to the liberty of any man, or in the least degree exceeding your province. It is, therefore, as a grievance, fairly none at all—nothing but what is essential, not only to the order, but to the liberty, of the whole community.

The petitioners are so sensible of the force of these arguments, that they do admit of one subscription—that is, to the Scripture. . . .

If the Church be, as Mr. Locke defines it, *a voluntary society,* &c., then it is essential to this voluntary society to exclude from her voluntary society any member she thinks fit, or to oppose the entrance of any upon such conditions as she thinks proper. For, otherwise, it would be a voluntary society acting contrary to her will, which is a contradiction in terms. And this is Mr. Locke's opinion, the advocate for the largest scheme of ecclesiastical and civil toleration to Protestants (for to Papists he allows no toleration at all).

They dispute only the extent of the subscription; they therefore tacitly admit the equity of the principle itself. Here they do not resort to the original rights of Nature, because it is manifest that those rights give as large a power of controverting every part of Scripture, or even the authority of the whole, as they do to the controverting any articles whatsoever. When a man requires you to sign an assent to Scripture, he requires you to assent to a doctrine as contrary to your natural understanding, and to your rights of free inquiry, as those who require your conformity to any one article whatsoever.

The subscription to Scripture is the most astonishing idea I ever heard, and will amount to just nothing at all. Gentlemen so acute have not, that I have heard, ever thought of answering a plain, obvious question: What is that Scripture to which they are content to subscribe? They do not think that a book becomes of divine authority because it is bound in blue morocco . . . The Bible is a vast collection of different treatises: a man who holds the divine authority of one may consider the other as merely human. What is his Canon? The Jewish? St. Jerome's? that of the Thirty-Nine Articles? Luther's? There are some who reject the Canticles; others, six of the Epistles; the Apocalypse has been suspected even as heretical, and was doubted of for many ages, and by many great men. As these narrow the Canon, others have enlarged it by admitting St. Barnabas's Epistles, the Apostolic Constitutions, to say nothing of many other Gospels. Therefore, to ascertain Scripture, you must have one article more; and you must define what that Scripture is which you mean to teach. . . .

The Scripture is no one summary of doctrines regularly digested, in which a man could not mistake his way. It is a most venerable, but most multifarious, collection of the records of the divine economy: a collection of an infinite variety —of cosmogony, theology, history, prophecy, psalmody, morality, apologue, allegory, legislation, ethics, carried through different books, by different authors, at different ages, for different ends and purposes. It is necessary to sort out what is intended for example, what only as narrative—what to be understood literally, what figuratively—where one precept is to be controlled and modified by another—what is used directly, and what only as an argument *ad hominem*—what is temporary, and what of perpetual obligation—what appropriated to one state and to one set of men, and what the general duty of all Christians. If we do not get some security for this, we not only permit, but we actually pay for, all the dangerous fanaticism which can be produced to corrupt our people, and to derange the public worship of the country. . . .

Speech
on
. . . the Relief of Protestant
Dissenters
[1773]

. . . The honorable gentleman thinks that the Dissenters enjoy a large share of liberty under a connivance; and he thinks that the establishing toleration by law is an attack upon Christianity.

The first of these is a contradiction in terms. Liberty under a connivance! Connivance is a relaxation from slavery, not a definition of liberty. What is connivance, but a state under which all slaves live? If I was to describe slavery, I would say, with those who *hate* it, it is living under will, not under law . . . The state of slavery and connivance is the same thing. If the liberty enjoyed be a liberty not of toleration, but of connivance, the only question is, whether establishing such by law is an attack upon Christianity. Toleration an attack upon Christianity! What, then! are we come to this pass, to suppose that nothing can support Christianity but the principles of persecution? Is that, then, the idea of establishment? . . . I am persuaded that toleration, so far from being an attack upon Christianity, becomes the best and surest support that possibly can be given to it. The Christian religion itself arose without establishment—it arose even without toleration; and whilst its own principles were not tolerated, it conquered all the powers of darkness, it conquered all the powers of the world. The moment it began to depart from these principles, it converted the establishment into tyranny; it subverted its foundations from that very hour. Zealous as I am for the principle of an establishment, so just an abhorrence do I conceive against whatever may shake it. I know nothing but the supposed necessity of persecution that can make an establishment disgusting. I would have toleration a part of establishment, as a principle favorable to Christianity, and as a part of Christianity.

All seem agreed that the law, as it stands, inflicting penalties on all religious teachers and on schoolmasters who do not sign the Thirty-Nine Articles of Religion, ought not to be executed. We are all agreed that *the law is not good:* for that, I presume, is undoubtedly the idea of a law that ought not to be executed. The question, therefore, is, whether in a well-constituted commonwealth . . . it is wise to retain those laws which it is not proper to execute. A penal law not ordinarily put in execution seems to me to be a very absurd and a very dangerous thing. For if its principle be right, if the object of its prohibitions and penalties be a real evil, then you do in effect permit that very evil, which not only the reason of the thing, but your very law, declares ought not to be permitted; and thus it reflects exceedingly on the wisdom, and consequently derogates not a little from the authority, of a legislature who can at once forbid and suffer, and in the same breath promulgate penalty and indemnity to the same persons and for the very same actions. But if the object of the law be no moral or political evil, then you ought not to hold even a terror to those whom you ought certainly not to punish: for if it is not right to hurt, it is neither right nor wise to menace. Such laws, therefore, as they must be defective either in justice or wisdom or both, so they cannot exist without a considerable degree of danger. Take them which way you will, they are pressed with ugly alternatives.

1st. All penal laws are either upon popular prosecution, or on the part of the crown. Now if they may be roused from their sleep, whenever a minister thinks proper, as instruments of oppression, then they put vast bodies of men into a state of slavery and court dependence; since their liberty of conscience and their power of executing their functions depend entirely on his will. I would have no man derive his means of continuing any function, or his being restrained from it, but from the laws only: they should be his only superior and sovereign lords.

2nd. They put statesmen and magistrates into an habit of playing fast and loose with the laws, straining or relaxing them as may best suit their political purposes—and in that light tend to corrupt the executive power through all its offices.

3rd. If they are taken up on popular actions, their operation in that light also is exceedingly evil. They become the instruments of private malice, private avarice, and not of public regulation; they nourish the worst of men to the prejudice of the best, punishing tender consciences, and rewarding informers.

Shall we . . . trust to the manners of the age? I am well pleased with the general manners of the times; but the desultory execution of penal laws, the thing I condemn, does not depend on the manners of the times. I would, however, have the laws tuned in unison with the manners. . . .

When any Dissenters, or any body of people, come here with a petition, it is not the number of people, but the reasonableness of the request, that should weigh with the House. . . . Toleration is good for all, or it is good for none.

The discussion this day is not between establishment on one hand and toleration on the other, but between those who, being tolerated themselves, refuse toleration to others. . . .

A magistrate, whenever he goes to put any restraint upon religious freedom, can only do it upon this ground—that the person dissenting does not dissent from the scruples of ill-informed conscience, but from a party ground of dissension, in order to raise a faction in the state. We give, with regard to rites and ceremonies, an indulgence to tender consciences. . . .

Whilst interior religion is within the jurisdiction of God alone, the external part, bodily action, is within the province of the chief governor. Hooker, and all the great lights of the Church, have constantly argued this to be a part within the province of the civil magistrate. . . .

I take toleration to be a part of religion. I do not know which I would sacrifice; I would keep them both: it is not necessary I should sacrifice either. I do not like the idea of tolerating the doctrines of Epicurus: but nothing in the world propagates them so much as the oppression of the poor, of the honest and candid disciples of the religion we profess in common—I mean revealed religion . . .

I would respect all conscience—all conscience that is really such, and which perhaps its very tenderness proves to be sincere. I wish to see the Established Church of England great and powerful; I wish to see her foundations laid low and deep . . . I would have her head raised up to that heaven to which she conducts us. I would have her open wide her hospitable gates by a noble and liberal comprehension, but I would have no breaches in her wall; I would have her cherish all those who are within, and pity all those who are without; I would have her a common blessing to the world, an example, if not an instructor, to those who have not the happiness to belong to her; I would have her give a lesson of peace to mankind, that a vexed and wandering generation might be taught to seek for repose and toleration in the maternal bosom of Christian charity, and not in the harlot lap of infidelity and indifference. Nothing has driven people more into that house of seduction than the mutual hatred of Christian congregations. Long may we enjoy our church under a learned and edifying episcopacy! But episcopacy may fail, and religion exist. The most horrid and cruel blow that can be offered to civil society is through atheism. Do not promote diversity; when you have it, bear it; have as many sorts of religion as you find in your country; there is a reasonable worship in them all. The others, the infidels, are outlaws of the constitution, not of this country, but of the human race. They are never, never to be supported, never to be tolerated. Under the systematic attacks of these people, I see some of the props of good government already begin to fail; I see propagated principles which will not leave to religion even a toleration. I see myself sinking every day under the attacks of these wretched people. How shall I arm myself against them? By uniting all those in affection, who are united in the belief of the great principles of the Godhead that made and sustains the world. They who hold revelation give double assurance to their country. Even the man who does not hold revelation, yet who wishes that it were proved to him, who observes a pious silence with regard to it, such a man, though not a Christian, is governed by religious principles. Let him be tolerated in this country. Let it be but a serious religion, natural or revealed, take what you can get. Cherish, blow up the slightest spark: one day it may be a pure and holy flame. By this proceeding you form an alliance offensive and defensive against those great ministers of darkness in the world who are endeavoring to shake all the works of God established in order and beauty. . . .

The honorable gentleman . . . would have us not only fight against infidelity, but fight at the same time with all the faith in the world except our own. In the moment we make a front against the common enemy, we have to combat with all those who are the natural friends of our cause. Strong as we are, we are not equal to this. The cause of the Church of England is included in that of religion, not that of religion in the Church of England. I will stand up at all times for the rights of conscience, as it is such—not for its particular modes against its general principles. . . .

*Speech
on . . .
the Petition of the Unitarian Society*
[1792]

•   •   •   •   •   •

I never govern myself, no rational man ever did govern himself, by abstractions and universals. I do not put abstract ideas wholly out of any question; because I well know that under that name I should dismiss principles, and that without the guide and light of sound, well-understood principles, all reasonings in politics, as in everything else, would be only a confused jumble of particular facts and details, without the means of drawing out any sort of theoretical or practical conclusion. A statesman differs from a professor in an university: the latter has only the general view of society; the former, the statesman, has a number of circumstances to combine with those general ideas, and to take into his consideration. Circumstances are infinite, are infinitely combined, are variable and transient: he who does not take them into consideration is not erroneous, but stark mad; *dat operam ut cum ratione insaniat;* he is metaphysically mad. A statesman, never losing sight of principles, is to be guided by circumstances; and judging contrary to the exigencies of the moment, he may ruin his country forever.

I go on this ground—that government, representing the society, has a general superintending control over all the actions and over all the publicly propagated doctrines of men, without which it never could provide adequately for all the wants of society: but then it is to use this power with an equitable discretion, the only bond of sovereign authority. For it is not, perhaps, so much by the assumption of unlawful powers as by the unwise or unwarrantable use of those which are most legal, that governments oppose their true end and object: for there is such a thing as tyranny, as well as usurpation. You can hardly state to me a case to which legislature is the most confessedly competent, in which, if the rules of benignity and prudence are not observed, the most mischievous and oppressive things may not be done. So that, after all, it is a moral and virtuous discretion, and not any abstract theory of right, which keeps governments faithful to their ends. Crude, unconnected truths are in the world of practice what falsehoods are in theory. A reasonable, prudent, provident, and moderate coercion may be a means of preventing acts of extreme ferocity and rigor: for by propagating excessive and extravagant doctrines, such extravagant disorders take place as require the most perilous and fierce corrections to oppose them.

It is not morally true that we are bound to establish in every country that form of religion which in *our* minds is most agreeable to truth, and conduces most to the eternal happiness of mankind. In the same manner, it is not true that we are, against the conviction of our own judgment, to establish a system of opinions and practices directly contrary to those ends, only because some majority of the people, told by the head, may prefer it. No conscientious man would willingly establish what he knew to be false and mischievous in religion, or in anything else. No wise man, on the contrary, would tyrannically set up his own sense so as to reprobate that of the great prevailing body of the community, and pay no regard to the established opinions and prejudices of mankind, or refuse to them the means of securing a religious instruction suitable to these prejudices. A great deal depends on the state in which you find men. . . .

An alliance between Church and State in a Christian commonwealth is, in my opinion, an idle and a fanciful speculation. An alliance is between two things that are in their nature distinct and independent, such as between two sovereign states. But in a Christian commonwealth the Church and the State are one and the same thing, being different integral parts of the same whole. For the Church has been always divided into two parts, the clergy and the laity—of which the laity is as much an essential integral part, and has as much its duties and privileges, as the clerical member, and in the rule, order, and government of the Church has its share. Religion is so far, in my opinion, from being out of the province or the duty of a Christian magistrate, that it is, and it ought to be, not only his care, but the principal thing in his care; because it is one of the great bonds of human society, and its object the supreme good, the ultimate end and object of man himself. The magistrate, who is a man, and charged with the concerns of men, and to whom very specially nothing human is remote and indifferent, has a right and a duty to watch over it with an unceasing vigilance, to protect, to promote, to forward it by every rational, just, and prudent means. It is principally his duty to prevent the abuses which grow out of every strong and efficient principle that actuates the human mind. As religion is one of the bonds of society, he ought not to suffer it to be made the pretext of destroying its peace, order, liberty, and its security. Above all, he ought strictly to look to it, when men begin to form new combinations, to be distinguished by new names, and especially when they mingle a political system with their religious opinions, true or false, plausible or implausible.

It is the interest, and it is the duty, and because it is the interest and the duty, it is the right of government to attend much to opinions; because, as opinions soon combine with passions, even when they do not produce them, they have much influence on actions. Factions are formed upon opinions, which factions become in effect bodies corporate in the state; nay, factions generate opinions, in order to become a centre of union, and to furnish watchwords to parties; and this may make it expedient for government to forbid things in themselves innocent and neutral. I am not fond of defining with precision what the ultimate rights of the sovereign supreme power, in providing for the safety of the commonwealth, may be, or may not extend to. It will signify very little what my notions or what their own notions on the subject may be; because, according to the exigence, they will take, in fact, the steps which seem to them necessary for the preservation of the whole: for as self-preservation in individuals is the first law of Nature, the same will prevail in societies, who will, right or wrong, make that an object paramount to all other rights whatsoever. There are ways and means by which a good man would not even save the commonwealth. . . . All things founded on the idea of danger ought in a great degree to be temporary. All policy is very suspicious that sacrifices any part to the ideal good of the whole. The object of the state is (as far as may be) the happiness of the whole. Whatever makes multitudes of men utterly miserable can never answer that object; indeed, it contradicts it wholly and entirely; and the happiness or misery of mankind, estimated by their feelings and sentiments, and not by any theories of their rights, is, and ought to be, the standard for the conduct of legislators towards the people. This naturally and necessarily conducts us to the peculiar and characteristic situation of a people, and to a knowledge of their opinions, prejudices, habits, and all the circumstances that diversify and color life. The first question a good statesman would ask himself, therefore, would be, How and in what circumstances do you find the society? and to act upon them. . . .

If religion only related to the individual, and was a question between God and the conscience, it would not be wise, nor in my opinion equitable, for human authority to step in. But when religion is embodied into faction, and factions have objects to pursue, it will and must, more or less, become a question of power between them. If even, when embodied into congregations, they limited their principle to their own congregations, and were satisfied themselves to abstain from what they thought unlawful, it would be cruel, in my opinion, to molest them in that tenet, and a consequent practice. But we know that they not only entertain these opinions, but entertain them with a zeal for propagating them by force, and employing the power of law and place to destroy establishments, if ever they should come to power sufficient to effect their purpose: that is, in other words, they declare they would persecute the heads of our Church; and the question is, whether you should keep them within the bounds of toleration, or subject yourself to their persecution. . . .

Their designs they declare to be to destroy the Established Church, and not to set up a new one of their own. . . . If they should find the State stick to the Church, the question is, whether they love the constitution in *State* so well as that they would not destroy the constitution of the State in order to destroy that of the Church. Most certainly they do not. . . .

Let them disband as a faction, and let them act as individuals, and when I see them with no other views than to enjoy their own conscience in peace, I, for one, shall most cheerfully vote for their relief. . . .

Whether anything be proper to be denied, which is right in itself, because it may lead to the demand of others which it is improper to grant? Abstractedly speaking, there can be no doubt that this question ought to be decided in the negative.

But as no moral questions are ever abstract questions, this, before I judge upon any abstract proposition, must be embodied in circumstances; for, since things are right or wrong, morally speaking, only by their relation and connection with other things, this very question of what it is politically right to grant depends upon this relation to its effects. It is the direct office of wisdom to look to the consequences of the acts we do . . . A man desires a sword: why should he be refused? A sword is a means of defence, and defence is the natural right of man—nay, the first of all his rights, and which comprehends them all. But if I know that the sword desired is to be employed to cut my own throat, common sense, and my own self-defence, dictate to me to keep out of his hands this natural right of the sword. But whether this denial be wise or foolish, just or unjust, prudent or cowardly, depends entirely on the state of the man's means. . . . See whether this be the case of these Dissenters, . . . who think that the national Church Establishment is itself a national grievance . . . The principle of your petitioners is no passive conscientious dissent, on account of an overscrupulous habit of mind: the dissent on their part is fundamental, goes to the very root; and it is at issue not upon this rite or that ceremony, on this or that school opinion, but upon this one question of an Establishment, as unchristian, unlawful, contrary to the Gospel and to natural right, Popish and idolatrous. These are the principles violently and fanatically held and pursued—taught to their children, who are sworn at the altar like Hannibal. The war is with the Establishment itself . . .

A Letter to
the Chairman of the Buckinghamshire
Meeting,
Held at Aylesbury, April 13, 1780,
on the Subject of
Parliamentary Reform

NOTE.

The meeting of the freeholders of the County of Buckingham, which occasioned the following Letter, was called for the purpose of taking into consideration a petition to Parliament for shortening the duration of Parliaments, and for a more equal representation of the people in the House of Commons.

. . . I will not deny that our Constitution may have faults, and that those faults, when found, ought to be corrected; but, on the whole, that Constitution has been our own pride, and an object of admiration to all other nations. It is not everything which appears at first view to be faulty, in such a complicated plan, that is to be determined to be so in reality. To enable us to correct the Constitution, the whole Constitution must be viewed together; and it must be compared with the actual state of the people, and the circumstances of the time. For that which taken singly and by itself may appear to be wrong, when considered with relation to other things, may be perfectly right—or at least such as ought to be patiently endured, as the means of preventing something that is worse. So far with regard to what at first view may appear a *distemper* in the Constitution. As to the *remedy* of that distemper an equal caution ought to be used; because this latter consideration is not single and separate, no more than the former. There are many things in reformation which would be proper to be done, if other things can be done along with them, but which, if they cannot be so accompanied, ought not to be done at all. I therefore wish, when any new matter of this deep nature is proposed to me, to have the whole scheme distinctly in my view, and full time to consider of it. Please God, I will walk with caution, whenever I am not able clearly to see my way before me.

I am now growing old. I have from my very early youth been conversant in reading and thinking upon the subject of our laws and Constitution, as well as upon those of other times and other countries; I have been for fifteen years a very laborious member of Parliament, and in that time have had great opportunities of seeing with my own eyes the working of the machine of our government, and remarking where it went smoothly and did its business, and where it checked in its movements, or where it damaged its work; I have also had and used the opportunities of conversing with men of the greatest wisdom and fullest experience in those matters; and I do declare to you most solemnly and most truly, that, on the result of all this reading, thinking, experience, and communication, I am not able to come to an immediate resolution in favor of a change of the groundwork of our Constitution, and in particular, that, in the present state of the country, in the present state of our representation, in the present state of our rights and modes of electing, in the present state of the several prevalent interests, in the present state of the affairs and manners of this country, the addition of an hundred knights of the shire, and hurrying election on election, will be things advantageous to liberty or good government. . . .

I most heartily wish that the deliberate sense of the kingdom on this great subject should be known. When it is known, it *must* be prevalent. It would be dreadful indeed, if there was any power in the nation capable of resisting its unanimous desire, or even the desire of any very great and decided majority of the people. The people may be deceived in their choice of an object; but I can scarcely conceive any choice they can make to be so very mischievous as the existence of any human force capable of resisting it. It will certainly be the duty of every man, in the situation to which God has called him, to give his best opinion and advice upon the matter: it will *not* be his duty, let him think what he will, to use any violent or any fraudulent means of counteracting the general wish, or even of employing the legal and constructive organ of expressing the people's sense against the sense which they do actually entertain.

In order that the real sense of the people should be known upon so great an affair as this, it is of absolute necessity that timely notice should be given—that the matter should be prepared in open committees, from a choice into which no class or description of men is to be excluded—and the subsequent county meetings should be as full and as well attended as possible. Without these precautions, the true sense of the people will ever be uncertain. Sure I am, that no precipitate resolution on a great change in the fundamental constitution of any country can ever be called the real sense of the people. . . .

*Speech
on
. . . the Duration
of Parliaments*
[1780]

It is always to be lamented, when men are driven to search into the foundations of the commonwealth. It is certainly necessary to resort to the theory of your government, whenever you propose any alteration in the frame of it—whether that alteration means the revival of some former antiquated and forsaken constitution of state, or the introduction of some new improvement in the commonwealth. The object of our deliberation is, to promote the good purposes for which elections have been instituted, and to prevent their inconveniences. If we thought frequent elections attended with no inconvenience, or with but a trifling inconvenience, the strong overruling principle of the Constitution would sweep us like a torrent towards them. But your remedy is to be suited to your disease, your present disease, and to your whole disease. That man thinks much too highly, and therefore he thinks weakly and delusively, of any contrivance of human wisdom, who believes that it can make any sort of approach to perfection. There is not, there never was, a principle of government under heaven, that does not, in the very pursuit of the good it proposes, naturally and inevitably lead into some inconvenience which makes it absolutely necessary to counterwork and weaken the application of that first principle itself, and to abandon something of the extent of the advantage you proposed by it, in order to prevent also the inconveniences which have arisen from the instrument of all the good you had in view.

To govern according to the sense and agreeably to the interests of the people is a great and glorious object of government. This object cannot be obtained but through the medium of popular election; and popular election is a mighty evil. It is such and so great an evil, that, though there are few nations whose monarchs were not originally elective, very few are now elected. They are the distempers of elections that have destroyed all free states. To cure these distempers is difficult, if not impossible; the only thing, therefore, left to save the commonwealth is, to prevent their return too frequently. The objects in view are, to have Parliaments as frequent as they can be without distracting them in the prosecution of public business: on one hand, to secure their dependence upon the people; on the other, to give them that quiet in their minds and that ease in their fortunes as to enable them to perform the most arduous and most painful duty in the world with spirit, with efficiency, with independency, and with experience, as real public counsellors, not as the canvassers at a perpetual election. . . .

This bill, I fear, would precipitate one of two consequences —I know not which most likely, or which most dangerous: either that the crown, by its constant, stated power, influence, and revenue, would wear out all opposition in elections, or that a violent and furious popular spirit would arise. I must see, to satisfy me, the remedies; I must see, from their operation in the cure of the old evil, and in the cure of those new evils which are inseparable from all remedies, how they balance each other, and what is the total result. The excellence of mathematics and metaphysics is, to have but one thing before you; but he forms the best judgment in all moral disquisitions who has the greatest number and variety of considerations in one view before him, and can take them in with the best possible consideration of the middle results of all. . . .

All are agreed that Parliaments should not be perpetual; the only question is, What is the most convenient time for their duration? . . . We are agreed, too, that the term ought not to be chosen most likely in its operation to spread corruption, and to augment the already overgrown influence of the crown. On these principles I mean to debate the question. It is easy to pretend a zeal for liberty. Those who think themselves not likely to be incumbered with the performance of their promises, either from their known inability or total indifference about the performance, never fail to entertain the most lofty ideas. They are certainly the most specious; and they cost them neither reflection to frame, nor pains to modify, nor management to support. The task is of another nature to those who mean to promise nothing that it is not in their intention, or may possibly be in their power to perform —to those who are bound and principled no more to delude the understandings than to violate the liberty of their fellow-subjects. Faithful watchmen we ought to be over the rights and privileges of the people. But our duty, if we are qualified for it as we ought, is to give them information, and not to receive it from them: we are not to go to school to them, to learn the principles of law and government. In doing so, we should not dutifully serve, but we should basely and scandalously betray the people, who are not capable of this service by nature, nor in any instance called to it by the Constitution. I reverentially look up to the opinion of the people, and with an awe that is almost superstitious. I should be ashamed to show my face before them, if I changed my ground as they cried up or cried down men or things or opinions—if I wavered and shifted about with every change, and joined in it or opposed as best answered any low interest or passion—if I held them up hopes which I knew I never intended, or promised what I well knew I could not perform. Of all these things they are perfect sovereign judges without appeal; but as to the detail of particular measures, or to any general schemes of policy, they have neither enough of speculation in the closet nor of experience in business to decide upon it. They can well see whether we are tools of a court or their honest servants. Of that they can well judge . . .

That the frequency of elections proposed by this bill has a tendency to increase the power and consideration of the electors, not lessen corruptibility, I do most readily allow: so far it is desirable. This is what it has: I will tell you now what it has not. 1st. It has no sort of tendency to increase their integrity and public spirit, unless an increase of power has an operation upon voters in elections, that it has in no other situation in the world, and upon no other part of mankind. 2nd. This bill has no tendency to limit the quantity of influence in the crown, to render its operation more difficult, or to counteract that operation which it cannot prevent in any way whatsoever. It has its full weight, its full range, and its uncontrolled operation on the electors exactly as it had before. 3rd. Nor, thirdly, does it abate the interest or inclination of ministers to apply that influence to the electors: on the contrary, it renders it much more necessary to them, if they seek to have a majority in Parliament, to increase the means of that influence, and redouble their diligence, and to sharpen dexterity in the application. The whole effect of the bill is, therefore, the removing the application of some part of the influence from the elected to the electors, and further to strengthen and extend a court interest already great and powerful in boroughs: here to fix their magazines and places of arms, and thus to make them the principal, not the secondary, theatre of their manœuvres for securing a determined majority in Parliament.

I believe nobody will deny that the electors are corruptible. They are men—it is saying nothing worse of them; many of them are but ill informed in their minds, many feeble in their circumstances, easily overreached, easily seduced. If they are many, the wages of corruption are the lower; and would to God it were not rather a contemptible and hypocritical adulation than a charitable sentiment, to say that there is already no debauchery, no corruption, no bribery, no perjury, no blind fury and interested faction among the electors in many parts of this kingdom!—nor is it surprising, or at all blamable, in that class of private men, when they see their neighbors aggrandized, and themselves poor and virtuous without that *éclat* or dignity which attends men in higher situations.

But admit it were true that the great mass of the electors were too vast an object for court influence to grasp or extend to, and that in despair they must abandon it; he must be very ignorant of the state of every popular interest, who does not know that in all the corporations, all the open boroughs, indeed in every district of the kingdom, there is some leading man, some agitator, some wealthy merchant or considerable manufacturer, some active attorney, some popular preacher, some money-lender, who is followed by the whole flock. This is the style of all free countries. . . .

These spirits, each of which informs and governs his own little orb, are neither so many, nor so little powerful, nor so incorruptible, but that a minister may, as he does frequently, find means of gaining them, and through them all their followers. To establish, therefore, a very general influence among electors will no more be found an impracticable project than to gain an undue influence over members of Parliament.

Therefore I am apprehensive that this bill, though it shifts the place of the disorder, does by no means relieve the Constitution. . . .

Theory, I know, would suppose that every general election is to the representative a day of judgment, in which he appears before his constituents to account for the use of the talent with which they intrusted him, and for the improvement he has made of it for the public advantage. It would be so, if every corruptible representative were to find an enlightened and incorruptible constituent. But the practice and knowledge of the world will not suffer us to be ignorant that the Constitution on paper is one thing, and in fact and experience is another. We must know that the candidate, instead of trusting at his election to the testimony of his behavior in Parliament, must bring the testimony of a large sum of money, the capacity of liberal expense in entertainments, the power of serving and obliging the rulers of corporations, of winning over the popular leaders of political clubs, associations, and neighborhoods. It is ten thousand times more necessary to show himself a man of power than a man of integrity, in almost all the elections with which I have been acquainted. Elections, therefore, become a matter of heavy expense; and if contests are frequent, to many they will become a matter of an expense totally ruinous, which no fortunes can bear, but least of all the landed fortunes, incumbered as they often, indeed as they mostly are, with debts, with portions, with jointures, and tied up in the hands of the possessor by the limitations of settlement. It is a material, it is in my opinion a lasting consideration, in all the questions concerning election. Let no one think the charges of elections a trivial matter.

The charge, therefore, of elections ought never to be lost sight of in a question concerning their frequency; because the grand object you seek is independence. Independence of mind will ever be more or less influenced by independence of fortune; and if every three years the exhausting sluices of entertainments, drinkings, open houses, to say nothing of bribery, are to be periodically drawn up and renewed—if government favors, for which now, in some shape or other, the whole race of men are candidates, are to be called for upon every occasion, I see that private fortunes will be washed away, and every, even to the least, trace of independence borne down by the torrent. I do not seriously think this Constitution, even to the wrecks of it, could survive five triennial elections. If you are to fight the battle, you must put on the armor of the ministry, you must call in the public to the aid of private money. . . . About the close of the last Parliament and the beginning of this, several agents for boroughs went about, and I remember well that it was in every one of their mouths, "Sir, your election will cost you three thousand pounds, if you are independent; but if the ministry supports you, it may be done for two, and perhaps for less." And, indeed, the thing spoke itself. Where a living was to be got for one, a commission in the army for another, a lift in the navy for a third, and custom-house offices scattered about without measure or number, who doubts but money may be saved? The Treasury may even add money: but, indeed, it is superfluous. A gentleman of two thousand a year, who meets another of the same fortune, fights with equal arms; but if to one of the candidates you add a thousand a year in places for himself, and a power of giving away as much among others, one must, or there is no truth in arithmetical demonstration, ruin his adversary, if he is to meet him and to fight with him every third year. It will be said I do not allow for the operation of character: but I do; and I know it will have its weight in most elections—perhaps it may be decisive in some; but there are few in which it will prevent great expenses.

The destruction of independent fortunes will be the consequence on the part of the candidate. What will be the consequence of triennial corruption, triennial drunkenness, triennial idleness, triennial lawsuits, litigations, prosecutions, triennial frenzy—of society dissolved, industry interrupted, ruined—of those personal hatreds that will never be suffered to soften, those animosities and feuds which will be rendered immortal, those quarrels which are never to be appeased—morals vitiated and gangrened to the vitals? I think no stable and useful advantages were ever made by the money got at elections by the voter, but all he gets is doubly lost to the public: it is money given to diminish the general stock of the community, which is in the industry of the subject. I am sure that it is a good while before he or his family settle again to their business. Their heads will never cool; the temptations of elections will be forever glittering before their eyes. They will all grow politicians; every one, quitting his business, will choose to enrich himself by his vote. They will all take the gauging-rod; new places will be made for them; they will run to the custom-house quay; their looms and ploughs will be deserted. . . .

Gentlemen . . . agree, that this would be the consequence of more frequent elections, if things were to continue as they are. But they think the greatness and frequency of the evil would itself be a remedy for it—that, sitting but for a short time, the member would not find it worth while to make such vast expenses, while the fear of their constituents will hold them the more effectually to their duty.

To this I answer, that experience is full against them. This is no new thing; we have had triennial Parliaments; at no period of time were seats more eagerly contested. The expenses of elections ran higher, taking the state of all charges, than they do now. The expense of entertainments was such, that an act, equally severe and ineffectual, was made against it; every monument of the time bears witness of the expense, and most of the acts against corruption in elections were then made; all the writers talked of it and lamented it. Will any one think that a corporation will be contented with a bowl of punch or a piece of beef the less, because elections are every three, instead of every seven years? Will they change their wine for ale, because they are to get more ale three years hence? . . .

It never can be otherwise. A seat in this House, for good purposes, for bad purposes, for no purposes at all, . . . will ever be a first-rate object of ambition in England. Ambition is no exact calculator. Avarice itself does not calculate strictly, when it games. One thing is certain—that in this political game the great lottery of power is that into which men will purchase with millions of chances against them. In Turkey, where the place, where the fortune, where the head itself are so insecure that scarcely any have died in their beds for ages, so that the bowstring is the natural death of bashaws, yet in no country is power and distinction (precarious enough, God knows, in all) sought for with such boundless avidity—as if the value of place was enhanced by the danger and insecurity of its tenure. Nothing will ever make a seat in this House not an object of desire to numbers by any means or at any charge, but the depriving it of all power and all dignity. This would do it. This is the true and only nostrum for that purpose. But an House of Commons without power and without dignity, either in itself or in its members, is no House of Commons for the purposes of this Constitution.

But they will be afraid to act ill, if they know that the day of their account is always near. I wish it were true; but it is not: here again we have experience, and experience is against us. The distemper of this age is a poverty of spirit and of genius: it is trifling, it is futile, worse than ignorant, superficially taught, with the politics and morals of girls at a boarding-school rather than of men and statesmen: but it is not yet desperately wicked, or so scandalously venal as in former times. . . .

The shortness of time in which they are to reap the profits of iniquity is far from checking the avidity of corrupt men; it renders them infinitely more ravenous. They rush violently and precipitately on their object; they lose all regard to decorum. The moments of profits are precious; never are men so wicked as during a general mortality. . . . It was so in the plague of London in 1665. It appears in soldiers, sailors, &c. Whoever would contrive to render the life of man much shorter than it is would, I am satisfied, find the surest receipt for increasing the wickedness of our nature.

Thus, in my opinion, the shortness of a triennial sitting would have the following ill effects: It would make the member more shamelessly and shockingly corrupt; it would increase his dependence on those who could best support him at his election; it would wrack and tear to pieces the fortunes of those who stood upon their own fortunes and their private interest; it would make the electors infinitely more venal; and it would make the whole body of the people, who are, whether they have votes or not, concerned in elections, more lawless, more idle, more debauched; it would utterly destroy the sobriety, the industry, the integrity, the simplicity of all the people, and undermine, I am much afraid, the deepest and best-laid foundations of the commonwealth. . . .

Speech

on
. . . *the Representation of the*
Commons in Parliament
[1782]

Mr. Speaker—We have now discovered, at the close of the eighteenth century, that the Constitution of England, which for a series of ages had been the proud distinction of this country, always the admiration and sometimes the envy of the wise and learned in every other nation—we have discovered that this boasted Constitution, in the most boasted part of it, is a gross imposition upon the understanding of mankind, an insult to their feelings, and acting by contrivances destructive to the best and most valuable interests of the people. Our political architects have taken a survey of the fabric of the British Constitution. It is singular that they report nothing against the crown, nothing against the lords: but in the House of Commons everything is unsound; it is ruinous in every part; it is infested by the dry rot, and ready to tumble about our ears without their immediate help. You know by the faults they find what are their ideas of the alteration. As all government stands upon opinion, they know that the way utterly to destroy it is to remove that opinion, to take away all reverence, all confidence from it; and then, at the first blast of public discontent and popular tumult, it tumbles to the ground.

In considering this question, they who oppose it oppose it on different grounds. One is in the nature of a previous question: that some alterations may be expedient, but that this is not the time for making them. The other is, that no essential alterations are at all wanting, and that neither *now* nor at *any* time is it prudent or safe to be meddling with the fundamental principles and ancient tried usages of our Constitution—that our representation is as nearly perfect as the necessary imperfection of human affairs and of human creatures will suffer it to be—and that it is a subject of prudent and honest use and thankful enjoyment, and not of captious criticism and rash experiment.

On the other side there are two parties, who proceed on two grounds, in my opinion, as they state them, utterly irreconcilable. The one is juridical, the other political. The one is in the nature of a claim of right, on the supposed rights of man as man: this party desire the decision of a suit. The other ground, as far as I can divine what it directly means, is, that the representation is not so politically framed as to answer the theory of its institution. As to the claim of *right*, the meanest petitioner, the most gross and ignorant, is as good as the best: in some respects his claim is more favorable, on account of his ignorance; his weakness, his poverty, and distress only add to his titles; he sues *in forma pauperis;* he ought to be a favorite of the court. But when the *other* ground is taken, when the question is political, when a new constitution is to be made on a sound theory of government, then the presumptuous pride of didactic ignorance is to be excluded from the counsel in this high and arduous matter, which often bids defiance to the experience of the wisest. The first claims a personal representation; the latter rejects it with scorn and fervor. The language of the first party is plain and intelligible; they who plead an absolute right cannot be satisfied with anything short of personal representation, because all *natural* rights must be the rights of individuals, as by *nature* there is no such thing as politic or corporate personality: all these ideas are mere fictions of law, they are creatures of voluntary institution; men as men are individuals, and nothing else. They, therefore, who reject the principle of natural and personal representation are essentially and eternally at variance with those who claim it. As to the first sort of reformers, it is ridiculous to talk to them of the British Constitution upon any or upon all of its bases: for they lay it down, that every man ought to govern, himself, and that, where he cannot go, himself, he must send his representative; that all other government is usurpation, and is so far from having a claim to our obedience, it is not only our right, but our duty, to resist it. Nine tenths of the reformers argue thus—that is, on the natural right.

It is impossible not to make some reflection on the nature of this claim, or avoid a comparison between the extent of the principle and the present object of the demand. If this claim be founded, it is clear to what it goes. The House of Commons, in that light, undoubtedly, is no representative of the people, as a collection of individuals. Nobody pretends it, nobody can justify such an assertion. When you come to examine into this claim of right, founded on the right of self-government in each individual, you find the thing demanded infinitely short of the principle of the demand. What! *one third* only of the legislature, and of the government no share at all? What sort of treaty of partition is this for those who have an inherent right to the whole? Give them all they ask, and your grant is still a cheat: for how comes only a third to be their younger-children's fortune in this settlement? How came they neither to have the choice of kings, or lords, or judges, or generals, or admirals, or bishops, or priests, or ministers, or justices of peace? Why, what have you to answer in favor of the prior rights of the crown and peerage but this: Our Constitution is a prescriptive constitution; it is a constitution whose sole authority is, that it has existed time out of mind? It is settled in these *two* portions against one, legislatively—and in the whole of the judicature, the whole of the federal capacity, of the executive, the prudential, and the financial administration, in one alone. Nor was your House of Lords and the prerogatives of the crown settled on any adjudication in favor of natural rights: for they could never be so partitioned. Your king, your lords, your judges, your juries, grand and little, all are prescriptive; and what proves it is the disputes, not yet concluded, and never near becoming so, when any of them first originated. Prescription is the most solid of all titles, not only to property, but, which is to secure that property, to government. They harmonize with each other, and give mutual aid to one another. It is accompanied with another ground of authority in the constitution of the human mind, presumption. It is a presumption in favor of any settled scheme of government against any untried project, that a nation has long existed and flourished under it. It is a better presumption even of the *choice* of a nation—far better than any sudden and temporary arrangement by actual election. Because a nation is not an idea only of local extent and individual momentary aggregation, but it is an idea of continuity which extends in time as well as in numbers and in space. And this is a choice not of one day or one set of people, not a tumultuary and giddy choice; it is a deliberate election of ages and of generations; it is a constitution made by what is ten thousand times better than choice; it is made by the peculiar circumstances, occasions, tempers, dispositions, and moral, civil, and social habitudes of the people, which disclose themselves only in a long space of time. It is a vestment which accommodates itself to the body. Nor is prescription of government formed upon blind, unmeaning prejudices. For man is a most unwise and a most wise being. The individual is foolish; the multitude, for the moment, is foolish, when they act without deliberation; but the species is wise, and, when time is given to it, as a species, it almost always acts right.

The reason for the crown as it is, for the lords as they are, is my reason for the commons as they are, the electors as they are. Now if the crown, and the lords, and the judicatures are all prescriptive, so is the House of Commons of the very same origin, and of no other. We and our electors have their powers and privileges both made and circumscribed by prescription, as much to the full as the other parts; and as such we have always claimed them, and on no other title. The House of Commons is a legislative body corporate by prescription, not made upon any given theory, but existing prescriptively—just like the rest. This prescription has made it essentially what it is, an aggregate collection of three parts, knights, citizens, burgesses. The question is, whether this has been always so, since the House of Commons has taken its present shape and circumstances, and has been an essential operative part of the Constitution—which, I take it, it has been for at least five hundred years.

This I resolve to myself in the affirmative: and then another question arises:—Whether this House stands firm upon its ancient foundations, and is not, by time and accidents, so declined from its perpendicular as to want the hand of the wise and experienced architects of the day to set it upright again, and to prop and buttress it up for duration;—whether it continues true to the principles upon which it has hitherto stood; —whether this be *de facto* the constitution of the House of Commons, as it has been since the time that the House of Commons has without dispute become a necessary and an efficient part of the British Constitution. To ask whether a thing which has always been the same stands to its usual principle seems to me to be perfectly absurd: for how do you know the principles, but from the construction? and if that remains the same, the principles remain the same. It is true that to say your Constitution is what it has been is no sufficient defence for those who say it is a bad constitution. It is an answer to those who say that it is a degenerate constitution. To those who say it is a bad one, I answer, Look to its effects. In all moral machinery, the moral results are its test.

On what grounds do we go to restore our Constitution to what it has been at some given period, or to reform and reconstruct it upon principles more conformable to a sound theory of government? A prescriptive government, such as ours, never was the work of any legislator, never was made upon any foregone theory. It seems to me a preposterous way of reasoning, and a perfect confusion of ideas, to take the theories which learned and speculative men have made from that government, and then, supposing it made on those theories which were made from it, to accuse the government as not corresponding with them. I do not vilify theory and speculation: no, because that would be to vilify reason itself. . . . No—whenever I speak against theory, I mean always a weak, erroneous, fallacious, unfounded, or imperfect theory; and one of the ways of discovering that it is a false theory is by comparing it with practice. This is the true touchstone of all theories which regard man and the affairs of men—Does it suit his nature in general?—does it suit his nature as modified by his habits?

The more frequently this affair is discussed, the stronger the case appears to the sense and the feelings of mankind. I have no more doubt than I entertain of my existence, that this very thing, which is stated as an horrible thing, is the means of the preservation of our Constitution whilst it lasts—of curing it of many of the disorders which, attending every species of institution, would attend the principle of an exact local representation, or a representation on the principle of numbers. If you reject personal representation, you are pushed upon expedience; and then what they wish us to do is, to prefer their speculations on that subject to the happy experience of this country, of a growing liberty and a growing prosperity for five hundred years. Whatever respect I have for their talents, this, for one, I will not do. Then what is the standard of expedience? Expedience is that which is good for the community, and good for every individual in it. Now this expedience is the *desideratum,* to be sought either without the experience of means or with that experience. If without, as in case of the fabrication of a new commonwealth, I will hear the learned arguing what promises to be expedient; but if we are to judge of a commonwealth actually existing, the first thing I inquire is, What has been *found* expedient or inexpedient? And I will not take their *promise* rather than the *performance* of the Constitution. . . .

But can you fairly and distinctly point out what one evil or grievance has happened which you can refer to the representative not following the opinion of his constituents? What one symptom do we find of this inequality? But it is not an arithmetical inequality with which we ought to trouble ourselves. If there be a moral, a political equality, this is the *desideratum* in our Constitution, and in every constitution in the world. Moral inequality is as between places and between classes. Now, I ask, what advantage do you find that the places which abound in representation possess over others in which it is more scanty, in security for freedom, in security for justice, or in any one of those means of procuring temporal prosperity and eternal happiness, the ends for which society was formed? Are the local interests of Cornwall and Wiltshire, for instance, their roads, canals, their prisons, their police, better than Yorkshire, Warwickshire, or Staffordshire? Warwick has members: is Warwick or Stafford more opulent, happy, or free than Newcastle, or than Birmingham? Is Wiltshire the pampered favorite, whilst Yorkshire, like the child of the bondwoman, is turned out to the desert? This is like the unhappy persons who live, if they can be said to live, in the statical chair—who are ever feeling their pulse, and who do not judge of health by the aptitude of the body to perform its functions, but by their ideas of what ought to be the true balance between the several secretions. Is a committee of Cornwall, &c., thronged, and the others deserted? No. You have an equal representation, because you have men equally interested in the prosperity of the whole, who are involved in the general interest and the general sympathy; and, perhaps, these places furnishing a superfluity of public agents and administrators, (whether in strictness they are representatives or not I do not mean to inquire, but they are agents and administrators,) they will stand clearer of local interests, passions, prejudices, and cabals than the others, and therefore preserve the balance of the parts, and with a more general view and a more steady hand than the rest.

In every political proposal we must not leave out of the question the political views and object of the proposer; and these we discover, not by what he says, but by the principles he lays down. "I mean," says he, "a moderate and temperate reform: that is, I mean to do as little good as possible." If the Constitution be what you represent it, and there be no danger in the change, you do wrong not to make the reform commensurate to the abuse. Fine reformer, indeed! generous donor! What is the cause of this parsimony of the liberty which you dole out to the people? Why all this limitation in giving blessings and benefits to mankind? You admit that there is an extreme in liberty, which may be infinitely noxious to those who are to receive it, and which in the end will leave them no liberty at all. I think so, too. They know it, and they feel it. The question is, then, What is the standard of that extreme? What that gentleman, and the associations, or some parts of their phalanxes, think proper? Then our liberties are in their pleasure; it depends on their arbitrary will how far I shall be free. I will have none of that freedom. If, therefore, the standard of moderation be sought for, I will seek for it. Where? Not in their fancies, nor in my own: I will seek for it where I know it is to be found—in the Constitution I actually enjoy. Here it says to an encroaching prerogative—"Your sceptre has its length; you cannot add an hair to your head, or a gem to your crown, but what an eternal law has given to it." Here it says to an overweening peerage—"Your pride finds banks that it cannot overflow": here to a tumultuous and giddy people—"There is a bound to the raging of the sea." Our Constitution is like our island, which uses and restrains its subject sea; in vain the waves roar. In that Constitution, I know, and exultingly I feel, both that I am free, and that I am not free dangerously to myself or to others. I know that no power on earth, acting as I ought to do, can touch my life, my liberty, or my property. I have that inward and dignified consciousness of my own security and independence, which constitutes, and is the only thing which does constitute, the proud and comfortable sentiment of freedom in the human breast. I know, too, and I bless God for, my safe mediocrity: I know, that, if I possessed all the talents of the gentlemen on the side of the House I sit, and on the other, I cannot, by royal favor, or by popular delusion, or by oligarchical cabal, elevate myself above a certain very limited point, so as to endanger my own fall, or the ruin of my country. I know there is an order that keeps things fast in their place: it is made to us, and we are made to it. Why not ask another wife, other children, another body, another mind?

The great object of most of these reformers is, to prepare the destruction of the Constitution, by disgracing and discrediting the House of Commons. For they think, (prudently, in my opinion,) that, if they can persuade the nation that the House of Commons is so constituted as not to secure the public liberty, not to have a proper connection with the public interests, so constituted as not either actually or virtually to be the representative of the people, it will be easy to prove that a government composed of a monarchy, an oligarchy chosen by the crown, and such a House of Commons, whatever good can be in such a system, can by no means be a system of free government.

The Constitution of England is never to have a quietus; it is to be continually vilified, attacked, reproached, resisted; instead of being the hope and sure anchor in all storms, instead of being the means of redress to all grievances, itself is the grand grievance of the nation, our shame instead of our glory. . . .

It suggests melancholy reflections, in consequence of the strange course we have long held, that we are now no longer quarrelling about the character, or about the conduct of men, or the tenor of measures, but we are grown out of humor with the English Constitution itself: this is become the object of the animosity of Englishmen. This Constitution in former days used to be the admiration and the envy of the world: it was the pattern for politicians, the theme of the eloquent, the meditation of the philosopher, in every part of the world. As to Englishmen, it was their pride, their consolation. By it they lived, for it they were ready to die. Its defects, if it had any, were partly covered by partiality, and partly borne by prudence. Now all its excellencies are forgot, its faults are now forcibly dragged into day, exaggerated by every artifice of representation. It is despised and rejected of men, and every device and invention of ingenuity or idleness set up in opposition or in preference to it. It is to this humor, and it is to the measures growing out of it, that I set myself (I hope not alone) in the most determined opposition. Never before did we at any time in this country meet upon the theory of our frame of government, to sit in judgment on the Constitution of our country, to call it as a delinquent before us, and to accuse it of every defect and every vice—to see whether it, an object of our veneration, even our adoration, did or did not accord with a preconceived scheme in the minds of certain gentlemen. Cast your eyes on the journals of Parliament. It is for fear of losing the inestimable treasure we have that I do not venture to game it out of my hands for the vain hope of improving it. I look with filial reverence on the Constitution of my country, and never will cut it in pieces, and put it into the kettle of any magician, in order to boil it, with the puddle of their compounds, into youth and vigor. On the contrary, I will drive away such pretenders; I will nurse its venerable age, and with lenient arts extend a parent's breath.

VI

INDIA AND THE IMPEACHMENT OF HASTINGS

Ninth Report
of the
Select Committee of the House of Commons
on
the Affairs of India
June 25, 1783

The affairs of India occupied Burke's attention from within the first few years of his entering Parliament, when debates in 1767 and 1769 established the right of the British government to regulate the internal actions and policies of the East India Company, until his retirement in 1794. Yet after the early debates, for over a decade few of the fundamental problems of India were brought before Parliament. In 1772 Warren Hastings became governor of Bengal. But at that time the American colonies occupied the center of the stage in dramas before Parliament. In March 1772 an East India judicature bill was introduced, but its provisions for some mild reforms of the Bengal administration were rejected. In April, General John Burgoyne asked that a select committee of inquiry in the House of Commons be established, to inform Parliament about Indian affairs, so that intelligent reforms could be passed. Burke and the Rockingham Whigs opposed Burgoyne's motion, because they were not yet aware of the nature and extent of British delinquencies in India, and therefore favored non-interference in the affairs of the East India Company; also, they feared that the inquiry was a preliminary step in putting the company's revenues under the Crown, which would further extend the power and abuses of royal patronage. Later, when Burke and his party learned how serious were the problems of India, and the irresponsibility of the East India Company administration, they supported the inquiry, and, of course, were accused of being opportunistic and inconsistent.

Burgoyne's select committee of inquiry was the first step toward introducing badly needed reform legislation to regulate the relationship between the British government and the East India Company. Burke was not a member of the original committee, which submitted two reports on India in the parliamentary session of 1772–73. At this time Burke was thought to be so well disposed toward the East India Company that in the summer of 1772 the company, through Sir George Colebrooke, offered Burke ten thousand pounds a year (the equivalent of almost two hundred and fifty thousand dollars today), to be chairman of a committee of supervisors to go out to India and reorganize its administration. After much deliberation Burke decided not to accept the offer.

Actually, Burke was somewhat critical of the East India directors for not reforming themselves, thus giving Lord North's administration the desired excuse for government intervention. On the first day of the new session of Parliament, Lord North had a secret committee elected to inquire into the East India Company's finances. With what Burke called "singular expedition" North's secret committee recommended that a restraining bill be passed, preventing the company from sending supervisors to India. Burke was convinced that the real intention of the government was not to reform abuses in the company's administration, but to gain control of its finances for purposes of patronage. North's restraining bill was passed over the protests of Burke's party.

In April 1773, the East India Company elected a new board of directors, and during the spring the company and the British government worked out a compromise settlement. The company doubled its grants to the government to four hundred thousand pounds, and remained substantially in charge of the administration of Indian affairs. These provisions were incorporated into the Loan Act and the Regulating Act, and were passed in June 1773. Burke opposed these bills, because he thought they extended royal patronage and were an invasion of the chartered rights of the East India Company. But between 1773 and 1783 he came to realize the extent of the abuses in India under the company, and its inability or unwillingness to reform its administration, so that gradually he became firmly committed to the intervention of Parliament and to the sovereignty of the British government over the territorial jurisdictions of the East India Company in India.

On December 1, 1780, agents representing 648 British subjects and some natives in Bengal wrote to Burke that they would shortly submit to Parliament petitions complaining of abuses in the Supreme Court of Bengal. They asked Burke to help them secure redress of their grievances. His activities in Indian affairs had by now earned him a reputation as an authority on India, and as one who also sympathized with the natives.

In January 1781 Burke began to take a very active part in behind-the-scenes discussions, including both administration and opposition leaders, concerning the relationship of the British government to India and the East India Company. Following these discussions the House of Commons voted to establish a select committee of fifteen members, to consider the Bengal petitions, and to recommend amending the provisions establishing courts in India in the Regulating Act of 1773. Burke was elected by his colleagues to the committee. On May 8, 1781, under his leadership in the law, the committee recommended that the rules of the Supreme Court of Bengal be revised to conform with the laws and customs of India.

After this initial assignment, the House of Commons extended the life and scope of the select committee to review the whole position of Britain in India. Soon Burke became more deeply immersed in Indian affairs than in any other concern of his entire political career. He knew that in the loss of the American colonies, the British Empire had suffered a major catastrophe in the West; now he considered solving the problems of India as identical with saving the British Empire in the East. Therefore, he considered India "the greatest object that ever can come before the Nation." This conviction is behind his famous statement in *A Letter to a Noble Lord* (1795), when he reviewed his political career to justify his pension after he had retired from Parliament:

If I were to call for a reward, (which I have never done,) it should be for those in which for fourteen years, without intermission, I showed the most industry, and had the least success; I mean in the affairs of India. They are those on which I value myself the most; most for the importance; most for the labour; most for the judgment; most for constancy and perseverance in the pursuit.

Late in 1781, after Sir Philip Francis had returned from India, where he had served on the Bengal council since 1774 in opposition to Hastings, new information was provided to the select committee. On February 5, 1782, the committee submitted its second report to Parliament, containing a detailed account of abuses of power under the East India Company, and of needed parliamentary action to protect the natives. A series of lesser reports amplified these points.

On June 25, 1783 appeared the *Ninth Report of the Select Committee of the House of Commons on the Affairs of India,* written by Burke. This report not only reviews Indian affairs since 1773, but also contains many of the essential ingredients that were to be found in subsequent discussions of Indian problems until the resolution of Hastings' impeachment trial in 1795.

L . . . OBSERVATIONS ON THE STATE OF THE
COMPANY'S AFFAIRS IN INDIA

In order to enable the House to adopt the most proper
means for regulating the British government in India, and for
promoting the happiness of the natives who live under its authority or influence, your Committee hold it expedient to collect into distinct points of view the circumstances by which
that government appeals to them to be most essentially disordered, and to explain fully the principles of policy and the
course of conduct by which the natives of all ranks and orders
have been reduced to their present state of depression and
misery. . . .

The plan adopted by your Committee is, first, to consider
the law regulating the East India Company, as it now stands—
and, secondly, to inquire into the circumstances of the two
great links of connection by which the territorial possessions
in India are united to this kingdom, namely, the Company's
commerce, and the government exercised under the charter
and under acts of Parliament. . . .

Your Committee observe, that this is the second attempt
made by Parliament for the reformation of abuses in the
Company's government. It appears, therefore, to them a necessary preliminary to this second undertaking, *to consider the
causes which, in their opinion,* have produced the failure of
the first—that the defects of the original plan may be supplied, its errors corrected, and such useful regulations as were
then adopted may be further explained, enlarged, and enforced.

The first design of this kind was formed in the session of
the year 1773. In that year, Parliament, taking up the consideration of the affairs of India, through two of its committees collected a very great body of details concerning the
interior economy of the Company's possessions, and concerning many particulars of abuse which prevailed at the time
when those committees made their ample and instructive reports. But it does not appear that the body of regulations enacted in that year, that is, in the East India Act of the thirteenth of his Majesty's reign, were altogether grounded on
that information, but were adopted rather on probable speculations and general ideas of good policy and good government. . . .

The first object of the policy of this act was to improve the constitution of the Court of Proprietors. In this case, as in almost all the rest, the remedy was not applied directly to the disease. The complaint was, that factions in the Court of Proprietors had shown, in several instances, a disposition to support the servants of the Company against the just coercion and legal prosecution of the Directors. Instead of applying a corrective to the distemper, a change was proposed in the constitution. By this reform, it was presumed that an interest would arise in the General Court more independent in itself, and more connected with the commercial prosperity of the Company. Under the new constitution, no proprietor, not possessed of a thousand pounds capital stock, was permitted to vote in the General Court: before the act, five hundred pounds was a sufficient qualification for one vote; and no value gave more. But as the lower classes were disabled, the power was increased in the higher: proprietors of three thousand pounds were allowed two votes; those of six thousand were entitled to three; ten thousand pounds was made the qualification for four. The votes were thus regulated in the scale and gradation of property. On this scale, and on some provisions to prevent occasional qualifications and splitting of votes, the whole reformation rested.

Several essential points, however, seem to have been omitted or misunderstood. No regulation was made to abolish the pernicious custom of voting by *ballot,* by means of which acts of the highest concern to the Company and to the state might be done by individuals with perfect impunity; and even the body itself might be subjected to a forfeiture of all its privileges for defaults of persons who, so far from being under control, could not be so much as known in any mode of legal cognizance. Nothing was done or attempted to prevent the operation of the interest of delinquent servants of the Company in the General Court, by which they might even come to be their own judges, and, in effect, under another description, to become the masters in that body which ought to govern them. Nor was anything provided to secure the independency of the proprietary body from the various exterior interests by which it might be disturbed, and diverted from the conservation of that pecuniary concern which the act laid down as the sole security for preventing a collusion between the General Court and the powerful delinquent servants in India. The whole of the regulations concerning the Court of Proprietors relied upon two principles, which have often proved fallacious: namely, that small numbers were a security against faction and disorder; and that integrity of conduct would follow the greater property. In no case could these principles be less depended upon than in the affairs of the East India Company. However, by wholly cutting off the lower, and adding to the power of the higher classes, it was supposed that the higher would keep their money in that fund to make profit—that the vote would be a secondary consideration, and no more than a guard to the property—and that therefore any abuse which tended to depreciate the value of their stock would be warmly resented by such proprietors.

If the ill effects of every misdemeanor in the Company's servants were to be *immediate,* and had a tendency to lower the value of the stock, something might justly be expected from the pecuniary security taken by the act. But from the then state of things, it was more than probable that proceedings ruinous to the permanent interest of the Company might commence in great lucrative advantages. Against this evil large pecuniary interests were rather the reverse of a remedy. Accordingly, the Company's servants have ever since covered over the worst oppressions of the people under their government, and the most cruel and wanton ravages of all the neighboring countries, by holding out, and for a time actually realizing, additions of revenue to the territorial funds of the Company, and great quantities of valuable goods to their investment.

But this consideration of mere income, whatever weight it might have, could not be the first object of a proprietor, in a body so circumstanced. The East India Company is not, like the Bank of England, a mere moneyed society for the sole purpose of the preservation or improvement of their capital; and therefore every attempt to regulate it upon the same principles must inevitably fail. When it is considered that a certain share in the stock gives a share in the government of so vast an empire, with such a boundless patronage, civil, military, marine, commercial, and financial, in every department of which such fortunes have been made as could be made nowhere else, it is impossible not to perceive that capitals far superior to any qualifications appointed to proprietors, or even to Directors, would readily be laid out for a participation in that power. The India proprietor, therefore, will always be, in the first instance, a politician; and the bolder his enterprise, and the more corrupt his views, the less will be his consideration of the price to be paid for compassing them. The new regulations did not reduce the number so low as not to leave the assembly still liable to all the disorder which might be supposed to arise from multitude. But if the principle had been well established and well executed, a much greater inconveniency grew out of the reform than that which had attended the old abuse: for if tumult and disorder be lessened by reducing the number of proprietors, private cabal and intrigue are facilitated at least in an equal degree; and it is cabal and corruption, rather than disorder and confusion, that was most dreaded in transacting the affairs of India. Whilst the votes of the smaller proprietors continued, a door was left open for the public sense to enter into that society: since that door has been closed, the proprietary has become, even more than formerly, an aggregate of private interests, which subsist at the expense of the collective body. At the moment of this revolution in the proprietary, as it might naturally be expected, those who had either no very particular interest in their vote or but a petty object to pursue immediately disqualified; but those who were deeply interested in the Company's patronage, those who were concerned in the supply of ships and of the other innumerable objects required for their immense establishments, those who were engaged in contracts with the Treasury, Admiralty, and Ordnance, together with the clerks in public offices, found means of securing qualifications at the enlarged standard. All these composed a much greater proportion than formerly they had done of the proprietary body.

Against the great, predominant, radical corruption of the Court of Proprietors the raising the qualification proved no sort of remedy. The return of the Company's servants into Europe poured in a constant supply of proprietors, whose ability to purchase the highest qualifications for themselves, their agents, and dependants could not be dubious. And this latter description form a very considerable, and by far the most active and efficient part of that body. To add to the votes, which is adding to the power in proportion to the wealth, of men whose very offences were supposed to consist in acts which lead to the acquisition of enormous riches, appears by no means a well-considered method of checking rapacity and oppression. In proportion as these interests prevailed, the means of cabal, of concealment, and of corrupt confederacy became far more easy than before. Accordingly, there was no fault with respect to the Company's government over its servants, charge or chargeable on the General Court as it originally stood, of which since the reform it has not been notoriously guilty. It was not, therefore, a matter of surprise to your Committee, that the General Court, so composed, has at length grown to such a degree of contempt both of its duty and of the permanent interest of the whole corporation as to put itself into open defiance of the salutary admonitions of this House, given for the purpose of asserting and enforcing the legal authority of their own body over their own servants. . . .

The second object of the act was the Court of Directors. Under the arrangement of the year 1773 that court appeared to have its authority much strengthened. It was made less dependent than formerly upon its constituents, the proprietary. The duration of the Directors in office was rendered more permanent, and the tenure itself diversified by a varied and intricate rotation. At the same time their authority was held high over their servants of all descriptions; and the only rule prescribed to the Council-General of Bengal, in the exercise of the large and ill-defined powers given to them, was that they were to yield obedience to the orders of the Court of Directors. As to the Court of Directors itself, it was left with very little regulations. The custom of ballot, infinitely the most mischievous in a body possessed of all the ordinary executive powers, was still left; and your Committee have found the ill effects of this practice in the course of their inquiries. Nothing was done to oblige the Directors to attend to the promotion of their servants according to their rank and merits. In judging of those merits nothing was done to bind them to any observation of what appeared on their records. Nothing was done to compel them to prosecution or complaint where delinquency became visible. The act, indeed, prescribed that no servant of the Company abroad should be eligible into the direction until two years after his return to England. But as this regulation rather presumes than provides for an inquiry into their conduct, a very ordinary neglect in the Court of Directors might easily defeat it, and a short remission might in this particular operate as a total indemnity. In fact, however, the servants have of late seldom attempted a seat in the direction—an attempt which might possibly rouse a dormant spirit of inquiry; but, satisfied with an interest in the proprietary, they have, through that name, brought the direction very much under their own control. . . .

The third object was a new judicial arrangement, the chief purpose of which was to form a strong and solid security for the natives against the wrongs and oppressions of British subjects resident in Bengal. An operose and expensive establishment of a Supreme Court was made, and charged upon the revenues of the country. The charter of justice was by the act left to the crown, as well as the appointment of the magistrates. The defect in the institution seemed to be this—that no rule was laid down, either in the act or the charter, by which the court was to judge. No descriptions of offenders or species of delinquency were properly ascertained, according to the nature of the place, or to the prevalent mode of abuse. Provision was made for the administration of justice in the remotest part of Hindostan as if it were a province of Great Britain. Your Committee have long had the constitution and conduct of this court before them, and they have not yet been able to discover very few instances (not one that appears to them of leading importance) of relief given to the natives against the corruptions or oppressions of British subjects in power—though they do find one very strong and marked instance of the judges having employed an unwarrantable extension or application of the municipal law of England, to destroy a person of the highest rank among those natives whom they were sent to protect. . . .

This court, which in its constitution seems not to have had sufficiently in view the necessities of the people for whose relief it was intended, and was, or thought itself, bound in some instances to too strict an adherence to the forms and rules of English practice, in others was framed upon principles perhaps too remote from the constitution of English tribunals. By the usual course of English practice, the far greater part of the redress to be obtained against oppressions of power is by process in the nature of civil actions. In these a trial by jury is a necessary part, with regard to the finding the offence and to the assessment of the damages. Both these were in the charter of justice left entirely to the judges. It was presumed, and not wholly without reason, that the British subjects were liable to fall into factions and combinations, in order to support themselves in the abuses of an authority of which every man might in his turn become a sharer. And with regard to the natives, it was presumed (perhaps a little too hastily) that they were not capable of sharing in the functions of jurors. But it was not foreseen that the judges were also liable to be engaged in the factions of the settlement—and if they should ever happen to be so engaged, that the native people were then without that remedy which obviously lay in the chance that the court and jury, though both liable to bias, might not easily unite in the same identical act of injustice. . . .

The fourth object of the act of 1773 was the Council-General. This institution was intended to produce uniformity, consistency, and the effective co-operation of all the settlements in their common defence. By the ancient constitution of the Company's foreign settlements, they were each of them under the orders of a President or Chief, and a Council, more or fewer, according to the discretion of the Company. Among those, Parliament (probably on account of the largeness of the territorial acquisitions, rather than the conveniency of the situation) chose Bengal for the residence of the controlling power, and, dissolving the Presidency, appointed a new establishment, upon a plan somewhat similar to that which had prevailed before . . . This establishment was composed of a Governor-General and four Counsellors, all named in the act of Parliament. They were to hold their offices for five years, after which term the patronage was to revert to the Court of Directors. In the mean time such vacancies as should happen were to be filled by that court, with the concurrence of the crown. The first Governor-General and one of the Counsellors had been old servants of the Company; the others were new men.

On this new arrangement the Courts of Proprietors and Directors considered the details of commerce as not perfectly consistent with the enlarged sphere of duty and the reduced number of the Council. Therefore, to relieve them from this burden, they instituted a new office, called the Board of Trade, for the subordinate management of their commercial concerns, and appointed eleven of the senior servants to fill the commission.

The powers given by the act to the new Governor-General and Council had for their direct object the kingdom of Bengal and its dependencies. Within that sphere (and it is not a small one) their authority extended over all the Company's concerns of whatever description. In matters of peace and war it seems to have been meant that the other Presidencies should be subordinate to their board. But the law is loose and defective, where it professes to restrain the subordinate Presidencies from making war without the consent and approbation of the Supreme Council. They are left free to act without it *in cases of imminent necessity,* or *where they shall have received special orders from the Company.* The first exception leaves it open to the subordinate to judge of the necessity of measures which, when taken, bind or involve the superior: the second refers a question of peace or war to two jurisdictions, which may give different judgments. With regard to their local administration, their powers were exceedingly and dangerously loose and undetermined. Their powers were not given directly, but in words of reference, in which neither the objects related to nor the mode of the relation were sufficiently expressed. Their legislative and executive capacities were not so accurately drawn, and marked by such strong and penal lines of distinction, as to keep these capacities separate. Where legislative and merely executive powers were lodged in the same hands, the legislative, which is the larger and the more ready for all occasions, was constantly resorted to. The Governor-General and Council, therefore, immediately gave constructions to their ill-defined authority which rendered it perfectly despotic—constructions which if they were allowed, no action of theirs ought to be regarded as criminal.

Armed as they were with an authority in itself so ample, and by abuse so capable of an unlimited extent, very few, and these very insufficient correctives, were administered. Ample salaries were provided for them, which indeed removed the necessity, but by no means the inducements to corruption and oppression. Nor was any barrier whatsoever opposed on the part of the natives against their injustice, except the Supreme Court of Judicature, which never could be capable of controlling a government with such powers, without becoming such a government itself.

There was, indeed, a prohibition against all concerns in trade to the whole Council, and against all taking of presents by any in authority. A right of prosecution in the King's Bench was also established; but it was a right the exercise of which is difficult, and in many, and those the most weighty cases, impracticable. No considerable facilities were given to prosecution in Parliament; nothing was done to prevent complaint from being far more dangerous to the sufferer than injustice to the oppressor. No overt acts were fixed, upon which corruption should be presumed in transactions of which secrecy and collusion formed the very basis; no rules of evidence nor authentic mode of transmission were settled in conformity to the unalterable circumstances of the country and the people.

One provision, indeed, was made for restraining the servants, in itself very wise and substantial: a delinquent once dismissed, could not be restored, but by the votes of three fourths of the Directors and three fourths of the proprietors: this was well aimed. But no method was settled for bringing delinquents to the question of removal: and if they should be brought to it, a door lay wide open for evasion of the law, and for a return into the service, in defiance of its plain intention—that is, by resigning to avoid removal; by which measure this provision of the act has proved as unoperative as all the rest. By this management a mere majority may bring in the greater delinquent, whilst the person removed for offences comparatively trivial may remain excluded forever.

The new Council nominated in the act was composed of two totally discordant elements, which soon distinguished themselves into permanent parties. One of the principal instructions which the three members of the Council sent immediately from England, namely, General Clavering, Colonel Monson, and Mr. Francis, carried out with them was, to *"cause the strictest inquiry to be made into all oppressions and abuses,"* among which *the practice of receiving presents from the natives,* at that time generally charged upon men in power, was principally aimed at.

Presents to any considerable value were justly reputed by the legislature, not as marks of attention and respect, but as bribes or extortions, for which either the beneficial and gratuitous duties of government were sold, or they were the price paid for acts of partiality, or, finally, they were sums of money extorted from the givers by the terrors of power. Against this system of presents, therefore, the new commission was in general opinion particularly pointed. In the commencement of reformation, at a period when a rapacious conquest had overpowered and succeeded to a corrupt government, an act of indemnity might have been thought advisable; perhaps a new account ought to have been opened; all retrospect ought to have been forbidden, at least to certain periods. If this had not been thought advisable, none in the higher departments of a suspected and decried government ought to have been kept in their posts, until an examination had rendered their proceedings clear, or until length of time had obliterated, by an even course of irreproachable conduct, the errors which so naturally grow out of a new power. But the policy adopted was different: it was to begin with *examples.* The cry against the abuses was strong and vehement throughout the whole nation, and the practice of presents was represented to be as general as it was mischievous. In such a case, indeed in any case, it seemed not to be a measure the most provident, without a great deal of previous inquiry, to place two persons, who from their situation must be the most exposed to such imputations, in the commission which was to inquire into their own conduct—much less to place one of them at the head of that commission, and with a casting vote in case of an equality. The persons who could not be liable to that charge were, indeed, three to two; but any accidental difference of opinion, the death of any one of them or his occasional absence or sickness, threw the whole power into the hands of the other two, who were Mr. Hastings and Mr. Barwell, one the President, and the other high in the Council of that establishment on which the reform was to operate. Thus those who were liable to process as delinquents were in effect set over the reformers; and that did actually happen which might be expected to happen from so preposterous an arrangement: a stop was soon put to all inquiries into their capital abuses. . . .

That which your Committee considers as the fifth and last of the capital objects of the act, and as the binding regulation of the whole, is the introduction (then for the first time) of the ministers of the crown into the affairs of the Company. The state claiming a concern and share of property in the Company's profits, the servants of the crown were presumed the more likely to preserve with a scrupulous attention the sources of the great revenues which they were to administer, and for the rise and fall of which they were to render an account.

The interference of government was introduced by this act in two ways: one by a control, in effect by a share, in the appointment to vacancies in the Supreme Council. The act provided that his Majesty's approbation should be had to the persons named to that duty. Partaking thus in the patronage of the Company, administration was bound to an attention to the characters and capacities of the persons employed in that high trust. The other part of their interference was by way of inspection. By this right of inspection, everything in the Company's correspondence from India, which related to the civil or military affairs and government of the Company, was directed by the act to be within fourteen days after the receipt laid before the Secretary of State, and everything that related to the management of the revenues was to be laid before the Commissioners of the Treasury. In fact, both descriptions of these papers have been generally communicated to that board.

It appears to your Committee that there were great and material defects in both parts of the plan. With regard to the approbation of persons nominated to the Supreme Council by the Court of Directors, no sufficient means were provided for carrying to his Majesty, along with the nomination, the particulars in the conduct of those who had been in the service before, which might render them proper objects of approbation or rejection. The India House possesses an office of record capable of furnishing, in almost all cases, materials for judging on the behavior of the servants in their progress from the lowest to the highest stations; and the whole discipline of the service, civil and military, must depend upon an examination of these records inseparably attending every application for an appointment to the highest stations. But in the present state of the nomination the ministers of the crown are not furnished with the proper means of exercising the power of control intended by the law, even if they were scrupulously attentive to the use of it. There are modes of proceeding favorable to neglect. Others excite inquiry and stimulate to vigilance. . . .

The temporary appointment by Parliament of the Supreme Council of India arose from an opinion that the Company, at that time at least, was not in a condition or not disposed to a proper exercise of the privileged which they held under their charter. It therefore behoved the Directors to be particularly attentive to their choice of Counsellors, on the expiration of the period during which their patronage had been suspended. The duties of the Supreme Council had been reputed of so arduous a nature as to require even a legislative interposition. They were called upon, by all possible care and impartiality, to justify Parliament at least as fully in the restoration of their privileges as the circumstances of the time had done in their suspension.

But interests have lately prevailed in the Court of Directors, which, by the violation of every rule, seemed to be resolved on the destruction of those privileges of which they were the natural guardians. Every new power given has been made the source of a new abuse; and the acts of Parliament themselves, which provide but imperfectly for the prevention of the mischief, have, it is to be feared, made provisions (contrary, without doubt, to the intention of the legislature) which operated against the possibility of any cure in the ordinary course.

In the original institution of the Supreme Council, reasons may have existed against rendering the tenure of the Counsellors in their office precarious. A plan of reform might have required the permanence of the persons who were just appointed by Parliament to execute it. But the act of 1780 gave a duration coexistent with the statute itself to a Council not appointed by act of Parliament, nor chosen for any temporary or special purpose; by which means the servants in the highest situation, let their conduct be never so grossly criminal, cannot be removed, unless the Court of Directors and ministers of the crown can be found to concur in the same opinion of it. The prevalence of the Indian factions in the Court of Directors and Court of Proprietors, and sometimes in the state itself, renders this agreement extremely difficult: if the principal members of the Direction should be in a conspiracy with any principal servant under censure, it will be impracticable; because the first act must originate there. The reduced state of the authority of this kingdom in Bengal may be traced in a great measure to that very natural source of independence. In many cases the instant removal of an offender from his power of doing mischief is the only mode of preventing the utter and perhaps irretrievable ruin of public affairs. In such a case the process ought to be simple, and the power absolute in one or in either hand separately. By contriving the balance of interests formed in the act, notorious offence, gross error, or palpable insufficiency have many chances of retaining and abusing authority, whilst the variety of representations, hearings, and conferences, and possibly the mere jealousy and competition between rival powers, may prevent any decision, and at length give time and means for settlements and compromises among parties, made at the expense of justice and true policy. But this act of 1780, not properly distinguishing judicial process from executive arrangements, requires in effect nearly the same degree of solemnity, delay, and detail for removing a political inconvenience which attends a criminal proceeding for the punishment of offences. It goes further, and gives the same tenure to all who shall succeed to vacancies which was given to those whom the act found in office.

Another regulation was made in the act, which has a tendency to render the control of delinquency or the removal of incapacity in the Council-General extremely difficult, as well as to introduce many other abuses into the original appointment of Counsellors. The inconveniences of a vacancy in that important office, at a great distance from the authority that is to fill it, were visible; but your Committee have doubts whether they balance the mischief which may arise from the power given in this act, of a provisional appointment to vacancies, not on the event, but on foresight. This mode of providing for the succession has a tendency to promote cabal, and to prevent inquiry into the qualifications of the persons to be appointed. An attempt has been actually made, in consequence of this power, in a very marked manner, to confound the whole order and discipline of the Company's service. Means are furnished thereby for perpetuating the powers of some given Court of Directors. They may forestall the patronage of their successors, on whom they entail a line of Supreme Counsellors and Governors-General. And if the exercise of this power should happen in its outset to fall into bad hands, the ordinary chances for mending an ill choice upon death or resignation are cut off.

In these provisional arrangements it is to be considered that the appointment is not in consequence of any marked event which calls strongly on the attention of the public, but is made at the discretion of those who lead in the Court of Directors, and may therefore be forward at times the most favorable to the views of partiality and corruption. Candidates have not, therefore, the notice that may be necessary for their claims; and as the possession of the office to which the survivors are to succeed seems remote, all inquiry into the qualifications and character of those who are to fill it will naturally be dull and languid.

Your Committee are not also without a grounded apprehension of the ill effect on any existing Council-General of all strong marks of influence and favor which appear in the subordinates of Bengal. This previous designation to a great and arduous trust, (the greatest that can be reposed in subjects,) when made out of any regular course of succession, marks that degree of countenance and support at home which may overshadow the existing government. That government may thereby be disturbed by factions, and led to corrupt and dangerous compliances. At best, when these Counsellors elect are engaged in no fixed employment, and have no lawful intermediate emolument, the natural impatience for their situations may bring on a traffic for resignations between them and the persons in possession, very unfavorable to the interests of the public and to the duty of their situations. . . .

Your Committee find that during the whole period which elapsed from 1773 to the commencement of 1782 disorders and abuses of every kind multiplied. Wars contrary to policy and contrary to public faith were carrying on in various parts of India. The allies, dependants, and subjects of the Company were everywhere oppressed; dissensions in the Supreme Council prevailed, and continued for the greater part of that time; the contests between the civil and judicial powers threatened that issue to which they came at last, an armed resistance to the authority of the king's court of justice; the order which by an act of Parliament the servants were bound to obey were avowedly and on principle contemned; . . .

In all this time the true state of the several Presidencies, and the real conduct of the British government towards the natives, was not at all known to Parliament: it seems to have been very imperfectly known even to ministers. Indeed, it required an unbroken attention, and much comparison of facts and reasonings, to form a true judgment on that difficult and complicated system of politics, revenue, and commerce, whilst affairs were only in their progress to that state which produced the present inquiries. Therefore, whilst the causes of their ruin were in the height of their operation, both the Company and the natives were understood by the public as in circumstances the most assured and most flourishing; insomuch that, whenever the affairs of India were brought before Parliament, as they were two or three times during that period, the only subject-matter of discussion anywise important was concerning the sums which might be taken out of the Company's surplus profits for the advantage of the state. Little was thought of but the disengagement of the Company from their debts in *England*, and to prevent the servants abroad from drawing upon them, so as that body might be enabled, without exiciting clamors here, to afford the contribution that was demanded. All descriptions of persons, either here or in India, looking solely to appearances at home, the reputation of the Directors depended on the keeping the Company's sales in a situation to support the dividend, that of the ministers depended on the most lucrative bargains for the Exchequer, and that of the servants abroad on the largest investments; until at length there is great reason to apprehend, that, unless some very substantial reform takes place in the management of the Company's affairs, nothing will be left for investment, for dividend, or for bargain, and India, instead of a resource to the public, may itself come, in no great length of time, to be reckoned amongst the public burdens.

In this manner the inspection of the ministers of the crown, the great cementing regulation of the whole act of 1773, has, along with all the others, entirely failed in its effect.

Your Committee, in observing on the failure of this act, do not consider the intrinsic defects or mistakes in the law itself as the sole cause of its miscarriage. The general policy of the nation with regard to this object has been, they conceive, erroneous; and no remedy by laws, under the prevalence of that policy, can be effectual. Before any remedial law can have its just operation, the affairs of India must be restored to their natural order. The prosperity of the natives must be previously secured, before any profit from them whatsoever is attempted. For as long as a system prevails which regards the transmission of great wealth to this country, either for the Company or the state, as its principal end, so long will it be impossible that those who are the instruments of that scheme should not be actuated by the same spirit for their own private purposes. It will be worse: they will support the injuries done in favor of those before whom they are to account. . . .

II.—CONNECTION OF GREAT BRITAIN WITH INDIA

In order to open more fully the tendency of the policy which has hitherto prevailed, and that the House may be enabled, in any regulations which may be made, to follow the tracks of the abuse, and to apply an appropriated remedy to a particular distemper, your Committee think it expedient to consider in some detail the manner in which India is connected with this kingdom—which is the second head of their plan.

The two great links by which this connection is maintained are, first, the East India Company's commerce, and, next, the government set over the natives by that company and by the crown. . . . The East India Company's trade is to be first considered, not only as it operates by itself, but as having a powerful influence over the general policy and the particular measures of the Company's government. Your Committee apprehend that the present state, nature, and tendency of this trade are not generally understood.

Until the acquisition of great territorial revenues by the East India Company, the trade with India was carried on upon the common principles of commerce—namely, by sending out such commodities as found a demand in the India market, and, where that demand was not adequate to the reciprocal call of the European market for Indian goods, by a large annual exportation of treasure, chiefly in silver. In some years that export has been as high as six hundred and eighty thousand pounds sterling. The other European companies trading to India traded thither on the same footing. . . . This influx of money, poured into India by an emulation of all the commercial nations of Europe, encouraged industry and promoted cultivation in a high degree, notwithstanding the frequent wars with which that country was harassed, and the vices which existed in its internal government. On the other hand, the export of so much silver was sometimes a subject of grudging and uneasiness in Europe, and a commerce carried on through such a medium to many appeared in speculation of doubtful advantage. But the practical demands of commerce bore down those speculative objections. The East India commodities were so essential for animating all other branches of trade, and for completing the commercial circle, that all nations contended for it with the greatest avidity. The English company flourished under this exportation for a very long series of years. The nation was considerably benefited both in trade and in revenue; and the dividends of the proprietors were often high, and always sufficient to keep up credit of the Company's stock in heart and vigor.

But at or very soon after the acquisition of the territorial revenues to the English company, the period of which may be reckoned as completed about the year 1765, a very great revolution took place in commerce as well as in dominion; and it was a revolution which affected the trade of Hindostan with all other European nations, as well as with that in whose favor and by whose power it was accomplished. From that time bullion was no longer regularly exported by the English East India Company to Bengal, or any part of Hindostan; and it was soon exported in much smaller quantities by any other nation. A new way of supplying the market for Europe, by means of the British power and influence, was invented: a species of trade (if such it may be called) by which it is absolutely impossible that India should not be radically and irretrievably ruined, although our possessions there were to be ordered and governed upon principles diametrically opposite to those which now prevail in the system and practice of the British company's administration.

A certain portion of the revenues of Bengal has been for many years set apart to be employed in the purchase of goods for exportation to England, and this is called *Investment.* The greatness of this investment has been the standard by which the merit of the Company's principal servants has been too generally estimated; and this main cause of the impoverishment of India has been generally taken as a measure of its wealth and prosperity. Numerous fleets of large ships, loaded with the most valuable commodities of the East, annually arriving in England, in a constant and increasing succession, imposed upon the public eye, and naturally gave rise to an opinion of the happy condition and growing opulence of a country whose surplus productions occupied so vast a space in the commercial world. This export from India seemed to imply also a reciprocal supply, by which the trading capital employed in those productions was continually strengthened and enlarged. But the payment of a tribute, and not a beneficial commerce to that country, wore this specious and delusive appearance.

The fame of a great territorial revenue, exaggerated, as is usual in such cases, beyond even its value, and the abundant fortunes of the Company's officers, military and civil, which flowed into Europe with a full tide, raised in the proprietors of East India stock a premature desire of partaking with their servants in the fruits of that splendid adventure. Government also thought they could not be too early in their claims for a share of what they considered themselves as entitled to in every foreign acquisition made by the power of this kingdom, through whatever hands or by whatever means it was made. These two parties, after some struggle, came to an agreement to divide between them the profits which their speculation proposed to realize in England from the territorial revenue in Bengal. About two hundred thousand pounds was added to the annual dividends of the proprietors. Four hundred thousand was given to the state, which, added to the old dividend, brought a constant charge upon the mixed interest of Indian trade and revenue of eight hundred thousand pounds a year. This was to be provided for at all events.

By that vast demand on the territorial fund, the correctives and qualifications which might have been gradually applied to the abuses in Indian commerce and government were rendered extremely difficult.

The practice of an investment from the revenue began in the year 1766. . . . The first investment was about five hundred thousand pounds, and care was taken afterwards to enlarge it. In the years 1767 and 1768 it arose to seven hundred thousand.

This new system of trade, carried on through the medium of power and public revenue, very soon produced its natural effects. The loudest complaints arose among the natives, and among all the foreigners who traded to Bengal. It must unquestionably have thrown the whole mercantile system of the country into the greatest confusion. With regard to the natives, no expedient was proposed for their relief. The case was serious with respect to European powers. The Presidency plainly represented to the Directors, that some agreement should be made with foreign nations for providing their investment to a certain amount, or that the deficiencies then subsisting must terminate in an open rupture with France. The Directors, pressed by the large payments in England, were not free to abandon their system; and all possible means of diverting the manufacturers into the Company's investment were still anxiously sought and pursued, until the difficulties of the foreign companies were at length removed by the natural flow of the fortunes of the Company's servants into Europe. . . .

But, with all these endeavors of the Presidency, the investment sunk in 1769, and they were even obliged to pay for a part of the goods to private merchants in the Company's bonds, bearing interest. It was plain that this course of business could not hold. . . .

The goods from Bengal, purchased from the territorial revenues, from the sale of European goods, and from the produce of the monopolies, for the four years which ended with 1780, when the investment from the surplus revenues finally closed, were never less than a million sterling, and commonly nearer twelve hundred thousand pounds. This million is the lowest value of the goods sent to Europe for which no satisfaction is made. . . .

The goods which are exported from Europe to India consist chiefly of military and naval stores, of clothing for troops, and of other objects for the consumption of the Europeans residing there; and, excepting . . . commodities of little comparative value, no sort of merchandise is sent from England that is in demand for the wants or desires of the native inhabitants.

When an account is taken of the intercourse (for it is not commerce) which is carried on between Bengal and England, the pernicious effects of the system of investment from revenue will appear in the strongest point of view. In that view, the whole exported produce of the country, so far as the Company is concerned, is not exchanged in the course of the barter, but is taken away without any return or payment whatsoever. In a commercial light, therefore, England becomes annually bankrupt to Bengal to the amount nearly of its whole dealing;

or rather, the country has suffered what is tantamount to an annual plunder of its manufactures and its produce to the value of twelve hundred thousand pounds. . . .

The companies of France, Holland, and Denmark . . . will be found to add their full proportion to the calamity brought upon Bengal by the destructive system of the ruling power; because the greater part of the capital of some of them, is furnished exactly as the British is, out of the revenues of the country. The civil and military servants of the English East India Company being restricted in drawing bills upon Europe, and none of them ever making or proposing an establishment in India, a very great part of their fortunes, well or ill gotten, is in all probability thrown, as fast as required, into the cash of these companies. . . .

But that the greatness of all these drains, and their effects, may be rendered more visible, your Committee have turned their consideration to the employment of those parts of the Bengal revenue which are not employed in the Company's own investments. . . . From the portion of that sum which goes to the support of civil government the natives are almost wholly excluded, as they are from the principal collections of revenue. With very few exceptions, they are only employed as servants and agents to Europeans, or in the inferior departments of collection, when it is absolutely impossible to proceed a step without their assistance. . . .

All the honorable, all the lucrative situations of the army, all the supplies and contracts of whatever species that belong to it, are solely in the hands of the English; so that whatever is beyond the mere subsistence of a common soldier and some officers of a lower rank, together with the immediate expenses of the English officers at their table, is sooner or later, in one shape or another, sent out of the country. . . .

III.—EFFECT OF THE REVENUE INVESTMENT ON THE COMPANY

Hitherto your Committee has considered this system of revenue investment, substituted in the place of a commerical link between India and Europe, so far as it affects India only: they are now to consider it as it affects the Company. So long as that corporation continued to receive a vast quantity of merchantable goods without any disbursement for the purchase, so long it possessed wherewithal to continue a dividend to pay debts, and to contribute to the state. But it must have been always evident to considerate persons, that this vast extraction of wealth from a country lessening in its resources in proportion to the increase of its burdens was not calculated for a very long duration. For a while the Company's servants kept up this investment, not by improving commerce, manufacture, or agriculture, but by forcibly raising the land-rents, on the principles and in the manner hereafter to be described. When these extortions disappointed or threatened to disappoint expectation, in order to purvey for the avarice which raged in England, they sought for expedients in breaches of all the agreements by which they were bound by any payment to the country powers, and in exciting disturbances among all the neighboring princes. Stimulating their ambition, and fomenting their mutual animosities, they sold to them reciprocally their common servitude and ruin. . . .

The investment has not been for any long time the natural product of the revenue of Bengal. When, by the vast charge and by the ill return of an evil political and military traffic, and by prodigal increases of establishments, and a profuse conduct in distributing agencies and contracts, they found themselves under difficulties, instead of being cured of their immoral and impolitic delusion, they plunged deeper into it, and were drawn from expedient to expedient for the supply of the investment into that endless chain of wars which this House by its resolutions has so justly condemned. At home these measures were sometimes countenanced, sometimes winked at, sometimes censured, but always with an acceptance of whatever profit they afforded.

At length the funds for the investment and for these wars together could no longer be supplied. . . .

By this failure a total revolution ensued, of the most extraordinary nature . . . the Council-General, in their letter of the 8th of April, 1782 . . . tell the Court of Directors, "that they had adopted a *new* method of keeping up the investment, by private subscribers . . . which will find *cargoes for their ships* on the usual terms of privilege, *at the risk of the individuals,* and is to be to them *according to the produce of the sales in England*" . . .

That the Indian trade may become a permanent vehicle of the private fortunes of the Company's servants is very probable—that is, as permanent as the means of acquiring fortunes in India; but that *some profit* will accrue to the Company is absolutely impossible. The Company are to bear all the charge outwards, and a very great part of that homewards; and their only compensation is the surplus commission on the sale of other people's goods. The nation will undoubtedly avoid great detriment, which would be the inevitable consequence of the total cessation of the trade with Bengal and the ships returning without cargoes. But if this temporary expedient should be improved into a system, no occasional advantages to be derived from it would be sufficient to balance the mischiefs of finding a great Parliamentary corporation turned into a vehicle for remitting to England the private fortunes of those for whose benefit the territorial possessions in India are in effect and substance under this project to be *solely* held.

By this extraordinary scheme the Company is totally overturned, and all its relations inverted. From being a body concerned in trade on their own account, and employing their servants as factors, the servants have at one stroke taken the whole trade into their own hands, on their own capital of 800,000*l.*, at their own risk, and the Company are become agents and factors to them, to sell by commission *their* goods for *their* profit. . . .

BRITISH GOVERNMENT IN INDIA

The other link by which India is bound to Great Britain is the government established there originally by the authority of the East India Company, and afterwards modified by Parliament by the acts of 1773 and 1780. This system of government appears to your Committee to be at least as much disordered, and as much perverted from every good purpose for which lawful rule is established, as the trading system has been from every just principle of commerce. Your Committee, in tracing the causes of this disorder through its effects, have first considered the government as it is constituted and managed within itself, beginning with its most essential and fundamental part, the order and discipline by which the supreme authority of this kingdom is maintained.

The British government in India being a subordinate and delegated power, it ought to be considered as a fundamental principle in such a system, that it is to be preserved in the strictest obedience to the government at home. Administration in India, at an immense distance from the seat of the supreme authority—intrusted with the most extensive powers—liable to the greatest temptations—possessing the amplest means of abuse—ruling over a people guarded by no distinct or well-ascertained privileges, whose language, manners, and radical prejudices render not only redress, but all complaint on their part, a matter of extreme difficulty—such an administration, it is evident, never can be made subservient to the interests of Great Britain, or even tolerable to the natives, but by the strictest rigor in exacting obedience to the commands of the authority lawfully set over it.

But your Committee find that this principle has been for some years very little attended to. . . . In proportion as the necessity of enforcing obedience grew stronger and more urgent, and in proportion to the magnitude and importance of the objects affected by disobedience, this rigor has been relaxed. Acts of disobedience have not only grown frequent, but systematic; and they have appeared in such instances, and are manifested in such a manner, as to amount, in the Company's servants, to little less than absolute independence, against which, on the part of the Directors, there is no struggle, and hardly so much as a protest to preserve a claim. . . .

The disobedience of Mr. Hastings has of late not only become uniform and systematical in practice, but has been in principle, also, supported by him, and by Mr. Barwell, late a member of the Supreme Council in Bengal, and now a member of this House.

In the Consultation of the 20th of July, 1778, Mr. Barwell gives it as his solemn and deliberate opinion, that, "while Mr. Hastings is in the government, the respect and dignity of his station should be supported. In these sentiments, I must decline an acquiescence in *any* order which has a *tendency* to bring the government into disrepute. As the Company have the means and power of forming their own administration in India, they may at pleasure place whom they please at the head; but in my opinion they are not authorized to treat a person in that post with *indignity*."

By treating them with indignity (in the particular cases wherein they have declined obedience to orders) they must mean those orders which imply a censure on any part of their conduct, a reversal of any of their proceedings, or, as Mr. Barwell expresses himself in words very significant, in any orders that have a *tendency* to bring *their* government into *disrepute*. The amplitude of this latter description, reserving to them the judgment of any orders which have so much as that *tendency*, puts them in possession of a complete independence, an independence including a despotic authority over the subordinates and the country. The very means taken by the Directors for enforcing their authority becomes, on this principle, a cause of further disobedience. It is observable, that their principles of disobedience do not refer to any local consideration, overlooked by the Directors, which might supersede their orders, or to any change of circumstances, which might render another course advisable, or even perhaps necessary—but it relates solely to their own interior feelings in matters relative to themselves, and their opinion of their own dignity and reputation. It is plain that they have wholly forgotten who they are, and what the nature of their office is. Mr. Hastings and Mr. Barwell are servants of the Company, and as such, by the duty inherent in that relation, as well as by their special covenants, were obliged to yield obedience to the orders of their masters. They have, as far as they were able, cancelled all the bonds of this relation, and all the sanctions of these covenants.

But in thus throwing off the authority of the Court of Directors, Mr. Hastings and Mr. Barwell have thrown off the authority of the whole legislative power of Great Britain; for, by the Regulating Act of the thirteenth of his Majesty, they are expressly "directed and required to pay due obedience to *all* such orders as they shall receive from the Court of Directors of the said United Company." Such is the declaration of the law. But Mr. Barwell declares that he declines obedience to *any* orders which he shall interpret to be indignities on a Governor-General. . . .

Mr. Hastings . . . from the habits of independent power, is carried to such a length as to consider a motion to obey the Court of Directors as a degradation of the executive government in his person. He looks upon a claim under that authority, and a complaint that it has produced no effects, as a piece of daring insolence which he is ashamed that the board has suffered. The behavior which your Committee consider as so intemperate and despotic he regards as a culpable degree of patience and forbearance. . . .

Mr. Hastings . . . in his principles . . . went further. Thinking himself assured of some extraordinary support, suitable to the open and determined defiance with which he was resolved to oppose the lawful authority of his superiors, and to exercise a despotic power, he no longer adhered to Mr. Barwell's distinction of the orders which had a tendency to bring his government into disrepute. This distinction afforded sufficient latitude to disobedience; but here he disdained all sorts of colors and distinctions. He directly set up an independent right to administer the government according to his pleasure; and he went so far as to bottom his claim to act independently of the Court of Directors on the very statute which commanded his obedience to them.

He declared roundly, "that he should *not* yield to the authority of the Court of Directors in *any* instance in which it should require his concession of the rights which he held under an act of Parliament." It is too clear to stand in need of proof, that he neither did nor could hold any authority that was not subject, in every particle of it, and in every instance in which it could be exercised, to the orders of the Court of Directors. . . .

Mr. Scott, who is authorized to defend Mr. Hastings, supported the same principles before your Committee by a comparison that avowedly reduces the Court of Directors to the state of a party against the servants. He declared, that, in his opinion, "it would be just *as absurd* to *deprive him* of the power of nominating his ambassador at Benares as it would be to force on *the ministry* of this country an ambassador from the *opposition*." Such is the opinion entertained in Bengal, and that but too effectually realized, of the relation between the principal servants of the Company and the Court of Directors. . . .

In England the authority is purely formal. In Bengal the power is positive and real. When they clash, their opposition serves only to degrade the authority that ought to predominate, and to exalt the power that ought to be dependent. . . .

Speech
(December 1, 1783)
upon
The Question for the Speaker's Leaving the
Chair in Order for the House to Resolve
Itself into a Committee
on
Mr. Fox's East India Bill

With the loss of the American colonies, the government of Lord North at last expired in March 1782, and the second Rockingham administration took its place. During April Parliament passed several resolutions condemning East India Company officials in Calcutta, Bombay, and Madras for dishonoring the British name by their abuse of office. Parliament ordered the Company's Court of Directors to recall Governor General Hastings and President Hornby of the Bombay council, and asked the King to remove Justice Impey from the Indian courts.

On July 1, unexpectedly, Rockingham suddenly died, and the King appointed Lord Shelburne as Prime Minister. A long-standing distrust of the new minister caused Charles James Fox to refuse to serve under him, and the Rockingham Whigs again went into opposition. The East India Company Court of Directors had agreed to recall Hastings, but when the East India Court of Proprietors discovered a friend in Shelburne they overruled the directors, and Hastings was reprieved. The reform of Indian affairs was not resumed again until April 1783, when a coalition of old and bitter enemies, Fox and North, compelled Shelburne's resignation. The much-criticized Fox-North coalition continued in office only until the defeat of Fox's East India Bill, on December 18, 1783.

Most of Fox's East India Bill was written by Burke, who allowed Fox to present it to Parliament. By 1783 Burke was thoroughly convinced that the East India Company was incurably corrupt, both in its destructive commercial dealings and in its government of India. He believed that British despotism in India could be removed only by founding the government upon principles that combined the universal ethical norms of the Natural Law with the ancient customs and local manners of life in India. Therefore, he conceived and drew up a bill that he thought would be the Magna Charta of India. The bill proposed to replace the East India Company directors with a commission of seven members, nominated by Fox from the House of Commons, who would rule India for four years, and be responsible to but not removable by the House of Commons.

The bill passed in the Commons, but certain of its provisions made it vulnerable to strong opposition both in and out of Parliament. The younger Pitt's Tories used the very arguments against Fox's bill that Burke and the Rockingham Whigs had used against the India bills of 1773: it would violate the chartered rights of the East India Company; for the legislature, rather than the King, to name an executive body independent of Parliament was clearly an unconstitutional innovation; the bill would give extensive Indian patronage to the House of Commons, whose minister, Fox, could use it as a party prerogative to corrupt Parliament. In short, despite Burke's sincere intentions, and the desperate condition of India that seemed to warrant his action, Fox's East India Bill was, in a sense, an *a priori* measure, contrary to Burke's own principle of prudence and to the spirit of the British constitution he so venerated. His very virtues as a legislator and as a man had betrayed him into this dilemma. He had acquired an encyclopedic knowledge of India, such as, in Macaulay's words, "certainly was never attained by any public man who had not quitted Europe," so that he knew in minute detail the extent to which India had been plundered by British avarice, and all the attendant cruelties. This, combined with his intense moral indignation against the indifference and collusion of officials in the East India Company, blinded him to the practical objections that would be raised against his bill. In one of his greatest speeches, Burke defended Fox's East India Bill in the House of Commons on December 1, 1783.

But the interests which rose against the measure included all the powerful returned East Indian nabobs, the directors and the owners of East India stock, the members of various chartered trade corporations, the political enemies of the Fox-North coalition, and above all the King. George III wished to get rid of the coalition. He placed such strong personal pressure on members of the House of Lords that the bill was roundly defeated on December 18. The King immediately dismissed the coalition ministers and appointed Pitt and his Tories to power. In 1784 Pitt's India bill was introduced, and Burke supported it.

. . . It is now to be determined whether the three years of laborious Parliamentary research, whether the twenty years of patient Indian suffering, are to produce a substantial reform in our Eastern administration; or whether our knowledge of the grievances has abated our zeal for the correction of them, and our very inquiry into the evil was only a pretext to elude the remedy which is demanded from us by humanity, by justice, and by every principle of true policy. Depend upon it, this business cannot be indifferent to our fame. It will turn out a matter of great disgrace or great glory to the whole British nation. We are on a conspicuous stage, and the world marks our demeanor.

I am therefore a little concerned to perceive the spirit and temper in which the debate has been all along pursued upon one side of the House. The declamation of the gentlemen who oppose the bill has been abundant and vehement; but they have been reserved and even silent about the fitness or unfitness of the plan to attain the direct object it has in view. By some gentlemen it is taken up (by way of exercise, I presume) as a point of law, on a question of private property and corporate franchise; by others it is regarded as the petty intrigue of a faction at court, and argued merely as it tends to set this man a little higher or that a little lower in situation and power. All the void has been filled up with invectives against coalition, with allusions to the loss of America, with the activity and inactivity of ministers. The total silence of these gentlemen concerning the interest and well-being of the people of India, and concerning the interest which this nation has in the commerce and revenues of that country, is a strong indication of the value which they set upon these objects.

It has been a little painful to me to observe the intrusion into this important debate of such company as *quo warranto,* and *mandamus,* and *certiorari:* as if we were on a trial about mayors and aldermen and capital burgesses, or engaged in a suit concerning the borough of Penryn, or Saltash, or St. Ives, or St. Mawes. Gentlemen have argued with as much heat and passion as if the first things in the world were at stake; and their topics are such as belong only to matter of the lowest and meanest litigation. It is not right, it is not worthy of us, in this manner to depreciate the value, to degrade the majesty, of this grave deliberation of policy and empire.

For my part, I have thought myself bound, when a matter of this extraordinary weight came before me, not to consider (as some gentlemen are so fond of doing) whether the bill originated from a Secretary of State for the Home Department or from a Secretary for the Foreign, from a minister of influence or a minister of the people, from Jacob or from Esau. I asked myself, and I asked myself nothing else, what part it was fit for a member of Parliament, who has supplied a mediocrity of talents by the extreme of diligence, and who has thought himself obliged by the research of years to wind himself into the inmost recesses and labyrinths of the Indian detail—what part, I say, it became such a member of Parliament to take, when a minister of state, in conformity to a recommendation from the throne, has brought before us a system for the better government of the territory and commerce of the East. In this light, and in this only, I will trouble you with my sentiments.

It is not only agreed, but demanded by the right honorable gentleman, and by those who act with him, that a *whole* system ought to be produced; that it ought not to be an *half-measure;* that it ought to be no *palliative,* but a legislative provision, vigorous, substantial, and effective—I believe that no man who understands the subject can doubt for a moment that those must be the conditions of anything deserving the name of a reform in the Indian government; that anything short of them would not only be delusive, but, in this matter, which admits no medium, noxious in the extreme.

To all the conditions proposed by his adversaries the mover of the bill perfectly agrees; and on his performance of them he rests his cause. On the other hand, not the least objection has been taken with regard to the efficiency, the vigor, or the completeness of the scheme. I am therefore warranted to assume, as a thing admitted, that the bills accomplish what both sides of the House demand as essential. The end is completely answered, so far as the direct and immediate object is concerned.

But though there are no direct, yet there are various collateral objections made: objections from the effects which this plan of reform for Indian administration may have on the privileges of great public bodies in England; from its probable influence on the constitutional rights, or on the freedom and integrity, of the several branches of the legislature.

Before I answer these objections, I must beg leave to observe, that, if we are not able to contrive some method of governing India *well,* which will not of necessity become the means of governing Great Britain *ill,* a ground is laid for their eternal separation, but none for sacrificing the people of that country to our Constitution. I am, however, far from being persuaded that any such incompatibility of interest does at all exist. On the contrary, I am certain that every means effectual to preserve India from oppression is a guard to preserve the British Constitution from its worst corruption. To show this, I will consider the objections, which, I think, are four.

1st, That the bill is an attack on the chartered rights of men.

2ndly, That it increases the influence of the crown.

3rdly, That it does *not* increase, but diminishes, the influence of the crown, in order to promote the interests of certain ministers and their party.

4thly, That it deeply affects the national credit.

As to the first of these objections, I must observe that the phrase of "the chartered rights *of men*" is full of affectation, and very unusual in the discussion of privileges conferred by charters of the present description. But it is not difficult to discover what end that ambiguous mode of expression, so often reiterated, is meant to answer.

The rights of *men*—that is to say, the natural rights of mankind—are indeed sacred things; and if any public measure is proved mischievously to affect them, the objection ought to be fatal to that measure, even if no charter at all could be set up against it. If these natural rights are further affirmed and declared by express covenants, if they are clearly defined and secured against chicane, against power and authority, by written instruments and positive engagements, they are in a still better condition: they partake not only of the sanctity of the object so secured, but of that solemn public faith itself which secures an object of such importance. Indeed, this formal recognition, by the sovereign power, of an original right in the subject, can never be subverted, but by rooting up the holding radical principles of government, and even of society itself. The charters which we call by distinction *great* are public instruments of this nature: I mean the charters of King John and King Henry the Third. The things secured by these instruments may, without any deceitful ambiguity, be very fitly called *the chartered rights of men*.

These charters have made the very name of a charter dear to the heart of every Englishman. But, Sir, there may be, and there are, charters, not only different in nature, but formed on principles *the very reverse* of those of the Great Charter. Of this kind is the charter of the East India Company. *Magna*

Charta is a charter to restrain power and to destroy monopoly. The East India charter is a charter to establish monopoly and to create power. Political power and commercial monopoly are *not* the rights of men; and the rights to them derived from charters it is fallacious and sophistical to call "the chartered rights of men." These chartered rights (to speak of such charters and of their effects in terms of the greatest possible moderation) do at least suspend the natural rights of mankind at large, and in their very frame and constitution are liable to fall into a direct violation of them.

It is a charter of this latter description (that is to say, a charter of power and monopoly) which is affected by the bill before you. The bill, Sir, does without question affect it: it does affect it essentially and substantially. But, having stated to you of what description the chartered rights are which this bill touches, I feel no difficulty at all in acknowledging the existence of those chartered rights in their fullest extent. They belong to the Company in the surest manner, and they are secured to that body by every sort of public sanction. They are stamped by the faith of Parliament: they have been bought for money, for money honestly and fairly paid; they have been bought for valuable consideration, over and over again.

I therefore freely admit to the East India Company their claim to exclude their fellow-subjects from the commerce of half the globe. I admit their claim to administer an annual territorial revenue of seven millions sterling, to command an army of sixty thousand men, and to dispose (under the control of a sovereign, imperial discretion, and with the due observance of the natural and local law) of the lives and fortunes of thirty millions of their fellow-creatures. All this they possess by charter, and by Acts of Parliament, (in my opinion,) without a shadow of controversy.

Those who carry the rights and claims of the Company the furthest do not contend for more than this; and all this I freely grant. But, granting all this, they must grant to me, in my turn, that all political power which is set over men, and that all privilege claimed or exercised in exclusion of them, being wholly artificial, and for so much a derogation from the natural equality of mankind at large, ought to be some way or other exercised ultimately for their benefit.

If this is true with regard to every species of political dominion and every description of commercial privilege, none of which can be original, self-derived rights, or grants for the mere private benefit of the holders, then such rights, or privileges, or whatever else you choose to call them, are all in the strictest sense *a trust:* and it is of the very essence of every trust to be rendered *accountable*—and even totally to *cease,* when it substantially varies from the purposes for which alone it could have a lawful existence.

This I conceive, Sir, to be true of trusts of power vested in the highest hands, and of such as seem to hold of no human creature. But about the application of this principle to subordinate *derivative* trusts I do not see how a controversy can be maintained. To whom, then, would I make the East India Company accountable? Why, to Parliament, to be sure—to Parliament, from whom their trust was derived—to Parliament, which alone is capable of comprehending the magnitude of its object, and its abuse, and alone capable of an effectual legislative remedy. The very charter, which is held out to exclude Parliament from correcting malversation with regard to the high trust vested in the Company, is the very thing which at once gives a title and imposes a duty on us to interfere with effect, wherever power and authority originating from ourselves are perverted from their purposes, and become instruments of wrong and violence.

If Parliament, Sir, had nothing to do with this charter, we might have some sort of Epicurean excuse to stand aloof, indifferent spectators of what passes in the Company's name in India and in London. But if we are the very cause of the evil, we are in a special manner engaged to the redress; and for us passively to bear with oppressions committed under the sanction of our own authority is in truth and reason for this House to be an active accomplice in the abuse.

That the power, notoriously grossly abused, has been bought from us is very certain. . . .

I ground myself, therefore, on this principle:—that, if the abuse is proved, the contract is broken, and we reënter into all our rights, that is, into the exercise of all our duties. Our own authority is, indeed, as much a trust originally as the Company's authority is a trust derivatively; and it is the use we make of the resumed power that must justify or condemn us in the resumption of it. When we have perfected the plan laid before us by the right honorable mover, the world will then see what it is we destroy, and what it is we create. By that test we stand or fall; and by that test I trust that it will be found, in the issue, that we are going to supersede a charter abused to the full extent of all the powers which it could abuse, and exercised in the plenitude of despotism, tyranny, and corruption—and that in one and the same plan we provide a real chartered security for *the rights of men*, cruelly violated under that charter.

This bill, and those connected with it, are intended to form the *Magna Charta* of Hindostan. Whatever the Treaty of Westphalia is to the liberty of the princes and free cities of the Empire, and to the three religions there professed—whatever the Great Charter, the Statute of Tallage, the Petition of Right, and the Declaration of Right are to Great Britain, these bills are to the people of India. Of this benefit I am certain their condition is capable: and when I know that they are capable of more, my vote shall most assuredly be for our giving to the full extent of their capacity of receiving; and no charter of dominion shall stand as a bar in my way to their charter of safety and protection.

The strong admission I have made of the Company's rights (I am conscious of it) binds me to do a great deal. I do not presume to condemn those who argue *a priori* against the propriety of leaving such extensive political powers in the hands of a company of merchants. I know much is, and much more may be, said against such a system. But, with my particular ideas and sentiments, I cannot go that way to work. I feel an insuperable reluctance in giving my hand to destroy any established institution of government, upon a theory, however plausible it may be. My experience in life teaches me nothing clear upon the subject. I have known merchants with the sentiments and the abilities of great statesmen, and I have seen persons in the rank of statesmen with the conceptions and character of peddlers. Indeed, my observation has furnished me with nothing that is to be found in any habits of life or education, which tends wholly to disqualify men for the functions of government, but that by which the power of exercising those functions is very frequently obtained: I mean a spirit and habits of low cabal and intrigue; which I have never, in one instance, seen united with a capacity for sound and manly policy.

To justify us in taking the administration of their affairs out of the hands of the East India Company, on my principles, I must see several conditions. 1st, The object affected by the abuse should be great and important. 2nd, The abuse affecting this great object ought to be a great abuse. 3rd, It ought to be habitual, and not accidental. 4th, It ought to be utterly incurable in the body as it now stands constituted. All this ought to be made as visible to me as the light of the sun, before I should strike off an atom of their charter. A right honorable gentleman has said, and said, I think, but once, and that very slightly, (whatever his original demand for a plan might seem to require,) that "there are abuses in the Company's government." If that were all, the scheme of the mover of this bill, the scheme of his learned friend, and his own scheme of reformation, (if he has any,) are all equally needless. There are, and must be, abuses in all governments. It amounts to no more than a nugatory proposition. But before I consider of what nature these abuses are, of which the gentleman speaks so very lightly, permit me to recall to your recollection the map of the country which this abused chartered right affects. This I shall do, that you may judge whether in that map I can discover anything like the first of my conditions: that is, whether the object affected by the abuse of the East India Company's power be of importance sufficient to justify the measure and means of reform applied to it in this bill.

With very few, and those inconsiderable intervals, the British dominion, either in the Company's name, or in the names of princes absolutely dependent upon the Company, extends from the mountains that separate India from Tartary to Cape Comorin, that is, one-and-twenty degrees of latitude!

In the northern parts it is a solid mass of land, about eight hundred miles in length, and four or five hundred broad. As you go southward, it becomes narrower for a space. It afterwards dilates; but, narrower or broader, you possess the whole eastern and northeastern coast of that vast country, quite from the borders of Pegu.—Bengal, Bahar, and Orissa, with Benares, (now unfortunately in our immediate possession,) measure 161,978 square English miles: a territory considerably larger than the whole kingdom of France. Oude, with its dependent provinces, is 53,286 square miles: not a great deal less than England. The Carnatic, with Tanjore and the Circars, is 65,948 square miles: very considerably larger than England. And the whole of the Company's dominions, comprehending Bombay and Salsette, amounts to 281,412 square miles: which forms a territory larger than any European dominion, Russia and Turkey excepted. Through all that vast extent of country there is not a man who eats a mouthful of rice but by permission of the East India Company.

So far with regard to the extent. The population of this great empire is not easy to be calculated. When the countries of which it is composed came into our possession, they were all eminently peopled, and eminently productive—though at that time considerably declined from their ancient prosperity. But since they are come into our hands!———! However, if we make the period of our estimate immediately before the utter desolation of the Carnatic, and if we allow for the havoc which our government had even then made in these regions, we cannot, in my opinion, rate the population at much less than thirty millions of souls: more than four times the number of persons in the island of Great Britain.

My next inquiry to that of the number is the quality and description of the inhabitants. This multitude of men does not consist of an abject and barbarous populace; much less of gangs of savages, like the Guaranies and Chiquitos, who wander on the waste borders of the River of Amazons or the Plate; but a people for ages civilized and cultivated—cultivated by all the arts of polished life, whilst we were yet in the woods. There have been (and still the skeletons remain) princes once of great dignity, authority, and opulence. There are to be found the chiefs of tribes and nations. There is to be found an ancient and venerable priesthood, the depository of their laws, learning, and history, the guides of the people whilst living and their consolation in death; a nobility of great antiquity and renown; a multitude of cities, not exceeded in population and trade by those of the first class in Europe; merchants and bankers, individual houses of whom have once vied in capital with the Bank of England, whose credit had often supported a tottering state, and preserved their governments in the midst of war and desolation; millions of ingenious manufacturers and mechanics; millions of the most diligent, and not the least intelligent, tillers of the earth. Here are to be found almost all the religions professed by men—the Braminical, the Mussulman, the Eastern and the Western Christian.

If I were to take the whole aggregate of our possessions there, I should compare it, as the nearest parallel I can find, with the Empire of Germany. Our immediate possessions I should compare with the Austrian dominions: and they would not suffer in the comparison. The Nabob of Oude might stand for the King of Prussia; the Nabob of Arcot I would compare, as superior in territory, and equal in revenue, to the Elector of Saxony. Cheit Sing, the Rajah of Benares, might well rank with the Prince of Hesse, at least; and the Rajah of Tanjore (though hardly equal in extent of dominion, superior in revenue) to the Elector of Bavaria. The Polygars and the North-

ern zemindars, and other great chiefs, might well class with
the rest of the princes, dukes, counts, marquises, and bishops
in the Empire; all of whom I mention to honor, and surely
without disparagement to any or all of those most respectable
princes and grandees.

All this vast mass, composed of so many orders and classes
of men, is again infinitely diversified by manners, by religion,
by hereditary employment, through all their possible combinations. This renders the handling of India a matter in an high
degree critical and delicate. But, oh, it has been handled
rudely indeed! Even some of the reformers seem to have
forgot that they had anything to do but to regulate the tenants
of a manor, or the shopkeepers of the next county town.

It is an empire of this extent, of this complicated nature, of
this dignity and importance, that I have compared to Germany and the German government—not for an exact resemblance, but as a sort of a middle term, by which India might
be approximated to our understandings, and, if possible, to
our feelings, in order to awaken something of sympathy for
the unfortunate natives, of which I am afraid we are not perfectly susceptible, whilst we look at this very remote object
through a false and cloudy medium.

My second condition necessary to justify me in touching
the charter is, whether the Company's abuse of their trust with
regard to this great object be an abuse of great atrocity. I shall
beg your permission to consider their conduct in two lights:
first the political, and then the commercial. . . .

These are some of my reasons, grounded on the abuse of
the external political trust of that body, for thinking myself
not only justified, but bound, to declare against those chartered rights which produce so many wrongs. I should deem
myself the wickedest of men, if any vote of mine could contribute to the continuance of so great an evil.

Now, Sir, according to the plan I proposed, I shall take notice of the Company's internal government, as it is exercised
first on the dependent provinces, and then as it affects those
under the direct and immediate authority of that body. And
here, Sir, before I enter into the spirit of their interior government, permit me to observe to you upon a few of the many
lines of difference which are to be found between the vices of
the Company's government and those of the conquerors who
preceded us in India, that we may be enabled a little the better
to see our way in an attempt to the necessary reformation.

The several irruptions of Arabs, Tartars, and Persians into

India were, for the greater part, ferocious, bloody, and wasteful in the extreme: our entrance into the dominion of that country was, as generally, with small comparative effusion of blood—being introduced by various frauds and delusions, and by taking advantage of the incurable, blind, and senseless animosity which the several country powers bear towards each other, rather than by open force. But the difference in favor of the first conquerors is this. The Asiatic conquerors very soon abated of their ferocity, because they made the conquered country their own. They rose or fell with the rise or fall of the territory they lived in. Fathers there deposited the hopes of their posterity; and children there beheld the monuments of their fathers. Here their lot was finally cast; and it is the natural wish of all that their lot should not be cast in a bad land. Poverty, sterility, and desolation are not a recreating prospect to the eye of man; and there are very few who can bear to grow old among the curses of a whole people. If their passion or their avarice drove the Tartar lords to acts of rapacity or tyranny, there was time enough, even in the short life of man, to bring round the ill effects of an abuse of power upon the power itself. If hoards were made by violence and tyranny, they were still domestic hoards; and domestic profusion, or the rapine of a more powerful and prodigal hand, restored them to the people. With many disorders, and with few political checks upon power, Nature had still fair play; the sources of acquisition were not dried up; and therefore the trade, the manufactures, and the commerce of the country flourished. Even avarice and usury itself operated both for the preservation and the employment of national wealth. The husbandman and manufacturer paid heavy interest, but then they augmented the fund from whence they were again to borrow. Their resources were dearly bought, but they were sure; and the general stock of the community grew by the general effort.

But under the English government all this order is reversed. The Tartar invasion was mischievous; but it is our protection that destroys India. It was their enmity; but it is our friendship. Our conquest there, after twenty years, is as crude as it was the first day. The natives scarcely know what it is to see the gray head of an Englishman. Young men (boys almost) govern there, without society and without sympathy with the natives. They have no more social habits with the people than if they still resided in England—nor, indeed, any species of intercourse, but that which is necessary to making a sudden fortune, with a view to a remote settlement. Animated with all the avarice of age and all the impetuosity of youth, they roll in one after another, wave after wave; and there is nothing before the eyes of the natives but an endless, hopeless prospect of new flights of birds of prey and passage, with appetites continually renewing for a food that is continually wasting. Every rupee of profit made by an Englishman is lost forever to India. With us are no retributory superstitions, by which a foundation of charity compensates, through ages, to the poor, for the rapine and injustice of a day. With us no pride erects stately monuments which repair the mischiefs which pride had produced, and which adorn a country out of its own spoils. England has erected no churches, no hospitals, no palaces, no schools; England has built no bridges, made no highroads, cut no navigations, dug out no reservoirs. Every other conqueror of every other description has left some monument, either of state or beneficence, behind him. Were we to be driven out of India this day, nothing would remain to tell that it had been possessed, during the inglorious period of our dominion, by anything better than the orang-outang or the tiger.

There is nothing in the boys we send to India worse than in the boys whom we are whipping at school, or that we see trailing a pike or bending over a desk at home. But as English youth in India drink the intoxicating draught of authority and dominion before their heads are able to bear it, and as they are full grown in fortune long before they are ripe in principle, neither Nature nor reason have any opportunity to exert themselves for remedy of the excesses of their premature power. The consequences of their conduct, which in good minds (and many of theirs are probably such) might produce penitence or amendment, are unable to pursue the rapidity of their flight. Their prey is lodged in England; and the cries of India are given to seas and winds, to be blown about, in every breaking up of the monsoon, over a remote and unhearing ocean. In India all the vices operate by which sudden fortune is acquired: in England are often displayed, by the same persons, the virtues which dispense hereditary wealth. Arrived in England, the destroyers of the nobility and gentry of a whole kingdom will find the best company in this nation at a board of elegance and hospitality. Here the manufacturer and husbandman will bless the just and punctual hand that in India has torn the cloth from the loom, or wrested the scanty portion of rice and salt from the peasant of Bengal, or wrung from him the very opium in which he forgot his oppressions and his oppressor. They marry into your families; they enter into your senate; they ease your estates by loans; they raise their value by demand; they cherish and protect your relations which lie heavy on your patronage; and there is scarcely an house in the kingdom that does not feel some concern and interest that makes all reform of our Eastern government appear officious and disgusting, and, on the whole, a most discouraging attempt. In such an attempt you hurt those who are able to return kindness or to resent injury. If you succeed, you save those who cannot so much as give you thanks. All these things show the difficulty of the work we have on hand: but they show its necessity, too. Our Indian government is in its best state a grievance. It is necessary that the correctives should be uncommonly vigorous, and the work of men sanguine, warm, and even impassioned in the cause. But it is an arduous thing to plead against abuses of a power which originates from your own country, and affects those whom we are used to consider as strangers.

I shall certainly endeavor to modulate myself to this temper; though I am sensible that a cold style of describing actions, which appear to me in a very affecting light, is equally contrary to the justice due to the people and to all genuine human feelings about them. I ask pardon of truth and Nature for this compliance. But I shall be very sparing of epithets either to persons or things. It has been said, (and, with regard to one of them, with truth,) that Tacitus and Machiavel, by their cold way of relating enormous crimes, have in some sort appeared not to disapprove them; that they seem a sort of professors of the art of tyranny; and that they corrupt the minds of their readers by not expressing the detestation and horror that naturally belong to horrible and detestable proceedings. But we are in general, Sir, so little acquainted with Indian details, the instruments of oppression under which the people suffer are so hard to be understood, and even the very names of the sufferers are so uncouth and strange to our ears, that it is very difficult for our sympathy to fix upon these objects. I am sure that some of us have come down stairs from the committee-room with impressions on our minds which to us were the inevitable results of our discoveries, yet, if we should venture to express ourselves in the proper language of our sentiments to other gentlemen not at all prepared to enter into the cause of them, nothing could appear more harsh and dissonant, more violent and unaccountable, than our language and behavior. All these circumstances are not, I confess, very

favorable to the idea of our attempting to govern India at all.
But there we are; there we are placed by the Sovereign Disposer; and we must do the best we can in our situation. The
situation of man is the preceptor of his duty. . . .

Such an universal proscription, upon any pretence, has few
examples. Such a proscription, without even a pretence of
delinquency, has none. It stands by itself. It stands as a monument to astonish the imagination, to confound the reason of
mankind. I confess to you, when I first came to know this
business in its true nature and extent, my surprise did a little
suspend my indignation. I was in a manner stupefied by the
desperate boldness of a few obscure young men, who, having
obtained, by ways which they could not comprehend, a power
of which they saw neither the purposes nor the limits, tossed
about, subverted, and tore to pieces, as if it were in the gambols of a boyish unluckiness and malice, the most established
rights, and the most ancient and most revered institutions, of
ages and nations. Sir, I will not now trouble you with any
detail with regard to what they have since done with these
same lands and landholders, only to inform you that nothing
has been suffered to settle for two seasons together upon any
basis, and that the levity and inconstancy of these mock legislators were not the least afflicting parts of the oppressions
suffered under their usurpation; nor will anything give stability to the property of the natives, but an administration in
England at once protecting and stable. The country sustains,
almost every year, the miseries of a revolution. . . .

In effect, Sir, every legal, regular authority, in matters of
revenue, of political administration, of criminal law, of civil
law, in many of the most essential parts of military discipline,
is laid level with the ground; and an oppressive, irregular,
capricious, unsteady, rapacious, and peculating despotism,
with a direct disavowal of obedience to any authority at home,
and without any fixed maxim, principle, or rule of proceeding
to guide them in India, is at present the state of your charter-
government over great kingdoms.

As the Company has made this use of their trust, I should
ill discharge mine, if I refused to give my most cheerful vote
for the redress of these abuses, by putting the affairs of so
large and valuable a part of the interests of this nation and of
mankind into some steady hands, possessing the confidence
and assured of the support of this House, until they can be
restored to regularity, order, and consistency.

I have touched the heads of some of the grievances of the

people and the abuses of government. But I hope and trust you will give me credit, when I faithfully assure you that I have not mentioned one fourth part of what has come to my knowledge in your committee; and further, I have full reason to believe that not one fourth part of the abuses are come to my knowledge, by that or by any other means. Pray consider what I have said only as an index to direct you in your inquiries.

If this, then, Sir, has been the use made of the trust of political powers, internal and external, given by you in the charter, the next thing to be seen is the conduct of the Company with regard to the commercial trust. And here I will make a fair offer:—If it can be proved that they have acted wisely, prudently, and frugally, as merchants, I shall pass by the whole mass of their enormities as statesmen. That they have not done this their present condition is proof sufficient. Their distresses are said to be owing to their wars. This is not wholly true. But if it were, is not that readiness to engage in wars, which distinguishes them, and for which the Committee of Secrecy has so branded their politics, founded on the falsest principles of mercantile speculation?

The principle of buying cheap and selling dear is the first, the great foundation of mercantile dealing. Have they ever attended to this principle? Nay, for years have they not actually authorized in their servants a total indifference as to the prices they were to pay?

A great deal of strictness in driving bargains for whatever we contract is another of the principles of mercantile policy. Try the Company by that test. Look at the contracts that are made for them. Is the Company so much as a good commissary to their own armies? I engage to select for you, out of the innumerable mass of their dealings, all conducted very nearly alike, one contract only the excessive profits on which during a short term would pay the whole of their year's dividend. I shall undertake to show that upon two others the inordinate profits given, with the losses incurred in order to secure those profits, would pay a year's dividend more.

It is a third property of trading-men to see that their clerks do not divert the dealings of the master to their own benefit. It was the other day only, when their Governor and Council taxed the Company's investment with a sum of fifty thousand pounds, as an inducement to persuade only seven members of their Board of Trade to give their *honor* that they would abstain from such profits upon that investment, as they must have violated their oaths, if they had made at all.

It is a fourth quality of a merchant to be exact in his accounts. What will be thought, when you have fully before you the mode of accounting made use of in the Treasury of Bengal? I hope you will have it soon. With regard to one of their agencies, when it came to the material part, the prime cost of the goods on which a commission of fifteen per cent was allowed, to the astonishment of the factory to whom the commodities were sent, the Accountant-General reports that he did not think himself authorized to call for *vouchers* relative to this and other particulars—because the agent was upon his *honor* with regard to them. A new principle of account upon honor seems to be regularly established in their dealings and their treasury, which in reality amounts to an entire annihilation of the principle of all accounts.

It is a fifth property of a merchant, who does not meditate a fraudulent bankruptcy, to calculate his probable profits upon the money he takes up to vest in business. Did the Company, when they bought goods on bonds bearing eight per cent interest, at ten and even twenty per cent discount, even ask themselves a question concerning the possibility of advantage from dealing on these terms?

The last quality of a merchant I shall advert to is the taking care to be properly prepared, in cash or goods in the ordinary course of sale, for the bills which are drawn on them. Now I ask, whether they have ever calculated the clear produce of any given sales, to make them tally with the four million of bills which are come and coming upon them, so as at the proper periods to enable the one to liquidate the other. No, they have not. They are now obliged to borrow money of their own servants to purchase their investment. The servants stipulate five per cent on the capital they advance, if their bills should not be paid at the time when they become due; and the value of the rupee on which they charge this interest is taken at two shillings and a penny. Has the Company ever troubled themselves to inquire whether their sales can bear the payment of that interest, and at that rate of exchange? Have they once considered the dilemma in which they are placed—the ruin of their credit in the East Indies, if they refuse the bills—the ruin of their credit and existence in England, if they accept them?

Indeed, no trace of equitable government is found in their politics, not one trace of commercial principle in their mercantile dealing: and hence is the deepest and maturest wisdom of Parliament demanded, and the best resources of this kingdom must be strained, to restore them—that is, to restore the countries destroyed by the misconduct of the Company, and to restore the Company itself, ruined by the consequences of their plans for destroying what they were bound to preserve.

I required, if you remember, at my outset, a proof that these abuses were habitual. But surely this is not necessary for me to consider as a separate head; because I trust I have made it evident beyond a doubt, in considering the abuses themselves, that they are regular, permanent, and systematical.

I am now come to my last condition, without which, for one, I will never readily lend my hand to the destruction of any established government, which is—that, in its present state, the government of the East India Company is absolutely incorrigible.

Of this great truth I think there can be little doubt, after all that has appeared in this House. It is so very clear, that I must consider the leaving any power in their hands, and the determined resolution to continue and countenance every mode and every degree of peculation, oppression, and tyranny, to be one and the same thing. I look upon that body incorrigible, from the fullest consideration both of their uniform conduct and their present real and virtual constitution.

If they had not constantly been apprised of all the enormities committed in India under their authority, if this state of things had been as much a discovery to them as it was to many of us, we might flatter ourselves that the detection of the abuses would lead to their reformation. I will go further. If the Court of Directors had not uniformly condemned every act which this House or any of its committees had condemned, if the language in which they expressed their disapprobation against enormities and their authors had not been much more vehement and indignant than any ever used in this House, I should entertain some hopes. If they had not, on the other hand, as uniformly commended all their servants who had done their duty and obeyed their orders as they had heavily censured those who rebelled, I might say, These people have been in an error, and when they are sensible of it they will mend. But when I reflect on the uniformity of their support to the objects of their uniform censure, and the state of insignificance and disgrace to which all of those have been reduced whom they approved, and that even utter ruin and premature death have been among the fruits of their favor, I must be convinced, that in this case, as in all others, hypocrisy is the only vice that never can be cured.

Attend, I pray you, to the situation and prosperity of Benfield, Hastings, and others of that sort. The last of these has been treated by the Company with an asperity of reprehension that has no parallel. They lament "that the power of disposing of their property for perpetuity should fall into such hands." Yet for fourteen years, with little interruption, he has governed all their affairs, of every description, with an absolute sway. He has had himself the means of heaping up immense wealth; and during that whole period, the fortunes of hundreds have depended on his smiles and frowns. He himself tells you he is incumbered with two hundred and fifty young gentlemen, some of them of the best families in England, all of whom aim at returning with vast fortunes to Europe in the prime of life. He has, then, two hundred and fifty of your children as his hostages for your good behavior; and loaded for years, as he has been, with the execrations of the natives, with the censures of the Court of Directors, and struck and blasted with resolutions of this House, he still maintains the most despotic power ever known in India. He domineers with an overbearing sway in the assemblies of his pretended masters; and it is thought in a degree rash to venture to name his offences in this House, even as grounds of a legislative remedy. . . .

Add to this, that, from the highest in place to the lowest, every British subject, who, in obedience to the Company's orders, has been active in the discovery of peculations, has been ruined. They have been driven from India. When they made their appeal at home, they were not heard; when they attempted to return, they were stopped. No artifice of fraud, no violence of power, has been omitted to destroy them in character as well as in fortune. . . .

When I accuse the Court of Directors of this habitual treachery in the use of reward and punishment, I do not mean to include all the individuals in that court. There have been, Sir, very frequently men of the greatest integrity and virtue amongst them; and the contrariety in the declarations and conduct of that court has arisen, I take it, from this—that the honest Directors have, by the force of matter of fact on the records, carried the reprobation of the evil measures of the servants in India. This could not be prevented, whilst these records stared them in the face; nor were the delinquents, either here or there, very solicitous about their reputation, as long as they were able to secure their power. The agreement of their partisans to censure them blunted for a while the edge of a severe proceeding. It obtained for them a character of impartiality, which enabled them to recommend with some sort of grace, what will always carry a plausible appearance, those treacherous expedients called moderate measures. Whilst these were under discussion, new matter of complaint came over, which seemed to antiquate the first. The same circle was here trod round once more; and thus through years they proceeded in a compromise of censure for punishment, until, by shame and despair, one after another, almost every man who preferred his duty to the Company to the interest of their servants has been driven from that court. . . .

Everything has followed in this order, and according to the natural train of events. I will close what I have to say on the incorrigible condition of the Company, by stating to you a few facts that will leave no doubt of the obstinacy of that corporation, and of their strength too, in resisting the reformation of their servants. By these facts you will be enabled to discover the sole grounds upon which they are tenacious of their charter.

It is now more than two years, that upon account of the gross abuses and ruinous situation of the Company's affairs, (which occasioned the cry of the whole world long before it was taken up here,) that we instituted two committees to inquire into the mismanagements by which the Company's affairs had been brought to the brink of ruin. These inquiries had been pursued with unremitting diligence, and a great body of facts was collected and printed for general information. In the result of those inquiries, although the committees consisted of very different descriptions, they were unanimous. They joined in censuring the conduct of the Indian administration, and enforcing the responsibility upon two men, whom this House, in consequence of these reports, declared it to be the duty of the Directors to remove from their stations, and recall to Great Britain—*"because they had acted in a manner repugnant to the honor and policy of this nation, and thereby brought great calamities on India and enormous expenses on the East India Company."*

Here was no attempt on the charter. Here was no question of their privileges. To vindicate their own honor, to support their own interests, to enforce obedience to their own orders—these were the sole object of the monitory resolution of this House. But as soon as the General Court could assemble, they assembled to demonstrate who they really were. Regardless of the proceedings of this House, they ordered the Directors not to carry into effect any resolution they might come to for the removal of Mr. Hastings and Mr. Hornby. The Directors, still retaining some shadow of respect to this House, instituted an inquiry themselves, which continued from June to October, and, after an attentive perusal and full consideration of papers, resolved to take steps for removing the persons who had been the objects of our resolution, but not without a violent struggle against evidence. Seven Directors went so far as to enter a protest against the vote of their court. Upon this the General Court takes the alarm: it reassembles; it orders the Directors to rescind their resolution, that is, not to recall Mr. Hastings and Mr. Hornby, and to despise the resolution of the House of Commons. Without so much as the pretence of looking into a single paper, without the formality of instituting any committee of inquiry, they superseded all the labors of their own Directors and of this House.

It will naturally occur to ask, how it was possible that they should not attempt some sort of examination into facts, as a color for their resistance to a public authority proceeding so very deliberately, and exerted, apparently at least, in favor of their own. The answer, and the only answer which can be given, is, that they were afraid that their true relation should be mistaken. They were afraid that their patrons and masters in India should attribute their support of them to an opinion of their cause, and not to an attachment to their power. They were afraid it should be suspected that they did not mean blindly to support them in the use they made of that power. They determined to show that they at least were set against reformation: that they were firmly resolved to bring the territories, the trade, and the stock of the Company to ruin, rather than be wanting in fidelity to their nominal servants and real masters, in the ways they took to their private fortunes. . . .

It has been said, If you violate this charter, what security has the charter of the Bank, in which public credit is so deeply concerned, and even the charter of London, in which the rights of so many subjects are involved? I answer, In the like case they have no security at all—no, no security at all. If the Bank should, by every species of mismanagement, fall into a state similar to that of the East India Company—if it should be oppressed with demands it could not answer, engagements which it could not perform, and with bills for which it could

not procure payment—no charter should protect the mismanagement from correction, and such public grievances from redress. If the city of London had the means and will of destroying an empire, and of cruelly oppressing and tyrannizing over
millions of men as good as themselves, the charter of the city
of London should prove no sanction to such tyranny and such
oppression. Charters are kept, when their purposes are maintained: they are violated, when the privilege is supported
against its end and its object.

Now, Sir, I have finished all I proposed to say, as my
reasons for giving my vote to this bill. If I am wrong, it is
not for want of pains to know what is right. This pledge, at
least, of my rectitude I have given to my country.

And now, having done my duty to the bill, let me say a word
to the author. I should leave him to his own noble sentiments,
if the unworthy and illiberal language with which he has been
treated, beyond all example of Parliamentary liberty, did not
make a few words necessary—not so much in justice to him
as to my own feelings. I must say, then, that it will be a distinction honorable to the age, that the rescue of the greatest
number of the human race that ever were so grievously oppressed from the greatest tyranny that was ever exercised has
fallen to the lot of abilities and dispositions equal to the task—
that it has fallen to one who has the enlargement to comprehend, the spirit to undertake, and the eloquence to support so
great a measure of hazardous benevolence. His spirit is not
owing to his ignorance of the state of men and things: he well
knows what snares are spread about his path, from personal
animosity, from court intrigues, and possibly from popular
delusion. But he has put to hazard his ease, his security, his
interest, his power, even his darling popularity, for the benefit
of a people whom he has never seen. This is the road that all
heroes have trod before him. He is traduced and abused for his
supposed motives. He will remember that obloquy is a necessary ingredient in the composition of all true glory: he will
remember that it was not only in the Roman customs, but it
is in the nature and constitution of things, that calumny and
abuse are essential parts of triumph. These thoughts will support a mind which only exists for honor under the burden of
temporary reproach. He is doing, indeed, a great good—such
as rarely falls to the lot, and almost as rarely coincides with
the desires, of any man. Let him use his time. Let him give
the whole length of the reins to his benevolence. He is now on
a great eminence, where the eyes of mankind are turned to

him. He may live long, he may do much; but here is the summit: he never can exceed what he does this day. . . .

For my own part, I am happy that I have lived to see this day; I feel myself overpaid for the labors of eighteen years, when, at this late period, I am able to take my share, by one humble vote, in destroying a tyranny that exists to the disgrace of this nation and the destruction of so large a part of the human species.

Speeches

in

the Impeachment

of

Warren Hastings, Esquire,
Late Governor General of Bengal
[1788]

For about a decade before 1783 Burke had studied Indian affairs with growing concern over the ruthless power politics being practiced by certain officers of the East India Company. Under charters granted by Parliament and the Indian Moguls, the East India Company had acquired enormous possessions of land, in which it enjoyed not merely a monopoly of commercial rights, but increasing political sovereignty. The company had its own military force and courts of law, and it levied and collected taxes and controlled the economic life of the whole of Bengal. By the 1770's, in Burke's words the East India Company had become "a state in the disguise of a merchant." The exploitation of India, carried on against the economic interests, the customs, manners, and laws of Indian life, and even against the basic ethical norms common to all men under the Natural Law, enabled greedy Englishmen to return home with enormous fortunes, with which they purchased the landed estates of impoverished gentry, or married into the aristocracy, and acquired an extensive influence in the public affairs of Britain. This last point was important to Burke, and has too often been dismissed lightly by his critics.

Sir Lewis Namier noted that the number of nabobs returned from India who were actually elected to Parliament was quite insignificant, and concluded that the hue and cry against the East Indian interests by the managers of Hastings' impeachment was one of Burke's unfounded myths. But Burke was not fearful of the direct political power of the English nabobs in Parliament. He feared their great wealth as an indirect power in demoralizing Parliament and in influencing public opinion throughout the nation. On the first day of his *Speech in Reply* (May 28, 1794), Burke noted the unanimity of the English nabobs on behalf of Hastings, and the extent and nature of their defense of him: "We cannot be insensible to the effects produced by the introduction of forty millions of money into this country from India. We know that the private fortunes which have been made there pervade this kingdom so universally that there is not a single parish in it unoccupied by the partisans of the defendant. . . . Under the shadow of his [Hastings'] crimes thousands of tongues are employed to justify the means by which these fortunes were made. When they cannot deny the facts, they attack the accusers—they attack their conduct, they attack their persons, they attack their language, in every possible manner." Burke feared that the following Hastings had acquired "by the oppression of the people of India" might become "too strong for the House of Commons itself." But these were conclusions to which he came after Hastings' trial began in February 1788. It is necessary to trace briefly the events which led to Burke's impeachment of Hastings.

From 1774 to 1783 Burke gradually became convinced that British misrule in India was largely the personal responsibility of Warren Hastings, the Governor General of Bengal and India. In 1774 Sir Philip Francis, a new member of the Bengal council sent out to reform abuses, began to send back critical reports on Hastings to John Bourke, a London merchant and relative of Burke. But Burke did not begin to believe in Hastings' delinquency until early in 1777, when reports reached Parliament that Lord George Pigot, Governor of Madras, had been deposed and imprisoned by a political group friendly to Hastings. Pigot had a reputation for great personal integrity, and in June 1777 Parliament directed Burke's kinsman, Will Burke, to sail for Madras to arrange the release and reinstatement of Pigot. But on reaching Madras in August Will discovered that Pigot had died in prison, and that his friendship with Sir Philip Francis put him out of favor with Hastings. In May 1778 he returned to England as agent in Parliament for the Raja of Tanjore, at two thousand pounds a year. Early in 1780, following a victory of the Hastings faction in electing members of the board of directors of the East India Company, Will returned to India to report to the Raja of Tanjore. In the fall of 1780 Edmund Burke worked on the General Court of Proprietors to defeat plans to bring the finances of Tanjore under company control. Whether his motive was a desire to help Will's cause or to prevent an extension of Hastings' power and avarice, or both, is still debatable. In November 1780 Lord Macartney, friendly to Hastings, was appointed Governor of Madras over Edmund's strong objections. Will's services to the Raja of Tanjore became even more a liability than an asset with the appointment of Paul Benfield, another agent of Hastings, to an administrative post in Madras. Those who had deposed Pigot were now officially established in his place. In all these political events and maneuverings Edmund Burke and Hastings were clearly in opposite camps.

Beginning in 1781, as a member of the Select Committee of the House, Burke continued to investigate Hastings' rule in India. As evidence of serious, systematic, and repeated abuses of power accumulated, he drew up the proceedings for Hastings' impeachment. The formal impeachment charges were made in 1786, and the impeachment trial before the House of Lords began on February 13, 1788 and lasted until June 16, 1794. The Lords acquitted Hastings in 1795.

Most historians have agreed that Burke allowed his passion and his prejudice against Hastings to seriously impair his sense of justice during portions of the trial. Burke did not allow enough for the natural difficulties of political administration over such a vast area, and blamed Hastings personally for abuses over which he had little control. This complex problem has yet to receive its final solution. But the impeachment itself was a notable achievement for Burke, even though the trial ended in acquittal, because it had a very sobering effect in raising the political morality of the British in India and throughout the Empire.

SPEECH

IN

OPENING THE IMPEACHMENT

FIRST DAY: FRIDAY, FEBRUARY 15, 1788

. . . With very few intermissions, the affairs of India have constantly engaged the attention of the Commons for more than fourteen years. We may safely affirm we have tried every mode of legislative provision before we had recourse to anything of penal process. It was in the year 1774 [1773?]

we framed an act of Parliament for remedy to the then existing disorders in India . . . Finding that the act of Parliament did not answer all the ends that were expected from it, we had, in the year 1782, recourse to a body of monitory resolutions. Neither had we the expected fruit from them. When, therefore, we found that our inquiries and our reports, our laws and our admonitions, were alike despised, that enormities increased in proportion as they were forbidden, detected, and exposed, . . . then it was time for the justice of the nation to recollect itself. To have forborne longer would not have been patience, but collusion . . .

The crimes with which we charge the prisoner at the bar are substantial crimes, . . . they are no errors or mistakes, such as wise and good men might possibly fall into . . . We know, as we are to be served by men, that the persons who serve us must be tried as men, and with a very large allowance indeed to human infirmity and human error. . . . But the crimes which we charge in these articles are not lapses, defects, errors of common human frailty, which, as we know and feel, we can allow for. We charge this offender with no crimes that have not arisen from passions which it is criminal to harbor—with no offences that have not their root in avarice, rapacity, pride, insolence, ferocity, treachery, cruelty, malignity of temper—in short, in [with?] nothing that does not argue a total extinction of all moral principle . . . We urge no crimes that were not crimes of forethought. We charge him with nothing that he did not commit upon deliberation—that he did not commit against advice, supplication, and remonstrance—that he did not commit against the direct command of lawful authority . . . The crimes of Mr. Hastings are crimes . . . not against forms, but against those eternal laws of justice which are our rule and our birthright. His offences are, not in formal, technical language, but in reality, in substance and effect, *high* crimes and high misdemeanors. . . .

My Lords, we have brought before you the first man of India, in rank, authority, and station. We have brought before you the chief of the tribe, the head of the whole body of Eastern offenders, a captain-general of iniquity, under whom all the fraud, all the peculation, all the tyranny in India are embodied, disciplined, arrayed, and paid. . . . We have brought before you such a person, that, if you strike at him with the firm and decided arm of justice, you will not have need of a great many more examples. You strike at the whole corps, if you strike at the head. . . .

When you consider the late enormous power of the prisoner
—when you consider his criminal, indefatigable assiduity in the
destruction of all recorded evidence—when you consider the
influence he has over almost all living testimony—when you
consider the distance of the scene of action—I believe your
Lordships, and I believe the world, will be astonished that so
much, so clear, so solid, and so conclusive evidence of all
kinds has been obtained against him. I have no doubt that in
nine instances in ten the evidence is such as would satisfy the
narrow precision supposed to prevail, and to a degree rightly
to prevail, in all subordinate power and delegated jurisdiction.
But your Lordships will maintain, what we assert and claim as
the right of the subjects of Great Britain, that you are not
bound by any rules of evidence, or any other rules whatever,
except those of natural, immutable, and substantial justice. . . .

My Lords, the powers which Mr. Hastings is charged with
having abused are the powers delegated to him by the East
India Company. The East India Company itself acts under two
very dissimilar sorts of powers, derived from two sources very
remote from each other. The first source of its power is under
charters which the crown of Great Britain was authorized by
act of Parliament to grant; the other is from several charters
derived from the Emperor of the Moguls, the person in whose
dominions they were chiefly conversant—particularly that great
charter by which, in the year 1765, they acquired the high-
stewardship of the kingdoms of Bengal, Bahar, and Orissa.
Under those two bodies of charters, the East India Company,
and all their servants, are authorized to act.

As to those of the first description, it is from the British
charters that they derive the capacity by which they are considered as a public body, or at all capable of any public function. It is from thence they acquire the capacity to take from
any power whatsoever any other charter, to acquire any other
offices, or to hold any other possessions. This, being the root
and origin of their power, renders them responsible to the
party from whom all their immediate and consequential powers are derived. As they have emanated from the supreme
power of this kingdom, the whole body and the whole train of
their servants, the corporate body as a corporate body, individuals as individuals, are responsible to the high justice of
this kingdom. In delegating great power to the East India Company, this kingdom has not released its sovereignty; on the contrary, the responsibility of the Company is increased by the

greatness and sacredness of the powers that have been intrusted to it. Attempts have been made abroad to circulate a
notion that the acts of the East India Company and their servants are not cognizable here. I hope on this occasion your
Lordships will show that this nation never did give a power
without annexing to it a proportionable degree of responsibility.

As to their other powers, the Company derives them from
the Mogul empire by various charters from that crown . . .
By that charter they bound themselves (and bound inclusively
all their servants) to perform all the duties belonging to that
new office, and to be held by all the ties belonging to that new
relation. If the Mogul empire had existed in its vigor, they
would have been bound, under that responsibility, to observe
the laws, rights, usages, and customs of the natives, and to
pursue their benefit in all things: for this duty was inherent
in the nature, institution, and purpose of the office which they
received. If the power of the sovereign from whom they derived these powers should by any revolution in human affairs
be annihilated or suspended, their duty to the people below
them, which was created under the Mogul charter, is not annihilated, is not even suspended; and for their responsibility in
the performance of that duty, they are thrown back upon that
country (thank God, not annihilated) from whence their original power, and all subsequent derivative powers, have flowed.
When the Company acquired that high office in India, an English corporation became an integral part of the Mogul empire.
When Great Britain virtually assented to that grant of office,
and afterwards took advantage of it, Great Britain guarantied
the performance of all its duties. Great Britain entered into a
virtual act of union with that country, by which we bound ourselves as securities to preserve the people in all the rights,
laws, and liberties which their natural, original sovereign was
bound to support, if he had been in condition to support them.
By the disposition of events, the two duties, flowing from two
different sources, are now united in one. The people of India,
therefore, come in the name of the Commons of Great Britain,
but in their own right, to the bar of this House, before the
supreme royal justice of this kingdom, from whence originally
all the powers under which they have suffered were derived.

It may be a little necessary, when we are stating the powers
the Company have derived from their charter, and which we
state Mr. Hastings to have abused, to state in as short and as
comprehensive words as I can . . . what the constitution of

that Company is—I mean chiefly, what it is in reference to its Indian service, the great theatre of the abuse. . . .

The East India Company had its origin about the latter end of the reign of Elizabeth, a period of projects, when all sorts of commercial adventures, companies, and monopolies were in fashion. At that time the Company was constituted with extensive powers for increasing the commerce and the honor of this country; because increasing its commerce, without increasing its honor and reputation, would have been thought at that time, and will be thought now, a bad bargain for the country. The powers of the Company were, under that charter, merely commercial. By degrees, as the theatre of operation was distant, as its intercourse was with many great, some barbarous, and all of them armed nations, nations in which not only the sovereign, but the subjects, were armed, it was found necessary to enlarge their powers. The first power they obtained was a power of naval discipline in their ships—a power which has been since dropped; the next was a power of law martial; the next was a power of civil, and, to a degree, of criminal jurisdiction, within their own factories, upon their own people and their own servants; the next was (and here was a stride indeed) the power of peace and war. Those high and almost incommunicable prerogatives of sovereignty, which were hardly ever known before to be parted with to any subjects, and which in several states were not wholly intrusted to the prince or head of the commonwealth himself, were given to the East India Company. That Company acquired these powers about the end of the reign of Charles the Second; and they were afterwards more fully, as well as more legally, given by Parliament after the Revolution. From this time, the East India Company was no longer merely a mercantile company, formed for the extension of the British commerce: it more nearly resembled a delegation of the whole power and sovereignty of this kingdom sent into the East. From that time the Company ought to be considered as a subordinate sovereign power: that is, sovereign with regard to the objects which it touched; subordinate with regard to the power from whence its great trust was derived.

Under these successive arrangements things took a course very different from their usual order. A new disposition took place, not dreamt of in the theories of speculative politicians, and of which few examples in the least resembling it have been seen in the modern world, none at all in the ancient. In other instances, a political body that acts as a commonwealth was first settled, and trade followed as a consequence of the protection obtained by political power; but here the course of affairs was reversed. The constitution of the Company began in commerce and ended in empire. Indeed, wherever the sovereign powers of peace and war are given, there wants but time and circumstance to make these powers supersede every other. The affairs of commerce will fall at last into their proper rank and situation. However primary in their original intention, they will become secondary. The possession, therefore, and the power of assertion of these great authorities coinciding with the improved state of Europe, with the improved state of arts in Europe, with the improved state of laws, and, what is much more material, the improved state of military discipline, more and more perfected every day with us—universal improvement in Europe coinciding with the general decay of Asia, (for the proud day of Asia is passed,) this improvement coinciding with the relaxation and dissolution of the Mogul government, with the decline of its warlike spirit, with the total disuse of the ancient strictness of the military discipline established by Tamerlane, the India Company came to be what it is, a great empire, carrying on, subordinately, a great commerce; it became that thing which was supposed by the Roman law irreconcilable to reason and propriety— *eundem negotiatorem et dominum:* the same power became the general trader, the same power became the supreme lord.

In this exalted situation, the India Company, however, still preserves traces of its original mercantile character. The whole exterior order of its political service is carried on upon a mercantile plan and mercantile principles. In fact, the East India Company in Asia is a state in the disguise of a merchant. Its whole service is a system of public offices in the disguise of a counting-house. Accordingly, the whole external order and series of the service, as I observed, is commercial; the principal, the inward, the real, is almost entirely political. . . .

SECOND DAY: SATURDAY, FEBRUARY 16, 1788

. . . My Lords, we conceive, that, when a British governor is sent abroad, he is sent to pursue the good of the people as much as possible in the spirit of the laws of this country, which in all respects intend their conservation, their happiness, and their prosperity. This is the principle upon which Mr. Hastings was bound to govern, and upon which he is to account for his conduct here. His rule was, what a British governor, intrusted with the power of this country, was bound to do or to forbear. If he has performed and if he has abstained as he ought, dismiss him honorably acquitted from your bar; otherwise condemn him. He may resort to other principles and to other maxims; but this country will force him to be tried by its laws. . . .

And, first, I am to state to your Lordships . . . the principles on which Mr. Hastings declares he has conducted his government—principles which he has avowed, first in several letters written to the East India Company, next in a paper of defence delivered to the House of Commons explicitly, and more explicitly in his defence before your Lordships. Nothing in Mr. Hastings's proceedings is so curious as his several defences; and nothing in the defences is so singular as the principles upon which he proceeds. Your Lordships will have to decide not only upon a large, connected, systematic train of misdemeanors, but an equally connected system of principles and maxims of government, invented to justify those misdemeanors. He has brought them forward and avowed them in the face of day. . . .

My Lords, we contend that Mr. Hastings, as a British governor, ought to govern on British principles, not by British forms—God forbid!—for if ever there was a case in which the letter kills and the spirit gives life, it would be an attempt to introduce British forms and the substance of despotic principles together into any country. No! We call for that spirit of equity, that spirit of justice, that spirit of protection, that spirit of lenity, which ought to characterize every British subject in power . . .

But he has told your Lordships, in his defence, that actions in Asia do not bear the same moral qualities which the same actions would bear in Europe.

My Lords, we positively deny that principle. I am authorized and called upon to deny it. And having stated at large what he means by saying that the same actions have not the same qualities in Asia and in Europe, we are to let your Lordships know that these gentlemen have formed a plan of *geographical morality,* by which the duties of men, in public and in private situations, are not to be governed by their relation to the great Governor of the Universe, or by their relation to mankind, but by climates, degrees of longitude, parallels, not of life, but of latitudes: as if, when you have crossed the equinoctial, all the virtues die . . .

This geographical morality we do protest against; Mr. Hastings shall not screen himself under it . . . the laws of morality are the same everywhere, and . . . there is no action which would pass for an act of extortion, of peculation, of bribery, and of oppression in England, that is not an act of extortion, of peculation, of bribery, and oppression in Europe, Asia, Africa, and all the world over. . . .

Mr. Hastings comes before your Lordships not as a British governor answering to a British tribunal, but as a subahdar, as a bashaw of three tails. He says, "I had an arbitrary power to exercise: I exercised it. Slaves I found the people: slaves they are—they are so by their constitution; and if they are, I did not make it for them. I was unfortunately bound to exercise this arbitrary power, and accordingly I did exercise it. It was disagreeable to me, but I did exercise it; and no other power can be exercised in that country." This, if it be true, is a plea in bar. . . .

His plea is, that he did govern there on arbitrary and despotic, and, as he supposes, Oriental principles. And as this plea is boldly avowed and maintained, and as, no doubt, all his conduct was perfectly correspondent to these principles, the principles and the conduct must be tried together. . . .

When in this speculative way he has established, or thinks he has, the vices of the government, he conceives he has found a sufficient apology for his own crimes. . . . He lays it down as a rule, that despotism is the genuine constitution of India, that a disposition to rebellion in the subject or dependent prince is the necessary effect of this despotism, and that jealousy and its consequences naturally arise on the part of the sovereign—that the government is everything, and the subject nothing . . .

But nothing is more false than that despotism is the constitution of any country in Asia that we are acquainted with. . . . He has declared his opinion, that he is a despotic prince, that he is to use arbitrary power; and of course all his acts are covered with that shield. *"I know,"* says he, *"the constitution of Asia only from its practice."* Will your Lordships submit to hear the corrupt practices of mankind made the principles of government? No! it will be your pride and glory to teach men intrusted with power, that, in their use of it, they are to conform to principles, and not to draw their principles from the corrupt practice of any man whatever. Was there ever heard, or could it be conceived, that a governor would dare to heap up all the evil practices, all the cruelties, oppressions, extortions, corruptions, briberies, of all the ferocious usurpers, desperate robbers, thieves, cheats, and jugglers, that ever had office, from one end of Asia to another, and, consolidating all this mass of the crimes and absurdities of barbarous domination into one code, establish it as the whole duty of an English governor? I believe that till this time so audacious a thing was never attempted by man.

He have arbitrary power! My Lords, the East India Company have not arbitrary power to give him; the king has no arbitrary power to give him; your Lordships have not; nor the Commons, nor the whole legislature. We have no arbitrary power to give, because arbitrary power is a thing which neither any man can hold nor any man can give. No man can lawfully govern himself according to his own will; much less can one person be governed by the will of another. We are all born in subjection—all born equally, high and low, governors and governed, in subjection to one great, immutable, preexistent law, prior to all our devices and prior to all our contrivances, paramount to all our ideas and all our sensations, antecedent to our very existence, by which we are knit and connected in the eternal frame of the universe, out of which we cannot stir.

This great law does not arise from our conventions or compacts; on the contrary, it gives to our conventions and compacts all the force and sanction they can have. It does not arise from our vain institutions. Every good gift is of God; all power is of God; and He who has given the power, and from whom alone it originates, will never suffer the exercise of it to be practised upon any less solid foundation than the power itself. If, then, all dominion of man over man is the effect of the Divine disposition, it is bound by the eternal laws of Him that gave it, with which no human authority can dispense—neither he that exercises it, nor even those who are subject to it; and if they were mad enough to make an express compact that should release their magistrate from his duty, and should declare their lives, liberties, and properties dependent upon, not rules and laws, but his mere capricious will, that covenant would be void. The acceptor of it has not his authority increased, but he has his crime doubled. Therefore can it be imagined, if this be true, that He will suffer this great gift of government, the greatest, the best, that was ever given by God to mankind, to be the plaything and the sport of the feeble will of a man, who, by a blasphemous, absurd, and petulant usurpation, would place his own feeble, contemptible, ridiculous will in the place of the Divine wisdom and justice?

The title of conquest makes no difference at all. No conquest can give such a right; for conquest, that is, force, cannot convert its own injustice into a just title, by which it may rule others at its pleasure. By conquest, which is a more immediate designation of the hand of God, the conqueror succeeds to all the painful duties and subordination to the power of God which belonged to the sovereign whom he has displaced, just as if he had come in by the positive law of some descent or some election. To this at least he is strictly bound: he ought to govern them as he governs his own subjects. . . .

Arbitrary power is not to be had by conquest. Nor can any sovereign have it by succession; for no man can succeed to fraud, rapine, and violence. Neither by compact, covenant, or submission—for men cannot covenant themselves out of their rights and their duties—nor by any other means, can arbitrary power be conveyed to any man. Those who give to others such rights perform acts that are void as they are given —good indeed and valid only as tending to subject themselves, and those who act with them, to the Divine displeasure; because morally there can be no such power. Those who give and those who receive arbitrary power are alike criminal; and there is no man but is bound to resist it to the best of his power, wherever it shall show its face to the world. . . .

Law and arbitrary power are in eternal enmity. Name me a magistrate, and I will name property; name me power, and I will name protection. It is a contradiction in terms, it is blasphemy in religion, it is wickedness in politics, to say that any man can have arbitrary power. In every patent of office the duty is included. For what else does a magistrate exist? To suppose for power is an absurdity in idea. Judges are guided and governed by the eternal laws of justice, to which we are all subject. We may bite our chains, if we will, but we shall be made to know ourselves, and be taught that man is born to be governed by law; and he that will substitute *will* in the place of it is an enemy to GOD.

Despotism does not in the smallest degree abrogate, alter, or lessen any one duty of any one relation of life, or weaken the force or obligation of any one engagement or contract whatsoever. Despotism, if it means anything that is at all defensible, means a mode of government bound by no written rules, and coerced by no controlling magistracies or well-settled orders in the state. But if it has no written law, it neither does nor can cancel the primeval, indefeasible, unalterable law of Nature and of nations; and if no magistracies control its exertions, those exertions must derive their limitation and direction either from the equity and moderation of the ruler, or from downright revolt on the part of the subject by rebellion, divested of all its criminal qualities. The moment a sovereign removes the idea of security and protection from his subjects, and declares that he is everything and they nothing, when he declares that no contract he makes with them can or ought to bind him, he then declares war upon them: he is no longer sovereign; they are no longer subjects.

No man, therefore, has a right to arbitrary power. . . .

Oriental governments know nothing of arbitrary power. I have taken as much pains as I could to examine into the constitutions of them. I have been endeavoring to inform myself at all times on this subject; of late my duty has led me to a more minute inspection of them; and I do challenge the whole race of man to show me any of the Oriental governors claiming to themselves a right to act by arbitrary will.

The greatest part of Asia is under Mahomedan governments. To name a Mahomedan government is to name a government by law. It is a law enforced by stronger sanctions than any law that can bind a Christian sovereign. Their law is believed to be given by God; and it has the double sanction of law and of religion, with which the prince is no more authorized to dispense than any one else. . . .

I must do justice to the East. I assert that their morality is equal to ours, in whatever regards the duties of governors, fathers, and superiors; and I challenge the world to show in any modern European book more true morality and wisdom than is to be found in the writings of Asiatic men in high trust, and who have been counsellors to princes. If this be the true morality of Asia, as I affirm and can prove that it is, the plea founded on Mr. Hastings's geographical morality is annihilated. . . .

That the people of Asia have no laws, rights, or liberty, is a doctrine that wickedly is to be disseminated through this country. But I again assert, every Mahomedan government is, by its principles, a government of law. . . .

Mr. Hastings has no refuge here. Let him run from law to law; let him fly from the common law and the sacred institutions of the country in which he was born; let him fly from acts of Parliament, from which his power originated; let him plead his ignorance of them, or fly in the face of them. Will he fly to the Mahomedan law? That condemns him. . . . Let him fly where he will, from law to law; law, I thank God,

meets him everywhere . . . I would as willingly have him
tried by the law of the Koran, or the Institutes of Tamerlane,
as on the common law or statute law of this kingdom. . . .

In Asia as well as in Europe the same law of nations prevails, the same principles are continually resorted to, and the
same maxims sacredly held and strenuously maintained, and,
however disobeyed, no man suffers from the breach of them
who does not know how and where to complain of that
breach . . . Asia is enlightened in that respect as well as Europe . . .

THIRD DAY: MONDAY, FEBRUARY 18, 1788

. . . The principles upon which Mr. Hastings governed his
conduct in India, and upon which he grounds his defence
. . . may all be reduced to one short word—*arbitrary power.*
. . . At the time he tells you he acted on the principles of
arbitrary power, he takes care to inform you that he was not
blind to the consequences. Mr. Hastings foresaw that the consequences of this system was corruption. An arbitrary system,
indeed, must always be a corrupt one. My Lords, there never
was a man who thought he had no law but his own will, who
did not soon find that he had no end but his own profit. Corruption and arbitrary power are of natural unequivocal generation, necessarily producing one another. Mr. Hastings fore-
sees the abusive and corrupt consequences, and then he
justifies his conduct upon the necessities of that system. These
are things which are new in the world; for there never was a
man, I believe, who contended for arbitrary power, . . . that
did not pretend, either that the system was good in itself, or
that by their conduct they had mitigated or had purified it, and
that the poison, by passing through their constitution, had acquired salutary properties. But if you look at his defence before the House of Commons, you will see that that very system
upon which he governed, and under which he now justifies
his actions, did appear to himself a system pregnant with a
thousand evils and a thousand mischiefs. . . .

We say, then, not only that he governed arbitrarily, but
corruptly—that is to say, that he was a giver and receiver of
bribes, and formed a system for the purpose of giving and
receiving them. . . .

In short, money is the beginning, the middle, and the end
of every kind of act done by Mr. Hastings: pretendedly for
the Company, but really for himself. . . .

It has been said of an ambassador, that he is a person employed to tell lies for the advantage of the court that sends him. His is patriotic bribery, and public-spirited corruption. He is a peculator for the good of his country. It has been said that private vices are public benefits. He goes the full length of that position, and turns his private peculation into a public good. This is what you are to thank him for. You are to consider him as a great inventor upon this occasion. Mr. Hastings improves on this principle. He is a robber in gross, and a thief in detail—he steals, he filches, he plunders, he oppresses, he extorts—all for the good of the dear East India Company—all for the advantage of his honored masters, the Proprietors . . .

If you sanction this practice, if, after all you have exacted from the people by your taxes and public imposts, you are to let loose your servants upon them, to extort by bribery and peculation what they can from them, for the purpose of applying it to the public service only whenever they please, this shocking consequence will follow from it. If your Governor is discovered in taking a bribe, he will say, "What is that to you? mind your business; I intend it for the public service." The man who dares to accuse him loses the favor of the Governor-General and the India Company. They will say, "The Governor has been doing a meritorious action, extorting bribes for our benefit, and you have the impudence to think of prosecuting him." So that the moment the bribe is detected, it is instantly turned into a merit: and we shall prove that this is the case with Mr. Hastings, whenever a bribe has been discovered. . . .

Fatally for the natives of India, every wild project and every corrupt sale of Mr. Hastings, and those whose example he followed, is covered with a pretended increase of revenue to the Company. Mr. Hastings would not pocket his bribe of 40,000*l.* for himself without letting the Company in as a sharer and accomplice. For the province of Rungpore, the object to which I mean in this instance to confine your attention, 7,000*l.* a year was added. . . .

If Mr. Hastings can forget his covenant, you may easily believe that Debi Sing had not a more correct memory; and accordingly, as soon as he came into the province, he instantly broke every covenant which he had entered into as a restraint on his avarice, rapacity, and tyranny, which, from the highest of the nobility and gentry to the lowest husbandmen, were afterwards exercised, with a stern and unrelenting impartiality, upon the whole people. . . .

It was not a rigorous collection of revenue, it was a savage war made upon the country. . . .

It is the nature of tyranny and rapacity never to learn moderation from the ill-success of first oppressions; on the contrary, all oppressors, all men thinking highly of the methods dictated by their nature, attribute the frustration of their desires to the want of sufficient rigor. Then they redouble the efforts of their impotent cruelty, which producing, as they must ever produce, new disappointments, they grow irritated against the objects of their rapacity; and then rage, fury, and malice, implacable because unprovoked, recruiting and reinforcing their avarice, their vices are no longer human. From cruel men they are transformed into savage beasts, with no other vestiges of reason left but what serves to furnish the inventions and refinements of ferocious subtlety, for purposes of which beasts are incapable and at which fiends would blush. . . .

And here, my Lords, began such a scene of cruelties and tortures as I believe no history has ever presented to the indignation of the world—such as I am sure, in the most barbarous ages, no politic tyranny, no fanatic persecution, has ever yet exceeded. . . .

FOURTH DAY: TUESDAY, FEBRUARY 19, 1788

. . . This shocking series of corruption, oppression, fraud, and chicanery . . . lasted for upwards of four years . . .

I charge all this villainy upon Warren Hastings . . .

I impeach him in the name of the Commons of Great Britain in Parliament assembled, whose Parliamentary trust he has betrayed.

I impeach him in the name of all the Commons of Great Britain, whose national character he has dishonored.

I impeach him in the name of the people of India, whose laws, rights, and liberties he has subverted, whose properties he has destroyed, whose country he has laid waste and desolate.

I impeach him in the name and by virtue of those eternal laws of justice which he has violated.

I impeach him in the name of human nature itself, which he has cruelly outraged, injured, and oppressed, in both sexes, in every age, rank, situation, and condition of life.

SPEECH
ON
THE SIXTH ARTICLE OF CHARGE
FOURTH DAY: THURSDAY, MAY 7, 1789

. . . Our liberty is as much in danger as our honor and our national character. We, who here appear representing the Commons of England, are not wild enough not to tremble both for ourselves and for our constituents at the effect of riches. . . . We dread the operation of money. Do we not know that there are many men who wait, and who indeed hardly wait, the event of this prosecution, to let loose all the corrupt wealth of India, acquired by the oppression of that country, for the corruption of all the liberties of this, and to fill the Parliament with men who are now the object of its indignation? To-day the Commons of Great Britain prosecute the delinquents of India: to-morrow the delinquents of India may be the Commons of Great Britain. We know, I say, and feel the force of money; and we now call upon your Lordships for justice in this cause of money. We call upon you for the preservation of our manners, of our virtues. We call upon you for our national character. We call upon you for our liberties; and hope that the freedom of the Commons will be preserved by the justice of the Lords.

SPEECH
IN
GENERAL REPLY
FIRST DAY: WEDNESDAY, MAY 28, 1794

. . . The next subject for your Lordships' consideration is the principle of the prisoner's defence. And here we must observe, that, either by confession or conviction, we are possessed of the facts, and perfectly agreed upon the matter at issue between us. In taking a view of the laws by which you are to judge, I shall beg leave to state to you upon what principles of law the House of Commons has criminated him, and upon what principles of law, or pretended law, he justifies himself: for these are the matters at issue between us; the matters of fact, as I have just said, being determined either by confession on his part or by proof on ours.

My Lords, we acknowledge that Mr. Hastings was invested with discretionary power; but we assert that he was bound to use that power according to the established rules of political morality, humanity, and equity. In all questions relating to foreign powers he was bound to act under the Law of Nature and under the Law of Nations, as it is recognized by the wisest authorities in public jurisprudence; in his relation to this country he was bound to act according to the laws and statutes of Great Britain, either in their letter or in their spirit; and we affirm, that in his relation to the people of India he was bound to act according to the largest and most liberal construction of their laws, rights, usages, institutions, and good customs; and we furthermore assert, that he was under an express obligation to yield implicit obedience to the Court of Directors. It is upon these rules and principles the Commons contend that Mr. Hastings ought to have regulated his government; and not only Mr. Hastings, but all other governors. It is upon these rules that he is responsible; and upon these rules, and these rules only, your Lordships are to judge.

My Lords, long before the Committee had resolved upon this impeachment, we had come, as I have told your Lordships, to forty-five resolutions, every one criminatory of this man, every one of them bottomed upon the principles which I have stated. We never will nor can we abandon them; and we therefore do not supplicate your Lordships upon this head, but claim and demand of right, that you will judge him upon those principles, and upon no other. If once they are evaded, you can have no rule for your judgment but your caprices and partialities.

Having thus stated the principles upon which the Commons hold him and all governors responsible, and upon which we have grounded our impeachment, and which must be the grounds of your judgment, . . . we will now tell you what are the grounds of his defence.

He first asserts, that he was possessed of an arbitrary and despotic power, restrained by no laws but his own will. He next says, that "the rights of the people he governed in India are nothing, and that the rights of the government are everything." The people, he asserts, have no liberty, no laws, no inheritance, no fixed property, no descendable estate, no subordinations in society, no sense of honor or of shame, and that they are only affected by punishment so far as punishment is a corporal infliction, being totally insensible of any difference between the punishment of man and beast. These are the principles of his Indian government, which Mr. Hastings has avowed in their full extent. Whenever precedents are required, he cites and follows the example of avowed tyrants, of Aliverdy Khân, Cossim Ali Khân, and Sujah Dowlah. With an avowal of these principles he was pleased first to entertain the House of Commons, the *active* assertors and conservators of the rights, liberties, and laws of his country; and then to insist upon them more largely and in a fuller detail before this awful tribunal, the *passive* judicial conservator of the same great interests. He has brought out these blasphemous doctrines in this great temple of justice, consecrated to law and equity for a long series of ages. He has brought them forth in Westminster Hall, in presence of all the Judges of the land, who are to execute the law, and of the House of Lords, who are bound as its guardians not to suffer the words "arbitrary power" to be mentioned before them. For I am not again to tell your Lordships, that arbitrary power is treason in the law—that to mention it with law is to commit a contradiction in terms. They cannot exist in concert; they cannot hold together for a moment. . . .

This is the account he gives of his power, and of the people subject to the British government in India. We deny that the act of Parliament gave him any such power; we deny that the India Company gave him any such power, or that they had ever any such power to give; we even deny that there exists in all the human race a power to make the government of any state dependent upon individual will. We disclaim, we reject all such doctrines with disdain and indignation; and we have brought them up to your Lordships to be tried at your bar. . . .

My Lords, the House of Commons has already well considered what may be our future moral and political condition, when the persons who come from that school of pride, insolence, corruption, and tyranny are more intimately mixed up with us of purer morals. Nothing but contamination can be the result, nothing but corruption can exist in this country, unless we expunge this doctrine out of the very hearts and souls of the people. It is not to the gang of plunderers and robbers of which I say this man is at the head, that we are only, or indeed principally, to look. Every man in Great Britain will be contaminated and must be corrupted, if you let loose among us whole legions of men, generation after generation, tainted with these abominable vices, and avowing these detestable principles. It is, therefore, to preserve the integrity and honor of the Commons of Great Britain th have brought this man to your Lordships' bar. .

But, my Lords, we all know that there has been arbitrary power in India—that tyrants have usurped it—and that, in some instances, princes otherwise meritorious have violated the liberties of the people, and have been lawfully deposed for such violation. I do not deny that there are robberies on Hounslow Heath—that there are such things as forgeries, burglaries, and murders; but I say that these acts are against law, and that whoever commit them commit illegal acts. When a man is to defend himself against a charge of crime, it is not instances of similar violation of law that is to be the standard of his defence. A man may as well say, "I robbed upon Hounslow Heath, but hundreds robbed there before me": to which I answer, "The law has forbidden you to rob there; and I will hang you for having violated the law, notwithstanding the long list of similar violations which you have produced as precedents." No doubt princes have violated the law of this country: they have suffered for it. Nobles have violated the law: their privileges have not protected them from punishment. Common people have violated the law: they have been hanged for it. I know no human being exempt from the law. The law is the security of the people of England; it is the security of the people of India; it is the security of every person that is governed, and of every person that governs. There is but one law for all, namely, that law which governs all law, the law of our Creator, the law of humanity, justice, equity—the Law of Nature and of Nations. So far as any laws fortify this primeval law, and give it more precision, more energy, more effect by their declarations, such laws enter into the sanctuary, and participate in the sacredness of its character. But the man who quotes as precedents the abuses of tyrants and robbers pollutes the very fountain of justice, destroys the foundations of all law, and thereby removes the only safeguard against evil men, whether governors or governed—the guard which prevents governors from becoming tyrants, and the governed from becoming rebels. . . .

SECOND DAY: FRIDAY, MAY 30, 1794

. . . Wherever existing laws were applicable, the prisoner at your bar was bound by the laws and statutes of this kingdom, as a British subject; and . . . whenever he exercised authority in the name of the Company, or in the name of his Majesty, or under any other name, he was bound by the laws and statutes of this kingdom, both in letter and spirit, so far

as they were applicable to him and to his case; and above
all, . . . he was bound by the act to which he owed his appointment, in all transactions with foreign powers, to act according to the known recognized rules of the Law of Nations,
whether these powers were really or nominally sovereign,
whether they were dependent or independent. . . .

On one side, your Lordships have the prisoner declaring
that the people have no laws, no rights, no usages, no distinctions of rank, no sense of honor, no property—in short, that
they are nothing but a herd of slaves, to be governed by the
arbitrary will of a master. On the other side, we assert that
the direct contrary of this is true. And to prove our assertion
we have referred you to the Institutes of Genghis Khân and
of Tamerlane; we have referred you to the Mahometan law,
which is binding upon all, from the crowned head to the
meanest subject—a law interwoven with a system of the wisest,
the most learned, and most enlightened jurisprudence that
perhaps ever existed in the world. We have shown you, that,
if these parties are to be compared together, it is not the rights
of the people which are nothing, but rather the rights of the
sovereign which are so. The rights of the people are everything, as they ought to be, in the true and natural order of
things. God forbid that these maxims should trench upon sovereignty, and its true, just, and lawful prerogative!—on the
contrary, they ought to support and establish them. The sovereign's rights are undoubtedly sacred rights, and ought to be
so held in every country in the world, because exercised for
the benefit of the people, and in subordination to that great
end for which alone God has vested power in any man or
any set of men. This is the law that we insist upon, and these
are the principles upon which your Lordships are to try the
prisoner at your bar. . . .

That your Lordships may be enabled to judge more fully
of the nature of this offence, let us see in what relation Cheyt
Sing stood with the Company. He was, my Lords, a person
clothed with every one of the attributes of sovereignty, under
a direct stipulation that the Company should not interfere in
his internal government. The military and civil authority, the
power of life and death, the whole revenue, and the whole
administration of the law, rested in him. Such was the sovereignty he possessed within Benares: but he was a subordinate sovereign dependent upon a superior, according to the
tenor of his compact, expressed or implied. Now, having contended, as we still contend, that the Law of Nations is the law

of India as well as of Europe, because it is the law of reason and the law of Nature, drawn from the pure sources of morality, of public good, and of natural equity, and recognized and digested into order by the labor of learned men, I will refer your Lordships to Vattel, Book I. Cap. 16, where he treats of the breach of such agreements, by the protector refusing to give protection, or the protected refusing to perform his part of the engagement. My design in referring you to this author is to prove that Cheyt Sing, so far from being blamable in raising objections to the unauthorized demand made upon him by Mr. Hastings, was absolutely bound to do so; nor could he have done otherwise, without hazarding the whole benefit of the agreement upon which his subjection and protection were founded. The law is the same with respect to both contracting parties: if the protected or protector does not fulfil with fidelity *each his separate stipulation*, the protected may resist the unauthorized demand of the protector, or the protector is discharged from his engagement; he may refuse protection, and declare the treaty broken. . . .

This was the rebellion, and the only rebellion; it was Warren Hastings's rebellion—a rebellion which arose from his own dreadful exaction, from his pride, from his malice and insatiable avarice—a rebellion which arose from his abominable tyranny, from his lust of arbitrary power, and from his determination to follow the examples of . . . all the gang of rebels who are the objects of his imitation. . . .

The whole country rose up in rebellion, and surely in justifiable rebellion. Every writer on the Law of Nations, every man that has written, thought, or felt upon the affairs of government, must write, know, think, and feel, that a people so cruelly scourged and oppressed, both in the person of their chief and in their own persons, were justified in their resistance. . . .

FOURTH DAY: THURSDAY, JUNE 5, 1794

. . . Your Lordships will find in the evidence before you that the inhabitants of the country were not only harassed in their fortunes, but cruelly treated in their persons. You have it upon Mr. Halhed's evidence, and it is not attempted, that I know of, to be contradicted, that the people were confined in open cages, exposed to the scorching heat of the sun, for pretended or real arrears of rent: it is indifferent which, because I consider all confinement of the person to support an arbitrary exaction to be an abomination not to be tolerated. They have endeavored, indeed, to weaken this evidence by an attempt to prove that a man day and night in confinement in an open cage suffers no inconvenience. And here I must beg your Lordships to observe the extreme unwillingness that appears in these witnesses. Their testimony is drawn from them drop by drop, their answers to our questions are never more than yes or no; but when they are examined by the counsel on the other side, it flows as freely as if drawn from a perennial spring: and such a spring we have in Indian corruption. We have, however, proved that in these cages the renters were confined till they could be lodged in the dungeons or mud forts. We have proved that some of them were obliged to sell their children, that others fled the country, and that these practices were carried to such an awful extent that Colonel Hannay was under the necessity of issuing orders against the unnatural sale and flight which his rapacity had occasioned.

The prisoner's counsel have attempted to prove that this had been a common practice in that country. And though possibly some person as wicked as Colonel Hannay might have been there before at some time or other, no man ever sold his children but under the pressure of some cruel exaction. Nature calls out against it. The love that God has implanted in the heart of parents towards their children is the first germ of that second conjunction which He has ordered to subsist between them and the rest of mankind. It is the first formation and first bond of society. It is stronger than all laws; for it is the law of Nature, which is the law of God. Never did a man sell his children who was able to maintain them. It is, therefore, not only a proof of his exactions, but a decisive proof that these exactions were intolerable.

Next to the love of parents for their children, the strongest instinct, both natural and moral, that exists in man, is the love of his country: an instinct, indeed, which extends even to the brute creation. All creatures love their offspring; next to that they love their homes: they have a fondness for the place where they have been bred, for the habitations they have dwelt in, for the stalls in which they have been fed, the pastures they have browsed in, and the wilds in which they have roamed. We all know that the natal soil has a sweetness in it beyond the harmony of verse. This instinct, I say, that binds all creatures to their country, never becomes inert in us, nor ever suffers us to want a memory of it. Those, therefore, who seek to fly their country can only wish to fly from oppression: and what other proof can you want of this oppression, when, as a witness has told you, Colonel Hannay was obliged to put bars and guards to confine the inhabitants within the country?

We have seen, therefore, Nature violated in its strongest principles. We have seen unlimited and arbitrary exaction avowed, on no pretence of any law, rule, or any fixed mode by which these people were to be dealt with. All these facts have been proved before your Lordships by costive and unwilling witnesses. In consequence of these violent and cruel oppressions, a general rebellion breaks out in the country, as was naturally to be expected. The inhabitants rise as if by common consent; every farmer, every proprietor of land, every man who loved his family and his country, and had not fled for refuge, rose in rebellion, as they call it. My Lords, they did rebel; it was a just rebellion. Insurrection was there just and legal, inasmuch as Colonel Hannay, in defiance of the laws and rights of the people, exercised a clandestine, illegal authority, against which there can be no rebellion in its proper sense. . . .

SEVENTH DAY: THURSDAY, JUNE 12, 1794

. . . My Lords, it was not corporal pain alone that these miserable women suffered. The unsatisfied cravings of hunger and the blows of the sepoys' bludgeons could touch only the physical part of their nature. But, my Lords, men are made of two parts—the physical part, and the moral. The former he has in common with the brute creation. Like theirs, our corporal pains are very limited and temporary. But the sufferings which touch our moral nature have a wider range, and are infinitely more acute, driving the sufferer sometimes to the extremities of despair and distraction. Man, in his moral nature, becomes, in his progress through life, a creature of prejudice, a creature of opinions, a creature of habits, and of sentiments growing out of them. These form our second nature, as inhabitants of the country and members of the society in which Providence has placed us. This sensibility of our moral nature is far more acute in that sex which, I may say without any compliment, forms the better and more virtuous part of mankind, and which is at the same time the least protected from the insults and outrages to which this sensibility exposes them. This is a new source of feelings, that often make corporal distress doubly felt; and it has a whole class of distresses of its own. These are the things that have gone to the heart of the Commons. . . .

Bengal, like every part of India subject to the British empire, contains . . . three distinct classes of people, forming three distinct social systems. The first is the Mahometans, which, about seven hundred years ago, obtained a footing in that country, and ever since has in a great degree retained its authority there. For the Mahometans had settled there long before the foundation of the Bengal empire, which was overturned by Tamerlane: so that this people, who are represented sometimes loosely as strangers, are people of ancient and considerable settlement in that country; and though, like Mahometan settlers in many other countries, they have fallen into decay, yet, being continually recruited from various parts of Tartary under the Mogul empire, and from various parts of Persia, they continue to be the leading and most powerful people throughout the peninsula; and so we found them there. These people, for the most part, follow no trades or occupation, their religion and laws forbidding them in the strictest manner to take usury or profit arising from money that is in any way lent; they have, therefore, no other means for their support but what arises from their adherence to and connection with the Mogul government and its viceroys. They enjoy under them various offices, civil and military—various employments in the courts of law, and stations in the army. Accordingly a prodigious number of people, almost all of them persons of the most ancient and respectable families in the country, are dependent upon and cling to the subahdars or viceroys of the several provinces. They, therefore, who oppress, plunder, and destroy the subahdars, oppress, rob, and destroy an immense mass of people. It is true that a supervening government, established upon another, always reduces a certain portion of the dependants upon the latter to want. You must distress, by the very nature of the circumstances of the case, a great number of people; but then it is your business, when, by the superiority which you have acquired, however you may have acquired it, . . . it is your business not to oppress those people with new and additional difficulties, but rather to console them in the state to which they are reduced, and to give them all the assistance and protection in your power.

The next system is composed of the descendants of the people who were found in the country by the Mahometan invaders. The system before mentioned comprehends the official interest, the judicial interest, the court interest, and the military interest. This latter body includes almost the whole landed interest, commercial interest, and moneyed interest of the country. For the Hindoos not being forbidden by their laws or religious tenets, as laid down in the Shaster, many of them became the principal money-lenders and bankers; and thus the Hindoos form the greatest part both of the landed and moneyed interest in that country.

The third and last system is formed of the English interest; which in reality, whether it appears directly or indirectly, is the governing interest of the whole country—of its civil and military interest, of its landed, moneyed, and revenue interest; and what to us is the greatest concern of all, it is this system which is responsible for the government of that country to the government of Great Britain. It is divided into two parts: one emanating from the Company, and afterwards regulated by act of Parliament; the other a judicial body, sent out by and acting under the authority of the crown itself. The persons composing that interest are those whom we usually call the servants of the Company. They enter into that service, as your Lordships know, at an early period of life, and they are promoted accordingly as their merit or their interest may provide for them. This body of men, with respect to its number, is so small as scarcely to deserve mentioning; but, from certain circumstances, the government of the whole country is fallen into their hands. Amongst these circumstances, the most important and essential are their having the public revenues and the public purse entirely in their own hands, and their having an army maintained by that purse, and disciplined in the European manner.

Such was the state of that country when Mr. Hastings was appointed Governor in 1772. Your Lordships are now to decide upon the manner in which he has comported himself with regard to all these three interests: first, whether he has made the ancient Mahometan families as easy as he could; secondly, whether he has made the Hindoo inhabitants, the zemindars and their tenants, as secure in their property and as easy in their tenure as he could; and lastly, whether he has made the English interest a blessing to the country, and, whilst it provided moderate, safe, and proper emoluments to the persons that were concerned in it, it kept them from oppression and rapine, and a general waste and ravage of the country: whether, in short, he made all these three interests pursue that one object which all interests and all governments ought to pursue, the advantage and welfare of the people under them.

My Lords, in support of our charge against the prisoner at your bar, that he acted in a manner directly the reverse of this, we have proved to you that his first acts of oppression were directed against the Mahometan government—that government which had been before, not only in name, but in effect, to the very time of his appointment, the real government of the country. . . . In this was comprehended the support of the whole mass of nobility—the soldiers, serving or retired—all the officers of the court, and all the women that were dependent upon them—the whole of the criminal jurisdiction of the country, and a very considerable part of the civil law and the civil government. These establishments formed the constitutional basis of their political government.

The Company never had . . . of right despotic power in that country, to overturn any of these establishments. The Mogul, who gave them their charters, could not give them such a power—he did not *de facto* give them such a power; the government of this country did not by act of Parliament, and the Company did not and could not by their delegation, give him such a power; the act by which he was appointed Governor did not give him such a power. If he exercised it, he usurped it; and therefore, every step we take in the examination of his conduct in Bengal, as in every step we take upon the same subject everywhere else, we look for the justification of his conduct to laws—the Law of Nations, the laws of this country, and the laws of the country he was sent to govern. . . .

EIGHTH DAY: SATURDAY, JUNE 14, 1794

My Lords, when we have shown plainly the utter extinction of the native Mahometan government, when we have shown the extinction of the native landed interest, what hope can there be for that afflicted country but in the servants of the Company? When we have shown the corrupt state of that service, what hope but from the Court of Directors, what hope but in the superintending control of British tribunals? I think as well of the body of my countrymen as any man can do. I do not think that any man sent out to India is sent with an ill purpose, or goes out with bad dispositions. No: I think the young men who go there are fair and faithful representatives of the people of the same age—uncorrupted, but corruptible from their age, as we all are. They are sent there young. There is but one thing held out to them—"You are going to make your fortune." The Company's service is to be the restoration of decayed noble families; it is to be the renovation of old, and the making of new ones. . . .

Mr. Hastings left these servants but this alternative: "Be starved, be depressed, be ruined, disappoint the hopes of your families, or be my slaves, be ready to be subservient to me in every iniquity I shall order you to commit, and to conceal everything I shall wish you to conceal." This was the state of the service. Therefore the Commons did well and wisely, when they sent us here, not to attack this or that servant who may have peculated, but to punish the man who was sent to reform abuses, and to make Bengal furnish to the world a brilliant example of British justice. . . .

We have stated and proved that Mr. Hastings did enter upon a systematic connivance at the peculation of the Company's servants, that he refused to institute any check whatever for the purpose of preventing corruption, and that he carried into execution no one measure of government agreeably to the positive and solemn engagements into which he had entered with the Directors. We therefore charge him, not only with his own corruptions, but with a systematic, premeditated corruption of the whole service, from the time when he was appointed, in the beginning of the year 1772, down to the year 1785, when he left it. He never attempted to detect any one single abuse whatever; he never endeavored once to put a stop to any corruption in any man, black or white, in any way whatever. . . .

My Lords, he desires an arbitrary power over the Company's servants to be given to him. God forbid arbitrary power should be given into the hands of any man! At the same time, God forbid, if by power be meant the ability to discover, to reach, to check, and to punish subordinate corruption, that he should not be enabled so to do, and to get at, to prosecute, and punish delinquency by law! But honesty only, and not arbitrary power, is necessary for that purpose. We well know, indeed, that a government requiring arbitrary power has been the situation in which this man has attempted to place us. . . .

We know that crimes of great magnitude, that acts of great tyranny, can but seldom be exercised, and only by a few persons. They are privileged crimes. They are the dreadful prerogatives of greatness, and of the highest situations only. But when a Governor-General descends into the muck and filth of peculation and corruption, when he receives bribes and extorts money, he does acts that are imitable by everybody. There is not a single man, black or white, from the highest to the lowest, that is possessed in the smallest degree of momentary authority, that cannot imitate the acts of such a Governor-General. Consider, then, what the consequences will be, when it is laid down as a principle of the service, that no man is to be called to account according to the existing laws, and that you must either give, as he says, arbitrary power, or suffer your government to be destroyed. . . .

He assumed arbitrary power, and turned in and out every servant at his pleasure. But did he by that arbitrary power correct any one corruption? Indeed, how could he? He does not say he did. For when a man gives ill examples in himself, when he cannot set on foot an inquiry that does not terminate in his own corruption, of course he cannot institute any inquiry into the corruption of the other servants. . . .

The subordinate servant . . . sees that the Governor-General is actuated by no other views—when he himself, as a farmer, is confidently assured of the corruptions of his superior—when he knows it to be laid down as a principle by the Governor-General, that no corruption is to be inquired into, and that, if it be not expressly laid down, yet that his conduct is such as to make it the same as if he had actually so laid it down—then, I say, every part of the service is instantly and totally corrupted. . . .

VII

THE FRENCH REVOLUTION

A Letter to M. Depont
[1789]

Early in 1773, in order to place his son in a school at Auxerre, Burke visited France. While in Paris he was well received in the *salon* of Madame du Deffand and in the circle of the Duchess of Luxembourg. At the rival *salon* of Mademoiselle Lespinasse, where the *philosophes* and "enlightened" wits gathered, he probably met Diderot, whose Bible of the Enlightenment, the *Encyclopedia,* was at last recently completed. Burke spoke with the Parisian freethinkers in religion and innovators in politics, whom he was to denounce in 1790 as "the sophisters, economists and calculators" of the new revolutionary order. After his return to England, on March 17, 1773, in his first speech in Parliament, he expressed his habitual deep distrust and fear of speculative rationalist philosophers, as men who would "degrade us into brutes." He noted that "the most horrid and cruel blow that can be offered to civil society is through atheism," and that "under the systematic attacks of these people, I see some of the props of good government already begin to fail; I see propagated principles which will not leave to religion even a toleration." Although the affairs of America, Ireland, and India were to absorb most of Burke's energy during the next fifteen years, his visit to France had convinced him that strong speculative intellectual forces in France were preparing for a great social convulsion.

Even four years before his visit to France, in his *Observations on . . . "The Present State of the Nation"* (1769), Burke had noted the serious economic problems of the French people: "Under such extreme straitness and distraction labors the whole body of their finances, so far does their charge outrun their supply in every particular, that no man, I believe, who has considered their affairs with any degree of attention or information but must hourly look for some extraordinary convulsion in that whole system: the effect of which on France, and even on all Europe, it is difficult to conjecture." Undoubtedly, the immediate occasion for Louis XVI's convocation of the States-General at Versailles in May 1789 was the chronic economic crises of France. But Burke was convinced that a silent revolution in philosophical principles, contrary to the principles on which European civilization had always stood, had preceded the political upheaval. There were ominous signs that the "extraordinary convulsion" he had long feared was about to overwhelm France, and even all Europe.

Although Burke was deeply apprehensive about the start of the French Revolution, it should be noted that his immediate public response to it was not hostile. When the Revolution began, he was prepared to allow events to determine the position he was to assume toward it. Burke was certainly aware that when Louis recognized a unicameral National Assembly, on June 27, 1789, in which the members voted not by corporate order but by head, that France was committed to a radically new political constitution. On July 14, angry at the dismissal of Necker, the Paris populace stormed the Bastille. This event was the prelude of much later mob violence throughout France. In August 1789, the National Assembly abolished all feudal privileges and issued a "Declaration of the Rights of Man and of the Citizen," the preamble to a new constitution. On October 5–6, a mob from Paris, under the leadership of the most radical demagogues, seized the royal family and brought them prisoners to Paris. To Burke, who always favored constitutional and peaceful methods of reforming serious inequities in civil society, such as existed in France, these swiftly moving events indicated that the constructive reformers were losing control of the events they had initiated. Nevertheless, as the following letter to his French friend, M. Depont, clearly reveals, up to October 1789 he still hoped that the French would establish a new social order based upon constitutional law and Natural Law, with justice and civil liberty for all its citizens.

. . . You may easily believe that I have had my eyes turned, with great curiosity, to the astonishing scene now displayed in France. It has certainly given rise in my mind to many reflections, and to some emotions. These are natural and unavoidable; but it would ill become me to be too ready in forming a positive opinion upon matters transacted in a country with the correct political map of which I must be very imperfectly acquainted. . . .

You hope, Sir, that I think the French deserving of liberty. I certainly do. I certainly think that all men who desire it deserve it. It is not the reward of our merit, or the acquisition of our industry. It is our inheritance. It is the birthright of our species. We cannot forfeit our right to it but by what forfeits our title to the privileges of our kind. I mean the abuse, or oblivion, of our rational faculties, and a ferocious indocility which makes us prompt to wrong and violence, destroys our social nature, and transforms us into something little better than the description of wild beasts. To men so degraded, a state of strong constraint is a sort of necessary substitute for freedom; since, bad as it is, it may deliver them in some measure from the worst of all slavery—that is, the despotism of their own blind and brutal passions.

You have kindly said that you began to love freedom from your intercourse with me. Permit me then to continue our conversation, and to tell you what the freedom is that I love, and that to which I think all men entitled. This is the more necessary because, of all the loose terms in the world, liberty is the most indefinite. It is not solitary, unconnected, individual, selfish liberty, as if every man was to regulate the whole of his conduct by his own will. The liberty I mean is *social* freedom. It is that state of things in which liberty is secured by the equality of restraint. A constitution of things in which the liberty of no one man, and no body of men, and no number of men, can find means to trespass on the liberty of any person, or any description of persons, in the society. This kind of liberty is, indeed, but another name for justice; ascertained by wise laws, and secured by well-constructed institutions. I am sure that liberty, so incorporated, and in a manner identified with justice, must be infinitely dear to everyone who is capable of conceiving what it is. But whenever a separation is made between liberty and justice, neither is, in my opinion, safe. I do not believe that men ever did submit, certain I am that they never ought to have submitted, to the arbitrary pleasure of one man; but, under circumstances in which the arbitrary pleasure of many persons in the community pressed with an intolerable hardship upon the just and equal rights of their fellows, such a choice might be made, as among evils. The moment *will* is set above reason and justice, in any community, a great question may arise in sober minds in what part or portion of the community that dangerous dominion of *will* may be the least mischievously placed.

If I think all men who cultivate justice entitled to liberty, and, when joined in states, entitled to a constitution framed to perpetuate and secure it, you may be assured, sir, that I think your countrymen eminently worthy of a blessing which is peculiarly adapted to noble, generous, and humane natures. Such I found the French when, more than fifteen years ago, I had the happiness, though but for too short a time, of visiting your country; and I trust their character is not altered since that period.

I have nothing to check my wishes towards the establishment of a solid and rational scheme of liberty in France. On the subject of the relative power of nations I may have my prejudices; but I envy internal freedom, security, and good order to none. When, therefore, I shall learn that, in France, the citizen, by whatever description he is qualified, is in a perfect state of legal security with regard to his life, to his property, to the uncontrolled disposal of his person, to the free use of his industry and his faculties: when I hear that he is protected in the beneficial enjoyment of the estates to which, by the course of settled law, he was born, or is provided with a fair compensation for them; that he is maintained in the full fruition of the advantages belonging to the state and condition of life in which he had lawfully engaged himself, or is supplied with a substantial, equitable, equivalent: when I am assured that a simple citizen may decently express his sentiments upon public affairs without hazard to his life or safety, even though against a predominant and fashionable opinion: when I know all this of France, I shall be as well pleased as everyone must be who has not forgot the general communion of mankind, nor lost his natural sympathy, in local and accidental connections.

If a constitution is settled in France upon those principles, and calculated for those ends, I believe there is no man in this country whose heart and voice would not go along with you. I am sure it will give me, for one, a heartfelt pleasure when I hear that, in France, the great public assemblies, the natural securities for individual freedom, are perfectly free themselves; when there can be no suspicion that they are under the coercion of a military power of any description; when it may be truly said that no armed force can be seen which is not called into existence by their creative voice, and which must not instantly disappear at their dissolving word; when such assemblies, after being freely chosen, shall proceed with the weight of magistracy, and not with the arts of candidates; when they do not find themselves under the necessity of feeding one part of the community at the grievous charge of other parts as necessitous as those who are so fed; when they are not obliged (in order to flatter those who have their lives in their disposal) to tolerate acts of doubtful influence on commerce and on agriculture; and for the sake of a precarious relief, under temporary scarcity, to sow (if I may be allowed the expression) the seeds of lasting want; when they are not compelled daily to stimulate an irregular and juvenile imagination for supplies which they are not in a condition firmly to demand; when they are not obliged to diet the state from hand to mouth, upon the casual alms of choice, fancy, vanity, or caprice, on which plan the value of the object to the public which receives often bears no sort of proportion to the loss of the individual who gives; when they are not necessitated to call for contributions to be estimated on the conscience of the contributor, by which the most pernicious sorts of exemptions and immunities may be established—by which virtue is taxed and vice privileged, and honor and public spirit are obliged to bear the burdens of craft, selfishness, and avarice; when they shall not be driven to be the instruments of the violence of others from a sense of their own weakness, and from a want of authority to assess equal and proportioned charges upon all, they are not compelled to lay a strong hand upon the possessions of a part; when, under the exigencies of the state (aggravated, if not caused, by the imbecility of their own government, and of all government), they are not obliged to resort to *confiscation* to supply the defect of *taxation,* and thereby to hold out a pernicious example, to teach the different descriptions of the community to prey upon one another; when they abstain religiously from all general and extra-judicial declarations concerning the property of the subject; when they look with horror upon all arbitrary decisions in their legislative capacity, striking at prescriptive right, long undisturbed possession, opposing an uninterrupted stream of regular judicial determinations, by which sort of decisions they are conscious no man's possession could be safe, and individual property, to the very idea, would be extinguished; when I see your great sovereign bodies, your now supreme power, in this condition of deliberative freedom, and guided by these or similar principles in acting and forbearing, I shall be happy to behold in assemblies whose name is venerable to my understanding and dear to my heart an authority, a dignity, a moderation, which, in all countries and governments, ought ever to accompany the collected reason and representative majesty of the commonwealth.

I shall rejoice no less in seeing a judicial power established in France correspondent to such a legislature as I have presumed to hint at, and worthy to second it in its endeavors to secure the freedom and property of the subject. When your courts of justice shall obtain an ascertained condition before they are made to decide on the condition of other men; when they shall not be called upon to take cognizance of public offenses whilst they themselves are considered only to exist as a tolerated abuse; when, under doubts of the legality of their rules of decision, their forms and modes of proceeding, and even of the validity of that system of authority to which they owe their existence; when, amidst circumstances of suspense, fear, and humiliation, they shall not be put to judge on the lives, liberties, properties, or estimation of their fellow-citizens; when they are not called upon to put any man to his trial upon undefined crimes of state, not ascertained by any previous rule, statute, or course of precedent; when victims shall not be snatched from the fury of the people to be brought before a tribunal, itself subject to the effects of the same fury, and where the acquittal of the parties accused might only place the judge in the situation of the criminal; when I see tribunals placed in this state of independence of everything but law, and with a clear law for their direction, as a true lover of equal justice (under the shadow of which alone true liberty can live) I shall rejoice in seeing such a happy order established in France, as much as I do in my consciousness that an order of the same kind, or one not very remote from it, has long been settled, and I hope on a firm foundation, in England. I am not so narrow-minded as to be unable to conceive that the same object may be attained in many ways, and perhaps in ways very different from those which we have followed in this country. If this real *practical* liberty, with a government powerful to protect, impotent to evade it, be established, or is in a fair train of being established in the democracy, or rather collection of democracies, which seem to be chosen for the future frame of society in France, it is not my having long enjoyed a sober share of freedom, under a qualified monarchy, that shall render me incapable of admiring and praising your system of republics. I should rejoice, even though England should hereafter be reckoned only as one among the happy nations, and should no longer retain her proud distinction, her monopoly of fame for a practical constitution, in which the grand secret had been found of reconciling a government of real energy for all foreign and all domestic purposes with the most perfect security to the liberty and safety of individuals. The government, whatever its name or form may be, that shall be found substantially and practically to unite these advantages will most merit the applause of all discerning men.

But if (for in my present want of information I must only speak hypothetically) neither your great assemblies, nor your judicatures, nor your municipalities, act, and forbear to act, in the particulars, upon the principles, and in the spirit that I have stated, I must delay my congratulations on your acquisition of liberty. You may have made a revolution, but not a reformation. You may have subverted monarchy, but not recovered freedom. . . .

*Reflections
on the
Revolution in France,
and on
the Proceedings in Certain Societies in
London Relative to That Event:
in a Letter
Intended to Have Been Sent to a Gentleman
in Paris
1790*

Under pressure from the Paris mobs, late in 1789 the National Assembly was forced to move from Versailles to Paris. More than three hundred of the more moderate deputies who had been present at Versailles failed to appear in Paris. Thus, leadership in the National Assembly passed into the hands of those deputies who were most eager for a complete and swift reform of France. A group of these deputies soon organized a private club called the *Société des Amis de la Constitution*. They met frequently at an old church previously occupied by Dominican monks in the Rue St. Honoré, nicknamed the Jacobins, and the society became known as the Jacobin Club. Individuals with no legal standing in the National Assembly were admitted into the Jacobins, and became prominent in its affairs. In order to facilitate the reforms and programs initiated in the Paris club, throughout the provinces of France an estimated sixty-eight hundred local Jacobin clubs were established, with perhaps a million members, who were kept informed through an extensive system of correspondence and newspapers of the determinations and policies made in Paris. Before long the superior organization and energy of the Jacobins dominated the National Assembly, which proceeded by edicts to demolish the entire traditional legal, political, religious, and social structure of France. It was at this point that Burke became convinced that the French Revolution was a destructive and evil force, aimed not at reforming economic and political inequities, but at founding French and European society anew, upon a basis of *a priori,* speculative Cartesian rationalism.

So long as the French Revolution confined itself to the internal affairs of France, Burke's convictions of its folly remained private. But his distrust was intensified into alarm when Englishmen began to express their strong approval of events across the Channel, and held up the National Assembly as a model to be followed by Britain. On February 9, 1790, during the debates in Parliament on budget estimates for the army, Burke reviewed all the violence that had characterized the French Revolution since June 1789. He pointed out particularly the measures which had subverted prescriptive property and established religious institutions. To follow the French example in Britain, Burke warned his countrymen, would end in the destruction of civil liberty under English constitutional law.

Burke's first concern for England grew out of an event that occurred on November 5, 1789. November 4, 1788 was the centennial date of the landing in England of the Prince of Orange, which act marked the triumph of the bloodless Revolution of 1688, which forced the abdication of James II. An association called the Revolution Society, composed of Protestant dissenters and Anglican Whigs, and including even some peers and members of Parliament, met annually in London on November 5 to celebrate the memory of the Revolution of 1688. The speaker in 1789 was the famous dissenting minister, Dr. Richard Price, whose sermon, "A Discourse on the Love of Our Country," praised the French Revolution as an extension of the principles of the English Revolution of 1688. Price's sermon was the red rag that drew Burke into the arena to do battle with the French Revolution. Burke had throughout his life admired the Revolution of 1688 as the most perfect example of a sound and constitutional method of making important changes in civil society. From his constitutional point of view, even the American Revolution differed strongly from the French Revolution, because the rebellion originated from the desire of the Colonies to preserve unimpaired their traditional constitutional rights as transplanted Englishmen, not from a desire to originate a new order of society. Nothing could be more false and mischievous than Dr. Price's confusion of the bloodless and constitutional events of 1688 with the violent and arbitrary innovations of the French Revolution. Burke's reply to Price's sermon was the origin of his most famous and influential work, which grew and developed for a year, until it was published in November 1790—the *Reflections on the Revolution in France, and on the proceedings in certain societies in London relative to that event.*

It may not be unnecessary to inform the reader that the following Reflections had their origin in a correspondence between the author and a very young gentleman at Paris, who did him the honor of desiring his opinion upon the important transactions which then, and ever since have, so much occupied the attention of all men. An answer was written some time in the month of October, 1789; but it was kept back upon prudential considerations. That letter is alluded to in the beginning of the following sheets. It has been since forwarded to the person to whom it was addressed. The reasons for the delay in sending it were assigned in a short letter to the same gentleman. This produced on his part a new and pressing application for the author's sentiments.

The author began a second and more full discussion on the subject. This he had some thoughts of publishing early in the last spring; but the matter gaining upon him, he found that what he had undertaken not only far exceeded the measure of a letter, but that its importance required rather a more detailed consideration than at that time he had any leisure to bestow upon it. However, having thrown down his first thoughts in the form of a letter, and, indeed, when he sat down to write, having intended it for a private letter, he found it difficult to change the form of address, when his sentiments had grown into a greater extent and had received another direction. A different plan, he is sensible, might be more favorable to a commodious division and distribution of his matter.

REFLECTIONS ON THE REVOLUTION IN FRANCE

. . . You imagined, when you wrote last, that I might possibly be reckoned among the approvers of certain proceedings in France, from the solemn public seal of sanction they have received from two clubs of gentlemen in London, called the Constitutional Society, and the Revolution Society.

I certainly have the honor to belong to more clubs than one in which the Constitution of this kingdom and the principles of the glorious Revolution are held in high reverence; and I reckon myself among the most forward in my zeal for maintaining that Constitution and those principles in their utmost purity and vigor. It is because I do so that I think it necessary for me that there should be no mistake. Those who cultivate the memory of our Revolution, and those who are attached to the Constitution of this kingdom, will take good care how they are involved with persons who, under the pretext of zeal towards the Revolution and Constitution, too frequently wander from their true principles, and are ready on every occasion to depart from the firm, but cautious and deliberate, spirit which produced the one and which presides in the other. . . .

I flatter myself that I love a manly, moral, regulated liberty as well as any gentleman . . . But I cannot stand forward, and give praise or blame to anything which relates to human actions and human concerns on a simple view of the object, as it stands stripped of every relation, in all the nakedness and solitude of metaphysical abstraction. Circumstances (which with some gentlemen pass for nothing) give in reality to every political principle its distinguishing color and discriminating effect. The circumstances are what render every civil and political scheme beneficial or noxious to mankind. Abstractedly speaking, government, as well as liberty, is good; yet could I, in common sense, ten years ago, have felicitated France on her enjoyment of a government, (for she then had a government,) without inquiry what the nature of that government was, or how it was administered? Can I now congratulate the same nation upon its freedom? Is it because liberty in the abstract may be classed amongst the blessings of mankind, that I am seriously to felicitate a madman who has escaped from the protecting restraint and wholesome darkness of his cell on his restoration to the enjoyment of light and liberty? Am I to congratulate a highwayman and murderer who has broke prison upon the recovery of his natural rights? . . .

When I see the spirit of liberty in action, I see a strong principle at work; and this, for a while, is all I can possibly know of it. The wild gas, the fixed air, is plainly broke loose: but we ought to suspend our judgment until the first effervescence is a little subsided, till the liquor is cleared, and until we see something deeper than the agitation of a troubled and frothy surface. I must be tolerably sure, before I venture publicly to congratulate men upon a blessing, that they have really received one. Flattery corrupts both the receiver and the giver; and adulation is not of more service to the people than to kings. I should therefore suspend my congratulations on the new liberty of France, until I was informed how it had been combined with government, with public force, with the discipline and obedience of armies, with the collection of an effective and well-distributed revenue, with morality and religion, with solidity and property, with peace and order, with civil and social manners. All these (in their way) are good things, too; and without them, liberty is not a benefit whilst it lasts, and is not likely to continue long. The effect of liberty to individuals is, that they may do what they please: we ought to see what it will please them to do, before we risk congratulations, which may be soon turned into complaints. Prudence would dictate this in the case of separate, insulated, private men. But liberty, when men act in bodies, is *power*. Considerate people, before they declare themselves, will observe the use which is made of *power*—and particularly of so trying a thing as *new* power in *new* persons, of whose principles, tempers, and dispositions they have little or no experience, and in situations where those who appear the most stirring in the scene may possibly not be the real movers. . . .

All circumstances taken together, the French Revolution is the most astonishing that has hitherto happened in the world. The most wonderful things are brought about in many instances by means the most absurd and ridiculous, in the most ridiculous modes, and apparently by the most contemptible instruments. Everything seems out of nature in this strange chaos of levity and ferocity, and of all sorts of crimes jumbled together with all sorts of follies. In viewing this monstrous tragi-comic scene, the most opposite passions necessarily succeed and sometimes mix with each other in the mind: alternate contempt and indignation, alternate laughter and tears, alternate scorn and horror.

It cannot, however, be denied that to some this strange scene appeared in quite another point of view. Into them it inspired no other sentiments than those of exultation and rapture. They saw nothing in what has been done in France but a firm and temperate exertion of freedom—so consistent, on the whole, with morals and with piety as to make it deserving not only of the secular applause of dashing Machiavelian politicians, but to render it a fit theme for all the devout effusions of sacred eloquence.

On the forenoon of the fourth of November last, Doctor Richard Price, a Non-Conforming minister of eminence, preached at the Dissenting meeting-house of the Old Jewry, to his club or society, a very extraordinary miscellaneous sermon, in which there are some good moral and religious sentiments, and not ill expressed, mixed up with a sort of porridge of various political opinions and reflections: but the Revolution in France is the grand ingredient in the caldron. . . .

I looked on that sermon as the public declaration of a man much connected with literary caballers and intriguing philosophers, with political theologians and theological politicians, both at home and abroad. I know they set him up as a sort of oracle; because, with the best intentions in the world, he naturally *philippizes,* and chants his prophetic song in exact unison with their designs.

That sermon is in a strain which I believe has not been heard in this kingdom, in any of the pulpits which are tolerated or encouraged in it, since the year 1648—when a predecessor of Dr. Price, the Reverend Hugh Peters, made the vault of the king's own chapel at St. James's ring with the honor and privilege of the saints, who, with the "high praises of God in their mouths, and a *two*-edged sword in their hands, were to execute judgment on the heathen, and punishments upon the *people;* to bind their *kings* with chains, and their *nobles* with fetters of iron." Few harangues from the pulpit, except in the days of your League in France, or in the days of our Solemn League and Covenant in England, have ever breathed less of the spirit of moderation than this lecture in the Old Jewry. . . .

This pulpit style, revived after so long a discontinuance, had to me the air of novelty, and of a novelty not wholly without danger. . . . If the noble *Seekers* should find nothing to satisfy their pious fancies in the old staple of the national Church, or in all the rich variety to be found in the well-assorted warehouses of the Dissenting congregations, Dr. Price advises them to improve upon Non-Conformity, and to set up, each of them, a separate meeting-house upon his own particular principles. It is somewhat remarkable that this reverend divine should be so earnest for setting up new churches, and so perfectly indifferent concerning the doctrine which may be taught in them. His zeal is of a curious character. It is not for the propagation of his own opinions, but of any opinions. It is not for the diffusion of truth, but for the spreading of contradiction. Let the noble teachers but dissent, it is no matter from whom or from what. This great point once secured, it is taken for granted their religion will be rational and manly. . . .

His doctrines affect our Constitution in its vital parts. He tells the Revolution Society, in this political sermon, that his Majesty "is almost the *only* lawful king in the world, because the *only* one who owes his crown to *the choice of his people.*" As to the kings of *the world,* all of whom (except one) this arch-pontiff of the *rights of men,* with all the plenitude and with more than the boldness of the Papal deposing power in its meridian fervor of the twelfth century, puts into one sweeping clause of ban and anathema, and proclaims usurpers by circles of longitude and latitude over the whole globe, it behooves them to consider how they admit into their territories these apostolic missionaries, who are to tell their subjects they are not lawful kings. That is their concern. It is ours, as a domestic interest of some moment, seriously to consider the solidity of the *only* principle upon which these gentlemen acknowledge a king of Great Britain to be entitled to their allegiance.

This doctrine, as applied to the prince now on the British throne, either is nonsense, and therefore neither true nor false, or it affirms a most unfounded, dangerous, illegal, and unconstitutional position. According to this spiritual doctor of politics, if his Majesty does not owe his crown to the choice of his people, he is no *lawful* king. Now nothing can be more untrue than that the crown of this kingdom is so held by his Majesty. Therefore, if you follow their rule, the king of Great Britain, who most certainly does not owe his high office to any form of popular election, is in no respect better than the rest of the gang of usurpers, who reign, or rather rob, all over the face of this our miserable world, without any sort of right or title to the allegiance of their people. The policy of this general doctrine, so qualified, is evident enough. The propagators of this political gospel are in hopes their abstract principle (their principle that a popular choice is necessary to the legal existence of the sovereign magistracy) would be overlooked, whilst the king of Great Britain was not affected by it. In the mean time the ears of their congregations would be gradually habituated to it, as if it were a first principle admitted without dispute. For the present it would only operate as a theory, pickled in the preserving juices of pulpit eloquence, and laid by for future use. . . . By this policy, whilst our government is soothed with a reservation in its favor, to which it has no claim, the security which it has in common with all governments, so far as opinion is security, is taken away. . . .

At some time or other, to be sure, all the beginners of dynasties were chosen by those who called them to govern. There is ground enough for the opinion that all the kingdoms of Europe were at a remote period elective, with more or fewer limitations in the objects of choice. But whatever kings might have been here or elsewhere a thousand years ago, or in whatever manner the ruling dynasties of England or France may have begun, the king of Great Britain is at this day king by a fixed rule of succession, according to the laws of his country; and whilst the legal conditions of the compact of sovereignty are performed by him, (as they are performed,) he holds his crown in contempt of the choice of the Revolution Society, who have not a single vote for a king amongst them, either individually or collectively. . . .

These gentlemen of the Old Jewry, in all their reasonings on the Revolution of 1688, have a revolution which happened in England about forty years before, and the late French Revolution, so much before their eyes and in their hearts, that they are constantly confounding all the three together. It is necessary that we should separate what they confound. We must recall their erring fancies to the *acts* of the Revolution which we revere, for the discovery of its true *principles*. If the *principles* of the Revolution of 1688 are anywhere to be found, it is in the statute called the *Declaration of Right*. . . .

This Declaration of Right . . . is the corner-stone of our Constitution, as reinforced, explained, improved, and in its fundamental principles forever settled. It is called "An act for declaring the rights and liberties of the subject, and for *settling* the *succession* of the crown." You will observe that these rights and this succession are declared in one body, and bound indissolubly together.

A few years after this period, a second opportunity offered for asserting a right of election to the crown. On the prospect of a total failure of issue from King William, and from the princess, afterwards Queen Anne, the consideration of the settlement of the crown, and of a further security for the liberties of the people, again came before the legislature. Did they this second time make any provision for legalizing the crown on the spurious Revolution principles of the Old Jewry? No. They followed the principles which prevailed in the Declaration of Right . . .

Unquestionably there was at the Revolution, in the person of King William, a small and a temporary deviation from the strict order of a regular hereditary succession; but it is against all genuine principles of jurisprudence to draw a principle from a law made in a special case and regarding an individual person. . . . If ever there was a time favorable for establishing the principle that a king of popular choice was the only legal king, without all doubt it was at the Revolution. Its not being done at that time is a proof that the nation was of opinion it ought not to be done at any time. . . .

In the very act in which, for a time, and in a single case, Parliament departed from the strict order of inheritance, in favor of a prince who, though not next, was, however, very near in the line of succession, it is curious to observe how Lord Somers, who drew the bill called the Declaration of Right, has comported himself on that delicate occasion. It is curious to observe with what address this temporary solution of continuity is kept from the eye; whilst all that could be found in this act of necessity to countenance the idea of an hereditary succession is brought forward, and fostered, and made the most of, by this great man, and by the legislature who followed him. Quitting the dry, imperative style of an act of Parliament, he makes the Lords and Commons fall to a pious legislative ejaculation, and declare that they consider it "as a marvellous providence, and merciful goodness of God to this nation, to preserve their said Majesties' *royal* persons most happily to reign over us *on the throne of their ancestors*, for which, from the bottom of their hearts, they return their humblest thanks and praises." . . .

The two Houses, in the act of King William, did not thank God that they had found a fair opportunity to assert a right to choose their own governors, much less to make an election the *only lawful* title to the crown. Their having been in a condition to avoid the very appearance of it, as much as possible, was by them considered as a providential escape. They threw a politic, well-wrought veil over every circumstance tending to weaken the rights which in the meliorated order of succession they meant to perpetuate, or which might furnish a precedent for any future departure from what they had then settled forever. . . .

They knew that a doubtful title of succession would but too much resemble an election, and that an election would be utterly destructive of the "unity, peace, and tranquillity of this nation," which they thought to be considerations of some moment. . . .

So far is it from being true that we acquired a right by the Revolution to elect our kings, that, if we had possessed it before, the English nation did at that time most solemnly renounce and abdicate it, for themselves, and for all their posterity forever. . . .

It is true, that, aided with the powers derived from force and opportunity, the nation was at that time, in some sense, free to take what course it pleased for filling the throne—but only free to do so upon the same grounds on which they might have wholly abolished their monarchy, and every other part of their Constitution. However, they did not think such bold changes within their commission. It is, indeed, difficult, perhaps impossible, to give limits to the mere *abstract* competence of the supreme power, such as was exercised by Parliament at that time; but the limits of a *moral* competence, subjecting, even in powers more indisputably sovereign, occasional will to permanent reason, and to the steady maxims of faith, justice, and fixed fundamental policy, are perfectly intelligible, and perfectly binding upon those who exercise any authority, under any name, or under any title, in the state. The House of Lords, for instance, is not morally competent to dissolve the House of Commons—no, nor even to dissolve itself, nor to abdicate, if it would, its portion in the legislature of the kingdom. Though a king may abdicate for his own person, he cannot abdicate for the monarchy. By as strong, or by a stronger reason, the House of Commons cannot renounce its share of authority. The engagement and pact of society, which generally goes by the name of the Constitution, forbids such invasion and such surrender. The constituent parts of a state are obliged to hold their public faith with each other, and with all those who derive any serious interest under their engagements, as much as the whole state is bound to keep its faith with separate communities: otherwise, competence and power would soon be confounded, and no law be left but the will of a prevailing force. On this principle, the succession of the crown has always been what it now is, an hereditary succession by law: in the old line it was a succession by the Common Law; in the new by the statute law, operating on the principles of the Common Law, not changing the substance, but regulating the mode and describing the persons. Both these descriptions of law are of the same force, and are derived from an equal authority, emanating from the common agreement and original compact of the state, . . and as such are equally binding on king, and people too, as long as the terms are observed, and they continue the same body politic.

It is far from impossible to reconcile, if we do not suffer ourselves to be entangled in the mazes of metaphysic sophistry, the use both of a fixed rule and an occasional deviation— the sacredness of an hereditary principle of succession in our government with a power of change in its application in cases of extreme emergency. . . .

A state without the means of some change is without the means of its conservation. Without such means it might even risk the loss of that part of the Constitution which it wished the most religiously to preserve. The two principles of conservation and correction operated strongly at the two critical periods of the Restoration and Revolution, when England found itself without a king. At both those periods the nation had lost the bond of union in their ancient edifice: they did not, however, dissolve the whole fabric. On the contrary, in both cases they regenerated the deficient part of the old Constitution through the parts which were not impaired. . . .

On this principle, the law of inheritance had admitted some amendment in the old time, and long before the era of the Revolution. . . . This is the spirit of our Constitution, not only in its settled course, but in all its revolutions. Whoever came in, or however he came in, whether he obtained the crown by law or by force, the hereditary succession was either continued or adopted. . . .

Do these new doctors of the rights of men presume to assert that King James the Second, who came to the crown as next of blood, according to the rules of a then unqualified succession, was not to all intents and purposes a lawful king of England, before he had done any of those acts which were justly construed into an abdication of his crown? If he was not, much trouble in Parliament might have been saved at the period these gentlemen commemorate. But King James was a bad king with a good title, and not an usurper. . . .

No experience has taught us that in any other course or method than that of an *hereditary crown* our liberties can be regularly perpetuated and preserved sacred as our *hereditary right*. An irregular, convulsive movement may be necessary to throw off an irregular, convulsive disease. But the course of succession is the healthy habit of the British Constitution. . . .

A few years ago I should be ashamed to overload a matter so capable of supporting itself by the then unnecessary support of any argument; but this seditious, unconstitutional doctrine is now publicly taught, avowed, and printed. The dislike I feel to revolutions, the signals for which have so often been given from pulpits—the spirit of change that is gone abroad—the total contempt which prevails with you, and may come to prevail with us, of all ancient institutions, when set in opposition to a present sense of convenience, or to the bent of a present inclination—all these considerations make it not unadvisable, in my opinion, to call back our attention to the true principles of our own domestic laws, that you, my French friend, should begin to know, and that we should continue to cherish them. We ought not, on either side of the water, to suffer ourselves to be imposed upon by the counterfeit wares which some persons, by a double fraud, export to you in illicit bottoms, as raw commodities of British growth, though wholly alien to our soil, in order afterwards to smuggle them back again into this country, manufactured after the newest Paris fashion of an improved liberty.

The people of England will not ape the fashions they have never tried, nor go back to those which they have found mischievous on trial. They look upon the legal hereditary succession of their crown as among their rights, not as among their wrongs—as a benefit, not as a grievance—as a security for their liberty, not as a badge of servitude. They look on the frame of their commonwealth, *such as it stands,* to be of inestimable value; and they conceive the undisturbed succession of the crown to be a pledge of the stability and perpetuity of all the other members of our Constitution.

I shall beg leave, before I go any further, to take notice of some paltry artifices which the abettors of election as the only lawful title to the crown are ready to employ, in order to render the support of the just principles of our Constitution a task somewhat invidious. These sophisters substitute a fictitious cause, and feigned personages, in whose favor they suppose you engaged, whenever you defend the inheritable nature of the crown. It is common with them to dispute as if they were in a conflict with some of those exploded fanatics of slavery who formerly maintained, what I believe no creature now maintains, "that the crown is held by divine, hereditary, and indefeasible right." These old fanatics of single arbitrary power dogmatized as if hereditary royalty was the only lawful government in the world—just as our new fanatics

of popular arbitrary power maintain that a popular election
is the sole lawful source of authority. The old prerogative
enthusiasts, it is true, did speculate foolishly, and perhaps impiously too, as if monarchy had more of a divine sanction
than any other mode of government—and as if a right to
govern by inheritance were in strictness *indefeasible* in every
person who should be found in the succession to a throne,
and under every circumstance, which no civil or political right
can be. But an absurd opinion concerning the king's hereditary right to the crown does not prejudice one that is rational,
and bottomed upon solid principles of law and policy. If all
the absurd theories of lawyers and divines were to vitiate the
objects in which they are conversant, we should have no law
and no religion left in the world. But an absurd theory on
one side of a question forms no justification for alleging a
false fact or promulgating mischievous maxims on the other.

The second claim of the Revolution Society is "a right of
cashiering their governors for *misconduct*." . . .

No government could stand a moment, if it could be blown
down with anything so loose and indefinite as an opinion of
"*misconduct*." They who led at the Revolution grounded
their virtual abdication of King James upon no such light and
uncertain principle. They charged him with nothing less than
a design, confirmed by a multitude of illegal overt acts, to
subvert the Protestant Church and State, and their *fundamental*, unquestionable laws and liberties: they charged him with
having broken the *original contract* between king and people.
This was more than *misconduct*. A grave and overruling necessity obliged them to take the step they took, and took with
infinite reluctance, as under that most rigorous of all laws.
Their trust for the future preservation of the Constitution was
not in future revolutions. The grand policy of all their regulations was to render it almost impracticable for any future
sovereign to compel the states of the kingdom to have again
recourse to those violent remedies. . . .

Dr. Price, in this sermon, condemns, very properly, the
practice of gross adulatory addresses to kings. Instead of this
fulsome style, he proposes that his Majesty should be told, on
occasions of congratulation, that "he is to consider himself
as more properly the servant than the sovereign of his people." . . .

Kings, in one sense, are undoubtedly the servants of the
people, because their power has no other rational end than

that of the general advantage; but it is not true that they are, in the ordinary sense, (by our Constitution, at least,) anything like servants—the essence of whose situation is to obey the commands of some other, and to be removable at pleasure. But the king of Great Britain obeys no other person; all other persons are individually, and collectively too, under him, and owe to him a legal obedience. The law, which knows neither to flatter nor to insult, calls this high magistrate, not our servant, as this humble divine calls him, but *"our sovereign lord the king"*; and we, on our parts, have learned to speak only the primitive language of the law, and not the confused jargon of their Babylonian pulpits.

As he is not to obey us, but we are to obey the law in him, our Constitution has made no sort of provision towards rendering him, as a servant, in any degree responsible. Our Constitution knows nothing of . . . any court legally appointed, nor of any process legally settled, for submitting the king to the responsibility belonging to all servants. In this he is not distinguished from the commons and the lords, who, in their several public capacities, can never be called to an account for their conduct; although the Revolution Society chooses to assert, in direct opposition to one of the wisest and most beautiful parts of our Constitution, that "a king is no more than the first servant of the public, created by it, *and responsible to it."* . . .

The ceremony of cashiering kings, of which these gentlemen talk so much at their ease, can rarely, if ever, be performed without force. It then becomes a case of war, and not of constitution. . . . The question of dethroning, or, if these gentlemen like the phrase better, "cashiering kings," will always be, as it has always been, an extraordinary question of state, and wholly out of the law: a question (like all other questions of state) of dispositions, and of means, and of probable consequences, rather than of positive rights. As it was not made for common abuses, so it is not to be agitated by common minds. The speculative line of demarcation, where obedience ought to end and resistance must begin, is faint, obscure, and not easily definable. It is not a single act or a single event which determines it. Governments must be abused and deranged indeed, before it can be thought of; and the prospect of the future must be as bad as the experience of the past. When things are in that lamentable condition, the nature of the disease is to indicate the remedy to those whom Nature has qualified to administer in extremities this critical, ambiguous, bitter potion to a distempered state. Times and occasions and provocations will teach their own lessons. The wise will determine from the gravity of the case; the irritable, from sensibility to oppression; the high-minded, from disdain and indignation at abusive power in unworthy hands; the brave and bold, from the love of honorable danger in a generous cause: but, with or without right, a revolution will be the very last resource of the thinking and the good.

The third head of right asserted by the pulpit of the Old Jewry, namely, the "right to form a government for ourselves," has, at least, as little countenance from anything done at the Revolution, either in precedent or principle, as the two first of their claims. .The Revolution was made to preserve our *ancient* indisputable laws and liberties, and that *ancient* constitution of government which is our only security for law and liberty. If you are desirous of knowing the spirit of our Constitution, and the policy which predominated in that great period which has secured it to this hour, pray look for both in our histories, in our records, in our acts of Parliament and journals of Parliament, and not in the sermons of the Old Jewry, and the after-dinner toasts of the Revolution Society. . . . The very idea of the fabrication of a new government is enough to fill us with disgust and horror. We wished at the period of the Revolution, and do now wish, to derive all we possess as *an inheritance from our forefathers.* Upon that body and stock of inheritance we have taken care not to inoculate any scion alien to the nature of the original plant. All the reformations we have hitherto made. have proceeded upon the principle of reference to antiquity . . .

Our oldest reformation is that of Magna Charta. . . .

You will observe, that, from Magna Charta to the Declaration of Right, it has been the uniform policy of our Constitution to claim and assert our liberties as an *entailed inheritance* derived to us from our forefathers, and to be transmitted to our posterity—as an estate specially belonging to the people of this kingdom, without any reference whatever to any other more general or prior right. By this means our Constitution preserves an unity in so great a diversity of its parts. We have an inheritable crown, an inheritable peerage, and a House of Commons and a people inheriting privileges, franchises, and liberties from a long line of ancestors.

This policy appears to me to be the result of profound reflection—or rather the happy effect of following Nature, which is wisdom without reflection, and above it. A spirit of innovation is generally the result of a selfish temper and confined views. People will not look forward to posterity, who never look backward to their ancestors. Besides, the people of England well know that the idea of inheritance furnishes a sure principle of conservation, and a sure principle of transmission, without at all excluding a principle of improvement. It leaves acquisition free; but it secures what it acquires. Whatever advantages are obtained by a state proceeding on these maxims are locked fast as in a sort of family settlement, grasped as in a kind of mortmain forever. By a constitutional policy working after the pattern of Nature, we receive, we hold, we transmit our government and our privileges, in the same manner in which we enjoy and transmit our property and our lives. The institutions of policy, the goods of fortune, the gifts of Providence, are handed down to us, and from us, in the same course and order. Our political system is placed in a just correspondence and symmetry with the order of the world, and with the mode of existence decreed to a permanent body composed of transitory parts—wherein, by the disposition of a stupendous wisdom, moulding together the great mysterious incorporation of the human race, the whole, at one time, is never old or middle-aged or young, but, in a condition of unchangeable constancy, moves on through the varied tenor of perpetual decay, fall, renovation, and progression. Thus, by preserving the method of Nature in the conduct of the state, in what we improve we are never wholly new, in what we retain we are never wholly obsolete. By adhering in this manner and on those principles to our forefathers, we are guided, not by the superstition of antiquarians, but by the spirit of philosophic analogy. In this choice of inheritance we have given to our frame of polity the image of a relation in blood: binding up the Constitution of our country with our dearest domestic ties; adopting our fundamental laws into the bosom of our family affections; keeping inseparable, and cherishing with the warmth of all their combined and mutually reflected charities, our state, our hearths, our sepulchres, and our altars.

Through the same plan of a conformity to Nature in our artificial institutions, and by calling in the aid of her unerring and powerful instincts to fortify the fallible and feeble contrivances of our reason, we have derived several other, and those no small benefits, from considering our liberties in the light of an inheritance. Always acting as if in the presence of canonized forefathers, the spirit of freedom, leading in itself to misrule and excess, is tempered with an awful gravity. This idea of a liberal descent inspires us with a sense of habitual native dignity, which prevents that upstart insolence almost inevitably adhering to and disgracing those who are the first acquirers of any distinction. By this means our liberty becomes a noble freedom. It carries an imposing and majestic aspect. It has a pedigree and illustrating ancestors. It has its bearings and its ensigns armorial. It has its gallery of portraits, its monumental inscriptions, its records, evidences, and titles. We procure reverence to our civil institutions on the principle upon which Nature teaches us to revere individual men: on account of their age, and on account of those from whom they are descended. All your sophisters cannot produce anything better adapted to preserve a rational and manly freedom than the course that we have pursued, who have chosen our nature rather than our speculations, our breasts rather than our inventions, for the great conservatories and magazines of our rights and privileges.

You might, if you pleased, have profited of our example, and have given to your recovered freedom a correspondent dignity. Your privileges, though discontinued, were not lost to memory. Your Constitution, it is true, whilst you were out of possession, suffered waste and dilapidation; but you possessed in some parts the walls, and in all the foundations, of a noble and venerable castle. You might have repaired those walls; you might have built on those old foundations. Your Constitution was suspended before it was perfected; but you had the elements of a Constitution very nearly as good as could be wished. In your old states you possessed that variety of parts corresponding with the various descriptions of which your community was happily composed; you had all that combination and all that opposition of interests, you had that action and counteraction, which, in the natural and in the political world, from the reciprocal struggle of discordant powers draws out the harmony of the universe. These opposed and conflicting interests, which you considered as so great a blemish in your old and in our present Constitution, interpose a salutary check to all precipitate resolutions. They render deliberation a matter, not of choice, but of necessity; they make all change a subject of *compromise*, which naturally begets moderation; they produce *temperaments*, preventing the sore evil of harsh, crude, unqualified reformations, and rendering all the headlong exertions of arbitrary power, in the few or in the many, forever impracticable. Through that diversity of members and interests, general liberty had as many securities as there were separate views in the several orders; whilst by pressing down the whole by the weight of a real monarchy, the separate parts would have been prevented from warping and starting from their allotted places.

You had all these advantages in your ancient states; but you chose to act as if you had never been moulded into civil society, and had everything to begin anew. You began ill, because you began by despising everything that belonged to you. . . . Respecting your forefathers, you would have been taught to respect yourselves. You would not have chosen to consider the French as a people of yesterday, as a nation of low-born, servile wretches until the emancipating year of 1789. . . . Or if, diffident of yourselves, and not clearly discerning the almost obliterated Constitution of your ancestors, you had looked to your neighbors in this land, who had kept alive the ancient principles and models of the old common law of Europe, meliorated and adapted to its present state—by following wise examples you would have given new examples of wisdom to the world. You would have rendered the cause of liberty venerable in the eyes of every worthy mind in every nation. You would have shamed despotism from the earth, by showing that freedom was not only reconcilable, but, as, when well disciplined, it is, auxiliary to law. You would have had an unoppressive, but a productive revenue. You would have had a flourishing commerce to feed it. You would have had a free Constitution, a potent monarchy, a disciplined army, a reformed and venerated clergy—a mitigated, but spirited nobility, to lead your virtue, not to overlay it; you would have had a liberal order of commons, to emulate and to recruit that nobility; you would have had a protected, satisfied, laborious, and obedient people, taught to seek and to recognize the happiness that is to be found by virtue in all conditions . . .

Compute your gains; see what is got by those extravagant and presumptuous speculations which have taught your leaders to despise all their predecessors, and all their contemporaries, and even to despise themselves, until the moment in which they became truly despicable. By following those false lights, France has bought undisguised calamities at a higher price than any nation has purchased the most unequivocal blessings. France has bought poverty by crime. France has not sacrificed her virtue to her interest; but she has abandoned her interest, that she might prostitute her virtue. All other nations have begun the fabric of a new government, or the reformation of an old, by establishing originally, or by enforcing with greater exactness, some rites or other of religion. All other people have laid the foundations of civil freedom in severer manners, and a system of a more austere and masculine morality. France, when she let loose the reins of regal authority, doubled the license of a ferocious dissoluteness in manners, and of an insolent irreligion in opinions and practices—and has extended through all ranks of life, as if she were communicating some privilege, or laying open some secluded benefit, all the unhappy corruptions that usually were the disease of wealth and power. This is one of the new principles of equality in France.

France, by the perfidy of her leaders, has utterly disgraced the tone of lenient council in the cabinets of princes, and disarmed it of its most potent topics. She has sanctified the dark, suspicious maxims of tyrannous distrust, and taught kings to tremble at (what will hereafter be called) the delusive plausibilities of moral politicians. Sovereigns will consider those who advise them to place an unlimited confidence in their people as subverters of their thrones—as traitors who aim at their destruction, by leading their easy good-nature, under specious pretences, to admit combinations of bold and faithless men into a participation of their power. This alone (if there were nothing else) is an irreparable calamity to you and to mankind. Remember that your Parliament of Paris told your king, that, in calling the states together, he had nothing to fear but the prodigal excess of their zeal in providing for the support of the throne. It is right that these men should hide their heads. It is right that they should bear their part in the ruin which their counsel has brought on their sovereign and their country. Such sanguine declarations tend to lull authority asleep—to encourage it rashly to engage in perilous adventures of untried policy—to neglect those provisions, preparations, and precautions which distinguish benevolence from imbecility, and without which no man can answer for the salutary effect of any abstract plan of government or of freedom. For want of these, they have seen the medicine of the state corrupted into its poison. They have seen the French rebel against a mild and lawful monarch, with more fury, outrage, and insult than ever any people has been known to rise against the most illegal usurper or the most sanguinary tyrant. Their resistance was made to concession; their revolt was from protection; their blow was aimed at a hand holding out graces, favors, and immunities.

This was unnatural. The rest is in order. They have found their punishment in their success. Laws overturned; tribunals subverted; industry without vigor; commerce expiring; the revenue unpaid, yet the people impoverished; a church pillaged, and a state not relieved; civil and military anarchy made the constitution of the kingdom; everything human and divine sacrificed to the idol of public credit, and national bankruptcy the consequence; and, to crown all, the paper securities of new, precarious, tottering power, the discredited paper securities of impoverished fraud and beggared rapine, held out as a currency for the support of an empire, in lieu of the two great recognized species that represent the lasting, conventional credit of mankind, which disappeared and hid themselves in the earth from whence they came, when the principle of property, whose creatures and representatives they are, was systematically subverted.

Were all these dreadful things necessary? Were they the inevitable results of the desperate struggle of determined patriots, compelled to wade through blood and tumult to the quiet shore of a tranquil and prosperous liberty? No! nothing like it. The fresh ruins of France, which shock our feelings wherever we can turn our eyes, are not the devastation of civil war: they are the sad, but instructive monuments of rash and ignorant counsel in time of profound peace. They are the display of inconsiderate and presumptuous, because unresisted and irresistible authority. . . .

This unforced choice, this fond election of evil, would appear perfectly unaccountable, if we did not consider the composition of the National Assembly: I do not mean its formal constitution, which, as it now stands, is exceptionable enough, but the materials of which in a great measure it is composed, which is of ten thousand times greater consequence than all the formalities in the world. If we were to know nothing of this assembly but by its title and function, no colors could paint to the imagination anything more venerable. . . . But no name, no power, no function, no artificial institution whatsoever, can make the men, of whom any system of authority is composed, any other than God, and Nature, and education, and their habits of life have made them. Capacities beyond these the people have not to give. . . .

After I had read over the list of the persons and descriptions elected into the *Tiers État,* nothing which they afterwards did could appear astonishing. Among them, indeed, I saw some of known rank, some of shining talents; but of any practical experience in the state not one man was to be found. The best were only men of theory. But whatever the distinguished few may have been, it is the substance and mass of the body which constitutes its character, and must finally determine its direction. . . .

Nothing can secure a steady and moderate conduct in such assemblies, but that the body of them should be respectably composed, in point of condition in life, of permanent property, of education, and of such habits as enlarge and liberalize the understanding.

In the calling of the States-General of France, the first thing that struck me was a great departure from the ancient course. I found the representation for the third estate composed of six hundred persons. They were equal in number to the representatives of both the other orders. If the orders were to act separately, the number would not, beyond the consideration of the expense, be of much moment. But when it became apparent that the three orders were to be melted down into one, the policy and necessary effect of this numerous representation became obvious. A very small desertion from either of the other two orders must throw the power of both into the hands of the third. In fact, the whole power of the state was soon resolved into that body. Its due composition became, therefore, of infinitely the greater importance.

Judge, Sir, of my surprise, when I found that a very great proportion of the Assembly (a majority, I believe, of the members who attended) was composed of practitioners in the law. It was composed, not of distinguished magistrates, who had given pledges to their country of their science, prudence, and integrity—not of leading advocates, the glory of the bar—not of renowned professors in universities—but for the far greater part, as it must in such a number, of the inferior, unlearned, mechanical, merely instrumental members of the profession. There were distinguished exceptions; but the general composition was of obscure provincial advocates, of stewards of petty local jurisdictions, country attorneys, notaries, and the whole train of the ministers of municipal litigation, the fomenters and conductors of the petty war of village vexation. From the moment I read the list, I saw distinctly, and very nearly as it has happened, all that was to follow. . . .

Whenever the supreme authority is vested in a body so

composed, it must evidently produce the consequences of supreme authority placed in the hands of men not taught habitually to respect themselves—who had no previous fortune
in character at stake—who could not be expected to bear with
moderation or to conduct with discretion a power which they
themselves, more than any others, must be surprised to find in
their hands. Who could flatter himself that these men, suddenly, and as it were by enchantment, snatched from the
humblest rank of subordination, would not be intoxicated
with their unprepared greatness? Who could conceive that
men who are habitually meddling, daring, subtle, active, of
litigious dispositions and unquiet minds, would easily fall back
into their old condition of obscure contention, and laborious,
low, and unprofitable chicane? . . . It was inevitable; it was
necessary; it was planted in the nature of things. They must
join (if their capacity did not permit them to *lead*) in any
project which could procure to them a *litigious constitution*—
which could lay open to them those innumerable lucrative
jobs which follow in the train of all great convulsions and
revolutions in the state, and particularly in all great and violent permutations of property. Was it to be expected that they
would attend to the stability of property, whose existence had
always depended upon whatever rendered property question-
able, ambiguous, and insecure? . . .

Well! but these men were to be tempered and restrained
by other descriptions, of more sober minds and more enlarged understandings. Were they, then, to be awed by the
supereminent authority and awful dignity of a handful of
country clowns, who have seats in that assembly, some of
whom are said not to be able to read and write—and by not a
greater number of traders, who, though somewhat more instructed, and more conspicuous in the order of society, had
never known anything beyond their counting-house? No! both
these descriptions were more formed to be overborne and
swayed by the intrigues and artifices of lawyers than to become their counterpoise. . . .

To the faculty of law was joined a pretty considerable proportion of the faculty of medicine. This faculty had not, any
more than that of the law, possessed in France its just estimation. Its professors, therefore, must have the qualities of
men not habituated to sentiments of dignity. But supposing
they had ranked as they ought to do, and as with us they do
actually, the sides of sick-beds are not the academies for
forming statesmen and legislators. Then came the dealers in

stocks and funds, who must be eager, at any expense, to change their ideal paper wealth for the more solid substance of land. To these were joined men of other descriptions, from whom as little knowledge of or attention to the interests of a great state was to be expected, and as little regard to the stability of any institution—men formed to be instruments, not controls.—Such, in general, was the composition of the *Tiers Etat* in the National Assembly; in which was scarcely to be perceived the slightest traces of what we call the natural landed interest of the country.

We know that the British House of Commons, without shutting its doors to any merit in any class, is, by the sure operation of adequate causes, filled with everything illustrious in rank, in descent, in hereditary and in acquired opulence, in cultivated talents, in military, civil, naval, and politic distinction, that the country can afford. But supposing, what hardly can be supposed as a case, that the House of Commons should be composed in the same manner with the *Tiers Etat* in France—would this dominion of chicane be borne with patience, or even conceived without horror? . . .

After all, if the House of Commons were to have an wholly professional and faculty composition, what is the power of the House of Commons, circumscribed and shut in by the immovable barriers of laws, usages, positive rules of doctrine and practice, counterpoised by the House of Lords, and every moment of its existence at the discretion of the crown to continue, prorogue, or dissolve us? The power of the House of Commons, direct or indirect, is, indeed, great . . . The power, however, of the House of Commons, when least diminished, is as a drop of water in the ocean, compared to that residing in a settled majority of your National Assembly. That assembly, since the destruction of the orders, has no fundamental law, no strict convention, no respected usage to restrain it. Instead of finding themselves obliged to conform to a fixed constitution, they have a power to make a constitution what shall conform to their designs. Nothing in heaven or upon earth can serve as a control on them. What ought to be the heads, the hearts, the dispositions, that are qualified, or that dare, not only to make laws under a fixed constitution, but at one heat to strike out a totally new consitution for a great kingdom, and in every part of it, from the monarch on the throne to the vestry of a parish? But

"Fools rush in where angels fear to tread."

In such a state of unbounded power, for undefined and undefinable purposes, the evil of a moral and almost physical inaptitude of the man to the function must be the greatest we can conceive to happen in the management of human affairs.

Having considered the composition of the third estate, as it stood in its original frame, I took a view of the representatives of the clergy. There, too, it appeared that full as little regard was had to the general security of property, or to the aptitude of the deputies for their public purposes, in the principles of their election. That election was so contrived as to send a very large proportion of mere country curates to the great and arduous work of new-modelling a state: men who never had seen the state so much as in a picture; men who knew nothing of the world beyond the bounds of an obscure village; who, immersed in hopeless poverty, could regard all property, whether secular or ecclesiastical, with no other eye than that of envy; among whom must be many who, for the smallest hope of the meanest dividend in plunder, would readily join in any attempts upon a body of wealth in which they could hardly look to have any share, except in a general scramble. Instead of balancing the power of the active chicaners in the other assembly, these curates must necessarily become the active coadjutors, or at best the passive instruments, of those by whom they had been habitually guided in their petty village concerns. . . .

To observing men it must have appeared from the beginning, that the majority of the third estate, in conjunction with such a deputation from the clergy as I have described, whilst it pursued the destruction of the nobility, would inevitably become subservient to the worst designs of individuals in that class. In the spoil and humiliation of their own order these individuals would possess a sure fund for the pay of their new followers. To squander away the objects which made the happiness of their fellows would be to them no sacrifice at all. Turbulent, discontented men of quality, in proportion as they are puffed up with personal pride and arrogance, generally despise their own order. One of the first symptoms they discover of a selfish and mischievous ambition is a profligate disregard of a dignity which they partake with others. To be attached to the subdivision, to love the little platoon we belong to in society, is the first principle (the germ, as it were) of public affections. It is the first link in the series by which we proceed towards a love to our country and to mankind. The interest of that portion of social arrangement is a trust in the hands of all those who compose it; and as none but bad men would justify it in abuse, none but traitors would barter it away for their own personal advantage. . . .

When men of rank sacrifice all ideas of dignity to an ambition without a distinct object, and work with low instruments and for low ends, the whole composition becomes low and base. Does not something like this now appear in France? Does it not produce something ignoble and inglorious: a kind of meanness in all the prevalent policy; a tendency in all that is done to lower along with individuals all the dignity and importance of the state? Other revolutions have been conducted by persons who, whilst they attempted or affected changes in the commonwealth, sanctified their ambition by advancing the dignity of the people whose peace they troubled. . . .

These disturbers were not so much like men usurping power as asserting their natural place in society. Their rising was to illuminate and beautify the world. Their conquest over their competitors was by outshining them. . . . I do not say that the virtues of such men were to be taken as a balance to their crimes; but they were some corrective to their effects. Such was . . . our Cromwell. Such were your whole race of Guises, Condés, and Colignys. Such the Richelieus, who in more quiet times acted in the spirit of a civil war. Such, as better men, and in a less dubious cause, were your Henry the Fourth, and your Sully, though nursed in civil confusions, and not wholly without some of their taint. It is a thing to be wondered at, to see how very soon France, when she had a moment to respire, recovered and emerged from the longest and most dreadful civil war that ever was known in any nation. Why? Because, among all their massacres, they had not slain the *mind* in their country. A conscious dignity, a noble pride, a generous sense of glory and emulation, was not extinguished. On the contrary, it was kindled and inflamed. The organs also of the state, however shattered, existed. All the prizes of honor and virtue, all the rewards, all the distinctions, remained. But your present confusion, like a palsy, has attacked the fountain of life itself. Every person in your country, in a situation to be actuated by a principle of honor, is disgraced and degraded, and can entertain no sensation of life, except in a mortified and humiliated indignation. . . . Believe me, Sir, those who attempt to level never equalize. In all societies consisting of various descriptions of citizens, some description must be uppermost. The levellers, therefore, only change and pervert the natural order of things: they load the edifice of society by setting up in the air what the solidity of the structure requires to be on the ground. . . .

There is no qualification for government but virtue and wisdom, actual or presumptive. Wherever they are actually found, they have, in whatever state, condition, profession, or trade, the passport of Heaven to human place and honor. Woe to the country which would madly and impiously reject the service of the talents and virtues, civil, military, or religious, that are given to grace and to serve it; and would condemn to obscurity everything formed to diffuse lustre and glory around a state! Woe to that country, too, that, passing into the opposite extreme, considers a low education, a mean, contracted view of things, a sordid, mercenary occupation, as a preferable title to command! . . . I do not hesitate to say that the road to eminence and power, from obscure condition, ought not to be made too easy, nor a thing too much of course. If rare merit be the rarest of all rare things, it ought to pass through some sort of probation. The temple of honor ought to be seated on an eminence. If it be opened through virtue, let it be remembered, too, that virtue is never tried but by some difficulty and some struggle.

Nothing is a due and adequate representation of a state, that does not represent its ability, as well as its property. But as ability is a vigorous and active principle, and as property is sluggish, inert, and timid, it never can be safe from the invasions of ability, unless it be, out of all proportion, predominant in the representation. It must be represented, too, in great masses of accumulation, or it is not rightly protected. The characteristic essence of property, formed out of the combined principles of its acquisition and conservation, is to be *unequal*. The great masses, therefore, which excite envy, and tempt rapacity, must be put out of the possibility of danger. Then they form a natural rampart about the lesser properties in all their gradations. The same quantity of property which is by the natural course of things divided among many has not the same operation. Its defensive power is weakened as it is diffused. In this diffusion each man's portion is less than what, in the eagerness of his desires, he may flatter himself to obtain by dissipating the accumulations of others. The plunder of the few would, indeed, give but a share inconceivably small in the distribution to the many. But the many are not capable of making this calculation; and those who lead them to rapine never intend this distribution.

The power of perpetuating our property in our families is one of the most valuable and interesting circumstances belonging to it, and that which tends the most to the perpetuation of society itself. It makes our weakness subservient to our virtue; it grafts benevolence even upon avarice. The possessors of family wealth, and of the distinction which attends hereditary possession, (as most concerned in it,) are the natural securities for this transmission. With us the House of Peers is formed upon this principle. It is wholly composed of hereditary property and hereditary distinction, and made, therefore, the third of the legislature, and, in the last event, the sole judge of all property in all its subdivisions. The House of Commons, too, though not necessarily, yet in fact, is always so composed, in the far greater part. Let those large proprietors be what they will, (and they have their chance of being amongst the best,) they are, at the very worst, the ballast in the vessel of the commonwealth. For though hereditary wealth, and the rank which goes with it, are too much idolized by creeping sycophants, and the blind, abject admirers of power, they are too rashly slighted in shallow speculations of the petulant, assuming, shortsighted coxcombs of philosophy. . . .

Your leaders in France began by affecting to admire, almost to adore, the British Constitution; but as they advanced, they came to look upon it with a sovereign contempt. The friends of your National Assembly amongst us have full as mean an opinion of what was formerly thought the glory of their country. The Revolution Society has discovered that the English nation is not free. . . .

These gentlemen value themselves on being systematic, and not without reason. They must therefore look on this gross and palpable defect of representation, this fundamental grievance, (so they call it,) as a thing not only vicious in itself, but as rendering our whole government absolutely *illegitimate,* and not at all better than a downright *usurpation.* Another revolution, to get rid of this illegitimate and usurped government, would of course be perfectly justifiable, if not absolutely necessary. . . .

Something they must destroy, or they seem to themselves to exist for no purpose. One set is for destroying the civil power through the ecclesiastical; another for demolishing the ecclesiastic through the civil. They are aware that the worst consequences might happen to the public in accomplishing this double ruin of Church and State; but they are so heated with their theories, that they give more than hints that this ruin, with all the mischiefs that must lead to it and attend it, and which to themselves appear quite certain, would not be unacceptable to them, or very remote from their wishes. . . .

It is no wonder, therefore, that, with these ideas of everything in their Constitution and government at home, either in Church or State, as illegitimate and usurped, or at best as a vain mockery, they look abroad with an eager and passionate enthusiasm. Whilst they are possessed by these notions, it is vain to talk to them of the practice of their ancestors, the fundamental laws of their country, the fixed form of a Constitution whose merits are confirmed by the solid test of long experience and an increasing public strength and national prosperity. They despise experience as the wisdom of unlettered men; and as for the rest, they have wrought under ground a mine that will blow up, at one grand explosion, all examples of antiquity, all precedents, charters, and acts of Parliament. They have "the rights of men." Against these there can be no prescription; against these no argument is binding: these admit no temperament and no compromise: anything withheld from their full demand is so much of fraud and injustice. Against these their rights of men let no government look for security in the length of its continuance, or in the justice and lenity of its administration. The objections of these speculatists, if its forms do not quadrate with their theories, are as valid against such an old and beneficent government as against the most violent tyranny or the greenest usurpation. They are always at issue with governments, not on a question of abuse, but a question of competency and a question of title. . . .

Far am I from denying in theory, full as far is my heart from withholding in practice, (if I were of power to give or to withhold,) the *real* rights of men. In denying their false claims of right, I do not mean to injure those which are real, and are such as their pretended rights would totally destroy. If civil society be made for the advantage of man, all the advantages for which it is made become his right. It is an institution of beneficence; and law itself is only beneficence acting by a rule. Men have a right to live by that rule; they have a right to justice, as between their fellows, whether their fellows are in politic function or in ordinary occupation. They have a right to the fruits of their industry, and to the means of making their industry fruitful. They have a right to the acquisitions of their parents, to the nourishment and improvement of their offspring, to instruction in life and to consolation in death. Whatever each man can separately do, without trespassing upon others, he has a right to do for himself; and he has a right to a fair portion of all which society, with all its combinations of skill and force, can do in his favor. In this partnership all men have equal rights; but not to equal things. He that has but five shillings in the partnership has as good a right to it as he that has five hundred pounds has to his larger proportion; but he has not a right to an equal dividend in the product of the joint stock. And as to the share of power, authority, and direction which each individual ought to have in the management of the state, that I must deny to be amongst the direct original rights of man in civil society; for I have in my contemplation the civil social man, and no other. It is a thing to be settled by convention.

If civil society be the offspring of convention, that convention must be its law. That convention must limit and modify all the descriptions of constitution which are formed under it. Every sort of legislative, judicial, or executory power are its creatures. They can have no being in any other state of things; and how can any man claim, under the conventions of civil society, rights which do not so much as suppose its existence —rights which are absolutely repugnant to it? One of the first motives to civil society, and which becomes one of its fundamental rules, is, *that no man should be judge in his own cause.* By this each person has at once divested himself of the first fundamental right of uncovenanted man, that is, to judge for himself, and to assert his own cause. He abdicates all right to be his own governor. He inclusively, in a great measure, abandons the right of self-defence, the first law of Nature. Men cannot enjoy the rights of an uncivil and of a civil state together. That he may obtain justice, he gives up his right of determining what it is in points the most essential to him. That he may secure some liberty, he makes a surrender in trust of the whole of it.

Government is not made in virtue of natural rights, which may and do exist in total independence of it—and exist in much greater clearness, and in a much greater degree of abstract perfection: but their abstract perfection is their practical defect. By having a right to everything they want everything. Government is a contrivance of human wisdom to provide for human *wants.* Men have a right that these wants should be provided for by this wisdom. Among these wants is to be reckoned the want, out of civil society, of a sufficient restraint upon their passions. Society requires not only that the passions of individuals should be subjected, but that even in the mass and body, as well as in the individuals, the inclinations of men should frequently be thwarted, their will controlled, and their passions brought into subjection. This can only be done *by a power out of themselves,* and not, in the exercise of its function, subject to that will and to those passions which it is its office to bridle and subdue. In this sense the restraints on men, as well as their liberties, are to be reckoned among their rights. But as the liberties and the restrictions vary with times and circumstances, and admit of infinite modifications, they cannot be settled upon any abstract rule; and nothing is so foolish as to discuss them upon that principle.

The moment you abate anything from the full rights of men each to govern himself, and suffer any artificial, positive limitation upon those rights, from that moment the whole organization of government becomes a consideration of convenience. This it is which makes the constitution of a state, and the due distribution of its powers, a matter of the most delicate and complicated skill. It requires a deep knowledge of human nature and human necessities, and of the things which facilitate or obstruct the various ends which are to be pursued by the mechanism of civil institutions. The state is to have recruits to its strength and remedies to its distempers. What is the use of discussing a man's abstract right to food or medicine? The question is upon the method of procuring and administering them. In that deliberation I shall always advise to call in the aid of the farmer and the physician, rather than the professor of metaphysics.

The science of constructing a commonwealth, or renovating it, or reforming it, is, like every other experimental science, not to be taught *a priori.* Nor is it a short experience that can instruct us in that practical science; because the real effects of moral causes are not always immediate, but that which in the first instance is prejudicial may be excellent in its remoter operation, and its excellence may arise even from the ill effects it produces in the beginning. The reverse also happens; and very plausible schemes, with very pleasing commencements, have often shameful and lamentable conclusions. In states there are often some obscure and almost latent causes, things which appear at first view of little moment, on which a very great part of its prosperity or adversity may most essentially depend. The science of government being, therefore, so practical in itself, and intended for such practical purposes, a matter which requires experience, and even more experience than any person can gain in his whole life, however sagacious and observing he may be, it is with infinite caution that any man ought to venture upon pulling down an edifice which has answered in any tolerable degree for ages the common purposes of society, or on building it up again without having models and patterns of approved utility before his eyes.

These metaphysic rights entering into common life, like rays of light which pierce into a dense medium, are, by the laws of Nature, refracted from their straight line. Indeed, in the gross and complicated mass of human passions and concerns, the primitive rights of men undergo such a variety of refractions and reflections that it becomes absurd to talk of them as if they continued in the simplicity of their original direction. The nature of man is intricate; the objects of society are of the greatest possible complexity: and therefore no simple disposition or direction of power can be suitable either to man's nature or to the quality of his affairs. When I hear the simplicity of contrivance aimed at and boasted of in any new political constitutions, I am at no loss to decide that the artificers are grossly ignorant of their trade or totally negligent of their duty. The simple governments are fundamentally defective, to say no worse of them. If you were to contemplate society in but one point of view, all these simple modes of polity are infinitely captivating. In effect each would answer its single end much more perfectly than the more complex is able to attain all its complex purposes. But it is better that the whole should be imperfectly and anomalously answered than that while some parts are provided for with great exactness, others might be totally neglected, or perhaps materially injured, by the over-care of a favorite member.

The pretended rights of these theorists are all extremes; and in proportion as they are metaphysically true, they are morally and politically false. The rights of men are in a sort of *middle*, incapable of definition, but not impossible to be discerned. The rights of men in governments are their advantages; and these are often in balances between differences of good—in compromises sometimes between good and evil, and sometimes between evil and evil. Political reason is a computing principle: adding, subtracting, multiplying, and dividing, morally, and not metaphysically or mathematically, true moral denominations.

By these theorists the right of the people is almost always sophistically confounded with their power. The body of the community, whenever it can come to act, can meet with no effectual resistance; but till power and right are the same, the whole body of them has no right inconsistent with virtue, and the first of all virtues, prudence. Men have no right to what is not reasonable, and to what is not for their benefit . . .

I never liked this continual talk of resistance and revolution, or the practice of making the extreme medicine of the Constitution its daily bread. It renders the habit of society dangerously valetudinary; it is taking periodical doses of mercury sublimate, and swallowing down repeated provocatives of cantharides to our love of liberty. . . .

Hypocrisy, of course, delights in the most sublime speculations; for, never intending to go beyond speculation, it costs nothing to have it magnificent. But even in cases where rather levity than fraud was to be suspected in these ranting speculations, the issue has been much the same. These professors, finding their extreme principles not applicable to cases which call only for a qualified, or, as I may say, civil and legal resistance, in such cases employ no resistance at all. It is with them a war or a revolution, or it is nothing. Finding their schemes of politics not adapted to the state of the world in which they live, they often come to think lightly of all public principle, and are ready, on their part, to abandon for a very trivial interest what they find of very trivial value. . . . They have some change in the Church or State, or both, constantly in their view. When that is the case, they are always bad citizens, and perfectly unsure connections. For, considering their speculative designs as of infinite value, and the actual arrangement of the state as of no estimation, they are, at best, indifferent about it. They see no merit in the good, and no fault in the vicious management of public affairs; they rather rejoice in the latter, as more propitious to revolution. They see no merit or demerit in any man, or any action, or any political principle, any further than as they may forward or retard their design of change; they therefore take up, one day, the most violent and stretched prerogative, and another time the wildest democratic ideas of freedom, and pass from the one to the other without any sort of regard to cause, to person, or to party. . . .

The worst of these politics of revolution is this: they tem-

per and harden the breast, in order to prepare it for the
desperate strokes which are sometimes used in extreme occasions. But as these occasions may never arrive, the mind receives a gratuitous taint; and the moral sentiments suffer not a
little, when no political purpose is served by the depravation.
This sort of people are so taken up with their theories about
the rights of man, that they have totally forgot his nature.
Without opening one new avenue to the understanding, they
have succeeded in stopping up those that lead to the heart.
They have perverted in themselves, and in those that attend
to them, all the well-placed sympathies of the human breast.

This famous sermon of the Old Jewry breathes nothing but
this spirit through all the political part. Plots, massacres, assassinations, seem to some people a trivial price for obtaining
a revolution. A cheap, bloodless reformation, a guiltless liberty, appear flat and vapid to their taste. There must be a
great change of scene; there must be a magnificent stage effect; there must be a grand spectacle to rouse the imagination,
grown torpid with the lazy enjoyment of sixty years' security,
and the still unanimating repose of public prosperity. The
preacher found them all in the French Revolution. This inspires a juvenile warmth through his whole frame. His enthusiasm kindles as he advances; and when he arrives at his
peroration, it is in a full blaze. . . .

Among the revolutions in France must be reckoned a considerable revolution in their ideas of politeness. In England we
are said to learn manners at second-hand from your side of
the water, and that we dress our behavior in the frippery of
France. If so, we are still in the old cut, and have not so far
conformed to the new Parisian mode of good breeding as to
think it quite in the most refined strain of delicate compliment
(whether in condolence or congratulation) to say, to the most
humiliated creature that crawls upon the earth, that great
public benefits are derived from the murder of his servants, the
attempted assassination of himself and of his wife, and the
mortification, disgrace, and degradation that he has personally suffered. . . .

History will record, that, on the morning of the sixth of
October, 1789, the king and queen of France, after a day of
confusion, alarm, dismay, and slaughter, lay down, under the
pledged security of public faith, to indulge nature in a few
hours of respite, to troubled, melancholy repose. From this
sleep the queen was first startled by the voice of the sentinel
at her door, who cried out to her to save herself by flight—

that this was the last proof of fidelity he could give—that they were upon him, and he was dead. Instantly he was cut down. A band of cruel ruffians and assassins, reeking with his blood, rushed into the chamber of the queen, and pierced with a hundred strokes of bayonets and poniards the bed, from whence this persecuted woman had but just time to fly almost naked, and, through ways unknown to the murderers, had escaped to seek refuge at the feet of a king and husband not secure of his own life for a moment.

This king, to say no more of him, and this queen, and their infant children, (who once would have been the pride and hope of a great and generous people,) were then forced to abandon the sanctuary of the most splendid palace in the world, which they left swimming in blood, polluted by massacre, and strewed with scattered limbs and mutilated carcasses. Thence they were conducted into the capital of their kingdom. . . .

It is now sixteen or seventeen years since I saw the queen of France, then the Dauphiness, at Versailles; and surely never lighted on this orb, which she hardly seemed to touch, a more delightful vision. I saw her just above the horizon, decorating and cheering the elevated sphere she just began to move in—glittering like the morning-star, full of life and splendor and joy. Oh! what a revolution! and what an heart must I have, to contemplate without emotion that elevation and that fall! Little did I dream, when she added titles of veneration to those of enthusiastic, distant, respectful love, that she should ever be obliged to carry the sharp antidote against disgrace concealed in that bosom! little did I dream that I should have lived to see such disasters fallen upon her in a nation of gallant men, in a nation of men of honor, and of cavaliers! I thought ten thousand swords must have leaped from their scabbards to avenge even a look that threatened her with insult. But the age of chivalry is gone. That of sophisters, economists, and calculators has succeeded; and the glory of Europe is extinguished forever. Never, never more, shall we behold that generous loyalty to rank and sex, that proud submission, that dignified obedience, that subordination of the heart, which kept alive, even in servitude itself, the spirit of an exalted freedom! The unbought grace of life, the cheap defence of nations, the nurse of manly sentiment and heroic enterprise, is gone! It is gone, that sensibility of principle, that chastity of honor, which felt a stain like a wound, which inspired courage whilst it mitigated ferocity, which ennobled whatever it touched, and under which vice itself lost half its evil by losing all its grossness!

This mixed system of opinion and sentiment had its origin in the ancient chivalry; and the principle, though varied in its appearance by the varying state of human affairs, subsisted and influenced through a long succession of generations, even to the time we live in. If it should ever be totally extinguished, the loss, I fear, will be great. It is this which has given its character to modern Europe. It is this which has distinguished it under all its forms of government, and distinguished it to its advantage, from the states of Asia, and possibly from those states which flourished in the most brilliant periods of the antique world. It was this, which, without confounding ranks, had produced a noble equality, and handed it down through all the gradations of social life. It was this opinion which mitigated kings into companions, and raised private men to be fellows with kings. Without force or opposition, it subdued the fierceness of pride and power; it obliged sovereigns to submit to the soft collar of social esteem, compelled stern authority to submit to elegance, and gave a domination, vanquisher of laws, to be subdued by manners.

But now all is to be changed. All the pleasing illusions which made power gentle and obedience liberal, which harmonized the different shades of life, and which by a bland assimilation incorporated into politics the sentiments which beautify and soften private society, are to be dissolved by this new conquering empire of light and reason. All the decent drapery of life is to be rudely torn off. All the superadded ideas, furnished from the wardrobe of a moral imagination, which the heart owns and the understanding ratifies, as necessary to cover the defects of our naked, shivering nature, and to raise it to dignity in our own estimation, are to be exploded, as a ridiculous, absurd, and antiquated fashion.

On this scheme of things, a king is but a man, a queen is but a woman, a woman is but an animal—and an animal not of the highest order. All homage paid to the sex in general as such, and without distinct views, is to be regarded as romance and folly. Regicide, and parricide, and sacrilege, are but fictions of superstition, corrupting jurisprudence by destroying its simplicity. The murder of a king, or a queen, or a bishop, or a father, are only common homicide—and if the people are by any chance or in any way gainers by it, a sort of homicide much the most pardonable, and into which we ought not to make too severe a scrutiny.

On the scheme of this barbarous philosophy, which is the offspring of cold hearts and muddy understandings, and which is as void of solid wisdom as it is destitute of all taste and elegance, laws are to be supported only by their own terrors, and by the concern which each individual may find in them from his own private speculations, or can spare to them from his own private interests. In the groves of *their* academy, at the end of every vista, you see nothing but the gallows. Nothing is left which engages the affections on the part of the commonwealth. On the principles of this mechanic philosophy, our institutions can never be embodied, if I may use the expression, in persons—so as to create in us love, veneration, admiration, or attachment. But that sort of reason which banishes the affections is incapable of filling their place. These public affections, combined with manners, are required sometimes as supplements, sometimes as correctives, always as aids to law. . . . There ought to be a system of manners in every nation which a well-formed mind would be disposed to relish. To make us love our country, our country ought to be lovely.

But power, of some kind or other, will survive the shock in which manners and opinions perish; and it will find other and worse means for its support. The usurpation, which, in order to subvert ancient institutions, has destroyed ancient principles, will hold power by arts similar to those by which it has acquired it. When the old feudal and chivalrous spirit of *fealty,* which, by freeing kings from fear, freed both kings and subjects from the precautions of tyranny, shall be extinct in the minds of men, plots and assassinations will be anticipated by preventive murder and preventive confiscation, and that long roll of grim and bloody maxims which form the political code of all power not standing on its own honor and the honor of those who are to obey it. Kings will be tyrants from policy, when subjects are rebels from principle.

When ancient opinions and rules of life are taken away, the loss cannot possibly be estimated. From that moment we have no compass to govern us, nor can we know distinctly to what port we steer. Europe, undoubtedly, taken in a mass, was in a flourishing condition the day on which your Revolution was completed. How much of that prosperous state was owing to the spirit of our old manners and opinions is not easy to say; but as such causes cannot be indifferent in their operation, we must presume, that, on the whole, their operation was beneficial.

We are but too apt to consider things in the state in which we find them, without sufficiently adverting to the causes by which they have been produced, and possibly may be upheld. Nothing is more certain than that our manners, our civilization, and all the good things which are connected with manners and with civilization, have, in this European world of ours, depended for ages upon two principles, and were, indeed, the result of both combined: I mean the spirit of a gentleman, and the spirit of religion. The nobility and the clergy, the one by profession, and the other by patronage, kept learning in existence, even in the midst of arms and confusions, and whilst governments were rather in their causes than formed. Learning paid back what it received to nobility and to priesthood, and paid it with usury, by enlarging their ideas, and by furnishing their minds. Happy, if they had all continued to know their indissoluble union, and their proper place! Happy, if learning, not debauched by ambition, had been satisfied to continue the instructor, and not aspired to be the master! Along with its natural protectors and guardians, learning will be cast into the mire and trodden down under the hoofs of a swinish multitude.

If, as I suspect, modern letters owe more than they are always willing to own to ancient manners, so do other interests which we value full as much as they are worth. Even commerce, and trade, and manufacture, the gods of our economical politicians, are themselves perhaps but creatures, are themselves but effects, which, as first causes, we choose to worship. They certainly grew under the same shade in which learning flourished. They, too, may decay with their natural protecting principles. With you, for the present at least, they all threaten to disappear together. Where trade and manufactures are wanting to a people, and the spirit of nobility and religion remains, sentiment supplies, and not always ill supplies, their place; but if commerce and the arts should be lost in an experiment to try how well a state may stand without these old fundamental principles, what sort of a thing must be a nation of gross, stupid, ferocious, and at the same time poor and sordid barbarians, destitute of religion, honor, or manly pride, possessing nothing at present, and hoping for nothing hereafter?

I wish you may not be going fast, and by the shortest cut, to that horrible and disgustful situation. Already there appears a poverty of conception, a coarseness and vulgarity, in all the proceedings of the Assembly and of all their instructors.

Their liberty is not liberal. Their science is presumptuous ignorance. Their humanity is savage and brutal.

It is not clear whether in England we learned those grand and decorous principles and manners, of which considerable traces yet remain, from you, or whether you took them from us. But to you, I think, we trace them best. . . . France has always more or less influenced manners in England; and when your fountain is choked up and polluted, the stream will not run long or not run clear with us, or perhaps with any nation. This gives all Europe, in my opinion, but too close and connected a concern in what is done in France. Excuse me, therefore, if I have dwelt too long on the atrocious spectacle of the sixth of October, 1789, or have given too much scope to the reflections which have arisen in my mind on occasion of the most important of all revolutions, which may be dated from that day: I mean a revolution in sentiments, manners, and moral opinions. As things now stand, with everything respectable destroyed without us, and an attempt to destroy within us every principle of respect, one is almost forced to apologize for harboring the common feelings of men.

Why do I feel so differently from the Reverend Dr. Price, and those of his lay flock who will choose to adopt the sentiments of his discourse?—For this plain reason: Because it is *natural* I should; because we are so made as to be affected at such spectacles with melancholy sentiments upon the unstable condition of mortal prosperity, and the tremendous uncertainty of human greatness; because in those natural feelings we learn great lessons; because in events like these our passions instruct our reason; because, when kings are hurled from their thrones by the Supreme Director of this great drama, and become the objects of insult to the base and of pity to the good, we behold such disasters in the moral as we should behold a miracle in the physical order of things. We are alarmed into reflection; our minds (as it has long since been observed) are purified by terror and pity; our weak, unthinking pride is humbled under the dispensations of a mysterious wisdom. Some tears might be drawn from me, if such a spectacle were exhibited on the stage. I should be truly ashamed of finding in myself that superficial, theatric sense of painted distress, whilst I could exult over it in real life. With such a perverted mind, I could never venture to show my face at a tragedy. People would think the tears that Garrick formerly, or that Siddons not long since, have extorted from me, were the tears of hypocrisy; I should know them to be the tears of folly.

Indeed, the theatre is a better school of moral sentiments than churches where the feelings of humanity are thus outraged. Poets who have to deal with an audience not yet graduated in the school of the rights of men, and who must apply themselves to the moral constitution of the heart, would not dare to produce such a triumph as a matter of exultation. There, where men follow their natural impulses, they would not bear the odious maxims of a Machiavelian policy, whether applied to the attainment of monarchical or democratic tyranny. They would reject them on the modern, as they once did on the ancient stage, where they could not bear even the hypothetical proposition of such wickedness in the mouth of a personated tyrant, though suitable to the character he sustained. No theatric audience in Athens would bear what has been borne in the midst of the real tragedy of this triumphal day: a principal actor weighing, as it were in scales hung in a shop of horrors, so much actual crime against so much contingent advantage—and after putting in and out weights, declaring that the balance was on the side of the advantages. They would not bear to see the crimes of new democracy posted as in a ledger against the crimes of old despotism, and the book-keepers of politics finding democracy still in debt, but by no means unable or unwilling to pay the balance. In the theatre, the first intuitive glance, without any elaborate process of reasoning, would show that this method of political computation would justify every extent of crime. They would see, that, on these principles, even where the very worst acts were not perpetrated, it was owing rather to the fortune of the conspirators than to their parsimony in the expenditure of treachery and blood. They would soon see that criminal means, once tolerated, are soon preferred. They present a shorter cut to the object than through the highway of the moral virtues. Justifying perfidy and murder for public benefit, public benefit would soon become the pretext, and perfidy and murder the end—until rapacity, malice, revenge, and fear more dreadful than revenge, could satiate their insatiable appetites. Such must be the consequences of losing, in the splendor of these triumphs of the rights of men, all natural sense of wrong and right. . . .

If it could have been made clear to me that the king and queen of France (those, I mean, who were such before the triumph) were inexorable and cruel tyrants, that they had formed a deliberate scheme for massacring the National Assembly, (I think I have seen something like the latter insinuated in certain publications,) I should think their captivity just. If this be true, much more ought to have been done, but done, in my opinion, in another manner. The punishment of real tyrants is a noble and awful act of justice; and it has with truth been said to be consolatory to the human mind. But if I were to punish a wicked king, I should regard the dignity in avenging the crime. Justice is grave and decorous, and in its punishments rather seems to submit to a necessity than to make a choice. . . .

I have often been astonished, considering that we are divided from you but by a slender dike of about twenty-four miles, and that the mutual intercourse between the two countries has lately been very great, to find how little you seem to know of us. I suspect that this is owing to your forming a judgment of this nation from certain publications, which do, very erroneously, if they do at all, represent the opinions and dispositions generally prevalent in England. The vanity, restlessness, petulance, and spirit of intrigue of several petty cabals, who attempt to hide their total want of consequence in bustle and noise, and puffing and mutual quotation of each other, makes you imagine that our contemptuous neglect of their abilities is a general mark of acquiescence in their opinions. No such thing, I assure you. Because half a dozen grasshoppers under a fern make the field ring with their importunate chink, whilst thousands of great cattle reposed beneath the shadow of the British oak chew the cud and are silent, pray do not imagine that those who make the noise are the only inhabitants of the field—that, of course, they are many in number—or that, after all, they are other than the little, shrivelled, meagre, hopping, though loud and troublesome insects of the hour. . . .

Thanks to our sullen resistance to innovation, thanks to the cold sluggishness of our national character, we still bear the stamp of our forefathers. We have not . . . lost the generosity and dignity of thinking of the fourteenth century; nor as yet have we subtilized ourselves into savages. We are not the converts of Rousseau; we are not the disciples of Voltaire; Helvétius has made no progress amongst us. Atheists are not our preachers; madmen are not our lawgivers. We know that *we* have made no discoveries, and we think that no discoveries are to be made, in morality—nor many in the great principles of government, nor in the ideas of liberty, which were understood long before we were born altogether as well as they will be after the grave has heaped its mould upon our presumption, and the silent tomb shall have imposed its law on our pert loquacity. In England we have not yet been completely embowelled of our natural entrails: we still feel within us, and we cherish and cultivate, those inbred sentiments which are the faithful guardians, the active monitors of our duty, the true supporters of all liberal and manly morals. We have not been drawn and trussed, in order that we may be filled, like stuffed birds in a museum, with chaff and rags, and paltry, blurred shreds of paper about the rights of man. We preserve the whole of our feelings still native and entire, unsophisticated by pedantry and infidelity. We have real hearts of flesh and blood beating in our bosoms. We fear God; we look up with awe to kings, with affection to Parliaments, with duty to magistrates, with reverence to priests, and with respect to nobility. Why? Because, when such ideas are brought before our minds, it is *natural* to be so affected; because all other feelings are false and spurious, and tend to corrupt our minds, to vitiate our primary morals, to render us unfit for rational liberty, and, by teaching us a servile, licentious, and abandoned insolence, to be our low sport for a few holidays, to make us perfectly fit for and justly deserving of slavery through the whole course of our lives.

You see, Sir, that in this enlightened age I am bold enough to confess that we are generally men of untaught feelings: that, instead of casting away all our old prejudices, we cherish them to a very considerable degree; and, to take more shame to ourselves, we cherish them because they are prejudices; and the longer they have lasted, and the more generally they have prevailed, the more we cherish them. We are afraid to put men to live and trade each on his own private stock of reason; because we suspect that the stock in each man is small, and that the individuals would do better to avail themselves of the general bank and capital of nations and of ages. Many of our men of speculation, instead of exploding general prejudices, employ their sagacity to discover the latent wisdom which prevails in them. If they find what they seek, (and they seldom fail,) they think it more wise to continue the prejudice, with the reason involved, than to cast away the coat of prejudice, and to leave nothing but the naked reason; because prejudice, with its reason, has a motive to give action to that reason, and an affection which will give it permanence. Prejudice is of ready application in the emergency; it previously engages the mind in a steady course of wisdom and virtue, and does not leave the man hesitating in the moment of decision, skeptical, puzzled, and unresolved. Prejudice renders a man's virtue his habit, and not a series of unconnected acts. Through just prejudice, his duty becomes a part of his nature.

Your literary men, and your politicians, and so do the whole clan of the enlightened among us, essentially differ in these points. They have no respect for the wisdom of others; but they pay it off by a very full measure of confidence in their own. With them it is a sufficient motive to destroy an old scheme of things, because it is an old one. As to the new, they are in no sort of fear with regard to the duration of a building run up in haste; because duration is no object to those who think little or nothing has been done before their time, and who place all their hopes in discovery. They conceive, very systematically, that all things which give perpetuity are mischievous, and therefore they are at inexpiable war with all establishments. They think that government may vary like modes of dress, and with as little ill effect; that there needs no principle of attachment, except a sense of present conveniency, to any constitution of the state. They always speak as if they were of opinion that there is a singular species of compact between them and their magistrates, which binds the magistrate, but which has nothing reciprocal in it, but that the majesty of the people has a right to dissolve it without any reason but its will. Their attachment to their country itself is only so far as it agrees with some of their fleeting projects: it begins and ends with that scheme of polity which falls in with their momentary opinion.

These doctrines, or rather sentiments, seem prevalent with your new statesmen. But they are wholly different from those on which we have always acted in this country. . . .

Formerly your affairs were your own concern only. We felt for them as men; but we kept aloof from them, because we were not citizens of France. But when we see the model held up to ourselves, we must feel as Englishmen, and, feeling, we must provide as Englishmen. . . .

We know, and, what is better, we feel inwardly, that religion is the basis of civil society, and the source of all good, and of all comfort. In England we are so convinced of this, that there is no rust of superstition, with which the accumulated absurdity of the human mind might have crusted it over in the course of ages, that ninety-nine in a hundred of the people of England would not prefer to impiety. We shall never be such fools as to call in an enemy to the substance of any system to remove its corruptions, to supply its defects, or to perfect its construction. If our religious tenets should ever want a further elucidation, we shall not call on Atheism to explain them. . . .

[We know, and it is our pride to know, that man is by his constitution a religious animal; that atheism is against, not only our reason, but our instincts; and that it cannot prevail long.] But if, in the moment of riot, and in a drunken delirium from the hot spirit drawn out of the alembic of hell, which in France is now so furiously boiling, we should uncover our nakedness, by throwing off that Christian religion which has hitherto been our boast and comfort, and one great source of civilization amongst us, and among many other nations, we are apprehensive (being well aware that the mind will not endure a void) that some uncouth, pernicious, and degrading superstition might take the place of it.

For that reason, before we take from our establishment the natural, human means of estimation, and give it up to contempt, as you have done, and in doing it have incurred the penalties you well deserve to suffer, we desire that some other may be presented to us in the place of it. We shall then form our judgment.

On these ideas, instead of quarrelling with establishments, as some do, who have made a philosophy and a religion of their hostility to such institutions, we cleave closely to them. We are resolved to keep an established church, an established monarchy, an established aristocracy, and an established democracy, each in the degree it exists, and in no greater. I shall show you presently how much of each of these we possess.

It has been the misfortune (not, as these gentlemen think it, the glory) of this age, that everything is to be discussed, as if the Constitution of our country were to be always a subject rather of altercation than enjoyment. For this reason, as well as for the satisfaction of those among you (if any such you have among you) who may wish to profit of examples, I venture to trouble you with a few thoughts upon each of these establishments. . . .

First I beg leave to speak of our Church Establishment, which is the first of our prejudices—not a prejudice destitute of reason, but involving in it profound and extensive wisdom. I speak of it first. It is first, and last, and midst in our minds.

For, taking ground on that religious system of which we are now in possession, we continue to act on the early received and uniformly continued sense of mankind. That sense not only, like a wise architect, hath built up the august fabric of states, but, like a provident proprietor, to preserve the structure from profanation and ruin, as a sacred temple, purged from all the impurities of fraud and violence and injustice and tyranny, hath solemnly and forever consecrated the commonwealth, and all that officiate in it. This consecration is made, that all who administer in the government of men, in which they stand in the person of God Himself, should have high and worthy notions of their function and destination; that their hope should be full of immortality; that they should not look to the paltry pelf of the moment, nor to the temporary and transient praise of the vulgar, but to a solid, permanent existence, in the permanent part of their nature, and to a permanent fame and glory, in the example they leave as a rich inheritance to the world.

Such sublime principles ought to be infused into persons of exalted situations, and religious establishments provided that may continually revive and enforce them. Every sort of moral, every sort of civil, every sort of politic institution, aiding the rational and natural ties that connect the human understanding and affections to the divine, are not more than necessary, in order to build up that wonderful structure, Man— whose prerogative it is, to be in a great degree a creature of his own making, and who, when made as he ought to be made, is destined to hold no trivial place in the creation. But whenever man is put over men, as the better nature ought ever to preside, in that case more particularly he should as nearly as possible be approximated to his perfection.

The consecration of the state by a state religious establishment is necessary also to operate with a wholesome awe upon free citizens; because, in order to secure their freedom, they must enjoy some determinate portion of power. To them, therefore, a religion connected with the state, and with their duty towards it, becomes even more necessary than in such societies where the people, by the terms of their subjection, are confined to private sentiments, and the management of their own family concerns. All persons possessing any portion of power ought to be strongly and awfully impressed with an idea that they act in trust, and that they are to account for their conduct in that trust to the one great Master, Author, and Founder of society.

This principle ought even to be more strongly impressed upon the minds of those who compose the collective sovereignty than upon those of single princes. Without instruments, these princes can do nothing. Whoever uses instruments, in finding helps, finds also impediments. Their power is therefore by no means complete; nor are they safe in extreme abuse. Such persons, however elevated by flattery, arrogance, and self-opinion, must be sensible, that, whether covered or not by positive law, in some way or other they are accountable even here for the abuse of their trust. If they are not cut off by a rebellion of their people, they may be strangled by the very janissaries kept for their security against all other rebellion. Thus we have seen the king of France sold by his soldiers for an increase of pay. But where popular authority is absolute and unrestrained, the people have an infinitely greater, because a far better founded, confidence in their own power. They are themselves in a great measure their own instruments. They are nearer to their objects. Besides, they are less under responsibility to one of the greatest controlling powers on earth, the sense of fame and estimation. The share of infamy that is likely to fall to the lot of each individual in public acts is small indeed: the operation of opinion being in the inverse ratio to the number of those who abuse power. Their own approbation of their own acts has to them the appearance of a public judgment in their favor. A perfect democracy is therefore the most shameless thing in the world. As it is the most shameless, it is also the most fearless. No man apprehends in his person that he can be made subject to punishment. Certainly the people at large never ought: for, as all punishments are for example towards the conservation of the people at large, the people at large can never become the subject of punishment by any human hand. It is therefore of infinite importance that they should not be suffered to imagine that their will, any more than that of kings, is the standard of right and wrong. They ought to be persuaded that they are full as little entitled, and far less qualified, with safety to themselves, to use any arbitrary power whatsoever; that therefore they are not, under a false show of liberty, but in truth to exercise an unnatural, inverted domination, tyrannically to exact from those who officiate in the state, not an entire devotion to their interest, which is their right, but an abject submission to their occasional will: extinguishing thereby, in all those who serve them, all moral principle, all sense of dignity, all use of judgment, and all consistency of character; whilst by the very same process they give themselves up a proper, a suitable, but a most contemptible prey to the servile ambition of popular sycophants or courtly flatterers.

When the people have emptied themselves of all the lust of selfish will, which without religion it is utterly impossible they ever should—when they are conscious that they exercise, and exercise perhaps in a higher link of the order of delegation, the power which to be legitimate must be according to that eternal, immutable law in which will and reason are the same —they will be more careful how they place power in base and incapable hands. In their nomination to office, they will not appoint to the exercise of authority as to a pitiful job, but as to a holy function; not according to their sordid, selfish interest, nor to their wanton caprice, nor to their arbitrary will; but they will confer that power (which any man may well tremble to give or to receive) on those only in whom they may discern that predominant proportion of active virtue and wisdom, taken together and fitted to the charge, such as in the great and inevitable mixed mass of human imperfections and infirmities is to be found.

When they are habitually convinced that no evil can be acceptable, either in the act or the permission, to Him whose essence is good, they will be better able to extirpate out of the minds of all magistrates, civil, ecclesiastical, or military, anything that bears the least resemblance to a proud and lawless domination.

But one of the first and most leading principles on which the commonwealth and the laws are consecrated is lest the temporary possessors and life-renters in it, unmindful of what they have received from their ancestors, or of what is due to their posterity, should act as if they were the entire masters; that they should not think it amongst their rights to cut off the entail or commit waste on the inheritance, by destroying at their pleasure the whole original fabric of their society: hazarding to leave to those who come after them a ruin instead of an habitation—and teaching these successors as little to respect their contrivances as they had themselves respected the institutions of their forefathers. By this unprincipled facility of changing the state as often and as much and in as many ways as there are floating fancies or fashions, the whole chain and continuity of the commonwealth would be broken; no one generation could link with the other; men would become little better than the flies of a summer.

And first of all, the science of jurisprudence, the pride of the human intellect, which, with all its defects, redundancies, and errors, is the collected reason of ages, combining the principles of original justice with the infinite variety of human concerns, as a heap of old exploded errors, would be no longer studied. Personal self-sufficiency and arrogance (the certain attendants upon all those who have never experienced a wisdom greater than their own) would usurp the tribunal. Of course no certain laws, establishing invariable grounds of hope and fear, would keep the actions of men in a certain course, or direct them to a certain end. Nothing stable in the modes of holding property or exercising function could form a solid ground on which any parent could speculate in the education of his offspring, or in a choice for their future establishment in the world. No principles would be early worked into the habits. As soon as the most able instructor had completed his laborious course of institution, instead of sending forth his pupil accomplished in a virtuous discipline fitted to procure him attention and respect in his place in society, he would find everything altered, and that he had turned out a poor creature to the contempt and derision of the world, ignorant of the true grounds of estimation. Who would insure a tender and delicate sense of honor to beat almost with the first pulses of the heart, when no man could know what would be the test of honor in a nation continually varying the standard of its coin? No part of life would retain its acquisitions. Barbarism with regard to science and literature, unskilfulness with regard to arts and manufactures, would infallibly succeed to the want of a steady education and settled principle; and thus the commonwealth itself would in a few generations crumble away, be disconnected into the dust and powder of individuality, and at length dispersed to all the winds of heaven.

To avoid, therefore, the evils of inconstancy and versatility, ten thousand times worse than those of obstinacy and the blindest prejudice, we have consecrated the state, that no man should approach to look into its defects or corruptions but with due caution; that he should never dream of beginning its reformation by its subversion; that he should approach to the faults of the state as to the wounds of a father, with pious awe and trembling solicitude. By this wise prejudice we are taught to look with horror on those children of their country who are prompt rashly to hack that aged parent in pieces and put him into the kettle of magicians, in hopes that by their poisonous weeds and wild incantations they may regenerate the paternal constitution and renovate their father's life.

Society is, indeed, a contract. Subordinate contracts for objects of mere occasional interest may be dissolved at pleasure; but the state ought not to be considered as nothing better than a partnership agreement in a trade of pepper and coffee, calico or tobacco, or some other such low concern, to be taken up for a little temporary interest, and to be dissolved by the fancy of the parties. It is to be looked on with other reverence; because it is not a partnership in things subservient only to the gross animal existence of a temporary and perishable nature. It is a partnership in all science, a partnership in all art, a partnership in every virtue and in all perfection. As the ends of such a partnership cannot be obtained in many generations, it becomes a partnership not only between those who are living, but between those who are living, those who are dead, and those who are to be born. Each contract of each particular state is but a clause in the great primeval contract of eternal society, linking the lower with the higher natures, connecting the visible and invisible world, according to a fixed compact sanctioned by the inviolable oath which holds all physical and all moral natures each in their appointed place. This law is not subject to the will of those who, by an obligation above them, and infinitely superior, are bound to submit their will to that law. The municipal corporations of that universal kingdom are not morally at liberty, at their pleasure, and on their speculations of a contingent improvement, wholly to separate and tear asunder the bands of their subordinate community, and to dissolve it into an unsocial, uncivil, unconnected chaos of elementary principles. It is the first and supreme necessity only, a necessity that is not chosen, but chooses, a necessity paramount to deliberation, that admits no discussion and demands no evidence, which alone can justify a resort to anarchy. This necessity is no exception to the rule; because this necessity itself is a part, too, of that moral and physical disposition of things to which man must be obedient by consent or force: but if that which is only submission to necessity should be made the object of choice, the law is broken, Nature is disobeyed, and the rebellious are outlawed, cast forth, and exiled, from this world of reason, and order, and peace, and virtue, and fruitful penitence, into the antagonist world of madness, discord, vice, confusion, and unavailing sorrow. . . .

Persuaded that all things ought to be done with reference, and referring all to the point of reference to which all should be directed, they think themselves bound, not only as individuals in the sanctuary of the heart, or as congregated in that personal capacity, to renew the memory of their high origin and cast, but also in their corporate character to perform their national homage to the Institutor and Author and Protector of civil society, without which civil society man could not by any possibility arrive at the perfection of which his nature is capable, nor even make a remote and faint approach to it. They conceive that He who gave our nature to be perfected by our virtue willed also the necessary means of its perfection: He willed, therefore, the state: He willed its connection with the source and original archetype of all perfection. They who are convinced of this His will, which is the law of laws and the sovereign of sovereigns, cannot think it reprehensible that this our corporate fealty and homage, that this our recognition of a signiory paramount, I had almost said this oblation of the state itself, as a worthy offering on the high altar of universal praise, should be performed, as all public, solemn acts are performed, in buildings, in music, in decoration, in speech, in the dignity of persons, according to the customs of mankind, taught by their nature—that is, with modest splendor, with unassuming state, with mild majesty and sober pomp. For those purposes they think some part of the wealth of the country is as usefully employed as it can be in fomenting the luxury of individuals. It is the public ornament. It is the public consolation. It nourishes the public hope. The poorest man finds his own importance and dignity in it, whilst the wealth and pride of individuals at every moment makes the man of humble rank and fortune sensible of his inferiority, and degrades and vilifies his condition. It is for the man in humble life, and to raise his nature, and to put him in mind of a state in which the privileges of opulence will cease, when he will be equal by nature, and may be more than equal by virtue, that this portion of the general wealth of his country is employed and sanctified. . . .

It is on some such principles that the majority of the people of England, far from thinking a religious national establishment unlawful, hardly think it lawful to be without one. . . .

This principle runs through the whole system of their polity. They do not consider their Church establishment as convenient, but as essential to their state: not as a thing heterogeneous and separable—something added for accommodation—what they may either keep up or lay aside, according to their temporary ideas of convenience. They consider it as the foundation of their whole Constitution, with which, and with every part of which, it holds an indissoluble union. Church and State are ideas inseparable in their minds, and scarcely is the one ever mentioned without mentioning the other.

Our education is so formed as to confirm and fix this impression. Our education is in a manner wholly in the hands of ecclesiastics, and in all stages from infancy to manhood. Even when our youth, leaving schools and universities, enter that most important period of life which begins to link experience and study together, and when with that view they visit other countries, instead of old domestics whom we have seen as governors to principal men from other parts, three fourths of those who go abroad with our young nobility and gentlemen are ecclesiastics: not as austere masters, nor as mere followers; but as friends and companions of a graver character, and not seldom persons as well born as themselves. With them, as relations, they most commonly keep up a close connection through life. By this connection we conceive that we attach our gentlemen to the Church; and we liberalize the Church by an intercourse with the leading characters of the country.

So tenacious are we of the old ecclesiastical modes and fashions of institution, that very little alteration has been made in them since the fourteenth or fifteenth century: adhering in this particular, as in all things else, to our old settled maxim, never entirely nor at once to depart from antiquity. We found these old institutions, on the whole, favorable to morality and discipline; and we thought they were susceptible of amendment, without altering the ground. We thought that they were capable of receiving and meliorating, and above all of preserving, the accessions of science and literature, as the order of Providence should successively produce them. And after all, with this Gothic and monkish education, (for such it is in the groundwork,) we may put in our claim to as ample and as early a share in all the improvements in science, in arts, and in literature, which have illuminated and adorned the modern world, as any other nation in Europe: we think one main cause of this improvement was our not despising the patrimony of knowledge which was left us by our forefathers.

It is from our attachment to a Church establishment, that the English nation did not think it wise to intrust that great fundamental interest of the whole to what they trust no part of their civil or military public service—that is, to the unsteady and precarious contribution of individuals. They go further. They certainly never have suffered, and never will suffer, the fixed estate of the Church to be converted into a pension, to depend on the Treasury, and to be delayed, withheld, or perhaps to be extinguished by fiscal difficulties: which difficulties may sometimes be pretended for political purposes, and are in fact often brought on by the extravagance, negligence, and rapacity of politicians. The people of England think that they have constitutional motives, as well as religious, against any project of turning their independent clergy into ecclesiastical pensioners of state. They tremble for their liberty, from the influence of a clergy dependent on the crown; they tremble for the public tranquillity, from the disorders of a factious clergy, if it were made to depend upon any other than the crown. They therefore made their Church, like their king and their nobility, independent.

From the united considerations of religion and constitutional policy, from their opinion of a duty to make a sure provision for the consolation of the feeble and the instruction of the ignorant, they have incorporated and identified the estate of the Church with the mass of *private property,* of which the state is not the proprietor, either for use or dominion, but the guardian only and the regulator. . . .

The Christian statesmen of this land would, indeed, first provide for the *multitude,* because it is the *multitude,* and is therefore, as such, the first object in the ecclesiastical institution, and in all institutions. They have been taught that the circumstances of the Gospel's being preached to the poor was one of the great tests of its true mission. They think, therefore, that those do not believe it who do not take care it should be preached to the poor. But as they know that charity is not confined to any one description, but ought to apply itself to all men who have wants, they are not deprived of a due and anxious sensation of pity to the distresses of the miserable great. . . .

The English people are satisfied, that to the great the consolations of religion are as necessary as its instructions. They, too, are among the unhappy. They feel personal pain and domestic sorrow. . . .

The people of England know how little influence the teachers of religion are likely to have with the wealthy and powerful of long standing, and how much less with the newly fortunate, if they appear in a manner no way assorted to those with whom they must associate, and over whom they must even exercise, in some cases, something like an authority. What must they think of that body of teachers, if they see it in no part above the establishment of their domestic servants? If the poverty were voluntary, there might be some difference. Strong instances of self-denial operate powerfully on our minds; and a man who has no wants has obtained great freedom and firmness, and even dignity. But as the mass of any description of men are but men, and their poverty cannot be voluntary, that disrespect which attends upon all lay poverty will not depart from the ecclesiastical. Our provident Constitution has therefore taken care that those who are to instruct presumptuous ignorance, those who are to be censors over insolent vice, should neither incur their contempt nor live upon their alms; nor will it tempt the rich to a neglect of the true medicine of their minds. For these reasons, whilst we provide first for the poor, and with a parental solicitude, we have not relegated religion (like something we were ashamed to show) to obscure municipalities or rustic villages. No! we will have her to exalt her mitred front in courts and parliaments. We will have her mixed throughout the whole mass of life, and blended with all the classes of society. The people of England will show to the haughty potentates of the world, and to their talking sophisters, that a free, a generous, an informed nation honors the high magistrates of its Church; that it will not suffer the insolence of wealth and titles, or any other species of proud pretension, to look down with scorn upon what they look up to with reverence, nor presume to trample on that acquired personal nobility which they intend always to be, and which often is, the fruit, not the reward, (for what can be the reward?) of learning, piety, and virtue. They can see, without pain or grudging, an archbishop precede a duke. They can see a bishop of Durham or a bishop of Winchester in possession of ten thousand pounds a year, and cannot conceive why it is in worse hands than estates to the like amount in the hands of this earl or that squire; although it may be true that so many dogs and horses are not kept by the former, and fed with the victuals which ought to nourish the children of the people. It is true, the whole Church revenue is not always employed, and to every shilling, in charity; nor perhaps ought it; but something is generally so employed. It is better to cherish virtue and humanity, by leaving much to free will, even with some loss to the object, than to attempt to make men mere machines and instruments of a political benevolence. The world on the whole will gain by a liberty without which virtue cannot exist. . . .

With these ideas rooted in their minds, the Commons of

Great Britain, in the national emergencies, will never seek their resource from the confiscation of the estates of the Church and poor. . . . There is not *one* public man in this kingdom, whom you wish to quote—no, not one, of any party or description—who does not reprobate the dishonest, perfidious, and cruel confiscation which the National Assembly has been compelled to make of that property which it was their first duty to protect. . . .

The robbery of your Church has proved a security to the possessions of ours. It has roused the people. They see with horror and alarm that enormous and shameless act of proscription. It has opened, and will more and more open, their eyes upon the selfish enlargement of mind and the narrow liberality of sentiment of insidious men, which, commencing in close hypocrisy and fraud, have ended in open violence and rapine. At home we behold similar beginnings. We are on our guard against similar conclusions.

I hope we shall never be so totally lost to all sense of the duties imposed upon us by the law of social union, as, upon any pretext of public service, to confiscate the goods of a single unoffending citizen. Who but a tyrant (a name expressive of everything which can vitiate and degrade human nature) could think of seizing on the property of men, unaccused, unheard, untried, by whole descriptions, by hundreds and thousands together? Who that had not lost every trace of humanity could think of casting down men of exalted rank and sacred function, some of them of an age to call at once for reverence and compassion—of casting them down from the highest situation in the commonwealth, wherein they were maintained by their own landed property, to a state of indigence, depression, and contempt? . . .

But this act of seizure of property, it seems, is a judgment in law, and not a confiscation. They have, it seems, found out in the academies of the Palais Royal and the Jacobins, that certain men had no right to the possessions which they held under law, usage, the decisions of courts, and the accumulated prescription of a thousand years. They say that ecclesiastics are fictitious persons, creatures of the state, whom at pleasure they may destroy, and of course limit and modify in every particular; that the goods they possess are not properly theirs, but belong to the state which created the fiction; and we are therefore not to trouble ourselves with what they may suffer in their natural feelings and natural persons on account of what is done towards them in this their constructive character. Of what import is it, under what names you injure men, and deprive them of the just emoluments of a profession in which they were not only permitted, but encouraged by the state to engage, and upon the supposed certainty of which emoluments they had formed the plan of their lives, contracted debts, and led multitudes to an entire dependence upon them? . . .

The arguments of tyranny are as contemptible as its force is dreadful. Had not your confiscators by their early crimes obtained a power which secures indemnity to all the crimes of which they have since been guilty, or that they can commit, it is not the syllogism of the logician, but the lash of the executioner, that would have refuted a sophistry which becomes an accomplice of theft and murder. The sophistic tyrants of Paris are loud in their declamations against the departed regal tyrants who in former ages have vexed the world. They are thus bold, because they are safe from the dungeons and iron cages of their old masters. Shall we be more tender of the tyrants of our own time, when we see them acting worse tragedies under our eyes? . . .

The enemies to property at first pretended a most tender, delicate, and scrupulous anxiety for keeping the king's engagements with the public creditor. These professors of the rights of men are so busy in teaching others, that they have not leisure to learn anything themselves; otherwise they would have known that it is to the property of the citizen, and not to the demands of the creditor of the state, that the first and original faith of civil society is pledged. The claim of the citizen is prior in time, paramount in title, superior in equity. The fortunes of individuals, whether possessed by acquisition, or by descent, or in virtue of a participation in the goods of some community, were no part of the creditor's security, expressed or implied. They never so much as entered into his head, when he made his bargain. He well knew that the public, whether represented by a monarch or by a senate, can pledge nothing but the public estate; and it can have no public estate, except in what it derives from a just and proportioned imposition upon the citizens at large. This was engaged, and nothing else could be engaged, to the public creditor. No man can mortgage his injustice as a pawn for his fidelity.

It is impossible to avoid some observation on the contradictions caused by the extreme rigor and the extreme laxity of this new public faith, which influenced in this transaction, and which influenced not according to the nature of the obliga-

tion, but to the description of the persons to whom it was engaged. No acts of the old government of the kings of France
are held valid in the National Assembly, except its pecuniary
engagements: acts of all others of the most ambiguous legality. The rest of the acts of that royal government are considered in so odious a light that to have a claim under its authority is looked on as a sort of crime. A pension, given as a
reward for service to the state, is surely as good a ground of
property as any security for money advanced to the state. It
is a better; for money is paid, and well paid, to obtain that
service. We have, however, seen multitudes of people under
this description in France, who never had been deprived of
their allowances by the most arbitrary ministers in the most
arbitrary times, by this assembly of the rights of men robbed
without mercy. They were told, in answer to their claim to the
bread earned with their blood, that their services had not
been rendered to the country that now exists.

This laxity of public faith is not confined to those unfortunate persons. The Assembly, with perfect consistency, it
must be owned, is engaged in a respectable deliberation how
far it is bound by the treaties made with other nations under
the former government; and their committee is to report
which of them they ought to ratify, and which not. By this
means they have put the external fidelity of this virgin state on
a par with its internal. . . .

By the vast debt of France a great moneyed interest has
insensibly grown up, and with it a great power. By the ancient usages which prevailed in that kingdom, the general
circulation of property, and in particular the mutual con-
vertibility of land into money and of money into land, had
always been a matter of difficulty. Family settlements, rather
more general and more strict than they are in England, the
jus retractûs, the great mass of landed property held by the
crown, and, by a maxim of the French law, held unalienably,
the vast estates of the ecclesiastic corporations—all these had
kept the landed and moneyed interests more separated in
France, less miscible, and the owners of the two distinct
species of property not so well disposed to each other as they
are in this country.

The moneyed property was long looked on with rather
an evil eye by the people. They saw it connected with their
distresses, and aggravating them. It was no less envied by the
old landed interests—partly for the same reasons that rendered
it obnoxious to the people, but much more so as it eclipsed,

by the splendor of an ostentatious luxury, the unendowed pedigrees and naked titles of several among the nobility. Even when the nobility, which represented the more permanent landed interest, united themselves by marriage (which sometimes was the case) with the other description, the wealth which saved the family from ruin was supposed to contaminate and degrade it. Thus the enmities and heart-burnings of these parties were increased even by the usual means by which discord is made to cease and quarrels are turned into friendship. In the mean time, the pride of the wealthy men, not noble, or newly noble, increased with its cause. They felt with resentment an inferiority the grounds of which they did not acknowledge. There was no measure to which they were not willing to lend themselves, in order to be revenged of the outrages of this rival pride, and to exalt their wealth to what they considered as its natural rank and estimation. They struck at the nobility through the crown and the Church. They attacked them particularly on the side on which they thought them the most vulnerable—that is, the possessions of the Church, which, through the patronage of the crown, generally devolved upon the nobility. The bishoprics and the great commendatory abbeys were, with few exceptions, held by that order.

In this state of real, though not always perceived, warfare between the noble ancient landed interest and the new moneyed interest, the greatest, because the most applicable, strength was in the hands of the latter. The moneyed interest is in its nature more ready for any adventure, and its possessors more disposed to new enterprises of any kind. Being of a recent acquisition, it falls in more naturally with any novelties. It is therefore the kind of wealth which will be resorted to by all who wish for change.

Along with the moneyed interest, a new description of men had grown up, with whom that interest soon formed a close and marked union: I mean the political men of letters. Men of letters, fond of distinguishing themselves, are rarely averse to innovation. Since the decline of the life and greatness of Louis the Fourteenth, they were not so much cultivated either by him, or by the Regent, or the successors to the crown; nor were they engaged to the court by favors and emoluments so systematically as during the splendid period of that ostentatious and not impolitic reign. What they lost in the old court protection they endeavored to make up by joining in a sort of incorporation of their own; to which the two academies of

France, and afterwards the vast undertaking of the Encyclo-
pædia, carried on by a society of these gentlemen, did not a
little contribute.

The literary cabal had some years ago formed something
like a regular plan for the destruction of the Christian religion. This object they pursued with a degree of zeal which
hitherto had been discovered only in the propagators of some
system of piety. They were possessed with a spirit of proselytism in the most fanatical degree—and from thence, by an
easy progress, with the spirit of persecution according to
their means. What was not to be done towards their great end
by any direct or immediate act might be wrought by a longer
process through the medium of opinion. To command that
opinion, the first step is to establish a dominion over those who
direct it. They contrived to possess themselves, with great
method and perseverance, of all the avenues to literary fame.
Many of them, indeed, stood high in the ranks of literature and
science. The world had done them justice, and in favor of
general talents forgave the evil tendency of their peculiar
principles. This was true liberality; which they returned by
endeavoring to confine the reputation of sense, learning, and
taste to themselves or their followers. I will venture to say
that this narrow, exclusive spirit has not been less prejudicial
to literature and to taste than to morals and true philosophy.
These atheistical fathers have a bigotry of their own; and they
have learnt to talk against monks with the spirit of a monk.
But in some things they are men of the world. The resources
of intrigue are called in to supply the defects of argument and
wit. To this system of literary monopoly was joined an unremitting industry to blacken and discredit in every way, and
by every means, all those who did not hold to their faction.
To those who have observed the spirit of their conduct it has
long been clear that nothing was wanted but the power of
carrying the intolerance of the tongue and of the pen into a
persecution which would strike at property, liberty, and life.

The desultory and faint persecution carried on against
them, more from compliance with form and decency than
with serious resentment, neither weakened their strength nor
relaxed their efforts. The issue of the whole was, that, what
with opposition, and what with success, a violent and malignant zeal, of a kind hitherto unknown in the world, had taken
an entire possession of their minds, and rendered their whole
conversation, which otherwise would have been pleasing and
instructive, perfectly disgusting. A spirit of cabal, intrigue,

and proselytism pervaded all their thoughts, words, and actions. And as controversial zeal soon turns its thoughts on force, they began to insinuate themselves into a correspondence with foreign princes—in hopes, through their authority, which at first they flattered, they might bring about the changes they had in view. To them it was indifferent whether these changes were to be accomplished by the thunderbolt of despotism or by the earthquake of popular commotion. The correspondence between this cabal and the late king of Prussia will throw no small light upon the spirit of all their proceedings. For the same purpose for which they intrigued with princes, they cultivated, in a distinguished manner, the moneyed interest of France; and partly through the means furnished by those whose peculiar offices gave them the most extensive and certain means of communication, they carefully occupied all the avenues to opinion.

Writers, especially when they act in a body and with one direction, have great influence on the public mind; the alliance, therefore, of these writers with the moneyed interest had no small effect in removing the popular odium and envy which attended that species of wealth. These writers, like the propagators of all novelties, pretended to a great zeal for the poor and the lower orders, whilst in their satires they rendered hateful, by every exaggeration, the faults of courts, of nobility, and of priesthood. They became a sort of demagogues. They served as a link to unite, in favor of one object, obnoxious wealth to restless and desperate poverty.

As these two kinds of men appear principal leaders in all the late transactions, their junction and politics will serve to account, not upon any principles of law or of policy, but as a *cause,* for the general fury with which all the landed property of ecclesiastical corporations has been attacked, and the great care which, contrary to their pretended principles, has been taken of a moneyed interest originating from the authority of the crown. All the envy against wealth and power was artificially directed against other descriptions of riches. On what other principle than that which I have stated can we account for an appearance so extraordinary and unnatural as that of the ecclesiastical possessions, which had stood so many successions of ages and shocks of civil violences, and were guarded at once by justice and by prejudice, being applied to the payment of debts comparatively recent, invidious, and contracted by a decried and subverted government?

Was the public estate a sufficient stake for the public debts?

Assume that it was not, and that a loss *must* be incurred somewhere. When the only estate lawfully possessed, and which the contracting parties had in contemplation at the time in which their bargain was made, happens to fail, who, according to the principles of natural and legal equity, ought to be the sufferer? Certainly it ought to be either the party who trusted, or the party who persuaded him to trust, or both; and not third parties who had no concern with the transaction. Upon any insolvency, they ought to suffer who were weak enough to lend upon bad security, or they who fraudulently held out a security that was not valid. Laws are acquainted with no other rules of decision. But by the new institute of the rights of men, the only persons who in equity ought to suffer are the only persons who are to be saved harmless: those are to answer the debt who neither were lenders nor borrowers, mortgagers nor mortgagees. . . .

Can one hear of the proscription of such persons, and the confiscation of their effects, without indignation and horror? He is not a man who does not feel such emotions on such occasions. He does not deserve the name of a free man who will not express them.

Few barbarous conquerors have ever made so terrible a revolution in property. None of the heads of the Roman factions, when they established *crudelem illam hastam* in all their auctions of rapine, have ever set up to sale the goods of the conquered citizen to such an enormous amount. . . .

These Roman confiscators, who were yet only in the elements of tyranny, and were not instructed in the rights of men to exercise all sorts of cruelties on each other without provocation, thought it necessary to spread a sort of color over their injustice. They considered the vanquished party as composed of traitors, who had borne arms, or otherwise had acted with hostility, against the commonwealth. They regarded them as persons who had forfeited their property by their crimes. With you, in your improved state of the human mind, there was no such formality. You seized upon five millions sterling of annual rent, and turned forty or fifty thousand human creatures out of their houses, because "such was your pleasure." The tyrant Harry the Eighth of England, as he was not better enlightened than the Roman Mariuses and Syllas, and had not studied in your new schools, did not know what an effectual instrument of despotism was to be found in that grand magazine of offensive weapons, the rights of men. When he resolved to rob the abbeys, as the club of the Jacobins have robbed all the ecclesiastics, he began by setting on foot a commission to examine into the crimes and abuses which prevailed in those communities. As it might be expected, his commission reported truths, exaggerations, and falsehoods. But truly or falsely, it reported abuses and offences. However, as abuses might be corrected, as every crime of persons does not infer a forfeiture with regard to communities, and as property, in that dark age, was not discovered to be a creature of prejudice, all those abuses (and there were enough of them) were hardly thought sufficient ground for such a confiscation as it was for his purposes to make. He therefore procured the formal surrender of these estates. All these operose proceedings were adopted by one of the most decided tyrants in the rolls of history, as necessary preliminaries, before he could venture, by bribing the members of his two servile Houses with a share of the spoil, and holding out to them an eternal immunity from taxation, to demand a confirmation of his iniquitous proceedings by an act of Parliament. Had fate reserved him to our times, four technical terms would have done his business, and saved him all this trouble; he needed nothing more than one short form of incantation:—*"Philosophy, Light, Liberality, the Rights of Men."*

I can say nothing in praise of those acts of tyranny, which no voice has hitherto ever commended under any of their false colors; yet in these false colors an homage was paid by despotism to justice. The power which was above all fear and all remorse was not set above all shame. Whilst shame keeps its watch, virtue is not wholly extinguished in the heart, nor will moderation be utterly exiled from the minds of tyrants. . . .

When all the frauds, impostures, violences, rapines, burnings, murders, confiscations, compulsory paper currencies, and every description of tyranny and cruelty employed to bring about and to uphold this Revolution have their natural effect, that is, to shock the moral sentiments of all virtuous and sober minds, the abettors of this philosophic system immediately strain their throats in a declamation against the old monarchical government of France. When they have rendered that deposed power sufficiently black, they then proceed in argument, as if all those who disapprove of their new abuses must of course be partisans of the old—that those who reprobate their crude and violent schemes of liberty ought to be treated as advocates for servitude. I admit that their necessities do compel them to this base and contemptible fraud. Nothing can reconcile men to their proceedings and projects but the supposition that there is no third option between them and some tyranny as odious as can be furnished by the records of history or by the invention of poets. This prattling of theirs hardly deserves the name of sophistry. It is nothing but plain impudence. Have these gentlemen never heard, in the whole circle of the worlds of theory and practice, of anything between the despotism of the monarch and the despotism of the multitude? Have they never heard of a monarchy directed by laws, controlled and balanced by the great hereditary wealth and hereditary dignity of a nation, and both again controlled by a judicious check from the reason and feeling of the people at large, acting by a suitable and permanent organ? Is it, then, impossible that a man may be found who, without criminal ill intention or pitiable absurdity, shall prefer such a mixed and tempered government to either of the extremes—and who may repute that nation to be destitute of all wisdom and of all virtue, which, having in its choice to obtain such a government with ease, *or rather to confirm it when actually possessed*, thought proper to commit a thousand crimes, and to subject their country to a thousand evils, in order to avoid it? Is it, then, a truth so universally acknowledged, that a pure democracy is the only tolerable form into which human society can be thrown, that a man is not permitted to hesitate about its merits, without the suspicion of being a friend to tyranny, that is, of being a foe to mankind?

I do not know under what description to class the present ruling authority in France. It affects to be a pure democracy, though I think it in a direct train of becoming shortly a mischievous and ignoble oligarchy. But for the present I admit it to be a contrivance of the nature and effect of what it pretends to. I reprobate no form of government merely upon abstract principles. There may be situations in which the purely democratic form will become necessary. There may be some (very few, and very particularly circumstanced) where it would be clearly desirable. This I do not take to be the case of France, or of any other great country. Until now, we have seen no examples of considerable democracies. The ancients were better acquainted with them. Not being wholly unread in the authors who had seen the most of those constitutions, and who best understood them, I cannot help concurring with their opinion, that an absolute democracy no more than absolute monarchy is to be reckoned among the legitimate forms of government. They think it rather the corruption and degeneracy than the sound constitution of a republic. If I recollect rightly, Aristotle observes, that a democracy has many striking points of resemblance with a tyranny. Of this I am certain, that in a democracy the majority of the citizens is capable of exercising the most cruel oppressions upon the minority, whenever strong divisions prevail in that kind of polity, as they often must—and that oppression of the minority will extend to far greater numbers, and will be carried on with much greater fury, than can almost ever be apprehended from the dominion of a single sceptre. In such a popular persecution, individual sufferers are in a much more deplorable condition than in any other. Under a cruel prince they have the balmy compassion of mankind to assuage the smart of their wounds, they have the plaudits of the people to animate their generous constancy under their sufferings: but those who are subjected to wrong under multitudes are deprived of all external consolation; they seem deserted by mankind, overpowered by a conspiracy of their whole species. . . .

Your government in France, though usually, and I think justly, reputed the best of the unqualified or ill-qualified monarchies, was still full of abuses. These abuses accumulated in a length of time, as they must accumulate in every monarchy not under the constant inspection of a popular representative. I am no stranger to the faults and defects of the subverted government of France; and I think I am not inclined by nature or policy to make a panegyric upon anything which is a just and natural object of censure. But the question is not now of the vices of that monarchy, but of its existence. Is it, then, true, that the French government was such as to be incapable or undeserving of reform, so that it was of absolute necessity the whole fabric should be at once pulled down, and the area cleared for the erection of a theoretic, experimental edifice in its place? All France was of a different opinion in the beginning of the year 1789. The instructions to the representatives to the States-General, from every district in that kingdom, were filled with projects for the reformation of that government, without the remotest suggestion of a design to destroy it. Had such a design been then even insinuated, I believe there would have been but one voice, and that voice for rejecting it with scorn and horror. Men have been sometimes led by degrees, sometimes hurried, into things of which, if they could have seen the whole together, they never would have permitted the most remote approach. When those instructions were given, there was no question but that abuses existed, and that they demanded a reform: nor is there now. In the interval between the instructions and the Revolution things changed their shape; and in consequence of that change, the true question at present is, whether those who would have reformed or those who have destroyed are in the right.

To hear some men speak of the late monarchy of France, you would imagine that they were talking of Persia bleeding under the ferocious sword of Thamas Kouli Khân—or at least describing the barbarous anarchic despotism of Turkey, where the finest countries in the most genial climates in the world are wasted by peace more than any countries have been worried by war, where arts are unknown, where manufactures languish, where science is extinguished, where agriculture decays, where the human race itself melts away and perishes under the eye of the observer. Was this the case of France? I have no way of determining the question but by a reference to facts. Facts do not support this resemblance. Along with much evil, there is some good in monarchy itself; and some corrective to its evil from religion, from laws, from manners, from opinions, the French monarchy must have received, which rendered it (though by no means a free, and therefore by no means a good constitution) a despotism rather in appearance than in reality. . . .

Indeed, when I consider the face of the kingdom of France, the multitude and opulence of her cities, the useful magnificence of her spacious high-roads and bridges, the opportunity of her artificial canals and navigations opening the conveniences of maritime communication through a solid continent of so immense an extent—when I turn my eyes to the stupendous works of her ports and harbors, and to her whole naval apparatus, whether for war or trade—when I bring before my view the number of her fortifications, constructed with so bold and masterly a skill, and made and maintained at so prodigious a charge, presenting an armed front and impenetrable barrier to her enemies upon every side—when I recollect how very small a part of that extensive region is without cultivation, and to what complete perfection the culture of many of the best productions of the earth have been brought in France—when I reflect on the excellence of her manufactures and fabrics, second to none but ours, and in some particulars not second—when I contemplate the grand foundations of charity, public and private—when I survey the state of all the arts that beautify and polish life—when I reckon the men she has bred for extending her fame in war, her able statesmen, the multitude of her profound lawyers and theologians, her philosophers, her critics, her historians and antiquaries, her poets and her orators, sacred and profane—I behold in all this something which awes and commands the imagination, which checks the mind on the brink of precipitate and indiscriminate censure, and which demands that we should very seriously examine what and how great are the latent vices that could authorize us at once to level so spacious a fabric with the ground. I do not recognize in this view of things the despotism of Turkey. Nor do I discern the character of a government that has been on the whole so oppressive, or so corrupt, or so negligent, as to be utterly unfit *for all reformation.* I must think such a government well deserved to have its excellences heightened, its faults corrected, and its capacities improved into a British Constitution. . . .

The advocates for this Revolution, not satisfied with exaggerating the vices of their ancient government, strike at the fame of their country itself, by painting almost all that could have attracted the attention of strangers, I mean their nobility and their clergy, as objects of horror. If this were only a libel, there had not been much in it. But it has practical consequences. Had your nobility and gentry, who formed the great body of your landed men and the whole of your military officers, resembled those of Germany, at the period when the Hanse towns were necessitated to confederate against the nobles in defence of their property—had they been like the Orsini and Vitelli in Italy, who used to sally from their fortified dens to rob the trader and traveller—had they been such as the Mamelukes in Egypt, or the Nayres on the coast of Malabar—I do admit that too critical an inquiry might not be advisable into the means of freeing the world from such a nuisance. The statues of Equity and Mercy might be veiled for a moment. The tenderest minds, confounded with the dreadful exigence in which morality submits to the suspension of its own rules in favor of its own principles, might turn aside whilst fraud and violence were accomplishing the destruction of a pretended nobility, which disgraced, whilst it persecuted, human nature. The persons most abhorrent from blood and treason and arbitrary confiscation might remain silent spectators of this civil war between the vices.

But did the privileged nobility who met under the king's precept at Versailles in 1789, or their constituents, deserve to be looked on as the Nayres or Mamelukes of this age, or as the Orsini and Vitelli of ancient times? If I had then asked the question, I should have passed for a madman. What have they since done, that they were to be driven into exile, that their persons should be hunted about, mangled, and tortured, their families dispersed, their houses laid in ashes, and that their order should be abolished, and the memory of it, if possible, extinguished, by ordaining them to change the very names by which they were usually known? Read their instructions to their representatives. They breathe the spirit of liberty as warmly, and they recommend reformation as strongly, as any other order. Their privileges relative to contribution were voluntarily surrendered; as the king, from the beginning, surrendered all pretence to a right of taxation. Upon a free constitution there was but one opinion in France. The absolute monarchy was at an end. It breathed its last without a groan, without struggle, without convulsion. All the struggle, all the dissension, arose afterwards, upon the preference of a despotic democracy to a government of reciprocal control. The triumph of the victorious party was over the principles of a British Constitution. . . .

I do not pretend to know France as correctly as some others; but I have endeavored through my whole life to make myself acquainted with human nature—otherwise I should be unfit to take even my humble part in the service of mankind. In that study I could not pass by a vast portion of our nature as it appeared modified in a country but twenty-four miles from the shore of this island. On my best observation, compared with my best inquiries, I found your nobility for the greater part composed of men of a high spirit, and of a delicate sense of honor, both with regard to themselves individually, and with regard to their whole corps, over whom they kept, beyond what is common in other countries, a censorial eye. They were tolerably well bred; very officious, humane, and hospitable; in their conversation frank and open; with a good military tone; and reasonably tinctured with literature, particularly of the authors in their own language. Many had pretensions far above this description. . . .

As to their behavior to the inferior classes, they appeared to me to comport themselves towards them with good-nature, and with something more nearly approaching to familiarity than is generally practised with us in the intercourse between the higher and lower ranks of life. To strike any person, even in the most abject condition, was a thing in a manner unknown, and would be highly disgraceful. Instances of other ill-treatment of the humble part of the community were rare; and as to attacks made upon the property or the personal liberty of the commons, I never heard of any whatsoever from *them*—nor, whilst the laws were in vigor under the ancient government, would such tyranny in subjects have been permitted. As men of landed estates, I had no fault to find with their conduct, though much to reprehend, and much to wish changed, in many of the old tenures. Where the letting of their land was by rent, I could not discover that their agreements with their farmers were oppressive; nor when they were in partnership with the farmer, as often was the case, have I heard that they had taken the lion's share. The proportions seemed not inequitable. There might be exceptions, but certainly they were exceptions only. I have no reason to believe that in these respects the landed noblesse of France were worse than the landed gentry of this country—certainly in no respect more vexatious than the landholders, not noble, of their own nation. In cities the nobility had no manner of power; in the country very little. You know, Sir, that much of the civil government, and the police in the most essential parts, was not in the hands of that nobility which presents itself first to our consideration. The revenue, the system and collection of which were the most grievous parts of the French government, was not administered by the men of the sword; nor were they answerable for the vices of its principle, or the vexations, where any such existed, in its management.

Denying, as I am well warranted to do, that the nobility had any considerable share in the oppression of the people, in cases in which real oppression existed, I am ready to admit that they were not without considerable faults and errors. A foolish imitation of the worst part of the manners of England, which impaired their natural character, without substituting in its place what perhaps they meant to copy, has certainly rendered them worse than formerly they were. Habitual dissoluteness of manners, continued beyond the pardonable period of life, was more common amongst them than it is with us; and it reigned with the less hope of remedy, though possibly with something of less mischief, by being covered with more exterior decorum. They countenanced too much that licentious philosophy which has helped to bring on their ruin. There was another error amongst them more fatal. Those of the commons who approached to or exceeded many of the nobility in point of wealth were not fully admitted to the rank and estimation which wealth, in reason and good policy, ought to bestow in every country—though I think not equally with that of other nobility. The two kinds of aristocracy were too punctiliously kept asunder: less so, however, than in Germany and some other nations.

This separation, as I have already taken the liberty of suggesting to you, I conceive to be one principal cause of the destruction of the old nobility. The military, particularly, was too exclusively reserved for men of family. But, after all, this was an error of opinion, which a conflicting opinion would have rectified. A permanent Assembly, in which the commons had their share of power, would soon abolish whatever was too invidious and insulting in these distinctions; and even the faults in the morals of the nobility would have been probably corrected, by the greater varieties of occupation and pursuit to which a constitution by orders would have given rise.

All this violent cry against the nobility I take to be a mere work of art. To be honored and even privileged by the laws, opinions, and inveterate usages of our country, growing out of the prejudice of ages, has nothing to provoke horror and indignation in any man. Even to be too tenacious of those privileges is not absolutely a crime. The strong struggle in every individual to preserve possession of what he has found to belong to him, and to distinguish him, is one of the securities against injustice and despotism implanted in our nature. It operates as an instinct to secure property, and to preserve communities in a settled state. What is there to shock in this? Nobility is a graceful ornament to the civil order. It is the Corinthian capital of polished society. . . . It is, indeed, one sign of a liberal and benevolent mind to incline to it with some sort of partial propensity. He feels no ennobling principle in his own heart, who wishes to level all the artificial institutions which have been adopted for giving a body to opinion and permanence to fugitive esteem. It is a sour, malignant, envious disposition, without taste for the reality, or for any image or representation of virtue, that sees with joy the unmerited fall of what had long flourished in splendor and in honor. I do not like to see anything destroyed, any void produced in society, any ruin on the face of the land. It was therefore with no disappointment or dissatisfaction that my inquiries and observations did not present to me any incorrigible vices in the noblesse of France, or any abuse which could not be removed by a reform very short of abolition.

Your noblesse did not deserve punishment; but to degrade is to punish.

It was with the same satisfaction I found that the result of my inquiry concerning your clergy was not dissimilar. It is no soothing news to my ears, that great bodies of men are incurably corrupt. It is not with much credulity I listen to any, when they speak evil of those whom they are going to plunder. I rather suspect that vices are feigned or exaggerated, when profit is looked for in their punishment. An enemy is a bad witness; a robber is a worse. Vices and abuses there were undoubtedly in that order, and must be. It was an old establishment, and not frequently revised. But I saw no crimes in the individuals that merited confiscation of their substance, nor those cruel insults and degradations, and that unnatural persecution, which have been substituted in the place of meliorating regulation.

If there had been any just cause for this new religious persecution, the atheistic libellers, who act as trumpeters to animate the populace to plunder, do not love anybody so much as not to dwell with complacence on the vices of the existing clergy. This they have not done. They find themselves obliged to rake into the histories of former ages (which they have ransacked with a malignant and profligate industry) for every instance of oppression and persecution which has been made by that body or in its favor, in order to justify, upon very iniquitous because very illogical principles of retaliation, their own persecutions and their own cruelties. After destroying all other genealogies and family distinctions, they invent a sort of pedigree of crimes. It is not very just to chastise men for the offences of their natural ancestors; but to take the fiction of ancestry in a corporate succession, as a ground for punishing men who have no relation to guilty acts, except in names and general descriptions, is a sort of refinement in injustice belonging to the philosophy of this enlightened age. The Assembly punishes men, many, if not most, of whom abhor the violent conduct of ecclesiastics in former times as much as their present persecutors can do, and who would be as loud and as strong in the expression of that sense, if they were not well aware of the purposes for which all this declamation is employed.

Corporate bodies are immortal for the good of the members, but not for their punishment. Nations themselves are such corporations. As well might we in England think of waging inexpiable war upon all Frenchmen for the evils which they have brought upon us in the several periods of our mutual hostilities. You might, on your part, think yourselves justified in falling upon all Englishmen on account of the unparalleled calamities brought upon the people of France by the unjust invasions of our Henrys and our Edwards. Indeed, we should be mutually justified in this exterminatory war upon each other, full as much as you are in the unprovoked persecution of your present countrymen, on account of the conduct of men of the same name in other times.

We do not draw the moral lessons we might from history. On the contrary, without care it may be used to vitiate our minds and to destroy our happiness. In history a great volume is unrolled for our instruction, drawing the materials of future wisdom from the past errors and infirmities of mankind. It may, in the perversion, serve for a magazine, furnishing offensive and defensive weapons for parties in Church and State, and supplying the means of keeping alive or reviving dissensions and animosities, and adding fuel to civil fury. History consists, for the greater part, of the miseries brought upon the world by pride, ambition, avarice, revenge, lust, sedition, hypocrisy, ungoverned zeal, and all the train of disorderly appetites, which shake the public with the same

> *"troublous storms that toss*
> *The private state, and render life unsweet."*

These vices are the *causes* of those storms. Religion, morals, laws, prerogatives, privileges, liberties, rights of men, are the *pretexts*. The pretexts are always found in some specious appearance of a real good. You would not secure men from tyranny and sedition by rooting out of the mind the principles to which these fraudulent pretexts apply? If you did, you would root out everything that is valuable in the human breast. As these are the pretexts, so the ordinary actors and instruments in great public evils are kings, priests, magistrates, senates, parliaments, national assemblies, judges, and captains. You would not cure the evil by resolving that there should be no more monarchs, nor ministers of state, nor of the Gospel—no interpreters of law, no general officers, no public councils. You might change the names: the things in some shape must remain. A certain *quantum* of power must always exist in the community, in some hands, and under some appellation. Wise men will apply their remedies to vices, not to names—to the causes of evil, which are permanent, not to the occasional organs by which they act, and the transitory modes in which they appear. Otherwise you will be wise historically, a fool in practice. Seldom have two ages the same fashion in their pretexts, and the same modes of mischief. Wickedness is a little more inventive. Whilst you are discussing fashion, the fashion is gone by. The very same vice assumes a new body. The spirit transmigrates; and, far from losing its principle of life by the change of its appearance, it is renovated in its new organs with the fresh vigor of a juvenile activity. It walks abroad, it continues its ravages, whilst you are gibbeting the carcass or demolishing the tomb. You are terrifying yourselves with ghosts and apparitions, whilst your house is the haunt of robbers. It is thus with all those who, attending only to the shell and husk of history, think they are waging war with intolerance, pride, and cruelty, whilst, under color of abhorring the ill principles of antiquated parties, they are authorizing and feeding the same odious vices in different factions, and perhaps in worse.

Your citizens of Paris formerly had lent themselves as the ready instruments to slaughter the followers of Calvin, at the infamous massacre of St. Bartholomew. What should we say to those who could think of retaliating on the Parisians of this day the abominations and horrors of that time? . . .

If your clergy, or any clergy, should show themselves vicious beyond the fair bounds allowed to human infirmity, and to those professional faults which can hardly be separated from professional virtues, though their vices never can countenance the exercise of oppression, I do admit that they would naturally have the effect of abating very much of our indignation against the tyrants who exceed measure and justice in their punishment. I can allow in clergymen, through all their divisions, some tenaciousness of their own opinion, some overflowings of zeal for its propagation, some predilection to their own state and office, some attachment to the interest of their own corps, some preference to those who listen with docility to their doctrines beyond those who scorn and deride them. I allow all this, because I am a man who have to deal with men, and who would not, through a violence of toleration, run into the greatest of all intolerance. I must bear with infirmities, until they fester into crimes.

Undoubtedly, the natural progress of the passions, from frailty to vice, ought to be prevented by a watchful eye and a firm hand. But is it true that the body of your clergy had passed those limits of a just allowance? From the general style of your late publications of all sorts, one would be led to believe that your clergy in France were a sort of monsters: an horrible composition of superstition, ignorance, sloth, fraud, avarice, and tyranny. But is this true? Is it true that the lapse of time, the cessation of conflicting interests, the woeful experience of the evils resulting from party rage, have had no sort of influence gradually to meliorate their minds? Is it true that they were daily renewing invasions on the civil power, troubling the domestic quiet of their country, and rendering the operations of its government feeble and precarious? Is it true that the clergy of our times have pressed down the laity with an iron hand, and were in all places lighting up the fires of a savage persecution? Did they by every fraud endeavor to increase their estates? Did they use to exceed the due demands on estates that were their own? Or, rigidly screwing up right into wrong, did they convert a legal claim into a vexatious extortion? When not possessed of power, were they filled with the vices of those who envy it? Were they inflamed with a violent, litigious spirit of controversy? Goaded on with the ambition of intellectual sovereignty, were they ready to fly in the face of all magistracy, to fire churches, to massacre the priests of other descriptions, to pull down altars, and to make their way over the ruins of subverted governments to an empire of doctrine, sometimes flattering, sometimes forcing, the consciences of men from the jurisdiction of public institutions into a submission to their personal authority, beginning with a claim of liberty and ending with an abuse of power?

These, or some of these, were the vices objected, and not wholly without foundation, to several of the churchmen of former times, who belonged to the two great parties which then divided and distracted Europe.

If there was in France, as in other countries there visibly is, a great abatement, rather than any increase of these vices, instead of loading the present clergy with the crimes of other men and the odious character of other times, in common equity they ought to be praised, encouraged, and supported, in their departure from a spirit which disgraced their predecessors, and for having assumed a temper of mind and manners more suitable to their sacred function.

When my occasions took me into France, towards the close of the late reign, the clergy, under all their forms, engaged a considerable part of my curiosity. So far from finding (except from one set of men, not then very numerous, though very active) the complaints and discontents against that body which some publications had given me reason to expect, I perceived little or no public or private uneasiness on their account. On further examination, I found the clergy, in general, persons of moderate minds and decorous manners: I include the seculars, and the regulars of both sexes. I had not the good fortune to know a great many of the parochial clergy: but in general I received a perfectly good account of their morals, and of their attention to their duties. With some of the higher clergy I had a personal acquaintance, and of the rest in that class a very good means of information. They were almost all of them persons of noble birth. They resembled others of their own rank; and where there was any difference, it was in their favor. They were more fully educated than the military noblesse—so as by no means to disgrace their profession by ignorance, or by want of fitness for the exercise of their authority. They seemed to me, beyond the clerical character, liberal and open, with the hearts of gentlemen and men of honor, neither insolent nor servile in their manners and conduct. They seemed to me rather a superior class—a set of men amongst whom you would not be surprised to find a Fénelon. I saw among the clergy in Paris (many of the description are not to be met with anywhere) men of great learning and candor; and I had reason to believe that this description was not confined to Paris. . . .

You had before your Revolution about a hundred and twenty bishops. A few of them were men of eminent sanctity, and charity without limit. When we talk of the heroic, of course we talk of rare virtue. I believe the instances of eminent depravity may be as rare amongst them as those of transcendent goodness. Examples of avarice and of licentiousness may be picked out, I do not question it, by those who delight in the investigation which leads to such discoveries. A man as old as I am will not be astonished that several, in every description, do not lead that perfect life of self-denial, with regard to wealth or to pleasure, which is wished for by all, by some expected, but by none exacted with more rigor than by those who are the most attentive to their own interests or the most indulgent to their own passions. When I was in France, I am certain that the number of vicious prelates was not great. Certain individuals among them, not distinguishable for the regularity of their lives, made some amends for their want of the severe virtues in their possession of the liberal, and were endowed with qualities which made them useful in the Church and State. I am told, that, with few exceptions, Louis the Sixteenth had been more attentive to character, in his promotions to that rank, than his immediate predecessor; and I believe (as some spirit of reform has prevailed through the whole reign) that it may be true. But the present ruling power has shown a disposition only to plunder the Church. It has punished *all* prelates: which is to favor the vicious, at least in point of reputation. It has made a degrading pensionary establishment, to which no man of liberal ideas or liberal condition will destine his children. It must settle into the lowest classes of the people. As with you the inferior clergy are not numerous enough for their duties, as these duties are beyond measure minute and toilsome, as you have left no middle classes of clergy at their ease, in future nothing of science or erudition can exist in the Gallican Church. To complete the project, without the least attention to the rights of patrons, the Assembly has provided in future an elective clergy: an arrangement which will drive out of the clerical profession all men of sobriety, all who can pretend to independence in their function or their conduct— and which will throw the whole direction of the public mind into the hands of a set of licentious, bold, crafty, factious, flattering wretches, of such condition and such habits of life as will make their contemptible pensions (in comparison of which the stipend of an exciseman is lucrative and honorable) an object of low and illiberal intrigue. Those officers whom they still call bishops are to be elected to a provision comparatively mean, through the same arts, (that is, electioneering arts,) by men of all religious tenets that are known or can be invented. The new lawgivers have not ascertained anything whatsoever concerning their qualifications, relative either to doctrine or to morals, no more than they have done with regard to the subordinate clergy; nor does it appear but that both the higher and the lower may, at their discretion, practise or preach any mode of religion or irreligion that they please. I do not yet see what the jurisdiction of bishops over their subordinates is to be, or whether they are to have any jurisdiction at all.

In short, Sir, it seems to me that this new ecclesiastical establishment is intended only to be temporary, and preparatory to the utter abolition, under any of its forms, of the Christian religion, whenever the minds of men are prepared for this last stroke against it by the accomplishment of the plan for bringing its ministers into universal contempt. They who will not believe that the philosophical fanatics who guide in these matters have long entertained such a design are utterly ignorant of their character and proceedings. These enthusiasts do not scruple to avow their opinion, that a state can subsist without any religion better than with one, and that they are able to supply the place of any good which may be in it by a project of their own—namely, by a sort of education they have imagined, founded in a knowledge of the physical wants of men, progressively carried to an enlightened self-interest, which, when well understood, they tell us, will identify with an interest more enlarged and public. . . .

Those of you who have robbed the clergy think that they shall easily reconcile their conduct to all Protestant nations, because the clergy whom they have thus plundered, degraded, and given over to mockery and scorn, are of the Roman Catholic, that is, of *their own* pretended persuasion. I have no doubt that some miserable bigots will be found here as well as elsewhere, who hate sects and parties different from their own more than they love the substance of religion, and who are more angry with those who differ from them in their particular plans and systems than displeased with those who attack the foundation of our common hope. These men will write and speak on the subject in the manner that is to be expected from their temper and character. . . .

The teachers who reformed our religion in England bore no sort of resemblance to your present reforming doctors in Paris. Perhaps they were (like those whom they opposed) rather more than could be wished under the influence of a party spirit; but they were most sincere believers; men of the most fervent and exalted piety; ready to die (as some of them did die) like true heroes in defence of their particular ideas of Christianity—as they would with equal fortitude, and more cheerfully, for that stock of general truth for the branches of which they contended with their blood. These men would have disavowed with horror those wretches who claimed a fellowship with them upon no other titles than those of their having pillaged the persons with whom they maintained controversies, and their having despised the common religion, for the purity of which they exerted themselves with a zeal which unequivocally bespoke their highest reverence for the substance of that system which they wished to reform. Many of their descendants have retained the same zeal, but (as less engaged in conflict) with more moderation. They do not forget that justice and mercy are substantial parts of religion. Impious men do not recommend themselves to their communion by iniquity and cruelty towards any description of their fellow-creatures.

We hear these new teachers continually boasting of their spirit of toleration. That those persons should tolerate all opinions, who think none to be of estimation, is a matter of small merit. Equal neglect is not impartial kindness. The species of benevolence which arises from contempt is no true charity. There are in England abundance of men who tolerate in the true spirit of toleration. They think the dogmas of religion, though in different degrees, are all of moment, and that amongst them there is, as amongst all things of value, a just ground of preference. They favor, therefore, and they tolerate. They tolerate, not because they despise opinions, but because they respect justice. They would reverently and affectionately protect all religions, because they love and venerate the great principle upon which they all agree, and the great object to which they are all directed. They begin more and more plainly to discern that we have all a common cause, as against a common enemy. They will not be so misled by the spirit of faction as not to distinguish what is done in favor of their subdivision from those acts of hostility which, through some particular description, are aimed at the whole corps in which they themselves, under another denomination, are included. . . .

You may suppose that we do not approve your confiscation of the revenues of bishops, and deans, and chapters, and parochial clergy possessing independent estates arising from land, because we have the same sort of establishment in England. . . . But it is in the principle of injustice that the danger lies, and not in the description of persons on whom it is first exercised. I see, in a country very near us, a course of policy pursued, which sets justice, the common concern of mankind, at defiance. With the National Assembly of France possession is nothing, law and usage are nothing. I see the National Assembly openly reprobate the doctrine of prescription, which one of the greatest of their own lawyers tells us, with great truth, is a part of the law of Nature. He tells us that the positive ascertainment of its limits, and its security from invasion, were among the causes for which civil society itself has been instituted. If prescription be once shaken, no species of property is secure, when it once becomes an object large enough to tempt the cupidity of indigent power. I see a practice perfectly correspondent to their contempt of this great fundamental part of natural law. . . . We entertain a high opinion of the legislative authority; but we have never dreamt that Parliaments had any right whatever to violate property, to overrule prescription, or to force a currency of their own fiction in the place of that which is real, and recognized by the law of nations. But you, who began with refusing to submit to the most moderate restraints, have ended by establishing an unheard-of despotism. . . .

Of all things, wisdom is the most terrified with epidemical fanaticism, because of all enemies it is that against which she is the least able to furnish any kind of resource. We cannot be ignorant of the spirit of atheistical fanaticism, that is inspired by a multitude of writings dispersed with incredible assiduity and expense, and by sermons delivered in all the streets and places of public resort in Paris. These writings and sermons have filled the populace with a black and savage atrocity of mind, which supersedes in them the common feelings of Nature, as well as all sentiments of morality and religion . . . The spirit of proselytism attends this spirit of fanaticism. They have societies to cabal and correspond at home and abroad for the propagation of their tenets. The republic of Berne, one of the happiest, the most prosperous, and the best-governed countries upon earth, is one of the great objects at the destruction of which they aim. I am told they have in some measure succeeded in sowing there the seeds of discontent. They are busy throughout Germany. Spain and Italy have not been untried. England is not left out of the comprehensive scheme of their malignant charity: and in England we find those who stretch out their arms to them, who recommend their example from more than one pulpit, and who choose, in more than one periodical meeting, publicly to correspond with them, to applaud them, and to hold them up as objects for imitation; who receive from them tokens of confraternity, and standards consecrated amidst their rites and mysteries; who suggest to them leagues of perpetual amity, at the very time when the power to which our Constitution has exclusively delegated the federative capacity of this kingdom may find it expedient to make war upon them.

It is not the confiscation of our Church property from this example in France that I dread, though I think this would be no trifling evil. The great source of my solicitude is, lest it should ever be considered in England as the policy of a state to seek a resource in confiscations of any kind, or that any one description of citizens should be brought to regard any of the others as their proper prey. Nations are wading deeper and deeper into an ocean of boundless debt. Public debts, which at first were a security to governments, by interesting many in the public tranquillity, are likely in their excess to become the means of their subversion. If governments provide for these debts by heavy impositions, they perish by becoming odious to the people. If they do not provide for them, they will be undone by the efforts of the most dangerous of all parties: I mean an extensive, discontented moneyed interest, injured and not destroyed. The men who compose this interest look for their security, in the first instance, to the fidelity of government; in the second, to its power. If they find the old governments effete, worn out, and with their springs relaxed, so as not to be of sufficient vigor for their purposes, they may seek new ones that shall be possessed of more energy; and this energy will be derived, not from an acquisition of resources, but from a contempt of justice. Revolutions are favorable to confiscation; and it is impossible to know under what obnoxious names the next confiscations will be authorized. I am sure that the principles predominant in France extend to very many persons, and descriptions of persons, in all countries, who think their innoxious indolence their security. This kind of innocence in proprietors may be argued into inutility; and inutility into an unfitness for their estates. Many parts of Europe are in open disorder. In many others there is a hollow murmuring under ground; a confused movement is felt, that threatens a general earthquake in the political world. Already confederacies and correspondences of the most extraordinary nature are forming in several countries. In such a state of things we ought to hold ourselves upon our guard. In all mutations (if mutations must be) the circumstance which will serve most to blunt the edge of their mischief, and to promote what good may be in them, is, that they should find us with our minds tenacious of justice and tender of property.

But it will be argued, that this confiscation in France ought not to alarm other nations. They say it is not made from wanton rapacity; that it is a great measure of national policy, adopted to remove an extensive, inveterate, superstitious mischief.—It is with the greatest difficulty that I am able to separate policy from justice. Justice is itself the great standing policy of civil society; and any eminent departure from it, under any circumstances, lies under the suspicion of being no policy at all.

When men are encouraged to go into a certain mode of life by the existing laws, and protected in that mode as in a lawful occupation—when they have accommodated all their ideas and all their habits to it—when the law had long made their adherence to its rules a ground of reputation, and their departure from them a ground of disgrace and even of penalty —I am sure it is unjust in legislature, by an arbitrary act, to offer a sudden violence to their minds and their feelings, forcibly to degrade them from their state and condition, and to stigmatize with shame and infamy that character and those customs which before had been made the measure of their happiness and honor. If to this be added an expulsion from their habitations and a confiscation of all their goods, I am not sagacious enough to discover how this despotic sport made of the feelings, consciences, prejudices, and properties of men can be discriminated from the rankest tyranny. . . .

There is something else than the mere alternative of absolute destruction or unreformed existence. . . . This is, in my opinion, a rule of profound sense, and ought never to depart from the mind of an honest reformer. I cannot conceive how any man can have brought himself to that pitch of presumption, to consider his country as nothing but *carte blanche,* upon which he may scribble whatever he pleases. A man full of warm, speculative benevolence may wish his society otherwise constituted than he finds it; but a good patriot, and a true politician, always considers how he shall make the most of the existing materials of his country. A disposition to preserve, and an ability to improve, taken together, would be my standard of a statesman. . . .

There are moments in the fortune of states, when particular men are called to make improvements by great mental exertion. In those moments, even when they seem to enjoy the confidence of their prince and country, and to be invested with full authority, they have not always apt instruments. A politician, to do great things, looks for a *power,* what our workmen call a *purchase;* and if he finds that power, in politics as in mechanics, he cannot be at a loss to apply it. In the monastic institutions, in my opinion, was found a great *power* for the mechanism of politic benevolence. There were revenues with a public direction; there were men wholly set apart and dedicated to public purposes, without any other than public ties and public principles—men without the possibility of converting the estate of the community into a private fortune —men denied to self-interests, whose avarice is for some community—men to whom personal poverty is honor, and implicit obedience stands in the place of freedom. In vain shall a man look to the possibility of making such things when he wants them. The winds blow as they list. These institutions are the products of enthusiasm; they are the instruments of wisdom. Wisdom cannot create materials; they are the gifts of Nature or of chance; her pride is in the use. The perennial existence of bodies corporate and their fortunes are things particularly suited to a man who has long views—who meditates designs that require time in fashioning, and which propose duration when they are accomplished. He is not deserving to rank high, or even to be mentioned in the order of great statesmen, who, having obtained the command and direction of such a power as existed in the wealth, the discipline, and the habits of such corporations as those which you have rashly destroyed, cannot find any way of converting it to the great and lasting benefit of his country. On the view of this subject, a thousand uses suggest themselves to a contriving mind. To destroy any power growing wild from the rank productive force of the human mind is almost tantamount, in the moral world, to the destruction of the apparently active properties of bodies in the material. . . . Did fifty thousand persons, whose mental and whose bodily labor you might direct, and so many hundred thousand a year of a revenue, which was neither lazy nor superstitious, appear too big for your abilities to wield? Had you no way of using the men, but by converting monks into pensioners? Had you no way of turning the revenue to account, but through the improvident resource of a spendthrift sale? If you were thus destitute of mental funds, the proceeding is in its natural course. Your politicians do not understand their trade; and therefore they sell their tools.

But the institutions savor of superstition in their very principle; and they nourish it by a permanent and standing influence.—This I do not mean to dispute; but this ought not to hinder you from deriving from superstition itself any resources which may thence be furnished for the public advantage. You derive benefits from many dispositions and many passions of the human mind which are of as doubtful a color, in the moral eye, as superstition itself. It was your business to correct and mitigate everything which was noxious in this passion, as in all the passions. But is superstition the greatest of all possible vices? In its possible excess I think it becomes a very great evil. It is, however, a moral subject, and of course admits of all degrees and all modifications. Superstition is the religion of feeble minds; and they must be tolerated in an intermixture of it, in some trifling or some enthusiastic shape or other, else you will deprive weak minds of a resource found necessary to the strongest. The body of all true religion consists, to be sure, in obedience to the will of the Sovereign of the world, in a confidence in His declarations, and in imitation of His perfections. The rest is our own. . . . Wisdom is not the most severe corrector of folly. They are the rival follies which mutually wage so unrelenting a war, and which make so cruel a use of their advantages, as they can happen to engage the immoderate vulgar, on the one side or the other, in their quarrels. Prudence would be neuter; but if, in the contention between fond attachment and fierce antipathy concerning things in their nature not made to produce such heats, a prudent man were obliged to make a choice of what errors and excesses of enthusiasm he would condemn or bear, perhaps he would think the superstition which builds to be more tolerable than that which demolishes—that which adorns a country, than that which deforms it—that which endows, than that which plunders—that which disposes to mistaken beneficence, than that which stimulates to real injustice—that which leads a man to refuse to himself lawful pleasures, than that which snatches from others the scanty subsistence of their self-denial. Such, I think, is very nearly the state of the question between the ancient founders of monkish superstition and the superstition of the pretended philosophers of the hour.

For the present I postpone all consideration of the supposed public profit of the sale, which, however, I conceive to be perfectly delusive. I shall here only consider it as a transfer of property. On the policy of that transfer I shall trouble you with a few thoughts.

In every prosperous community something more is produced than goes to the immediate support of the producer. This surplus forms the income of the landed capitalist. It will be spent by a proprietor who does not labor. But this idleness is itself the spring of labor, this repose the spur to industry. The only concern for the state is, that the capital taken in rent from the land should be returned again to the industry from whence it came, and that its expenditure should be with the least possible detriment to the morals of those who expend it and to those of the people to whom it is returned.

In all the views of receipt, expenditure, and personal employment, a sober legislator would carefully compare the possessor whom he was recommended to expel with the stranger who was proposed to fill his place. Before the inconveniences are incurred which *must* attend all violent revolutions in property through extensive confiscation, we ought to have some rational assurance that the purchasers of the confiscated property will be in a considerable degree more laborious, more virtuous, more sober, less disposed to extort an unreasonable proportion of the gains of the laborer, or to consume on themselves a larger share than is fit for the measure of an individual—or that they should be qualified to dispense the surplus in a more steady and equal mode, so as to answer the purposes of a politic expenditure, than the old possessors, call those possessors bishops, or canons, or commendatory abbots, or monks, or what you please. The monks are lazy. Be it so. Suppose them no otherwise employed than by singing in the choir. They are as usefully employed as those who neither sing nor say—as usefully even as those who sing upon the stage. They are as usefully employed as if they worked from dawn to dark in the innumerable servile, degrading, unseemly, unmanly, and often most unwholesome and pestiferous occupations to which by the social economy so many wretches are inevitably doomed. If it were not generally pernicious to disturb the natural course of things, and to impede in any degree the great wheel of circulation which is turned by the strangely directed labor of these unhappy people, I should be infinitely more inclined forcibly to rescue them from their miserable industry than violently to disturb the tranquil repose of monastic quietude. Humanity, and perhaps policy, might better justify me in the one than in the other. It is a subject on which I have often reflected, and never reflected without feeling from it. I am sure that no consideration, except the necessity of submitting to the yoke of luxury and the despotism of fancy, who in their own imperious way will distribute the surplus product of the soil, can justify the toleration of such trades and employments in a well-regulated state. But for this purpose of distribution, it seems to me that the idle expenses of monks are quite as well directed as the idle expenses of us lay loiterers.

When the advantages of the possession and of the project are on a par, there is no motive for a change. But in the present case, perhaps, they are not upon a par, and the difference is in favor of the possession. It does not appear to me that the expenses of those whom you are going to expel do in fact take a course so directly and so generally leading to vitiate and degrade and render miserable those through whom they pass as the expenses of those favorites whom you are intruding into their houses. Why should the expenditure of a great landed property, which is a dispersion of the surplus product of the soil, appear intolerable to you or to me, when it takes its course through the accumulation of vast libraries, which are the history of the force and weakness of the human mind —through great collections of ancient records, medals, and coins, which attest and explain laws and customs—through paintings and statues, that, by imitating Nature, seem to extend the limits of creation—through grand monuments of the dead, which continue the regards and connections of life beyond the grave—through collections of the specimens of Nature, which become a representative assembly of all the classes and families of the world, that by disposition facilitate, and by exciting curiosity open, the avenues to science? If by great permanent establishments all these objects of expense are better secured from the inconstant sport of personal caprice and personal extravagance, are they worse than if the same tastes prevailed in scattered individuals? Does not the sweat of the mason and carpenter, who toil in order to partake the sweat of the peasant, flow as pleasantly and as salubriously in the construction and repair of the majestic edifices of religion as in the painted booths and sordid sties of vice and luxury? as honorably and as profitably in repairing those sacred works which grow hoary with innumerable years as on the momentary receptacles of transient voluptuousness—in opera-houses, and brothels, and gaming-houses, and club-houses, and obelisks in the Champ de Mars? Is the surplus product of the olive and the vine worse employed in the frugal sustenance of persons whom the fictions of a pious imagination raise to dignity by construing in the service of God than in pampering the innumerable multitude of those who are degraded by being made useless domestics, subservient to the pride of man? Are the decorations of temples an expenditure less worthy a wise man than ribbons, and laces, and national cockades, and petit maisons, and petit soupers, and all the innumerable fopperies and follies in which opulence sports away the burden of its superfluity?

We tolerate even these—not from love of them, but for fear of worse. We tolerate them, because property and liberty, to a degree, require that toleration. But why proscribe the other, and surely, in every point of view, the more laudable use of estates? Why, through the violation of all property, through an outrage upon every principle of liberty, forcibly carry them from the better to the worse?

This comparison between the new individuals and the old corps is made upon a supposition that no reform could be made in the latter. But, in a question of reformation, I always consider corporate bodies, whether sole or consisting of many, to be much more susceptible of a public direction, by the power of the state, in the use of their property, and in the regulation of modes and habits of life in their members, than private citizens ever can be, or perhaps ought to be; and this seems to me a very material consideration for those who undertake anything which merits the name of a politic enterprise. . . .

A Letter

to

a Member of the National Assembly,

in

Answer to Some Objections to His

Book on French Affairs

1791

The success of Burke's *Reflections* made many Englishmen and Frenchmen aware for the first time of the dangers inherent in certain of the principles underlying the French Revolution. But the force of Burke's political argument and his literary eloquence also provoked a bitter counteroffensive. At least forty replies to the *Reflections* appeared in Britain alone. On the Continent one of the earliest rejoinders was a letter published on November 17, 1790, written by a member of the National Assembly, M. de Menonville. He expressed agreement with Burke's general principles and political viewpoint, but criticized him for not having offered an alternative plan of action. In January 1791, he answered this criticism by publishing *A Letter to a Member of the National Assembly.*

Burke declined on grounds of moral prudence to offer any plans to the National Assembly. "Permit me to say," he wrote, "that if I were as confident as I ought to be diffident in my own loose general ideas, I never should venture to broach them, if but at twenty leagues' distance from the centre of your affairs. I must see with my own eyes; I must in a manner touch with my own hands, not only the fixed, but momentary circumstances, before I could venture to suggest any political project whatsoever. I must know the power and disposition to accept, to execute, to persevere. I must see all the aids and all the obstacles. I must see the means of correcting the plan, where correctives would be wanted. I must see the things: I must see the men. Without a concurrence and adaptation of these to the design, the very best speculative projects might become not only useless but mischievous." Addressing himself directly to de Menonville, Burke concluded: "Sir, the proposition of plans without an attention to circumstances is the very cause of all your misfortunes; and never shall you find me aggravating, by the infusion of any speculations of mine, the evils which have arisen from the speculation of others."

But the main purpose of his reply was to attack the widely held belief that the violence and excesses of the revolutionaries were merely accidents and blunders of well-intentioned men. Burke was by this time convinced that the men guiding the Revolution were corrupted in principle, and were prepared to destroy every vestige of traditional civil society in order to reconstruct the social order according to their speculative theories. As proof of his conviction, he noted that the revolutionists proposed to construct a new educational system, based upon Rousseau's theory of human nature.

Thirty-five years earlier, in his *Vindication of Natural Society* (1756), Burke had shown his intense dislike of theories of man's natural goodness in a supposed state of simple society. In his book reviews in the *Annual Register,* in 1759 and 1762, he had raised serious doubts about the practicality of Rousseau's theories, and had attacked his "paradoxes" as literary sensationalism. In the intervening years before the French Revolution Burke had looked with grave mistrust upon the character of Rousseau. Along with the rationalist philosophers of the Enlightenment, Rousseau had been the object of his attack in the *Reflections.* Burke had noted that "the paradoxes of eloquent writers, brought forth purely as a sport of fancy, to try their talents, to rouse attention, and to excite surprise," were being taken seriously by the revolutionists:

"These paradoxes become with them serious grounds of action, upon which they proceed in regulating the most important concerns of the state. Cicero ludicrously describes Cato as endeavoring to act in the commonwealth upon the school paradoxes which exercised the wits of the junior students in the Stoic philosophy. If this were true of Cato, these gentlemen copy after him in the manner of some persons who lived

about his time. . . . Mr. Hume told me that he had from Rousseau himself the secret of his principles of composition. That acute, though eccentric observer, had perceived, that, to strike and interest the public, the marvellous must be produced; that the marvellous of the heathen mythology had long since lost its effects; that giants, magicians, fairies, and heroes of romance, which succeeded, had exhausted the portion of credulity which belonged to their age; that now nothing was left to a writer but that species of the marvellous, which might be produced, and with as great an effect as ever, though in another way—that is, the marvellous in life, in manners, in characters, and in extraordinary situations, giving rise to new and unlooked-for strokes in politics and morals. I believe, that, were Rousseau alive, and in one of his lucid intervals, he would be shocked at the practical frenzy of his scholars, who in their paradoxes are servile imitators, and even in their incredulity discover an implicit faith.

Thus did Burke write in the *Reflections.* In his *Letter to a Member of the National Assembly,* his attack on Rousseau as a philosopher is the climax of his lifelong skepticism toward speculative theory based upon an assumed antithesis between "art" and "nature," and upon a system of ethics based on Romantic sensibility.

Sir—I had the honor to receive your letter of the 17th of November last, in which, with some exceptions, you are pleased to consider favorably the letter I have written on the affairs of France. . . .

As to the cavils which may be made on some part of my remarks with regard to the *gradations* in your new Constitution, you observe justly that they do not affect the substance of my objections. . . .

I published my thoughts on that Constitution, that my countrymen might be enabled to estimate the wisdom of the plans which were held out to their imitation. . . .

I am unalterably persuaded that the attempt to oppress, degrade, impoverish, confiscate, and extinguish the original gentlemen and landed property of a whole nation cannot be justified under any form it may assume. . . .

The indulgence of a sort of undefined hope, an obscure confidence, that some lurking remains of virtue, some degree of shame, might exist in the breasts of the oppressors of France, has been among the causes which have helped to bring on the common ruin of king and people. There is no

safety for honest men, but by believing all possible evil of evil
men, and by acting with promptitude, decision, and steadiness
on that belief. I well remember, at every epocha of this wonderful history, in every scene of this tragic business, that,
when your sophistic usurpers were laying down mischievous
principles, and even applying them in direct resolutions, it
was the fashion to say that they never intended to execute
those declarations in their rigor. This made men careless in
their opposition, and remiss in early precaution. By holding
out this fallacious hope, the imposters deluded sometimes one
description of men, and sometimes another, so that no means
of resistance were provided against them, when they came
to execute in cruelty what they had planned in fraud.

There are cases in which a man would be ashamed not to
have been imposed on. There is a confidence necessary to
human intercourse, and without which men are often more
injured by their own suspicions than they would be by the
perfidy of others. But when men whom we *know* to be wicked
impose upon us, we are something worse than dupes. When
we know them, their fair pretences become new motives for
distrust. There is one case, indeed, in which it would be
madness not to give the fullest credit to the most deceitful of
men—that is, when they make declarations of hostility against
us.

I find that some persons entertain other hopes, which I confess appear more specious than those by which at first so
many were deluded and disarmed. They flatter themselves
that the extreme misery brought upon the people by their
folly will at last open the eyes of the multitude, if not of their
leaders. Much the contrary, I fear. As to the leaders in this
system of imposture—you know that cheats and deceivers
never can repent. The fraudulent have no resource but in
fraud. They have no other goods in their magazine. They have
no virtue or wisdom in their minds, to which, in a disappointment concerning the profitable effects of fraud and cunning,
they can retreat. The wearing out of an old serves only to put
them upon the invention of a new delusion. Unluckily, too,
the credulity of dupes is as inexhaustible as the invention of
knaves. They never give people possession; but they always
keep them in hope. Your state doctors do not so much as pretend that any good whatsoever has hitherto been derived from
their operations, or that the public has prospered in any one
instance under their management. The nation is sick, very
sick, by their medicines. But the charlatan tells them that what

is past cannot be helped;—they have taken the draught, and they must wait its operation with patience;—that the first effects, indeed, are unpleasant, but that the very sickness is a proof that the dose is of no sluggish operation;—that sickness is inevitable in all constitutional revolutions;—that the body must pass through pain to ease;—that the prescriber is not an empiric who proceeds by vulgar experience, but one who grounds his practice on the sure rules of art, which cannot possibly fail. . . .

The people of France, almost generally, have been taught to look for other resources than those which can be derived from order, frugality, and industry. They are generally armed; and they are made to expect much from the use of arms. . . . Besides this, the retrograde order of society has something flattering to the dispositions of mankind. The life of adventurers, gamesters, gypsies, beggars, and robbers is not unpleasant. It requires restraint to keep men from falling into that habit. The shifting tides of fear and hope, the flight and pursuit, the peril and escape, the alternate famine and feast of the savage and the thief, after a time, render all course of slow, steady, progressive, unvaried occupation, and the prospect only of a limited mediocrity at the end of long labor, to the last degree tame, languid, and insipid. Those who have been once intoxicated with power, and have derived any kind of emolument from it, even though but for one year, never can willingly abandon it. They may be distressed in the midst of all their power; but they will never look to anything but power for their relief. . . .

The more active and stirring part of the lower orders having got government and the distribution of plunder into their hands, they will use its resources in each municipality to form a body of adherents. These rulers and their adherents will be strong enough to overpower the discontents of those who have not been able to assert their share of the spoil. The unfortunate adventurers in the cheating lottery of plunder will probably be the least sagacious or the most inactive and irresolute of the gang. If, on disappointment, they should dare to stir, they will soon be suppressed as rebels and mutineers by their brother rebels. . . .

From the forced repentance of invalid mutineers and disbanded thieves you can hope for no resource. Government itself, which ought to constrain the more bold and dexterous of these robbers, is their accomplice. . . .

Till the justice of the world is awakened, such as these will go on, without admonition, and without provocation, to every extremity. . . . They do not commit crimes for their designs; but they form designs that they may commit crimes. It is not their necessity, but their nature, that impels them. They are modern philosophers, which when you say of them, you express everything that is ignoble, savage, and hard-hearted.

Besides the sure tokens which are given by the spirit of their particular arrangements, there are some characteristic lineaments in the general policy of your tumultuous despotism, which, in my opinion, indicate, beyond a doubt, that no revolution whatsoever *in their disposition* is to be expected: I mean their scheme of educating the rising generation, the principles which they intend to instil and the sympathies which they wish to form in the mind at the season in which it is the most susceptible. Instead of forming their young minds to that docility, to that modesty, which are the grace and charm of youth, to an admiration of famous examples, and to an averseness to anything which approaches to pride, petulance, and self-conceit, (distempers to which that time of life is of itself sufficiently liable,) they artificially foment these evil dispositions, and even form them into springs of action. Nothing ought to be more weighed than the nature of books recommended by public authority. So recommended, they soon form the character of the age. Uncertain indeed is the efficacy, limited indeed is the extent, of a virtuous institution. But if education takes in *vice* as any part of its system, there is no doubt but that it will operate with abundant energy, and to an extent indefinite. The magistrate, who in favor of freedom thinks himself obliged to suffer all sorts of publications, is under a stricter duty than any other well to consider what sort of writers he shall authorize, and shall recommend by the strongest of all sanctions, that is, by public honors and rewards. He ought to be cautious how he recommends authors of mixed or ambiguous morality. He ought to be fearful of putting into the hands of youth writers indulgent to the peculiarities of their own complexion, lest they should teach the humors of the professor, rather than the principles of the science. He ought, above all, to be cautious in recommending any writer who has carried marks of a deranged understanding: for where there is no sound reason, there can be no real virtue; and madness is ever vicious and malignant.

The Assembly proceeds on maxims the very reverse of these. The Assembly recommends to its youth a study of the bold experimenters in morality. Everybody knows that there is a great dispute amongst their leaders, which of them is the best resemblance of Rousseau. In truth, they all resemble him. His blood they transfuse into their minds and into their manners. Him they study; him they meditate; him they turn over in all the time they can spare from the laborious mischief of the day or the debauches of the night. Rousseau is their canon of holy writ; in his life he is their canon of Polycletus; he is their standard figure of perfection. To this man and this writer, as a pattern to authors and to Frenchmen, the foundries of Paris are now running for statues, with the kettles of their poor and the bells of their churches. If an author had written like a great genius on geometry, though his practical and speculative morals were vicious in the extreme, it might appear that in voting the statue they honored only the geometrician. But Rousseau is a moralist or he is nothing. It is impossible, therefore, putting the circumstances together, to mistake their design in choosing the author with whom they have begun to recommend a course of studies.

Their great problem is, to find a substitute for all the principles which hitherto have been employed to regulate the human will and action. They find dispositions in the mind of such force and quality as may fit men, far better than the old morality, for the purposes of such a state as theirs, and may go much further in supporting their power and destroying their enemies. They have therefore chosen a selfish, flattering, seductive, ostentatious vice, in the place of plain duty. True humility, the basis of the Christian system, is the low, but deep and firm foundation of all real virtue. But this, as very painful in the practice, and little imposing in the appearance, they have totally discarded. Their object is to merge all natural and all social sentiment in inordinate vanity. In a small degree, and conversant in little things, vanity is of little moment. When full-grown, it is the worst of vices, and the occasional mimic of them all. It makes the whole man false. It leaves nothing sincere or trustworthy about him. His best qualities are poisoned and perverted by it, and operate exactly as the worst. When your lords had many writers as immoral as the object of their statue (such as Voltaire and others) they chose Rousseau, because in him that peculiar vice which they wished to erect into ruling virtue was by far the most conspicuous.

We have had the great professor and founder of *the philosophy of vanity* in England. As I had good opportunities of knowing his proceedings almost from day to day, he left

no doubt on my mind that he entertained no principle, either
to influence his heart or to guide his understanding, but *vanity*.
With this vice he was possessed to a degree little short of madness. It is from the same deranged, eccentric vanity, that this,
the insane Socrates of the National Assembly, was impelled
to publish a mad confession of his mad faults, and to attempt
a new sort of glory from bringing hardily to light the obscure
and vulgar vices which we know may sometimes be blended
with eminent talents. He has not observed on the nature of
vanity who does not know that it is omnivorous—that it has no
choice in its food—that it is fond to talk even of its own faults
and vices, and what will excite surprise and draw attention,
and what will pass at worst for openness and candor.

It was this abuse and perversion, which vanity makes even
of hypocrisy, which has driven Rousseau to record a life not
so much as checkered or spotted here and there with virtues,
or even distinguished by a single good action. It is such a life
he chooses to offer to the attention of mankind. It is such a life
that, with a wild defiance, he flings in the face of his Creator,
whom he acknowledges only to brave. Your Assembly, knowing how much more powerful example is found than precept,
has chosen this man (by his own account without a single virtue) for a model. To him they erect their first statue. From
him they commence their series of honors and distinctions.

It is that new-invented virtue which your masters canonize
that led their moral hero constantly to exhaust the stores of
his powerful rhetoric in the expression of universal benevolence, whilst his heart was incapable of harboring one spark
of common parental affection. Benevolence to the whole species, and want of feeling for every individual with whom the
professors come in contact, form the character of the new
philosophy. Setting up for an unsocial independence, this their
hero of vanity refuses the just price of common labor, as well
as the tribute which opulence owes to genius, and which,
when paid, honors the giver and the receiver; and then he
pleads his beggary as an excuse for his crimes. He melts with
tenderness for those only who touch him by the remotest relation, and then, without one natural pang, casts away, as a
sort of offal and excrement, the spawn of his disgustful
amours, and sends his children to the hospital of foundlings.
The bear loves, licks, and forms her young: but bears are not
philosophers. Vanity, however, finds its account in reversing
the train of our natural feelings. Thousands admire the senti-

mental writer; the affectionate father is hardly known in his parish.

Under this philosophic instructor in *the ethics of vanity*, they have attempted in France a regeneration of the moral constitution of man. Statesmen like your present rulers exist by everything which is spurious, fictitious, and false—by everything which takes the man from his house, and sets him on a stage—which makes him up an artificial creature, with painted, theatric sentiments, fit to be seen by the glare of candle-light, and formed to be contemplated at a due distance. Vanity is too apt to prevail in all of us, and in all countries. To the improvement of Frenchmen, it seems not absolutely necessary that it should be taught upon system. But it is plain that the present rebellion was its legitimate offspring, and it is piously fed by that rebellion with a daily dole.

If the system of institution recommended by the Assembly is false and theatric, it is because their system of government is of the same character. To that, and to that alone, it is strictly conformable. To understand either, we must connect the morals with the politics of the legislators. Your practical philosophers, systematic in everything, have wisely began at the source. As the relation between parents and children is the first among the elements of vulgar, natural morality, they erect statues to a wild, ferocious, low-minded, hard-hearted father, of fine general feelings—a lover of his kind, but a hater of his kindred. Your masters reject the duties of this vulgar relation, as contrary to liberty, as not founded in the social compact, and not binding according to the rights of men; because the relation is not, of course, the result of *free election* —never so on the side of the children, not always on the part of the parents.

The next relation which they regenerate by their statues to Rousseau is that which is next in sanctity to that of a father. They differ from those old-fashioned thinkers who considered pedagogues as sober and venerable characters, and allied to the parental. . . . In this age of light they teach the people that preceptors ought to be in the place of gallants. They systematically corrupt a very corruptible race, (for some time a growing nuisance amongst you,)—a set of pert, petulant literators, to whom, instead of their proper, but severe, unostentatious duties, they assign the brilliant part of men of wit and pleasure, of gay, young, military sparks, and danglers at toilets. They call on the rising generation in France to take a sympathy in the adventures and fortunes, and they endeavor to engage their sensibility on the side, of pedagogues who betray the most awful family trusts and vitiate their female pupils. They teach the people that the debauchers of virgins, almost in the arms of their parents, may be safe inmates in their house, and even fit guardians of the honor of those husbands who succeed legally to the office which the young literators had preoccupied without asking leave of law or conscience.

Thus they dispose of all the family relations of parents and children, husbands and wives. Through this same instructor, by whom they corrupt the morals, they corrupt the taste. Taste and elegance, though they are reckoned only among the smaller and secondary morals, yet are of no mean importance in the regulation of life. A moral taste is not of force to turn vice into virtue; but it recommends virtue with something like the blandishments of pleasure, and it infinitely abates the evils of vice. Rousseau, a writer of great force and vivacity, is totally destitute of taste in any sense of the word. Your masters, who are his scholars, conceive that all refinement has an aristocratic character. The last age had exhausted all its powers in giving a grace and nobleness to our natural appetites, and in raising them into a higher class and order than seemed justly to belong to them. Through Rousseau, your masters are resolved to destroy these aristocratic prejudices. The passion called love has so general and powerful an influence, it makes so much of the entertainment, and indeed so much of the occupation, of that part of life which decides the character forever, that the mode and the principles on which it engages the sympathy and strikes the imagination become of the utmost importance to the morals and manners of every society. Your rulers were well aware of this; and in their system of changing your manners to accommodate them to their politics, they found nothing so convenient as Rousseau. Through him they teach men to love after the fashion of philosophers: that is, they teach to men, to Frenchmen, a love without gallantry—a love without anything of that fine flower of youthfulness and gentility which places it, if not among the virtues, among the ornaments of life. Instead of this passion, naturally allied to grace and manners, they infuse into their youth an unfashioned, indelicate, sour, gloomy, ferocious medley of pedantry and lewdness—of metaphysical speculations blended with the coarsest sensuality. Such is the general morality of the passions to be found in their famous philosopher, in his famous work of philosophic gallantry, the *Nouvelle Éloise*.

When the fence from the gallantry of preceptors is broken down, and your families are no longer protected by decent pride and salutary domestic prejudice, there is but one step to a frightful corruption. The rulers in the National Assembly are in good hopes that the females of the first families in France may become an easy prey to dancing-masters, fiddlers, pattern-drawers, friseurs, and valets-de-chambre, and other active citizens of that description, who, having the entry into your houses, and being half domesticated by their situation, may be blended with you by regular and irregular relations. By a law they have made these people their equals. By adopting the sentiments of Rousseau they have made them your rivals. In this manner these great legislators complete their plan of levelling, and establish their rights of men on a sure foundation.

I am certain that the writings of Rousseau lead directly to this kind of shameful evil. I have often wondered how he comes to be so much more admired and followed on the Continent than he is here. Perhaps a secret charm in the language may have its share in this extraordinary difference. We certainly perceive, and to a degree we feel, in this writer, a style glowing, animated, enthusiastic, at the same time that we find it lax, diffuse, and not in the best taste of composition—all the members of the piece being pretty equally labored and expanded, without any due selection or subordination of parts. He is generally too much on the stretch, and his manner has little variety. We cannot rest upon any of his works, though they contain observations which occasionally discover a considerable insight into human nature. But his doctrines, on the whole, are so inapplicable to real life and manners, that we never dream of drawing from them any rule for laws or conduct, or for fortifying or illustrating anything by a reference to his opinions. . . .

Perhaps bold speculations are more acceptable because more new to you than to us, who have been long since satiated with them. We continue, as in the two last ages, to read, more generally than I believe is now done on the Continent, the authors of sound antiquity. These occupy our minds; they give us another taste and turn; and will not suffer us to be more than transiently amused with paradoxical morality. It is not that I consider this writer as wholly destitute of just notions. Amongst his irregularities, it must be reckoned that he is sometimes moral, and moral in a very sublime strain. But the *general spirit and tendency* of his works is mischievous—and the more mischievous for this mixture: for perfect depravity of sentiment is not reconcilable with eloquence; and the mind (though corruptible, not complexionally vicious) would reject and throw off with disgust a lesson of pure and unmixed evil. These writers make even virtue a pander to vice.

However, I less consider the author than the system of the Assembly in perverting morality through his means. This I confess makes me nearly despair of any attempt upon the minds of their followers, through reason, honor, or conscience. The great object of your tyrants is to destroy the gentlemen of France; and for that purpose they destroy, to the best of their power, all the effect of those relations which may render considerable men powerful or even safe. To destroy that order, they vitiate the whole community. That no means may exist of confederating against their tyranny, by the false sympathies of this *Nouvelle Éloise* they endeavor to subvert those principles of domestic trust and fidelity which form the discipline of social life. They propagate principles by which every servant may think it, if not his duty, at least his privilege, to betray his master. By these principles, every considerable father of a family loses the sanctuary of his house. . . . They destroy all the tranquillity and security of domestic life: turning the asylum of the house into a gloomy prison, where the father of the family must drag out a miserable existence, endangered in proportion to the apparent means of his safety—where he is worse than solitary in a crowd of domestics, and more apprehensive from his servants and inmates than from the hired, bloodthirsty mob without doors who are ready to pull him to the *lanterne*.

It is thus, and for the same end, that they endeavor to destroy that tribunal of conscience which exists independently of edicts and decrees. Your despots govern by terror. They know that he who fears God fears nothing else; and therefore they eradicate from the mind, through their Voltaire, their Helvétius, and the rest of that infamous gang, that only sort of fear which generates true courage. Their object is, that their fellow-citizens may be under the dominion of no awe but that of their Committee of Research and of their *lanterne*. . . .

An Appeal
from
the New to the Old Whigs,
in Consequence of Some Late
Discussions in Parliament
Relative to the
Reflections on the French Revolution
1791

Late in 1790 there was a general election in Britain, in which the Tories, under the younger Pitt, defeated the Whig minority. In order to win support from electors who favored an extensive reform of the House of Commons, and social changes in general, Charles James Fox and other liberal Whig leaders committed themselves increasingly to an endorsement of the changes made by the French Revolution. To Burke it appeared that in praising the events in France, his own party leaders were violating the great political principles of government inherited from the Revolution of 1688, to which the Whigs had traditionally adhered. He believed that such seventeenth-century Whigs as Sir John Hawles, General Stanhope, Sir Joseph Jekyl, and Sir Robert Eyre, who helped to bring about the Revolution of 1688, had also determined the constitutional form of the British government, and described 1688 as "that period of our history . . . when the constitution was settled on its actual foundation." Burke had always regarded the Rockingham Whigs as standing in a direct line of descent from the Whigs of 1688, by way of their successors—Shrewsbury, Sir Robert Walpole, the Pelhams, and Newcastle, all of whom believed in a constitutional hereditary monarchy, limited in its powers and prerogatives by the balanced orders of the Commons and Lords. To Burke, 1688 was a revolution "not made but prevented," that is, it prevented the executive branch, in the person of James II, from subverting the traditional balance of power between Crown, Commons, and Lords, in favor of the Crown. During the 1770's, apart from party politics, Burke's opposition to the extension of the prerogatives of George III was based upon precisely the same principle and interpretation of the British constitution. The Revolution of 1688 maintained the traditional structure of the English state, but qualified by positive law the condition under which the hereditary executive branch would be held, in having the King a member of the Church of England. It did not make the monarchy elective rather than hereditary. His views of the Revolution of 1688, and of the balanced powers of the English constitution, were unimpeachable articles of political faith to Burke during his entire public life.

But among the Rockingham Whigs there had always been individuals, led by Charles James Fox, whose opposition to monarchical power, like that of other liberal Whigs, had rested not upon a balance of power under the constitution, but upon a moderated version of the radical doctrine of popular sovereignty. These Whigs had little reverence for the Church or Crown, nor for Burke's conception of a "manly, moral, regulated liberty" under the traditions of the common law. Like many rationalists of the Enlightenment, they regarded "liberty" as a political abstraction, and interpreted the Revolution of 1688 in the spirit of Dr. Price, simply as the triumph of England's general or popular will. Therefore, they were quick to draw analogies between the English and French revolutions.

It was perhaps inevitable that sooner or later there would be a quarrel between Burke and Fox over the interpretations of the two revolutions. On April 15, 1791, in a speech in the House of Commons, Fox praised the new French constitution as "the most stupendous and glorious edifice of liberty which had been erected on the foundation of human integrity in any time or country." Burke was deeply disturbed by this eulogy, because he had read the new French constitution, in which Article Six based all law, and therefore all human rights, upon "*la volonté générale.*" In the English and American constitutions, as Burke well knew, the tyranny of the majority was circumscribed by law, because the state was regarded as existing in order to protect pre-existing natural rights to life, liberty, and property, so that the power of the state was itself limited. But Article Six of the French constitution defined the supreme law as the general will, and in effect denied that men had any natural rights beyond those which the state, in the name of the general will, wished to allow. Since the National Assembly was a unicameral body, any group which could dominate it could for all practical purposes decide arbitrarily which rights citizens were to have or be denied. In the speeches of many of the deputies, before the new French constitution was adopted, the authority of the general will had been proclaimed as superior to the natural rights of men.

Burke saw in the new French constitution an instrument for the subversion of government under the Natural Law, and for the perfection of a popular totalitarian tyranny over the French nation, by any triumphant faction in the National Assembly.

On May 6, 1791, during the debate on the Quebec Bill, Burke replied to Fox by attacking the French constitution as fundamentally different from the old Whig principles of 1688. While he was speaking, Fox's friends and even Fox himself attacked him, and after one of the most violent and bitter quarrels ever witnessed in the House of Commons, he formally broke his friendship with Fox. Burke refused to be reconciled, and on May 12 the *Morning Chronicle*, which spoke for Fox, wrote that "the great and firm body of the Whigs of England, true to their principles, have decided on the dispute between Mr. Fox and Mr. Burke; and the former is declared to have maintained the pure doctrines by which they are bound together and upon which they have invariably acted." Burke found himself rejected by his own party, which he had guided and served for over twenty-five years.

Defeated and embittered, Burke journeyed to Margate to write *An Appeal from the New to the Old Whigs*, which was published in August 1791. This work is probably the most calm and closely reasoned of his writings on the French Revolution. It is a brilliant defense of his political consistency as an "old Whig," whose adherence to the principles of constitutional sovereignty in the Revolution of 1688 and the American Revolution led him to attack the "new Whig" principles of popular sovereignty in the French Revolution. In the process of defending his political consistency under a limited constitutional monarchy, he expounded more fully his Aristotelian conception of "the people" as a corporate political body.

At the time that Burke wrote his *Appeal* he was rejected by his whole party and alienated from much of the English nation. But shortly after his work came off the press, events across the Channel did more than his words to show that he was right in contrasting the bloodless and moderate Revolution of 1688 with that of France. The mob violence, the wanton massacre of persons and pillage of property, the wholesale proscription of the clergy and nobility, the aggressive military actions of the revolutionists, and finally the execution of Louis XVI in January 1793, drew much of the British public to Burke's views. He had predicted the essential course of the Revolution to the letter. Within two years many of the Whigs abandoned Fox, and ultimately Burke and the Duke of Portland led the more conservative Whigs into a coalition with the Tories of Pitt in their war against the Revolution.

. . . It is certainly well for Mr. Burke that there are impartial men in the world. To them I address myself, pending the appeal which on his part is made from the living to the dead, from the modern Whigs to the ancient. . . .

If the party had denied his doctrines to be the current opinions of the majority in the nation, they would have put the question on its true issue. . . . His censurers will find, on the trial, that the author is as faithful a representative of the general sentiment of the people of England, as any person amongst them can be of the ideas of his own party.

The French Revolution can have no connection with the objects of any parties in England formed before the period of that event, unless they choose to imitate any of its acts, or to consolidate any principles of that Revolution with their own opinions. The French Revolution is no part of their original contract. . . . But if any considerable number of British subjects, taking a factious interest in the proceedings of France, begin publicly to incorporate themselves for the subversion of nothing short of the *whole* Constitution of this kingdom—to incorporate themselves for the utter overthrow of the body of its laws, civil and ecclesiastical, and with them of the whole system of its manners, in favor of the new Constitution and of the modern usages of the French nation—I think no party principle could bind the author not to express his sentiments strongly against such a faction. . . .

He had undertaken to demonstrate, by arguments which he thought could not be refuted, and by documents which he was sure could not be denied, that no comparison was to be made between the British government and the French usurpation.—That they who endeavored madly to compare them were by no means making the comparison of one good system with another good system, which varied only in local and circumstantial differences; much less that they were holding out to us a superior pattern of legal liberty, which we might substitute in the place of our old, and, as they describe it, superannuated Constitution. He meant to demonstrate that the French scheme was not a comparative good, but a positive evil.—That the question did not at all turn, as it had been stated, on a parallel between a monarchy and a republic. He denied that the present scheme of things in France did at all deserve the respectable name of a republic: he had therefore no comparison between monarchies and republics to make.—That what was done in France was a wild attempt to methodize anarchy, to perpetuate and fix disorder. . . .

The excellencies of the British Constitution had already exercised and exhausted the talents of the best thinkers and the most eloquent writers and speakers that the world ever saw. But in the present case a system declared to be far better, and which certainly is much newer, (to restless and unstable minds no small recommendation,) was held out to the admiration of the good people of England. In that case it was surely thought proper for those who had far other thoughts of the French Constitution to scrutinize that plan which has been recommended to our imitation by active and zealous factions at home and abroad. . . .

When we praise our Revolution of 1688, though the nation in that act was on the defensive, and was justified in incurring all the evils of a defensive war, we do not rest there. We always combine with the subversion of the old government the happy settlement which followed. When we estimate that Revolution, we mean to comprehend in our calculation both the value of the thing parted with and the value of the thing received in exchange.

The burden of proof lies heavily on those who tear to pieces the whole frame and contexture of their country, that they could find no other way of settling a government fit to obtain its rational ends, except that which they have pursued by means unfavorable to all the present happiness of millions of people, and to the utter ruin of several hundreds of thousands. In their political arrangements, men have no right to put the well-being of the present generation wholly out of the question. Perhaps the only moral trust with any certainty in our hands is the care of our own time. With regard to futurity, we are to treat it like a ward. We are not so to attempt an improvement of his fortune as to put the capital of his estate to any hazard.

It is not worth our while to discuss, like sophisters, whether in no case some evil for the sake of some benefit is to be tolerated. Nothing universal can be rationally affirmed on any moral or any political subject. Pure metaphysical abstraction does not belong to these matters. The lines of morality are not like the ideal lines of mathematics. They are broad and deep as well as long. They admit of exceptions; they demand modifications. These exceptions and modifications are not made by the process of logic, but by the rules of prudence. Prudence is not only the first in rank of the virtues political and moral, but she is the director, the regulator, the standard of them all. Metaphysics cannot live without definition; but

Prudence is cautious how she defines. Our courts cannot be more fearful in suffering fictitious cases to be brought before them for elicting their determination on a point of law than prudent moralists are in putting extreme and hazardous cases of conscience upon emergencies not existing. Without attempting, therefore, to define, what never can be defined, the case of a revolution in government, this, I think, may be safely affirmed—that a sore and pressing evil is to be removed, and that a good, great in its amount and unequivocal in its nature, must be probable almost to certainty, before the inestimable price of our own morals and the well-being of a number of our fellow-citizens is paid for a revolution. If ever we ought to be economists even to parsimony, it is in the voluntary production of evil. Every revolution contains in it something of evil.

It must always be, to those who are the greatest amateurs, or even professors, of revolutions, a matter very hard to prove, that the late French government was so bad that nothing worse in the infinite devices of men could come in its place. They who have brought France to its present condition ought to prove also, by something better than prattling about the Bastile, that their subverted government was as incapable as the present certainly is of all improvement and correction. How dare they to say so who have never made that experiment? They are experimenters by their trade. They have made an hundred others, infinitely more hazardous.

The English admirers of the forty-eight thousand republics which form the French federation praise them not for what they are, but for what they are to become. They do not talk as politicians, but as prophets. But in whatever character they choose to found panegyric on prediction, it will be thought a little singular to praise any work, not for its own merits, but for the merits of something else which may succeed to it. When any political institution is praised, in spite of great and prominent faults of every kind, and in all its parts, it must be supposed to have something excellent in its fundamental principles. . . .

The gentlemen of the party . . . have . . . publicly represented him as . . . disgracing his whole public life by a scandalous contradiction of every one of his own acts, writings, and declarations. . . .

On their ideas, the new Whig party have . . . acted as became them. The author of the Reflections, however, on his part, cannot, without great shame to himself, . . . admit the truth or justice of the charges which have been made upon him . . . He must believe, if he does not mean wilfully to abandon his cause and his reputation, that principles fundamentally at variance with those of his book are fundamentally false. . . . He is very unwilling to suppose that the doctrines of some books lately circulated are the principles of the party; though, from the vehement declarations against his opinions, he is at some loss how to judge otherwise. . . .

I pass to the next head of charge—Mr. Burke's inconsistency. . . . This is the great gist of the charge against him. It is not so much that he is wrong in his book (that, however, is alleged also) as that he has therein belied his whole life. I believe, if he could venture to value himself upon anything, it is on the virtue of consistency that he would value himself the most. Strip him of this, and you leave him naked indeed. . . .

He who thinks that the British Constitution ought to consist of the three members, of three very different natures, of which it does actually consist, and thinks it his duty to preserve each of those members in its proper place and with its proper proportion of power, must (as each shall happen to be attacked) vindicate the three several parts on the several principles peculiarly belonging to them. He cannot assert the democratic part on the principles on which monarchy is supported, nor can he support monarchy on the principles of democracy, nor can he maintain aristocracy on the grounds of the one or of the other or of both. All these he must support on grounds that are totally different, though practically they may be, and happily with us they are, brought into one harmonious body. A man could not be consistent in defending such various, and, at first view, discordant, parts of a mixed Constitution, without that sort of inconsistency with which Mr. Burke stands charged.

As any one of the great members of this Constitution happens to be endangered, he that is a friend to all of them chooses and presses the topics necessary for the support of the part attacked, with all the strength, the earnestness, the vehemence, with all the power of stating, of argument, and of coloring, which he happens to possess, and which the case demands. He is not to embarrass the minds of his hearers, or to incumber or overlay his speech, by bringing into view at once (as if he were reading an academic lecture) all that may and ought, when a just occasion presents itself, to be said in favor of the other members. At that time they are out of the court; there is no question concerning them. Whilst he opposes his defence on the part where the attack is made, he presumes that for his regard to the just rights of all the rest he has credit in every candid mind. He ought not to apprehend that his raising fences about popular privileges this day will infer that he ought on the next to concur with those who would pull down the throne; because on the next he defends the throne, it ought not to be supposed that he has abandoned the rights of the people. . . .

If the principles of a mixed Constitution be admitted, he wants no more to justify to consistency everything he has said and done during the course of a political life just touching to its close. I believe that gentleman has kept himself more clear of running into the fashion of wild, visionary theories, or of seeking popularity through every means, than any man perhaps ever did in the same situation.

He was the first man who, on the hustings, at a popular election, rejected the authority of instructions from constituents—or who, in any place, has argued so fully against it. Perhaps the discredit into which that doctrine of compulsive instructions under our Constitution is since fallen may be due in a great degree to his opposing himself to it in that manner and on that occasion.

The reforms in representation, and the bills for shortening the duration of Parliaments, he uniformly and steadily opposed for many years together, in contradiction to many of his best friends. These friends, however, in his better days, when they had more to hope from his service and more to fear from his loss than now they have, never chose to find any inconsistency between his acts and expressions in favor of liberty and his votes on those questions. But there is a time for all things.

Against the opinion of many friends, even against the solicitation of some of them, he opposed those of the Church clergy who had petitioned the House of Commons to be discharged from the subscriptions. Although he supported the Dissenters in their petition for the indulgence which he had refused to the clergy of the Established Church, in this, as he was not guilty of it, so he was not reproached with inconsistency. At the same time he promoted, and against the wish of several, the clause that give the Dissenting teachers another subscription in the place of that which was then taken away. Neither at that time was the reproach of inconsistency brought against him. People could then distinguish between a difference in conduct under a variation of circumstances and an inconsistency in principle. It was not then thought necessary to be freed of him as of an incumbrance.

These instances, a few among many, are produced as an answer to the insinuation of his having pursued high popular courses which in his late book he has abandoned. Perhaps in his whole life he has never omitted a fair occasion, with whatever risk to him of obloquy as an individual, with whatever detriment to his interest as a member of opposition, to assert the very same doctrines which appear in that book. . . .

At his first offering himself to Bristol, where he was almost sure he should not obtain, on that or any occasion, a single Tory vote, (in fact, he did obtain but one,) and rested wholly on the Whig interest, he thought himself bound to tell to the electors, both before and after his election, exactly what a representative they had to expect in him.

"The *distinguishing* part of our Constitution," he said, "is its liberty. To preserve that liberty inviolate is the *peculiar* duty and *proper* trust of a member of the House of Commons. But the liberty, the *only* liberty, I mean is a liberty connected with *order;* and that not only exists *with* order and virtue, but cannot exist at all *without* them. It inheres in good and steady government, as in *its substance and vital principle*."

The liberty to which Mr. Burke declared himself attached is not French liberty. That liberty is nothing but the rein given to vice and confusion. Mr. Burke was then, as he was at the writing of his Reflections, awfully impressed with the difficulties arising from the complex state of our Constitution and our empire, and that it might require in different emergencies different sorts of exertions, and the successive call upon all the various principles which uphold and justify it. . . .

Seventeen years ago, he spoke, not like a partisan of one particular member of our Constitution, but as a person strongly, and on principle, attached to them all. He thought these great and essential members ought to be preserved, and preserved each in its place—and that the monarchy ought not only to be secured in its peculiar existence, but in its pre-eminence too, as the presiding and connecting principle of the whole. Let it be considered whether the language of his book, printed in 1790, differs from his speech at Bristol in 1774.

With equal justice his opinions on the American war are introduced, as if in his late work he had belied his conduct and opinions in the debates which arose upon that great event. On the American war he never had any opinions which he has seen occasion to retract, or which he has ever retracted. He, indeed, differs essentially from Mr. Fox as to the cause of that war. Mr. Fox has been pleased to say that the Americans rebelled "because they thought they had not enjoyed liberty enough." This cause of the war, *from him,* I have heard of for the first time. It is true that those who stimulated the nation to that measure did frequently urge this topic. They contended that the Americans had from the beginning aimed at independence—that from the beginning they meant wholly to throw off the authority of the crown, and to break their connection with the parent country. This Mr. Burke never believed. When he moved his second conciliatory proposition, in the year 1776, he entered into the discussion of this point at very great length, and, from nine several heads of presumption, endeavored to prove the charge upon that people not to be true.

If the principles of all he has said and wrote on the occasion be viewed with common temper, the gentlemen of the party will perceive, that, on a supposition that the Americans had rebelled merely in order to enlarge their liberty, Mr. Burke would have thought very differently of the American cause. What might have been in the secret thoughts of some of their leaders it is impossible to say. As far as a man so locked up as Dr. Franklin could be expected to communicate his ideas, I believe he opened them to Mr. Burke. It was, I think, the very day before he set out for America that a very long conversation passed between them, and with a greater air of openness on the Doctor's side than Mr. Burke had observed in him before. In this discourse Dr. Franklin lamented, and with apparent sincerity, the separation which he feared was inevitable between Great Britain and her colonies. He certainly spoke of it as an event which gave him the greatest concern. America, he said, would never again see such happy days as she had passed under the protection of England. He observed, that ours was the only instance of a great empire in which the most distant parts and members had been as well governed as the metropolis and its vicinage, but that the Americans were going to lose the means which secured to them this rare and precious advantage. The question with them was not, whether they were to remain as they had been before the troubles—for better, he allowed, they could not hope to be—but whether they were to give up so happy a situation without a struggle. Mr. Burke had several other conversations with him about that time, in none of which, soured and exasperated as his mind certainly was, did he discover any other wish in favor of America than for a security to its *ancient* condition. Mr. Burke's conversation with other Americans was large, indeed, and his inquiries extensive and diligent. Trusting to the result of all these means of information, but trusting much more in the public presumptive indications I have just referred to, and to the reiterated solemn declarations of their Assemblies, he always firmly believed that they were purely on the defensive in that rebellion. He considered the Americans as standing at that time, and in that controversy, in the same relation to England as England did to King James the Second in 1688. He believed that they had taken up arms from one motive only: that is, our attempting to tax them without their consent—to tax them for the purposes of maintaining civil and military establishments. If this attempt of ours could have been practically established, he thought, with them, that their Assemblies would become totally useless—that, under the system of policy which was then pursued, the Americans could have no sort of security for their laws or liberties, or for any part of them—and that the very circumstance of *our* freedom would have augmented the weight of *their* slavery.

Considering the Americans on that defensive footing, he thought Great Britain ought instantly to have closed with them by the repeal of the taxing act. He was of opinion that our general rights over that country would have been preserved by this timely concession. When, instead of this, a Boston Port Bill, a Massachusetts Charter Bill, a Fishery Bill, an Intercourse Bill, I know not how many hostile bills, rushed out like so many tempests from all points of the compass, and were accompanied first with great fleets and armies of English, and followed afterwards with great bodies of foreign troops, he thought that their cause grew daily better, because daily more defensive—and that ours, because daily more offensive, grew daily worse. He therefore, in two motions, in two successive years, proposed in Parliament many concessions beyond what he had reason to think in the beginning of the troubles would ever be seriously demanded.

So circumstanced, he certainly never could and never did wish the colonists to be subdued by arms. He was fully persuaded, that, if such should be the event, they must be held in that subdued state by a great body of standing forces, and perhaps of foreign forces. He was strongly of opinion that such armies, first victorious over Englishmen, in a conflict for English constitutional rights and privileges, and afterwards habituated (though in America) to keep an English people in a state of abject subjection, would prove fatal in the end to the liberties of England itself; that in the mean time this military system would lie as an oppressive burden upon the national finances; that it would constantly breed and feed new discussions, full of heat and acrimony, leading possibly to a new series of wars; and that foreign powers, whilst we continued in a state at once burdened and distracted, must at length obtain a decided superiority over us. On what part of his late publication, or on what expression that might have escaped him in that work, is any man authorized to charge Mr. Burke with a contradiction to the line of his conduct and to the current of his doctrines on the American war? The pamphlet is in the hands of his accusers: let them point out the passage, if they can. . . .

Is it because he did not wish the Americans to be subdued by arms, that he must be inconsistent with himself, if he reprobates the conduct of those societies in England, who, alleging no one act of tyranny or oppression, and complaining of no hostile attempt against our ancient laws, rights, and usages, are now endeavoring to work the destruction of the crown of this kingdom, and the whole of its Constitution? Is he obliged, from the concessions he wished to be made to the colonies, to keep any terms with those clubs and federations who hold out to us, as a pattern for imitation, the proceedings in France, in which a king, who had voluntarily and formally divested himself of the right of taxation, and of all other species of arbitrary power, has been dethroned? Is it because Mr. Burke wishes to have America rather conciliated than vanquished, that he must wish well to the army of republics which are set up in France—a country wherein not the people, but the monarch, was wholly on the defensive, (a poor, indeed, and feeble defensive,) to preserve *some fragments* of the royal authority against a determined and desperate body of conspirators, whose object it was, with whatever certainty of crimes, with whatever hazard of war, and every other species of calamity, to annihilate the *whole* of that authority, to level all ranks, orders, and distinctions in the state, and utterly to destroy property, not more by their acts than in their principles?

Mr. Burke has been also reproached with an inconsistency between his late writings and his former conduct, because he had proposed in Parliament several economical, leading to several constitutional reforms. Mr. Burke thought, with a majority of the House of Commons, that the influence of the crown at one time was too great; but after his Majesty had, by a gracious message, and several subsequent acts of Parliament, reduced it to a standard which satisfied Mr. Fox himself, and, apparently at least, contented whoever wished to go farthest in that reduction, is Mr. Burke to allow that it would be right for us to proceed to indefinite lengths upon that subject? that it would therefore be justifiable in a people owing allegiance to a monarchy, and professing to maintain it, not to *reduce,* but wholly to *take away all* prerogative and *all* influence whatsoever? Must his having made, in virtue of a plan of economical regulation, a reduction of the influence of the crown compel him to allow that it would be right in the French or in us to bring a king to so abject a state as in function not to be so respectable as an undersheriff, but in person not to differ from the condition of a mere prisoner? One would think that such a thing as a medium had never been heard of in the moral world.

This mode of arguing from your having done *any* thing in a certain line to the necessity of doing *every* thing has political consequences of other moment than those of a logical fallacy. If no man can propose any diminution or modification of an invidious or dangerous power or influence in government, without entitling friends turned into adversaries to argue him into the destruction of all prerogative, and to a spoliation of the whole patronage of royalty, I do not know what can more effectually deter persons of sober minds from engaging in any reform, nor how the worst enemies to the liberty of the subject could contrive any method more fit to bring all correctives on the power of the crown into suspicion and disrepute.

If, say his accusers, the dread of too great influence in the crown of Great Britain could justify the degree of reform which he adopted, the dread of a return under the despotism of a monarchy might justify the people of France in going much further, and reducing monarchy to its present nothing. —Mr. Burke does not allow that a sufficient argument *ad hominem* is inferable from these premises. If the horror of the excesses of an absolute monarchy furnishes a reason for abolishing it, no monarchy once absolute (all have been so at one period or other) could ever be limited. It must be destroyed; otherwise no way could be found to quiet the fears of those who were formerly subjected to that sway. But the principle of Mr. Burke's proceeding ought to lead him to a very different conclusion—to this conclusion—that a monarchy is a thing perfectly susceptible of reform, perfectly susceptible of a balance of power, and that, when reformed and balanced, for a great country it is the best of all governments. The example of our country might have led France, as it has led him, to perceive that monarchy is not only reconcilable to liberty, but that it may be rendered a great and stable security to its perpetual enjoyment. No correctives which he proposed to the power of the crown could lead him to approve of a plan of a republic (if so it may be reputed) which has no correctives, and which he believes to be incapable of admitting any. No principle of Mr. Burke's conduct or writings obliged him from consistency to become an advocate for an exchange of mischiefs; no principle of his could compel him to justify the setting up in the place of a mitigated monarchy a new and far more despotic power, under which there is no trace of liberty, except what appears in confusion and in crime. . . .

So far as to the attack on Mr. Burke in consequence of his reforms.

To show that he has in his last publication abandoned those principles of liberty which have given energy to his youth, and in spite of his censors will afford repose and consolation to his declining age, those who have thought proper in Parliament to declare against his book ought to have produced something in it which directly or indirectly militates with any rational plan of free government. It is something extraordinary, that they whose memories have so well served them with regard to light and ludicrous expressions, which years had consigned to oblivion, should not have been able to quote a single passage in a piece so lately published, which contradicts anything he has formerly ever said in a style either ludicrous or serious. They quote his former speeches and his former votes, but not one syllable from the book. It is only by a collation of the one with the other that the alleged inconsistency can be established. But as they are unable to cite any such contradictory passage, so neither can they show anything in the general tendency and spirit of the whole work unfavorable to a rational and generous spirit of liberty; unless a warm opposition to the spirit of levelling, to the spirit of impiety, to the spirit of proscription, plunder, murder, and cannibalism, be adverse to the true principles of freedom.

The author of that book is supposed to have passed from extreme to extreme; but he has always kept himself in a medium. This charge is not so wonderful. It is in the nature of things, that they who are in the centre of a circle should appear directly opposed to those who view them from any part of the circumference. In that middle point, however, he will still remain, though he may hear people who themselves run beyond Aurora and the Ganges cry out that he is at the extremity of the West.

In the same debate Mr. Burke was represented by Mr. Fox as arguing in a manner which implied that the British Constitution could not be defended, but by abusing all republics ancient and modern. He said nothing to give the least ground for such a censure. He never abused all republics. He has never professed himself a friend or an enemy to republics or to monarchies in the abstract. He thought that the circumstances and habits of every country, which it is always perilous and productive of the greatest calamities to force, are to decide upon the form of its government. There is nothing in his nature, his temper, or his faculties which should make him an enemy to any republic, modern or ancient. Far from it. He has studied the form and spirit of republics very early in life; he has studied them with great attention, and with a mind undisturbed by affection or prejudice. He is, indeed, convinced that the science of government would be poorly cultivated without that study. But the result in his mind from that investigation has been and is, that neither England nor France, without infinite detriment to them, as well in the event as in the experiment, could be brought into a republican form; but that everything republican which can be introduced with safety into either of them must be built upon a monarchy— built upon a real, not a nominal monarchy, *as its essential basis;* that all such institutions, whether aristocratic or democratic, must originate from their crown, and in all their proceedings must refer to it; that by the energy of that mainspring alone those republican parts must be set in action, and from thence must derive their whole legal effect, (as amongst us they actually do,) or the whole will fall into confusion. These republican members have no other point but the crown in which they can possibly unite.

This is the opinion expressed in Mr. Burke's book. He has never varied in that opinion since he came to years of discretion. . . .

To fortify the imputation of a desertion from his principles, his constant attempts to reform abuses have been brought forward. It is true, it has been the business of his strength to reform abuses in government, and his last feeble efforts are employed in a struggle against them. Politically he has lived in that element; politically he will die in it. Before he departs, I will admit for him that he deserves to have all his titles of merit brought forth, as they have been, for grounds of condemnation, if one word justifying or supporting abuses of any sort is to be found in that book which has kindled so much indignation in the mind of a great man. On the contrary, it spares no existing abuse. Its very purpose is to make war with abuses—not, indeed, to make war with the dead, but with those which live, and flourish, and reign.

The *purpose* for which the abuses of government are brought into view forms a very material consideration in the mode of treating them. The complaints of a friend are things very different from the invectives of an enemy. The charge of abuses on the late monarchy of France was not intended to lead to its reformation, but to justify its destruction. They who have raked into all history for the faults of kings, and who have aggravated every fault they have found, have acted consistently, because they acted as enemies. No man can be a friend to a tempered monarchy who bears a decided hatred to monarchy itself. He, who, at the present time, is favorable or even fair to that system, must act towards it as towards a friend with frailties who is under the prosecution of implacable foes. I think it a duty, in that case, not to inflame the public mind against the obnoxious person by any exaggeration of his faults. It is our duty rather to palliate his errors and defects, or to cast them into the shade, and industriously to bring forward any good qualities that he may happen to possess. But when the man is to be amended, and by amendment to be preserved, then the line of duty takes another direction. When his safety is effectually provided for, it then becomes the office of a friend to urge his faults and vices with all the energy of enlightened affection, to paint them in their most vivid colors, and to bring the moral patient to a better habit. Thus I think with regard to individuals; thus I think with regard to ancient and respected governments and orders of men. A spirit of reformation is never more consistent with itself than when it refuses to be rendered the means of destruction. . . . These revolutionists, indeed, may be well thought to vary in their conduct. He is, however, far from accusing them, in this variation, of the smallest degree of inconsistency. He is persuaded that they are totally indifferent at which end they begin the demolition of the Constitution. Some are for commencing their operations with the destruction of the civil powers, in order the better to pull down the ecclesiastical —some wish to begin with the ecclesiastical, in order to facilitate the ruin of the civil; some would destroy the House of Commons through the crown, some the crown through the House of Commons, and some would overturn both the one and the other through what they call the people. But I believe that this injured writer will think it not at all inconsistent with his present duty or with his former life strenuously to oppose all the various partisans of destruction, let them begin where or when or how they will. No man would set his face more determinedly against those who should attempt to deprive them, or any description of men, of the rights they possess. No man would be more steady in preventing them from abusing those rights to the destruction of that happy order under which they enjoy them. As to their title to anything further, it ought to be grounded on the proof they give of the safety with which power may be trusted in their hands. When they attempt without disguise, not to win it from our affections, but to force it from our fears, they show, in the character of their means of obtaining it, the use they would make of their dominion. That writer is too well read in men not to know how often the desire and design of a tyrannic domination lurks in the claim of an extravagant liberty. . . .

The attacks on the author's consistency relative to France are (however grievous they may be to his feelings) in a great degree external to him and to us, and comparatively of little moment to the people of England. The substantial charge upon him is concerning his doctrines relative to the Revolution of 1688. Here it is that they who speak in the name of the party have thought proper to censure him the most loudly and with the greatest asperity. Here they fasten, and, if they are right in their fact, with sufficient judgment in their selection. If he be guilty in this point, he is equally blamable, whether he is consistent or not. If he endeavors to delude his countrymen by a false representation of the spirit of that leading event, and of the true nature and tenure of the government formed in consequence of it, he is deeply responsible, he is an enemy to the free Constitution of the kingdom. But he is not guilty in any sense. I maintain that in his Reflections he has stated the Revolution and the Settlement upon their true principles of legal reason and constitutional policy. . . .

His construction is in perfect harmony with that of the ancient Whigs, to whom, against the sentence of the modern, on his part, I here appeal. . . .

These new Whigs hold that the sovereignty, whether exercised by one or many, did not only originate *from* the people, (a position not denied nor worth denying or assenting to,) but that in the people the same sovereignty constantly and unalienably resides; that the people may lawfully depose kings, not only for misconduct, but without any misconduct at all; that they may set up any new fashion of government for themselves, or continue without any government, at their pleasure; that the people are essentially their own rule, and their will the measure of their conduct; that the tenure of magistracy is not a proper subject of contract, because magistrates have duties, but no rights; and that, if a contract *de facto* is made with them in one age, allowing that it binds at all, it only binds those who are immediately concerned in it, but does not pass to posterity. These doctrines concerning *the people* (a term which they are far from accurately defining, but by which, from many circumstances, it is plain enough they mean their own faction, if they should grow, by early arming, by treachery, or violence, into the prevailing force) tend, in my opinion, to the utter subversion, not only of all government, in all modes, and to all stable securities to rational freedom, but to all the rules and principles of morality itself.

I assert that the ancient Whigs held doctrines totally different from those I have last mentioned. I assert, that the foundations laid down by the Commons, on the trial of Dr. Sacheverell, for justifying the Revolution of 1688, are the very same laid down in Mr. Burke's Reflections—that is to say, a breach of the *original contract*, implied and expressed in the Constitution of this country, as a scheme of government fundamentally and inviolably fixed in King, Lords, and Commons;—that the fundamental subversion of this ancient Constitution, by one of its parts, having been attempted, and in effect accomplished, justified the Revolution;—that it was justified *only* upon the *necessity* of the case, as the *only* means left for the recovery of that *ancient* Constitution formed by the *original contract* of the British state, as well as for the future preservation of the *same* government. . . .

The factions now so busy amongst us, in order to divest men of all love for their country, and to remove from their minds all duty with regard to the state, endeavor to propagate an opinion, that the *people*, in forming their commonwealth, have by no means parted with their power over it. This is an impregnable citadel, to which these gentlemen retreat, whenever they are pushed by the battery of laws and usages and positive conventions. Indeed, it is such, and of so great force, that all they have done in defending their outworks is so much time and labor thrown away. Discuss any of their schemes, their answer is, It is the act of the *people,* and that is sufficient. Are we to deny to a *majority* of the people the right of altering even the whole frame of their society, if such should be their pleasure? They may change it, say they, from a monarchy to a republic to-day, and to-morrow back again from a republic to a monarchy; and so backward and forward as often as they like. They are masters of the commonwealth, because in substance they are themselves the commonwealth. The French Revolution, say they, was the act of the majority of the people; and if the majority of any other people, the people of England, for instance, wish to make the same change, they have the same right.

Just the same, undoubtedly. That is, none at all. Neither the few nor the many have a right to act merely by their will, in any matter connected with duty, trust, engagement, or obligation. The Constitution of a country being once settled upon some compact, tacit or expressed, there is no power existing of force to alter it, without the breach of the covenant, or the consent of all the parties. Such is the nature of a contract. And the votes of a majority of the people, whatever their infamous flatterers may teach in order to corrupt their minds, cannot alter the moral any more than they can alter the physical essence of things. The people are not to be taught to think lightly of their engagements to their governors; else they teach governors to think lightly of their engagements towards them. In that kind of game, in the end, the people are sure to be losers. To flatter them into a contempt of faith, truth, and justice is to ruin them; for in these virtues consists their whole safety. To flatter any man, or any part of mankind, in any description, by asserting that in engagements he or they are free, whilst any other human creature is bound, is ultimately to vest the rule of morality in the pleasure of those who ought to be rigidly submitted to it—to subject the sovereign reason of the world to the caprices of weak and giddy men.

But, as no one of us men can dispense with public or private faith, or with any other tie of moral obligation, so neither can any number of us. The number engaged in crimes, instead of turning them into laudable acts, only augments the quantity and intensity of the guilt. I am well aware that men love to hear of their power, but have an extreme disrelish to be told of their duty. This is of course; because every duty is a limitation of some power. Indeed, arbitrary power is so much to the depraved taste of the vulgar, of the vulgar of every description, that almost all the dissensions which lacerate the commonwealth are not concerning the manner in which it is to be exercised, but concerning the hands in which it is to be placed. Somewhere they are resolved to have it. Whether they desire it to be vested in the many or the few depends with most men upon the chance which they imagine they themselves may have of partaking in the exercise of that arbitrary sway, in the one mode or in the other.

It is not necessary to teach men to thirst after power. But it is very expedient that by moral instruction they should be taught, and by their civil constitutions they should be compelled, to put many restrictions upon the immoderate exercise of it, and the inordinate desire. The best method of obtaining these two great points forms the important, but at the same time the difficult problem to the true statesman. He thinks of the place in which political power is to be lodged with no other attention than as it may render the more or the less practicable its salutary restraint and its prudent direction. For this reason, no legislator, at any period of the world, has willingly placed the seat of active power in the hands of the multitude; because there it admits of no control, no regulation, no steady direction whatsoever. The people are the natural control on authority; but to exercise and to control together is contradictory and impossible.

As the exorbitant exercise of power cannot, under popular sway, be effectually restrained, the other great object of political arrangement, the means of abating an excessive desire of it, is in such a state still worse provided for. The democratic commonwealth is the foodful nurse of ambition. Under the other forms it meets with many restraints. Whenever, in states which have had a democratic basis, the legislators have endeavored to put restraints upon ambition, their methods were as violent as in the end they were ineffectual—as violent, indeed, as any the most jealous despotism could invent. . . .

I cannot too often recommend it to the serious consideration of all men who think civil society to be within the province of moral jurisdiction, that, if we owe to it any duty, it is not subject to our will. Duties are not voluntary. Duty and will are even contradictory terms. Now, though civil society might be at first a voluntary act, (which in many cases it undoubtedly was,) its continuance is under a permanent standing covenant, coexisting with the society; and it attaches upon every individual of that society, without any formal act of his own. This is warranted by the general practice, arising out of the general sense of mankind. Men without their choice derive benefits from that association; without their choice they are subjected to duties in consequence of these benefits; and without their choice they enter into a virtual obligation as binding as any that is actual. Look through the whole of life and the whole system of duties. Much the strongest moral obligations are such as were never the results of our option. I allow, that, if no Supreme Ruler exists, wise to form, and potent to enforce, the moral law, there is no sanction to any contract, virtual or even actual, against the will of prevalent power. On that hypothesis, let any set of men be strong enough to set their duties at defiance, and they cease to be duties any longer. . . . Taking it for granted that I do not write to the disciples of the Parisian philosophy, I may assume that the awful Author of our being is the Author of our place in the order of existence—and that, having disposed and marshalled us by a divine tactic, not according to our will, but according to His, He has in and by that disposition virtually subjected us to act the part which belongs to the place assigned us. We have obligations to mankind at large, which are not in consequence of any special voluntary pact. They arise from the relation of man to man, and the relation of man to God, which relations are not matters of choice. On the contrary, the force of all the pacts which we enter into with any particular person or number of persons amongst mankind depends upon those prior obligations. In some cases the subordinate relations are voluntary, in others they are necessary—but the duties are all compulsive. When we marry, the choice is voluntary, but the duties are not matter of choice: they are dictated by the nature of the situation. Dark and inscrutable are the ways by which we come into the world. The instincts which give rise to this mysterious process of Nature are not of our making. But out of physical causes, unknown to us, perhaps unknowable, arise moral duties, which, as we are able perfectly to comprehend, we are bound indispensably to perform. Parents may not be consenting to their moral relation; but, consenting or not, they are bound to a long train of burdensome duties towards those with whom they have never made a convention of any sort. Children are not consenting to their relation; but their relation, without their actual consent, binds them to its duties—or rather it implies their consent, because the presumed consent of every rational creature is in unison with the predisposed order of things. Men come in that manner into a community with the social state of their parents, endowed with all the benefits, loaded with all the duties of their situation. If the social ties and ligaments, spun out of those physical relations which are the elements of the commonwealth, in most cases begin, and always continue, independently of our will, so, without any stipulation on our own part, are we bound by that relation called our country, which comprehends (as it has been well said) "all the charities of all." Nor are we left without powerful instincts to make this duty as dear and grateful to us as it is awful and coercive. Our country is not a thing of mere physical locality. It consists, in a great measure, in the ancient order into which we are born. We may have the same geographical situation, but another country; as we may have the same country in another soil. The place that determines our duty to our country is a social, civil relation. . . .

I admit, indeed, that in morals, as in all things else, difficulties will sometimes occur. Duties will sometimes cross one another. Then questions will arise, which of them is to be placed in subordination? which of them may be entirely superseded? . . . Duties, at their extreme bounds, are drawn very fine, so as to become almost evanescent. In that state some shade of doubt will always rest on these questions, when they are pursued with great subtilty. But the very habit of stating these extreme cases is not very laudable or safe; because, in general, it is not right to turn our duties into doubts. They are imposed to govern our conduct, not to exercise our ingenuity; and therefore our opinions about them ought not to be in a state of fluctuation, but steady, sure, and resolved.

Amongst these nice, and therefore dangerous points of casuistry, may be reckoned the question so much agitated in the present hour—Whether, after the people have discharged themselves of their original power by an habitual delegation, no occasion can possibly occur which may justify the resumption of it? This question, in this latitude, is very hard to affirm or deny: but I am satisfied that no occasion can justify such a resumption, which would not equally authorize a dispensation with any other moral duty, perhaps with all of them together. However, if in general it be not easy to determine concerning the lawfulness of such devious proceedings, which must be ever on the edge of crimes, it is far from difficult to foresee the perilous consequences of the resuscitation of such a power in the people. The practical consequences of any political tenet go a great way in deciding upon its value. Political problems do not primarily concern truth or falsehood. They relate to good or evil. What in the result is likely to produce evil is politically false; that which is productive of good, politically true.

Believing it, therefore, a question at least arduous in the theory, and in the practice very critical, it would become us to ascertain as well as we can what form it is that our incantations are about to call up from darkness and the sleep of ages. When the supreme authority of the people is in question, before we attempt to extend or to confine it, we ought to fix in our minds, with some degree of distinctness, an idea of what it is we mean, when we say, the PEOPLE.

In a state of *rude* Nature there is no such thing as a people. A number of men in themselves have no collective capacity. The idea of a people is the idea of a corporation. It is wholly artificial, and made, like all other legal fictions, by common agreement. What the particular nature of that agreement was is collected from the form into which the particular society has been cast. Any other is not *their* covenant. When men, therefore, break up the original compact or agreement which gives its corporate form and capacity to a state, they are no longer a people—they have no longer a corporate existence— they have no longer a legal coactive force to bind within, nor a claim to be recognized abroad. They are a number of vague, loose individuals, and nothing more. With them all is to begin again. Alas! they little know how many a weary step is to be taken before they can form themselves into a mass which has a true politic personality.

We hear much, from men who have not acquired their hardiness of assertion from the profundity of their thinking, about the omnipotence of a *majority,* in such a dissolution of an ancient society as hath taken place in France. But amongst men so disbanded there can be no such thing as majority or minority, or power in any one person to bind another. The power of acting by a majority, which the gentlemen theorists seem to assume so readily, after they have violated the contract out of which it has arisen, (if at all it existed,) must be grounded on two assumptions: first, that of an incorporation produced by unanimity; and secondly, an unanimous agreement that the act of a mere majority (say of one) shall pass with them and with others as the act of the whole.

We are so little affected by things which are habitual, that we consider this idea of the decision of a *majority* as if it were a law of our original nature. But such constructive whole, residing in a part only, is one of the most violent fictions of positive law that ever has been or can be made on the principles of artificial incorporation. Out of civil society Nature knows nothing of it; nor are men, even when arranged according to civil order, otherwise than by very long training, brought at all to submit to it. The mind is brought far more easily to acquiesce in the proceedings of one man, or a few, who act under a general procuration for the state, than in the vote of a victorious majority in councils in which every man has his share in the deliberation. For there the beaten party are exasperated and soured by the previous contention, and mortified by the conclusive defeat. This mode of decision, where wills may be so nearly equal, where, according to circumstances, the smaller number may be the stronger force, and where apparent reason may be all upon one side, and on the other little else than impetuous appetite—all this must be the result of a very particular and special convention, confirmed afterwards by long habits of obedience, by a sort of discipline in society, and by a strong hand, vested with stationary, permanent power to enforce this sort of constructive general will. . . .

If men dissolve their ancient incorporation in order to regenerate their community, in that state of things each man has a right, if he pleases, to remain an individual. Any number of individuals, who can agree upon it, have an undoubted right to form themselves into a state apart and wholly independent. If any of these is forced into the fellowship of another, this is conquest and not compact. On every principle which supposes society to be in virtue of a free covenant, this compulsive incorporation must be null and void. . . .

As in the abstract it is perfectly clear, that, out of a state of civil society, majority and minority are relations which can have no existence, and that, in civil society, its own specific conventions in each corporation determine what it is that constitutes the people, so as to make their act the signification of the general will—to come to particulars, it is equally clear that neither in France nor in Enlgand has the original or any subsequent compact of the state, expressed or implied, constituted *a majority of men, told by the head,* to be the acting people of their several communities. And I see as little of policy or utility as there is of right, in laying down a principle that a majority of men told by the head are to be considered as the people, and that as such their will is to be law. What policy can there be found in arrangements made in defiance of every political principle? To enable men to act with the weight and character of a people, and to answer the ends for which they are incorporated into that capacity, we must suppose them (by means immediate or consequential) to be in that state of habitual social discipline in which the wiser, the more expert, and the more opulent conduct, and by conducting enlighten and protect, the weaker, the less knowing, and the less provided with the goods of fortune. When the multitude are not under this discipline, they can scarcely be said to be in civil society. . . .

A true natural aristocracy is not a separate interest in the state, or separable from it. It is an essential integrant part of any large body rightly constituted. It is formed out of a class of legitimate presumptions, which, taken as generalities, must be admitted for actual truths. To be bred in a place of estimation; to see nothing low and sordid from one's infancy; to be taught to respect one's self; to be habituated to the censorial inspection of the public eye; to look early to public opinion; to stand upon such elevated ground as to be enabled to take a large view of the wide-spread and infinitely diversified combinations of men and affairs in a large society; to have leisure to read, to reflect, to converse; to be enabled to draw the court and attention of the wise and learned, wherever they are to be found; to be habituated in armies to command and to obey; to be taught to despise danger in the pursuit of honor and duty; to be formed to the greatest degree of vigilance, foresight, and circumspection, in a state of things in which no fault is committed with impunity and the slightest mistakes draw on the most ruinous consequences; to be led to a guarded and regulated conduct, from a sense that you are considered as an instructor of your fellow-citizens in their highest concerns, and that you act as a reconciler between God and man; to be employed as an administrator of law and justice, and to be thereby amongst the first benefactors of mankind; to be a professor of high science, or of liberal and ingenuous art; to be amongst rich traders, who from their success are presumed to have sharp and vigorous understandings, and to possess the virtues of diligence, order, constancy, and regularity, and to have cultivated an habitual regard to commutative justice: these are the circumstances of men that form what I should call a *natural* aristocracy, without which there is no nation.

The state of civil society which necessarily generates this aristocracy is a state of Nature—and much more truly so than a savage and incoherent mode of life. For man is by nature reasonable; and he is never perfectly in his natural state, but when he is placed where reason may be best cultivated and most predominates. Art is man's nature. We are as much, at least, in a state of Nature in formed manhood as in immature and helpless infancy. Men, qualified in the manner I have just described, form in Nature, as she operates in the common modification of society, the leading, guiding, and governing part. It is the soul to the body, without which the man does not exist. . . .

When great multitudes act together, under that discipline of Nature, I recognize the PEOPLE. I acknowledge something that perhaps equals, and ought always to guide, the sovereignty of convention. In all things the voice of this grand chorus of national harmony ought to have a mighty and decisive influence. But when you disturb this harmony—when you break up this beautiful order, this array of truth and Nature, as well as of habit and prejudice—when you separate the common sort of men from their proper chieftains, so as to form them into an adverse army—I no longer know that venerable object called the people in such a disbanded race of deserters and vagabonds. . . .

To apply this to our present subject. When the several orders, in their several bailliages, had met in the year 1789, (such of them, I mean, as had met peaceably and constitutionally,) to choose and to instruct their representatives, so organized and so acting, (because they were organized and were acting according to the conventions which made them a people,) they were the *people* of France. They had a legal and a natural capacity to be considered as that people. But observe, whilst they were in this state, that is, whilst they were a people, in no one of their instructions did they charge or even hint at any of those things which have drawn upon the usurping Assembly and their adherents the detestation of the rational and thinking part of mankind. . . . Their instructions purported the direct contrary to all those famous proceedings which are defended as the acts of the people. Had such proceedings been expected, the great probability is, that the people would then have risen, as to a man, to prevent them. The whole organization of the Assembly was altered, the whole frame of the kingdom was changed, before these things could be done. . . .

After the weighty and respectable part of the people had been murdered, or driven by the menaces of murder from their houses, or were dispersed in exile into every country in Europe—after the soldiery had been debauched from their officers—after property had lost its weight and consideration, along with its security—after voluntary clubs and associations of factious and unprincipled men were substituted in the place of all the legal corporations of the kingdom arbitrarily dissolved—after freedom had been banished from those popular meetings whose sole recommendation is freedom—after it had come to that pass that no dissent dared to appear in any of them, but at the certain price of life—after even dissent had been anticipated, and assassination became as quick as suspicion—such pretended ratification by addresses could be no act of what any lover of the people would choose to call by their name. It is that voice which every successful usurpation, as well as this before us, may easily procure, even without making (as these tyrants have made) donatives from the spoil of one part of the citizens to corrupt the other.

The pretended *rights of man*, which have made this havoc, cannot be the rights of the people. For to be a people, and to have these rights, are things incompatible. The one supposes the presence, the other the absence, of a state of civil society. The very foundation of the French commonwealth is false and self-destructive; nor can its principles be adopted in any country, without the certainty of bringing it to the very same condition in which France is found. . . .

The whole scheme of our mixed Constitution is to prevent any one of its principles from being carried as far as, taken by itself, and theoretically, it would go. Allow that to be the true policy of the British system, then most of the faults with which that system stands charged will appear to be, not imperfections into which it has inadvertently fallen, but excellencies which it has studiously sought. To avoid the perfections of extreme, all its several parts are so constituted as not alone to answer their own several ends, but also each to limit and control the others; insomuch that, take which of the principles you please, you will find its operation checked and stopped at a certain point. The whole movement stands still rather than that any part should proceed beyond its boundary. From thence it results that in the British Constitution there is a perpetual treaty and compromise going on, sometimes openly, sometimes with less observation. To him who contemplates the British Constitution, as to him who contemplates the subordinate material world, it will always be a matter of his most curious investigation to discover the secret of this mutual limitation. . . .

They who have acted, as in France they have done, upon a scheme wholly different, and who aim at the abstract and unlimited perfection of power in the popular part, can be of no service to us in any of our political arrangements. . . . Our fabric is so constituted, one part of it bears so much on the other, the parts are so made for one another, and for nothing else, that to introduce any foreign matter into it is to destroy it. . . .

The British Constitution has not been struck out at an heat by a set of presumptuous men, like the Assembly of pettifoggers run mad in Paris.

> *"'T is not the hasty product of a day,*
> *But the well-ripened fruit of wise delay."*

It is the result of the thoughts of many minds in many ages. It is no simple, no superficial thing, nor to be estimated by superficial understandings. An ignorant man, who is not fool enough to meddle with his clock, is, however, sufficiently confident to think he can safely take to pieces and put together, at his pleasure, a moral machine of another guise, importance, and complexity, composed of far other wheels and springs and balances and counteracting and coöperating powers. Men little think how immorally they act in rashly meddling with what they do not understand. Their delusive good intention is no sort of excuse for their presumption. They who truly mean well must be fearful of acting ill. The British Constitution may have its advantages pointed out to wise and reflecting minds, but it is of too high an order of excellence to be adapted to those which are common. It takes in too many views, it makes too many combinations, to be so much as comprehended by shallow and superficial understandings. Profound thinkers will know it in its reason and spirit. The less inquiring will recognize it in their feelings and their experience. They will thank God they have a standard, which, in the most essential point of this great concern, will put them on a par with the most wise and knowing. . . .

Rational and experienced men tolerably well know, and have always known, how to distinguish between true and false liberty, and between the genuine adherence and the false pretence to what is true. But none, except those who are profoundly studied, can comprehend the elaborate contrivance of a fabric fitted to unite private and public liberty with public force, with order, with peace, with justice, and, above all, with the institutions formed for bestowing permanence and stability, through ages, upon this invaluable whole.

Place, for instance, before your eyes such a man as Montesquieu. Think of a genius not born in every country or every time: a man gifted by Nature with a penetrating, aquiline eye—with a judgment prepared with the most extensive erudition—with an Herculean robustness of mind, and nerves not to be broken with labor—a man who could spend twenty years in one pursuit. Think of a man like the universal patriarch in Milton (who had drawn up before him in his prophetic vision the whole series of the generations which were to issue from his loins): a man capable of placing in review, after having brought together from the East, the West, the North, and the South, from the coarseness of the rudest barbarism to the most refined and subtle civilization, all the schemes of government which had ever prevailed amongst mankind, weighing, measuring, collating, and comparing them all, joining fact with theory, and calling into council, upon all this infinite assemblage of things, all the speculations which have fatigued the understandings of profound reasoners in all times. Let us then consider, that all these were but so many preparatory steps to qualify a man, and such a man, tinctured with no national prejudice, with no domestic affection, to admire, and to hold out to the admiration of mankind, the Constitution of England. . . .

A Letter
to
William Elliot, Esq.,
Occasioned by
the Account Given in a Newspaper of the
Speech Made in the House of Lords
by the **** of *******
in the Debate
concerning Lord Fitzwilliam
1795

Shortly after he retired from Parliament, in the following letter to his friend Elliot, Burke looked back upon the origin of the French Revolution, and its nature, and reviewed his role in and reasons for opposing it. This letter has biographical and philosophical significance for an understanding of Burke and the French Revolution.

BEACONSFIELD, MAY 26, 1795.

. . . In the long series of ages which have furnished the matter of history, never was so beautiful and so august a spectacle presented to the moral eye as Europe afforded the day before the Revolution in France. I knew, indeed, that this prosperity contained in itself the seeds of its own danger. In one part of the society it caused laxity and debility; in the other it produced bold spirits and dark designs. A false philosophy passed from academies into courts; and the great themselves were infected with the theories which conducted to their ruin. Knowledge, which in the two last centuries either did not exist at all, or existed solidly on right principles and in chosen hands, was now diffused, weakened, and perverted. General wealth loosened morals, relaxed vigilance, and increased presumption. Men of talent began to compare, in the partition of the common stock of public prosperity, the proportions of the dividends with the merits of the claimants. As usual, they found their portion not equal to their estimate (or perhaps to the public estimate) of their own worth. When it was once discovered by the Revolution in France that a struggle between establishment and rapacity could be maintained, though but for one year and in one place, I was sure that a practicable breach was made in the whole order of things, and in every country. Religion, that held the materials of the fabric together, was first systematically loosened. All other opinions, under the name of prejudices, must fall along with it; and property, left undefended by principles, became a repository of spoils to tempt cupidity, and not a magazine to furnish arms for defence. I knew, that, attacked on all sides by the infernal energies of talents set in action by vice and disorder, authority could not stand upon authority alone. It wanted some other support than the poise of its own gravity. Situations formerly supported persons. It now became necessary that personal qualities should support situations. . . .

I wished to warn the people against the greatest of all evils— a blind and furious spirit of innovation, under the name of reform. I was, indeed, well aware that power rarely reforms itself. So it is, undoubtedly, when all is quiet about it. But I was in hopes that provident fear might prevent fruitless penitence. I trusted that danger might produce at least circumspection. I flattered myself, in a moment like this, that nothing would be added to make authority top-heavy—that the very moment of an earthquake would not be the time chosen for adding a story to our houses. I hoped to see the surest of all reforms, perhaps the only sure reform—the ceasing to do ill. In the mean time I wished to the people the wisdom of knowing how to tolerate a condition which none of their efforts can render much more than tolerable. It was a condition, however, in which everything was to be found that could enable them to live to Nature, and, if so they pleased, to live to virtue and to honor.

I do not repent that I thought better of those to whom I wished well than they will suffer me long to think that they deserved. Far from repenting, I would to God that new faculties had been called up in me, in favor not of this or that man, or this or that system, but of the general, vital principle, that, whilst it was in its vigor, produced the state of things transmitted to us from our fathers, but which, through the joint operation of the abuses of authority and liberty, may perish in our hands. I am not of opinion that the race of men, and the commonwealths they create, like the bodies of individuals, grow effete and languid and bloodless, and ossify, by the necessities of their own conformation, and the fatal operation of longevity and time. These analogies between bodies natural and politic, though they may sometimes illustrate arguments, furnish no argument of themselves. They are but too often used, under the color of a specious philosophy, to find apologies for the despair of laziness and pusillanimity, and to excuse the want of all manly efforts, when the exigencies of our country call for them the more loudly.

How often has public calamity been arrested on the very brink of ruin by the seasonable energy of a single man! Have we no such man amongst us? I am as sure as I am of my being, that one vigorous mind, without office, without situation, without public functions of any kind, (at a time when the want of such a thing is felt, as I am sure it is,) I say, one such man, confiding in the aid of God, and full of just reliance in his own fortitude, vigor, enterprise, and perseverance, would first draw to him some few like himself, and then that multitudes, hardly thought to be in existence, would appear and troop about him. . . .

Even in solitude, something may be done for society. The meditations of the closet have infected senates with a subtle frenzy, and inflamed armies with the brands of the Furies. The cure might come from the same source with the distemper. I would add my part to those who would animate the people (whose hearts are yet right) to new exertions in the old cause.

Novelty is not the only source of zeal. Why should not a Maccabæus and his brethren arise to assert the honor of the ancient law and to defend the temple of their forefathers with as ardent a spirit as can inspire any innovator to destroy the monuments of the piety and the glory of ancient ages? It is not a hazarded assertion, it is a great truth, that, when once things are gone out of their ordinary course, it is by acts out of the ordinary course they can alone be reëstablished. . . . I would persuade a resistance both to the corruption and to the reformation that prevails. It will not be the weaker, but much the stronger, for combating both together. A victory over real corruptions would enable us to baffle the spurious and pretended reformations. I would not wish to excite, or even to tolerate, that kind of evil spirit which evokes the powers of hell to rectify the disorders of the earth. No! I would add my voice with better, and, I trust, more potent charms, to draw down justice and wisdom and fortitude from heaven, for the correction of human vice, and the recalling of human error from the devious ways into which it has been betrayed. I would wish to call the impulses of individuals at once to the aid and to the control of authority. By this, which I call the true republican spirit, paradoxical as it may appear, monarchies alone can be rescued from the imbecility of courts and the madness of the crowd. This republican spirit would not suffer men in high place to bring ruin on their country and on themselves. It would reform, not by destroying, but by saving, the great, the rich, and the powerful. Such a republican spirit we perhaps fondly conceive to have animated the distinguished heroes and patriots of old, who knew no mode of policy but religion and virtue. These they would have paramount to all constitutions; they would not suffer monarchs, or senates, or popular assemblies, under pretences of dignity or authority or freedom, to shake off those moral riders which reason has appointed to govern every sort of rude power. . . . The great must submit to the dominion of prudence and of virtue, or none will long submit to the dominion of the great. . . .

VIII

DEFENSE OF HIS LIFE

A
Letter to a Noble Lord
on
the Attacks Made upon Mr. Burke and His Pension, in the House of Lords,
by
the Duke of Bedford and the Earl of Lauderdale, Early in the Present Session of Parliament 1795

As soon as the trial of Warren Hastings was concluded, in the summer of 1794, Burke applied for the Chiltern Hundreds, which signalized his retirement from the House of Commons. In the split with Fox over the French Revolution, he had led the remnants of the Rockingham party, the Portland Whigs, into an anti-revolutionary alliance with the Tory government of the younger Pitt. Partly from political gratitude and partly from a recognition of Burke's services to the state for thirty years, including his writings in defense of Britain against revolutionary France, Pitt agreed to reward him by making him a peer, with the title Lord Beaconsfield. The title was to carry with it a pension of twenty-five hundred pounds for the life of Burke and his wife.

However, in the midst of these arrangements, in August 1794, Burke's son Richard died suddenly after a brief and unexpected illness. As he had no other child to whom he could transmit his title, the proposal for a peerage was dropped. Burke's anguish and pathos over the death of his son is expressed in one of the most moving passages in his *Letter to a Noble Lord:* "The storm has gone over me; and I lie like one of those old oaks which the late hurricane has scattered about me. I am stripped of all my honors, I am torn up by the roots, and lie prostrate on the earth. . . . I am alone. I have none to meet my enemies in the gate. . . . I live in an inverted order. They who ought to have succeeded me are gone before me. They who should have been to me as posterity are in the place of ancestors." Burke survived the tragedy of his son's death by less than three years.

Meanwhile, the living had to be provided for, and Burke's always entangled financial affairs were more desperate than at any period of his life. To expedite matters, and to avoid political recriminations in Parliament, Pitt had the pension conferred directly by the Crown, rather than through a vote of Parliament. Naturally, Burke's pension was attacked in the opposition press by English Jacobins who favored an appeasement of revolutionary France, and disliked him for his attack on the Revolution. Early in 1795, when the liberal Whig opposition to Pitt was aroused against the Treason and Sedition Bills, Burke's pension was again attacked in Parliament, as a means of embarrassing Pitt. In particular, the Duke of Bedford and the Earl of Lauderdale were most vehement against it, arguing that it required the consent of Parliament, that it was excessive, and that it contradicted the very principles of economy which Burke himself had championed in 1780 in his attempt to reform the King's power through patronage and pensions. As the inheritor of vast wealth which originated from grants from the Crown, whose ancestor had shared in the spoils from monasteries confiscated by Henry VIII, the Duke of Bedford was perhaps the last person in England who should protest against grants from the Crown. In the contrast between the origins, nature, and extent of the Duke of Bedford's fortune and his own pension, Burke saw his opening, and in his *Letter to a Noble Lord* delivered a defense of his life and whole political career which John Morley considered "the most splendid repartee in the English language." Burke's brilliant reply to his detractors is written in the form of a public letter to his friend Earl Fitzwilliam.

My Lord—I could hardly flatter myself with the hope that so very early in the season I should have to acknowledge obligations to the Duke of Bedford and to the Earl of Lauderdale. These noble persons have lost no time in conferring upon me that sort of honor which it is alone within their competence, and which it is certainly most congenial to their nature and their manners, to bestow.

To be ill spoken of, in whatever language they speak, by the zealots of the new sect in philosophy and politics, of which these noble persons think so charitably, and of which others think so justly, to me is no matter of uneasiness or surprise. To have incurred the displeasure of the Duke of Orleans or the Duke of Bedford, to fall under the censure of Citizen Brissot or of his friend the Earl of Lauderdale, I ought to consider as proofs, not the least satisfactory, that I have produced some part of the effect I proposed by my endeavors. I have labored hard to earn what the noble Lords are generous enough to pay. Personal offence I have given them none. The part they take against me is from zeal to the cause. It is well—it is perfectly well. I have to do homage to their justice. I have to thank the Bedfords and the Lauderdales for having so faithfully and so fully acquitted towards me whatever arrear of debt was left undischarged by the Priestleys and the Paines.

Some, perhaps, may think them executors in their own wrong: I at least have nothing to complain of. They have gone beyond the demands of justice. They have been (a little, perhaps, beyond their intention) favorable to me. They have been the means of bringing out by their invectives the handsome things which Lord Grenville has had the goodness and condescension to say in my behalf. Retired as I am from the world, and from all its affairs and all its pleasures, I confess it does kindle in my nearly extinguished feelings a very vivid satisfaction to be so attacked and so commended. It is soothing to my wounded mind to be commended by an able, vigorous, and well-informed statesman, and at the very moment when he stands forth, with a manliness and resolution worthy of himself and of his cause, for the preservation of the person and government of our sovereign, and therein for the security of the laws, the liberties, the morals, and the lives of his people. To be in any fair way connected with such things is indeed a distinction. No philosophy can make me above it: no melancholy can depress me so low as to make me wholly insensible to such an honor.

Why will they not let me remain in obscurity and inaction? Are they apprehensive, that, if an atom of me remains, the sect has something to fear? Must I be annihilated, lest, like old John Zisca's, my skin might be made into a drum, to animate Europe to eternal battle against a tyranny that threatens to overwhelm all Europe and all the human race?

My Lord, it is a subject of awful meditation. Before this of France, the annals of all time have not furnished an instance of a *complete* revolution. That revolution seems to have extended even to the constitution of the mind of man. It has this of wonderful in it, that it resembles what Lord Verulam says of the operations of Nature: It was perfect, not only in its elements and principles, but in all its members and its organs, from the very beginning. The moral scheme of France furnishes the only pattern ever known which they who admire will *instantly* resemble. It is, indeed, an inexhaustible repertory of one kind of examples. In my wretched condition, though hardly to be classed with the living, I am not safe from them. They have tigers to fall upon animated strength; they have hyenas to prey upon carcasses. The national menagerie is collected by the first physiologists of the time; and it is defective in no description of savage nature. They pursue even such as me into the obscurest retreats, and haul them before their revolutionary tribunals. Neither sex, nor age, nor the sanctuary of the tomb, is sacred to them. . . .

In one thing I can excuse the Duke of Bedford for his attack upon me and my mortuary pension: He cannot readily comprehend the transaction he condemns. What I have obtained was the fruit of no bargain, the production of no intrigue, the result of no compromise, the effect of no solicitation. The first suggestion of it never came from me, mediately or immediately, to his Majesty or any of his ministers. It was long known that the instant my engagements would permit it, and before the heaviest of all calamities had forever condemned me to obscurity and sorrow, I had resolved on a total retreat. I had executed that design. I was entirely out of the way of serving or of hurting any statesman or any party, when the ministers so generously and so nobly carried into effect the spontaneous bounty of the crown. Both descriptions have acted as became them. When I could no longer serve them, the ministers have considered my situation. When I could no longer hurt them, the revolutionists have trampled on my infirmity. My gratitude, I trust, is equal to the manner in which the benefit was conferred. It came to me, indeed, at a time of life, and in a state of mind and body, in which no circumstance of fortune could afford me any real pleasure. But this was no fault in the royal donor, or in his ministers, who were pleased, in acknowledging the merits of an invalid servant of the public, to assuage the sorrows of a desolate old man. . . .

Loose libels ought to be passed by in silence and contempt. By me they have been so always. I knew, that, as long as I remained in public, I should live down the calumnies of malice and the judgments of ignorance. If I happened to be now and then in the wrong, (as who is not?) like all other men, I must bear the consequence of my faults and my mistakes. The libels of the present day are just of the same stuff as the libels of the past. But they derive an importance from the rank of the persons they come from, and the gravity of the place where they were uttered. In some way or other I ought to take some notice of them. To assert myself thus traduced is not vanity or arrogance. It is a demand of justice; it is a demonstration of gratitude. If I am unworthy, the ministers are worse than prodigal. On that hypothesis, I perfectly agree with the Duke of Bedford. . . .

I refuse all revolutionary tribunals, where men have been put to death for no other reason than that they had obtained favors from the crown. I claim, not the letter, but the spirit of the old English law—that is, to be tried by my peers. I decline his Grace's jurisdiction as a judge. I challenge the Duke of Bedford as a juror to pass upon the value of my services. Whatever his natural parts may be, I cannot recognize in his few and idle years the competence to judge of my long and laborious life. If I can help it, he shall not be on the inquest of my *quantum meruit*. Poor rich man! he can hardly know anything of public industry in its exertions, or can estimate its compensations when its work is done. . . .

His Grace thinks I have obtained too much. I answer, that my exertions, whatever they have been, were such as no hopes of pecuniary reward could possibly excite; and no pecuniary compensation can possibly reward them. Between money and such services, if done by abler men than I am, there is no common principle of comparison: they are quantities incommensurable. Money is made for the comfort and convenience of animal life. It cannot be a reward for what mere animal life must, indeed, sustain, but never can inspire. With submission to his Grace, I have not had more than sufficient. As to any noble use, I trust I know how to employ as well as he a much greater fortune than he possesses. In a more confined application, I certainly stand in need of every kind of relief and easement much more than he does. When I say I have not received more than I deserve, is this the language I hold to Majesty? No! Far, very far, from it! Before that presence I claim no merit at all. Everything towards me is favor and bounty. One style to a gracious benefactor; another to a proud and insulting foe.

His Grace is pleased to aggravate my guilt by charging my acceptance of his Majesty's grant as a departure from my ideas and the spirit of my conduct with regard to economy. If it be, my ideas of economy were false and ill-founded. But they are the Duke of Bedford's ideas of economy I have contradicted, and not my own. If he means to allude to certain

bills brought in by me on a message from the throne in 1782,
I tell him that there is nothing in my conduct that can contradict either the letter or the spirit of those acts. Does he
mean the Pay-Office Act? I take it for granted he does not.
The act to which he alludes is, I suppose, the Establishment
Act. I greatly doubt whether his Grace has ever read the one
or the other. The first of these systems cost me, with every
assistance which my then situation gave me, pains incredible.
I found an opinion common through all the offices, and general in the public at large, that it would prove impossible to
reform and methodize the office of paymaster-general. I undertook it, however; and I succeeded in my undertaking.
Whether the military service, or whether the general economy
of our finances have profited by that act, I leave to those who
are acquainted with the army and with the treasury to judge.

An opinion full as general prevailed also, at the same time,
that nothing could be done for the regulation of the civil list
establishment. The very attempt to introduce method into it,
and any limitations to its services, was held absurd. I had not
seen the man who so much as suggested one economical principle or an economical expedient upon that subject. Nothing
but coarse amputation or coarser taxation were then talked
of, both of them without design, combination, or the least
shadow of principle. Blind and headlong zeal or factious fury
were the whole contribution brought by the most noisy, on
that occasion, towards the satisfaction of the public or the relief of the crown.

Let me tell my youthful censor, that the necessities of that
time required something very different from what others then
suggested or what his Grace now conceives. Let me inform
him, that it was one of the most critical periods in our annals.

Astronomers have supposed, that, if a certain comet, whose
path intersected the ecliptic, had met the earth in some (I
forget what) sign, it would have whirled us along with it, in
its eccentric course, into God knows what regions of heat and
cold. Had the portentous comet of the Rights of Man, (which
"from its horrid hair shakes pestilence and war," and "with
fear of change perplexes monarchs,") had that comet crossed
upon us in that internal state of England, nothing human could
have prevented our being irresistibly hurried out of the highway of heaven into all the vices, crimes, horrors, and miseries
of the French Revolution.

Happily, France was not then Jacobinized. Her hostility was
at a good distance. We had a limb cut off, but we preserved

the body: we lost our colonies, but we kept our Constitution. There was, indeed, much intestine heat; there was a dreadful fermentation. Wild and savage insurrection quitted the woods, and prowled about our streets in the name of Reform. Such was the distemper of the public mind, that there was no madman, in his maddest ideas and maddest projects, who might not count upon numbers to support his principles and execute his designs.

Many of the changes, by a great misnomer called Parliamentary Reforms, went, not in the intention of all the professors and supporters of them, undoubtedly, but went in their certain, and, in my opinion, not very remote effect, home to the utter destruction of the Constitution of this kingdom. Had they taken place, not France, but England, would have had the honor of leading up the death-dance of democratic revolution. Other projects, exactly coincident in time with those, struck at the very existence of the kingdom under any Constitution. There are who remember the blind fury of some and the lamentable helplessness of others; here, a torpid confusion, from a panic fear of the danger—there, the same inaction, from a stupid insensibility to it; here, well-wishers to the mischief—there, indifferent lookers-on. At the same time, a sort of National Convention, dubious in its nature and perilous in its example, nosed Parliament in the very seat of its authority—sat with a sort of superintendence over it—and little less than dictated to it, not only laws, but the very form and essence of legislature itself. In Ireland things ran in a still more eccentric course. Government was unnerved, confounded, and in a manner suspended. Its equipoise was totally gone. . . .

At that time I was connected with men of high place in the community. They loved liberty as much as the Duke of Bedford can do; and they understood it at least as well. Perhaps their politics, as usual, took a tincture from their character, and they cultivated what they loved. The liberty they pursued was a liberty inseparable from order, from virtue, from morals, and from religion—and was neither hypocritically nor fanatically followed. They did not wish that liberty, in itself one of the first of blessings, should in its perversion become the greatest curse which could fall upon mankind. To preserve the Constitution entire, and practically equal to all the great ends of its formation, not in one single part, but in all its parts, was to them the first object. Popularity and power they regarded alike. These were with them only different means of obtaining that object, and had no preference over each other in their minds, but as one or the other might afford a surer or a less certain prospect of arriving at that end. It is some consolation to me, in the cheerless gloom which darkens the evening of my life, that with them I commenced my political career, and never for a moment, in reality nor in appearance, for any length of time, was separated from their good wishes and good opinion.

By what accident it matters not, nor upon what desert, but just then, and in the midst of that hunt of obloquy which ever has pursued me with a full cry through life, I had obtained a very considerable degree of public confidence. I know well enough how equivocal a test this kind of popular opinion forms of the merit that obtained it. I am no stranger to the insecurity of its tenure. I do not boast of it. It is mentioned to show, not how highly I prize the thing, but my right to value the use I made of it. I endeavored to turn that short-lived advantage to myself into a permanent benefit to my country. . . . He is an ill-furnished undertaker who has no machinery but his own hands to work with. . . . I consulted and sincerely coöperated with men of all parties who seemed disposed to the same ends, or to any main part of them. Nothing to prevent disorder was omitted: when it appeared, nothing to subdue it was left uncounselled nor unexecuted, as far as I could prevail. At the time I speak of, and having a momentary lead, so aided and so encouraged, and as a feeble instrument in a mighty hand—I do not say I saved my country; I am sure I did my country important service. There were few, indeed, that did not at that time acknowledge it—and that time was thirteen years ago. It was but one voice, that no man in the kingdom better deserved an honorable provision should be made for him.

So much for my general conduct through the whole of the portentous crisis from 1780 to 1782, and the general sense then entertained of that conduct by my country. But my character as a reformer, in the particular instances which the Duke of Bedford refers to, is so connected in principle with my opinions on the hideous changes which have since barbarized France, and, spreading thence, threaten the political and moral order of the whole world, that it seems to demand something of a more detailed discussion.

My economical reforms were not, as his Grace may think, the suppression of a paltry pension or employment, more or less. Economy in my plans was, as it ought to be, secondary, subordinate, instrumental. I acted on state principles. I found a great distemper in the commonwealth, and according to the nature of the evil and of the object I treated it. The malady was deep; it was complicated, in the causes and in the symptoms. Throughout it was full of contra-indicants. On one hand, government, daily growing more invidious from an apparent increase of the means of strength, was every day growing more contemptible by real weakness. Nor was this dissolution confined to government commonly so called. It extended to Parliament, which was losing not a little in its dignity and estimation by an opinion of its not acting on worthy motives. On the other hand, the desires of the people (partly natural and partly infused into them by art) appeared in so wild and inconsiderate a manner with regard to the economical object, (for I set aside for a moment the dreadful tampering with the body of the Constitution itself,) that, if their petitions had literally been complied with, the state would have been convulsed, and a gate would have been opened through which all property might be sacked and ravaged. Nothing could have saved the public from the mischiefs of the false reform but its absurdity, which would soon have brought itself, and with it all real reform, into discredit. This would have left a rankling wound in the hearts of the people, who would know they had failed in the accomplishment of their wishes, but who, like the rest of mankind in all ages, would impute the blame to anything rather than to their own proceedings. But there were then persons in the world who nourished complaint, and would have been thoroughly disappointed, if the people were ever satisfied. I was not of that humor. I wished that they *should* be satisfied. It was my aim to give to the people the substance of what I knew they desired, and what I thought was right, whether they desired it or not, before it had been modified for them into senseless petitions. I knew that there is a manifest, marked distinction, which ill men with ill designs, or weak men incapable of any design, will constantly be confounding—that is, a marked distinction between change and reformation. The former alters the substance of the objects themselves, and gets rid of all their essential good as well as of all the accidental evil annexed to them. Change is novelty; and whether it is to operate any one of the effects of reformation at all, or whether it may not contradict the very principle upon which reformation is desired, cannot be certainly known beforehand. Reform is not a change in the substance or in the primary modification of the object, but a direct application of a remedy to the grievance complained of. So far as that is removed, all is sure. It stops there; and if it fails, the substance which underwent the operation, at the very worst, is but where it was. . . .

It cannot at this time be too often repeated, line upon line, precept upon precept, until it comes into the currency of a proverb—*To innovate is not to reform.* The French revolutionists complained of everything; they refused to reform anything; and they left nothing, no, nothing at all, *unchanged.* The consequences are *before* us—not in remote history, not in future prognostication: they are about us; they are upon us. They shake the public security; they menace private enjoyment. They dwarf the growth of the young; they break the quiet of the old. If we travel, they stop our way. They infest us in town; they pursue us to the country. Our business is interrupted, our repose is troubled, our pleasures are saddened, our very studies are poisoned and perverted, and knowledge is rendered worse than ignorance, by the enormous evils of this dreadful innovation. The Revolution harpies of France, sprung from Night and Hell, or from that chaotic Anarchy which generates equivocally "all monstrous, all prodigious things," cuckoo-like, adulterously lay their eggs, and brood over, and hatch them in the nest of every neighboring state. These obscene harpies, who deck themselves in I know not what divine attributes, but who in reality are foul and ravenous birds of prey, (both mothers and daughters,) flutter over our heads, and souse down upon our tables, and leave nothing unrent, unrifled, unravaged, or unpolluted with the slime of their filthy offal. . . .

If his Grace can contemplate the result of this complete innovation, or, as some friends of his will call it, *reform,* in the whole body of its solidity and compound mass, at which, as Hamlet says, the face of heaven glows with horror and indignation, and which, in truth, makes every reflecting mind and every feeling heart perfectly thought-sick, without a thorough abhorrence of everything they say and everything they do, I am amazed at the morbid strength or the natural infirmity of his mind.

It was, then, not my love, but my hatred to innovation, that produced my plan of reform. Without troubling myself with the exactness of the logical diagram, I considered them as things substantially opposite. It was to prevent that evil, that I proposed the measures which his Grace is pleased, and I am not sorry he is pleased, to recall to my recollection. I had (what I hope that noble Duke will remember in all his operations) a state to preserve, as well as a state to reform. I had a people to gratify, but not to inflame or to mislead. I do not claim half the credit for what I did as for what I prevented from being done. In that situation of the public mind, I did not undertake, as was then proposed, to new-model the House of Commons or the House of Lords, or to change the authority under which any officer of the crown acted, who was suffered at all to exist. Crown, lords, commons, judicial system, system of administration, existed as they had existed before, and in the mode and manner in which they had always existed. My measures were, what I then truly stated them to the House to be, in their intent, healing and mediatorial. A complaint was made of too much influence in the House of Commons: I reduced it in both Houses; and I gave my reasons, article by article, for every reduction, and showed why I thought it safe for the service of the state. I heaved the lead every inch of way I made. A disposition to expense was complained of: to that I opposed, not mere retrenchment, but a system of economy, which would make a random expense, without plan or foresight, in future, not easily practicable. I proceeded upon principles of research to put me in possession of my matter, on principles of method to regulate it, and on principles in the human mind and in civil affairs to secure and perpetuate the operation. I conceived nothing arbitrarily, nor proposed anything to be done by the will and pleasure of others or my own—but by reason, and by reason only. I have ever abhorred, since the first dawn of my understanding to this its obscure twilight, all the operations of opinion, fancy, inclination, and will, in the affairs of government, where only a sovereign reason, paramount to all forms of legislation and administration, should dictate. Government is made for the very purpose of opposing that reason to will and to caprice, in the reformers or in the reformed, in the governors or in the governed, in kings, in senates, or in people. . . .

But do I justify his Majesty's grace on these grounds? I think them the least of my services. The time gave them an occasional value. What I have done in the way of political economy was far from confined to this body of measures. I did not come into Parliament to con my lesson. I had earned my pension before I set my foot in St. Stephen's Chapel. I was prepared and disciplined to this political warfare. The first session I sat in Parliament, I found it necessary to analyze the whole commercial, financial, constitutional, and foreign interests of Great Britain and its empire. A great deal was then done; and more, far more, would have been done, if more had been permitted by events. Then, in the vigor of my manhood, my constitution sunk under my labor. Had I then died, (and I seemed to myself very near death,) I had then earned for those who belonged to me more than the Duke of Bedford's ideas of service are of power to estimate. But, in truth, these services I am called to account for are not those on which I value myself the most. If I were to call for a reward, (which I have never done,) it should be for those in which for fourteen years without intermission I showed the most industry and had the least success: I mean in the affairs of India. They are those on which I value myself the most: most for the importance, most for the labor, most for the judgment, most for constancy and perseverance in the pursuit. Others may value them most for the *intention*. In that, surely, they are not mistaken.

Does his Grace think that they who advised the crown to make my retreat easy considered me only as an economist? That, well understood, however, is a good deal. If I had not deemed it of some value, I should not have made political economy an object of my humble studies from my very early youth to near the end of my service in Parliament, even before (at least to any knowledge of mine) it had employed the thoughts of speculative men in other parts of Europe. At that time it was still in its infancy in England, where, in the last century, it had its origin. Great and learned men thought my studies were not wholly thrown away, and deigned to communicate with me now and then on some particulars of their immortal works. Something of these studies may appear incidentally in some of the earliest things I published. The House has been witness to their effect, and has profited of them, more or less, for above eight-and-twenty years.

To their estimate I leave the matter. I was not, like his Grace of Bedford, swaddled and rocked and dandled into a legislator: *"Nitor in adversum"* is the motto for a man like me. I possessed not one of the qualities nor cultivated one of the arts that recommend men to the favor and protection of the great. I was not made for a minion or a tool. As little did I follow the trade of winning the hearts by imposing on the understandings of the people. At every step of my progress in life, (for in every step was I traversed and opposed,) and at every turnpike I met, I was obliged to show my passport, and again and again to prove my sole title to the honor of being useful to my country, by a proof that I was not wholly unac-

quainted with its laws and the whole system of its interests
both abroad and at home. Otherwise, no rank, no toleration
even, for me. I had no arts but manly arts. On them I have
stood, and, please God, in spite of the Duke of Bedford and
the Earl of Lauderdale, to the last gasp will I stand.

Had his Grace condescended to inquire concerning the person whom he has not thought it below him to reproach, he
might have found, that, in the whole course of my life, I have
never, on any pretence of economy, or on any other pretence, so much as in a single instance, stood between any man
and his reward of service or his encouragement in useful talent and pursuit, from the highest of those services and pursuits to the lowest. On the contrary, I have on an hundred
occasions exerted myself with singular zeal to forward every
man's even tolerable pretensions. I have more than once had
good-natured reprehensions from my friends for carrying the
matter to something bordering on abuse. This line of conduct,
whatever its merits might be, was partly owing to natural
disposition, but I think full as much to reason and principle.
I looked on the consideration of public service or public ornament to be real and very justice; and I ever held a scanty and
penurious justice to partake of the nature of a wrong. I held
it to be, in its consequences, the worst economy in the world.
In saving money I soon can count up all the good I do; but
when by a cold penury I blast the abilities of a nation, and
stunt the growth of its active energies, the ill I may do is
beyond all calculation. Whether it be too much or too little,
whatever I have done has been general and systematic. I have
never entered into those trifling vexations and oppressive details that have been falsely and most ridiculously laid to my
charge.

Did I blame the pensions given to Mr. Barré and Mr. Dunning between the proposition and execution of my plan? No!
surely, no! Those pensions were within my principles. I assert it, those gentlemen deserved their pensions, their titles—
all they had; and if more they had, I should have been but
pleased the more. They were men of talents; they were men of
service. . . . I have never heard the Earl of Lauderdale complain of these pensions. He finds nothing wrong till he comes
to me. This is impartiality, in the true, modern, revolutionary
style. . . .

It may be new to his Grace, but I beg leave to tell him that
mere parsimony is not economy. It is separable in theory
from it; and in fact it may or it may not be a *part* of economy,

according to circumstances. Expense, and great expense, may be an essential part in true economy. If parsimony were to be considered as one of the kinds of that virtue, there is, however, another and an higher economy. Economy is a distributive virtue, and consists, not in saving, but in selection. Parsimony requires no providence, no sagacity, no powers of combination, no comparison, no judgment. Mere instinct, and that not an instinct of the noblest kind, may produce this false economy in perfection. The other economy has larger views. It demands a discriminating judgment, and a firm, sagacious mind. It shuts one door to impudent importunity, only to open another, and a wider, to unpresuming merit. If none but meritorious service or real talent were to be rewarded, this nation has not wanted, and this nation will not want, the means of rewarding all the service it ever will receive, and encouraging all the merit it ever will produce. No state, since the foundation of society, has been impoverished by that species of profusion. Had the economy of selection and proportion been at all times observed, we should not now have had an overgrown Duke of Bedford, to oppress the industry of humble men, and to limit, by the standard of his own conceptions, the justice, the bounty, or, if he pleases, the charity of the crown.

His Grace may think as meanly as he will of my deserts in the far greater part of my conduct in life. It is free for him to do so. There will always be some difference of opinion in the value of political services. But there is one merit of mine which he, of all men living, ought to be the last to call in question. I have supported with very great zeal, and I am told with some degree of success, those opinions, or, if his Grace likes another expression better, those old prejudices, which buoy up the ponderous mass of his nobility, wealth, and titles. I have omitted no exertion to prevent him and them from sinking to that level to which the meretricious French faction his Grace at least coquets with omit no exertion to reduce both. I have done all I could to discountenance their inquiries into the fortunes of those who hold large portions of wealth without any apparent merit of their own. I have strained every nerve to keep the Duke of Bedford in that situation which alone makes him my superior. Your Lordship has been a witness of the use he makes of that preëminence.

But be it that this is virtue; be it that there is virtue in this well-selected rigor: yet all virtues are not equally becoming to all men and at all times. There are crimes, undoubtedly there are crimes, which in all seasons of our existence ought to put a generous antipathy in action—crimes that provoke an indignant justice, and call forth a warm and animated pursuit. But all things that concern what I may call the preventive police of morality, all things merely rigid, harsh, and censorial, the antiquated moralists at whose feet I was brought up would not have thought these the fittest matter to form the favorite virtues of young men of rank. What might have been well enough, and have been received with a veneration mixed with awe and terror, from an old, severe, crabbed Cato, would have wanted something of propriety in the young Scipios, the ornament of the Roman nobility, in the flower of their life. But the times, the morals, the masters, the scholars, have all undergone a thorough revolution. It is a vile, illiberal school, this new French academy of the *sans-culottes*. There is nothing in it that is fit for a gentleman to learn. . . .

The awful state of the time, and not myself, or my own justification, is my true object in what I now write, or in what I shall ever write or say. It little signifies to the world what becomes of such things as me, or even as the Duke of Bedford. What I say about either of us is nothing more than a vehicle, as you, my Lord, will easily perceive, to convey my sentiments on matters far more worthy of your attention. It is when I stick to my apparent first subject that I ought to apologize, not when I depart from it. I therefore must beg your Lordship's pardon for again resuming it after this very short digression—assuring you that I shall never altogether lose sight of such matter as persons abler than I am may turn to some profit.

The Duke of Bedford conceives that he is obliged to call the attention of the House of Peers to his Majesty's grant to me, which he considers as excessive and out of all bounds.

I know not how it has happened, but it really seems, that, whilst his Grace was meditating his well-considered censure upon me, he fell into a sort of sleep. Homer nods, and the Duke of Bedford may dream; and as dreams (even his golden dreams) are apt to be ill-pieced and incongruously put together, his Grace preserved his idea of reproach to *me*, but took the subject-matter from the crown grants *to his own family.* This is "the stuff of which his dreams are made." In that way of putting things together his Grace is perfectly in the right. The grants to the House of Russell were so enormous as not only to outrage economy, but even to stagger credibility. The Duke of Bedford is the leviathan among all the creatures of the crown. He tumbles about his unwieldy bulk, he plays and frolics in the ocean of the royal bounty. Huge as he is, and whilst "he lies floating many a rood," he is still a creature. His ribs, his fins, his whalebone, his blubber, the very spiracles through which he spouts a torrent of brine against his origin, and covers me all over with the spray, everything of him and about him is from the throne. Is it for *him* to question the dispensation of the royal favor?

I really am at a loss to draw any sort of parallel between the public merits of his Grace, by which he justifies the grants he holds, and these services of mine, on the favorable construction of which I have obtained what his Grace so much disapproves. In private life I have not at all the honor of acquaintance with the noble Duke; but I ought to presume, and it costs me nothing to do so, that he abundantly deserves the esteem and love of all who live with him. But as to public service, why, truly, it would not be more ridiculous for me to compare myself, in rank, in fortune, in splendid descent, in youth, strength, or figure, with the Duke of Bedford, than to make a parallel between his services and my attempts to be useful to my country. It would not be gross adulation, but uncivil irony, to say that he has any public merit of his own to keep alive the idea of the services by which his vast landed pensions were obtained. My merits, whatever they are, are original and personal: his are derivative. It is his ancestor, the original pensioner, that has laid up this inexhaustible fund of merit which makes his Grace so very delicate and exceptious about the merit of all other grantees of the crown. Had he permitted me to remain in quiet, I should have said, " 'T is his estate: that's enough. It is his by law: what have I to do with it or its history?" He would naturally have said, on his side, " 'T is this man's fortune. He is as good now as my ancestor was two hundred and fifty years ago. I am a young man with very old pensions; he is an old man with very young pensions: that's all."

Why will his Grace, by attacking me, force me reluctantly to compare my little merit with that which obtained from the crown those prodigies of profuse donation by which he tramples on the mediocrity of humble and laborious individuals? . . .

Well, then, since the new grantees have war made on them by the old, . . . let us turn our eyes to history, in which great men have always a pleasure in contemplating the heroic origin of their house.

The first peer of the name, the first purchaser of the grants, was a Mr. Russell, a person of an ancient gentleman's family, raised by being a minion of Henry the Eighth. As there generally is some resemblance of character to create these relations, the favorite was in all likelihood much such another as his master. The first of those immoderate grants was not taken from the ancient demesne of the crown, but from the recent confiscation of the ancient nobility of the land. The lion, having sucked the blood of his prey, threw the offal carcass to the jackal in waiting. Having tasted once the food of confiscation, the favorites became fierce and ravenous. This worthy favorite's first grant was from the lay nobility. The second, infinitely improving on the enormity of the first, was from the plunder of the Church. In truth, his Grace is somewhat excusable for his dislike to a grant like mine, not only in its quantity, but in its kind, so different from his own.

Mine was from a mild and benevolent sovereign: his from Henry the Eighth.

Mine had not its fund in the murder of any innocent person of illustrious rank,* or in the pillage of any body of unoffending men. His grants were from the aggregate and consolidated funds of judgments iniquitously legal, and from possessions voluntarily surrendered by the lawful proprietors with the gibbet at their door.

The merit of the grantee whom he derives from was that of being a prompt and greedy instrument of a *levelling* tyrant, who oppressed all descriptions of his people, but who fell with particular fury on everything that was *great and noble.* Mine has been in endeavoring to screen every man, in every class, from oppression, and particularly in defending the high and eminent, who, in the bad times of confiscating princes, confiscating chief governors, or confiscating demagogues, are the most exposed to jealousy, avarice, and envy.

The merit of the original grantee of his Grace's pensions was in giving his hand to the work, and partaking the spoil, with a prince who plundered a part of the national Church of his time and country. Mine was in defending the whole of the national Church of my own time and my own country, and the whole of the national Churches of all countries, from the principles and the examples which lead to ecclesiastical pillage, thence to a contempt of *all* prescriptive titles, thence to

* See the history of the melancholy catastrophe of the Duke of Buckingham. Temp. Hen. VIII.

the pillage of *all* property, and thence to universal desolation.

The merit of the origin of his Grace's fortune was in being a favorite and chief adviser to a prince who left no liberty to their native country. My endeavor was to obtain liberty for the municipal country in which I was born, and for all descriptions and denominations in it. Mine was to support with unrelaxing vigilance every right, every privilege, every franchise, in this my adopted, my dearer, and more comprehensive country; and not only to preserve those rights in this chief seat of empire, but in every nation, in every land, in every climate, language, and religion, in the vast domain that still is under the protection, and the larger that was once under the protection, of the British crown.

His founder's merits were, by arts in which he served his master and made his fortune, to bring poverty, wretchedness, and depopulation on his country. Mine were under a benevolent prince, in promoting the commerce, manufactures, and agriculture of his kingdom—in which his Majesty shows an eminent example, who even in his amusements is a patriot, and in hours of leisure an improver of his native soil.

His founder's merit was the merit of a gentleman raised by the arts of a court and the protection of a Wolsey to the eminence of a great and potent lord. His merit in that eminence was, by instigating a tyrant to injustice, to provoke a people to rebellion. My merit was, to awaken the sober part of the country, that they might put themselves on their guard against any one potent lord, or any greater number of potent lords, or any combination of great leading men of any sort, if ever they should attempt to proceed in the same courses, but in the reverse order—that is, by instigating a corrupted populace to rebellion, and, through that rebellion, introducing a tyranny yet worse than the tyranny which his Grace's ancestor supported, and of which he profited in the manner we behold in the despotism of Henry the Eighth.

The political merit of the first pensioner of his Grace's house was that of being concerned as a counsellor of state in advising, and in his person executing, the conditions of a dishonorable peace with France—the surrendering the fortress of Boulogne, then our outguard on the Continent. By that surrender, Calais, the key of France, and the bridle in the mouth of that power, was not many years afterwards finally lost. My merit has been in resisting the power and pride of France, under any form of its rule; but in opposing it with the greatest zeal and earnestness, when that rule appeared in the worst form it could assume—the worst, indeed, which the prime cause and principle of all evil could possibly give it. It was my endeavor by every means to excite a spirit in the House, where I had the honor of a seat, for carrying on with early vigor and decision the most clearly just and necessary war that this or any nation ever carried on, in order to save my country from the iron yoke of its power, and from the more dreadful contagion of its principles—to preserve, while they can be preserved, pure and untainted, the ancient, inbred integrity, piety, good-nature, and good-humor of the people of England, from the dreadful pestilence which, beginning in France, threatens to lay waste the whole moral and in a great degree the whole physical world, having done both in the focus of its most intense malignity.

The labors of his Grace's founder merited the "curses, not loud, but deep," of the Commons of England, on whom *he* and his master had effected a *complete Parliamentary Reform,* by making them, in their slavery and humiliation, the true and adequate representatives of a debased, degraded, and undone people. My merits were in having had an active, though not always an ostentatious share, in every one act, without exception, of undisputed constitutional utility in my time, and in having supported, on all occasions, the authority, the efficiency, and the privileges of the Commons of Great Britain. . . .

Thus stands the account of the comparative merits of the crown grants which compose the Duke of Bedford's fortune as balanced against mine. In the name of common sense, why should the Duke of Bedford think that none but of the House of Russell are entitled to the favor of the crown? Why should he imagine that no king of England has been capable of judging of merit but King Henry the Eighth? Indeed, he will pardon me, he is a little mistaken: all virtue did not end in the first Earl of Bedford . . .

Had it pleased God to continue to me the hopes of succession, I should have been, according to my mediocrity and the mediocrity of the age I live in, a sort of founder of a family: I should have left a son, who, in all the points in which personal merit can be viewed, in science, in erudition, in genius, in taste, in honor, in generosity, in humanity, in every liberal sentiment and every liberal accomplishment, would not have shown himself inferior to the Duke of Bedford, or to any of those whom he traces in his line. . . .

But a Disposer whose power we are little able to resist, and whose wisdom it behoves us not at all to dispute, has ordained it in another manner, and (whatever my querulous weakness might suggest) a far better. The storm has gone over me; and I lie like one of those old oaks which the late hurricane has scattered about me. I am stripped of all my honors, I am torn up by the roots, and lie prostrate on the earth. There, and prostrate there, I most unfeignedly recognize the Divine justice, and in some degree submit to it. But whilst I humble myself before God, I do not know that it is forbidden to repel the attacks of unjust and inconsiderate men. . . . I am alone. I have none to meet my enemies in the gate. Indeed, my Lord, I greatly deceive myself, if in this hard season I would give a peck of refuse wheat for all that is called fame and honor in the world. . . . But we are all of us made to shun disgrace, as we are made to shrink from pain and poverty and disease. It is an instinct; and under the direction of reason, instinct is always in the right. I live in an inverted order. They who ought to have succeeded me are gone before me. They who should have been to me as posterity are in the place of ancestors. . . .

The crown has considered me after long service: the crown has paid the Duke of Bedford by advance. He has had a long credit for any service which he may perform hereafter. He is secure, and long may he be secure, in his advance, whether he performs any services or not. But let him take care how he endangers the safety of that Constitution which secures his own utility or his own insignificance, or how he discourages those who take up even puny arms to defend an order of things which, like the sun of heaven, shines alike on the useful and the worthless. His grants are ingrafted on the public law of Europe, covered with the awful hoar of innumerable ages. They are guarded by the sacred rules of prescription, found in that full treasury of jurisprudence from which the jejuneness and penury of our municipal law has by degrees been enriched and strengthened. This prescription I had my share . . . in bringing to its perfection. The Duke of Bedford will stand as long as prescriptive law endures—as long as the great, stable laws of property, common to us with all civilized nations, are kept in their integrity, and without the smallest intermixture of the laws, maxims, principles, or precedents of the Grand Revolution. They are secure against all changes but one. The whole Revolutionary system, institutes, digest, code, novels, text, gloss, comment, are not only not the same, but they are the very reverse, and the reverse fundamentally, of all the laws on which civil life has hitherto been upheld in all the governments of the world. The learned professors of the Rights of Man regard prescription not as a title to bar all claim set up against old possession, but they look on prescription as itself a bar against the possessor and proprietor. They hold an immemorial possession to be no more than a long continued and therefore an aggravated injustice.

Such are *their* ideas, such *their* religion, and such *their* law. But as to *our* country and *our* race, as long as the well-compacted structure of our Church and State, the sanctuary, the holy of holies of that ancient law, defended by reverence, defended by power, a fortress at once and a temple, shall stand inviolate on the brow of the British Sion—as long as the British monarchy, not more limited than fenced by the orders of the state, shall, like the proud Keep of Windsor, rising in the majesty of proportion, and girt with the double belt of its kindred and coëval towers, as long as this awful structure shall oversee and guard the subjected land—so long the mounds and dikes of the low, fat, Bedford level will have nothing to fear from all the pickaxes of all the levellers of France. As long as our sovereign lord the king, and his faithful subjects, the lords and commons of this realm—the triple cord which no man can break—the solemn, sworn, constitutional frank-pledge of this nation—the firm guaranties of each other's being and each other's right—the joint and several securities, each in its place and order, for every kind and every quality of property and of dignity—as long as these endure, so long the Duke of Bedford is safe, and we are all safe together—the high from the blights of envy and the spoliations of rapacity, the low from the iron hand of oppression and the insolent spurn of contempt. . . .

But if the rude inroad of Gallic tumult, with its sophistical rights of man to falsify the account, and its sword as a make-weight to throw into the scale, shall be introduced into our city by a misguided populace, set on by proud great men, themselves blinded and intoxicated by a frantic ambition, we shall all of us perish and be overwhelmed in a common ruin. If a great storm blow on our coast, it will cast the whales on the strand, as well as the periwinkles. His Grace will not survive the poor grantee he despises—no, not for a twelvemonth. If the great look for safety in the services they render to this Gallic cause, it is to be foolish even above the weight of privilege allowed to wealth. If his Grace be one of these whom they endeavor to proselytize, he ought to be aware of the character of the sect whose doctrines he is invited to embrace. With them insurrection is the most sacred of revolutionary duties to the state. Ingratitude to benefactors is the first of revolutionary virtues. Ingratitude is, indeed, their four cardinal virtues compacted and amalgamated into one; and he will find it in everything that has happened since the commencement of the philosophic Revolution to this hour. If he pleads the merit of having performed the duty of insurrection against the order he lives in, (God forbid he ever should!) the merit of others will be to perform the duty of insurrection against him. If he pleads (again God forbid he should, and I do not suspect he will) his ingratitude to the crown for its creation of his family, others will plead their right and duty to pay him in kind. They will laugh, indeed they will laugh, at his parchment and his wax. His deeds will be drawn out with the rest of the lumber of his evidence-room, and burnt to the tune of *Ça ira* in the courts of Bedford (then Equality) House.

Am I to blame, if I attempt to pay his Grace's hostile reproaches to me with a friendly admonition to himself? Can I be blamed for pointing out to him in what manner he is like to be affected, if the sect of the cannibal philosophers of France should proselytize any considerable part of this people, and, by their joint proselytizing arms, should conquer that government to which his Grace does not seem to me to give all the support his own security demands? Surely it is proper that he, and that others like him, should know the true genius of this sect—what their opinions are—what they have done, and to whom—and what (if a prognostic is to be formed from the dispositions and actions of men) it is certain they will do hereafter. He ought to know that they have sworn assistance, the only engagement they ever will keep, to all in this country who bear a resemblance to themselves, and who think, as such, that *the whole duty of man* consists in destruction. They are a misallied and disparaged branch of the House of Nimrod. They are the Duke of Bedford's natural hunters; and he is their natural game. Because he is not very profoundly reflecting, he sleeps in profound security: they, on the contrary, are always vigilant, active, enterprising, and, though far removed from any knowledge which makes men estimable or useful, in all the instruments and resources of evil their leaders are not meanly instructed or insufficiently furnished. In the French Revolution everything is new, and, from want of preparation to meet so unlooked-for an evil, everything is dangerous. Never before this time was a set of literary men converted into a gang of robbers and assassins; never before did a den of bravoes and banditti assume the garb and tone of an academy of philosophers.

Let me tell his Grace, that an union of such characters, monstrous as it seems, is not made for producing despicable enemies. But if they are formidable as foes, as friends they are dreadful indeed. The men of property in France, confiding in a force which seemed to be irresistible because it had never been tried, neglected to prepare for a conflict with their enemies at their own weapons. They were found in such a situation as the Mexicans were, when they were attacked by the dogs, the cavalry, the iron, and the gunpowder of an handful of bearded men, whom they did not know to exist in Nature. This is a comparison that some, I think, have made; and it is just. In France they had their enemies within their houses. They were even in the bosoms of many of them. But they had not sagacity to discern their savage character. They seemed tame, and even caressing. They had nothing but *douce humanité* in their mouth. They could not bear the punishment of the mildest laws on the greatest criminals. The slightest severity of justice made their flesh creep. The very idea that war existed in the world disturbed their repose. Military glory was no more, with them, than a splendid infamy. Hardly would they hear of self-defence, which they reduced within such bounds as to leave it no defence at all. All this while they meditated the confiscations and massacres we have seen. Had any one told these unfortunate noblemen and gentlemen how and by whom the grand fabric of the French monarchy under which they flourished would be subverted, they would not have pitied him as a visionary, but would have turned from him as what they call a *mauvais plaisant*. Yet we have seen what has happened. The persons who have suffered from the cannibal philosophy of France are so like the Duke of Bedford, that nothing but his Grace's probably not speaking quite so good French could enable us to find out any difference. A great many of them had as pompous titles as he, and were of full as illustrious a race; some few of them had fortunes as ample; several of them, without meaning the least disparagement to the Duke of Bedford, were as wise, and as virtuous, and as valiant, and as well educated, and as complete in all the lineaments of men of honor, as he is; and to all this they had added the powerful outguard of a military profession, which, in its nature, renders men somewhat more cautious than those who have nothing to attend to but the lazy enjoyment of undisturbed possessions. But security was their ruin. They are dashed to pieces in the storm, and our shores are covered with the wrecks. If they had been aware that such a thing might happen, such a thing never could have happened.

I assure his Grace, that, if I state to him the designs of his enemies in a manner which may appear to him ludicrous and impossible, I tell him nothing that has not exactly happened, point by point, but twenty-four miles from our own shore. I assure him that the Frenchified faction, more encouraged than others are warned by what has happened in France, look at him and his landed possessions as an object at once of curiosity and rapacity. He is made for them in every part of their double character. As robbers, to them he is a noble booty; as speculatists, he is a glorious subject for their experimental philosophy. He affords matter for an extensive analysis in all the branches of their science, geometrical, physical, civil, and political. These philosophers are fanatics: independent of any interest, which, if it operated alone, would make them much more tractable, they are carried with such an headlong rage towards every desperate trial that they would sacrifice the whole human race to the slightest of their experiments. I am better able to enter into the character of this description of men than the noble Duke can be. I have lived long and variously in the world. Without any considerable pretensions to literature in myself, I have aspired to the love of letters. I have lived for a great many years in habitudes with those who professed them. I can form a tolerable estimate of what is likely to happen from a character chiefly dependent for fame and fortune on knowledge and talent, as well in its morbid and perverted state as in that which is sound and natural. Naturally, men so formed and finished are the first gifts of Providence to the world. But when they have once thrown off the fear of God, which was in all ages too often the case, and the fear of man, which is now the case, and when in that state they come to understand one another, and to act in corps, a more dreadful calamity cannot arise out of hell to scourge mankind. Nothing can be conceived more hard than the heart of a thorough-bred metaphysician. It comes nearer to the cold malignity of a wicked spirit than to the frailty and passion of a man. It is like that of the Principle of Evil himself, incorporeal, pure, unmixed, dephlegmated, defecated evil. It is no easy operation to eradicate humanity from the human breast. What Shakspeare calls the "compunctious visitings of Nature" will sometimes knock at their hearts, and protest against their murderous speculations. But they have a means of compounding with their nature. Their humanity is not dissolved; they only give it a long prorogation. They are ready to declare that they do not think two thousand years too long a period for the good that they pursue. It is remarkable that they never see any way to their projected good but by the road of some evil. Their imagination is not fatigued with the contemplation of human suffering through the wild waste of centuries added to centuries of misery and desolation. Their humanity is at their horizon—and, like the horizon, it always flies before them. The geometricians and the chemists bring, the one from the dry bones of their diagrams, and the other from the soot of their furnaces, dispositions that make them worse than indifferent about those feelings and habitudes which are the supports of the moral world. Ambition is come upon them suddenly; they are intoxicated with it, and it has rendered them fearless of the danger which may from thence arise to others or to themselves. These philosophers consider men in their experiments no more than they do mice in an air-pump or in a recipient of mephitic gas. Whatever his Grace may think of himself, they look upon him, and everything that belongs to him, with no more regard than they do upon the whiskers of that little long-tailed animal that has been long the game of the grave, demure, insidious, spring-nailed, velvet-pawed, green-eyed philosophers, whether going upon two legs or upon four.

His Grace's landed possessions are irresistibly inviting to an agrarian experiment. They are a downright insult upon the rights of man. They are more extensive than the territory of many of the Grecian republics; and they are without comparison more fertile than most of them. There are now republics in Italy, in Germany, and in Switzerland, which do not possess anything like so fair and ample a domain. There is scope for seven philosophers to proceed in their analytical experiments upon Harrington's seven different forms of republics, in the acres of this one Duke. Hitherto they have been wholly unproductive to speculation—fitted for nothing but to fatten bullocks, and to produce grain for beer, still more to stupefy the dull English understanding. Abbé Sieyès has whole nests of pigeon-holes full of constitutions ready-made, ticketed, sorted, and numbered, suited to every season and every fancy: some with the top of the pattern at the bottom, and some with the bottom at the top; some plain, some flowered; some distin-

guished for their simplicity, others for their complexity; some
of blood color, some of *boue de Paris;* some with directories,
others without a direction; some with councils of elders and
councils of youngsters, some without any council at all; some
where the electors choose the representatives, others where
the representatives choose the electors; some in long coats,
and some in short cloaks; some with pantaloons, some without breeches; some with five-shilling qualifications, some totally unqualified. So that no constitution-fancier may go un-
suited from his shop, provided he loves a pattern of pillage,
oppression, arbitrary imprisonment, confiscation, exile, revolutionary judgment, and legalized premeditated murder, in
any shapes into which they can be put. What a pity it is that
the progress of experimental philosophy should be checked
by his Grace's monopoly! Such are their sentiments, I assure
him; such is their language, when they dare to speak; and
such are their proceedings, when they have the means to
act.

Their geographers and geometricians have been some time
out of practice. It is some time since they have divided their
own country into squares. That figure has lost the charms of
its novelty. They want new lands for new trials. It is not only
the geometricians of the Republic that find him a good subject: the chemists have bespoke him, after the geometricians
have done with him. As the first set have an eye on his Grace's
lands, the chemists are not less taken with his buildings. They
consider mortar as a very anti-revolutionary invention, in its
present state, but, properly employed, an admirable material
for overturning all establishments. They have found that the
gunpowder of *ruins* is far the fittest for making other *ruins*,
and so *ad infinitum*. They have calculated what quantity of
matter convertible into nitre is to be found in Bedford House,
in Woburn Abbey, and in what his Grace and his trustees
have still suffered to stand of that foolish royalist, Inigo Jones,
in Covent Garden. Churches, play-houses, coffee-houses, all
alike, are destined to be mingled, and equalized, and blended
into one common rubbish . . .

While the Morveaux and Priestleys are proceeding with
these experiments upon the Duke of Bedford's houses, the
Sieyès, and the rest of the analytical legislators and constitu-
tion-venders, are quite as busy in their trade of decomposing
organization, in forming his Grace's vassals into primary assemblies, national guards, first, second, and third requisition-
ers, committees of research, conductors of the travelling

guillotine, judges of revolutionary tribunals, legislative hangmen, supervisors of domiciliary visitation, exactors of forced loans, and assessors of the maximum.

The din of all this smithery may some time or other possibly wake this noble Duke, and push him to an endeavor to save some little matter from their experimental philosophy. If he pleads his grants from the crown, he is ruined at the outset. If he pleads he has received them from the pillage of superstitious corporations, this indeed will stagger them a little, because they are enemies to all corporations and to all religion. However, they will soon recover themselves, and will tell his Grace, or his learned council, that all such property belongs to the *nation*—and that it would be more wise for him, if he wishes to live the natural term of a *citizen,* (that is, according to Condorcet's calculation, six months on an average,) not to pass for an usurper upon the national property. This is what the *serjeants*-at-law of the rights of man will say to the puny *apprentices* of the common law of England.

Is the genius of philosophy not yet known? You may as well think the garden of the Tuileries was well protected with the cords of ribbon insultingly stretched by the National Assembly to keep the sovereign *canaille* from intruding on the retirement of the poor King of the French as that such flimsy cobwebs will stand between the savages of the Revolution and their natural prey. Deep philosophers are no triflers; brave *sans-culottes* are no formalists. They will no more regard a Marquis of Tavistock than an Abbot of Tavistock; the Lord of Woburn will not be more respectable in their eyes than the Prior of Woburn; they will make no difference between the superior of a Covent Garden of nuns and of a Covent Garden of another description. They will not care a rush whether his coat is long or short—whether the color be purple, or blue and buff. They will not trouble *their* heads with what part of *his* head his hair is cut from; and they will look with equal respect on a tonsure and a crop. Their only question will be that of their Legendre, or some other of their legislative butchers: How he cuts up; how he tallows in the caul or on the kidneys.

Is it not a singular phenomenon, that, whilst the *sans-culotte* carcass-butchers and the philosophers of the shambles are pricking their dotted lines upon his hide, and, like the print of the poor ox that we see in the shop-windows at Charing Cross, alive as he is, and thinking no harm in the world, he is divided into rumps, and sirloins, and briskets, and into all sorts of pieces for roasting, boiling, and stewing, that, all the while they are measuring *him*, his Grace is measuring *me*—is invidiously comparing the bounty of the crown with the deserts of the defender of his order, and in the same moment fawning on those who have the knife half out of the sheath? Poor innocent!

> *"Pleased to the last, he crops the flowery food,*
> *And licks the hand just raised to shed his blood."* . . .

A SELECTED BIBLIOGRAPHY

"Edmund Burke and the Law of Nations," *The American Journal of International Law*, Vol. 47, No. 3, July 1953, pp. 397-413.

"Dr. Wu and Justice Holmes: A Reappraisal on Natural Law," *The University of Detroit Law Journal*, Vol. XVII, No. 3, March 1955, pp. 149-170.

"Edmund Burke and the Natural Law," *The University of Detroit Law Journal*, Vol. XXXIII, No. 2, January 1956, pp. 150-190.

"Edmund Burke, New York Agent," *Fordham Law Review*, Vol. XXV, No. 2, Summer 1956, pp. 402-406.

"Beyond the Dreams of Avarice," *Fordham Law Review*, Vol. XXVI, No. 3, Autumn 1957, pp. 602-604.

"The Present Impasse of the Idea of Progress," *Modern Age*, Vol. 2, No. 1, Winter 1957-58, pp. 62-75.

Edmund Burke and the Natural Law (Ann Arbor: University of Michigan Press, 1958), 311 pp. Second edition, Ann Arbor Paperbacks, 1965.

"Fountain of Justice: A Study in the Natural Law," *The University of Detroit Law Journal*, Vol. 35, No. 4, April 1958, pp. 550-558.

"Naturrecht und Politik," *Die Krone*, June 1, 1958, p. 5.

Anthology selections: Passages from *Edmund Burke and the Natural Law*, in *Cases on Jurisprudence* (American Casebook Series), (St. Paul, Minnesota: West Publishing Co., 1958, pp. 189-90; 625-26; 695 and 698.

Article-review of *Burke and the Nature of Politics: The Age of the American Revolution*, by Carl B. Cone, *Thought*, Summer 1958, pp. 308-10.

"Foreword" and editor of the "Jurisprudence Issue" of *The University of Detroit Law Journal*, Vol. 36, No. 2, December 1958, pp. 117-60.

Review of *The World of the Polis* and *Plato and Aristotle*, by Eric Voegelin, *Modern Age*, Vol. 3, No. 2, Spring, 1959, pp. 189-96.

"Burke's Letters," *Modern Age*, Vol. 3, Summer, 1959, pp. 329-30.

The Burke Newsletter, Editor and contributor. Vol. I, No. 1, Summer, 1959, through Vol. II, No. 3, Winter, 1960-61, pp. 1-42, in *Modern Age*. Vol. II, No. 4, Spring, 1961, through Vol. VIII, No. 3, Spring, 1967, pp. 43-747, published by the University of Detroit Press. Name of journal changed to *Studies in Burke and His Time*. Vol. IX, No. 1, Fall, 1967, through Vol. XII, No. 3, Spring, 1971, pp. 751-1956, published by Alfred University, Alfred, New York. Editorial Advisor, *Studies in Burke and His Time*, Vol XIII, No. 1, Fall, 1972 through Vol. XVI, No. 3, 1975, pp. 1957 ff., published by Alfred University. Editorial Advisor, *Studies in Burke and His Time*, Vol. 17, No. 1, Winter, 1976 ff., published by Texas Tech University.

"The Law School in Relation to General Education," in *The Law Schools Look Ahead* (Ann Arbor: University of Michigan Law School, 1959), pp. 221-24.

"Elective Franchise" and "Education," in *Report to Governor John B. Swainson on Constitutional Revision*, March, 1961, pp. 7-9 and 31-34.

Review of *The Correspondence of Edmund Burke*, ed. George H. Guttridge, Vol. III (1774-1778), *The Burke Newsletter*, Spring-Summer, 1961, II, p. 51.

Review of *The Gazetteer, 1735-1797*, by Robert L.

Haig, *The Burke Newsletter*, Spring-Summer, 1961, II, pp. 51-52.

Review of *Reflections With Edmund Burke*, ed. Timothy P. Sheehan, *The Burke Newsletter*, Spring-Summer, 1961, II, p. 51.

"Burke and the Sensibility of Rousseau," *Thought*, Vol. XXXVI, No. 141, Summer, 1961, pp. 246-76.

"The Basis of Burke's Political Conservatism," *Modern Age*, Vol. V, No. 3, Summer, 1961, pp. 263-74.

"Wetterleuchten der Revolution: Edmund Burkes erste Auseinandersetzungen mit Jean-Jacques Rousseau," *Osterreichische Akademische Blatter*, Vol. II, No. 7-8, Summer, 1961, pp. 5-7.

Review of *Samuel Johnson the Moralist*, by Robert Voitle, *The Burke Newsletter*, Vol. III, No. 1, Fall, 1961, pp. 66-69.

Review of *Burke, Disraeli, and Churchill: The Politics of Perseverance*, by Stephen Graubard, *The Burke Newsletter*, Vol. III, No. 1, Fall, 1961, pp. 65-66.

A Methodology for Studying the Services of Local Government (Detroit: The Southeastern Michigan Metropolitan Community Research Corporation, 1961), 165 pp.

Review of *The Brave New World of the Enlightenment*, by Louis I. Bredvold, *The Burke Newsletter*, Vol. III, No. 4, Summer, 1962, pp. 148-57. Also reviewed in *University Bookman*, Vol. II, No. 3, Fall, 1962.

Review of *English Literature—1660-1800: A Bibliography of Modern Studies, Compiled for Philological Quarterly*, Vol III, 1951-56, and Vol. IV, 1957-60, *The Burke Newsletter*, Vol. IV, No. 1, Fall, 1962, pp. 177-78.

Review of *Yorkshire and English National Politics, 1783-1784*, by N.C. Phillips, *The Burke Newsletter*, Vol. IV, No. 1, Fall, 1962, pp. 174-77.

"Burke's Prose Style," *The Burke Newsletter*, Vol. IV, No. 2, Winter, 1962-63, pp. 181-84.

Review of *The Burke-Paine Controversy: Texts and Criticism*, ed. by Ray B. Browne (New York: Harcourt, Brace and World, 1963), *The Burke Newsletter*, Vol. IV, No. 2, Winter, 1962-63, pp. 193-95.

Edmund Burke: Selected Writings and Speeches, ed. and with introduction and notes, (New York: Doubleday and Co., 1963), 586 pp. An Anchor Paperback.

"A Reply to Donald J. Greene's 'Samuel Johnson and Natural Law,' " *The Journal of British Studies*, Vol. II, May, 1963, pp. 76-83; and a further reply, *The Journal of British Studies*, Vol. III, Nov. 1963, pp. 158-64. A final reply in a letter to the editor, *The Journal of British Studies*, Vol. IV, May, 1965, pp. 149-57.

Review of *The English Press in Politics, 1760-1774*, by Robert R. Rea, *The Burke Newsletter*, Vol. IV, No. 3 and 4, Spring-Summer, 1963, pp. 226-28.

Review of *The Idea of Order: Contributions to a Philosophy of Politics*, by Hans Barth, trans. by Ernest W. Hankamer and William M. Newell (D. Reidel Co., Dordrecht, Holland, 1960), *The Burke Newsletter*, Vol. IV, No. 3 and 4, Spring-Summer, 1963, pp. 221-23.

Review of *The London Daily Press, 1772-1792*, by Lucyle Werkmeister, *The Burke Newsletter*, Vol. IV, No. 3 and 4, Spring-Summer, 1963, pp. 228-33.

Review of *The Correspondence of Edmund Burke*, ed. John A. Woods, Vol. IV (1778-1782), *The Burke Newsletter*, Vol. V, No. 2, Winter, 1963-64, pp. 292-95.

"Edmund Burke in the Twentieth Century," *Bucknell Review*, Vol. XII, No. 2, May, 1964, pp 65-89.

The Predicament of Modern Politics, ed Harold J. Spaeth (Detroit: The University of Detroit Press,

1964), comments on pp. 31-32; 38-39, 84 and 89-90.

Review of *The Language of Politics in the Age of Wilkes and Burke,* by James T. Boulton, *The Burke Newsletter,* Vol. V, No. 3 and 4, Spring-Summer, 1964, pp. 340-45.

The Relevance of Edmund Burke, ed. by Peter J. Stanlis (New York: P.J. Kenedy & Sons, 1964), 134 pp. (Essays on Burke by Peter J. Stanlis, C.P. Ives, Francis Canavan and Ross J.S. Hoffman, with an introduction by Louis I. Bredvold).

Review of *Edmund Burke: Speech on Conciliation with the Colonies,* ed. by Jeffrey Hart (Henry Regnery Co., Chicago, 1964), *The Burke Newsletter,* Vol. VI, No. 2, Winter, 1964-65, pp. 406-08.

"A Report on the Conference on British Studies," *The Burke Newsletter,* Vol. VI, No. 3, Spring, 1965, pp. 434-37.

Review of *Individualism, Collectivism and Political Power,* by Ervin Laszlo (Martinus Nijhoff: The Hague, 1963), in *American Political Science Review,* Vol. LIX, No. 1, March, 1965.

Review of *Burke and the Nature of Politics: The Age of the French Revolution,* by Carl B. Cone (University of Kentucky Press, Lexington, Ky., 1964), *Modern Age,* Vol. 9, No. 2, Spring, 1965, pp. 203-204.

Edmund Burke and the Natural Law, Second Edition, 1965.

"Robert Frost: Individualistic Democrat," *The Intercollegiate Review,* Vol. 2, No. 1, September, 1965, pp. 27-32.

Review of *The Correspondence of Edmund Burke,* ed. by Holden Furber, Vol. V (1783-1789), *The Burke Newsletter,* Vol. VIII, No. 2, Winter, 1965-66, pp. 538-41.

"A Report on the CBS Symposium: 'Man Versus

Society in Eighteenth-Century Britain,'" *The Burke Newsletter*, Vol. VIII, No. 2, Winter, 1966-67, pp. 652-62.

Edmund Burke, the Enlightenment and the Modern World, ed. Peter J. Stanlis (Detroit: The University of Detroit Press, 1967), xviii, 129 pp. Introduction by Louis I. Bredvold. Papers of a symposium on Edmund Burke, November 11-12, 1965, at the University of Detroit. Contributors: Thomas H.D. Mahoney, Robert A. Smith, Harvey C. Mansfield, Jr., Peter J. Stanlis, and Walter D. Love.

Review of *A Newspaper History of England, 1792-1793*, by Lucyle Werkmeister (Lincoln, Nebraska: University of Nebraska Press, 1967), *Studies in Burke and His Time*, Vol. IX, No. 3, Spring, 1968, pp. 971-80.

"The College Administrative Apparatus," *The University Bookman*, Vol. IX, No. 1, Autumn, 1968, pp. 3-11.

"Edmund Burke and Revolution," *The Intercollegiate Review*, Vol. 7, No. 5, Summer, 1971, pp. 215-25.

"Introduction," to Japanese translation of Edmund Burke, *The Sublime and Beautiful*, trans. and ed. by Noritada Nabeshima (Tokyo: Riso-Sha, 1973).

"America is Hard to See," *The University Bookman*, Vol. XIII, No. 3, Spring, 1973, pp. 52-60.

"Robert Frost: The Individual and Society," *The Intercollegiate Review*, Vol. 8, No. 5, Summer, 1973, pp. 211-34. Japanese translation, 1976.

Robert Frost: The Individual and Society (Rockford, Illinois: Rockford College Press, 1973), 88 pp.

"The Modern Social Consciousness," *The Occasional Review*, Vol. I, No. 1, February, 1974, pp. 81-98.

"A Preposterous Way of Reasoning: Frederick

Dreyer's 'Edmund Burke: The Philosopher in Action,'" *Studies in Burke and His Time*, Vol. XV, No. 3, Spring, 1974, pp. 265-75.

"Robert Frost's Masques and the Classic American Tradition," in *Frost Centennial Essays*, ed. Jac Tharpe (Jackson, Miss.: University Press of Mississippi, 1974), pp. 441-68.

"Robert Frost," in *Contemporary Literary Criticism* (Detroit: Gale Research Co., 1975), pp. 174-75.

Edmund Burke on Conciliation with the Colonies and Other Papers on the American Revolution, ed. Peter J. Stanlis, (Lunenberg, Vermont: The Stinehaur Press, 1975), 269 pp. A Limited Editions Club volume Bicentennial Celebration selection.

"Robert Frost: Politics in Theory and Practice," *Frost Centennial Essays*, Vol. II, ed. Jac Tharpe (Jackson, Mississippi: University Press of Mississippi, 1976), pp. 48-82.

Review of *Robert Frost: Modern Poetics and the Landscape of Self*, by Frank Lentricchia (Durham, North Carolina: Duke University Press, 1975), in *The New England Quarterly*, June 1976, pp. 320-322.

"The Aesthetic Theory of Eliseo Vivas," in *Viva Vivas*, ed. Henry Regnery (Indianapolis, Indiana: Liberty Press, 1976), pp. 139-183.

"British Views of the American Revolution: A Conflict over 'Rights' of Sovereignty," in *Early American Literature*, Spring 1977, pp. 191-201.

"Reflections on Dinwiddy on Mill on Burke on Prescription," *Studies in Burke and His Time*, Spring, 1977.

"Acceptable in Heaven's Sight: Robert Frost at Bread Loaf, 1939-1941," *Frost Centennial Essays*, Vol. III, ed. Jac Tharpe (Jackson, Mississippi: University Press of Mississippi, 1978), pp. 179-311. (A literary memoir consisting of three years of conversations with Robert Frost, based on a friendship of twenty-three years).

"Orestes Brownson's *The American Republic* Today," in *No Divided Allegiance: Essays in Brownson's Thought,* ed. Leonard Gilhooley (New York: Fordham University Press, 1980), pp. 142-162.

"Misinterpreting Burke," a review-article on *Edmund Burke and the Critique of Political Radicalism,* by Michael Freeman, in *Modern Age,* Vol. 25, No. 3, Summer 1981, pp. 301-304.

"Edmund Burke, The Perennial Political Philosopher," *Modern Age,* Vol. 26, Summer/Fall, Numbers 3-4, 1982, pp. 325-329.

Edmund Burke: A Bibliography of Secondary Studies to 1982, by Peter J. Stanlis and Clara I. Gandy, with a foreword by William B. Todd (New York: Garland Publishing Co., 1983), 357 pp.

Work in Progress: "Constitutional Liberty in Western Civilization: The American Republic," (The annual Andrew R. Cecil Lecture at the Universtiy of Texas, to be published in spring 1984).